Global Trends in Intelligent Computing Research and Development

B.K. Tripathy
VIT University, India

D.P. Acharjya
VIT University, India

A volume in the Advances in
Computational Intelligence and Robotics
(ACIR) Book Series

An Imprint of IGI Global

Managing Director:	Lindsay Johnston
Production Manager:	Jennifer Yoder
Development Editor:	Austin DeMarco
Acquisitions Editor:	Kayla Wolfe
Typesetter:	Lisandro Gonzalez
Cover Design:	Jason Mull

Published in the United States of America by
Information Science Reference (an imprint of IGI Global)
701 E. Chocolate Avenue
Hershey PA 17033
Tel: 717-533-8845
Fax: 717-533-8661
E-mail: cust@igi-global.com
Web site: http://www.igi-global.com

Library of Congress Cataloging-in-Publication Data

Global trends in intelligent computing research and development / B.K. Tripathy and D.P. Acharjya, editors.
     pages cm
 Includes bibliographical references and index.
 Summary: "This book brings together recent advances and indepth knowledge in the fields of knowledge representation and computational intelligence, highlighting the theoretical advances and their applications to real life problems"-- Provided by publisher.
  ISBN 978-1-4666-4936-1 (hardcover) -- ISBN 978-1-4666-4937-8 (ebook) -- ISBN 978-1-4666-4938-5 (print & perpetual access) 1. Engineering--Data processing. 2. Science--Data processing. 3. Artificial intelligence. I. Tripathy, B. K., 1957- editor of compilation. II. Acharjya, D. P., 1969- editor of compilation.
 TA345.G56 2013
 006.3--dc23
                                                2013038556

This book is published in the IGI Global book series Advances in Computational Intelligence and Robotics (ACIR) (ISSN: 2327-0411; eISSN: 2327-042X)

British Cataloguing in Publication Data
A Cataloguing in Publication record for this book is available from the British Library.

All work contributed to this book is new, previously-unpublished material. The views expressed in this book are those of the authors, but not necessarily of the publisher.

For electronic access to this publication, please contact: eresources@igi-global.com.

Advances in Computational Intelligence and Robotics (ACIR) Book Series

ISSN: 2327-0411
EISSN: 2327-042X

MISSION

While intelligence is traditionally a term applied to humans and human cognition, technology has progressed in such a way to allow for the development of intelligent systems able to simulate many human traits. With this new era of simulated and artificial intelligence, much research is needed in order to continue to advance the field and also to evaluate the ethical and societal concerns of the existence of artificial life and machine learning.

The **Advances in Computational Intelligence and Robotics (ACIR) Book Series** encourages scholarly discourse on all topics pertaining to evolutionary computing, artificial life, computational intelligence, machine learning, and robotics. ACIR presents the latest research being conducted on diverse topics in intelligence technologies with the goal of advancing knowledge and applications in this rapidly evolving field.

COVERAGE

- Adaptive & Complex Systems
- Agent Technologies
- Artificial Intelligence
- Cognitive Informatics
- Computational Intelligence
- Natural Language Processing
- Neural Networks
- Pattern Recognition
- Robotics
- Synthetic Emotions

IGI Global is currently accepting manuscripts for publication within this series. To submit a proposal for a volume in this series, please contact our Acquisition Editors at Acquisitions@igi-global.com or visit: http://www.igi-global.com/publish/.

Titles in this Series

For a list of additional titles in this series, please visit: www.igi-global.com

Mathematics of Uncertainty Modeling in the Analysis of Engineering and Science Problems
S. Chakraverty (National Institute of Technology - Rourkela, India)
Information Science Reference • copyright 2014 • 442pp • H/C (ISBN: 9781466649910) • US $195.00 (our price)

Global Trends in Intelligent Computing Research and Development
B.K. Tripathy (VIT University, India) and D.P. Acharjya (VIT University, India)
Information Science Reference • copyright 2014 • 340pp • H/C (ISBN: 9781466649361) • US $195.00 (our price)

Exploring Innovative and Successful Applications of Soft Computing
Antonio D. Masegosa (Universidad de Granada, Spain) Pablo J. Villacorta (Universidad de Granada, Spain) Carlos Cruz-Corona (Universidad de Granada, Spain) M. Socorro García-Cascales (Universidad Politécnica de Cartagena, Spain) María T. Lamata (Universidad de Granada, Spain) and José L. Verdegay (Universidad de Granada, Spain)
Information Science Reference • copyright 2014 • 375pp • H/C (ISBN: 9781466647855) • US $190.00 (our price)

Research Developments in Computer Vision and Image Processing Methodologies and Applications
Rajeev Srivastava (Indian Institute of Technology (BHU), India) S. K. Singh (Indian Institute of Technology (BHU), India) and K. K. Shukla (Indian Institute of Technology (BHU), India)
Information Science Reference • copyright 2014 • 388pp • H/C (ISBN: 9781466645585) • US $195.00 (our price)

Handbook of Research on Novel Soft Computing Intelligent Algorithms Theory and Practical Applications
Pandian M. Vasant (Petronas University of Technology)
Information Science Reference • copyright 2014 • 1004pp • H/C (ISBN: 9781466644502) • US $495.00 (our price)

Intelligent Technologies and Techniques for Pervasive Computing
Kostas Kolomvatsos (University of Athens, Greece) Christos Anagnostopoulos (Ionian University, Greece) and Stathes Hadjiefthymiades (University of Athens, Greece)
Information Science Reference • copyright 2013 • 351pp • H/C (ISBN: 9781466640382) • US $195.00 (our price)

Mobile Ad Hoc Robots and Wireless Robotic Systems Design and Implementation
Raul Aquino Santos (University of Colima, Mexico) Omar Lengerke (Universidad Autónoma de Bucaramanga, Colombia) and Arthur Edwards-Block (University of Colima, Mexico)
Information Science Reference • copyright 2013 • 344pp • H/C (ISBN: 9781466626584) • US $190.00 (our price)

Intelligent Planning for Mobile Robotics Algorithmic Approaches
Ritu Tiwari (ABV – Indian Institute of Information, India) Anupam Shukla (ABV – Indian Institute of Information, India) and Rahul Kala (School of Systems Engineering, University of Reading, UK)
Information Science Reference • copyright 2013 • 322pp • H/C (ISBN: 9781466620742) • US $195.00 (our price)

DISSEMINATOR OF KNOWLEDGE

www.igi-global.com

701 E. Chocolate Ave., Hershey, PA 17033
Order online at www.igi-global.com or call 717-533-8845 x100
To place a standing order for titles released in this series, contact: cust@igi-global.com
Mon-Fri 8:00 am - 5:00 pm (est) or fax 24 hours a day 717-533-8661

My beloved father Sri Hadu Tripathy

B. K. Tripathy
VIT University, India

My beloved father Sri Gouri Sankar Acharjya

D. P. Acharjya
VIT University, India

Table of Contents

Section 1
Classification and Clustering

    Manish Joshi, North Maharashtra University, India
    Pawan Lingras, Saint Mary's University Halifax, Canada
    Gajendra Wani, Bhusawal Arts, Science, and Commerce College, India
    Peng Zhang, Saint Mary's University Halifax, Canada

    Sourav De, University Institute of Technology, University of Burdwan, India
    Siddhartha Bhattacharyya, RCC Institute of Information Technology, India
    Susanta Chakraborty, Bengal Engineering and Science University, India

    V. Susheela Devi, Indian Institute of Science, India

    Sandip Dey, Camellia Institute of Technology, India
    Siddhartha Bhattacharyya, RCC Institute of Information Technology, India
    Ujjwal Maulik, Jadavpur University, India

Section 2
Foundations of Knowledge Representation

Section 3
Foundations of Computational Intelligence

Detailed Table of Contents

Section 1
Classification and Clustering

This chapter proposes an approach that uses time series clustering and time series prediction techniques to forecast future demand for each product in an inventory management system. A stability and seasonality analysis of the time series is proposed to identify groups of products (local groups) exhibiting similar sales patterns. The details of the experimental techniques and results for obtaining optimal inventory predictions are shared in this chapter.

This chapter depicts the parallel version of the OptiMUSIG (ParaOptiMUSIG) activation function with the optimized class responses for the individual features with a parallel self-organizing neural network architecture to segment true color images. A genetic algorithm-based optimization technique has been employed to yield the optimized class responses in parallel. Comparison of the proposed method with the existing non-optimized method is applied on two real life true color images and is demonstrated with the help of three standard objective functions as they are employed to measure the quality of the segmented images.

This chapter focuses on a few key applications in the field of classification and clustering. Techniques of soft computing have been used to solve these applications. The first application finds a new similarity measure for time series data, combining some available similarity measures. The weight to be given to these similarity measures is found using a genetic algorithm. The other applications discussed are for pattern clustering. A Particle Swarm Optimization (PSO) algorithm has been used for clustering. A modification of the PSO using genetic operators has been suggested.

This chapter presents a Quantum Inspired Genetic Algorithm (QIGA). The QIGA adopted the inherent principles of quantum computing and has been applied on three gray level test images to determine their optimal threshold values. Quantum random interference based on chaotic map models and later quantum crossover, quantum mutation, and quantum shift operation have been applied in the proposed QIGA. In addition, the performance analysis have been made between the proposed QIGA with the conventional GA and later with QEA proposed by Han et al. that reveals its time efficacy compare to GA along with the drawbacks in QEA.

# Chapter 5

This chapter has discussed some important issues such as pre-processing of gene expression data, curse of dimensionality, feature extraction/selection, and measuring or estimating classifier performance. In most classifier design strategies, the gene or feature selection is an integral part of the classifier; as such, it must be a part of the cross-validation process that is used to estimate the classifier prediction performance. Furthermore, this chapter discusses important properties such as generalizability or sensitivity to overtraining, built-in feature selection, ability to report prediction strength, and transparency of different approaches to provide a quick and concise reference.

# Chapter 6

Cancer has been identified as the leading cause of death, and hence, it is an urgent need for a more effective methodology to understand, prevent, and cure cancer. Microarray technology provides a useful basis of achieving this goal, with cluster analysis of gene expression data leading to the discrimination of patients, identification of possible tumor subtypes, and individualized treatment. This chapter discusses the basis of weighted dimensional space and different approaches to soft subspace clustering. A number of state-of-the-art techniques of cluster ensembles are also included in this chapter, such that a combination of soft subspace clustering and ensemble models can be customized to different requirements.

Section 2
Foundations of Knowledge Representation

The classical rule mining techniques based on crisp sets have bad experience of "sharp boundary problems" while mining rule from numerical data. Fuzzy rule mining approaches eliminate these problems and generate more human understandable rules. Several quality measures are used in order to quantify the quality of these discovered rules. However, most of these objectives are conflicting to each other and hence fuzzy rule mining problems are modeled as multi-objective optimization problem rather than single objective. Due to the ability of finding diverse trade-off solutions for several objectives in a single run, multi-objective genetic algorithms are popularly employed in rule mining. This chapter discusses the multi-objective genetic-fuzzy approaches in rule mining along with their advantages and disadvantages.

# Chapter 8

Impreciseness and uncertainties are major concerns while analyzing data from large databases. Fuzzy set of Zadeh and Rough sets of Pawlak are two major popular models to handle impreciseness and uncertainties. This is further extended and hybridized by many researchers in different directions. The introduction of fuzzy logic and the approximate reasoning obtained through it are more realistic as it is close to the human beings reason out. Again, equality of crisp sets is too restricted from application point of view and so concepts of approximate equalities were introduced using rough sets. These notions were further generalized by Tripathy. This chapter provides a comprehensive study of all these forms of approximate equalities and illustrates their applicability through several examples.

# Chapter 9

Case-based reasoning may be defined as a model of reasoning that incorporates problem solving, understanding, and learning, and integrates all of them with memory processes. It focuses on the human problem solving approach such as how people learn new skills and generate solutions about new situations based on their past experience. This book chapter provides the basic idea of case based reasoning and a few typical applications.

# Chapter 10

Real coded Genetic Algorithms (GAs) are most effective techniques for solving continuous optimization problems. Researchers used the Laplace Crossover (LX) and Power Mutation (PM) in the GA cycle (namely LX-PM) efficiently for solving optimization problems. This chapter discusses a local search technique, namely Quadratic Approximation (QA). Further, QA is hybridized with LX-PM in order to improve its efficiency and efficacy. The hybrid system (H-LX-PM) is validated over LX-PM through a test bed of 22 unconstrained and 15 constrained typical benchmark problems. In addition, a few applications of GA are highlighted as the scope for future research.

Formal Concept Analysis (FCA) analyzes the data, which is represented in the form of a formal context, that describe the relationship between a particular set of objects and a particular set of attributes. It produces hierarchically ordered clusters called formal concepts and basis of attribute dependencies, called attribute implications. Several algorithms are proposed in the literature to extract the formal concepts from a given context. This chapter analyzes, demonstrates, and compare few standard algorithms that extract the formal concepts

The data structure "r-Train" (Train) where r is a natural number is a new kind of powerful robust data structure which can store homogeneous data dynamically in a flexible way, in particular for large amounts of data. However, it cannot store heterogeneous data. The advanced data structure "r-Atrain" (Atrain) is logically almost analogous to the data structure r-train (train) with an advanced level of construction to accommodate heterogeneous data of large volumes. It is important to note that none of these two new data structures is a competitor of the other. By default, any heterogeneous data structure can work as a homogeneous data structure too. However, for working with huge volume of homogeneous data, train is more suitable than atrain. This chapter discusses in detail about heterogeneous data structure, r-Atrain, and accommodating large volumes of data.

The whole mathematical scenario has been changed with the advent of the rough set theory, a powerful tool to deal with uncertainty and incompleteness in an information system. On the other end, soft set has emerged as an advanced mathematical tool to deal with data associated with uncertainty. This chapter endeavors to forge a connection between soft set and rough set and maps a new model rough soft set to address the challenges of vagueness and impreciseness. This chapter is a new attempt to construct the relationship between a rough set, soft set, and fuzzy set to form a hybrid soft set.

This chapter presents a novel system for drawing geometric diagrams on the Braille medium in order to make the diagrams tactile and accessible by the blind people. The computer graphics algorithms for drawing digital shapes have been suitably modified to make them work for the Braille environment. The goodness of the diagrams is measured by quantifying approximation errors in these diagrams. This chapter further demonstrates how computational intelligence can be embedded in the system to develop an intelligent teaching-learning aid for the blind, especially for teaching them figure-based subjects like geometry, physics, engineering drawing, etc.

  Sasanko Sekhar Gantayat, GMR Institute of Technology, India
  B. K. Tripathy, VIT University, India

This chapter discusses list theory-based relational database models using position function approach and illustrates how query processing can be realized for some of the relational algebraic operations. Petri nets are graphical and mathematical modeling tools applicable to many systems. Analysis of Petri nets using extended bag theoretic relational algebra is due to Kim and Kim. This chapter also provides a clear idea about list theoretic relational algebra (LRA) and analyzes Petri nets using this LRA.

  Pinaki Majumdar, M.U.C. Women's College, India & Visva-Bharati University, India

This chapter provides the advancements that took place in the last 14 years in the field of soft sets theory. The notions of generalized fuzzy soft sets are defined, and their properties are studied. A notion of mapping, called soft mapping, in soft set is introduced. In addition, some real life applications of hybrid soft sets like medical diagnosis, decision-making, etc. are discussed. It also addresses measurement of similarity of soft sets.

Section 4
Information Science and Neural Network

  J. Abdul Jaleel, Al Azhar College of Engineering and Technology, India
  Anish Benny, Amal Jyothi College of Engineering, India
  David K. Daniel, VIT University, India

The control of pH is of great importance in chemical processes, biotechnological industries, and many other areas. High performance and robust control of pH neutralization is difficult to achieve due to the nonlinear and time-varying process characteristics. The process gain varies at higher order of magnitude over a small range of pH. This chapter uses the adaptive and neural control techniques for the pH neutralization process for a strong acid-strong base system. The simulation results are analyzed to show that an adaptive controller can be perfectly tuned and a properly trained neural network controller may outperform an adaptive controller.

Chapter 18

Bertram C. Brookes theorized that a Shannon-Hartley's logarithmic-like measure could be applied to both information and recipient knowledge structure in order to satisfy his "Fundamental Equation of Information Science." To date, this idea has remained almost forgotten. This chapter introduces a novel quantitative approach that shows that a Shannon-Hartley's log-like model can represent a feasible solution for the cognitive process of retention of information described by Brookes.

Preface

The vast amount of data collected by different organizations all over the world across a wide variety of fields today has no utility unless these are analyzed to get useful information. This necessitates the development of techniques that can be used to facilitate the process of analysis. The development of powerful computers is a boon to implement these techniques leading to automated systems. The transformation of data into knowledge is by no means an easy task. Moreover, these data may involve uncertainty in many different forms. Many different models, like fuzzy sets, rough sets, soft sets, neural networks, their generalizations, and hybrid models obtained by combining two or more of these models, have been found to be fruitful in representing data. These models are also very fruitful for analysis. More often than not, the high dimensional data are reduced to include only the important characteristics necessary from a particular study point of view or depending upon the application area. Therefore, reduction techniques have been developed. Often, the data collected have missing values. These values need to be generated or the tuples having these missing values are eliminated from the data set before analysis. The later approach sometimes leads to loss of information and hence not preferred.

Our intention in editing this book is to offer concepts and methods of knowledge representation and computational intelligence in a precise and clear manner to the research community. In editing the book, our attempt is to provide frontier advancements in knowledge representation and computational intelligence, the conceptual basis required to achieve in depth knowledge in the field of computer science and information technology. It will help those researchers who have interest in this field to keep insight into different concepts and their importance for applications in real life. This has been done to make the edited book more flexible and to stimulate further interest in topics.

The topics to be discussed are theoretical foundations of computational intelligence, knowledge representation, and computational intelligence for knowledge representation. Hybrid intelligent techniques and real life applications that give stress on the basic knowledge on computational techniques; its development stages to present day technology is also discussed in different parts of the edited book. These parts will broadly be distributed over the topics rough sets, fuzzy sets and neural network, knowledge discovery in databases, data mining, soft set, genetic algorithm, soft computing, and their applications in real life situations.

Knowledge representation is a sub area of Artificial Intelligence concerned with understanding, designing, and implementing ways of representing information in computers so that programs (agents) can use this information to derive information that is implied by it, to converse with people in natural languages, to decide what to do next to plan future activities, and to solve problems in areas that normally require human expertise. Deriving information that is implied by the information already present is a form of reasoning. Knowledge representation schemes are useless without the ability to reason with them.

Data mining automates the process of finding predictive information in large databases. Questions that traditionally required extensive hands-on analysis can now be answered directly from the data quickly. A typical example of a predictive problem is targeted marketing. Data mining uses data on past promotional mailings to identify the targets most likely to maximize return on investment in future mailings. Other predictive problems include forecasting bankruptcy and other forms of default and identifying segments of a population likely to respond similarly to given events. The most commonly used techniques in data mining such as artificial neural network, decision trees, genetic algorithm, nearest neighbor method, evolutionary algorithms, and rule induction will be stressed.

The book is comprised of four sections. The first section is an attempt to provide an insight on classification and clustering. It presents variety of real life applications based on classification and clustering. The second section discusses theoretical foundations on knowledge representation, and section three provides information on computational intelligence. The final section discusses information science and application of neural network in bio-sciences. Each section provides the current research trends in the concerned field of study.

Optimal inventory prediction is one of the important issues faced by owners of retail chain stores. Determination of how, when, and what quantities of products are to be reordered is a key to running a profitable business. Several attempts have been made to develop a generic forecasting model for accurate inventory prediction for all products. In chapter 1, progression analysis technique is used, which reveals that most of the stable products of successive years come from the list of stable products of previous years. It is concluded that clustering driven stability analysis can be used as one of the handy tools for better inventory prediction.

The purpose of segmentation is to detect relevant and meaningful data by means of removal of redundancy embedded therein. Image segmentation is one of the major application areas of segmentation as it is a process of segregating an image space into multiple non-overlapping meaningful homogeneous regions (i.e. pixels of each region are homogeneous to each other with respect to some characteristics whereas the union of any two regions is not). The 2nd chapter is concerned with the segmentation of true color images and is aimed to segment true color images into a different number of classes with help of the optimized class boundaries for individual color components. The proposed genetic algorithm-based optimization techniques has been applied to generate these color components in parallel.

Soft Computing techniques generally refer to the techniques, which use some method of search to solve the problem. It differs from conventional computing in that it is tolerant of imprecision, uncertainty, partial truth, and approximation. It also refers to techniques, which mimic the methods used by human beings and animals. Some of the soft computing techniques are evolutionary computation, neural networks, particle swarm optimization, ant colony optimization, and fuzzy computing. Chapter 3 provides specific applications where the techniques mentioned above have been used. The applications are in the fields of supervised and unsupervised learning, namely classification and clustering have been discussed.

Chapter 4 presents a Quantum Inspired Genetic Algorithm (QIGA). The QIGA adopted the inherent principles of quantum computing and has been applied on three gray level test images to determine their optimal threshold values. Quantum random interference based on chaotic map models and later quantum crossover, quantum mutation, and quantum shift operation have been applied in the proposed QIGA. The basic features of quantum computing like qubit, superposition of states, coherence and decoherence, etc. help to espouse parallelism and time discreteness in QIGA. Finally, the optimum threshold value has been derived through the quantum measurement phase. In the proposed QIGA, the selected evaluation metrics are Wu's algorithm, Renyi's algorithm, Yen's algorithm, Johannsen's algorithm, Silva's algorithm, and finally, Linear index of fuzziness and the selected gray level images are Baboon, Peppers and Corridor. The conventional Genetic Algorithm (GA) and Quantum Evolutionary Algorithm (QEA) proposed by Han et al. have been run on the same set of images and evaluation metrics with the same parameters as QIGA. Finally, the performance analysis has been made between the proposed QIGA with the conventional GA and later with QEA proposed by Han et al. that reveals its time efficacy compare to GA along with the drawbacks in QEA.

As computer and database technologies advance rapidly, data accumulates at a speed unmatchable to human's capacity of data processing. Data mining as a multidisciplinary topic obtained from databases, machine learning, and statistics is efficient in transforming mountains of data into nuggets. Researchers and practitioners realize that, to use effectively data mining tools, data pre-processing is highly essential. Feature selection or dimensionality reduction is one of the important and frequently used techniques in data pre-processing for data mining and bio-informatics applications. In contrast to other dimensionality reduction techniques, feature selection techniques preserve the original semantics of the variables, hence offering the advantage of interpretability by a domain expert. Feature selection has been a fertile field of research and development since 1970s in statistical pattern recognition, machine learning, and data mining, and is widely applied to many fields such as text categorization, image retrieval, customer relationship management, intrusion detection, and genomic analysis. The main objective chapter 5 is to make researchers aware of the benefits, and in some cases even the necessity of applying feature selection techniques in Bioinformatics domain, highlighting the efforts given by the bioinformatics community in developing novel and adapted procedures.

There is an urgent need for a more effective methodology to understand, prevent, and cure cancer. Microarray technology provides a useful basis of achieving this goal, with cluster analysis of gene expression data leading to the discrimination of patients, identification of possible tumor subtypes and individualized treatment. Chapter 6 provides a survey of significant developments in this direction in order to prevent cancer.

Chapter 7 discusses the hybridization of fuzzy techniques with genetic algorithms, which is very fruitful in many application areas. Multiobjective optimization is also another recent technique instead of single objective optimization because of its utility in real life scenario. In this chapter, multi-objective genetic-fuzzy association rule mining approaches and multi-objective genetic-fuzzy approaches in associative classification have been presented and some of the application areas of this approach have been discussed.

Ever since their inception, rough sets have been found to be a fruitful model to capture imprecision in data and have many useful applications in different fields including computer science. Equality of sets in the mathematical sense is too stringent to be applied in real life situations. Most importantly, it does not include user knowledge in deciding the equality of two sets. In order to incorporate user knowledge in deciding the equality of two sets, Novotny and Pawlak used rough sets to define a set of approximate equalities. By adding three more types of rough set-based approximate equalities, Tripathy et al. studies it further and extended these notions to study the approximate equalities of fuzzy sets, intuitionistic fuzzy sets also. Further, the same has been extended to generalize rough set models like covering based rough sets and multigranular rough sets. In chapter 8, all the notions of approximate equalities have been presented in chronological order; several properties of all these notions have been presented and their applicability is discussed with suitable examples and comparative analysis. Approximate reasoning is an integral part of human reasoning in day to day live. The notion of approximate reasoning has been discussed using the notions of approximate equalities and is reflected in all the real life examples provided.

Case-Based Reasoning (CBR) is an offspring of research into cognitive science starting with the work of Prof. Roger Schank and his students at Yale University. CBR may be defined as a model of reasoning that incorporates problem solving, understanding and learning, and integrates all of them with memory processes. CBR is a general Artificial Intelligence paradigm for reasoning from experience, and learning from problem solving. It involves analogical reasoning, problem solving, and experimental learning. Chapter 9 provides basic idea of case-based reasoning, with an eye on its up to date status and its applications. This chapter will be useful to researchers in computer science, electrical engineering, system science, and information technology as both a textbook. Researchers and practitioners in industry and R&D laboratories working in such fields as system design, control, pattern recognition, data mining, vision, and machine intelligence will also benefit.

A Genetic Algorithm (GA) is a search heuristic that mimics the process of natural selection and is used to generate useful solutions optimization and search problems. It is a subclass of Evolutionary Algorithms (EA), which generate solutions to optimization problems using techniques inspired by natural evolution, such as inheritance, mutation, selection, and crossover. Using simple GAs sometimes puts the simulation suffering from getting trapped in local minima and sometimes results in premature convergence. A solution to this is the use of hybrid versions of GA. Chapter 10 provides the hybridization process through the set of benchmark functions both of unconstrained and constrained optimization problems. It also discusses some probable networking optimization application.

Knowledge discovery from data is very important from the utility point of view of the available data. Formal Concept Analysis (FCA) is a mathematical framework that offers conceptual data analysis and knowledge discovery. Chapter 11 analyzes, demonstrates, and compares a few standard algorithms that extract the formal concepts.

Data structures provide the ability to computers to fetch and store data efficiently at any place in its memory. The data structures record and array are based on computing the addresses of data items with arithmetic operations, while the linked data structures are based on storing addresses of data items within the structure itself. Chapter 12 introduces two new data structures called "r-Train" (or "Train" in short) and "r-Atrain" (or "Atrain" in short), which are very suitable for storing huge volume of data. The natural number r is suitably predefined and fixed by the programmer depending upon the problem under consideration and also upon the organization or industry for which the problem is posed. While train stores homogeneous data, atrain is suitable for the purpose of storing heterogeneous data. The term "Atrain" is an abbreviation for "Advanced train." The two data structures r-train and r-atrain do not have any conflict, which is evident from their functionalities.

Soft set is one of the latest additions to the list of imprecise models to capture uncertainty in data. It has been a practice to develop hybrid models by combining two or models. This provides models, which are better than the individual ones as they capture the important characteristics of the individual models. Therefore, researchers have tried to find hybrid models of soft sets with earlier models like the fuzzy set, rough set, and intuitionistic fuzzy sets. Chapter 13 provides a detailed account of some such hybrid models and their properties.

In the study of different science and engineering subjects, we often encounter texts or problems that are essentially illustrated by figures or diagrams. To understand (and also solve) a problem, the representative diagrams are not a mere convenience but also an inherent component in a person's cognitive representation of a scientific text or problem. Therefore, diagrams are as important for blind people as they are for sighted people. However, generating and communicating graphics for blind people, in the context of a subject, is not as straightforward as it is for sighted people. Chapter 14 presents a novel system for drawing geometric diagrams on the Braille medium in order to make the diagram tactile for blind people. The algorithms for drawing digital shapes have been suitably modified to make them work for the Braille environment. The goodness of the diagrams is measured by computing errors in these diagrams. This chapter further demonstrates how the system is helpful for embedding computational intelligence in developing a teaching or learning aid for the blind, especially for teaching them figure-based subjects like geometry, physics, engineering drawing, etc.

List or array is one of the most important data structures in computer science. In fact, functional programming completely depends upon theory of lists. From the mathematical point of view, a list is a generalization of the notion of bags or multisets, which in turn is a generalization of the fundamental notion of sets. Extending the idea of characteristic function of a set and that of the count function of a bag, the notion of position function of a list was introduced by Tripathy et al. in 2001. Relational models are the best-known form of models to represent and manipulate databases and the theory is very rich. An approach to develop relational models using lists was also proposed by Tripathy et al. in 2012 and many related operations like selection and projection have been introduced and studied. Chapter 15 presents all these with informational examples to illustrate the concepts developed. A similar study for the bag theoretic relational algebra for Petri net models was in existence. This has been extended to a more efficient theory of list theoretic relational algebra and Petri net operations have been elaborated in this chapter.

In chapter 13 of this volume, the imprecise model of soft sets has been considered. The content of chapter 16 is in a sense complementary to the contents of that chapter. Besides the preliminary notions about soft sets and some operations on them, a particular type of generalization of soft sets, called generalized fuzzy soft set has been discussed. Many concepts in soft set theory like the soft mapping, soft group, soft ring, soft topology, and soft entropy have been discussed. Most importantly, this chapter discusses some applications of soft sets.

Several attempts have been made for the development of a good dynamic model of pH neutralization process. The nonlinear characteristics and complexity of a pH neutralization plant creates major problems in this process. Among the four types of the pH process, the strong acid-strong base pH process is the most nonlinear. pH control is an interesting and challenging research subject which has led to a large number of motivating and interesting published papers. Out of the various control strategies used for pH control, chapter 17 emphasizes simulation-based pH control. This chapter discusses an adequate dynamic nonlinear pH neutralization model, based on physical and chemical principles that can represent the real pH neutralization plant. This model also facilitates the design, development, and implementation of advanced form of controllers. The research work in this direction mainly concerns about the use of a combined feedback/feed forward system and a highly robust feedback system as an overall control structure and the implementation and testing of the designed controller using latest computer tools. All these have been presented in this chapter.

Equality for the information-knowledge duality is widely known as the fundamental equation of information science. A Shannon-like solution for the fundamental equation of information science is desirable, and in this connection, Brookes's contributions to information science are indisputable. Based on Brookes's premises, information (an outside stimulus) is considered as an element that provokes changes in the cognitive structure (framework) of an individual. In chapter 18, a possible quantitative treatment for information, in accordance with a suggestion by Bawden, combining physical and cognitive aspects, is presented. Further, the treatment in this chapter shows that there is a relationship between Brookes's qualitative equation and Shannon's quantitative equation, and that this relationship can indicate the similarity of both viewpoints.

We strove to keep the book reader-friendly. By a problem solving approach, researchers learn the material through real life examples that provide the motivation behind the concepts and their relation to real world problems. At the same time, readers must discover a solution for the non-trivial aspect of the solution. We trust and hope that the book will help the readers to further carry out their research in different directions.

B. K. Tripathy
VIT University, India

D. P. Acharjya
VIT University, India

Acknowledgment

While writing, contributors have referred to several books and journals, and we take this opportunity to thank all those authors and publishers. In addition, we are also thankful to VIT University, India, for providing facilities to complete this project. We are extremely thankful to the editorial board and reviewers for their support during the process of evaluation. Last but not the least, we thank the production team of IGI Global for encouraging us and extending their cooperation and help for a timely completion of this edited book.

B. K. Tripathy
VIT University, India

D. P. Acharjya
VIT University, India

Section 1
Classification and Clustering

Chapter 1
Clustering–Based Stability and Seasonality Analysis for Optimal Inventory Prediction

Manish Joshi
North Maharashtra University, India

Gajendra Wani
Bhusawal Arts, Science, and Commerce College, India

Pawan Lingras
Saint Mary's University Halifax, Canada

Peng Zhang
Saint Mary's University Halifax, Canada

ABSTRACT

This chapter exemplifies how clustering can be a versatile tool in real life applications. Optimal inventory prediction is one of the important issues faced by owners of retail chain stores. Researchers have made several attempts to develop a generic forecasting model for accurate inventory prediction for all products. Regression analysis, neural networks, exponential smoothing, and Autoregressive Integrated Moving Average (ARIMA) are some of the widely used time series prediction techniques in inventory management. However, such generic models have limitations. The authors propose an approach that uses time series clustering and time series prediction techniques to forecast future demand for each product in an inventory management system. A stability and seasonality analysis of the time series is proposed to identify groups of products (local groups) exhibiting similar sales patterns. The details of the experimental techniques and results for obtaining optimal inventory predictions are shared in this chapter.

1. INTRODUCTION

This chapter exemplifies how clustering can be a versatile tool in real life applications. Traditionally, clustering techniques group similar patterns, which can be used for creating profiles. We show how clustering can be a very useful first step in prediction. Optimal inventory prediction is one of the important issues faced by owners of retail chain stores. Determination of how, when and what quantities of products are to be reordered is a key to running a profitable business. Researchers have

DOI: 10.4018/978-1-4666-4936-1.ch001

made several attempts to develop a generic forecasting model for accurate inventory prediction for all products. The demand quantity of a particular item or a group of related items can be considered as a time series. Time series prediction techniques that predict future values of a time series plays a critical role in forecasting quantity demand in business operations. Regression analysis, neural networks, exponential smoothing and autoregressive integrated moving average (ARIMA) are some of the widely used time series prediction techniques in inventory management.

Many researchers focus on finding a generic forecasting solution for all the products. However, products are distinguished by their seasonal sales patterns and volatilities in sales demand. One generic solution may not always be able to predict the most accurate demand for each product. Hence, these approaches are not always successful.

Limitations of generic forecasting model are overcome by developing specialized or targeted forecasting models. A variety of prediction techniques are combined with clustering to develop inventory prediction models. Clustering facilitate to explore stability underneath temporal variations. This chapter describes stability and seasonality analysis used to develop inventory prediction model.

We also elaborate on the effectiveness of stability analysis by applying it to a larger volume of data and further analyze stability for multiple years. We demonstrate that a group of stable products obtained using stability analysis is similar for different years. We also share our observations regarding how stable products from a particular year carry forward to subsequent years. A cross tabulation is used for trend analysis that emphasizes importance of stability analysis for multiple years.

The details of the experimental techniques and results for obtaining optimal inventory predictions are shared in this chapter. We elaborate usefulness of clustering in sales forecasting of objects that show similar sales patterns.

The experimental data set is obtained from an independent small retail chain of specialty stores. Information of customers, products, and their business operations from January 2005 to December 2009 is used for experimentation. More than 600,000 sales transactions are recorded in 60 months. In total, there are 25,378 distinct customers and 15,045 different products. Table 1 shows specific characteristics of the data set.

The chapter is organized into eight sections. Section 2 presents related research work of researchers who are exploring Data Mining and related techniques to enhance inventory prediction. Section 3 discusses the limitation of Generic Forecasting Model for inventory prediction. This section demonstrates two such cases in a real world retail store, which show how generic forecasting model can fail. Section 4 introduces some statistical measures obtained by preprocessing the data before the actual process of cluster analysis. Sections 5 and 6, present detailed description of clustering based Stability and Seasonality analysis. Section 7 reveals whether stable products for a year are also present in the list of stable products for subsequent years. We put forward our conclusions regarding the process of use of clustering for optimal inventory prediction in Section 8.

2. RELATED WORKS

As discussed in introduction, several models for inventory management have been proposed by a number of researchers. Varieties of time series

Table 1. An overview of experimental data set

Attribute	2005	2006	2007	2008	2009
Number of products	5782	7567	8034	8948	9409
Number of customers	4203	6159	10501	11548	13247
Number of transactions	55774	99852	75664	131499	147995

prediction techniques have been experimented. But use of clustering to group products exhibiting similar sales pattern followed by an appropriate time series prediction model is experimented by very few researchers.

(Ray, 1982) modeled monthly sales forecasting of chemical food in an inventory control system with ARIMA.

(Sorjamaa, A., Hao J., Reyhani, N., Ji, Y. & Lendasse, A., 2007) suggested that there are two main types of time series forecasting: short-term and long-term forecasting. While short-term forecasting refers to one period ahead prediction, long-term forecasting refers to multiple periods ahead predictions.

(Tseng, F. M., Yu, H. C., & Tzeng, G. H., 2002) proposed a hybrid forecasting model - SARIMABP, which combines the seasonal time series ARIMA (SARIMA) and the neural network back propagation (BP) models.

(Snyder, R. D., Koehler, A. B., & Ord, J. Keith, 2002) conducted the study of exponential smoothing models with single source of error and multiple sources of errors on weekly sales figures. This showed that exponential smoothing remains appropriate under general conditions, where the variance is allowed to grow or contract with corresponding movements in the underlying level.

(Mehrez, A., & Hu, M. Y., 1992) in their review analyzed results of 16 various forecasting models which were clustered along four defined dimensions. Mehrez et al. found that none of the forecasting methods have demonstrated the expected advantage. They recommended more specific knowledge as a prerequisite to assign a forecasting method to specific data. In our approach we propose to form cluster of products before applying any forecasting model.

(Stefanovic, N.,Stefanovic, D., & Radenkovic, B.) used clustering as a basis for supply chain inventory forecasting. In order to obtain out-of-stock forecasts at the store/product level clustering is used as a first phase followed by decision trees and neural network mining algorithms. Stores

that have similar aggregate sales patterns across the chain are clustered in this case whereas we propose to concentrate on forming local groups of products based on their sales pattern.

Similar to our work, (Kumar, M.,& Patel, N., 2010) also show the importance of clustering products prior to prediction. While they develop a single model for the entire cluster, we actually identify the best techniques for each cluster. Our clustering is also more versatile. Kumar et al. use clustering to identify the seasonality of the products.

We use seasonality analysis as well as stability analysis. The stability allows us to identify the best prediction period for each product. We also identify products that do not need any prediction, since they are only sold in single or pair of periods.

3. DOES GENERIC MODEL FIT BEST?

In this section, we illustrate that a generic model is not the best solution for forecasting and also discuss our proposed model. The first subsection explains about determination of a generic model for the dataset. The second subsection demonstrates with help of case studies how a generic model could not generate an optimal solution for certain products. The final subsection depicts our proposal to overcome the problem.

Deriving a Generic Model

Simple Exponential Smoothing, Holt's Exponential Smoothing, Brown's Exponential Smoothing, Damp Trend Exponential Smoothing, and Autoregressive Integrated Moving Average (ARIMA) inventory forecasting models are applied on the dataset. Mean absolute percentage error (MAPE) is one of the popularly used statistical evaluation metrics. It is applied to evaluate various inventory forecasting models used in this study.

Time series prediction technique as the best fit solution for a product if it has the lowest MAPE compared with other time series prediction techniques. A generic optimal solution is the time series prediction model that most frequently appeared to be the best fit solution in the entire product set. Due to the large number of computations, inventory forecasting is not performed at week level. Table 2 illustrates generic optimal solutions at month and quarter level in 2005 and 2006.

It compares frequencies of the best-fit solutions' occurrences. For example, in 2005, the occurrence frequency of Damp Trend Exponential Smoothing (1771) is the highest. That is, it is the best-fit solution for 1771 products. Thus, Damp Trend Exponential Smoothing is the generic optimal solution for the entire product set at month level in 2005. Autoregressive Integrated Moving Average (ARIMA) is the generic optimal solution at month level in 2006 since it is the best-fit solution for the most number of products (2360). The generic optimal solution at quarter level in 2005 is Holt's Exponential Smoothing, which is the same as the generic optimal solution in 2006.

Evaluating Generic Model

Following two case studies reveal whether derived generic model is really able to outperform all remaining models for various groups of products.

Case 1: The generic optimal solution at quarter level is Holt's Exponential Smoothing in 2005, as shown in Table 2. However, Brown's Exponential Smoothing is the optimal solution for a typical group (named G-05Q20) consisting of 135 products. Brown's Exponential Smoothing is the best-fit solution for all products within this group. The comparison of MAPE values of time series prediction models for products of the group G-05Q20 is displayed in Table 3. MAPE values associated with Brown's Exponential Smoothing (7.50035) are lower than Holt's Exponential Smoothing values (7.541999), which is the generic optimal solution. All products in this group G-05Q20 exhibit similar sales pattern.

Case 2: In case-1 the usefulness of a generic model was tested. Furthermore, this case study indicates whether use of any inventory forecasting model is at all required for products with strong sales pattern. For example, products that are sold same number of times in each quarter forms a stable quarterly group. A simple solution is to keep these products at the stable quantity for all the quarters. Similarly, seasonal sales groups may also have very strong sales patterns. A closer

Table 2. Generic solutions in 2005 and 2006

Year	2005		2006	
Level	Monthly	Quarterly	Monthly	Quarterly
Simple Exponential Smoothing	688	765	958	991
Holt's Exponential Smoothing	948	**1703**	1200	**2009**
Brown's Exponential Smoothing	580	1077	1085	1586
Damp Trend Exponential Smoothing	**1771**	914	1922	1279
Autoregressive Integrated Moving Average	1750	1370	**2360**	1788
Generic Optimal Solutions	Damp Trend Exponential Smoothing	Holt's Exponential Smoothing	Autoregressive Integrated Moving Average	Holt's Exponential Smoothing

Table 3. MAPE comparison results for products in a group G-05Q20

Simple Exponential Smoothing	Holt's Exponential Smoothing	Brown's Exponential Smoothing	Damp Trend Exponential Smoothing	Autoregressive Integrated Moving Average
7.716615	7.541999	**7.50035**	7.541548	7.6875

look at our dataset uncovers the fact that some products were only sold in July in 2006 (group G-06M60). The MAPE comparison results for these products show high MAPE values for all the prediction techniques (Table 4). It suggests that applying any prediction models to forecast products with strong sales pattern might produce incorrect predictions.

Proposed Approach

Products have their own sales patterns. Some products are sold throughout a whole year, while others are sold seasonally. Moreover, some products may share the same patterns. Seasonal selling distributions are clearly shown for some products. Categorizing products, based on their sales patterns, may ease inventory management. Following description shows how to discover products that are mostly sold in certain month(s) or quarter(s). Products are considered as single period selling products if their selling ratios in one period are high. Here, the ratio is calculated as Equation 1:

$$\frac{Pk}{TS - Pk} \quad (1)$$

Where Pk is the sales quantity in period k, TS is the total sales quantity throughout the year. The ratio is considered high if its value is greater than 10. Table 5 illustrates the distribution of single quarter selling products. For instance, in 2006, 800 products were mostly sold in the first quarter, 336 products are mostly sold in the second quarter, etc. Table 6 illustrates the distribution of single month selling products.

Above two case studies and the information of products' sales pattern provide a strong motivation for a better combined inventory management strategy that includes in-depth analysis of dataset prior to application of any time series prediction model. The study proposes to use time series

Table 4. MAPE comparison results for products in group G-06M60

Simple Exponential Smoothing	Holt's Exponential Smoothing	Brown's Exponential Smoothing	Damp Trend Exponential Smoothing	Autoregressive Integrated Moving Average
9.248119	9.247283	9.243259	9.249918	**9.243056**

Table 5. The distribution of single quarter selling products

Quarters	Quarter 1	Quarter 2	Quarter 3	Quarter 4
Number of products (2005)	478	292	332	662
Number of products (2006)	800	336	306	579

Table 6. The distribution of single month selling products

Months	Jan	Feb	Mar	Apr	May	Jun	Jul	Aug	Sep	Oct	Nov	Dec
Number of products (2005)	132	156	106	79	96	74	104	92	91	108	115	300
Number of products (2006)	491	93	99	110	76	105	85	91	81	92	127	188

clustering techniques, using algorithms such as K-Means and EM, to categorize products into several reasonable groups based on product sales patterns.

4. PREPROCESSING

In preprocessing, some statistical measures like z-score, A and P are obtained before actual processing of cluster analysis. In order to perform stability study, two reasonable criteria are used: the mean of absolute z-score and the percentage of non-zero values. The mean of absolute z-score score, denoted by A, is:

$$z = \frac{x - \mu}{\sigma} \qquad (2)$$

$$A = \frac{\Sigma z}{n} \qquad (3)$$

where x is the value of data object, which is the sales quantity of a given period, μ is the mean of the population, σ is the standard deviation of the population and n is the total number of data objects. The value of A indicates how stable the product is based on periodical sales quantities. The lower the value of A, the more stable the product. The percentage of non-zero values, denoted by P, is:

$$P = \frac{m}{n} \qquad (4)$$

where m is the number of data objects with any non-zero sales quantity. The value of P indicates the frequency of the product sold in corresponding periods. Therefore, the range of value P is from 0 to 1. Zero means that the product has no sales records in any period. One means that the product has been sold in every period. Products with higher values of P are considered to be sold more often, which makes them more stable.

Table 7 shows a sample of time series clustering data sets used for monthly stability analysis. For example, product 'PId625' has a higher value of P compared to product 'PIdLiv'. That is, PId625 has been sold more often than PIdLiv. In addition, the A value of PId625, 0.8114, is lower than the A value of PIdLiv, which is 0.8862. Therefore, PId625 is more stable than PIdLiv. The stability analysis is performed in two tiers. Tier-1 clustering

Table 7. A sample of time series clustering data set

Product ID	Percentage of Non Zero Value P	Mean of Absolute z Score (A)
PId689	1.0000	0.7878
PId876	0.4167	0.9592
PId624	1.0000	0.7556
PId200	0.6667	0.8402
PId117	1.0000	0.7903
PId625	0.7500	0.8114
PId772	1.0000	0.8140
PId871	1.0000	0.8456
PId631	1.0000	0.6627
PId635	1.0000	0.8951
PId774	1.0000	0.7690
PId600	0.0833	0.5528
PId626	1.0000	0.7791
PId693	1.0000	0.8405
PId872	1.0000	0.8052
PIdLiv	0.5833	0.8862

analysis figures out broad stable groups. Tier 2 clustering further analyzes the most appropriate stable group to determine a list of stable products.

5. STABILITY ANALYSIS

In this section stability analysis is performed as weekly, monthly and quarterly. In first subsection weekly stable product are identified for the year 2006. In second subsection monthly stable product are identified for the year 2008 whereas in third subsection quarterly stable product are identified for the year 2005.

Products are called stable if their sales quantities change negligibly over allotted periods. On the other hand, products are defined as unstable if their sales quantities change greatly with time. The products are categorized based on their stabilities of sales quantity in three levels: weekly, monthly and quarterly.

This stability analysis is carried out from "the least" to "the greatest", that is, the experiment starts with weekly sales quantities analysis, and then follows by monthly and quarterly sales quantities analysis. The K-Means and EM algorithms are applied to the three level analyses. The possible categorizing results are weekly stable products, monthly stable products, quarterly stable products, and unstable products. Each level of analysis categorizes products into two groups: a stable and an unstable group. Moreover, stable weekly products can be considered as stable monthly products, and stable monthly products as stable quarterly products. Unstable products of lower level are further processed for higher level of stability analysis. Hence, monthly stability analysis on unstable weekly products is performed.

Figure 1 illustrates the above mentioned process of stability analysis and seasonality analysis.

The process of grouping products to obtain weekly and monthly stable products is discussed in the following two subsections.

Figure 1. Procedural steps to obtain stable and seasonal products

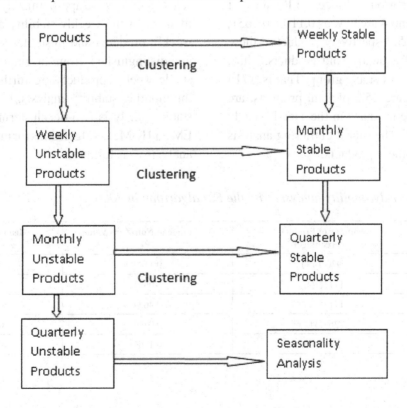

Weekly Stability Analysis

If products' sales quantities are approximately the same in all weeks, they are called stable weekly products. This subsection describes two tier clustering analysis to identify weekly stable products. Tier-1 clustering analysis figures out broad stable groups. Tier-2 clustering analysis further analyzes the most appropriate stable group to determine a list of stable products.

Tier-1 Weekly Stability Analysis

The goal of the Tier-1 time series clustering is to define stable groups from the noisy data set. The stability analysis starts with the EM algorithm. Table 8 shows the EM clustering results of the Tier-1 2006 weekly stability analysis.

According to the results, 6767 products are clustered based on their weekly sales quantities and 5 groups (clusters) are generated as an optimal clustering solution. Among them, Cluster 2 has the highest value of P (0.4644), which means that products in this group were sold more often than products in other groups. Since the P values of Clusters 0, 1, 3 and 4 are low, as 0.1103, 0.0651, 0.0261 and 0.1765, respectively, products in these groups are not frequently sold products. Thus, Cluster 2 is the most stable group. That is, 1714 products, which are 25% of total products, are considered stable products in the Tier-1 weekly stability analysis. The Tier-2 clustering analysis is performed on these products.

Tier-2 Weekly Stability Analysis

In the Tier-2 clustering analysis, time series clustering techniques, such as EM and K-Means, are applied. The normalized data set is clustered with the EM algorithm. However, the K-Means algorithm is used as an alternative solution to facilitate the Tier-2 clustering tasks when EM clustering results are not descriptive. Moreover, the number of output clusters is defined as 5 to distinguish products into finer groups, such as very stable, relatively stable, normal, relatively unstable and unstable groups.

Table 9 shows the Tier-2 clustering results carried on 1714 products (Cluster 2) filtered in the Tier-1 2006 weekly stability analysis. The results show that Cluster 5 is the most stable group since it has the highest P value (0.9285) and reasonable A value (0.7659). Therefore, 32 products are categorized as weekly stable products in 2006.

Monthly Stability Analysis

Products are considered stable monthly if their sales quantities are approximately the same in all months. In the weekly stability analysis, stable weekly products and unstable weekly products are distinguished from original data set. Unstable weekly products are further analyzed in the monthly stability analysis. Likewise weekly stability analysis, two-tier clustering analysis with EM and K-Means algorithms for monthly stability analysis is as follows.

Table 8. Tier-1 weekly stability analysis with the EM algorithm in 2006

Product Group	Number of Products (Percentage)	Percentage of Non-Zero Values (P)	Mean of Absolute z-Score (A)
Cluster 0	970(14%)	0.1103	0.6078
Cluster 1	1111(16%)	0.0651	0.4852
Cluster 2	1714(25%)	0.4644	0.8244
Cluster 3	2269(34%)	0.0261	0.3132
Cluster 4	703(10%)	0.1765	0.723

Table 9. Tier-2 weekly stability analysis with the EM algorithm in 2006

Product Group	Number of Products (Percentage)	Percentage of Non-Zero Values (P)	Mean of Absolute z-Score (A)
Cluster 0	346 (20%)	0.2965	0.8499
Cluster 1	209 (12%)	0.8319	0.8121
Cluster 2	368 (21%)	0.3998	0.8761
Cluster 3	71 (4%)	0.3473	0.7888
Cluster 4	140 (8%)	0.5273	0.8319
Cluster 5	**32 (2%)**	**0.9285**	**0.7659**
Cluster 6	275(16%)	0.6275	0.7782
Cluster 7	273 (16%)	0.2393	0.8104

Tier-1 Monthly Stability Analysis

Table 10 shows the EM clustering results of the Tier-1 2008 monthly stability analysis. In total, 3619 products are clustered based on their monthly sales quantities. The optimal clustering solution categorizes products into 7 groups (clusters). Cluster 1 has the highest value of P (0.9415), which means products in this group were sold more often than the others. The A value (0.0669) in Cluster 1 is reasonable. Thus, products in Cluster 1 are the most stable products in terms of monthly sales quantities in 2008. Therefore, 528 products, which are 15% of total products, are to be analyzed in the Tier-2 monthly stability analysis.

Tier-2 Monthly Stability Analysis

The Tier-2 EM clustering is built upon the results of the Tier-1 2008 monthly stability analysis (528 products). The result is illustrated in Table 11. Statistically, the results show that one big group of all the products is the optimal solution. It does not meet the group refinement goal of the Tier-2 stability analysis. In this case, the K-Means is used algorithm to categorize products into 5 groups. The K-Means clustering results are shown in Table 12. According to the results, Clusters 1, 2, 3 are the most stable groups since its P value (1.0) is the highest. Therefore, 259 (98+60+101) products are categorized as stable monthly products in 2008.

Table 10. Tier-1 monthly stability analysis with the EM algorithm in 2008

Product Group	Number of Products (Percentage)	Percentage of Non-Zero Values (P)	Mean of Absolute z-Score (A)
Cluster 0	503 (14%)	0.6293	0.8364
Cluster 1	**528 (15%)**	**0.9415**	**0.8334**
Cluster 2	236 (7%)	0.7723	0.7064
Cluster 3	506(14%)	0.1739	0.7313
Cluster 4	510(14%)	0.2852	0.8454
Cluster 5	884(24%)	0.0836	0.5528
Cluster 6	452(12%)	0.4282	0.9271

Table 11. Tier-2 monthly stability analysis with the EM algorithm in 2008

Product Group	Number of Products (Percentage)	Percentage of Non-Zero Values (P)	Mean of Absolute z-Score (A)
Cluster 0	528 (100%)	0.9402	0.8318

Table 12. Tier-2 monthly stability analysis with the K-Means algorithm in 2008

Product Group	Number of Products (Percentage)	Percentage of Non-Zero Values (P)	Mean of Absolute z-Score (A)
Cluster 0	159 (30%)	0.9167	0.8267
Cluster 1	98(19%)	1.0	0.8226
Cluster 2	60(11%)	1.0	0.7707
Cluster 3	101(19%)	1.0	0.8825
Cluster 4	110(21%)	0.8333	0.8342

Quarterly Stability Analysis

Products, which have stable sales quantity in each quarter, are considered quarterly stable products. In addition, stable weekly and stable monthly products can be considered quarterly stable products. Here, quarterly stability analysis is applied on unstable monthly products. Again, two tiers of analyses with EM and K-Means algorithms are performed in the Tier-2 quarterly stability analysis.

Tier-1 Quarterly Stability Analysis

Tables 13 and 14 illustrate EM and K-Means clustering results of the Tier-1 quarterly stabil-

ity analysis in 2005 respectively. The optimal clustering results show that only two clusters (groups) are distinguished from data set in 2005. Moreover, the stable groups have 2689 (48%) products in 2005. Statistically, the results are correct as clustering data objects based on their statistic values. However, they do not meet the reality of the real world inventory management. In the real world, stable products do not represent high proportions of total products. This could be caused by the fact that the value of P is limited as 0, 0.25, 0.5, 0.75 and 1.

As an alternative time-series clustering algorithm, K-Means is applied on quarterly stability analysis in 2005. We categorize products into 7

Table 13. Tier-1 quarterly stability analysis with the EM algorithm in 2005

Product Group	Number of Products (Percentage)	Percentage of Non-Zero Values (P)	Mean of Absolute z-Score (A)
Cluster 0	2689 (48%)	0.8472	0.898
Cluster 1	2929 (52%)	0.8944	0.354

Table 14. Tier-1 quarterly stability analysis with the K-Means algorithm in 2005

Product Group	Number of Products (Percentage)	Percentage of Non-Zero Values (P)	Mean of Absolute z-Score (A)
Cluster 0	563 (10%)	0.8331	0.75
Cluster 1	1736 (31%)	0.866	0.25
Cluster 2	777 (14%)	0.8102	1
Cluster 3	1193 (21%)	0.9364	0.5
Cluster 4	799 (14%)	0.9207	1
Cluster 5	218 (4%)	0.6325	0.7764
Cluster 6	332 (6%)	0.9201	0.75

groups (clusters). In this way, we could distinguish products based on their stability levels, such as very stable, relatively stable, stable, normal, unstable, relatively unstable and very unstable. Table 14 show K-Means clustering results of quarterly stability analysis in 2005. According to the results, in 2005, Cluster 2 is a very stable quarterly group since it has the optimal P value (1) and an acceptable A value (0.8102). Cluster 5 can be considered another very stable group since it's A value is the lowest and P value (0.7764) is acceptable. To avoid losing stable quarterly products, 777+218=995 products will be analyzed in the Tier-2 2005 quarterly stability analysis.

Tier-2 Quarterly Stability Analysis

The Tier-2 EM clustering results of these 995 products in the Tier-1 2005 quarterly stability analysis are shown in Table 15. Obviously, Cluster 1 is the most stable group because it has the optimal values of A (0) and P (1). Therefore, 23 products are categorized as stable quarterly products in 2005.

6. SEASONALITY ANALYSIS

In this section we perform monthly seasonality analysis in two-tiers. Within the group of unstable products, `seasonal patterns' is considered as another criterion to further categorize products. That is, unstable products are categorized into groups based on their monthly and quarterly sales patterns. K-Means and EM clustering algorithms are applied again to cluster products. Products are considered seasonal products if their sales quantities periodically change with time. If products' selling ratios in one period are high, they are called single period selling products. In addition, products, which were mostly sold in two periods, are called two-period selling products.

We perform monthly and quarterly seasonality analysis, to discover products' sales patterns. Similar to stability analysis, two tiers of clustering analysis is performed for each level of seasonality analyses. That is, the Tier-1 clustering analysis indicates reasonable seasonal groups and the Tier-2 clustering analysis categorizes these seasonal groups into finer groups. Since the amount of computation in seasonality analysis is rather intensive, the K-Means algorithm is chosen to facilitate seasonality analysis.

Monthly Seasonality Analysis

Products are considered single month selling products if they were mostly sold in one month. Similarly, products that were mostly sold in two months are considered two-months selling products.

Tier-1 Monthly Seasonality Analysis

The Tier-1 2006 monthly seasonality analysis results are illustrated in Table 16. In 2006, Cluster

Table 15. Tier-2 quarterly stability analysis with the EM algorithm in 2005

Product Group	Number of Products (Percentage)	Percentage of Non-Zero Values (P)	Mean of Absolute z-Score (A)
Cluster 0	195 (20%)	0.7071	0.75
Cluster 1	23 (2%)	0	1
Cluster 2	0 (0%)	0.8527	1
Cluster 3	691 (69%)	0.823	1
Cluster 4	86 (9%)	0.7071	0.9339

5 is a single month selling group in January since the normalized sales quantity in January (11.4969) is extremely high. The numbers of products sold in their selling month (January) are extremely high. In addition, these products were rarely sold in off selling months. Clusters 0, 1, 3, 6 and 9 are also single month selling products in May, June, November, July and March, 2006. Products in Cluster 7 were mostly sold in two-months: April (4.581) and August (5.0619). Cluster 2 seems to have a high sales quantity in December. In addition, quite a few sales were made in February. This could be a typical fuzzy group. The Tier-2 monthly seasonality analysis may categorize these products into finer groups.

Tier-2 Monthly Seasonality Analysis

The Tier-1 clustering analysis above provides us with several reasonable groups. The Tier-2 clustering analysis is performed based on these groups so that to identify their sales patterns and categorize them into finer groups. Here, products are categorized into 5 groups based on their seasonality's in monthly sales quantities. Typical Tier-2 monthly seasonality analysis results are discussed below.

The Tier-1 2006 monthly seasonality analysis indicates that Cluster 2 is a fuzzy group. Products in Cluster 2 are further analyzed in the Tier-2 monthly seasonality analysis and the clustering results are shown in Table 17. The results show that products in Cluster 1 are single month selling products in February, 2006. Cluster 0 is also a single month selling group, where products were sold mostly in December. Clusters 2, 3 and 4 are really two-months selling groups in October-December, January-December and August-December, respectively.

Similar to monthly seasonality analysis quarterly seasonality analysis is completed. This study analyzes a retail chain data set for seasonality. The EM and K-Means clustering algorithms are used to facilitate product analyses. According to

Table 16. Tier-1 monthly seasonality analysis in 2006

	Product Groups									
	C-0	**C-1**	**C-2**	**C-3**	**C-4**	**C-5**	**C-6**	**C-7**	**C-8**	**C-9**
Number of Products (%)	216 (3%)	300 (4%)	514 (7%)	341 (5%)	3599 (48%)	564 (8%)	114 (2%)	354 (5%)	1157 (16%)	287 (4%)
Jan	0.489	0.334	0.367	0.429	1.512	11.497	0.089	0.2912	0.7566	0.6418
Feb	0.362	0.229	2.444	0.178	1.016	0.0777	0.003	0.2895	0.4381	0.7014
Mar	0.101	0.432	0.095	0.013	1.024	0.0369	0.100	0.1506	0.4295	8.1342
Apr	0.835	0.253	0.205	0.209	0.958	0.0502	0.057	4.8473	0.6801	0.5225
May	8.157	0.333	0.079	0.075	0.921	0.0209	0.117	0.0779	0.6475	0.484
Jun	0.042	8.221	0.096	0.070	0.894	0.034	0.194	0.1621	0.8398	0.124
Jul	0.380	0.382	0.068	0.093	0.532	0.0679	10.98	0.0879	2.5253	0.2118
Aug	0.396	0.279	0.188	0.411	0.795	0.0242	0.148	5.1765	1.0027	0.3297
Sept	0.390	0.434	0.292	0.326	0.872	0.0594	0.087	0.4115	2.3278	0.3309
Oct	0.206	0.242	0.422	0.639	1.471	0.0064	0.041	0.2417	0.7339	0.1765
Nov	0.285	0.333	0.386	8.538	0.998	0.0525	0.076	0.1457	0.803	0.2025
Dec	0.359	0.528	7.361	1.019	1.008	0.0729	0.109	0.1181	0.8157	0.1408

Table 17. Tier-2 2006 monthly seasonality analysis

	Product Groups				
	C-0	**C-1**	**C-2**	**C-3**	**C-4**
Number of Products(%)	328 (64%)	92 (18%)	43 (8%)	31 (6%)	20 (4%)
Jan	0.101	0	0.0856	**4.8906**	0
Feb	0.4512	**11.902**	0.0558	0.129	0.35
Mar	0.1107	0	0.186	0.0968	0
Apr	0.2901	0	0	0.0968	0.36
May	0.0983	0	0.0558	0	0.3
Jun	0.1284	0	0	0	0.3557
Jul	0.0855	0	0.1395	0	0.05
Aug	0.0519	0	0	0.043	**3.9105**
Sept	0.3569	0	0.2601	0.4731	0.3545
Oct	0.0734	0	**4.3521**	0	0.2945
Nov	0.4707	0.0326	0.6004	0.1742	0.4848
Dec	**9.782**	0.0652	**6.2645**	**6.0965**	**5.5399**

the analysis, 3 stable groups are identified at three levels: weekly (32 products), monthly (87 products) and quarterly (23 products) in 2005. Similarly, in 2006, stable weekly (21 products), monthly (26 products) and quarterly (32 products) groups are identified. There are 50 seasonal groups, including 1485 products, located in 2005 and 49 seasonal groups, including 2194 products, located in 2006. Figures 2 and 3 illustrate product distributions in 2005 and 2006, respectively. Product groups and numbers of products they contained are labeled in the Figures. It can be observed that sales patterns of more than 50% of products have been identified through product analyses.

A comparison between generic optimal solutions and local optimal solutions for specific groups reveals that local optimal solutions out-

Figure 2. Product distribution in 2005

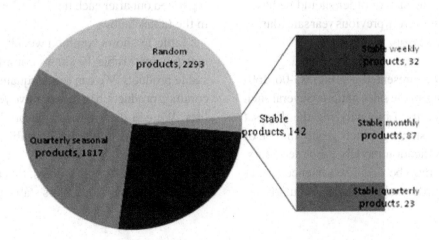

Figure 3. Product distribution in 2006

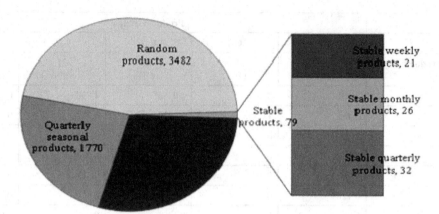

performed generic optimal solutions based on the lower MAPE criterion. The group G-05Q20 represented in case study-1 of section 3 is a local group that exhibits seasonal sells pattern. All 135 products in this group are sold mostly in quarter 1. Hence the generic model could not obtain optimal solution. A different model suits best and generates the optimal solution for products of this group. Simple inventory management strategies are proposed to control seasonal inventories, such as groups discussed in case study-1.

1. Carry very few seasonal products in their off-sales periods. The inventory in off season should be based on quantities from previous year sales during off-season.
2. Order a lot of seasonal products in their sales periods. The size of order should be based on quantities from previous year sales during the same season.

Case study-2 presented a group (G-06M60) that has a strong stable sales pattern. Several such groups are identified by analyzing the data set thoroughly. For stable products group, the use of time series predication models is not necessary. Sometimes it may be disguised. Hence, better strategy is to order stable products regularly for

the pertinent period. The size of order should be stable and based on quantities that came forward as a result of stability analysis.

7. PROGRESSION ANALYSIS

The motivation of the study is to check if the stable products of a certain year carried forward to the next year or not. We listed the common products in successive years and the results thereof are presented in two different tables.

We obtained weekly and monthly stable products for years 2005 to 2009. Appropriate preprocessing and clustering is applied to identify local groups exhibiting weekly and monthly stable sales pattern. The number of distinct products separated out after each tier of clustering is listed in the tables below.

Table 18 shows common weekly stable products whereas Table 19 shows common monthly stable products. We can see adequate numbers of common products in two successive years' product lists. We can determine stable products for the coming year using the list of stable products of previous year.

It is evident from the tables, that at least 33% products from previous years stable products are

Table 18. Weekly stability analysis: common stable products

Year	Number of Products Filtered in Tier-1	Number of Stable Products Obtained Using Tier-2	Number of Common Stable Products	Retention From Previous Year (%)
2005	1366	113		
2006	1714	32	0 (05 06)	0
2007	900	47	1 (06 07)	3.13
2008	1290	177	46 (07 08)	97.87
2009	452	119	105 (08 09)	59.32

Table 19. Monthly stability analysis: common stable products

Year	Number of Products Filtered in Tier-1	Number of Stable Products Obtained Using Tier-2	Number of Common Stable Products	Retention from Previous Year (%)
2005	639	252		
2006	1738	594	188 (05 06)	74.60
2007	423	211	95 (06 07)	15.99
2008	528	259	71 (07 08)	33.65
2009	625	348	136 (08 09)	52.51

retained in the next years monthly stable products (except for year 2005 to 2006). Similarly, except for year 2005 and 2006 more than 59% weekly stable products are also retained. This trend can be useful to determine stable products for the coming year.

In summary, we can say that it is possible to predict weekly as well monthly stable products at the start of every new year. We further explored the transactions to derive cross table analysis that depicts common stable products for all the years. The year wise cross table information of common weekly stable products (Table 20) and common monthly stable products (Table 21) provides insight of the core of products that are common stable products throughout all the years.

For 2005 and 2006, we determined that 188 products are common monthly stable products.

Table 20. Year-wise cross table of common weekly stable products

Years	2006	2007	2008	2009
2005	0	0	0	0
2006		1	2	1
2007			46	34
2008				105

Table 21. Year-wise cross table of common monthly stable products

Years	2006	2007	2008	2009
2005	188	56	39	45
2006		95	105	106
2007			71	95
2008				136

Interestingly, out of 56 common monthly stable products for 2005 and 2007, 51 products are from the previous year's list of 188 common stable products. Similarly for year 2005 and 2008, 32 out 39 products belong to primary list of 188 common stable products. 41 out of 45 common monthly stable products for year 2005 and 2009 are present in the 2005-2006 common monthly stable product list. It indicates that, we can formulate a list of common weekly/monthly stable products that remains common throughout several years and such list constitutes a core of products.

One can easily underline the importance of having a list of products that are weekly or monthly stable. We obtained a list of such common products (core), which led to an overall improved inventory prediction.

8. CONCLUSION

Products in a retail store tend to exhibit different sales patterns. Some of the products sell more or less uniformly day after day. These products demonstrate the most stable sales pattern. Another group of products may sell more or less uniformly throughout the year. While their sales patterns may be similar from week to week, they may show significant daily variations. Similarly, some products may have a stable sales pattern from month to month, with fluctuating daily or weekly demand. Identification of these patterns can be referred to as stability analysis.

Identification of weekly and monthly stable products does help in inventory management. We tested whether stable products (weekly as well as monthly) of a year carries to the next years. We tested our hypothesis on a larger volume of data set having more than 620,000 transaction span over a period of five years (2005 to 2009). We found that more than one third of last year's stable products continue to follow the same sales pattern i.e. weekly or monthly stability trend.

Our progression analysis reveals that most of the stable products of successive years come from the list of stable products of previous years. We can conclude that clustering driven stability analysis can be used as one of the handy tools for better inventory prediction. We are emphasizing the importance of studying the clustering over multiple years to determine the stability trend. Even though different stores might have different trends, the analysis we propose certainly demonstrated stability despite of temporal variations in successive years of transactions.

Our experiments were based on data from a specialty store that is prone to significant innovations of new products and was in a growth phase. A more traditional and stable retail business may find even fewer variations in the clustering driven stability analysis.

REFERENCES

Aviv, Y. (2003). A time series framework for supply-chain inventory management. *Operations Research*, *51*, 210–227. doi:10.1287/opre.51.2.210.12780

Billah, B., King, M. L., Snyder, R. D., & Koehler, A. B. (2006). Exponential smoothing model selection for forecasting. *International Journal of Forecasting*, *22*, 239–247. doi:10.1016/j.ijforecast.2005.08.002

Chatterjee, S., & Hadi, A. S. (2006). *Regression analysis of example* (4th ed.). Hoboken, NJ: Wiley-Interscience. doi:10.1002/0470055464

Contreras, J., Espnola, R., Nogales, F. J., & Conejo, A. J. (2003). ARIMA models to predict next day electricity prices. *IEEE Transactions on Power Systems*, *18*(3), 1014–1021. doi:10.1109/TPWRS.2002.804943

Dempster, A., Laird, N., & Rubin, D. (1977). Maximum likelihood from incomplete data via the EM algorithm. *Journal of the Royal Statistical Society. Series B. Methodological*, *39*(1).

Gardner, E. S., McKenzie, J. R., & McKenzie, E. D. (1989). Seasonal exponential smoothing with damped trends. *Management Science, 35*(3), 372–376. doi:10.1287/mnsc.35.3.372

Gershenfeld, N. A., & Weigend, A. S. (1993). The future of time series. In *Time series prediction: Forecasting the future and understanding the past.* Reading, MA: Addison-Wesley.

Harrison, P. J. (1967). Exponential smoothing and short-term sales forecasting. *Management Science, 13*(11), 821–842. doi:10.1287/mnsc.13.11.821

Hogarth, R. M., & Makridakis, S. (1981). Forecasting and planning: An evaluation. *Management Science, 27*(2), 115–138. doi:10.1287/mnsc.27.2.115

Joshi, M., Lingras, P., Wani, G., & Zheng, P. (2011). Clustering based stability despite of temporal variations. In *Proceedings of the International Conference on Information Technology, Systems and Management (ITSM 2011),* (pp. 306-311). Macmillan Publisher.

Kruger, G. A. (2005). A statistician looks at inventory management. *Quality Progress, 38*(2), 36.

Kumar, M., & Patel, N. (2010). Using clustering to improve sales forecasts in retail merchandising. *Annals of Operations Research, 174*(1), 33–46. doi:10.1007/s10479-008-0417-z

Lawrence, J. (1993). *Introduction to neural networks: Design, theory, and applications.* California Scientific Software Press.

Lingras, P., Zhong, M., & Sharma, S. (2008). Evolutionary regression and neural imputations of missing values. *STUDFUZZ, 226,* 151–163.

MacQueen, J. (1967). Some methods for classification and analysis of multivariate observations. In *Proceedings of Fifth Berkeley Symposium on Mathematical Statistics and Probability,* (pp. 281-297). IEEE.

Mehrez, A., & Hu, M. Y. (1992). A clustering analysis of forecasting methods in a multiobjective inventory system. *International Journal of Production Economics, 27*(1), 1–8. doi:10.1016/0925-5273(92)90121-M

Ray, W. D. (1982). ARIMA forecasting models in inventory control. *The Journal of the Operational Research Society, 33*(6), 567–574.

Silver, E. A., Pyke, D. F., & Peterson, R. (1998). *Inventory management and production planning and scheduling* (3rd ed.). Hoboken, NJ: John Wiley & Sons.

Snyder, R. D., Koehler, A. B., & Ord, J. K. (2002). Forecasting for inventory control with exponential smoothing. *International Journal of Forecasting, 18*(1), 5–18. doi:10.1016/S0169-2070(01)00109-1

Sorjamaa, A., Hao, J., Reyhani, N., Ji, Y., & Lendasse, A. (2007). Methodology for long-term prediction of time series. *Neurocomputing, 70*(16-18), 2861–2869. doi:10.1016/j.neucom.2006.06.015

Stefanovic, N.,Stefanovic, D., & Radenkovic, B. (n.d.). Application of data mining for supply chain inventory forecasting. *Applications and Innovations in Intelligent Systems, 15,* 175-188.

Taylor, J. W. (2003). Short-term electricity demand forecasting using double seasonal exponential smoothing. *The Journal of the Operational Research Society, 54*(8), 799–805. doi:10.1057/palgrave.jors.2601589

Tseng, F. M., Yu, H. C., & Tzeng, G. H. (2002). Combining neural network model with seasonal time series ARIMA model. *Technological Forecasting and Social Change, 69,* 71–87. doi:10.1016/S0040-1625(00)00113-X

Zhang, P., Joshi, M., & Lingras, P. (2011). Use of stability and seasonality analysis for optimal inventory prediction models. *Journal of Intelligent Systems, 20*(2), 20. doi:10.1515/jisys.2011.009

KEY TERMS AND DEFINITIONS

Cluster: A collection of data objects that are similar to one another and thus can be treated collectively as one group.

Clustering: Clustering is a technique to group similar patterns, which can be used for creating profiles.

Inventory Prediction: Inventory prediction is a technique which predicts the future inventory demand based on historical and current demand.

Seasonal Products: Products are considered seasonal product if their sales quantities periodically change with time.

Seasonality Analysis: The process of identification of seasonal products is referred as Seasonality Analysis.

Stability Analysis: The process of identification of stable products and unstable products is referred as Stability Analysis.

Stable Products: Products are called stable if their sales quantities change negligibly over allotted periods.

Time Series: A time series is a chronological sequence of observations on a particular variable.

Unstable Products: Products are called unstable if their sales quantities changed greatly with time.

Chapter 2
Efficient Color Image Segmentation by a Parallel Optimized (ParaOptiMUSIG) Activation Function

Sourav De
University Institute of Technology, University of Burdwan, India

Siddhartha Bhattacharyya
RCC Institute of Information Technology, India

Susanta Chakraborty
Bengal Engineering and Science University, India

ABSTRACT

The optimized class responses from the image content has been applied to generate the optimized version of MUSIG (OptiMUSIG) activation function for a multilayer self organizing neural network architecture to effectively segment multilevel gray level intensity images. This chapter depicts the parallel version of the OptiMUSIG (ParaOptiMUSIG) activation function with the optimized class responses for the individual features with a parallel self-organizing neural network architecture to segment true color images. A genetic algorithm-based optimization technique has been employed to yield the optimized class responses in parallel. Comparison of the proposed method with the existing non-optimized method is applied on two real life true color images and is demonstrated with the help of three standard objective functions as they are employed to measure the quality of the segmented images. Results evolved by the ParaOptiMUSIG activation function are superior enough in comparison with the conventional nonoptimized MUSIG activation applied separately on the color gamut.

DOI: 10.4018/978-1-4666-4936-1.ch002

INTRODUCTION

Segmentation has a pivotal role in different areas ranging from statistics, computer science, engineering, biology to social sciences and economics. Segmentation means the act of partitioning of patterns into disjoint groups or segments such that similar patterns will belong to the same segment while dissimilar patterns will belong to different segments. These similar groups are also referred as clusters. The purpose of segmentation is to detect relevant and meaningful data by means of removal of redundancy embedded therein. Some of the basic criteria of segmentation are based on the variety of data representation, proximity measurement between data elements and grouping of data elements. Some metrics are responsible for the determination of similarity or dissimilarity of patterns. The problem of segmentation can be analytically presented as follows (Das, 2008; Lucchese, 2001): suppose that a d-dimensional pattern $\mathbf{x}$ is denoted as $\mathbf{x} = (x_1, x_2, .., x_d)$, where d denotes the number of features to represent the pattern. The pattern set consists of n elements and it is presented as $P = \{\mathbf{x_1}, \mathbf{x_2} \ldots \mathbf{x_n}\}$ in which the ith pattern in this set is denoted as $\mathbf{x_i} = (x_{i,1}, x_{i,2}, \ldots, x_{i,d})$. Based on some features, the process of segmentation comprises in determining the segments $S_1, S_2, \ldots, S_K$ such that every $\mathbf{x_n}$ belongs to one of these segments and no $\mathbf{x_n}$ belongs to two regions at the same time, i. e. $\bigcup_{i=1}^{K} S_i = P$ and $S_i \cap S_j = \phi \; \forall i \neq j$ (Das, 2008). Different techniques have been applied to segment the set of patterns using all of the aforementioned properties.

Image segmentation is one of the major application areas of segmentation as it is a process of segregating an image space into multiple non-overlapping meaningful homogeneous regions i. e. pixels of each region are homogeneous to each other with respect to some characteristics whereas the union of any two regions is not. It plays a key role in image analysis and pattern recognition and also has other application areas like, machine vision, biometric measurements, medical imaging etc. for the purpose of detecting, recognition or tracking of objects (Das, 2008; Tao, 2007). Color images comprises much more information than the gray level images as color image expresses much more image features than gray scale images (Cheng, 2001). Hence, more complicated segmentation techniques are required to deal with color images as the underlying data exhibits information in primary color components and their admixtures. Nonlinearity in the representation of colors in the color spectrum is another challenge in the processing of color images. In fact, each pixel of color image is characterized either by information in three primary color components, viz., red (R), green (G) and blue (B) or by a number of combinations of R, G, B chromatic components. Thus, processing and understanding of a color image amounts to processing of all the combinations of the primary color components in a true color image. In recent years, it has been detected that color image segmentation has become one of the major investigation areas due to demanding needs.

Review of Literature

Different image segmentation techniques are basically classified into two categories, viz. classical algorithm based approaches and soft computing techniques based approaches (Bhattacharyya, 2011a). Several classical approaches of image segmentation and analysis have been reported in the literature (Gonzalez, 2002; Chen, 2001). Classical image segmentation approaches can be generally relegated into three major categories, i. e., feature space based segmentation, image domain based segmentation and graph based segmentation. In feature space based techniques, image segmentation is achieved by capturing the global characteristics of the image through the selection and calculation of the image features, viz. gray level, color level, texture, to name a few (Gonzalez, 2002; Jacobs, 2000). Histogram thresholding technique is a very common technique in this arena. The histogram thresholding of a color image relies on the peaks or valleys in three color histograms or a three dimensional histogram. A segmentation method to extract regions within a image has been presented by thresholding the HSV histograms of a color image (Androutsos, 1998). A color image segmentation method has been presented by pixel classification in a hybrid color space which is adjusted to analyze the image (Vandenbroucke, 2003). A hybrid color image segmentation technique is proposed by Tan (Tan, 2011) on the basis of histogram thresholding and fuzzy *c*-means algorithm. In this method, the histogram thresholding method has been employed to determine the consistent regions in the color image. The resultant image is again treated with the fuzzy *c*-means algorithm for the betterment of the compactness of the segments. The drawback of the histogram thresholding technique is that this technique overlooks all the spatial relationship information and the detailed edge information of the images except the pixel intensity. Split and merge, region growing, edge detection, etc. are the examples of image domain based segmentation techniques based on the strategy of spatial grouping (Gonzalez, 2002). The working principle of region-based technique is based on the region entities or on the spatial information of the regions. A region growing image segmentation approach, named JSEG, has been proposed by Deng *et al.* (Deng, 1999). This method comprises of color quantization on the basis of the pixel labels of the color images and spatial segmentation. The image segmentation criterion of this method uses the color map employed on the *J*-image and the resultant high and low values in *J*-images denote the possible boundaries and centers of the regions. Ruzon *et al.* (Ruzon, 1999) designed a compass operator to compare color distributions and detect edges in color images. In this method, the color distribution of each pixel in compared on the both side of the region using the Earth Mover's distance (EMD) (Rubner, 1998), a robust histogram-

matching method. But the computational running time of this method is high (Maxwell, 2003). Out of the existing image enhancement procedures, the normalized cut - a graph-theoretic approach has become very popular over the years for addressing the problem of image segmentation. A good overview of the image segmentation using normalized cut is depicted in (Tao, 2007). An image segmentation approach on the basis of normalized cut (Ncut) by figuring out an eigen-system of equations has been proposed by Shi *et al.* (Shi, 2000). The cost function, named as ratio cut, which is based on the graph reduction method is employed to segment color images efficiently (Wang, 2003a). Tao *et al.* (Tao, 2007) pointed out the discontinuity property of the color images that can be preserved by the mean shift algorithm to form the segmented regions and after that the normalized cut has been employed on the segmented regions to reduce the complexity of the process.

The image segmentation techniques using classical approaches always demand some *a priori* knowledge regarding the feature space and its distribution in the image data. These are the limitations of these approaches. But the nonclassical approaches viz. the neuro-fuzzy-genetic approaches work on the underlying data regardless of the distribution and operating parameters. Neural networks are very much favorite tool of the researchers for the processing of the color images as neural networks have different important properties like high degree of parallelism, nonlinear mapping, ability of approximation, adaptation, graceful degradation, error tolerance etc. Several works have been reported where different neural network architectures have been used in this regard (Egmont, 2002; Sammouda, 2004). The competitive learning (CL) is applied for online color clustering on the basis of the least sum of squares criterion (Uchiyama, 1994). This CL method efficiently converges to a local optimum solution for color clustering. Wang *et al.* (Wang, 2003b) proposed a two-stage clustering approach using competitive learning (CL) for fast clustering. The local density centers of the clustering data are identified by the CL and after that an iterative Gravitation Neural Network is applied to agglomerate the resulting codewords in a parallel fashion. Self organizing maps (SOM) (Vesanto, 2000; Jiang, 2004) which are efficient to retrieve the dominant color content of images have been widely employed to color image segmentation arena (Ong, 2002). An ensemble of multiple SOM networks (Jiang, 2004) are employed for color image segmentation in which segmentation is accomplished by the different SOM networks on the basis of the color and spatial features of the image pixels. Finally, the desired output is derived by combining the clustered outputs. The primitive clustering results are generated by training the SOM on the basis of a training set of five-dimensional vectors (R, G, B, and x, y) in (Jiang, 2003). The isolated pixels are eliminated during the segmentation of the image which is done by merging the scattered blocks. In (Arajo, 2009), a fast convergent network named Local Adaptive Receptive Field Self-organizing Map (LARFSOM) is employed to segment color images efficiently. Neural networks are also able categorize content based images efficiently (Park, 2004). In this method, the region segmentation technique is employed to extract the objects from the background and after that the back propagation algorithm is applied in the neural network for feature extraction.

The varied amount of vagueness manifested in the color image intensity gamut can be efficiently handled by fuzzy set theory and fuzzy logic. Fuzzy set theory and fuzzy logic are very much familiar technique in the field of image processing and image classification. A good literature survey of the color image segmentation using fuzzy logic is presented in the literature (Cheng, 2001; Bhattacharyya, 2011). Yang *et al.* (Yang, 2002) proposed an eigen based fuzzy C-means (FCM) clustering algorithm to segment color images. In this method, the eigen space is formed by dividing the selected color pixels of the image. Color image segmentation is achieved by combining the eigen space transform and the FCM method. A fuzzy min-max neural network based color image segmentation technique (FMMIS) is proposed by Estevez *et al.* (Estevez, 2005) to detect the image artifacts. The minimum bounded rectangle (MBR) for each object, present in an image, is determined in this method and then the method grows boxes around starting seed pixels to delineate different object regions in the image. Fuzzy logic in combination with the seeded region growing method is applied for color image segmentation in (Kang, 2009). The initial seed in this method is selected with the proposed fuzzy edge detection method which has been used to detect the connected edges.

Genetic algorithms (GAs) (Goldberg, 1989) are an efficient optimization technique as it has faith on the accumulation of the evidence rather than on the domain dependent knowledge. GAs are ideal for those problems that does not have any knowledge about the domain theories of the problem or it is difficult to formulate the problem. Due to generality of the GAs, they are applied to solve the image segmentation problem without knowing the segmentation techniques used and only requires a segmentation quality measurement criterion. An extensive and detailed work of image segmentation using GAs is depicted by Bhanu *et al.* (Bhanu, 1995). Ramos *et al.* (Ramos, 2004) presented an image segmentation using genetic algorithm. The GAs in combination with the classical fuzzy c-means algorithm (FCM) is applied for color image segmentation and the objective function of the FCM is modified by considering the spatial information of image data and the intensity inhomogeneities (Ballerina, 2004). This image segmentation method does not require the prefiltering step to eliminate the background. Medical image segmentation can be handled by the genetic algorithm though the medical images have poor image contrast and artifacts that result in missing or diffuse organ/tissue boundaries (Maulik, 2009). An unsupervised color image segmentation method by genetic algorithm is presented in (Zingaretti, 2002) as it executes multipass thresholding. Different thresholds are applied in different iterations of the genetic algorithm to segment a wide variety of non-textured images successfully. Pignalberi *et al.* (Pignalberi, 2003) projected a method to segment out surfaces of 3D objects, but this method could be employed to segmentation of 2D images as well.

Scope of Work

In this chapter, we are concerned with the segmentation of true color images. The multilayer self organizing neural network (MLSONN) architecture was presented by Ghosh *et al.* (Ghosh, 1993). This network extracts binary objects from a noisy binary image scene by applying some fuzzy measures of the outputs in the output layer of the network architecture. The standard backpropagation algorithm (Haykin, 1999; Rojas, 1996) is employed to adjust the neighborhood topology based interconnection weights of the network with a view to derive a stable solution. The use of the standard bilevel sigmoidal activation function by this network curtails its application in the multilevel domain. Pure color objects can be extracted from a noisy background using the parallel version of the multilayer self organizing neural network (PSONN) architecture (Bhattacharyya, 2003; Bhattacharyya, 2007). This network comprises of three independent and parallel MLSONNs in which each individual MLSONN is employed to process the individual color components. Bhattacharyya *et al.* (Bhattacharyya, 2008) innovated the multilevel sigmoidal (MUSIG) activation function to guide the self supervised parallel self organizing neural network (PSONN) architecture for true color image segmentation. Since the utilized activation functions use fixed and uniform thresholding parameters, they assume homogeneous image information content. The optimized MUSIG (OptiMUSIG) activation function (De, 2010a) has been generated by a genetic algorithm based optimization procedure. This function integrates the heterogeneous image information content in the MUSIG activation function to segment multilevel gray scale images. The parallel version of the OptiMUSIG (ParaOptiMUSIG) activation function (De, 2012; De, 2010b) is applied in the PSONN architecture to segment true color images. A standard objective function, correlation coefficient (ρ), has been applied to demonstrate the efficiency and effectivity of the ParaOptiMUSIG activation function in (De, 2012). It is to be noted that the most widely discerned limitation of correlation coefficient (ρ) is that it is computationally intensive. This evaluation function is often unable to differentiate two images those are totally heterogeneous to each other and it is also very much sensitive to image skewing, fading, etc. The correlation coefficient may become undetermined, due to division by zero, if one of the test images has constant, uniform intensity.

This chapter is aimed to segment true color images into different number of classes with help of the optimized class boundaries for individual color components. The proposed genetic algorithm based optimization techniques has been applied to generate these color components in parallel. The individual color component is transferred to individual SONNs in the PSONN architecture (Bhattacharyya, 2003; Bhattacharyya, 2007) by differentiating the input true color images into different color components. However, different activation functions are applied for different SONNs. The parallel version of the optimized MUSIG (ParaOptiMUSIG) activation function for the PSONN is designed with the optimized class boundaries for all the color components. These optimized class boundaries are determined from the image context. Finally, the sink layer of the PSONN architecture fuses the processed color component information into a processed color image. The application of the proposed genetic algorithm-based ParaOptiMUSIG activation function approach is demonstrated using true color version of the Lena and Baboon images. The image segmentation evaluation index like, entropy-based index (Chi, 2011; Zhang, 2004) or quantitative-based index (Chi, 2011; Borsotti, 1998) are very much efficient to assess the quality of the image segmentation results. A lower quantitative value or entropy value signifies better segmentations. Three measures, viz., F due to Liu and Yang (Liu, 1994) and F' and Q due to Borsotti *et al.* (Borsotti, 1998) have been applied separately to evaluate the segmentation efficiency of the proposed approach.

MATHEMATICAL PREREQUISITES

An overview of the formal definition of image segmentation and image segmentation validity indices is provided in this section.

The Image Segmentation Problem

Basically, the necessity of the image segmentation is to segregate an image into different homogeneous object regions on the basis of the intensity, spatial coordinates, shape, object textures, etc. like different object centric features. Different literatures in the research arena introduce a number of definitions of the image segmentation problem. A region growing perspective of the image segmentation problem using equivalence relations (Bhattacharyya, 2011b; Liu, 1985) was introduced by Wan *et al.* (Wan, 2003). These equivalence relations, both positive and negative equivalence relations, were also applied into the k-means clustering algorithm (Bhattacharyya, 2011b; Wagstaf, 2001). The concepts of relational object models and equivalence relations have been employed for the purpose of recognition and clustering (Hillel, 2006; Hillel, 2003). In this section, we illustrate the definition of the image segmentation problem.

Definition of Image Segmentation

Let, the intensity values of an image (I) of size $p \times q$ may be denoted as (Bhattacharyya, 2011b) $\aleph = n_{ij}, i \leq p, j \leq q$. An image consists of a spe-

cific permutation of the intensity values, n_{ij}, depending on the intensity distribution. Let, the image may be segmented into K number of target segments/classes. The image segmentation method can be represented as a function (c) and can be denoted as (Bhattacharyya, 2011b)

$$c: \aleph \rightarrow [0...K]. \tag{1}$$

Classification of a gray scale image that has the intensity levels in a range of 0 to 255 into K segments denotes the clustering of gray levels $g_k, 0 \leq k \leq K$ such that (Bhattacharyya, 2011b)

$$0 = g_0 \leq g_1 \leq ... \leq g_k \leq ... \leq g_{K-1} \leq g_K = 255. \tag{2}$$

The kth segment comprises with all the pixels with gray levels in $[g_{k-1}, g_k) = s_k$. The following conditions will be maintained in the individual classes in a K class classified image (Bhattacharyya, 2011b)

- $s_k \cap s_l = \phi$ for $k \neq l, 1 \leq k, l \leq K$
- $\bigcup_{k-1}^{K} s_k = [0...255]$

If the class composition of the image (I) denoted as (Bhattacharyya, 2011b) $S_{(I)} = s_k, 1 \leq k \leq K$, then the objective of the segmentation task is to find out an optimum choice (Bhattacharyya, 2011b) $S_I^* = s_k^*, 1 \leq k \leq K$

Suppose, the number of pixels in class k, $1 \leq k \leq K$ in $S_{(I)}$ is referred as u_k (Bhattacharyya, 2011b). The optimum class sizes

$$u_k^*, 1 \leq k \leq K$$

in S_I^* are represented as (Bhattacharyya, 2011b)

$$\sum_{k=1}^{K} u_k^* = p \times q \tag{3}$$

Let, $\aleph_k = \{n_{ij} \in \aleph \mid c(p_{ij}) = k\}$ (Bhattacharyya, 2011b). An equivalence relation $\sim$ makes an equivalence partition of $\aleph$ into K many classes $\aleph_k$, $1 \leq k \leq K$ with the following conditions (Bhattacharyya, 2011b).

- $\aleph_k \cap \aleph_k = \phi, \forall k \neq l, 1 \leq k, l \leq K$
- $\bigcup_{k-1}^{K} \aleph_k = \aleph$

The segmentation process reduces to detecting the optimum partition $\{\aleph_k, 1 \leq k \leq K\}$ of $\aleph$, which is going to be inducted by the choice of S_I^*.

Image Segmentation Evaluation Indices

An overview of three different empirical measures to determine the quality of the segmented images is provided in this subsection.

F (M) Measure

Liu and Yang (Liu, 1994) proposed a quantitative evaluation function (EF), $F(M)$, denoted as

$$F\left(M\right) = \sqrt{N} \sum_{re=1}^{N} \frac{e_{re}^2}{\sqrt{S_{re}}} \qquad (4)$$

where, the entire image is denoted as M and N signifies the number of arbitrarily shaped regions of the image. RE_{re} represents the number of pixels in region re. The area of the re region is represented as $S_{re} = |RE_{re}|$. e_{re}^2, the squared color error of region re, is given as (Liu, 1994)

$$e_{re}^2 = \sum_{v \in (R,G,B)} \sum_{px \in RE_{re}} \left(C_v\left(px\right) - \widehat{C_v}(RE_{re})\right)^2 \qquad (5)$$

Here, $\widehat{C_v}\left(RE_{re}\right)$ is the average value of feature v (*R*ed, *G*reen or *B*lue) of a pixel px in region re and denoted as (Liu, 1994)

$$\widehat{C_v}\left(RE_{re}\right) = \frac{\sum_{px \in RE_{re}} C_v(px)}{S_{re}} \qquad (6)$$

where, $C_v(px)$ denotes the value of component v for pixel px.

F′ (M) Measure

Borsotti *et al.* (Borsotti, 1998) suggested another EF, $F'(M)$, that improved the performance of Liu and Yang's method (Liu, 1994). It is represented as

$$F'(M) = \frac{1}{1000.S_M} \sqrt{\sum_{u=1}^{Maxarea} \left[N\left(u\right)\right]^{1+\frac{1}{u}}} \sum_{r=1}^{N} \frac{e_{re}^2}{\sqrt{S_{re}}} \qquad (7)$$

where, S_M is the area of an image (M) to be segmented. *Maxarea* is represented as the area of the largest region in the segmented image. $N(u)$ denotes the number of regions in the segmented image having an area of exactly u.

Q (M) Measure

Borsotti *et al.* (Borsotti, 1998) proposed another EF, $Q(M)$, defined as

$$Q\left(M\right) = \frac{1}{1000.S_M} \sqrt{N} \sum_{re=1}^{N} \left[\frac{e_{re}^2}{1 + \log S_{re}} + \left(\frac{N\left(S_{re}\right)}{S_{re}}\right)^2\right] \qquad (8)$$

where, $N(S_{re})$ stands for the number of regions having an area S_{re}.

These measures have been applied as different objective functions for the proposed genetic algorithm based optimization procedure to design the optimized multilevel sigmoidal activation function that is to be used for segmenting true color images using a PSONN architecture (Bhattacharyya, 2003; Bhattacharyya, 2007).

PARALLEL SELF ORGANIZING NEURAL NETWORK (PSONN) ARCHITECTURE

Three independent single three-layer self organizing neural network (SONN) architecture for component level processing constitute the parallel version of the self organizing neural network (PSONN) (Bhattacharyya, 2003; Bhattacharyya, 2007) in addition with a source layer for inputs to the network and a sink layer for generating the final network output. This network can be employed for extracting pure color objects from a pure color image (Bhattacharyya, 2003). The source layer disperses the primary color component information of true color images into the three parallel SONN architectures. After processing of each color components at these three parallel SONN architectures, the sink layer fuses and generates the final pure color output images. However, the three parallel self organizing neural network architectures operate in a self supervised mode on multiple shades of color component information (Bhattacharyya, 2003). The linear indices of fuzziness of the color component information obtained at the respective output layers are employed to calculate the system errors. The respective interlayer interconnection weights using the standard backpropagation algorithm (Haykin, 1999; Rojas, 1996) are adjusted with these system errors. This method of self supervision is proceeded on until the system errors at the output layers of the three independent SONNs fall below some tolerable limits. The extracted color component outputs are produced by the corresponding output layers of three independent SONN architectures. Finally, the extracted pure color output image is developed by mixing the segmented component outputs at

the sink layer of the PSONN network architecture (Bhattacharyya, 2003; Bhattacharyya, 2007). Basically, the object and the background regions in the input image are segregated on the basis of the intensity features of the pixels of different regions. The PSONN network architecture (Bhattacharyya, 2003; Bhattacharyya, 2007) is not capable to segment multilevel input images i. e. inputs which consist of different heterogeneous shades of image pixel intensity levels. This is solely due to the fact that the constituent primitives/SONNs resort to the use of the standard bilevel sigmoidal activation functions. However, the problem of these network architectures can be facilitated by resorting to a modified PSONN network architecture. For this reason, Bhattacharyya *et al.* (Bhattacharyya, 2008) introduced a multilevel version of the generalized bilevel sigmoidal activation function. The novelty of the multilevel sigmoidal (MUSIG) activation (Bhattacharyya, 2008) function consists of its ability to map inputs into multiple output levels and capable to segment true color images efficiently. The detailed review of the architecture and operational characteristics of the PSONN network architecture can be found in the article (Bhattacharyya, 2003; Bhattacharyya, 2007).

PARALLEL OPTIMIZED MULTILEVEL SIGMOIDAL (PARAOPTIMUSIG) ACTIVATION FUNCTION

Segmentation of the true color images, using a PSONN architecture (Bhattacharyya, 2003; Bhattacharyya, 2007) by optimized embedding functional characteristics in the constituent SONN primitives obtained from the true color image context is the main objective of this chapter. The three coupled SONNs are applied to process the R, G and B color components after decomposing the inherent color components. Each color component of a particular pixel is segregated into different class levels in parallel. For a particular pixel after segmentation, the individual segmented class levels of the individual color components are aggregated to generate the segmented image.

In a general overview, this method can be regarded as a problem of segmentation of a multidimensional dataset, where the segmentation of every feature can be carried out simultaneously in parallel. The resultant segmented value of that datapoint is thereby obtained through the combination of all the features in the parallel segmentation process. It has been observed in most of the cases that the selection of the different class levels for the segmentation of such a dataset can be usually influenced heuristically from the histograms of the k features of the dataset. In those cases heterogeneity of the underlying information is generally ignored as the data points in a real life dataset generally manifest a fair amount of heterogeneity and the class levels generally differ from one dataset to another. Such a heuristic approach does not always reflect the true essence of information content underneath. Thus, like the single dimensional dataset, the heterogeneity characteristics of the data points of that dataset can be integrated in the segmentation process.

Among the different techniques for segmenting datasets, neural network is quite efficient enough to manage the segmentation of the multidimensional data points of the dataset due to its parallelism characteristics. Thus, the processing of the multidimensional feature of the data points can be undertaken in parallel. The individual neural networks are employed to process the individual feature of the multidimensional data points in parallel and independently. In particular for a kth dimensional dataset, one can either employ an ensemble of competitive neural networks (Ceccarelli, 1997; Azimi, 1993) with a voting mechanism or a collection of neural networks connected in parallel (Bhattacharyya, 2007) assigned for each and every feature of the data points in the dataset to decide on the final segmentation procedure.

The neural networks reach their goals by updating the network weights dynamically. Basically, the performance of the neural network architectures depend on the activation/transfer functions of the neural networks. The standard bilevel sigmoidal activation function is one of the commonly used activation function in neural networks as the function generates the bipolar responses [0(low)/1(high)] corresponding to input information. This function is unable to classify the data features into multiple levels. It will be quite helpful if the activation function has the capability to handle multilevel characteristics of the dataset instead of including multiple layers for multilevel datasets.

In order to generate multilevel outputs corresponding to the multiple scales of the data points, the multilevel form of the sigmoidal activation function is denoted as multilevel sigmoidal (MUSIG) activation function (Bhattacharyya, 2008) and the generalized form of the MUSIG activation function is denoted as (Bhattacharyya, 2008)

$$f_{MUSIG}\left(x; \alpha_\xi, cl_\xi\right) = \sum_{\xi=1}^{K-1} \frac{1}{\alpha_\xi + e^{-\lambda\left[x-(\xi-1)cl_\xi-\theta\right]}} \quad (9)$$

where α_ξ represents the multilevel class responses. α_ξ is represented by (Bhattacharyya, 2008)

$$\alpha_\xi = \frac{C_N}{cl_\xi - cl_{\xi-1}} \quad (10)$$

where, ξ denotes the feature class index ($1 \leq \xi < K$) and K is the total number of feature classes. The transfer characteristics of the MUSIG activation function is also checked by the ξ parameter. The feature contributions of the ξth and $(\xi-1)^{th}$ classes are represented by the cl_ξ and $cl_{\xi-1}$, respectively. The maximum fuzzy membership of the feature contribution of neighborhood geometry is denoted as C_N. The threshold parameter (θ) in the MUSIG activation function is fixed and uniform.

However, the class boundaries (cl_ξ) used by the MUSIG activation function are chosen randomly from the feature histograms of the input data points and this function is totally independent of the nature and distribution of the operated dataset. The class levels of the data points can be incorporated in the characteristics neuronal activations by the optimized class boundaries derived from the dataset. The optimized version of the MUSIG activation (OptiMUSIG) (De, 2010a) function, using optimized class boundaries, can be represented as (De, 2010a)

$$f_{OptiMUSIG} = \sum_{\xi_{opt}=1}^{K-1} \frac{1}{\alpha_{\xi_{opt}} + e^{-\lambda\left[x-(\xi-1)cl_{\xi_{opt}}-\theta_{var}\right]}} \qquad (11)$$

where, $cl_{\xi_{opt}}$ are the optimized feature contributions corresponding to optimized class boundaries. $\alpha_{\xi_{opt}}$ are the respective optimized multilevel class responses. θ_{var} is a variable threshold and it depends on the optimized class boundaries and is represented as (De, 2010a)

$$\theta_{var} = cl_{\xi_{opt-1}} + \frac{cl_{\xi_{opt}} - cl_{\xi_{opt-1}}}{2} \qquad (12)$$

Each individual SONN primitive of PSONN architecture (Bhattacharyya, 2003; Bhattacharyya, 2007) is activated with the OptiMUSIG activation function with appropriate optimized parameter settings. The parallel representation of the Opti-MUSIG (ParaOptiMUSIG) activation function is referred as (De, 2010b)

$$f_{ParaOptiMUSIG} = \sum_{t\in\{t_1,t_2,..,t_n\}} f_{t_{OptiMUSIG}} \qquad (13)$$

where $\{t_1, t_2, ..., t_n\}$ denotes the different layers of the parallel self organizing neural network (PSONN) (Bhattacharyya, 2003; Bhattacharyya, 2007) architecture and $f_{t_{OptiMUSIG}}$ denotes the Opti-MUSIG activation function for one layer of the network (De, 2010b). The collection of the Opti-MUSIG functions of different layers is denoted by the $\sum$ sign. The genetic algorithm is applied in parallel to generate the optimized class boundaries for different OptiMUSIG activation functions of different layers. A designed ParaOptiMUSIG activation function for the different R, G, B color components for $K = 8$ classes with the optimized color levels to process the individual color components is shown in Figure 1. In the same way, the three different MUSIG activation functions are employed in parallel to process the different R, G, B color components for $K = 8$ classes of the constituent component networks. It is discernible from Figure 1 and 2 that the transition lobes of the constituent R, G, B components of the ParaOptiMUSIG activation function in Figure 1 are sharply and distinctly spread from each other as compared to the heuristically designed R, G, B collections in the MUSIG activation function in Figure 2. Thus, the applicability of the ParaOptiMUSIG activation function is more appropriate for the true color images than the MUSIG activation functions for the same as far as the incorporation of the heterogeneity of the images under consideration.

PARAOPTIMUSIG ACTIVATION FUNCTION BASED COLOR IMAGE SEGMENTATION SCHEME

This section describes the proposed true color image segmentation technique by ParaOptiMUSIG activation function with a PSONN architecture in detail. The different phases of this technique are discussed elaborately in the following subsections.

Figure 1. ParaOptiMUSIG activation function applied for R, G and B color components with optimized class responses for K = 8 classes

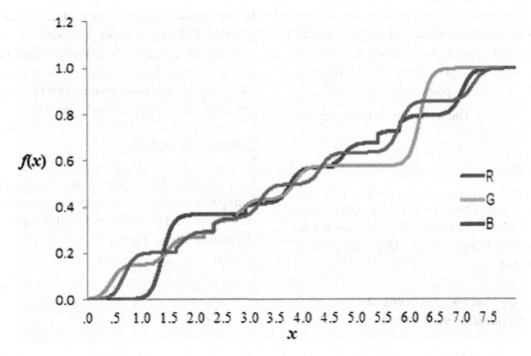

Figure 2. Three MUSIG activation function applied in parallel for R, G and B color components for K = 8 classes

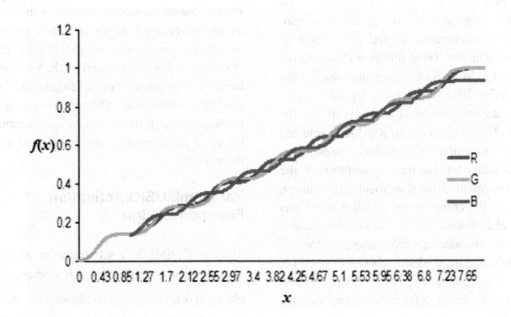

Optimized Class Boundaries Generation for True Color Images

In this most important phase of the proposed approach, a GA-based optimization procedure is applied to generate the optimized class boundaries ($cl_{\xi_{opt}}$) of the proposed ParaOptiMUSIG activation function. The procedure employed in this phase is as follows.

Input Phase

The pixel intensity levels of the true color image and the number of classes (K) to be segmented are supplied as inputs to this GA based optimization procedure.

Chromosome Representation and Population Generation

A binary encoding technique for the chromosomes is applied for originating the optimized class boundaries from the input true color image information content. Each pixel intensity of the true color image information is differentiated into three color components, viz. red, green and blue color components. Three different chromosome pools are produced for the three individual color components. Each chromosome pool is used to generate the optimized class levels for the individual color component. Randomly selected binary combinations of eight bits represent the class boundary level of the segmentation. If the image is segmented into K segments in the image, the size of the chromosome equals $K{\times}8{\times}3$ bits and the class boundaries for the individual color component encoded in a chromosome in the initial population are randomly chosen to obtain K distinct class boundaries from the image content. A population size of 200 has been employed for this treatment.

Fitness Computation

In this phase, three segmentation evaluation criterias (F, F', Q) given in Equations 4, 7 and 8 respectively, are applied separately as the fitness functions. These functions are applied to evaluate the quality of the segmented images in this genetic algorithm based optimization procedure.

Genetic Operators

In the selection phase, a proportionate fitness selection operator is employed to select the reproducing chromosomes. The selection probability of the ith chromosome is evaluated as

$$p_i = \frac{f_i}{\sum\limits_{j=1}^{n} f_j} \tag{14}$$

where f_i is the fitness value of the ith chromosome and n is the population size. The cumulative fitness p_i of each chromosome is evaluated by adding individual fitnesses in ascending order. Subsequently, the crossover and mutation operators are applied to evolve a new population. In this approach, the crossover probability is equal to 0.8. A single point crossover operation is applied to generate the new pool of chromosomes. The mutation probability is taken as 0.1 in this approach. After mutation, the child chromosomes are propagated to form the new generation.

ParaOptiMUSIG Activation Function Design

The ParaOptiMUSIG activation function is designed by the optimized class boundaries ($cl_{\xi_{opt}}$) obtained from the previous phase. The optimized class boundaries for individual color component in the selected chromosomes are applied to generate the individual OptiMUSIG activation function for that color component, viz. the class boundaries for the red component is employed to generate OptiMUSIG activation function for red and so on. The ParaOptiMUSIG function is derived by collection of the individual OptiMUSIG functions generated for the individual color components using Equation 13.

Input of True Color Image Pixel Values to the Source Layer of the PSONN Architecture

In this phase, the source layer of the PSONN architecture is fed with the pixel intensity levels of the true color image. The number of neurons in the source layer of the PSONN architecture is same as the number of the pixels in the processed image.

Distribution of the Color Component Images to Three Individual SONNs

The individual primary color components are differentiated from the pixel intensity levels of the input true color image and the three individual three-layer component SONNs are used for these individual primary color components, viz. the red component is applied to one SONN, the green component to another SONN and the remaining SONN accepts the blue component information at their respective input layers. The fixed interconnections of the respective SONNs with the source layer are responsible for this scenario.

Segmentation of Color Component Images by Individual SONNs

The corresponding SONN architecture channelized by the projected ParaOptiMUSIG activation function at the individual primitives/neurons is applied to segment the individual color components of the true color images. Depending on the number of transition lobes of the ParaOptiMUSIG activa-

tion function the neurons of the different layers of individual three-layer SONN architecture yield different input color component level responses. The system errors are evaluated by the subnormal linear index of fuzziness (Bhattacharyya, 2008) at the corresponding output layers of the individual SONNs since the network has no *a priori* knowledge about the outputs. The standard backpropagation algorithm (Haykin, 1999; Rojas, 1996) is then applied to adjust the interconnection weights between the different layers to minimize the errors. The respective output layers of the independent SONNs render the final color component images when the self supervisions of the corresponding networks achieve stabilization.

Fusion of Individual Segmented Component Outputs into a True Color Image at the Sink Layer of the PSONN Architecture

The segmented outputs derived at the three output layers of the three independent three-layer SONN architectures are fused at the sink layer of the PSONN architecture to deduce the segmented true color image. The number of segments is a combination of the number of transition lobes of the designed ParaOptiMUSIG activation functions applied during component level segmentation.

EXPERIMENTAL RESULTS

In this chapter, two real life true color images viz. Lena and Baboon each of dimensions 256 × 256 have been used to demonstrate the purported true color image segmentation approach using the ParaOptiMUSIG activation function in connection with the PSONN architecture. The ParaOptiMUSIG activation function has been prepared with a fixed slope, $\lambda = \{2, 4\}$ for $K = \{4, 6, 8\}$ classes. In this chapter, the results are reported with a fixed slope $\lambda = 4$ in combination with $\{6, 8\}$ classes. In the following sections, the quantifiable performance analysis of the proposed GA based ParaOptiMUSIG activation function and the corresponding segmented outputs are depicted, respectively. The segmentation derived by the conventional MUSIG activation function with same number of class responses and with heuristic class levels is compared with the proposed approach. Segmentation efficiency of the conventional MUSIG activation function as regards to its efficacy in the segmentation of true color test images are elaborated in the following sections.

Quantitative Performance Analysis of Segmentation

Three evaluation functions (F, F' and Q) have been employed separately to demonstrate the quantitative measures of the efficiency of the proposed ParaOptiMUSIG and the conventional MUSIG activation functions for $K = \{6, 8\}$ in this section. The ParaOptiMUSIG activation function based experimental evaluation results have been discussed in the following subsection and the corresponding results deduced with the conventional fixed class response based MUSIG activation function are illustrated in the next subsection.

ParaOptiMUSIG Activation Function based Segmentation Evaluation

The genetic algorithm based optimization procedure generates the optimized sets of class boundaries $cl_{\xi_{opt}}$ on the basis of three evaluation function (F, F' and Q) for different number of classes. These are tabulated in Tables 1-6 (in the Appendix) for the two test images. The first column of these tables shows the name of the image. The evaluation functions (EF_{op}) which are treated as the fitness functions in this proposed approach are shown in the second columns of these tables and the optimized set of class boundaries are accounted in the fourth column of the tables. Two set of results per evaluation function of each test

image are reported. The last columns of the tables show the quality measures η [graded on a scale of 1 (best) to 2 (worst)] obtained by the segmentation of the test images based on the corresponding set of optimized class boundaries. The bold-faced result in each table denotes the best values obtained by the proposed approach for easy reckoning. These quality measures are applied to compare with the quality measures those are derived with the heuristically selected class boundary based conventional MUSIG activation function.

Segmentation Evaluation by MUSIG Activation Function

In the same manner, the second column of the Tables 1 through 6 (in the Appendix) are tabulated with the evaluation functions (EF_{fx}) corresponding to the heuristically selected class boundaries with the conventional MUSIG activation function. The corresponding quality measures assessed after the segmentation process along with the boldfaced best results are also shown alongside. It is quite observable from these tables that the fitness values derived by the ParaOptiMUSIG activation function are better than those obtained by the conventional MUSIG activation function.

True Color Image Segmentation Outputs

The segmented true color output images obtained with the proposed GA based optimized approach and those obtained with the heuristically chosen class boundaries according to the quantitative measure, are demonstrated in this section.

ParaOptiMUSIG Guided Segmented Outputs

The proposed ParaOptiMUSIG activation function based PSONN architecture is applied to generate the segmented multilevel test images for $K = 8$

and corresponding to the best segmentation quality measures (F, F', Q) achieved, are shown in Figures 3 through 8 (in the Appendix).

MUSIG Guided Segmented Outputs

The segmented multicolor test images obtained with the conventional MUSIG activation function based PSONN architecture characterized by fixed class responses for $K = 8$ and with different segmentation quality measures (F, F', Q) achieved, are presented in Figures 9 through 14 (in the Appendix).

It is quite clear from the derived results that the ParaOptiMUSIG activation function overwhelms its conventional MUSIG counterpart in respect of the segmentation quality of the images for the different number of classes. It is also be evident that the ParaOptiMUSIG function incorporates the image heterogeneity as it can handle a wide variety of image intensity distribution prevalent in real life.

CONCLUSION

A segmentation procedure of true color images has been demonstrated with the parallel self organizing neural network (PSONN) architecture in this chapter. A parallel optimized multilevel MUSIG activation function is described to introduce the multiscaling capabilities in the network. In this chapter, it has been noted that the fixed and heuristic class responses are employed in the MUSIG activation function. The MUSIG activation function is unaware of the underneath information of the image data. A parallel version of the optimized MUSIG (ParaOptiMUSIG) activation function is purported with the optimized class boundaries by incorporating the intensity gamut immanent in the input images. The optimized class boundaries are deduced by a genetic algorithm based optimization procedure with three different entropy based objective functions. These functions are treated

as measures of image segmentation quality. The performance of the proposed ParaOptiMUSIG activation function for the segmentation of real life true color images indicate superior performance as compared to the conventional MUSIG activation function with fixed and heuristic class levels.

This color image segmentation method is done on the basis of single objective based parallel OptiMUSIG (ParaOptiMUSIG) activation function. The derived segmented color image for one evaluation function may or may not generate better result for another evaluation function. A set of alternative solutions may yield instead of a single optimal solution when we consider different criterions of a problem at a go. Multiple segmentation evaluation measures will be optimized simultaneously to overcome the problem. The authors are working in this direction.

REFERENCES

Androutsos, D., Plataniotis, K. N., & Venetsanopoulos, A. N. (1998). Distance measures for color image retrieval. *Proceedings IEEE Conference Image Processing, 2*, 770-774.

Araújo, A. R. F., & Costa, D. C. (2009). Local adaptive receptive field self-organizing map for image color segmentation. *Image and Vision Computing, 27*(9), 1229–1239. doi:10.1016/j.imavis.2008.11.014

Azimi-Sadjadi, M. R., Ghaloum, S., & Zoughi, R. (1993). Terrain classification in SAR images using principal component analysis and neural networks. *IEEE Transactions on Geoscience and Remote Sensing, 31*(2), 511–515. doi:10.1109/36.214928

B-Hillel. A., Hertz, T., Shental, N., & Weinshall, D. (2003). Learning distance functions using equivalence relations. In *Proceedings of the 20th International Conference on Machine Learning (ICML-2003)*. Washington, DC: ICML.

B-Hillel. A., & Weinshall, D. (2006). Subordinate class recognition using relational object models. In Advances in Neural Information Processing Systems. Cambridge, MA: MIT Press.

Ballerini, L., Bocchi, L., & Johansson, C. (2004). Image segmentation by a genetic fuzzy c-means algorithm using color and spatial information. *Applications of Evolutionary Computing, 3005,* 260–269. doi:10.1007/978-3-540-24653-4_27

Bhanu, B., Lee, S., & Ming, J. (1995). Adaptive image segmentation using a genetic algorithm. *IEEE Transactions on Systems, Man, and Cybernetics, 25*(12), 1543–1567. doi:10.1109/21.478442

Bhattacharyya, S. (2011a). A brief survey of color image preprocessing and segmentation techniques. *Journal of Pattern Recognition Research, 1*(1), 120–129. doi:10.13176/11.191

Bhattacharyya, S., & Dasgupta, K. (2003). Color object extraction from a noisy background using parallel multilayer self-organizing neural networks. *Proceedings of CSI-YITPA (E), 2003,* 32-36.

Bhattacharyya, S., Dutta, P., & Maulik, U. (2008). Self organizing neural network (SONN) based gray scale object extractor with a multilevel sigmoidal (MUSIG) activation function. *Foundations of Computing and Decision Sciences, 33*(2), 131–165.

Bhattacharyya, S., Dutta, P., Maulik, U., & Nandi, P. K. (2007). Multilevel activation functions for true color image segmentation using a self supervised parallel self organizing neural network (PSONN) architecture: A comparative study. *International Journal on Computer Sciences, 2*(1).

Bhattacharyya, S., Maulik, U., & Dutta, P. (2011b). Multilevel image segmentation with adaptive image context based thresholding. *Applied Soft Computing, 11,* 946–962. doi:10.1016/j.asoc.2010.01.015

Borsotti, M., Campadelli, P., & Schettini, R. (1998). Quantitative evaluation of color image segmentation results. *Pattern Recognition Letters, 19,* 741–747. doi:10.1016/S0167-8655(98)00052-X

Ceccarelli, M., & Petrosino, A. (1997). Multi-feature adaptive classifiers segmentation for SAR image. *Journal of Neuro-Computing, 14,* 345–363.

Chen, H.-C., Chien, W.-J., & Wang, S.-J. (2004). Contrast-based color image segmentation. *IEEE Signal Processing Letters, 11*(7), 641–644. doi:10.1109/LSP.2004.830116

Cheng, H. D., Jiang, X. H., Sun, Y., & Wang, J. (2001). Color image segmentation: Advances and prospects. *Pattern Recognition, 34*(12), 2259–2281. doi:10.1016/S0031-3203(00)00149-7

Chi, D. (2011). Self-organizing map-based color image segmentation with k-means clustering and saliency map. *ISRN Signal Processing, 2011.* doi:10.5402/2011/393891

Das, S., Abraham, A., & Konar, A. (2008). Automatic clustering using an improved differential evolution algorithm. *IEEE Transactions on Systems, Man, and Cybernetics. Part A, Systems and Humans, 38*(1), 218–237. doi:10.1109/TSMCA.2007.909595

De, S., Bhattacharyya, S., & Chakraborty, S. (2010b). True color image segmentation by an optimized multilevel activation function. In *Proceedings of 2010 IEEE International Conference on Computational Intelligence and Computing Research,* (pp. 545-548). IEEE.

De, S., Bhattacharyya, S., & Chakraborty, S. (2012). Color image segmentation using parallel OptiMUSIG activation function. *Applied Soft Computing Journal, 12*(10), 3228–3236. doi:10.1016/j.asoc.2012.05.011

De, S., Bhattacharyya, S., & Dutta, P. (2010a). Efficient gray level image segmentation using an optimized MUSIG (OptiMUSIG) activation function. *International Journal of Parallel. Emergent and Distributed Systems, 26*(1), 1–39.

Deng, Y., Manjunath, B. S., & Shin, H. (1999). Color image segmentation. In *Proceedings of IEEE Conference Computer Vision Pattern Recognition*, (pp. 1021-1025). IEEE.

Egmont-Petersen, M., & de Ridder, D. (2002). Image processing using neural networks - A review. *Pattern Recognition, 35*(10), 2279–2301. doi:10.1016/S0031-3203(01)00178-9

Estevez, P. A., Flores, R. J., & Perez, C. A. (2005). Color image segmentation using fuzzy min-max neural networks. *Proceedings of IEEE International Joint Conference on Neural Networks, 5,* 3052-3057.

Ghosh, A., Pal, N. R., & Pal, S. K. (1993). Self-organization for object extraction using a multilayer neural network and fuzziness measures. *IEEE Transactions on Fuzzy Systems, 1*(1), 54–68. doi:10.1109/TFUZZ.1993.390285

Goldberg, D. E. (1989). *Genetic algorithm in search optimization and machine learning*. Reading, MA: Addison-Wesley.

Gonzalez, R. C., & Woods, R. E. (2002). *Digital image processing*. Upper Saddle River, NJ: Prentice Hall.

Haykin, S. (1999). *Neural networks: A comprehensive foundation*. Upper Saddle River, NJ: Prentice Hall.

Jacobs, D. W., Weinshall, D., & Gdalyahu, Y. (2000). Classification with nonmetric distances: Image retrieval and class representation. *IEEE Transactions on Pattern Analysis and Machine Intelligence, 22*(6), 583–600. doi:10.1109/34.862197

Jiang, Y., Chen, K. J., & Zhou, Z. H. (2003). SOM-based image segmentation. In *Proceedings of 9th Conf. Rough Sets, Fuzzy Sets, Data Mining and Granular Computing*, (pp. 640-643). IEEE.

Jiang, Y., & Zhou, Z. (2004). SOM ensemble-based image segmentation. *Neural Processing Letters, 20*(3), 171–178. doi:10.1007/s11063-004-2022-8

Kang, C. C., & Wang, W. J. (2009). *Fuzzy based seeded region growing for image segmentation*. Paper presented at the 2009 Annual Meeting of the North American Fuzzy Information Processing Society. New York, NY.

Liu, C. L. (1985). *Elements of discrete mathematics* (2nd ed.). New York: McGraw-Hill.

Liu, J., & Yang, Y. H. (1994). Multi-resolution color image segmentation. *IEEE Transactions on Pattern Analysis and Machine Intelligence, 16*(7), 689–700. doi:10.1109/34.297949

Lucchese, L., & Mitra, S. K. (2001). Color image segmentation: A state-of-art survey. *Image Processing, Vision, and Pattern Recognition, 67*(2), 207–221.

Maulik, U. (2009). Medical image segmentation using genetic algorithms. *Proceedings of 16th Annual International Conference of the IEEE Engineering in Medicine and Biology Society, 13*(2), 166-173.

Maxwell, B. A., & Brubaker, S. J. (2003). Texture edge detection using the compass operator. *University of Pennsylvania Law Review in British Machine Vision Conference, 154*(3), 477.

Ong, S. H., Yeo, N. C., Lee, K. H., Venkatesh, Y. V., & Cao, D. M. (2002). Segmentation of color images using a two-stage self-organizing network. *Image and Vision Computing*, *20*, 279–289. doi:10.1016/S0262-8856(02)00021-5

Park, S. B., Lee, J. W., & Kim, S. K. (2004). Content-based image classification using a neural network. *Pattern Recognition Letters*, *25*, 287–300. doi:10.1016/j.patrec.2003.10.015

Pignalberi, G., Cucchiara, R., Cinque, L., & Levialdi, S. (2003). Tuning range image segmentation by genetic algorithm. *EURASIP Journal on Applied Signal Processing*, *8*, 780–790. doi:10.1155/S1110865703303087

Ramos, V., & Muge, F. (2004). Image colour segmentation by genetic algorithms. *Pattern Recognition*, 125–129.

Rojas, R. (1996). *Neural networks: A systematic introduction*. Berlin: Springer-Verlag.

Rubner, Y., Tomasi, C., & Guibas, L. J. (1998). A metric for distributions with applications to image databases. In *Proceedings International Conference on Computer Vision*, (pp. 59-66). ICV.

Ruzon, M. A., & Tomasi, C. (1999). Color edge detection with the compass operator. *Computer Vision Pattern Recognition*, *2*, 511–514.

Sammouda, M., Sammouda, R., Niki, N., & Benaichouche, M. (2004). Tissue color images segmentation using artificial neural networks. In *Proceedings of IEEE International Symposium on Biomedical Imaging: Nano to Macro*, (pp. 145-148). IEEE.

Shi, J., & Malik, J. (2000). Normalized cuts and image segmentation. *IEEE Transactions on Pattern Analysis and Machine Intelligence*, *22*(8), 888–905. doi:10.1109/34.868688

Tan, K. S., & Isa, N. A. M. (2011). Color image segmentation using histogram thresholding Fuzzy C-means hybrid approach. *Pattern Recognition*, *44*, 1–15.

Tao, W., Jin, H., & Zhang, Y. (2007). Color image segmentation based on mean shift and normalized cuts. *IEEE Transactions on Systems, Man, and Cybernetics. Part B, Cybernetics*, *37*(5), 1382–1389. doi:10.1109/TSMCB.2007.902249 PMID:17926718

Uchiyama, T., & Arbib, M. A. (1994). Color image segmentation using competitive learning. *IEEE Transactions on Pattern Analysis and Machine Intelligence*, *16*(12), 1197–1206. doi:10.1109/34.387488

Vandenbroucke, N., Macaire, L., & Postaire, J. G. (2003). Color image segmentation by pixel classification in an adapted hybrid color space: Application to soccer image analysis. *Computer Vision and Image Understanding*, *90*(2), 190–216. doi:10.1016/S1077-3142(03)00025-0

Vesanto, J., & Alhoniemi, E. (2000). Clustering of the self-organizing map. *IEEE Transactions on Pattern Analysis and Machine Intelligence*, *11*(3), 586–600. PMID:18249787

Wagstaf, K., Cardie, C., Rogers, S., & Schroedl, S. (2001). Constrained K-means clustering with back-ground knowledge. In *Proceedings of the 18th International Conference on Machine Learning*. San Francisco: Morgan Kaufmann.

Wan, S.-Y., & Higgins, W. E. (2003). Symmetric region growing. *IEEE Transactions on Image Processing*, *12*(8), 1–9. PMID:18237875

Wang, J.-H., Rau, J.-D., & Liu, W.-J. (2003b). Two-stage clustering via neural networks. *IEEE Transactions on Neural Networks*, *14*(3), 606–615. doi:10.1109/TNN.2003.811354 PMID:18238042

Wang, S., & Siskind, J. M. (2003). Image segmentation with ratio cut. *IEEE Transactions on Pattern Analysis and Machine Intelligence, 25*(6), 675–690. doi:10.1109/TPAMI.2003.1201819

Yang, J., Hao, S., & Chung, P. (2002). Color image segmentation using fuzzy *C*-means and eigenspace projections. *Signal Processing, 82*(3), 461–472. doi:10.1016/S0165-1684(01)00196-7

Zhang, H., Fritts, J. E., & Goldman, S. A. (2004). An entropy-based objective evaluation method for image segmentation. In *Proceedings of SPIE Storage and Retrieval Methods and Applications for Multimedia*, (pp. 38–49). SPIE.

Zingaretti, P., Tascini, G., & Regini, L. (2002). Optimising the colour image segmentation. In *Proceedings VIII Convegno dell Associazione Italiana per Intelligenza Artificiale*. Academic Press.

ADDITIONAL READING

Bezdek, J. C. (1981). *Pattern Recognition with Fuzzy Objective Function Algorithms*. New York: Plenum. doi:10.1007/978-1-4757-0450-1

Bhattacharyya, S., & Dasgupta, K. (2003). Color Object Extraction From A Noisy Background Using Parallel Multilayer Self-Organizing Neural Networks, *Proceedings of CSI-YITPA (E) 2003*, 32-36.

Bhattacharyya, S., Dutta, P., & Maulik, U. (2008). Self organizing neural network (SONN) based gray scale object extractor with a multilevel sigmoidal (MUSIG) activation function. *Foundations of Computing and Decision Sciences, 33*(2), 131–165.

Bhattacharyya, S., Dutta, P., Maulik, U., & Nandi, P. K. (2007), Multilevel activation functions for true color image segmentation using a self supervised parallel self organizing neural network (PSONN) architecture: A comparative study, *International Journal on Computer Sciences, 2* (1), 09-21, ISSN 1306-4428.

Borsotti, M., Campadelli, P., & Schettini, R. (1998). Quantitative evaluation of color image segmentation results. *Pattern Recognition Letters, 19*, 741–747. doi:10.1016/S0167-8655(98)00052-X

Das, S., Abraham, A., & Konar, A. (2008). Automatic Clustering Using an Improved Differential Evolution Algorithm. *IEEE Transactions on Systems, Man, and Cybernetics. Part A, Systems and Humans, 38*(1), 218–237. doi:10.1109/TSMCA.2007.909595

Davies, D. L., & Bouldin, D. W. (1979). A cluster separation measure. *IEEE Transactions on Pattern Recognition and Machine Intelligence, 1*, 224–227. doi:10.1109/TPAMI.1979.4766909 PMID:21868852

De, S., Bhattacharyya, S., & Chakraborty, S. (2010b) True Color Image Segmentation by an Optimized Multilevel Activation Function, *Proceedings of 2010 IEEE International Conference on Computational Intelligence and Computing Research*, 545-548.

De, S., Bhattacharyya, S., & Dutta, P. (2010a). Efficient Gray Level Image Segmentation Using An Optimized MUSIG (OptiMUSIG) Activation Function, *International Journal of Parallel. Emergent and Distributed Systems, 26*(1), 1–39. doi: doi:10.1080/17445760903546618

Egmont-Petersen, M., & Ridder, de D. (2002). Image processing using neural networks - a review. *Pattern Recognition, 35*(10), 2279–2301. doi:10.1016/S0031-3203(01)00178-9

Ghosh, A., Pal, N. R., & Pal, S. K. (1993). Self-organization for object extraction using a multilayer neural network and fuzziness measures. *IEEE Transactions on Fuzzy Systems*, *1*(1), 54–68. doi:10.1109/TFUZZ.1993.390285

Gonzalez, R. C., & Woods, R. E. (2002). *Digital Image Processing*. Prentice Hall.

Haykin, S. (1999). *Neural Networks: A Comprehensive Foundation*. Upper Saddle River, NJ: Prentice Hall.

Jahne, B. (1993). *Digital Image Processing* (2nd ed.). New York: Springer-Verlag. doi:10.1007/978-3-662-21817-4

Jain, A. K., Murty, M. N., & Flynn, P. J. (1999). Data Clustering: A Review. *ACM Computing Surveys*, *31*(3). doi:10.1145/331499.331504

Jain, K. (1989). *Fundamentals of Digital Image Processing*. Upper Saddle River, NJ: Prentice-Hall.

Kohonen, T. (1989). *Self-Organization and Associative Memory*. Berlin, Germany: Springer-Verlag. doi:10.1007/978-3-642-88163-3

Rojas, R. (1996). *Neural Networks: A Systematic Introduction*. Berlin: Springer-Verlag.

Shi, J., & Malik, J. (2000). Normalized cuts and image segmentation. *IEEE Transactions on Pattern Analysis and Machine Intelligence*, *22*(8), 888–905. doi:10.1109/34.868688

Zhang, H., Fritts, J. E., & Goldman, S. A. (2004) An entropy-based objective evaluation method for image segmentation, *Proceedings of SPIE Storage and Retrieval Methods and Applications for Multimedia*, 38–49.

Zhang, Y. (1996). A survey on evaluation methods for image segmentation. *Pattern Recognition*, *29*(8), 1335–1346. doi:10.1016/0031-3203(95)00169-7

KEY TERMS AND DEFINITIONS

Fuzzy Set: A soft computing model to determine the ambiguity, vagueness and uncertainty in real world knowledge bases.

Genetic Algorithm: A probabilistic search technique for achieving an optimum solution to combinatorial problems that works in the principles of genetics.

Image Segmentation: It is a process to collect the image pixels, similar to one another within the same segment, dissimilar to the objects in other segments with respect to some features.

Optimization: A technique for determining single or more feasible solutions which corresponds to minimum or maximum values of single or more objective functions.

Self-Organizing Feature Map: A topology maintaining artificial neural network architecture capable of learning through self-supervision of incident input features.

APPENDIX

Table 1. Optimized and fixed class boundaries and evaluated segmentation quality measures, F, for 6 classes of Lena and Baboon image

Image	EF	Set	Class Levels	η
Lena	F_{op}	1	R={43, 78, 114, 239, 251, 255}	**0.522 (1)**
			G={0, 18, 31, 163, 203, 255}	
			B={32, 48, 162, 183, 193, 238}	
		2	R={43, 71, 77, 103, 212, 255}	0.527 (2)
			G={0, 121, 150, 195, 210, 255}	
			B={32, 53, 157, 176, 204, 238}	
	F_{fx}	1	R={43, 90, 100, 115, 140, 255}	1.000 (2)
			G={0, 20, 130, 150, 160, 255}	
			B={32, 70, 105, 120, 160, 238}	
		2	**R={43, 125, 130, 210, 230, 255}**	**0.707 (1)**
			G={0, 80, 100, 135, 200, 255}	
			B={32, 140, 155, 200, 230, 238}	
Baboon	F_{op}	1	**R={0, 20, 39, 61, 204, 255}**	**0.491 (1)**
			G={0, 15, 53, 187, 200, 255}	
			B={0, 10, 169, 206, 213, 255}	
		2	R={0, 16, 35, 81, 238, 255}	0.495 (2)
			G={0, 29, 41, 159, 194, 255}	
			B={0, 10, 186, 218, 233, 255}	
	F_{fx}	1	**R={0, 25, 75, 130, 140, 255}**	**0.796 (1)**
			G={0, 30, 90, 170, 210, 255}	
			B={0, 40, 80, 160, 200, 255}	
		2	R={0, 80, 90, 190, 240, 255}	1.000 (2)
			G={0, 60, 95, 185, 200, 255}	
			B={0, 50, 100, 230, 235, 255}	

Table 2. Optimized and fixed class boundaries and evaluated segmentation quality measures, F', for 6 classes of Lena and Baboon image

Image	EF	Set	Class Levels	η
Lena	F'_{op}	1	R={43, 72, 172, 206, 223, 255}	0.571 (2)
			G={0, 60, 174, 196, 223, 255}	
			B={32, 66, 82, 157, 163, 238}	
		2	**R={43, 78, 95, 132, 233, 255}**	**0.501 (1)**
			G={0, 21, 43, 69, 132, 255}	
			B={32, 48, 54, 118, 134, 238}	
	F'_{fx}	1	R={43, 80, 130, 180, 205, 255}	0.734 (1)
			G={0, 25, 35, 135, 159, 255}	
			B={32, 85, 135, 175, 179, 238}	
		2	**R={43, 75, 120, 140, 182, 255}**	**1.000 (2)**
			G={0, 50, 85, 90, 177, 255}	
			B={32, 60, 150, 180, 190, 238}	
Baboon	F'_{op}	1	**R={0, 43, 170, 212, 233, 255}**	**0.497 (1)**
			G={0, 24, 79, 181, 201, 255}	
			B={0, 54, 79, 194, 203, 255}	
		2	R={0, 62, 124, 182, 184, 255}	0.533 (2)
			G={0, 15, 44, 55, 132, 255}	
			B={0, 5, 92, 122, 213, 255}	
	F'_{fx}	1	**R={0, 21, 75, 115, 136, 255}**	**0.632 (1)**
			G={0, 24, 147, 177, 200, 255}	
			B={0, 21, 62, 125, 202, 255}	
		2	R={0, 70, 116, 151, 165, 255}	1.000 (2)
			G={0, 41, 157, 180, 200, 255}	
			B={0, 53, 88, 145, 162, 255}	

Table 3. Optimized and fixed class boundaries and evaluated segmentation quality measures, Q, for 6 classes of Lena and Baboon image

Image	EF	Set	Class Levels	η
Lena	Q_{op}	1	**R={43, 130, 171, 187, 204, 255}**	**0.608 (1)**
			G={0, 97, 111, 129, 172, 255}	
			B={32, 81, 99, 105, 197, 238}	
		2	R={43, 147, 188, 204, 221, 255}	0.628 (2)
			G={0, 117, 131, 149, 193, 255}	
			B={32, 50, 96, 119, 124, 238}	
	Q_{fx}	1	R={43, 45, 85, 135, 200, 255}	1.000 (2)
			G={0, 44, 87, 137, 210, 255}	
			B={32, 41, 82, 134, 212, 238}	
		2	**R={43, 80, 17, 206, 220, 255}**	**0.828 (1)**
			G={0, 115, 176, 192, 207, 255}	
			B={32, 85, 130, 150, 180, 238}	
Baboon	Q_{op}	1	R={0, 95, 110, 129, 174, 255}	0.655 (2)
			G={0, 37, 72, 120, 181, 255}	
			B={0, 36, 68, 84, 107, 255}	
		2	**R={0, 78, 130, 149, 172, 255}**	**0.611 (1)**
			G={0, 80, 92, 108, 147, 255}	
			B={0, 37, 74, 80, 125, 255}	
	Q_{fx}	1	**R={0, 158, 170, 185, 221, 255}**	**0.859 (1)**
			G={0, 66, 106, 159, 228, 255}	
			B={0, 93, 124, 129, 139, 255}	
		2	R={0, 36, 144, 201, 219, 255}	1.000 (2)
			G={0, 54, 69, 146, 190, 255}	
			B={0, 51, 117, 122, 151, 255}	

Table 4. Optimized and fixed class boundaries and evaluated segmentation quality measures, F, for 8 classes of Lena and Baboon image

Image	EF	Set	Class Levels	η
Lena	F_{op}	1	**R={43, 81, 129, 133, 174, 203, 254, 255}**	**0.676 (1)**
			G={0, 12, 74, 128, 155, 209, 217, 255}	
			B={32, 50, 60, 124, 170, 174, 206, 238}	
		2	R={43, 90, 92, 107, 125, 238, 244, 255}	0.713 (2)
			G={0, 4, 59, 121, 129, 145, 157, 255}	
			B={32, 60, 108, 153, 175, 176, 206, 238}	
	F_{fx}	1	**R={43, 70, 120, 130, 150, 170, 190, 255}**	**0.866 (1)**
			G={0, 20, 140, 180, 190, 210, 230, 255}	
			B={32, 50, 80, 90, 140, 150,160, 238}	
		2	R={43, 90, 118, 126, 136, 161, 175, 255}	1.000 (2)
			G={0, 51, 121, 167, 176, 200, 210, 255}	
			B={32, 43, 84, 98, 138, 165, 172, 238}	
Baboon	F_{op}	1	**R={0, 44, 47, 66, 88, 231, 239, 255}**	**0.065 (1)**
			G={0, 11, 70, 116, 123, 137, 148, 255}	
			B={0, 23, 97, 165, 199, 200, 224, 255}	
		2	R={0, 32, 53, 197, 204, 246, 249, 255}	0.069 (2)
			G={0, 31, 86, 94, 108, 118, 183, 255}	
			B={0, 61, 129, 163, 164, 188, 234, 255}	
	F_{fx}	1	**R={0, 50, 60, 80, 100, 240, 250, 255}**	**0.827 (1)**
			G={0, 15, 40, 100, 160, 170, 190, 255}	
			B={0, 40, 50, 110, 115, 220, 230, 255}	
		2	R={0, 70, 90, 125, 135, 155, 180, 255}	1.000 (2)
			G={0, 10, 25, 85, 145, 180, 195, 255}	
			B={0, 20, 40,50, 95, 125, 205, 255}	

Table 5. Optimized and fixed class boundaries and evaluated segmentation quality measures, F', for 8 classes of Lena and Baboon image

Image	EF	Set	Class Levels	η
Lena	F_{op}'	1	**R={43, 90, 92, 107, 125, 238, 244, 255}**	**0.046 (1)**
			G={0, 18, 131, 134, 156, 171, 200, 255}	
			B={32, 57, 122, 150, 176, 185, 193, 238}	
		2	R={43, 73, 92, 114, 123, 166, 246, 255}	0.054 (2)
			G={0, 93, 94, 148, 150, 212, 225, 255}	
			B={32, 54, 77, 113, 139, 166, 191, 238}	
	F_{fx}'	1	R={43, 75, 95, 125, 155, 185, 215, 255}	1.000 (2)
			G={0, 40, 70, 100, 130, 160, 200, 255}	
			B={32, 60, 105, 135, 175, 195, 215, 238}	
		2	**R={43, 100, 128, 141, 163, 179, 190, 255}**	**0.101 (1)**
			G={0, 50, 70, 89, 145, 206, 210, 255}	
			B={32, 53, 75, 106, 111, 121, 160, 238}	
Baboon	F_{op}'	1	**R={0, 17, 59, 62, 81, 103, 246, 255}**	**0.516 (1)**
			G={0, 24, 83, 129, 136, 150, 161, 255}	
			B={0, 39, 113, 181, 215, 216, 240, 255}	
		2	R={0, 23, 83, 88, 101, 203, 241, 255}	0.587 (2)
			G={0, 27, 29, 64, 99, 185, 192, 255}	
			B={0, 29, 46, 141, 199, 203, 244, 255}	
	F_{fx}'	1	**R={0, 21, 75, 95, 125, 165, 190, 255}**	**0.089 (1)**
			G={0, 24, 72, 97, 127, 163, 200, 255}	
			B={0, 21, 70, 92, 124, 158, 202,255}	
		2	R={0, 20, 80, 85, 98, 180, 200, 255}	1.000 (2)
			G={0, 18, 32, 102, 153, 170, 205, 255	
			B={0, 45, 50, 100, 120, 140, 190, 255}	

Table 6. Optimized and fixed class boundaries and evaluated segmentation quality measures, Q, for 8 classes of Lena and Baboon images

Image	EF	Set	Class Levels	η
Lena	Q_{op}	1	R={43, 141, 166, 167, 202, 208, 220, 255}	0.601 (2)
			G={0, 36, 48, 64, 136, 147, 182, 255}	
			B={32, 49, 79, 93, 109, 139, 206, 238}	
		2	**R={43, 167, 173, 207, 209, 224, 241, 255}**	**0.581 (1)**
			G={0, 45, 48, 71, 83, 115, 158, 255}	
			B={32, 61, 89, 91, 124, 132, 157, 238}	
	Q_{fx}	1	**R={43, 75, 95, 125, 155, 185, 215, 255}**	**0.833 (1)**
			G={0, 40, 70, 100, 130, 160, 200, 255}	
			B={32, 60, 105, 135, 175, 195, 215, 238}	
		2	R={43, 45, 65, 85, 135, 175, 200, 255}	1.000 (2)
			G={0, 14, 62, 87, 137, 173, 210, 255}	
			B={32, 41, 60, 82, 134, 168, 212, 238}	
Baboon	Q_{op}	1	R={0, 47, 73, 96, 116, 129, 177, 255}	0.575 (2)
			G={0, 71, 96, 113, 134, 161, 189, 255}	
			B={0, 54, 122, 124, 148, 162, 195, 255}	
		2	**R={0, 58, 108, 112, 125, 128, 219, 255}**	**0.538 (1)**
			G={0, 27, 46, 89, 146, 158, 165, 255}	
			B={0, 47, 71, 91, 113, 124, 162, 255}	
	Q_{fx}	1	**R={0, 50, 60, 90, 100, 110, 150, 255}**	**0.787 (1)**
			G={0, 60, 110, 160, 170, 185, 200, 255}	
			B={0, 10, 20, 60, 80, 150, 220, 255}	
		2	R={0, 21, 40, 62, 115, 138, 180, 255}	1.000 (2)
			G={0, 22, 30, 104, 120, 140, 200, 255}	
			B={0, 10, 30, 120, 200, 210, 220, 255}	

Figure 3. 8-class segmented 256 × 256 Lena image with the optimized class levels referring to (a) set 1 (b) set 2 of Table 4 for the quality measure F with ParaOptiMUSIG activation function

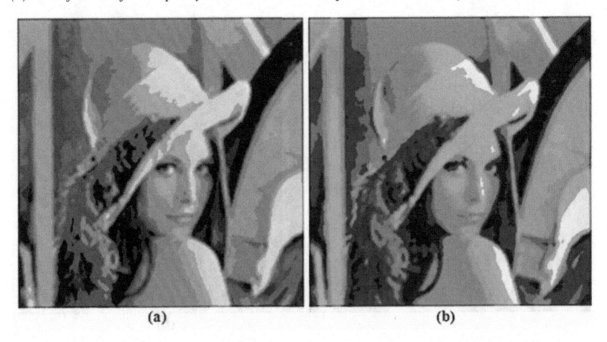

(a)　　　　　　　　　　　　(b)

Figure 4. 8-class segmented 256 × 256 Lena image with the optimized class levels referring to (a) set 1 (b) set 2 of Table 5 for the quality measure F' with ParaOptiMUSIG activation function

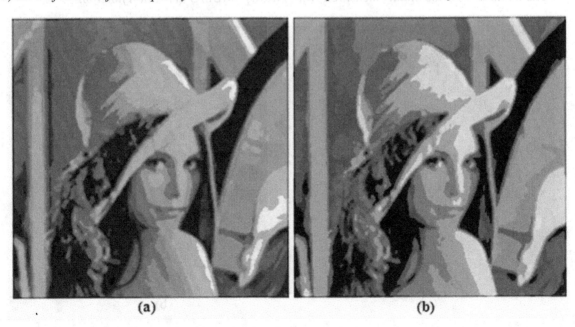

(a)　　　　　　　　　　　　(b)

Figure 5. 8-class segmented 256 × 256 Lena image with the optimized class levels referring to (a) set 1 (b) set 2 of Table 6 for the quality measure Q with ParaOptiMUSIG activation function

(a)   (b)

Figure 6. 8-class segmented 256 × 256 Baboon image with the optimized class levels referring to (a) set 1 (b) set 2 of Table 4 for the quality measure F with ParaOptiMUSIG activation function

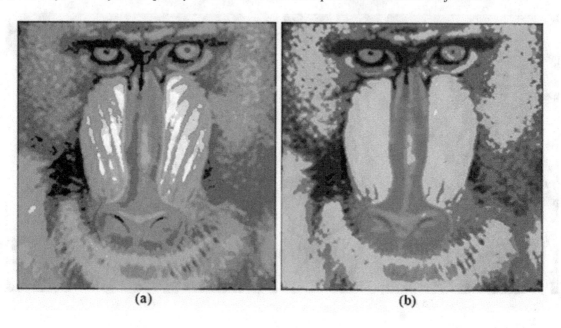

(a)   (b)

Figure 7. 8-class segmented 256 × 256 Baboon image with the optimized class levels referring to (a) set 1 (b) set 2 of Table 5 for the quality measure F' with ParaOptiMUSIG activation function

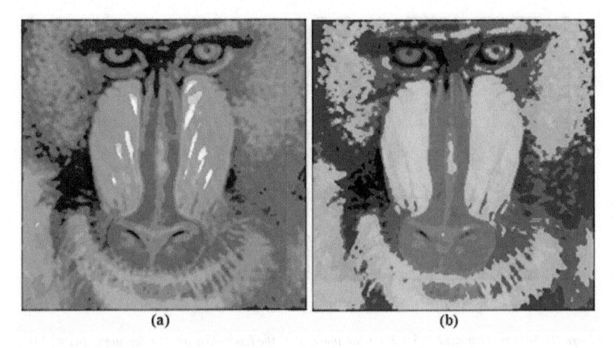

(a)   (b)

Figure 8. 8-class segmented 256 × 256 Baboon image with the optimized class levels referring to (a) set 1 (b) set 2 of Table 6 for the quality measure Q with ParaOptiMUSIG activation function

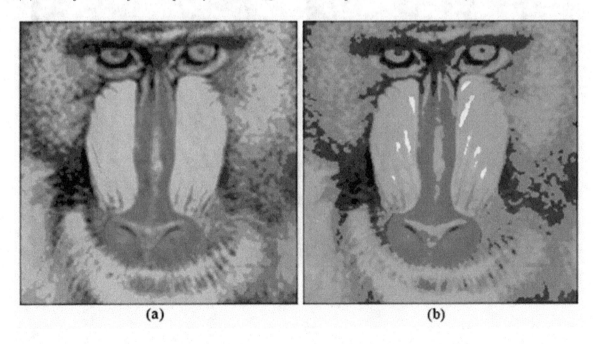

(a)   (b)

Figure 9. 8-class segmented 256 × 256 Lena image with the fixed class levels referring to (a) set 1 (b) set 2 of Table 4 for the quality measure F with MUSIG activation function

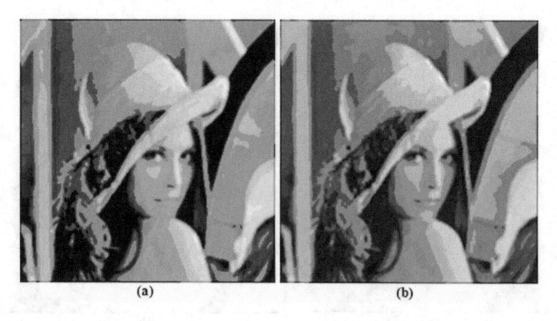

Figure 10. 8-class segmented 256 × 256 Lena image with the fixed class levels referring to (a) set 1 (b) set 2 of Table 5 for the quality measure F' with MUSIG activation function

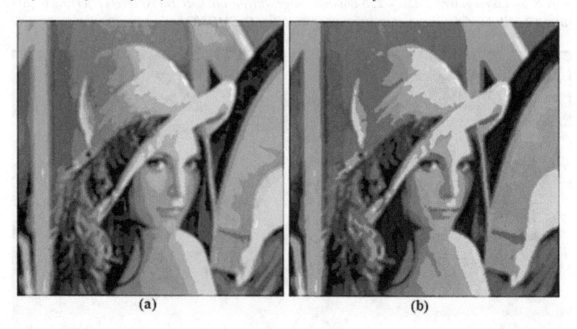

Figure 11. 8-class segmented 256 × 256 Lena image with the fixed class levels referring to (a) set 1 (b) set 2 of Table 6 for the quality measure Q with MUSIG activation function

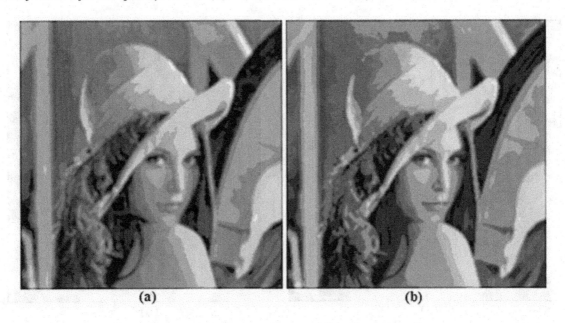

(a)   (b)

Figure 12. 8-class segmented 256 × 256 Baboon image with the fixed class levels referring to (a) set 1 (b) set 2 of Table 4 for the quality measure F with MUSIG activation function

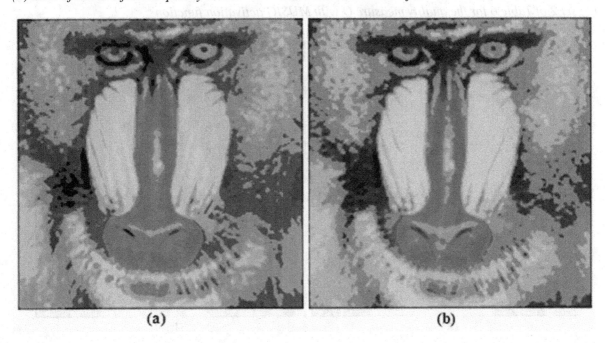

(a)   (b)

Figure 13. 8-class segmented 256 × 256 Baboon image with the fixed class levels referring to (a) set 1 (b) set 2 of Table 5 for the quality measure F' with MUSIG activation function

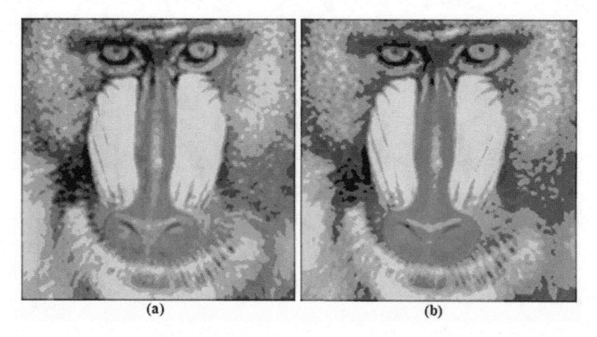

(a)   (b)

Figure 14. 8-class segmented 256 × 256 Baboon image with the fixed class levels referring to (a) set 1 (b) set 2 of Table 6 for the quality measure Q with MUSIG activation function

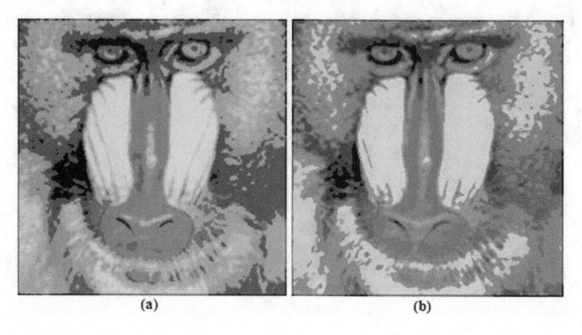

(a)   (b)

Chapter 3
Learning Using Soft Computing Techniques

V. Susheela Devi
Indian Institute of Science, India

ABSTRACT

This chapter focuses on a few key applications in the field of classification and clustering. Techniques of soft computing have been used to solve these applications. The first application finds a new similarity measure for time series data, combining some available similarity measures. The weight to be given to these similarity measures is found using a genetic algorithm. The other applications discussed are for pattern clustering. A Particle Swarm Optimization (PSO) algorithm has been used for clustering. A modification of the PSO using genetic operators has been suggested. In addition, simultaneous clustering and feature selection and simultaneous clustering and feature weighting has been discussed. Results have been given for all the techniques showing the improvement achieved using these techniques.

1. INTRODUCTION

Soft Computing techniques generally refer to the techniques which use some method of search to solve the problem. It differs from conventional computing in that it is tolerant of imprecision, uncertainty, partial truth and approximation. It also refers to techniques which mimic the methods used by human beings and animals.

Some of the soft computing techniques are evolutionary computation, neural networks, particle swarm optimization, ant colony optimization, and fuzzy computing. This chapter talks about specific applications where the techniques mentioned above have been used. The applications are in the fields of supervised and unsupervised learning namely classification and clustering.

There are a number of classification methods like nearest neighbour, decision tree, support vector machines, rule based systems etc. It is also possible to use soft computing techniques like neural networks, evolutionary computations,

DOI: 10.4018/978-1-4666-4936-1.ch003

particle swarm optimization etc. for carrying out classification. Even techniques for feature selection, feature extraction and prototype selection can be carried out using these techniques.

When the class labels of patterns are fuzzy, it means that each pattern belongs to each class with a membership value. When we use fuzzy classification techniques, we get the fuzzy membership value of each test pattern to every class which has to be defuzzified to get the crisp class label.

A rough set consists of two parts, the upper approximation which consists of objects which definitely belong to the set and the lower approximation which consists of objects which might belong to the set. In the context of pattern classification, each class is a rough set which has some patterns which belong to its upper approximation and some patterns which belong to its lower approximation. From the point of view of a pattern, it can belong to the upper approximation of one class or the lower approximation of more than one class.

Clustering can also be carried out using soft techniques like genetic algorithms, simulated annealing, particle swarm optimization etc.

The chapter will discuss the following topics:

1. Use of genetic algorithms for time series classification (Dohare & Devi, 2011).
2. Use of PSO for classification and clustering.
3. Modified PSO with genetic operators for clustering(Swetha & Devi, 2012).
4. Use of PSO for feature selection and clustering simultaneously(Swetha & Devi, 2012).
5. Use of PSO for feature weighting and clustering simultaneously(Swetha & Devi, 2012)

2. GENETIC ALGORITHMS FOR TIME SERIES CLASSIFICATION

Distance-based time series classification can be done using a distance measure. There are a number of distance measures each of them have

their own strengths and weaknesses. The distance measure used is crucial to the performance of the classification algorithm. The method discussed in this section, combines a number of distance measures by assigning weights to each one. The weights assigned are found by using a genetic algorithm.

Time series data consists of multivariate data where the values of one or more variable is in the form of a sequence. Time series data are found everywhere, for example, weather data, stocks and share prices, energy consumption at a place etc. These consist of data which vary in time. Generally, a time series

$$t = [t_1, ..., t_r],$$

is an ordered set of r data points which are typically measured at successive points of time spaced at uniform time intervals. A time series could be a pattern which belongs to a particular class. The problem of time series classification is to learn a classifier C, which is a function that maps a time series t to a class label l, that is, $C(t) = l$ where l L, the set of class labels.

There are three basic methods of carrying out time series classification:

- **Distance Based Classification:** Distance based methods computes the distance or similarity between pairs of time series. The distance function, which measures the similarity between sequences, determines the quality of the classification significantly(Ding et.al,2008)(Keogh & Kasetty, 2002)(Xi et.al,2006).
- **Feature Based Classification:** Feature based methods transform time series data into feature vectors and then apply conventional classification methods. Feature selection plays an important role in these methods as it decreases the dimensionality of the data (Lesh, Zaki & Ogihara, 1999; Chuzhanova, Jones & Margetts, 1998).

- **Model Based Classification:** Model based methods use a model such as Hidden Markov Model (HMM) or other statistical models to classify time series data (Yashnenko, Silvescu & Honavar, 2005; Lewis, 1998).

The distance based methods, use a similarity metric. The choice of the similarity affects the performance of the classification algorithm. The time and space complexity of the classification algorithm is also affected by the similarity metric used(Ding et.al., 2008). Some well known similarity measures for time series data are Euclidean distance (ED), Dynamic time warping distance (DTW)(Ratanamahatana & Keogh, 2008), Longest Common Sub-sequence (LCSS), etc. The standard One Nearest Neighbor (1NN) classifier has often been found to perform better than any other classifier for time series classification(Keogh and Kasetty, 2002). We combine different similarity measures to form a new weighted similarity measure and use a 1NN classifier to carry out the classification. Our work has been carried out for time series data where finding a good similarity measure is non trivial. This is because the similarity is to be found not between two points, but two curves.

Stochastic optimization methods are optimization methods which generate and use random variables. In many of the problems the random variables appear in the formulation of the optimization problem itself. For some non-linear optimization problems, conventional calculus-based techniques cannot be used. In such cases, stochastic search techniques are a good alternative. These techniques are iterative and employ one or more current solutions at each step. The current solution(s) are evaluated and operators are applied to perturb the current solution(s) to get the next solution. The operators used are explorative and exploitative so that a number of promising candidate solutions are evaluated while searching in the problem space. Hence the stochastic search technique gives an experimental way out to find the solution to problems which are impossible

to solve using the deterministic approach. One such stochastic search technique namely genetic algorithm(GA) is used here.

The approach in this work (Dohare & Devi, 2010) is as follows:

1. Use GA to find weights $w_1, w_2, \ldots, w_n$ for n similarity measures $S_1, S_2, \ldots, S_n$.
   a. Set $w_1, w_2, \ldots, w_n$ to a value between 0-1 at random for m strings.
   b. repeat for it iterations,
      i. Use $S = w_1.s_1 + w_2.s_2 + \ldots + w_n.s_n$ to classify validation set. Set fitness as the classification accuracy.
      ii. Use selection, crossover and mutation to get a new population of strings.
   c. Set $w_1, w_2, \ldots, w_n$ as the values from the string in the final population giving best fitness.
2. Set $S_{new} = s_1.w_1 + s_2.w_2 + \ldots + s_n.w_n$
3. Use S_{new} and 1NN to classify the test data set and measure the classification accuracy.

2.1 Similarity Measures Used

To find S_{new}, 8 similarity measures were used and a weighted similarity measure found by using a genetic algorithm to find the weights. If we have two time series:

$$x = (x_1, x_2, ..., x_n)$$

$$y = (y_1, y_2, ..., y_n)$$

$s(x, y)$ denotes the similarity between the x and y. The eight similarity measures used by us are given below:

1. **Euclidean Distance (L_2 norm):** Euclidean distance is a widely used similarity measure. The distance from x to y is given by:

$$s_1(x,y) = \sqrt{\sum_{t=1}^{n}(x_i - y_i)^2}$$

2. **Manhattan Distance (L_1 norm):** The distance function is given by:

$$s_2(x,y) = \sum_{t=1}^{n} |(x_i - y_i)|$$

3. **Maximum Norm (L_∞ norm):** The infinity norm distance is also called Chebyshev distance. The distance function is given by:

$$s_3(x,y) = \max(|(x_1 - y_1)|,$$
$$|(x_2 - y_2)|, \cdots, |(x_n - y_n)|)$$

4. **Mean Dissimilarity:** Fink and Pratt(2004) proposed a similarity measure between two numbers a and b as:

$$sim(a,b) = 1 - \frac{|a-b|}{|a|+|b|}$$

They define two similarities, mean similarity and root mean square similarity. We use the above similarity measure to define a distance function:

$$disim(a,b) = \frac{|a-b|}{|a|+|b|}$$

and then define Mean dissimilarity as:

$$s_4(x,y) = \sqrt{\frac{1}{n}\sum_{t=1}^{n} dissim(x_i, y_i)^2}$$

where

$$disim(x_i, y_i) = \frac{|x_i - y_i|}{|x_i|+|y_i|}$$

5. **Root Mean Square Dissimilarity:** By using the above similarity measure, we define Root Mean Square Dissimilarity as:

$$s_5(x,y) = \sqrt{\frac{1}{n}\sum_{i=1}^{n} disim(x_i, y_i)^2}$$

6. **Peak Dissimilarity:** In addition to above similarity measures, Fink and Pratt(2004) also define peak similarity between two numbers a and b as:

$$psim(a,b) = 1 - \frac{|a-b|}{2.\max(|a|,|b|)}$$

and then define peak dissimilarity as

$$peakdisim(x_i, y_i) = \frac{|x_i - y_i|}{2.\max(|x_i|,|y_i|)}$$

The peak dissimilarity between two time series p and q is given by:

$$s_6(x,y) = \frac{1}{n}.\sum_{i=1}^{n} peakdisim(x_i, y_i)$$

7. **Cosine Distance:** Cosine similarity finds the cosine of the angle between two vectors. The cosine similarity, θ, between two time series x and y is represented using a dot product and magnitude as:

$$\cos(\theta) = \frac{x.y}{||x||||y||}$$

and cosine dissimilarity as:

$$s_7(x,y) = 1 - \cos(\theta)$$

8. **Dynamic Time Warping Distance (DTW):**
First we need to create a matrix of size |x| × |y| where each element is the squared distance, $d(x_i, y_j) = (x_i - y_j)^2$, between every pair of point in x and y. Every possible warping between two time series, is a path P, though the matrix. A warping path P, is a contiguous set of matrix elements that characterizes a mapping between x and y where k^{th} element of P is defined as $p_k = (i,j)_k$. We want the best path that minimizes the warping cost:

$$s_8(x,y) = DTW(x,y) = \min\left\{\sqrt{\sum_{k=1}^{K} p_k \Big/ K}\right.$$

where

$$\max(|x|,|y|) \le K < |x| + |y| - 1$$

This path can be found using dynamic programming to evaluate the following recurrence which defines the cumulative distance $\lambda(i,j)$. The recursive function $\lambda(i,j)$ gives us the minimum cost path:

$$\lambda(i,j) = d(x_i, y_i)$$
$$+ \min\{\lambda(i-1, j-1), \lambda(i-1, j), \lambda(i, j-1)\}$$

2.2 Implementation and Results

Eight benchmark datasets were used from the UCI data repository. In each case the best weights for eight similarity measures was found and is detailed in Table 1.

Table 1 shows that in most cases the DTW gives good results and therefore the weight w_8 for DTW is high. But in some cases, DTW does very poorly. This can be seen from this table where w_8 for ECG200 is 0. The weight w_2 is 0.9 for coffee and 0.79 for Lightning-2 but is very low or 0 for other data sets. Looking at this table, it can be seen that the weights vary over the datasets and different similarity measures give good results with different datasets.

Table 2 gives the classification accuracy obtained using the combined similarity measure and 1NN on the eight datasets.

It can be seen from the table that in most cases, the new combined similarity measure is doing well as compared with the other similarity measures.

3. USE OF PSO FOR CLASSIFICATION AND CLUSTERING

Clustering is partitioning of the dataset into sub-partitions so that patterns belonging to the same sub-partition are similar in some sense and patterns belonging to different sub-partitions are

Table 1. Weights assigned to eight similarity measures after 10 iterations in genetic algorithms

Dataset	S1	s2	s3	s4	s5	s6	s7	s8
Control Chart	0.72	0.29	0.33	0.18	0.12	0.61	0.31	0.82
Coffee	0.74	0.9	0.9	0.1	0.03	0.03	0.06	0.70
Beef	0.95	0.09	0	0.48	0	0.62	0.58	0.73
OliveOil	0.7	0	0.79	0	0	0	0.58	0.67
Lightning-2	0.90	0.75	0.79	0.09	0.21	0.09	0.71	0.97
Lightning-7	0.95	0.06	0.09	0.81	0.95	0.29	0.38	0.99
Trace	0.62	0.08	0.28	0.39	0.14	0.47	0.23	0.98
ECG200	0.052	0	0.21	0	0	0.98	0.90	0

Table 2. Comparison of the new combined similarity measure and best similarity measures

Dataset	Size	1NN-GA (%)(mean ± st.dev.)	Best Similarity Measure
Control Chart	600	99.07 ± 0.37	DTW (99.33)
Coffee	56	87.50 ± 2.06	L_∞ norm (89.28)
Beef	60	54.45 ± 1.92	ED, L_∞ norm (53.33)
OliveOil	121	82.67 ± 4.37	DTW (86.67)
Lightning-2	121	87.54 ± 1.47	DTW (85.25)
Lightning-7	143	69.28 ± 2.97	DTW (72.6)
Trace	200	100.0 ± 0.00	DTW (100)
ECG200	200	90.00 ± 1.15	peakdisim (91)

dissimilar in some sense. Usually the similarity between patterns is measured in terms of a distance measure. So the distance between patterns in the same sub-partition is smaller and the distance between patterns in different sub-partitions is larger.

Many heuristic approaches have been applied to solve the data clustering problem. Recently, many soft computing algorithms such as genetic algorithms(GA) (Tseng & Yang, 2001; Bezdek et.al., 1994), Simulated annealing(Selim & Al-sultan, 1991) Tabu search(Al-Sultan, 1995), Ant colony Optimization(Shelokar, Jayaraman & Kulkarni, 2004; Jaffer & Shivakumar, 2010) and Particle Swarm Optimization(Omran, Engelbrecht & Salman, 2006; van der Merwe & Engelbrecht, 2003) have been used for clustering.

Particle swarm optimizer(PSO) was introduced by Kennedy & Eberhart(1995). The particle swarm optimizer(PSO) is based on swarm intelligence which emulates the behaviour of a flock searching over a solution space. The swarm converges to the most promising regions.

Particle Swarm Optimization(PSO) is a population based search algorithm based on the simulation of the social behaviour of a flock of birds. A flock of birds move over time to finally regroup in an optimal formation. This concept is used to find the optimal solution to a problem.

In PSO, individuals in the swarm move through the search space. Changes in the position of particles are based on the social psychological tendency of individuals to emulate the success of other individuals. The change in the position of a particle is influenced by the experience, or knowledge, of its neighbours and its own experience(or knowledge). As a consequence of this, the particles stochastically visit successful regions of the search space . The self organizing behaviour of a species of living being such as a flock of birds, a school of fish or a herd of sheep is modeled. In these social groups, even though individuals do not have any knowledge of the global behaviour of the entire group, they move together optimally based on local interaction between individuals. Even though each individual behaves in a simple way, complex collective behaviour emerges.

The PSO has been used to solve classification and clustering problems. PSO consists of a set of particles that represent candidate solutions to the problem. Each particle consists of a position in space. At every iteration each particle moves with a velocity which depends on the best solution encountered by the particle thus far (pbest) and the best solution of all the particles in the neighbourhood (gbest). Each particle i calculates the velocity by which it moves as follows:

$$v_i(t+1) = \omega v_i(t) + c_1 r_1(t)(y_i(t) - x_i(t)) + c_2 r_2(t)(y_i(t) - x_i(t))$$

The new position of the particle will be

$$x_i(t+1) = x_i(t) + v_i(t+1)$$

where ω is the inertia weight which provides the necessary diversity to the swarm by changing the momentum of the particle to avoid the stagnation of particles at the local optima. Research conducted by Eberhart shows improvement in search efficiency through decreasing the value of inertia weight from a higher to a lower value. The inertia weight can be set to

$$[0.5 + (R_{nd}/2.0)]$$

c_1 and c_2 are social parameters that are bound between 0 and 2 and are generally known as the acceleration coefficients for the particles to move about in the solution space and to pull towards the pbest and gbest positions. r_1 and r_2 are random numbers with uniform distribution U[0,1] $\hat{y}$ is the global best position.

The PSO has been used to solve classification and clustering problems. Prototype selection is the process of selecting a subset of the training patterns to be used instead of the training set. One method of doing this is to have as many elements as the number of training patterns in an individual in the swarm. Each element corresponds to a particular training pattern. If this element has a value of 1, it means that the individual is in the prototypes selected. On the contrary, if it is 0, it means that the individual is not in the prototype set. Each individual in the swarm is evaluated by finding the performance of the selected prototypes in classifying a validation data set.

Clustering is partitioning of the dataset into sub-partitions so that patterns belonging to the same sub-partition are similar in some sense and patterns belonging to different sub-partitions are dissimilar in some sense. Usually the similarity between patterns is measured in terms of a distance measure. So the distance between patterns in the same sub-partition is smaller and the distance between patterns in different sub-partitions is larger.

For carrying out clustering using PSO, each individual in the swarm consists of as many elements as the number of patterns in the dataset. Each element takes on a value varying from 1 to c where c is the number of clusters. So if an element has a value of k, it means that it belongs to the kth cluster. Each individual in the swarm is evaluated by using a cluster evaluation method such as the Sum of Squared Error(SSE). If there are N patterns $X_1, ..., X_N$ where each pattern has r features making the ith pattern $X_i = \{x_1, ...x_r\}$, then SSE will be

$$SSE = \sum_{k=1}^{c} \sum_{\forall X_t \in C_k} d(X_t, m_k)^2$$

where C_k refers to the kth cluster, m_k gives the centroid of the kth cluster and $d(i,j)$ refers to the distance between points i and j.

2.1 Modified PSO with GA for Pattern Clustering

When PSO is used for clustering, each particle in the swarm has as many elements as the number of patterns. If we have c clusters, each element in the swarm takes a value between 1 and c and gives the cluster number to which that pattern belongs.

If we have data points $X = (X_1, X_2, ...,X_N)$ then the ith particle S_i is represented as

$$S_i = (y_1, y_2, ..., y_N)$$

where y_j refers to the cluster to which X_j belongs. y_j takes a value between 1 and c.

The centroid of each cluster j is calculated as

$$m_j = \frac{\sum_{X_i \in C_j} X_i}{|C_j|} \forall j = 1,...,c$$

where m_j refers to the centroid of the jth cluster and it is the sum of all the patterns assigned to the cluster C_j divided by number of patterns assigned to cluster C_j. The centroid of the entire dataset is m which is given by

$$m = \frac{\sum_{i=1}^{N} X_i}{N}$$

The fitness value of particle i is measured as

$$fitness[i] = \frac{\sum_{j=1}^{k}\left[\frac{X_i \in C_j d(X_i, m_j)}{|C_j|}\right]}{\left[\sum_{j=1}^{k} d(m_j, m)\right]}$$

Both GA and PSO can be used to solve optimization problems. A search is carried out to find the best solution to the problem. The approach in the two methods vary in the way they are perceived. Both methods work with a number of candidate solutions. In PSO, the candidate solutions are in the form of individuals in a swarm whereas in GA, they are strings in a generation. When it comes to the next generation, new strings are found by using the operators of selection, crossover and mutation on the previous generation. In the PSO, new individuals do not get generated but the same particles move to new positions with a velocity which depends on its best position and the global best.

Combining GA operations like selection, crossover and mutation with the PSO can give better results since the focused selection of GA can be combined with the movement of the particles towards the optimal solution. It has been suggested in Eberhart & Kennedy(1995) and Angeline(1998) that a hybrid combination of GA and PSO could produce a robust optimization strategy. In Abdel-Khader(2010), a hybrid

PSO has been used where in each iteration some of the particles are updated using PSO and the rest of the particles are modified using GA. It is suggested by us in Swetha & Devi(2012) that good results can be obtained by using GA in some iterations on all the patterns and using PSO in the other iterations on all the patterns. By using a validation set, the best combination of PSO+GA was found. Figure 1 gives the flowchart of this combined method.

GA is known for its randomized focused search. In this method as shown in Fig(1), in every iteration either the entire set of particles are updated using a PSO or the entire set is passed to the GA and the next generation of particles are generated. The population size of the GA-PSO algorithm is set to N. The initial N particles are randomly generated and their fitness function is calculated. These N particles are then fed into the PSO search algorithm. In each iteration, the particle adjusts the vector position in the vector space according to its own experience and those of its neighbours. The fitness function is recalculated and the particles created by PSO are used as the new population. When the particles go into the GA loop, selection, crossover and mutation is carried out to get the new population of particles. When selection is carried out, particles having higher fitness have a higher probability of going into the next generation. This will weed out particles with low fitness. At the same time, the local best of each particle is also maintained as it is required when the particles are updated using PSO. When crossover is carried out between two particles, both these particles will keep track of the local best as the better of the two local best positions of the two particles. The fitness function is recalculated again and the process is repeated for the prescribed number of iterations (tmax) or until the convergence criteria are met.

The algorithm is as follows:

Figure 1. Flowchart for PSO+GA algorithm

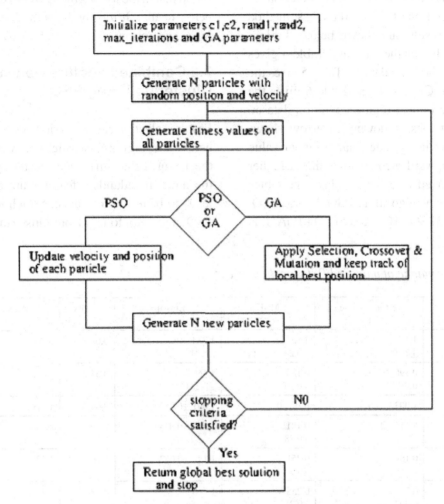

1. Initialize each particle to have *N* elements where each element is set randomly to a number between 1 and *k* where *k* is the number of clusters.
2. For t=1 to tmax do
3. Run step *a* or step *b*.
   a. PSO
      i. For each particle S do a) Calculate the fitness b) Update local best position.
      ii. Update the global best position
      iii. Update the velocity and position of particles
   b. GA
      i. Use selection, crossover and mutation to generate the new population.
      ii. While doing this, keep track of local best for each particle

The decision to be taken here is the iterations where PSO is carried out and the iterations where the GA operators are used. A validation set has been used and the performance is checked for 1PSO+1GA(1 iteration of PSO and 1 iteration of GA), 3PSO+1GA(3 iterations of PSO and 1 iteration of GA), and 5PSO+1GA (5 iterations of PSO and 1 iteration of GA) and the best method is used. The results are shown below. Table 3 gives the results for the Iris data. Table 4 gives the results for the wine dataset. Table 5 gives the results for the CMC dataset. Table 6 gives the results for the optical digit recognition dataset. In all these tables, a downward arrow shows that a lower value is better than a higher value whereas an upward arrow shows that a higher value is preferred to a lower value. The tables compare Kmeans algorithm, PSO, hybrid PSO, 1PSO+1GA, 3PSO+1GA and 5PSO+1GA. It is found that in most cases the 1PSO+1GA is giving better results. It mostly gives the lowest fitness, MSE and entropy and the highest purity value.

3.2 Combined Feature Selection and Clustering Using PSO

Feature selection can be carried out on the dataset before carrying out clustering. This will only retain the features that influence clustering accuracy the most. If redundant features are removed, it leads to better performance. So while using the PSO algorithm to carry out clustering, simulta-

Table 3. Performance of modified PSO for the Iris data

Methods	Fitness Value ↓	MSE ↓	Entropy ↓	Purity ↑	Avg CPU Time
Kmeans	1.125 ±0.19	1.023 ±0.20	1.234 ±0.21	0.66	0.20s
PSO	0.190± 0.06	0.189 ±0.16	1.169 ±0.23	0.64	1.24s
Hybrid PSO	1.003 ±0.09	0.89 ±0.22	1.091 ±0.052	0.68	1.82s
1PSO+1GA	0.176 ±0.12	0.181 ±0.18	1.172 ±0.048	0.80	2.28s
3PSO+1GA	0.189 ±0.23	0.251 ±0.30	1.172 ±0.082	0.76	2.53s
5PSO+1GA	0.266 ±0.11	0.258 ±0.25	1.210 ±0.156	0.74	2.73s

Table 4. Performance of modified PSO for the Wine data

Methods	Fitness Value ↓	MSE ↓	Entropy ↓	Purity ↑	Avg CPU Time
Kmeans	1.102 ±0.16	1.025 ±0.10	1.365 ±0.78	0.65	0.65s
PSO	0.282 ±0.02	0.263 ±0.03	1.321 ±0.21	0.58	1.82s
Hybrid PSO	0.235 ±0.17	0.172 ±0.07	1.356 ±0.46	0.56	2.82s
1PSO+1GA	0.163 ±0.18	0.150 ±0.13	1.299 ±0.32	0.73	3.01s
3PSO+1GA	0.170 ±0.14	0.158 ±0.50	1.315 ±0.21	0.63	3.53s
5PSO+1GA	0.181 ±0.15	0.162 ±0.20	1.320 ±0.19	0.61	3.73s

Table 5. Performance of modified PSO for the CMC data

Methods	Fitness Value ↓	MSE ↓	Entropy ↓	Purity ↑	Avg CPU Time
Kmeans	1.125 ±0.19	1.023 ±0.20	1.234 ±0.21	0.66	0.20s
PSO	0.190 ±0.07	0.189 ±0.01	1.169 ±0.20	0.64	1.24s
Hybrid PSO	1.003 ±0.09	0.89 ±0.22	1.091 ±0.52	0.68	1.82s
1PSO+1GA	0.176 ±0.12	0.181 ±0.18	1.172 ±0.048	0.80	2.28s
3PSO+1GA	0.489 ±0.23	0.512 ±0.30	1.172 ±0.82	0.76	2.53s
5PSO+1GA	0.566 ±0.11	0.580 ±0.25	1.210 ±0.156	0.74	2.73s

Table 6. Performance of modified PSO for the Optimal Digit Recognition data

Methods	Fitness Value ↓	MSE ↓	Entropy ↓	Puri-ty ↑	Avg CPU Time
Kmeans	3.160 ±0.89	3.023 ±0.64	2.722 ±0.18	0.62	512.89s
PSO	2.334 ±0.75	2.266 ±0.16	2.346 ±0.54	0.68	716.36s
Hybrid PSO	2.210 ±0.21	2.172 ±0.15	2.249 ±0.48	0.63	938.63s
1PSO+1GA	1.921 ±0.24	1.835 ±0.54	1.946 ±0.51	0.70	923.82s
3PSO+1GA	2.116 ±0.23	2.091 ±0.26	2.003 ±0.56	0.69	947.58s
5PSO+1GA	2.361 ±0.19	2.125 ±0.22	2.182 ±0.29	0.612	983.21s

neously feature selection can also be carried out (Swetha & Devi, 2012). This method using PSO is described in this section and results presented. Another paper which carries out simultaneous feature selection and clustering uses mixture models(Law, Figueiredo & Jain, 2001). In the particles in the swarm, we had n elements if n is the number of patterns to be clustered which took a value between 1 and k if there were k clusters. Additionally, we need to include d elements if there are d features. These elements take on the values 1 or 0 depending on whether the feature is present or absent. The PSO+FS algorithm is as given below:

1. Initialize every particle to have n+d elements where the first n elements have random values between 1 and k. The next d elements are randomly set to 0 or 1 and pertain to the features selected.

2. For t= 1 to tmax do
    a. For each particle S do
        i.   Calculate the fitness of the particle
        ii. Update local best position of the particle
    b. Update the global best position of the particles
    c. Update the particles velocity and position
3. Report the best string generated which gives the clustering of the patterns and the features selected.

The fitness value calculation is as follows:
The fitness is

$$fit = \frac{\sum_{j=1}^{k} \frac{\sum_{\forall y \in C_j} d(y, m_j)}{|C_j|}}{\sum_{j=1}^{k} d(m_j, m)} \text{,}$$

the centroid is

$$m = \frac{\sum_y y}{n}$$

and the distance between two points a and b is given by

$$d(a,b) = \sqrt{z_1 (a_1 - b_1)^2 + z_2 \left(a_2 - b_2\right)^2 + \cdots}$$

where $z_j \in (0,1)$ and is 0 if the jth feature is absent and 1 if the jth feature is present. A clustering which has a lower value of fitness is a better clustering of the points. The numerator of fit gives the sum of squared error of all points from its centroid and the denominator gives the between class distance.

3.3 Simultaneous Feature Weighting and Clustering Using Particle Swarm Optimization

In a dataset, each feature can have a different weighting depending on its significance in the classification or clustering problem. A feature which is more discriminative is more significant and will be given a higher weight. For clustering the data, we also simultaneously carry out feature weighting(Swetha & Devi,2012). A particle swarm optimization has been used. Whereas in the previous section the presence or absence of a feature is represented by a 1 or 0 in the particle, in this case the values are real values which lie between 0 and 1. The algorithm is given below:

1. Initialize every particle to have n+d elements where the first n elements have random values between 1 and k. The next d elements are randomly set to real values between 0 and 1 and pertain to the weights given to the features selected.
2. For t= 1 to t_{max} do
    a. For each particle S do
        i.   Calculate the fitness of the particle
        ii. Update local best position of the particle
    b. Update the global best position of the particles
    c. Update the particles velocity and position
3. Report the best string generated which gives the clustering of the patterns and the features selected.

The fitness function used in this case is the same as the one for simultaneous feature selection and clustering. Here the z_j takes real values between 0 and 1.

3.4 Results

The results obtained are given in the tables below. Table 7 gives the results for the wine dataset. Table 8 gives the results for the CMC dataset. Table 9 gives the results for the page-blocks dataset. Table 10 gives the results for the mammographic masses data. Table 11 gives the results for the digit recognition data. The performance metrics chosen are the fitness value, mean square error (MSE), entropy and purity. The results of clustering using kmeans, only PSO, PSO with feature selection(PSO with FS) and PSO with feature weighting(PSO with FW) have been carried out so that PSO with FS and PSO with FW can be compared to each other and with the other two methods.

It can be seen from the Tables that PSO with FW is giving the best performance followed by PSO with FS in most cases. The time taken for PSO with FW and PSO with FS is higher than that for PSO and k-means algorithm. The better performance more than makes up for the extra time required.

4. SUMMARY

A number of applications of GA and PSO to pattern classification and clustering have been discussed in this chapter. These algorithms give robust optimization techniques which can be used for applications in different fields of study. These

Table 7. Results of simultaneous clustering and feature selection(PSO with FS) and simultaneous clustering and feature weighting(PSP with FW) for Wine data having 13 features

Methods	Fitness Value ↓	MSE ↓	Entropy ↓	Puri-ty ↑	Avg CPU Time
Kmeans	1.102 ±0.06	1.025 ±0.01	1.365 ±0.78	0.65	0.65s
PSO	0.282 ±0.02	0.263 ±0.03	1.321 ±0.30	0.58	1.82s
PSO with FS	0.076 ±0.06	0.089 ±0.09	1.260 ±0.09	0.80	2.03s
PSO with FW	0.048±0.03	0.066±0.03	1.257 ±0.24	0.95	2.93s

Table 8. Results of simultaneous clustering and feature selection(PSO with FS) and simultaneous clustering and feature weighting(PSO with FW) for CMC data having 9 features

Methods	Fitness Value ↓	MSE ↓	Entropy ↓	Puri-ty ↑	Avg CPU Time
Kmeans	1.125 ±0.06	1.023 ±0.01	1.234 ±0.78	0.66	0.20s
PSO	0.190 ±0.02	0.189 ±0.03	1.169 ±0.30	0.64	1.24s
PSO with FS	0.092 ±0.06	1.043 ±0.09	1.320 ±0.09	0.83	10.39s
PSO with FW	0.056 ±0.03	0.320 ±0.06	1.138 ±0.02	0.97	11.36s

Table 9. Results of simultaneous clustering and feature selection(PSO with FS) and simultaneous clustering and feature weighting(PSO with FW) for page-blocks data having 10 features

Methods	Fitness Value ↓	MSE ↓	Entropy ↓	Purity ↑	Avg CPU Time
Kmeans	1.901±0.192	2.004±0.34	1.721±0.18	0.53	42.31s
PSO	1.036±0.08	1.823±0.29	1.524±0.41	0.60	55.22s
PSO with FS	0.210 ±0.07	0.309±0.08	1.173±0.22	0.76	60.02s
PSO with FW	0.192±0.08	0.159±0.06	1.062±0.10	0.85	61.34s

Table 10. Results of simultaneous clustering and feature selection(PSO with FS) and simultaneous clustering and feature weighting(PSO with FW) for mammographic masses data having 5 features

Methods	Fitness Value ↓	MSE ↓	Entropy ↓	Puri-ty ↑	Avg CPU Time
Kmeans	1.009 ±0.06	1.182 ±0.01	1.351 ±0.78	0.53	0.92s
PSO	0.300 ±0.02	1.035 ±0.03	1.231 ±0.03	0.60	1.64s
PSO with FS	0.052 ±0.06	0.108 ±0.09	1.085 ±0.09	0.90	2.05s
PSO with FW	0.014 ±0.05	0.096 ±0.02	1.005 ±0.71	0.93	2.12s

Table 11. Results of simultaneous clustering and feature selection(PSO withFS) and simultaneous clustering and feature weighting(PSO with FW) for digit recognition data having 64 features

Methods	Fitness Value ↓	MSE ↓	Entropy ↓	Puri-ty ↑	Avg CPU Time
Kmeans	3.16 ± 0.89	3.023 ± 0.64	2.722 ± 0.18	0.73	312.89s
PSO	2.334 ± 0.75	2.005 ± 0.48	1.946 ± 0.54	0.68	923.82s
PSO with FS	1.351 ± 0.33	1.318 ± 0.29	1.761 ± 0.51	0.87	1002.8s
PSO with FW	1.192 ± 0.52	1.283 ± 0.30	1.532 ± 0.88	0.85	983.88s

methods work well even in situations where the objective function or the constraints cannot be expressed properly. The evaluation of the strings in GA and individuals in PSO is crucial to the working of the algorithms. Domain knowledge is required for this evaluation. Besides GA and PSO, it is also possible to use other stochastic search techniques such as simulated annealing and tabu search.

Use of GA to form a new distance measure as a weighted sum of some existing distance measures is found to give good results. It is necessary to find the weights for every dataset used. The use of PSO for clustering has been discussed. Modifying the PSO with GA operators works well. Simultaneous feature selection and clustering and simultaneous feature weighting and clustering has been shown to give good results. These methods are very amenable to finding the optimal clustering simultaneously with feature selection or feature weighting.

5. SCOPE FOR FUTURE WORK

This chapter has shown how soft computing techniques can be used in the field of pattern classification and clustering. Only a few representative techniques have been described. There is immense scope to use soft computing techniques for a number of applications. It is to be noted that whenever genetic algorithms can be used, it is also possible to use other stochastic search techniques such as simulated annealing, tabu search and PSO. The optimal string for simultaneous clustering feature selection or simultaneous clustering and feature weighting can also be done using other stochastic search techniques besides PSO. It is also possible to use fuzzy and rough techniques to carry out learning. Thus it can be seen that what has been described in this chapter is just the tip of the iceberg and there is a lot more which can be explored.

REFERENCES

Abdel-Kader, R. F. (2010). Genetically improved PSO algorithm for efficient data clustering. In *Proceedings of the 2010 Second International Conference on Machine Learning and Computing,* (pp. 71-75). ICMLC.

Al-Sultan, K. S. (1995). A tabu search approach to the clustering algorithm. *Pattern Recognition, 28*(9), 1443–1451. doi:10.1016/0031-3203(95)00022-R

Angeline, P. J. (1998). Evolutionary optimization versus particle swarm optimization: Philosophy and performance differences. In *Proceedings of the 7th International Conference on Evolutionary Programming VII,* (pp. 601-610). Springer-Verlag.

Bezdek, J. C., Boggavaparu, S., Hall, L. O., & Bensaid, A. (1994). Genetic algorithm guided clustering. In *Proceedings of IEEE Congress on Evolutionary Computation* (pp. 34-40). IEEE.

Chuzhanova, N. A., Jones, A. J., & Margetts, S. (1998). Feature selection for genetic sequence classification. *Bioinformatics (Oxford, England), 14*(2), 139–143. doi:10.1093/bioinformatics/14.2.139 PMID:9545445

Ding, H., Trajeevski, G., Scheuermann, P., Wang, X., & Keogh, E. (2008). Querying and mining of time series data: Experimental comparison of representations and distance measures. *Proceedings VLDB Endow., 1*, 1542–1552.

Dohare, D., & Devi, V. S. (2011). Combination of similarity measures for time series classification using genetic algorithms. In *Proceedings of IEEE Congress on Evolutionary Computation.* New Orleans, LA: IEEE.

Eberhart, R. C., & Kennedy, J. (1995). A new optimizer using particle swarm theory. In *Proceedings of Sixth International Symposium on Micro Machine and Human Science* (pp. 39-43). Academic Press.

Fink, E., & Pratt, K. B. (2004). Indexing of compressed time series. In *Data mining in time series databases* (pp. 51–78). Singapore: World Scientific. doi:10.1142/9789812565402_0003

Jafar, O. A. M., & Shivakumar, R. (2010). Ant-based clustering algorithms: A brief survey. *International Journal of Computer Theory and Engineering, 2*(5), 1793–8201.

Kennedy, J., & Eberhart, R. C. (1995). Particle swarm optimization. *Neural Networks, 4*, 1942–1948.

Law, M. H. C., Figueiredo, M. A. T., & Jain, A. K. (2004). Simultaneous feature selection and clustering using mixture models. *Pattern Analysis and Machine Intelligence, 26,* 1154–1166. doi:10.1109/TPAMI.2004.71 PMID:15742891

Lewis, D. D. (1998). Naive (Bayes) at forty: The independence assumption in information retrieval. In *Proceedings of the 10th European Conference on Machine Learning* (pp. 4-15). London, UK: Academic Press.

Omran, M. G. H., Engelbrecht, A. P., & Salman, A. (2006). Particle swarm optimization for pattern recognition and image processing. *Studies in Computational Intelligence, 34,* 125–151. doi:10.1007/978-3-540-34956-3_6

Ratanamahatana, C. A., & Keogh, E. (2004). Making time-series classification more accurate using learned constraints. In *Proceedings of SDM 04: SIAM International Conference on Data Mining.* SIAM.

Selim, S. Z., & Alsultan, K. (1991). A simulated annealing algorithm for the clustering problem. *Pattern Recognition, 24*(10), 1003–1008. doi:10.1016/0031-3203(91)90097-O

Shelokar, P. S., Jayaraman, V. K., & Kulkarni, B. D. (2004). An ant colony approach for clustering. *Analytica Chimica Acta, 509*(2), 187–195. doi:10.1016/j.aca.2003.12.032

Swetha, K. P., & Devi, V. S. (2012a). Modified particle swarm optimization for pattern clustering. In *Proceedings of the International Conference on Neural Information Processing,* (pp. 496-503). Doha, Qatar: ICONIP.

Swetha, K. P., & Devi, V. S. (2012b). Simultaneous feature selection and clustering using particle swarm optimization. In *Proceedings of the International Conference on Neural Information Processing,* (pp. 509-515). Doha, Qatar: ICONIP.

Swetha, K. P., & Devi, V. S. (2012c). Feature weighting for clustering by particle swarm optimization. In *Proceedings of the Sixth International Conference on Genetic and Evolutionary Computing,* (pp. 441-444). ICGEC.

Ding, H., Trajeevski, G., Scheuermann, P., Wang, X., & Keogh, E. (n.d.). *Querying and mining of time series data: Experimental comparison of representations and distance measures.* Academic Press.

Keogh, E., & Kasetty, S. (2002). On the need for time series data mining benchmark: A survey and empirical demonstration. [ACM.]. *Proceedings of SIGKDD, 02,* 102–111.

Tseng, L. Y., & Yang, S. B. (2001). A genetic approach to the automatic clustering problem. *Pattern Recognition, 34,* 415–424. doi:10.1016/S0031-3203(00)00005-4

van der Merwe, D. W., & Engelbrecht, A. P. (2003). Data clustering using particle swarm optimization. *Congress on Evolutionary Computation, 1,* 215–220.

Xi, X., Keogh, E., Shelton, C., Wei, L., & Ratanamahatana, C. A. (2006). Fast time series classification using numerosity reduction. In *Proceedings of ICML06* (pp. 1033-1040). ICML.

Lesh, N., Zaki, M. J., & Ogihara, M. (1999). Mining features for sequence classification. In *Proceedings of the Fifth ACM SIGKDD International Conference on Knowledge Discovery and Data Mining,* (pp. 342-346). New York: ACM.

Yakhnenko, O., Silvescu, A., & Honavar, V. (2005). Discriminatively trained Markov model for sequence classification. In *Proceedings of the Fifth IEEE International Conference on Data Mining,* (pp. 498-505). Washington, DC: IEEE.

KEY TERMS AND DEFINITIONS

Clustering: The task of grouping a set of patterns so that patterns in the same group are more similar to each other than to patterns in other groups.

Data Mining: The analysis of large quantities of data to extract previously unknown interesting patterns in the data.

Feature Selection: Process of selecting a subset of the features available for use in the classification or clustering algorithm.

Genetic Algorithms: Computational method which mimics the process of natural selection and genetics to carry out optimization and search.

Particle Swarm Optimization: Computational method which mimics the social behaviour of a flock of birds to carry out optimization.

Pattern Recognition: The assignment of a class label to an input pattern.

Soft Computing: Finds inexact solutions to computationally hard problems and in many cases mimics the behaviour of human beings and animals.

Chapter 4
Chaotic Map Model–Based Interference Employed in Quantum–Inspired Genetic Algorithm to Determine the Optimum Gray Level Image Thresholding

Sandip Dey
Camellia Institute of Technology, India

Siddhartha Bhattacharyya
RCC Institute of Information Technology, India

Ujjwal Maulik
Jadavpur University, India

ABSTRACT

In this chapter, a Quantum-Inspired Genetic Algorithm (QIGA) is presented. The QIGA adopted the inherent principles of quantum computing and has been applied on three gray level test images to determine their optimal threshold values. Quantum random interference based on chaotic map models and later quantum crossover, quantum mutation, and quantum shift operation have been applied in the proposed QIGA. The basic features of quantum computing like qubit, superposition of states, coherence and decoherence, etc. help to espouse parallelism and time discreteness in QIGA. Finally, the optimum threshold value has been derived through the quantum measurement phase. In the proposed QIGA, the selected evaluation metrics are Wu's algorithm, Renyi's algorithm, Yen's algorithm, Johannsen's algorithm, Silva's algorithm, and finally, linear index of fuzziness, and the selected gray level images are Baboon, Peppers, and Corridor. The conventional Genetic Algorithm (GA) and Quantum Evolutionary Algorithm (QEA) proposed by Han et al. have been run on the same set of images and evaluation metrics with the same parameters as QIGA. Finally, the performance analysis has been made between the proposed QIGA with the conventional GA and later with QEA proposed by Han et al., which reveals its time efficacy compared to GA along with the drawbacks in QEA.

DOI: 10.4018/978-1-4666-4936-1.ch004

INTRODUCTION

All the animals are in inherent race aiming to control over environmental resources. The evolution can be determined by the competent. The rule of nature advocates that the better participants in all respect would be able to survive and scatter their own genetic material among the others. Artificial intelligence, a branch of computer science, embraces the evolutionary computations that mostly involve the optimization problems which are poles apart from each other. Basically Evolutionary Algorithms (EAs) can be considered as very good examples of stochastic search and optimization methods that always tag on the rules of natural biological evolution (Han, 2002). Since the last decade, researchers throughout the world are working on EAs that includes the optimization problems serving various objectives (Kim, 2006). Unlike the traditional optimization methods, the applications of EAs are vast and provide very successful results especially for solving complex optimization problems. EAs can deal with a number of participants in chorus which proves its parallelism capability. It has a very quick response for adapting different problems that in turn make a very good result (Han, 2002).

There are numerous evolutionary computation methods to develop various optimization techniques. Some of them are Genetic Algorithm (GA) developed by Fraser (Fraser, 1957), Bremermann (Bremermann, 1962) and Holland (Holland, 1975), evolution strategies (ES) developed by Rechenberg (Rechenberg, 1973), Schwefel (Schwefel, 1995) and evolutionary programming (EP) developed by Fogel (Fogel, 1966). These methods have the strengths of their own and also suffer from various weaknesses. The most non ignorable problem crops up to fit in are that; these methods take lot of times especially for the convergence for optimization of complex problems (Han, 2002).

EAs work on the principle of survival for the fittest. A selection is made at each generation based on the objective functions (or fitness functions). After the completion of each generation some strong vectors would be able to survive and some will not. The upshot of each iteration results better solution by the evolution mechanism, incorporated by the evolutionary algorithm (Han, 2002).

Image segmentation plays a very important role in image processing. This is mainly used in pattern recognition. Segmentation is the process which partitions a whole image into number of homogenous subsets called regions where each region possesses a different well-defined property. If an image I is partitioned into a number of non-empty regions, $R_1, R_2, \ldots, R_n$ then the following properties must hold (Pal, 1993).

$$\bigcup_{j=1}^{n} R_j = I \tag{1}$$

$$R_j \cap R_k = \phi \quad \forall \quad j \neq k \tag{2}$$

Segmentation is the earliest and most widely used method for image thresholding. The purpose of using thresholding is to distinguish an image into objects (foreground O) and its background (B) (Sahoo, 1997). In practice, there exist various algorithms that may be used to determine the threshold values of images. Let $I = \left[I_{pq} \right]_{m \times n}$ be a given image where each (p, q) consists of any gray value L with the following properties (Jawahar, 1997):

$$I_{pq} \in \{0, 1, 2, \ldots, L-1\} \tag{3}$$

$$O = \{I_{pq} | I_{pq} > T\} \tag{4}$$

$$O = \{I_{pq} \big| I_{pq} \leq T\} \qquad (5)$$

where, T represents the selected threshold value.

Quantum Computing (QC) is a method that has been envisaged from the principles of quantum physics. It is one of the most demanding topics of research in this twenty-first century. The Schrödinger equation (SE) is the sole resource from where the dynamic processes of QC can be described. QC is more efficient and faster while compared with the classical computing (Han, 2002). Richard Feynman discovered some inherent problems of classical computing. The basic classical computers are very inefficient to serve the quantum mechanical activities. He observed that these problems can be solved efficiently if quantum effects can be put into consideration (Talbi, 2004). QC is more fast and its efficiency is much more than the classical one because it uses its parallelism capability that in turn make the algorithms to run exponentially faster than its counterparts (Talbi, 2006 ; Reiffel, 2000). It may be very useful for solving different kinds of problems especially for problems that may need larger solution space. So it provides the flexibility to the designer to design more powerful algorithms. These algorithms could be made in such a way that it can solve different complex optimization problems. From the beginning of the last decade researchers are trying to construct such algorithms that can be run efficiently on QC. Though these machines are not available yet, the concept is that the aforesaid quantum algorithms could be run on these machines with very high efficiency while invented (Han, 2002). So the attention of the researchers turns into combining quantum algorithm with the conventional evolutionary algorithms which could be fit for quantum computer. Some of the typical quantum

algorithms may include Grover's database search algorithm (Grover, 1996) and Shor's quantum factoring algorithm (Shor, 1996).

Quantum inspired evolutionary computing acts according as the principles of QC. The basis of QC is quantum bits (qubits) and superposition of states. Like the conventional computer where the bit (0 or 1) is the smallest unit, the qubit acts similar for QC. The only difference for qubit is that instead of using 0 or 1, it is represented by the linear superposition of the basic two states with a probability constraint. Comparing to a classical computer, where for an n bit system, 2^n states are formed for an n-dimensional vector space whereas, for n-qubits QC, the state space will be of n-dimensions. The effect of this exponential growth of state space between classical computers and a QC makes the QC exponentially faster to perform any sort of actions. Like the conventional computer, the backbone of QC's architecture is a collection of gates called Q-gate. A primitive example of Q-gate is the CNOT gate which can be used to perform operation on the state of one qubit by other qubit. Other examples of Q-gates may include Hadamard gate and rotation gate (Hey, 1999).

The structure of the chapter is arranged as follows. Section 2 is about quantum computing rudiments. Section 3 describes the solution of the *NP*-Complete problem on quantum machines. Section 4 presents the detail of quantum evolutionary algorithm. Section 5 discusses about image thresholding. Section 6 presents the evaluation metrics that are used in the proposed QIGA to find optimum threshold value of three gray level test images. The proposed quantum inspired genetic algorithm is presented in Section 7. The experimental results of the proposed QIGA and the comparison with the conventional GA (Holland, 1975 ; Reeves, 1993) and later with the algorithm proposed by Han *et al.* (Han, 2002) is presented in Section 8. Finally, some conclusions regarding the proposed QIGA are presented in Section 9.

2. QUANTUM COMPUTING RUDIMENTS

QC follows the principles of quantum mechanics that in turn make it faster to perform any task. The basic features of QC are described as following subsections.

2.1 Qubit

A quantum bit or qubit is the smallest unit for a two-state quantum computer. A qubit is used to store information for a QC (Hey, 1999). In QC, the two-state vector $|0\rangle$ and $|1\rangle$ of a quantum bit is used for bit representation where

$$|0\rangle = \begin{bmatrix} 1 \\ 0 \end{bmatrix} \text{ and } |1\rangle = \begin{bmatrix} 0 \\ 1 \end{bmatrix} \tag{6}$$

Paul Dirac introduced the bracket notation for qubit representation (Araujo, 2008). We may define a qubit by "0" state, "1" state or any superposition (i.e., linear combination) of these two state vectors as

$$|\psi\rangle = \alpha|0\rangle + \beta|1\rangle \tag{7}$$

α and β are complex numbers and the normalization of the qubit state must follow the equation given by

$$|\alpha|^2 + |\beta|^2 = 1 \tag{8}$$

The probabilities of measuring $|0\rangle$ and $|1\rangle$ are $|\alpha|^2$ and $|\beta|^2$ respectively. For a quantum system having n qubits, the basis of the state space can be written as

$$\underbrace{|000\cdots0\rangle}_{n \ qubits}, \underbrace{|000\cdots1\rangle}_{n \ qubits}, \cdots, \underbrace{|111\cdots1\rangle}_{n \ qubits}$$

If ξ is the angle measured to define the qubit phase, it is given by

$$\xi = \arctan\left(\beta \middle/ \alpha\right) \tag{9}$$

The dot product of α and β is defined as (Araujo, 2008).

$$d = \alpha.\beta \tag{10}$$

2.2 Quantum Gate

Like the classical computer, there are different gates called quantum gates in QC that can process information. Some of the quantum gates are Hadamard gate, rotation gate, NOT gate, Controlled NOT gate etc. (Hey, 1999 ; Araujo, 2008). One feature of these gates is that they perform unitary operation.

Let U be the unitary operator, the inverse of it must be equal to adjoint i.e., $U^+ = U^{-1}$ and also it holds the relation given by

$$UU^+ = U^+U = I \tag{11}$$

For Hermitian operator H, the unitary operator holds the following equation

$$U = e^{iHt} \tag{12}$$

The Q-gates that perform transformation operation are responsible for preserving it's orthogonally. One of the basic features of quantum transformations is that in addition to be unitary, they are also reversible.

2.3 Quantum Entanglement

Entanglement is as an appealing feature of quantum states. Quantum entanglement can be employed in quantum computing to demonstrate the approach that different qubits can be turned into correlations with each other such that they can interact regardless of their locations. The entanglement of participating qubits assures to be in one state (say $|0\rangle$) for a particular qubit while the other is in other state (say $|1\rangle$), no matter how far apart they are. It signifies that correlation can exist between different qubits so that if one qubit is in the $|0\rangle$ state, another will be in the $|1\rangle$ state. Entanglement can be calculated, altered, and even sanitized if necessary (Bhattacharyya, 2011).

2.4 Quantum Coherence and Decoherence

The concepts of coherence and decoherence are analogous to linear superposition of the constituent basic states. It is obvious to have the existence of coherence between two participating wave functions, $|\psi\rangle$ as given in (7) while a constant phase relationship is retained between them. Similarly, decoherence comes into existence while the aforesaid phase relationship comes to an end or the linear superposition of the ingredient basis states are forced to be destroyed. In all participating states, $|\alpha|^2$ and $|\beta|^2$ are the required probabilities for collapsing to the states $|1\rangle$ and $|0\rangle$ when decoherence occurs.

3. NP-COMPLETE PROBLEMS AND QUANTUM COMPUTING

A P class problem of its first kind of NP-Complete problem can be solved with a finite number of computational steps which can be determined by a polynomial p^j where, p is supposed to be the input size and j is a constant. The efficiency to solve these kinds of problems is very high.

In another class of problems known as NP, an exhaustive searching is being continued until a given arrangement satisfies the solution of the given problem in polynomial-time. So, it can be stated that $P \subseteq NP$. NP-complete problems are the subclass of NP. For each NP-hard problem an NP-complete problem can be found out that can be transformed to NP-hard problem in a given polynomial time.

Quantum computers are capable to store and process a huge amount compare to its classical counterparts. It can process all possible combinations of solutions of a given problem simultaneously. For certain kind of problems, it performs with a very high efficacy. All P class problems can be solved with high efficiency in a given polynomial-time. For other NP-complete problems it may not sustain its approbation. Deutsch et al. have clarified in their paper that some classically hard problems can have efficient solution (Deutsch, 1992).

4. QUANTUM EVOLUTIONARY ALGORITHM

The principles and activities of Quantum Evolutionary Algorithm (QEA) (Han, 2002) are analogous to the concept of QC such as qubit and superposition of states. The basic characteristics of this algorithm are based on population dynamics that are maintained and updated from generation to generation through a given evaluation function. With each and every generation of population,

QEA finds the best individuals that suit the evaluation function from the current population and exclude the others. Before describing the QEA, we need to describe the probabilistic representation of qubit.

4.1 Quantum Inspired Representation

A quantum evolutionary algorithm (QEA) (Han, 2002 ; Araujo, 2008) may have many representation mechanisms viz. numerical representation, symbolic representation or binary representation (Hinterding, 1999). Unlike digital computer where the smallest bit is represented by either "0" or "1", QEA uses a different probabilistic representation using qubit which may be in "0" state or "1" state. In addition to that it can be represented as the superposition of two states. The definition and representation of qubit or qubit individual is constructed by a number of qubit strings as defined as follows:

- **Representation 1:** The smallest unit of information a QC holds is qubit which is defined by a pair of complex numbers (α, β) as shown below:

$$r = \begin{bmatrix} \alpha \\ \beta \end{bmatrix} \qquad (13)$$

where, α and β are the complex numbers, which satisfies Equations 10, 11 and 12. Geometrically, an angle θ can be measured and defined as $\cos(\theta) = |\alpha|$ and $\sin(\theta) = |\beta|$ such that Equation (10) is satisfied, since (Han, 2002)

$$\left[\cos(\theta)\right]^2 + \left[\sin(\theta)\right]^2 = 1 \qquad (14)$$

- **Representation 2:** A Q-bit individual as a collection of m numbers of Q-bit string, is defined as follows:

$$s = \begin{bmatrix} \alpha_1 & \alpha_2 & \alpha_3 & \cdots & \alpha_m \\ \beta_1 & \beta_2 & \beta_3 & \cdots & \beta_m \end{bmatrix} \qquad (15)$$

For s, each α_i and β_i must hold the relation $|\alpha_i|^2 + |\beta_i|^2 = 1$ for $i = 1, 2, \ldots, m$.

The superposition principle of qubits of all possible states enhances the capacity of storing the information about different states together. Let us assume that we represent one particular individual by three qubits $(m = 3)$ as follows:

$$= \begin{bmatrix} \dfrac{1}{\sqrt{2}} & \dfrac{1}{\sqrt{2}} & \dfrac{1}{2} \\ \dfrac{1}{\sqrt{2}} & -\dfrac{1}{\sqrt{2}} & \dfrac{\sqrt{3}}{2} \end{bmatrix} \qquad (16)$$

According to Equation 16, the states can be represented as

$$t = +\left(\frac{1}{4}\right)\left|000\right\rangle + \left(\frac{\sqrt{3}}{4}\right)\left|001\right\rangle - \left(\frac{1}{4}\right)\left|010\right\rangle$$

$$-\left(\frac{\sqrt{3}}{4}\right)\left|011\right\rangle + \left(\frac{1}{4}\right)\left|100\right\rangle - \left(\frac{1}{4}\right)\left|101\right\rangle$$

$$-\left(\frac{1}{4}\right)\left|110\right\rangle - \left(\frac{\sqrt{3}}{4}\right)\left|111\right\rangle \qquad (17)$$

From the Equation 17, it is clear that there are 9 states namely,

$$\underset{3 \; qubits}{\left|000\right\rangle}, \underset{3 \; qubits}{\left|001\right\rangle}, \ldots, \underset{3 \; qubits}{\left|111\right\rangle}$$

which have probabilities

$$\frac{1}{16}, \frac{3}{16}, \frac{1}{16}, \frac{3}{16}, \frac{1}{16}, \frac{1}{16}, \frac{1}{16}$$

and $\dfrac{3}{16}$ respectively. One q-individual is sufficient to represent these 9 different states as shown in 16 whereas 9 different strings viz.

$$(000), (001), \ldots, (111)$$

are needed for its equivalent classical representation (Han, 2002 ; Araujo, 2008).

4.2 QEA Description

The quantum evolutionary algorithm (QEA) (Han, 2002 ; Araujo, 2008) which is probabilistic in nature, is presented and described in this subsection. In QEA, a population of qubit individuals of size n generated at generation u is defined as

$$R(u) = \left\{ r_1^u, r_2^u, \ldots, r_n^u \right\}$$

where; each q-individual r_j^u is defined as

$$r_j^u = \begin{bmatrix} \alpha_{j1}^u & \alpha_{j2}^u & \alpha_{j3}^u & \ldots & \alpha_{jm}^u \\ \beta_{j1}^u & \beta_{j2}^u & \beta_{j3}^u & \ldots & \beta_{jm}^u \end{bmatrix} \qquad (18)$$

Here m denotes the number of qubits that is set for determining the string length of each q-individual for $j = 1, 2, \ldots, n$. In the first generation, the population of n individual is generated by initializing each

$$\alpha_i^0 = \beta_i^0 = \frac{1}{\sqrt{2}}$$

For

$$i = 1, 2, \ldots, m \quad \forall \quad r_j^0 = r_j^u \big| u = 0$$

for $j = 1, 2, \ldots, n$. This initialization indicates that with the same probability, the superposition for all possible states may occurs. In $R(u)$ the states of q-individuals gives a binary solution P_u. Let

$$P_u = \left\{ y_1^u, y_2^u, \ldots, y_n^u \right\}$$

is obtained at generation u where each y_i^u for $i = 1, 2, \ldots, n$ is a binary string of length m i.e., $y_i^u = a_1 a_2 a_3 \ldots a_m$ and each a_j for $j = 1, 2, \ldots, m$ where, m is either 0 or 1. In the observation process, a random number between 0 and 1 is generated for each $\left(\alpha_k, \beta_k \right)^T$ where, for every qubit in the population $R(u)$. If $r \geq |\beta|^2$, the qubit is set as 0; otherwise it is set as 1.

Different Q-gates are implemented in the QC to update the q-individuals in $R(u)$. After successful completion of a predefined number of generations, the best solution (if not being improved for a long time) is taken and all the solutions are replaced by the best solution, b. The algorithm for QEA is specified in Figure 1 (Han, 2002 ; Araujo, 2008).

QEA has various application areas. It can be used for solving combinatorial optimization problems like knapsack problem and many others (Han, 2002). For optimization, QEA initiates a random search. As the algorithm runs, the probability of getting a solution increases and QEA commences a local search. At the end of some runs it is observed that the probability of the solution converges to 1 which means instead of starting with a local search, it initiates a global search. After some generations, it will automatically be converted to the local search for optimization. QEA implements some rotation gates for performing the required operations according to some predefined lookup tables to maintain the population diversity.

Despite lots of advantages, QEA also have certain disadvantages. The coding and decoding process in QEA is not convenient to adopt in an easy manner. In addition to this, the algorithm

Figure 1. Quantum evolutionary algorithm

begin

$c \longleftarrow 0$

Initialize $R(0)$ with n individuals

Observing the state of $R(0)$ create $P(0)$

for *each element* $x \in P(0)$ **do**

Evaluate $Fitness(x)$ using fitness function

Copy the elements of $P(0)$ into $B(0)$

repeat

$c \longleftarrow c+1$

Observing the states of $R(t-1)$, create $P(t)$

for $x \in P(t)$ **do**

Evaluate $Fitness(x)$ using fitness function

Update the elements of $R(t)$ using Q-gate

Probability constraints are applied for computation

The best solution among $B(t-1)$ and $P(t)$ is stored into $B(t)$

The best solution b is stored in $B(t)$

if *(no better solution is obtained for several predefined generations)* **then**

Replace b with all the solutions of $B(t)$

possesses very low search efficiency while it is applied for any optimization process relating to numerical methods. QEA is also unable for adapting the dimensions and precisions for the numerical problems of optimization. The main disadvantage for QEA is that it has to depend on look up tables which are always prerequisites for solving combinatorial optimization problems to be optimized. These defects of QEA delimit its use in real time situations. However, QEA finds wide applications as cited in (Han, 2002 ; Araujo, 2008 ; Hossain, 2010) .

5. IMAGE THRESHOLDING

This section deals with the different facets of image thresholding in practice.

5.1 Thresholding: Purpose, Application and Optimization

In image processing, the most commonly used segmentation process is thresholding. Thresholding is the method used to distinguish objects with its background in an image. Its purpose is to convert any gray level image to binary image. Each Pixel intensity is compared with a predefined intensity value called threshold for the entire image and grouped into either foreground class or background class. The member of the foreground class possesses the pixel intensity values greater than or equal to the threshold, whereas the members of background class have lesser pixel intensity values than the threshold (or vice versa) (Bhattacharyya, 2011). One use of thresholding is in optical character recognition where the characters from the document image are to be extracted and recognized (Sathya, 2010 ; Lázaro, 2010) . In video change, a threshold is used to determine the change which may occur between the current images with the background image which was established before (Su, 2006). In certain industrial applications, it may require to make a system that may automatically make a visual inspection for the electronics components. Thresholding may be used in such cases for detecting such components (Alteanu, 2005). Some real-time applications where image segmentation (for moving objects) is employed for efficient compression to separate texture with contour are reported in (Chen, 2004).

In medical system, sometime Magnetic Resonance Image (MRI) is prescribed to detect the deformities in the brain region. Image thresholding may give a magnificent solution to these problems (Atkins, 1998 ; Doelken, 2008) . Other applications for image processing are biomedical image analysis, text enhancement, and automatic target recognition (Anagnostopoulos) etc. This can be used as a popular tool to locate addresses written on envelopes (Yeh, 1986). This tool can also be used in different real-time application like robotics, object tracking, automobiles laser range finding. Thresholding is employed in Optical Character Recognition (OCR) (Sezgin, 2004) and Non-Destructive Testing (NDT) (Sezgin, 2004) where image analysis and image segmentation put an important role such as some defective materials need to have ultrasonic inspection. Some typical

examples of this type may include Carbon-Fibre Reinforced (CFRP) (Maldague, 1994), Thermal inspection of Glass-Fibre Reinforced (GFRP) (Sezgin, 2004), checking for surface roughness of metal and ceramics, to inspect depth of coating in steel plates and eddy current inspection of fuselage cracks and aircraft wheels (Trier, 1995) .

There are two types of thresholding methods viz., local and global methods. In former one, more than one threshold values exist across the entire image neighborhoods, whereas there is a fixed threshold for the later method (Bazi, 2007). Thresholding can be employed as an effective tool for segmentation from the histogram viewpoint. It has a single lobe in unimodal histogram, whereas multimodal histogram deals with multiple lobes. So, the results are obtained by a tight coupling between the thresholding and numerous heuristic optimization algorithms that may establish the thresholding as a classical optimization problem.

5.2 Thresholding Methods

The methods that are broadly used in different thresholding algorithms can be differentiated into six categories as follows (Han, 2002 ; Sezgin, 2004):

1. Histogram shape-based methods,
2. Object attribute-based methods,
3. Histogram entropy-based methods,
4. Clustering-based methods,
5. Spatial methods,
6. Local adaptation-based methods.

Each individual category is illustrated below. In category (1), an optimum threshold is obtained based on the histogram's shape properties. From the histogram, a peak value is detected. The objects are categorized by iterative smoothing of the histogram shape (Wu, 1998).

For the next category, a similarity between the gray level and binarized image is measured.

Different form of attributes namely, edge matching (Venkatesh, 1995), grey-level moments (O'Gorman, 1994), connectivity (Pal, 1988), fuzzy compactness (Liu, 1994), texture analysis (Russ, 1987), stability of segmented objects (Yanni, 1994) etc are considered.

For histogram entropy-based methods, the entropy of the distribution of gray level is calculated. Entropy is calculated from the foreground (object) and background gray level distribution. Then the resulting entropy is taken by optimizing the above calculated values using various methods (Sezgin, 2004).

For category number (4), a clustering analysis is done for the gray level data by setting the cluster number to two for the two lobes of the histogram assuming they are distinct. Several methods have been developed so far for clustering-based methods. Some authors considered the midpoint of the histogram peaks (Srikanthan, 2001). On some occasions some algorithms demand the fitting of the mixture of Gaussians. Some other method of this category is fuzzy clustering thresholding method (Jawahar, 1997).

The algorithms for the category (5), gray-level distribution is considered. In addition to this, it may take the pixels from the neighborhood. The neighboring pixels may be considered in terms of context probabilities, co-occurrence probabilities, correlation function, 2D entropy (Niblack, 1986).

For local adaptation, the algorithms are constructed by considering different parameters about each pixel of an image whose threshold value is to be calculated. These parameters may include some statistics like variance, range and some other parameter regarding surface fitting of the neighborhood of the pixels. Many local adaptation methods have been proposed by different authors so far. Some typical example may include Niblack (Sauvola, 2000), Sauvola (Yen, 1995) to name a few.

6. EVALUATION METRICS

In the proposed QIGA six measures have been considered as the evaluation metrics. In (Sezgin, 2004), the authors have presented various thresholding techniques in details. The selected evaluation metrics for this paper are Wu's algorithm (Wu, 1998), Renyi's algorithm (Sahoo, 1997), Yen's algorithm (Yen, 1995), Johannsen's algorithm (Johannsen, 1982), Silva's algorithm (Silva, 2006) and Linear Index of Fuzziness (Huang, 1995 ; Tizhoosh, 2005). The first five measures are entropy-based of gray scale images while the last one is based on soft computing approach. Let us consider the probability distribution of pixels frequencies of a gray scale image as given by

$$p_j = \frac{n_j}{N}, j \in \left[0, 255\right] \qquad (19)$$

and

$$P_T = \sum_{j=0}^{T} p_j \qquad (20)$$

where, n_j is the number of pixels in the given image, N is the total pixels in the image. P_T is a measure which is computed by totaling the probability distributions up to the threshold value T. The selected algorithms are described in the following subsections in details.

6.1 Wu's Algorithm

Wu, Songde and Hanquing proposed this entropy-based algorithm (Wu, 1998). The authors have made two probability distributions for the object and its background of the selected gray scale image as given by (Wu, 1998)

$$E : p(j) = \frac{p_j}{P_T}, j \in [0, T]$$

$$F : p(j) = \frac{p_j}{P_T}, j \in [T+1, 255] \qquad (21)$$

The values of p_j and P_T are obtained by the Equations 19 and 20 respectively. Two entropies have been considered for foreground and background probability distributions as given by (Wu, 1998)

$$H_b(T) = -\sum_{j=0}^{T} p_j \log(p_j) \qquad (22)$$

and

$$H_f(T) = -\sum_{j=T+1}^{255} p_j \log(p_j) \qquad (23)$$

where, $H_f(T)$ and $H_b(T)$ represent foreground and background entropy. For getting the optimum threshold, the authors has minimized the differences of the aforesaid class entropies as given by (Wu, 1998)

$$W(T) = |H_b(T) - H_f(T)| \qquad (24)$$

6.2 Renyi's Algorithm

This is a entropy-based thresholding method (Sahoo, 1997 ; Sezgin, 2004) which employs two probability distributions, one for the object and other for the background for a gray level image.

Let us assume that $p_0, p_1, \ldots, p_{255}$ are the given probability distributions for a gray level image. The object class (D_1) and background class (D_2) are derived from the above probability distributions as given by

$$D_1 : \frac{p_0}{p(D_1)}, \frac{p_1}{p(D_1)}, \ldots, \frac{p_T}{p(D_1)}$$

$$D_2 : \frac{p_{T+1}}{p(D_2)}, \frac{p_{T+2}}{p(D_2)}, \ldots, \frac{p_{255}}{p(D_2)}$$

where,

$$p(D_1) = \sum_{j=0}^{T} p_j, p(D_2) = \sum_{j=T+1}^{255} p_j \qquad (25)$$

and

$$p(D_1) + p(D_2) = 1 \qquad (26)$$

The Renyi entropy can be defined in related to the foreground and background image distribution with some parameter ρ as depicted below (Sahoo, 1997).

$$H_f^\rho = \frac{1}{1-\rho} \ln \left(\sum_{j=0}^{T} \left[\frac{p_j}{p(D_1)} \right]^\rho \right) \qquad (27)$$

$$H_b^\rho = \frac{1}{1-\rho} \ln \left(\sum_{j=T+1}^{255} \left[\frac{p_j}{p(D_2)} \right]^\rho \right) \qquad (28)$$

The optimum threshold of gray level image can be obtained by maximizing $\left\{H_f^\rho + H_b^\rho\right\}$. In the proposed QIGA, the value of ρ is assumed to be 0.5.

6.3 Yen's Algorithm

This entropy-based algorithm proposed by Yen, Chang and Chang (Sezgin, 2004 ; Yen, 1995) has the same thought as Kapur (Johannsen, 1982) for determining the foreground and background image distributions.

The authors defined the entropic correlation by (Yen, 1995)

$$EC\left(T\right) = Y_b^T\left(T\right) + Y_f^T\left(T\right)$$

$$= -\log\left(\sum_{j=0}^{T}\left[\frac{p_j}{p\left(D_1\right)}\right]^2\right)$$

$$-\log\left(\sum_{j=T+1}^{255}\left[\frac{p_j}{p\left(D_2\right)}\right]^2\right)$$

(29)

where, the values of $p\left(D_1\right)$ and $p\left(D_2\right)$ are obtained by the equation 25. Maximizing $EC\left(T\right)$ yields to optimum threshold of test image using the given evaluation function. The equations 27 and 28 are transformed to the functions $Y_b^T\left(T\right)$ and $Y_f^T\left(T\right)$ while $\rho = 2$ (Sezgin, 2004 ; Johannsen, 1982) .

6.4 Johannsen's Algorithm

Johannsen and Bille have proposed this algorithm (Johannsen, 1982). To obtain the optimal threshold of a given gray scale image, the algorithm minimize the expression given by (Johannsen, 1982)

$$J\left(T\right) = J_b\left(T\right) + J_f\left(T\right)$$

$$= \log\left(P_T\right) + \frac{1}{P_T}\left\{E\left(p_T\right) + E\left(P_{T-1}\right)\right\}$$

$$+ \log\left(1 - P_{T-1}\right) + \frac{1}{1 - P_{T-1}}\left\{E\left(p_T\right) + E\left(1 - P_T\right)\right\}$$

(30)

where,

$$E\left(p\right) = -p\log\left(p\right)$$

and the values of p_j and P_T are obtained by the Equations 19 and 20 respectively (Silva, 2006) .

6.5 Silva's Algorithm

The algorithm by Silva, Lins and Rocha (Silva,, 2006) performs a statistical measure. For this reason entropy is calculated between the gray level distributions with its binary version of the test image. Let S be the entropy of the gray scale image as given by (Silva, 2006)

$$S = \sum_{j=0}^{255} p_j \log_2\left(p_j\right)$$

(31)

Firstly, the *priori probability distribution* namely,

$$\left\{p_0, p_1, \ldots, p_{255}\right\}$$

is obtained with the Equation 19. The value of T is calculated by the posteriori probability distributions $\left\{P_T, 1 - P_T\right\}$ for $P_T \leq 0.5$ which is the associated with the entropy based distribution as given by

$$S'\left(T\right) = h\left(P_T\right)$$

(31)

where,

$$h(p) = -p \log_2(p) - (1-p) \log_2(1-p)$$

and the value of P_T is obtained by the Equation 21.

A loss factor β is determined by the equation given by

$$\beta\left(\frac{S}{\log(256)}\right) = -\frac{3}{7}\left(\frac{S}{\log(256)}\right) + 0.8$$

if

$$\frac{S}{\log(256)} < 0.7$$

$$= \left(\frac{S}{\log(256)}\right) - 0.2, \text{ if } \frac{S}{\log(256)} \geq 0.7 \quad (33)$$

Finally, the optimum threshold of the gray level image is determined by minimizing $|E(T)|$, given by

$$|E(T)| = \left| \frac{S'(T)}{\left(\frac{S}{\log(256)}\right)} - \beta\left(\frac{S}{\log(256)}\right) \right| \quad (34)$$

6.6 Linear Index of Fuzziness

The fuzzy measures can be defined as the measurement of degree such that a gray level, g, fits in the object with its background (Sezgin, 2004). The term index of fuzziness has been proposed by Huang and Wang. Huang *et al.* used this mea-

sure by computing the distance between the gray scale image and its corresponding binary version (Huang, 1995; Tizhoosh, 2005). Let us consider a given gray scale image of the dimension $C \times D$ has L gray levels $g \in [0, 1, ..., L]$. For a subset $B \subseteq Y$ and the membership function $\mu_Y(g)$, the linear index of fuzziness γ_l is defined by (Huang, 1995)

$$\gamma_l = \frac{2}{CD} \sum_{g=0}^{L-1} h(g) \times \min\{\mu_B(g), 1 - \mu_B(g)\}$$
$$(35)$$

where, $h(g)$ represents the histogram of the data set. The optimum threshold can be obtained by minimizing γ_l (Huang, 1995 ; Tizhoosh, 2005).

7. QUANTUM INSPIRED GENETIC ALGORITHM

It is very common practice for any researcher to design quantum-inspired evolutionary algorithms from the principle of quantum computers (Han, 2002). Han et al. proposed a QEA using the concept of qubits having some probability constraints and superposition of states. A concept of Q-gate with the above principles to enhance the better solution space capability was also demonstrated in this work. Talbi *et al.* proposed another algorithmic approach based on quantum GA to solve the TSP problem (Talbi, 2004). The same concept was used to construct another algorithm for image registration (Talbi, 2006). In this algorithm, interference played an important role that was incorporated using a rotation gate with the consultation of a predefined lookup table. This is the limitation of the proposed algorithm as because it may not be possible to predict always the best solution beforehand (Bhattacharyya, 2011).

In this article, we have proposed another quantum-inspired genetic algorithm (QIGA) which comprises the phases as illustrated in the flow diagram in Figure1. The steps of the algorithm are detailed in the following subsections.

7.1 Generation and Initialization of Population

This is the first phase of the proposed QIGA. In this phase, an initial population of four chromosomes is generated and initialized with qubit elements. An L level gray-scale image has L number of intensity levels i.e.,

$$L = \left\{ 0, 1, 2, ..., L-1 \right\}$$

At the starting phase, a $L \times L$ matrix with two superposed quantum states $\left| \psi \right\rangle$, $i = 1, 2$ is formed for encoding the intensity values of the given image. Each single quantum chromosome is represented as (Talbi, 2004 ; Bhattacharyya, 2011).

$$\left| \psi \right\rangle = \begin{bmatrix} \alpha_{11} \left\langle \psi_1 \right| + \beta_{11} \left\langle \psi_2 \right| \cdots \alpha_{1L} \left\langle \psi_1 \right| + \beta_{1L} \left\langle \psi_2 \right| \\ \alpha_{21} \left\langle \psi_1 \right| + \beta_{21} \left\langle \psi_2 \right| \cdots \alpha_{2L} \left\langle \psi_1 \right| + \beta_{2L} \left\langle \psi_2 \right| \\ \cdots\cdots\cdots\cdots\cdots\cdots\cdots\cdots\cdots\cdots \\ \cdots\cdots\cdots\cdots\cdots\cdots\cdots\cdots\cdots\cdots \\ \alpha_{L1} \left\langle \psi_1 \right| + \beta_{L1} \left\langle \psi_2 \right| \cdots \alpha_{LL} \left\langle \psi_1 \right| + \beta_{LL} \left\langle \psi_2 \right| \end{bmatrix}$$

(36)

where, $\left| \alpha_{ij} \right|^2$ and $\left| \beta_{ij} \right|^2$ are the required probabilities for measuring the state $\left| 0 \right\rangle$ and $\left| 1 \right\rangle$ respectively for the qubits and $i, j = 1, 2, ..., L$.

7.2 Random Quantum Interference

Each element in the L × L matrix is formed with two quantum states in superposed fashion and each of them must satisfy the equation given by

$$\left| \alpha_{ij} \right|^2 + \left| \beta_{ij} \right|^2 = 1$$

(37)

where, $i, j = 1, 2, ..., L$.

Quantum interference must be performed in each of the qubits such that Equation (37) must be satisfied. A typical example of 6 chromosomes after interference is shown in Figure 2 where, $(0.2395)^2 + (0.9708)^2 = 1, (-0.1523)^2 + (0.9883)^2 = 1$ etc.

One very important aspect about random quantum interference is that its performance is solely dependent on the following two phases. The initially generated chromosomes must undergo the following two phases to yield the quantum interference.

Generate the Equivalence Random Chaotic Maps for All Participating Qubit States

In the proposed QIGA, this phase is considered to be very important as it initiates random quantum interference of the participating qubits. The quantum states which are represented in terms of a real chaotic map undergo the quantum interference (Bhattacharyya, 2011). We can consider that the QIGA maintain dynamic time discreteness and this quantum system demonstrates transformations U and V, which should abide by the properties like (1) Automorphism, (2) Endomorphism, (3) Flow and (4) Semiflow (Web-source,2000; Bhattacharyya, 2011). The real chaotic map can estimate this qubit representation (Bhattacharyya, 2011). If we consider a measure space $\left(Y; A; \mu \right)$ and if $h \in L^1 \left(Y; A; \mu \right)$, then for μ-*a.a.* and $y \in Y$, the following rules hold.

- **For Automorphism:** Assuming U be an automorphism then (Bhattacharyya, 2011 ; Image)

$$\lim_{n \to \infty} \frac{1}{n} \sum_{k=0}^{n-1} h\left(U^k y \right) = \lim_{n \to \infty} \frac{1}{n} \sum_{k=0}^{n-1} h\left(U^{-k} y \right) \quad (38)$$

i.e.,

Figure 2. The proposed algorithm

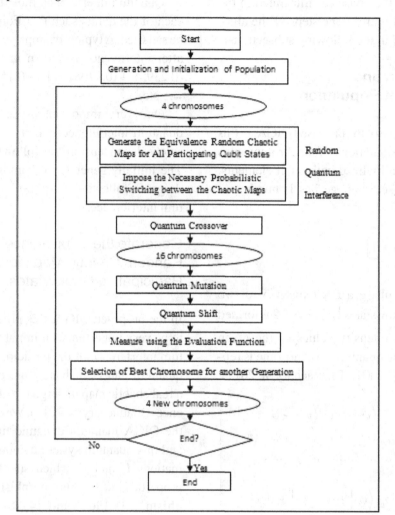

$$\frac{1}{2n+1}\sum_{k=-n}^{n}h\left(U^{k}y\right)\overset{def}{=}\overline{h}\left(y\right) \tag{39}$$

- **For Endomorphism:** Assuming U be an endomorphism then (Bhattacharyya, 2011 ; Image)

$$\lim_{n\to\infty}\frac{1}{n}\sum_{k=0}^{n-1}h\left(U^{k}y\right)\overset{def}{=}\overline{h}\left(y\right) \tag{40}$$

- **For Flow:** Assuming $\left\{U^{t}\right\}_{t\in R}$ (R is in the measurement space) be an flow then (Bhattacharyya, 2011 ; Image)

$$\lim_{t\to\infty}\frac{1}{t}\int_{0}^{t}h\left(U^{\tau}y\right)d\tau=\lim_{t\to\infty}\frac{1}{t}\int_{0}^{t}h\left(U^{-\tau}y\right)d\tau \tag{41}$$

i.e.,

$$\lim_{t\to\infty}\frac{1}{2t}\int_{-t}^{t}h\left(U^{\tau}y\right)d\tau\overset{def}{=}\overline{h}\left(y\right) \tag{42}$$

- **For Semiflow:** Assuming $\left\{V^{t}\right\}_{t\in R^{+}}$ (R is in the measurement space) be an semiflow then (Bhattacharyya, 2011 ; Image)

$$\lim_{t \to \infty} \frac{1}{2t} \int h\left(V^\tau y\right) d\tau \overset{def}{=} \bar{h}\left(y\right) \tag{43}$$

Moreover, the following relations also hold.

$$\bar{h}\left(Uy\right) = \bar{h}\left(y\right)$$

or

$$\bar{h}\left(U^t y\right) = \bar{h}\left(y\right)$$

or

$$\bar{h}\left(V^t y\right) = \bar{h}\left(y\right) \tag{44}$$

Any transformation that satisfies the Equations 38, 40, 41 and 43 is known to be invariant w.r.t. the above properties. When the measure $\mu\left(A\right)$ of any invariant set A is either 0 or 1, then this system is called ergodic (Websource,2000) . We may regard the participating qubit

$$\left(\left|\psi\right\rangle = \alpha_j \left|\psi_j\right\rangle + \beta_j \left|\psi_j\right\rangle, j = 1,2\right)$$

to follow a dynamical ergodic system. Boyarsky and Góra used Birkhoff's Ergodic theorem as a tool to set up the equivalence between the quantum state and chaotic map (Websource,2000) .

Therefore, some invariant point transformation, S can be applied to the qubits to make them over to a corresponding assortment of chaotic maps

$$S = \left\{t_1, t_2, I, p_1, p_2, 1 - p_1, 1 - p_2\right\}$$

(Websource,2000) where,

$$\tau_j\left(j = 1,2\right) = h \circ S \circ h^{-1}$$

is said to be nonlinear point transformations differentially conjugate to S and I is known as identity map. The two weighting probabilities p_1 and p_2 of τ_1 and τ_2 respectively are determined by

$$p_j = \frac{a_j f_j}{\sum_{j=1}^{2} a_j f_j} \tag{45}$$

where, a_j are the positive constants and

$$f_j = \left|\psi_j\right\rangle \left\langle\psi_j\right| = \psi_j^* \psi_j$$

are pdf corresponding to each τ_j (Bhattacharyya, 2011).

Impose the Necessary Probabilistic Switching between the Chaotic Maps

Here, a necessary probabilistic switching is applied between the maps. The outcome of this switching may be the cause of alteration of states of the maps which is formed by the participating qubits. It capitulate the expected interference between the states which may be due to the superposition effect among two wave functions when applied in some orderly manner. So, the innovation of the proposed method reveals the reality of not maintaining any predefined order to regulate the interference process. Rather the randomness which is gained due to the probabilistic transformation S from the last phase, makes it simple.

7.3 Quantum Crossover

In this phase, a random position is chosen for crossover two different chromosomes. Based on a predefined crossover probability, crossover is performed between a set of two chromosomes at the selected particular position. Figure 3 shows a

Figure 3. Quantum Interference

0.1119	0.2395	0.2232	0.9883	0.9950	-0.1532
0.9937	0.9708	0.9747	-0.1523	0.0987	0.9881

Figure 4. Quantum crossover

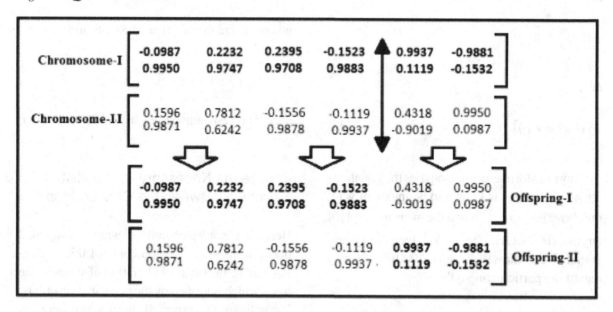

crossover between two chromosomes. At the end of this phase, a new set of 12 chromosomes are created. It makes a pool of total 16 chromosomes for next phase.

7.4 Quantum Mutation

In this phase, the quantum mutation is performed on each chromosome based on the values of two different parameters. The first parameter is called *mutethrs* which is the probability of deciding whether a particular chromosome will be selected for mutation or not. The second parameter,

muteprob decides for each line in the chromosome whether it will be mutated with another line or not. The portrayal of quantum mutation is shown in Figure 5.

7.5 Quantum Shift

Along with the aforesaid quantum crossover and quantum mutation, this phase also improve the population diversity of chaotic maps. This shift operation performs a random shifting in some chromosomes in the population. In this phase, a group of chromosomes in the population are selected for

Figure 5. Quantum mutation

begin

Let *cr* be the population of chromosomes and *L* be the gray-level of the image.

for *each* chromosome $x \in cr$ **do**

Generate a real random number $r_1 \in [0,1]$.

if $(r_1 \leq \text{mutethrs})$ **then**
for *each* line $j \in x$ **do**

Generate another real random number $r_2 \in [0,1]$.

if $(r_2 \leq \text{muteprob})$ **then**

Generate an integer random number $k \in [0,1]$.

Mutate line number k with the line number j within x

quantum shifting based on a predefined shifting probability, *shift_thrs* . The route of quantum shifting is depicted in Figure 6.

7.6 Measure Using the Evaluation Function

In quantum measurement phase, the fitness of chromosomes is computed for selected evaluation functions. The proposed algorithm adopts the measurement procedure from (Talbi, 2004). The aim is to destruct that superposition of states and preserve some states for further information. Here a random number (N) is generated and a compared with the probability obtained in all β_{ij} positions of Equation 36 where

$$i, j = 1, 2, ..., L$$

All those β_{ij} position of Equation 36 satisfying $|\beta_{ij}|^2 > N$ indicates the required possible solutions.

Let us demonstrate the procedure of determining the optimum threshold value with an example. Let a gray scale image has L possible gray level,

$$L = \{0, 1, 2, ..., L-1\}$$

To have the best possible solution, we compare a randomly generated number N with all p_2 values as obtained by the Equation 45. Let us assume

Figure 6.Quantum shift

```
begin
  Let cr be the population of chromosomes and L be the gray-level of the image.
  for each chromosome x ∈ cr do
      Generate a real random number r1 ∈ [0,1].
      if (r1 ≤ shift_thrs) then
          Generate a random integer, r2 ∈ [1, floor(L/3)].
          Generate a random position, j ∈ [1, L − r2].
          Generate another random number, s ∈ [1, L − r2 − j].
          Perform shifting of r2 lines starting from the j_th position according to s.
```

that after successful completion of all the predefined runs, we get the position $(15, 7)$ which satisfies $|p_2|^2 > N$. Note that N is the randomly generated number. This typical example is depicted as a solution matrix in Figure 7. Here, the value for this particular position is set to 1 and the values for all other positions are set to 0. So the optimum threshold value is obtained as $(15 \times 7) = 105$ (shown by circle) in Figure 7.

Figure 7. The solution matrix

$$
\begin{array}{c c}
\text{Level} & \begin{array}{ccccccccc} 0 & 1 & 2 & 3 & 4 \cdots & 7 & 8 & 9 \cdots & L \end{array} \\
\theta = \begin{array}{c} 0 \\ 1 \\ 2 \\ \vdots \\ 15 \\ 16 \\ 17 \\ \vdots \\ L \end{array} & \begin{bmatrix} 0 & 0 & 0 & 0 & 0 \cdots & 0 & 0 & 0 \cdots & 0 \\ 0 & 0 & 0 & 0 & 0 \cdots & 0 & 0 & 0 \cdots & 0 \\ 0 & 0 & 0 & 0 & 0 \cdots & 0 & 0 & 0 \cdots & 0 \\ \cdots & & & & & & & & \\ 0 & 0 & 0 & 0 & 0 \cdots & \textcircled{1} & 0 & 0 \cdots & 0 \\ 0 & 0 & 0 & 0 & 0 \cdots & 0 & 0 & 0 \cdots & 0 \\ 0 & 0 & 0 & 0 & 0 \cdots & 0 & 0 & 0 \cdots & 0 \\ \cdots & & & & & & & & \\ 0 & 0 & 0 & 0 & 0 \cdots & 0 & 0 & 0 \cdots & 0 \end{bmatrix}
\end{array}
$$

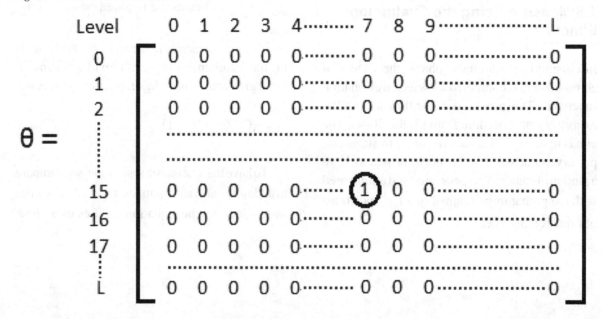

7.7 Selection of Best Chromosome for Another Generation

The fitness of each chromosome is evaluated using different methods. At the prior of each generation, four chromosomes are selected from a pool of chromosomes based on selection criteria. Out of these four chromosomes, three best chromosomes are taken according to fitness values and another one is randomly chosen from the rest. These four chromosomes are preserved to run for the next generation. The whole process is repeated until the stopping criterion is not fulfilled. QIGA stop executing when there is no further improvement for a predefined number of iterations.

8. EXPERIMENTAL RESULTS

8.1 Results of the Proposed QIGA and Conventional GA

In this article, three gray scale test images of dimension 256×256 have been selected for the proposed QIGA algorithm. These are Baboon (intensity dynamic range varies from 0 and 236) (Websource,2000), Peppers (intensity dynamic range varies from 0 and 239) (Websource,2000) and Corridor (intensity dynamic range varies from 0 and 255) (Websource,2000) . The proposed QIGA has been run using six different evaluation metrics to obtain the optimum threshold of the selected test images. The selected metrics are Wu's algorithm (Wu, 1998), Renyi's algorithm (Sahoo, 1997), Yen's algorithm (Yen, 1995), Johannsen's algorithm (Johannsen, 1982), Silva's algorithm (Silva, 2006) and Linear Index of Fuzziness (Huang, 1995 ; Tizhoosh, 2005) . The optimum threshold values for each measure have been documented for 10 different runs having 500 iterations each. The conventional GA has also been executed for 10 different runs having 500

iterations each for same set of evaluation functions and test images as stated above. The results have been documented.

The results of QIGA and GA for different six evaluation functions are listed in Tables 1 through 6. Each tables show three different parameters viz., fitness value $\left(\mu\right)$, optimum threshold $\left(\theta\right)$ and the execution time $\left(t\right)$ (in seconds) both for QIGA and the conventional genetic algorithm (GA). The tables also depict the optimum threshold value $\left(\theta_{op}\right)$ for each evaluation function.

A mathematical deduction can be made for the proposed QIGA and the conventional GA. Let us assume that the QIGA is working on two qubit states and the dimensions of each test images are $e \times f$. The total size QIGA takes is

$$Y = 2 \times e \times f \times g \times 8 = 16efg$$

bits where the pixel intensity size of each test image is assumes to be g. Under the same condition as in QIGA, the total size for the conventional GA can be calculated as $Z = e \times f \times g \times 8 = 8efg$ bits. So,

$$\frac{Z}{Y} = \frac{8efg}{16efg} = \frac{1}{2}$$

But in practical 16 and 8192 chromosomes have been taken for the proposed QIGA and the conventional GA respectively. The selected chromosomes for QIGA are of double data type whereas it is integer data type (as $2^8 = 256$) for GA. The dimension of each test image is 256×256. So, the total size for the proposed QIGA is

$$16 \times 2 \times 256 \times 256 \times 8 \times 8 = 134217728$$

bits whereas the size for conventional GA is

$$8192 \ \times 8 \times 4 \times 8 = 2097152 \text{ bits.}$$

Table 1. Experimental results of QIGA and GA (Holland, 1975 ; Reeves, 1993) for three gray scale images using Wu's method (Wu, 1998)

TN	Baboon QIGA			Baboon GA			Peppers QIGA			Peppers GA			Corridor QIGA			Corridor GA		
	θ	v	t	θ	v	t	θ	v	t	θ	v	t	θ	v	t	θ	v	t
1	134	0.0480	350	134	0.0480	1329	125	0.0179	348	125	0.0179	886	136	0.0084	346	136	0.0084	556
2	134	0.0480	349	134	0.0480	1209	125	0.0179	353	125	0.0179	1077	136	0.0084	346	136	0.0084	766
3	134	0.0480	348	134	0.0480	997	125	0.0179	349	125	0.0179	908	136	0.0084	345	136	0.0084	689
4	134	0.0480	346	134	0.0480	967	125	0.0179	348	125	0.0179	895	136	0.0084	347	136	0.0084	747
5	134	0.0480	346	134	0.0480	1001	125	0.0179	347	125	0.0179	991	136	0.0084	347	136	0.0084	802
6	134	0.0480	347	134	0.0480	1116	125	0.0179	347	125	0.0179	1055	136	0.0084	345	136	0.0084	739
7	134	0.0480	349	134	0.0480	897	125	0.0179	345	125	0.0179	1011	136	0.0084	346	136	0.0084	741
8	134	0.0480	349	134	0.0480	1018	125	0.0179	346	125	0.0179	943	136	0.0084	346	136	0.0084	752
9	134	0.0480	348	134	0.0480	884	125	0.0179	348	125	0.0179	1072	136	0.0084	347	136	0.0084	809
10	134	0.0480	350	134	0.0480	1109	125	0.0179	347	125	0.0179	994	136	0.0084	345	136	0.0084	840
θ_{op}	134			134			125			125			136			136		
v_{op}		0.0480			0.0480			0.0179			0.0179			0.0084			0.0084	

Table 2. Experimental results of QIGA and GA (Holland, 1975 ; Reeves, 1993) for three gray scale images using Renyi's method (Sahoo, 1997)

TN	Baboon						Peppers						Corridor					
	QIGA			GA			QIGA			GA			QIGA			GA		
	θ	υ	t	θ	υ	t	θ	υ	t	θ	υ	t	θ	υ	t	θ	υ	t
1	108	8.9564	346	108	8.9564	3329	98	9.3140	344	98	9.3140	3978	138	9.3174	343	138	9.3174	3334
2	108	8.9564	343	108	8.9564	3102	98	9.3140	345	98	9.3140	3554	138	9.3174	344	138	9.3174	3014
3	108	8.9564	345	108	8.9564	3401	98	9.3140	345	98	9.3140	2997	138	9.3174	345	138	9.3174	2864
4	108	8.9564	345	108	8.9564	2806	98	9.3140	344	98	9.3140	3447	138	9.3174	344	138	9.3174	2678
5	108	8.9564	344	108	8.9564	2924	98	9.3140	343	98	9.3140	3100	138	9.3174	344	138	9.3174	3421
6	108	8.9564	343	108	8.9564	3278	98	9.3140	346	98	9.3140	3248	138	9.3174	345	138	9.3174	3178
7	108	8.9564	344	108	8.9564	3124	98	9.3140	344	98	9.3140	3278	138	9.3174	344	138	9.3174	3328
8	108	8.9564	344	108	8.9564	3178	98	9.3140	345	98	9.3140	3079	138	9.3174	344	138	9.3174	3452
9	108	8.9564	346	108	8.9564	3233	98	9.3140	346	98	9.3140	3002	138	9.3174	346	138	9.3174	3125
10	108	8.9564	344	108	8.9564	3212	98	9.3140	343	98	9.3140	3212	138	9.3174	344	138	9.3174	2907
θ_{op}	108			108			98			98			138			138		
υ_{op}	8.9564			8.9564			9.3140			9.3140			9.3174			9.3174		

Table 3. Experimental results of QIGA and GA (Holland, 1975 ; Reeves, 1993) for three gray scale images using Yen's method (Yen, 1995)

TN	Baboon QIGA			Baboon GA			Peppers QIGA			Peppers GA			Corridor QIGA			Corridor GA		
	θ	v	t	θ	v	t	θ	v	t	θ	v	t	θ	v	t	θ	v	t
1	108	8.5512	345	108	8.5512	410	95	8.9983	346	95	8.9983	444	151	7.3945	345	151	7.3945	409
2	108	8.5512	344	108	8.5512	425	95	8.9983	348	95	8.9983	431	151	7.3945	345	151	7.3945	432
3	108	8.5512	344	108	8.5512	509	95	8.9983	346	95	8.9983	425	151	7.3945	344	151	7.3945	429
4	108	8.5512	345	108	8.5512	512	95	8.9983	347	95	8.9983	426	151	7.3945	344	151	7.3945	430
5	108	8.5512	343	108	8.5512	424	95	8.9983	345	95	8.9983	501	151	7.3945	345	151	7.3945	437
6	108	8.5512	344	108	8.5512	434	95	8.9983	346	95	8.9983	486	151	7.3945	343	151	7.3945	416
7	108	8.5512	345	108	8.5512	463	95	8.9983	345	95	8.9983	437	151	7.3945	344	151	7.3945	424
8	108	8.5512	344	108	8.5512	455	95	8.9983	347	95	8.9983	419	151	7.3945	345	151	7.3945	437
9	108	8.5512	346	108	8.5512	439	95	8.9983	348	95	8.9983	440	151	7.3945	345	151	7.3945	513
10	108	8.5512	345	108	8.5512	430	95	8.9983	345	95	8.9983	416	151	7.3945	343	151	7.3945	471
θ_{op}	108			108			95			95			151			151		
v_{op}	8.5512			8.5512			8.9983			8.9983			7.3945			7.3945		

Table 4. Experimental results of QIGA and GA (Holland, 1975; Reeves, 1993) for three gray scale images using Johannsen's method (Johannsen, 1982)

TN	Baboon						Peppers						Corridor					
	QIGA			GA			QIGA			GA			QIGA			GA		
	θ	v	t	θ	v	t	θ	v	t	θ	v	t	θ	v	t	θ	v	t
1	118	0.1484	345	118	0.1484	407	137	0.0714	342	137	0.0714	444	47	0.0276	345	47	0.0276	409
2	118	0.1484	344	118	0.1484	412	137	0.0714	343	137	0.0714	421	47	0.0276	346	47	0.0276	405
3	118	0.1484	343	118	0.1484	441	137	0.0714	344	137	0.0714	434	47	0.0276	346	47	0.0276	419
4	118	0.1484	343	118	0.1484	437	137	0.0714	342	137	0.0714	408	47	0.0276	345	47	0.0276	425
5	118	0.1484	344	118	0.1484	490	137	0.0714	344	137	0.0714	434	47	0.0276	345	47	0.0276	436
6	118	0.1484	344	118	0.1484	431	137	0.0714	344	137	0.0714	405	47	0.0276	347	47	0.0276	471
7	118	0.1484	344	118	0.1484	430	137	0.0714	344	137	0.0714	419	47	0.0276	345	47	0.0276	469
8	118	0.1484	345	118	0.1484	442	137	0.0714	343	137	0.0714	451	47	0.0276	346	47	0.0276	409
9	118	0.1484	344	118	0.1484	416	137	0.0714	343	137	0.0714	431	47	0.0276	347	47	0.0276	461
10	118	0.1484	343	118	0.1484	422	137	0.0714	342	137	0.0714	410	47	0.0276	346	47	0.0276	467
θ_{op}	118			118			137			137			47			47		
v_{op}	0.1484			0.1484			0.0714			0.0714			0.0276			0.0276		

Table 5. Experimental results of QIGA and GA (Holland, 1975 ; Reeves, 1993) for three gray scale images using Silva's method (Silva, 2006)

TN	Baboon						Peppers						Corridor					
	QIGA			GA			QIGA			GA			QIGA			GA		
	θ	v	t	θ	v	t	θ	v	t	θ	v	t	θ	v	t	θ	v	t
1	135	0.3391	346	135	0.3391	485	126	0.4242	346	126	0.4242	511	128	0.3611	342	128	0.3611	449
2	135	0.3391	347	135	0.3391	497	126	0.4242	348	126	0.4242	502	128	0.3611	343	128	0.3611	483
3	135	0.3391	347	135	0.3391	413	126	0.4242	349	126	0.4242	490	128	0.3611	344	128	0.3611	486
4	135	0.3391	348	135	0.3391	455	126	0.4242	347	126	0.4242	477	128	0.3611	344	128	0.3611	476
5	135	0.3391	345	135	0.3391	462	126	0.4242	348	126	0.4242	469	128	0.3611	342	128	0.3611	503
6	135	0.3391	346	135	0.3391	461	126	0.4242	348	126	0.4242	470	128	0.3611	343	128	0.3611	482
7	135	0.3391	348	135	0.3391	424	126	0.4242	346	126	0.4242	523	128	0.3611	344	128	0.3611	506
8	135	0.3391	347	135	0.3391	429	126	0.4242	347	126	0.4242	512	128	0.3611	344	128	0.3611	439
9	135	0.3391	347	135	0.3391	431	126	0.4242	345	126	0.4242	448	128	0.3611	342	128	0.3611	470
10	135	0.3391	345	135	0.3391	430	126	0.4242	346	126	0.4242	453	128	0.3611	343	128	0.3611	481
θ_{op}	135			135			126			126			128			128		
v_{op}		0.3391			0.3391			0.4242			0.4242			0.3611			0.3611	

Table 6. Experimental results of QIGA and GA (Holland, 1975 ; Reeves, 1993) for three gray scale images using Linear Index of Fuzziness (Huang, 1995 ; Tizhoosh, 2005)

TN	Baboon QIGA θ	v	t	Baboon GA θ	v	t	Peppers QIGA θ	v	t	Peppers GA θ	v	t	Corridor QIGA θ	v	t	Corridor GA θ	v	t
1	128	0.2963	350	128	0.2963	2511	128	0.2397	356	128	0.2397	2763	128	0.1666	348	128	0.1666	2614
2	128	0.2963	353	128	0.2963	2636	128	0.2397	354	128	0.2397	2802	128	0.1666	347	128	0.1666	2473
3	128	0.2963	352	128	0.2963	2914	128	0.2397	353	128	0.2397	2337	128	0.1666	346	128	0.1666	2531
4	128	0.2963	354	128	0.2963	2007	128	0.2397	352	128	0.2397	2642	128	0.1666	346	128	0.1666	2782
5	128	0.2963	354	128	0.2963	2714	128	0.2397	354	128	0.2397	2843	128	0.1666	347	128	0.1666	2701
6	128	0.2963	353	128	0.2963	2466	128	0.2397	354	128	0.2397	2774	128	0.1666	345	128	0.1666	2146
7	128	0.2963	352	128	0.2963	2435	128	0.2397	352	128	0.2397	2559	128	0.1666	345	128	0.1666	2348
8	128	0.2963	351	128	0.2963	2676	128	0.2397	353	128	0.2397	2502	128	0.1666	346	128	0.1666	2635
9	128	0.2963	355	128	0.2963	2778	128	0.2397	354	128	0.2397	2364	128	0.1666	347	128	0.1666	2443
10	128	0.2963	354	128	0.2963	2586	128	0.2397	353	128	0.2397	2548	128	0.1666	346	128	0.1666	2475
θ_{op}	128			128			128			128			128			128		
v_{op}		0.2963			0.2963			0.2397			0.2397			0.1666			0.1666	

Therefore, it can be concluded that the size for GA is

$$\frac{134217728}{2097152} = 64$$

times bigger than that of QIGA. While considering the time efficacy, it can be concluded that QIGA is better than its GA counterpart. The convergence curves of the proposed QIGA are shown in Figure 11. The thresholded images for the selected metrics are shown in Figures 8 through 10.

Figure 8. Thresholded images of Baboon, Peppers and Corridor using Wu's method (Wu, 1998) in Figures 8(a), 8(b), 8(c) and Renyi's method (Sahoo, 1997) in Figures 8(d), 8(e), 8(f) with θ_{op} for QIGA

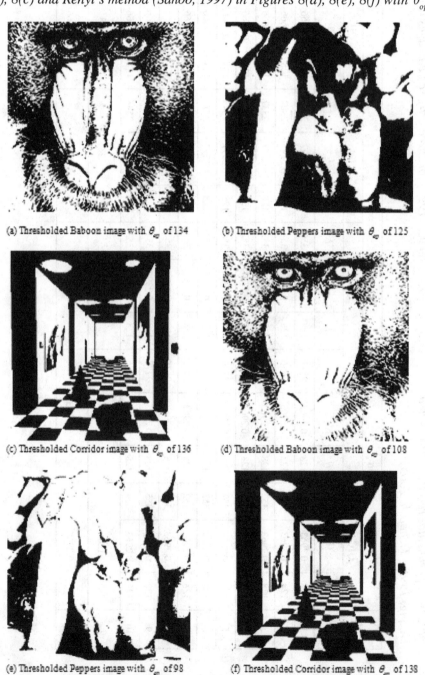

(a) Thresholded Baboon image with θ_{op} of 134

(b) Thresholded Peppers image with θ_{op} of 125

(c) Thresholded Corridor image with θ_{op} of 136

(d) Thresholded Baboon image with θ_{op} of 108

(e) Thresholded Peppers image with θ_{op} of 98

(f) Thresholded Corridor image with θ_{op} of 138

Figure 9. Thresholded images of Baboon, Peppers and Corridor using Yen's method (Yen, 1995) in Figures 9(a), 9(b), 9(c) and Johannsen's method (Johannsen, 1982) in Figures 9(d), 9(e), 9(f) with θ_{op} for QIGA

(a) Thresholded Baboon image with θ_{op} of 108

(b) Thresholded Peppers image with θ_{op} of 95

(c) Thresholded Corridor image with θ_{op} of 151

(d) Thresholded Baboon image with θ_{op} of 118

(e) Thresholded Peppers image with θ_{op} of 137

(f) Thresholded Corridor image with θ_{op} of 47

Figure 10. Thresholded images of Baboon, Peppers and Corridor using Silva's method (Silva, 2006) in Figures 10(a),10(b),10(c) and Linear Index of Fuzziness (Huang, 1995 ; Tizhoosh, 2005) in Figures10(d),10(e),10(f) with θ_{op} for QIGA

(a) Thresholded Baboon image with θ_{op} of 135   (b) Thresholded Peppers image with θ_{op} of 126

(c) Thresholded Corridor image with θ_{op} of 128   (d) Thresholded Baboon image with θ_{op} of 128

(e) Thresholded Peppers image with θ_{op} of 128   (f) Thresholded Corridor image with θ_{op} of 128

8.2 Results Obtained with QEA

The QEA, proposed by Han *et al.* (Han, 2002), has also been applied on the same test images using the same evaluation functions as QIGA. The results obtained with 10 different having 500 iterations each has been documented for QEA. For QEA (Han, 2002), 6 different heuristically made predefined lookup tables have been used for its quantum random interference. As QEA has been applied on three different test images, 2 lookup tables have been used for each image using each evaluation function. For this purpose, two different thresholds have been picked up heuristically between the dynamic intensity ranges of each of the selected image. The intensity dynamic range varies from 0 to 236 for Baboon, 0 to 239 for peppers and 0 to 255 for Corridor. The preferred threshold vales for Baboon are $118 \left(= 2 \times 59\right)$ and $120 \left(= 6 \times 20\right)$, for Peppers are $120 \left(= 3 \times 40\right)$ and $124 \left(= 4 \times 31\right)$ whereas for Corridor are $125 \left(= 5 \times 25\right)$ and $128 \left(= 4 \times 32\right)$ respectively. The required lookup tables have been produced accordingly for quantum random interference. Only the average and best results for 10 different runs using each of the particular metric are documented and listed in Tables 7 through 12. The convergence curves for the six methods in QEA are depicted in Figure 11. Finally, the thresholded images for each of the selected methods are shown in Figures 12 through 14.

8.3 Performance Analysis of the Proposed QIGA, Conventional GA and Algorithm Proposed by Han et al.

This section describes the performance analysis between the proposed QIGA, the conventional GA (Reeves, 1993) and the algorithm proposed by Han *et al.* (Han, 2002 ; Araujo, 2008). As said before, all the above mentioned algorithms have been applied and executed for 10 different runs with 500 iterations each. As the proposed QIGA is inspired by QC, its performance is greatly prejudiced by the inherent features of QC. For the quantum random interference, only probabilistic qubit states have been used. As parallelism is a big part in QC, the proposed QIGA becomes very much time efficient compared to conventional GA which has been shown in the corresponding tables in the above subsection. Han *et al* used heuristically set up predefined look up table for its quantum random interference (Han, 2002) which in turn shows a great flaw in practical. In addition to this, different rotation gates have been used for its random quantum interference rotation in QEA (Han, 2002).

As the proposed QIGA is only influenced by the probabilistic approach for its random interference, no such rogation gates are required. The approach of Han *et al.* proposed by QEA (Han, 2002 ; Araujo, 2008) is that it initiates its random searching with a global search. It then converts to a local searching technique until the required probability for best fit qubit individual converges to 1. It may establish the exploration and exploitation (Han, 2002) for this said algorithm. The convergence curves as shown in Figure 11 and Figure 15 prove that the time intervene in global searching in the proposed QIGA is very less as compared to QEA proposed by Han *et al.* (Han, 2002 ; Araujo, 2008). Again the Figure 11 through 13 show the behavioral patterns of QEA proposed by Han et al. (Han, 2002 ; Araujo, 2008) for six evaluation metrics applied for determination of optimal threshold value of the selected test images. The behavioral patterns of QIGA for the same have been described in Figure 11.

Therefore, the searching mechanism is better in QIGA than that of QEA (Han, 2002 ; Araujo,

Table 7. Experimental results of QEA (Han, 2002) for three gray scale images using Wu's method (Wu, 1998)

TN	Baboon 118 θ	Baboon 118 v	Baboon 118 t	Baboon 120 θ	Baboon 120 v	Baboon 120 t	Peppers 120 θ	Peppers 120 v	Peppers 120 t	Peppers 124 θ	Peppers 124 v	Peppers 124 t	Corridor 125 θ	Corridor 125 v	Corridor 125 t	Corridor 128 θ	Corridor 128 v	Corridor 128 t
Average	134	0.0480	346	134	0.0480	346	125	0.0179	345	125	0.0179	344	136	0.0084	344	136	0.0084	345
Best	134	0.0480	344	134	0.0480	344	125	0.0179	343	125	0.0179	342	136	0.0084	343	136	0.0084	344
θ_{op}	134						125						136					
υ_{op}	0.0480						0.0179						0.0084					

Table 8. Experimental results of QEA (Han, 2002) for three gray scale images using Renyi's method (Sahoo, 1997)

TN	Baboon 118 θ	Baboon 118 v	Baboon 118 t	Baboon 120 θ	Baboon 120 v	Baboon 120 t	Peppers 120 θ	Peppers 120 v	Peppers 120 t	Peppers 124 θ	Peppers 124 v	Peppers 124 t	Corridor 125 θ	Corridor 125 v	Corridor 125 t	Corridor 128 θ	Corridor 128 v	Corridor 128 t
Average	108	8.9564	346	108	8.9564	345	98	9.3140	344	98	9.3140	344	138	9.3174	343	138	9.3174	344
Best	108	8.9564	343	108	8.9564	344	98	9.3140	342	98	9.3140	343	138	9.3174	342	138	9.3174	342
θ_{op}	108						98						138					
υ_{op}	8.9564						9.3140						9.3174					

Table 9. Experimental results of QEA (Han, 2002) for three gray scale images using Yen's method (Yen, 1995)

TN	Baboon						Peppers						Corridor					
	118			120			120			124			125			128		
	θ	v	t	θ	v	t	θ	v	t	θ	v	t	θ	v	t	θ	v	t
Average	108	8.5512	345	108	8.5512	344	95	8.9983	346	95	8.9983	344	151	7.3945	345	151	7.3945	344
Best	108	8.5512	344	108	8.5512	343	95	8.9983	344	95	8.9983	342	151	7.3945	343	151	7.3945	342
θ_{op}	108						95						151					
v_{op}	8.5512						8.9983						7.3945					

Table 10. Experimental results of QEA (Han, 2002) for three gray scale images using Johannsen's method (Johannsen, 1982)

TN	Baboon						Peppers						Corridor					
	118			120			120			124			125			128		
	θ	v	t	θ	v	t	θ	v	t	θ	v	t	θ	v	t	θ	v	t
Average	118	0.1484	344	118	0.1484	345	137	0.0714	344	137	0.0714	344	47	0.0276	345	47	0.0276	344
Best	118	0.1484	343	118	0.1484	343	137	0.0714	343	137	0.0714	342	47	0.0276	343	47	0.0276	342
θ_{op}	118						137						47					
v_{op}	0.1484						0.0714						0.0276					

Table 11. Experimental results of QEA (Han, 2002) for three gray scale images using Silva's method (Silva, 2006)

TN	Baboon 118			Baboon 120			Peppers 120			Peppers 124			Corridor 125			Corridor 128		
	θ	v	t	θ	v	t	θ	v	t	θ	v	t	θ	v	t	θ	v	t
Average	135	0.3391	346	135	0.3391	344	126	0.4242	345	126	0.4242	345	128	0.3611	344	128	0.3611	344
Best	135	0.3391	345	135	0.3391	342	126	0.4242	344	126	0.4242	342	128	0.3611	343	128	0.3611	343
θ_{op}	135						126						128					
v_{op}	0.3391						0.4242						0.3611					

Table 12. Experimental results of QEA (Han, 2002) for three gray scale images using Linear Index of Fuzziness (Huang, 1995 ; Tizhoosh, 2005)

TN	Baboon 118			Baboon 120			Peppers 120			Peppers 124			Corridor 125			Corridor 128		
	θ	v	t	θ	v	t	θ	v	t	θ	v	t	θ	v	t	θ	v	t
Average	128	0.2963	348	128	0.2963	346	128	0.2397	345	128	0.2397	346	128	0.1666	346	128	0.1666	345
Best	128	0.2963	346	128	0.2963	344	128	0.2397	344	128	0.2397	344	128	0.1666	345	128	0.1666	342
θ_{op}	128						128						128					
v_{op}	0.2963						0.2397						0.1666					

Figure 11. (a) Convergence curves for Wu's method (Wu, 1998) and Renyi's method (Sahoo, 1997) for QIGA (b) Convergence curves for Johannsen's method (Johannsen, 1982) and Yen's method (Yen, 1995) for QIGA (c) Convergence curves for Silva's method (Silva, 2006) and Linear Index of Fuzziness (Huang, 1995 ; Tizhoosh, 2005) for QIGA

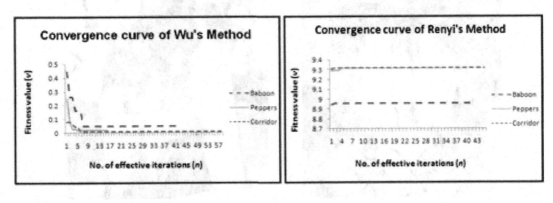

(a)

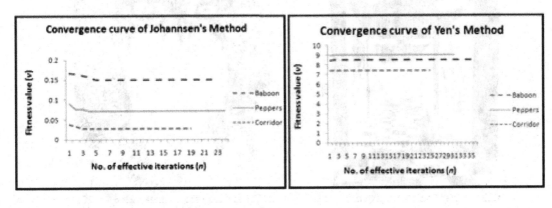

(b)

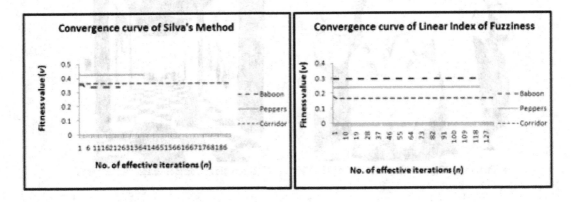

(c)

Figure 12. Thresholded images of Baboon, Peppers and Corridor using Wu's method (Wu, 1998) in Figures 12(a),12(b),12(c) and Renyi's method (Sahoo, 1997) in Figures 12(d), 12(e), 12(f) with θ_{op} for QEA

(a) Thresholded Baboon image with θ_{op} of 134

(b) Thresholded Peppers image with θ_{op} of 125

(c) Thresholded Corridor image with θ_{op} of 136

(d) Thresholded Baboon image with θ_{op} of 108

(e) Thresholded Peppers image with θ_{op} of 98

(f) Thresholded Corridor image with θ_{op} of 138

Figure 13. Thresholded images of Baboon, Peppers and Corridor using Yen's method (Yen, 1995) in Figures 13(a), 13(b), 13(c) and Johannsen's method (Johannsen, 1982) in Figures 13(d), 13(e), 13(f) with θ_{op} for QEA

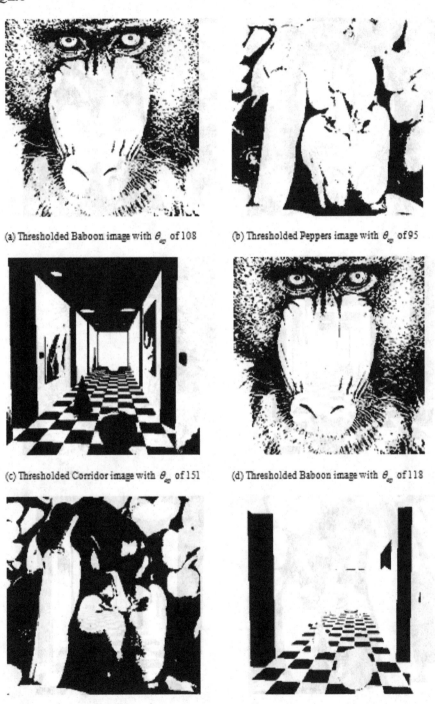

(a) Thresholded Baboon image with θ_{op} of 108

(b) Thresholded Peppers image with θ_{op} of 95

(c) Thresholded Corridor image with θ_{op} of 151

(d) Thresholded Baboon image with θ_{op} of 118

(e) Thresholded Peppers image with θ_{op} of 137

(f) Thresholded Corridor image with θ_{op} of 47

Figure 14. Thresholded images of Baboon, Peppers and Corridor using Silva's method (Silva, 2006) in Figures 14(a),14(b),14(c) and Linear Index of Fuzziness (Huang, 1995 ; Tizhoosh, 2005) in Figures14(d),14(e),14(f) with θ_{op} for QEA

(a) Thresholded Baboon image with θ_{op} of 135

(b) Thresholded Peppers image with θ_{op} of 126

(c) Thresholded Corridor image with θ_{op} of 128

(d) Thresholded Baboon image with θ_{op} of 128

(e) Thresholded Peppers image with θ_{op} of 128

(f) Thresholded Corridor image with θ_{op} of 128

Figure 15. (a) Convergence curves for Wu's method (Wu, 1998) and Renyi's method (Sahoo, 1997) for QIGA for QEA (b) Convergence curves for Johannsen's method (Johannsen, 1982) and Yen's method (Yen, 1995) for QIGA for QEA (c) Convergence curves for Silva's method (Silva, 2006) and Linear Index of Fuzziness (Huang, 1995 ; Tizhoosh, 2005) for QIGA for QEA

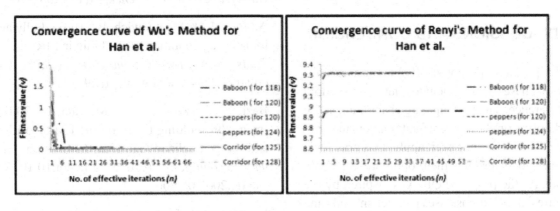

(a)

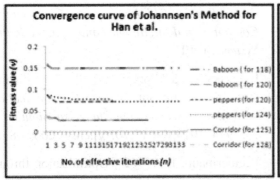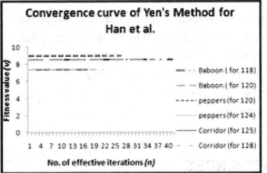

(b)

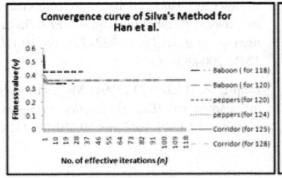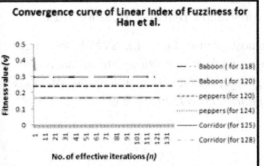

(c)

2008). These inherent features of QC also facilitate QIGA to outperform QEA in this application regarding thresholding optimization.

9. DISCUSSIONS AND CONCLUSION

In this paper, the proposed QIGA comprises number of phases which includes quantum random interference. The participating chaotic maps use Birkhoffs Ergodic theorem for its random interference. The QIGA has been applied on gray level images to determine their optimum threshold value. As the proposed QIGA is inspired by the features of QC, it possesses parallelism and time discreteness which in turn resort to time efficacy compared to its classical counterpart. Unlike the QEA, proposed by Han et al. which have used predefined heuristically made lookup table for its quantum random interference, this proposed QIGA uses probabilistic random interference that may obviates encouraging avenues.

The application of the proposed QIGA on pure and true color images is the future research area of the authors.

REFERENCES

Alteanu, D., Ristic, D., & Graser, A. (2005). Content based threshold adaptation for image processing in industrial application. In *Proceedings of 2005 International Conference Control and Automation*. Budapest, Hungary: IEEE.

Anagnostopoulos, G. (n.d.). SVM-based target recognition from synthetic aperture radar images using target region outline descriptors. *Methods & Applications, 71*, 2934–2939.

Araujo, T., Nedjah, N., & Mourelle, L. (2008). Quantum-inspired evolutionary state assignment for synchronous finite state machines. *Journal of Universal Computer Science, 14*(15), 2532–2548.

Atkins, M., & Mackiewich, B. (1998). Fully automatic segmentation of the brain in MRI. *IEEE Transactions on Medical Imaging, 17*(1), 98–107. doi:10.1109/42.668699 PMID:9617911

Bazi, Y., Bruzzone, L., & Melgani, F. (2007). Image thresholding based on the EM algorithm and the generalized Gaussian distribution. *Pattern Recognition, 40*, 619–634. doi:10.1016/j.patcog.2006.05.006

Bhattacharyya, S., & Dey, S. (2011). An efficient quantum inspired genetic algorithm with chaotic map model based interference and fuzzy objective function for gray level image thresholding. In *Proceedings of 2011, International Conference on Computational Intelligence and Communication Systems*. IEEE.

Boyarsky, A., & G'ora, P. (2010). A random map model for quantum interference. *Communications in Nonlinear Science and Numerical Simulation, 15*, 1974–1979. doi:10.1016/j.cnsns.2009.08.018

Bremermann, H. (1962). Optimization through evolution and recombination. In *Self-organizing systems*. Washington, DC: Spartan Books.

Chen, S., Huang, Y., Hsieh, B., Ma, S., & Chen, L. (2004). Fast video segmentation algorithm with shadow cancellation: Global motion compensation and adaptive threshold techniques. *IEEE Transactions on Multimedia, 6*, 732–748. doi:10.1109/TMM.2004.834868

Delp, E., & Mitchell, O. (1991). Moment-preserving quantization. *IEEE Transactions on Communications, 39*, 1549–1558. doi:10.1109/26.111432

Deutsch, D., & Jozsa, R. (1992). Rapid solution of problems by quantum computation. *Royal Society of London Proceedings Series, 439*(1907), 553–558.

Doelken, M., Stefan, H., Pauli, E., Stadlbauer, A., Struffert, T., & Engelhorn, T. et al. (2008). Hammen. T. 1H-MRS profile in MRI positive-versus MRI negative patients with temporal lobe epilepsy. *Seizure, 17*, 490–497. doi:10.1016/j.seizure.2008.01.008 PMID:18337128

Fogel, L., Owens, A., & Walsh, M. (1966). *Artificial intelligence through simulated evolution*. New York: Wiley.

Fraser, A. (1957). Simulation of genetic systems by automatic digital computers. *Australian Journal of Biological Sciences, 10*, 484–491.

Grover, L. (1996). A fast quantum mechanical algorithm for database search. In *Proceedings of 28th ACM Symposium on Theory of Computing*, (pp. 212–219). ACM.

Han, K., & Kim, J. (2002). Quantum-inspired evolutionary algorithm for a class combinational optimization. *IEEE Transactions on Evolutionary Computation, 6*(6), 580–593. doi:10.1109/TEVC.2002.804320

Hey, T. (1999). Quantum computing: An introduction. *IEEE Computing & Control Engineering, 10*, 105–112. doi:10.1049/cce:19990303

Hinterding, R. (1999). Representation, constraint satisfaction and the knapsack problem. In *Proceedings of 2008 Congress on Evolutionary Computation. Piscataway*. IEEE Press.

Holland, J. (1975). *Adaptation in natural and artificial systems*. Ann Arbor, MI: University of Michigan Press.

Hossain, M., Hossain, M., & Hashem, M. (2010). A generalizes hybrid real-coded quantum evolutionary algorithm based on particle swarm theory with arithmetic crossover. [IJCSIT]. *International Journal of Computer Science & Information TECHNOLOGY, 2*(4). doi:10.5121/ijcsit.2010.2415

Huang, L., & Wang, G. M. (1995). Image thresholding by minimizing the measures of fuzziness. *Pattern Recognition, 28*, 41–51. doi:10.1016/0031-3203(94)E0043-K

Jawahar, C., Biswas, P., & Ray, A. (1997). Investigations on fuzzy thresholding based on fuzzy clustering. *Pattern Recognition, 30*, 1605–1613. doi:10.1016/S0031-3203(97)00004-6

Johannsen, G., & Bille, J. (1982). A threshold selection method using information measures. [ICPR.]. *Proceedings of ICPR, 82*, 140–143.

Kim, Y., Kim, J., & Han, K. (2006). Quantum-inspired multiobjective evolutionary algorithm for multiobjective 0/1 knapsack problems. In *Proceedings of 2006 IEEE Congress on Evolutionary Computation*. IEEE.

L`azaro, J., Mart`ın, J., Arias, J., Astarloa, A., & Cuadrado, C. (2010). Neuro semantic thresholding using OCR software for high precision OCR applications. *Image and Vision Computing, 28*(4), 571–578. doi:10.1016/j.imavis.2009.09.011

Liu, Y., & Srihari, S. (1994). Document image binarization based on texture analysis. *Proceedings of 1994 SPIE, 2181*, 254–263.

Maldague, X. (1994). *Advances in signal processing for non destructive evaluation of materials IV*. Berlin: Springer. doi:10.1007/978-94-011-1056-3

Niblack, W. (1986). *An introduction to image processing*. Englewood Cliffs, NJ: Prentice-Hall.

O'Gorman, L. (1994). Binarization and multi-thresholding of document images using connectivity. *Graph. Models Image Process, 56*, 494–506. doi:10.1006/cgip.1994.1044

Pal, N., & Bhandari, D. (1993). Image thresholding: Some new techniques. *Signal Processing, 33*, 139–158. doi:10.1016/0165-1684(93)90107-L

Pal, S., & Rosenfeld, A. (1988). Image enhancement and thresholding by optimization of fuzzy compactness. *Pattern Recognition Letters, 7*, 77–86. doi:10.1016/0167-8655(88)90122-5

Rechenberg, I. (1973). *Evolutionsstrategie: Optimierung technischer systeme nach prinzipien der biologishen evolution.* Stuttgart, Germany: Frommann-Holzbog.

Reeves, C. (1993). Using genetic algorithms with small populations. In *Proceedings of Fifth International Conference on Genetic Algorithms.* Morgan Kaufman.

Reiffel, E., & Polak, W. (2000). *An introduction to quantum computing for non-physicists.* Retrieved from arxive.org.quant-ph/9809016v2

Russ, J. (1987). Automatic discrimination of features in gray-scale images. *Journal of Microscopy, 148*, 263–277. doi:10.1111/j.1365-2818.1987.tb02872.x

Sahoo, P., Wilkins, C., & Yeager, J. (1997). Threshold selection using Renyi's entropy. *Pattern Recognition, 30*, 71–84. doi:10.1016/S0031-3203(96)00065-9

Sathya, P., & Kayalvizhi, R. (2010). Development of a new optimal multilevel thresholding using improved particle swarm optimization algorithm for image segmentation. *International Journal of Electronics Engineering, 1*(2), 63–67.

Sauvola, J., & Pietaksinen, M. (2000). Adaptive document image binarization. *Pattern Recognition, 33*, 225–236. doi:10.1016/S0031-3203(99)00055-2

Schwefel, H. (1995). *Evolution and optimum seeking.* New York: Wiley.

Sezgin, M., & Sankur, B. (2004). Survey over image thresholding techniques and quantitative performance evaluation. *Journal of Electronic Imaging, 13*(1), 146–165. doi:10.1117/1.1631315

Shor, P. (1998). *Quantum computing.* Retrieved from http://east.camel.math.ca/EMIS/journals/DMJDMV/xvolicm/00/Shor.MAN.html

Silva, J., Lins, R., & Rocha, V., Jr. (2006). Binarizing and filtering historical documents with back-to-front interference. In *Proceedings of SAC ACM Symposium on Applied Computing.* ACM.

Srikanthan, T., & Asari, K. (2001). Automatic segmentation algorithm for the extraction of lumen region and boundary from endoscopic images. *Medical & Biological Engineering & Computing, 39*, 8–14. doi:10.1007/BF02345260 PMID:11214277

Su, C., & Amer, A. (2006). A real-time adaptive thresholding for video change detection. In *Proceedings of 2006 IEEE International Conference, Image Processing.* Atlanta, GA: IEEE.

Talbi, H., Draa, A., & Batouche, M. (2004). A new quantum-inspired genetic algorithm for solving the travelling salesman problem. In *Proceedings of IEEE International Conference on Industrial Technology.* IEEE.

Talbi, H., Draa, A., & Batouche, M. (2006). A novel quantum-inspired evolutionary algorithm for multi-sensor image registration. *The International Arab Journal of Information Technology, 3*(1), 9–15.

Tizhoosh, H. (2005). Image thresholding using type II fuzzy sets. *Pattern Recognition, 38,* 2363–2372. doi:10.1016/j.patcog.2005.02.014

Trier, O., & Jain, A. (1995). Goal-directed evaluation of binarization methods. *IEEE Transactions on Pattern Analysis and Machine Intelligence, 17,* 1191–1201. doi:10.1109/34.476511

Venkatesh, S., Rosin, P., & Hanqing, L. (1995). Dynamic threshold determination by local and global edge evaluation. *CVGIP: Graph. Models Image Process., 57,* 146–160. doi:10.1006/gmip.1995.1015

WebSource. (2000). Retrieved from http://www.math.tau.ac.il/~turkel/images.html

Wu, L., Songde, M., & Hanqing, L. (1998). An effective entropic thresholding for ultrasonic imaging. In *Proceedings of 1998 Intl. Conf. Patt. Recog.,* (pp. 1522–1524). IEEE.

Yanni, M., & Horne, E. (1994). A new approach to dynamic thresholding. In *Proceedings of 1994 EUSIPCO' 94: 9th European Conf. Sig. Process.,* (pp. 34–44). EUSIPCO.

Yeh, P., Antoy, S., Litcher, A., & Rosenfeld, A. (1986). *Address location on envelopes.* University of Maryland.

Yen, J., Chang, F., & Chang, S. (1995). A new criterion for automatic multilevel thresholding. *IEEE Transactions on Image Processing, 4,* 370–378. doi:10.1109/83.366472 PMID:18289986

ADDITIONAL READING

Bhattacharyya, S., & Dey, S. (2011) An Efficient Quantum Inspired Genetic Algorithm with Chaotic Map Model based Interference and Fuzzy Objective Function for Gray Level Image Thresholding, *Proceedings of 2011, International Conference on Computational Intelligence and Communication Systems, Gwalior, India,* 121-125.

Boyarsky, A., & G'ora, P. (2010). A random map model for quantum interference. *Communications in Nonlinear Science and Numerical Simulation, 15,* 1974–1979. doi:10.1016/j.cnsns.2009.08.018

Deutsch D., & Jozsa, R. (1992) Rapid Solution of Problems by Quantum Computation, *Royal Society of London Proceedings Series, 439(1907),* 553–558

Han, K., & Kim, J. (2002). Quantum-Inspired Evolutionary Algorithm for a Class Combinational Optimization. *IEEE Transactions on Evolutionary Computation, 6(6),* 580–593. doi:10.1109/TEVC.2002.804320

Hinterding, R. (1999) Representation, constraint satisfaction and the knapsack problem, *Proceedings of 2008 Congress on Evolutionary Computation. Piscataway, NJ: IEEE Press, 2,* 1286–1292

Huang, L., & Wang, G. M. (1995). Image thresholding by minimizing the measures of fuzziness. *Pattern Recognition, 28,* 41–51. doi:10.1016/0031-3203(94)E0043-K

Jawahar, C., Biswas, P., & Ray, A. (1997). Investigations on Fuzzy Thresholding Based On Fuzzy Clustering. *Pattern Recognition, 30,* 1605–1613. doi:10.1016/S0031-3203(97)00004-6

Kim, Y., Kim, J., & Han, K. (2006) Quantum-inspired Multiobjective Evolutionary Algorithm for Multiobjective 0/1 Knapsack Problems. *Proceedings of 2006 IEEE Congress on Evolutionary Computation, Sheraton Vancouver Wall Centre Hotel, Vancouver, BC, Canada,* 16–21

Russ, J. (1987). Automatic discrimination of features in gray-scale images. *Journal of Microscopy, 148,* 263–277. doi:10.1111/j.1365-2818.1987.tb02872.x

Sahoo, P., Wilkins, C., & Yeager, J. (1997). Threshold Selection Using Renyi's Entropy. *Pattern Recognition, 30,* 71–84. doi:10.1016/S0031-3203(96)00065-9

Talbi, H., Draa, A., & Batouche, M. (2004) A New Quantum-Inspired Genetic Algorithm for Solving the Travelling Salesman Problem, *Proceedings of IEEE International Conference on Industrial Technology (ICIT'04), 3,* 1192–1197

KEY TERMS AND DEFINITIONS

Chaotic Map: The quantum states of any quantum individual are represented in terms of a real chaotic map used for quantum interference.

Genetic Algorithm: A meta-heuristic optimization search technique based on the principles of genetics.

Gray Level Image Thresholding: A method used to differentiate objects with its background in a gray level image. It is employed to convert any gray level image to its binary version.

Probabilistic Representation: The basis of quantum bits in quantum computer is to maintain some basic properties based on some assigned probabilities.

Quantum Computing: Quantum computing is a method that is visualized from the principles of quantum physics. It may be more advantageous than using its classical part.

Quantum Inspired Evolutionary Algorithms: A kind of algorithm that works according to the principles of quantum computing.

Quantum Interference: The quantum states which are represented in terms of a real chaotic map undergo the quantum interference to generate new states.

Chapter 5
Feature Selection Algorithms for Classification and Clustering in Bioinformatics

Sujata Dash
Gandhi Institute for Technology, India

Bichitrananda Patra
KMBB College of Engineering and Technology, India

ABSTRACT

This chapter discusses some important issues such as pre-processing of gene expression data, curse of dimensionality, feature extraction/selection, and measuring or estimating classifier performance. Although these concepts are relatively well understood among the technical people such as statisticians, electrical engineers, and computer scientists, they are relatively new to biologists and bioinformaticians. As such, it was observed that there are still some misconceptions about the use of classification methods. For instance, in most classifier design strategies, the gene or feature selection is an integral part of the classifier, and as such, it must be a part of the cross-validation process that is used to estimate the classifier prediction performance. Simon (2003) discussed several studies that appeared in prestigious journals where this important issue is overlooked, and optimistically biased prediction performances were reported. Furthermore, the authors have also discuss important properties such as generalizability or sensitivity to overtraining, built-in feature selection, ability to report prediction strength, and transparency of different approaches to provide a quick and concise reference. The classifier design and clustering methods are relatively well established; however, the complexity of the problems rooted in the microarray technology hinders the applicability of the classification methods as diagnostic and prognostic predictors or class-discovery tools in medicine.

DOI: 10.4018/978-1-4666-4936-1.ch005

1. INTRODUCTION

As computer and database technologies advance rapidly, data accumulates in a speed unmatchable to the human's capacity of data processing. Data mining (Sanjay Chawla, 2010; J. Han and M. Kamber, 2001) as a multidisciplinary from databases, machine learning and statistics, is efficient in transforming the mountains of data into nuggets. Researchers and practitioners realize that, to use effectively data mining tools, data pre-processing is highly essential (M.A. Hall, 2000). Feature selection or dimensionality reduction is one of the important and frequently used techniques in data pre-processing for data mining and bio-informatics applications.

In contrast to other dimensionality reduction techniques like those based on projection (e.g. principal component analysis) or compression, feature selection techniques do not alter the original features of the variables, but merely selects a subset of them. Thus, they preserve the original semantics of the variables, hence offering the advantage of interpretability by a domain expert. It reduces the number of features, removes irrelevant, redundant, or noisy data and brings immediate effects for applications such as improving execution time of a data mining algorithm, improving mining performance such as classification accuracy and result comprehensibility.

Feature selection has been a fertile field of research and development since 1970s in statistical pattern recognition (Michael D Swartz, et al., 2008; P. Mitra et al., 2002), machine learning (Jennifer G. Dy and Carla E. Brodley, 2004; Jianqing Fan et al., 2009A. L. Blum and P. Langley, 1997; G. H. John et al, 1994) and data mining (M. Dash et al, 2002) and widely applied to many fields such as text categorization (E. Leopold and J. Kindermann, 2002) image retrieval (Y. Rui et al., 1999), customer relationship management (K. S. Ng and H. Liu, 2000), intrusion detection (W. Lee et al., 2000) and genomic analysis (E. Xing et al., 2001).

The main aim of this chapter is to make researchers aware of the benefits, and in some cases even the necessity of applying feature selection techniques in Bioinformatics domain, highlighting the efforts given by the bioinformatics community in developing novel and adapted procedures. This chapter is organized into six sections. Section 2 describes the basic steps associated with feature selection techniques. Section 3 demonstrates the different feature selection algorithms considering the evaluation criteria involved. Section 4 demonstrates the classifier performance and section 5 demonstrates the unsupervised classification methods. Section 6 concludes the chapter with discussion on current trends and future direction.

2. FEATURE SELECTION TECHNIQUES

As many pattern recognition techniques were originally not designed to cope with large amounts of irrelevant features, combining them with FS (Feature Selection) techniques has become a necessity in many applications (H. Liu and L. Liu, 2005). The objectives of feature selection are manifold, the most important ones being:

1. To avoid over fitting and improve model performance, i.e. prediction performance in the case of supervised classification and better cluster detection in the case of clustering,
2. To provide faster and more cost-effective models, and
3. To gain a deeper insight into the underlying processes that generated the data.

However, the advantages of feature selection techniques come at a certain price, as the search for a subset of relevant features introduces an additional layer of complexity in the modelling task. Instead of just optimizing the parameters of the model for the full feature subset, we now need to find the optimal model parameters for the optimal feature subset, as there is no guarantee that the optimal parameters for the full feature set are equally optimal for the optimal feature subset (W. Daelemans et al., 2003). As a result, the search in the model hypothesis space is augmented by another dimension: the one of finding the optimal subset of relevant features. Feature selection techniques differ from each other in the way they incorporate this search in the added space of feature subsets in the model selection.

Feature Selection is a process that selects a subset of original features. A typical feature selection process consists of four basic steps: subset generation, subset evaluation, stopping criterion and result validation (S. Das, 2001) which is shown in figure.1 and explained in detail. Feature selection can be found in many areas of data mining such as classification, clustering, association rules and regression. In this chapter, we focus on feature selection algorithms for classification with labelled data (S. Das, 2001) and clustering with unlabelled data (H. Liu and L. Yu., 2005).

The purpose of feature selection can be broadly categorized into visualization, data understanding, data cleaning, redundancy removal and performance enhancement. Feature selection algorithms are designed with different *evaluation criteria,* broadly classified into three categories such as the *filter model* (M. Dash et al, 2002; M. A. Hall, 2000), the wrapper model (Y.Kim et al., 2000, R. S. Dash and B. N. Patra, 2012) and the *embedded model* (S. Das, 2001). To enhance the

mining performance, algorithms in the wrapper model should be preferred than those in the filter model as they are better suited to the mining algorithms (Liu et al., 2002; Li et al., 2004; Sun et al., 2005; Lai et al., 2006; Ma, 2006; Swartz et al., 2008; Murie et al., 2009). Sometimes, algorithms in the hybrid model are needed to serve more complicated purposes.

Subset Generation

Subset generation is essentially a process of heuristic search, with each state in the search space specifying a candidate subset for evaluation. The nature of this process is determined by two basic issues. First, one must decide the search starting point (or points) which in turn influences the search direction. Search may start with an empty set and successively add features (i.e., forward), or start with a full set and successively remove features (i.e., backward), or start with both ends and add and remove features simultaneously (i.e., bidirectional). Search may also start with a randomly selected subset in order to avoid being trapped into local optima (Inza et al., 2004). Second, one must decide a search strategy. For a data set with N features, there exist 2^N candidate subsets. This search space is exponentially prohibitive for exhaustive search with even a moderate N. Therefore, different strategies for search have been explored, such as complete, sequential, and random search.

Figure 1. Four key steps of feature selection

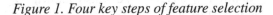
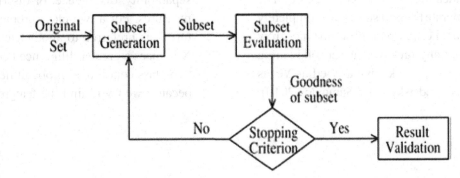

Complete Search

It guarantees to find the optimal result according to the evaluation criterion used. Different heuristic functions can be used to reduce the search space without jeopardizing the chances of finding the optimal result. Hence, although the order of the search space is $O(2^N)$ a smaller number of subsets are evaluated. Some examples are branch and bound (Zheng Zhao and Huan Liu, 2007), and beam search (W. Lee, 2000).

Sequential Search

It gives completeness and thus the risks losing optimal subsets. There are many variations to the greedy hill-climbing approach, such as the sequential forward selection, sequential backward elimination, and bidirectional selection (H. Liu and L. Liu, 2005). All these approaches add or remove features one at a time. Another alternative is to add (or remove) p features in one step and remove (or add) q features in the next step (p > q). Algorithms with sequential search are simple to implement and fast in producing results as the order of the search space is usually $O(N^2)$ or less.

Random Search

It starts with a randomly selected subset and proceeds in two different ways. One is to follow the sequential search, which injects randomness into the above classical sequential approaches. Examples are random-start hill-climbing and simulated annealing (W. Lee, et al., 2000). The other is to generate the next subset in a completely random manner i.e. a current subset does not grow or shrink from any previous subset following a deterministic rule, also known as the Las Vegas algorithm (V. Gorodetsky and V. Samoylov, 2010).

For all these approaches, the use of randomness helps to escape local optima in the search space, and optimality of the selected subset depends on the resources available.

Subset Evaluation

As we mentioned earlier, each newly generated subset needs to be evaluated by an evaluation criterion. The goodness of a subset is always determined by a certain criterion i.e., an optimal subset selected using one criterion may not be optimal according to another criterion. An evaluation criterion can be broadly categorized into two groups based on their dependency on mining algorithms that will finally be applied on the selected feature subset (H.V. Nguyen and V. Gopalkrishnan, 2010). We discuss the two groups of evaluation criteria below.

Independent Criteria

Typically, an independent criterion is used in algorithms of the filter model. It tries to evaluate the goodness of a feature or feature subset by exploiting the intrinsic characteristics of the training data without involving any mining algorithm. Some popular independent criteria are distance measures, information measures, dependency measures, and consistency measures (J. Weston et al., 2003; M.A. Hall, 2000; H. Liu and H. Motoda, 2007; H. Liu and L. Liu, 2005).

- **Distance Measures:** Are also known as separability, divergence, or discrimination measures. For a two-class problem, a feature X is preferred to another feature Y if X induces a greater difference between the two-class conditional probabilities than Y, because we try to find the feature that can separate the two classes as far as possible. X and Y are indistinguishable if the difference is zero.

- **Information Measures:** Typically determine the information gain from a feature. The information gain from a feature X is defined as the difference between the prior uncertainty and expected posterior uncertainty using X. Feature X is preferred to feature Y if the information gain from X is greater than that from Y.

- **Dependency Measures:** Are also known as correlation measures or similarity measures. They measure the ability to predict the value of one variable from the value of another. In feature selection for classification, we look for how strongly a feature is associated with the class. A feature X is preferred to another feature Y if the association between feature X and class C is higher than the association between Y and C. In feature selection for clustering, the association between two random features measures the similarity between the two.

- **Consistency Measures:** Are characteristically different from the above measures because of their heavy reliance on the class information and the use of the Min-Features bias (J. Weston et al., 2003) in selecting a subset of features. These measures attempt to find a minimum number of features that separate classes as consistently as the full set of features can. An inconsistency is defined as two instances having the same feature values but different class labels.

Dependent Criteria

A subset to determine which features are selected. It usually gives superior performance as it finds features better suited to the predetermined mining algorithm, but it also tends to be more computationally expensive, and may not be suitable for other mining algorithms (E. Xing et al., 2001). For example, in a task of classification, predictive accuracy is widely used as the primary measure. It can be used as a dependent criterion for feature selection. As features are selected by the classifier that later on dependent criterion used in the wrapper model requires a predetermined mining algorithm in feature selection and uses the performance of the mining algorithm in predicting the class labels of unseen instances. Accuracy is normally high, but it is computationally rather costly to estimate accuracy for every feature subset (H. Liu and Motoda, 1998).

In a task of clustering, the wrapper model of feature selection tries to evaluate the goodness of a feature subset by the quality of the clusters resulted from applying the clustering algorithm on the selected subset. There exist a number of heuristic criteria for estimating the quality of clustering results, such as cluster compactness, scatter separability, and maximum likelihood. Recent work on developing dependent criteria in feature selection for clustering can be found in (Wang et al., 2003; Duda et al., 2001).

Stopping Criteria

A stopping criterion determines when the feature selection process should stop. Some frequently used stopping criteria are:

1. The search completes.
2. Some given bound is reached, where a bound can be a specified number i.e., minimum number of features or maximum number of iterations.
3. Subsequent addition or deletion of any feature does not produce a better subset.
4. A sufficiently good subset is selected e.g., a subset may be sufficiently good if its classification error rate is less than the allowable error rate for a given task.

Result Validation

A straightforward way of result validation is to directly measure the result using prior knowledge about the data. If we know the relevant features beforehand, we can compare this known set of features with the selected features. Knowledge on the irrelevant or redundant features can also help. We do not expect them to be selected. In real-world applications, however, we usually do not have such prior knowledge. Hence, we have to rely on some indirect methods by monitoring the change of mining performance with the change of features. For example, if we use classification error rate as a performance indicator for a mining task, for a selected feature subset, we can simply conduct the "before-and-after" experiment to compare the error rate of the classifier learned on the full set of features and that learned on the selected subset (H. Liu and L. Yu, 2005).

3. SELECTION ALGORITHMS

In the process of feature selection, the training data can be either labelled, unlabeled or partially labelled, leading to the development of supervised, unsupervised and semi-supervised feature selection algorithms. In the evaluation process, a supervised feature selection algorithm (Weston et al., 2003; Song et al., 2007; Zhang et al., 2008; Kohbalan Moorthy et al., 2013; Jiarui Ding et al., 2011) determines features' relevance by evaluating their correlation with the class or their utility for achieving accurate prediction, and without labels, an unsupervised feature selection algorithm may exploit data variance or data distribution in its evaluation of features' relevance (Dash and Liu, 2000; Dy and Brodley, 2004; He et al., 2005). A semi-supervised feature selection algorithm (Zhao and Liu, 2007c; Xu et al., 2009) uses a small amount of labelled data as additional information to improve unsupervised feature selection.

Depending on how and when the utility of selected features is evaluated, different strategies can be adopted, which broadly fall into three categories: *filter, wrapper and embedded models.* Filter model evaluates the relevance of features by looking only at the intrinsic properties of the data. In most cases a feature relevance score is calculated, and low scoring features are removed. Afterwards, this subset of features is presented as input to the classification algorithm. Depending on how and when the utility of selected features is evaluated, different strategies can be adopted, which broadly fall into three categories: filter, wrapper and embedded models. To evaluate the utility of features, in the evaluation step, feature selection algorithms of filter model rely on analyzing the general characteristics of data and evaluating features without involving any learning algorithm. On the other hand, feature selection algorithms of wrapper model require a predetermined learning algorithm and use its performance on the provided features in the evaluation step to identify relevant feature.

Advantages of filter algorithms are that they easily scale to very high-dimensional datasets, computationally simple and fast, and are independent of the classification algorithm. As a result, feature selection needs to be performed only once, and then different classifiers can be evaluated. A common disadvantage of filter methods is that they do not interact with the classifier and the proposed algorithms are univariate. This means that each feature is considered separately, thereby ignoring feature dependencies, which may lead to worse classification performance when compared to other types of feature selection techniques.

This domination of the univariate approach can be explained by a number of reasons:

1. The output provided by univariate feature rankings is intuitive and easy to understand;
2. The gene ranking output could fulfil the objectives and expectations that bio-domain

experts have when wanting to subsequently validate the result by laboratory techniques or in order to explore literature searches. The experts could not feel the need for selection techniques that take into account gene interactions;

3. The possible unawareness of subgroups of gene expression domain experts about the existence of data analysis techniques to select genes in a multivariate way;

4. The extra computation time needed by multivariate gene selection techniques.

Some of the simplest heuristics for the identification of differentially expressed genes include setting a threshold on the observed fold change differences in gene expression between the states under study, and the detection of the threshold point in each gene that minimizes the number of training sample misclassification (threshold number of misclassification, TNoM (Lee JW et al,

2005). However, a wide range of new or adapted univariate feature ranking techniques has since then been developed. These techniques can be divided into two classes: parametric and model-free methods (see Table 1).

Parametric methods assume a given distribution from which the samples (observations) have been generated. The two sample t-test and ANOVA are among the most widely used techniques in microarray studies, although the usage of their basic form, possibly without justification of their main assumptions, is not advisable (Irizarry RA et al., 2003). Modifications of the standard t-test to better deal with the small sample size and inherent noise of gene expression datasets include a number of t- or t-test like statistics (differing primarily in the way the variance is estimated) and a number of Bayesian frameworks (Dobbin K and Simon R, 2005). Although Gaussian assumptions have dominated the field, other types of parametrical ap-

Table 1. A taxonomy of feature selection techniques. For each feature selection type, we highlight a set of characteristics which can guide the choice for a technique suited to the goals and resources of practitioners in the field.

	Model search		Advantages	Disadvantages	Examples
Filter	FS space → Classifier	Univariate	Fast Scalable Independent of the classifier	Ignores feature dependencies Ignores interaction with the classifier	Chi-square Euclidean distance t-test Information gain, Gain ratio [6]
		Multivariate	Models feature dependencies Independent of the classifier Better computational complexity than wrapper methods	Slower than univariate techniques Less scalable than univariate techniques Ignores interaction with the classifier	Correlation based feature selection (CFS) [45] Markov blanket filter (MBF) [62] Fast correlation based feature selection (FCBF) [136]
Wrapper	FS space Hypothesis space Classifier	Deterministic	Simple Interacts with the classifier Models feature dependencies Less computationally intensive than randomized methods	Risk of over fitting More prone than randomized algorithms to getting stuck in a local optimum (greedy search) Classifier dependent selection	Sequential forward selection (SFS) [60] Sequential backward elimination (SBE) [60] Plus q take-away r [33] Beam search [106]
		Randomized	Less prone to local optima Interacts with the classifier Models feature dependencies	Computationally intensive Classifier dependent selection Higher risk of overfitting than deterministic algorithms	Simulated annealing Randomized hill climbing [110] Genetic algorithms [50] Estimation of distribution algorithms [52]
Embedded	FS U Hypothesis space Classifier		Interacts with the classifier Better computational complexity than wrapper methods Models feature dependencies	Classifier dependent selection	Decision trees Weighted naïve Bayes [28] Feature selection using the weight vector of SVM [44, 125]

proaches can also be found in the literature, such as regression modelling approaches (Jiang et al,2003) and Gamma distribution models (Braga-Neto and Dougherty, 2004).

Due to the uncertainty about the true underlying distribution of many gene expression scenarios, and the difficulties to validate distributional assumptions because of small sample sizes, non-parametric or model-free methods have been widely proposed as an attractive alternative to make less stringent distributional assumptions (Z. Zhao and H.Liu.,2007). Many model-free metrics, frequently borrowed from the statistics field, have demonstrated their usefulness in many gene expression studies, including the Wilcoxon rank-sum test (Jiang et al,2003), the between-within classes sum of squares (BSS/WSS) and the rank products method.

In order to overcome the problem of ignoring feature dependencies, a number of multivariate filter techniques were introduced, aiming at the incorporation of feature dependencies to some degree. The application of multivariate filter methods ranges from simple bivariate interactions (B. Taskar et al, 2006) towards more advanced solutions exploring higher order interactions, such as correlation based feature selection (CFS) (Sanjay Chawla, 2010) and several variants of the Markov blanket filter method (Dbbin K et al,2005). The Minimum Redundancy - Maximum Relevance (MRMR) (Jaeger. J.et al., 2005) and Uncorrelated Shrunken Centroid (USC) (Yang. J. et al.,2003) algorithms are two other solid multivariate filter procedures, highlighting the advantage of using multivariate methods over univariate procedures in the gene expression domain.

Feature selection using wrapper or embedded methods offers an alternative way to perform a multivariate gene subset selection, incorporating the classifier's bias into the search and thus offering an opportunity to construct more accurate classifiers. In the context of microarray analysis, most wrapper methods use population based, randomized search heuristics (M.A. Esseghir,

2010; Jianqing Fan et al, 2009), although also a few examples use sequential search techniques (Freudenberg J. et al., 2004).

Instead of choosing one particular FS method, and accepting its outcome as the final subset, different FS methods can be combined using ensemble FS approaches. Based on the evidence that there is often not a single universally optimal feature selection technique (Getz G. et al.,2003; J. Ding et al., 2012), and due to the possible existence of more than one subset of features that discriminates the data equally well (Yang J. et al., 2002), model combination approaches such as boosting have been adapted to improve the robustness and stability of final, discriminative methods (Alizadeh AA et al.,2001). Novel ensemble techniques in the microarray and mass spectrometry domains include averaging over multiple single feature subsets (Heesung Lee et al, 2009), integrating a collection of univariate differential gene expression purpose statistics via a distance synthesis scheme (Getz G. et al.,2003), using different runs of a genetic algorithm to asses relative importance's of each feature (Zheng Zhao et al., 2010), computing the Kolmogorov- Smirnov test in different bootstrap samples to assign a probability of being selected to each peak (Getz G and Domany E., 2003), and a number of Bayesian averaging approaches (S. Dash and B. N. P atra, 2013, Yang J. et al., 2002). Furthermore, methods based on a collection of decision trees (e.g. random forests) can be used in an ensemble FS way to assess the relevance of each feature (Halvorsen OJ et al., 2005, S. Dash and B. N. Patra, 2012).

A Generalized Filter Algorithm

See Algorithm 1.

Wrapper Algorithm

It wraps the model hypothesis search within the feature subset search. In this setup, a search procedure in the space of possible feature subsets is

Algorithm 1.

```
input:    D(F_0, F_1, ..., F_{n-1})  // a training data set with N features
          S_0                        // a subset from which to start the search
          δ                          // a stopping criterion
output:   S_best                     // an optimal subset
01  begin
02      initialize: S_best = S_0;
03      γ_best = eval(S_0, D, M); // evaluate S_0 by an independent measure M
04      do begin
05          S = generate(D); // generate a subset for evaluation
06          γ = eval(S, D, M); // evaluate the current subset S by M
07          if (γ is better than γ_best)
08              γ_best = γ;
09              S_best = S;
10          end until (δ is reached);
11          return S_best;
12  end;
```

defined, and various subsets of features are generated and evaluated (S. Dash and B. N. Patra, 2012). The evaluation of a specific subset of features is obtained by training and testing a specific classification model, rendering this approach tailored to a specific classification algorithm. To search the space of all feature subsets, a search algorithm is then "wrapped" around the classification model. However, as the space of feature subsets grows exponentially with the number of features, heuristic search methods are used to guide the search for an optimal subset. These search methods can be divided in two classes: deterministic and randomized search algorithms. Advantages of wrapper approaches include the interaction between feature subset search and model selection, and the ability to take into account feature dependencies. A common drawback of these techniques is that they have a higher risk of over fitting than filter techniques and are very computationally intensive, especially building the classifier has a high computational cost.

A Generalized Wrapper Algorithm

See Algorithm 2.

Embedded Algorithm

Algorithms of the embedded model, e.g., C4.5 (Quinlan, 1993), LARS (Efron et al., 2004), 1-norm sup-port vector machine (Zhu et al., 2003), and sparse logistic regression (Cawley et al., 2007), incorporate feature selection as a part of the model fitting/training process, and features utility is obtained based on analyzing their utility for optimizing the objective function of the learning model. On the other hand, researcher also recognized that compared to the filter model, feature selection algorithms of the wrapper and embedded models can usually select features that result in higher learning performance for a particular learning model, which is used in the feature selection process. Comparing with the wrapper model, feature selection algorithms

Algorithm 2.

```
input:      D(F_0, F_1, ..., F_{n-1})   // a training data set with N features
            S_0                          // a subset from which to start the search
            δ                            // a stopping criterion
output:     S_best                       // an optimal subset
01  begin
02      initialize: S_best = S_0;
03      γ_best = eval(S_0, D, A); // evaluate S_0 by a mining algorithm A
04      do begin
05          S = generate(D); // generate a subset for evaluation
06          γ = eval(S, D, A); // evaluate the current subset S by A
07          if (γ is better than γ_best)
08              γ_best = γ;
09              S_best = S;
10      end until (δ is reached);
11      return S_best;
12  end;
```

of embedded model are usually more efficient, since they look into the structure of the involved learning model and use its properties to guide feature evaluation and search. In recent years, the embedded model is gaining increasing interests in feature selection research due to its superior performance. Currently, most embedded feature selection algorithms are designed by applying L0 norm (Weston et al., 2003) or L1 norm (Liu et al., 2009; Zhu et al., 2003; Zhao et al., 2010b) as a constraint to existing learning models to achieve a sparse solution. When the constraint is of L1 norm form, and the original problem is convex, existing optimization techniques can be applied to obtain the unique global optimal solution for the regularized problem in a very efficient way (Liu et al., 2009).

Although the wrapper approaches have been extensively studied in the pattern classification literature, they are not widely used in the feature selection phase of gene expression profile classifier design. However, these approaches because of their multivariate nature i.e., they consider the joint distribution of the features can detect genes with weak effects but possibly strong interactions. (S. Dash and B.N. Patra, 2012) demonstrate the benefits of wrapper feature selection approaches in the gene expression profile and proteomic mass spectrometry analysis, respectively. (S. Dash and B. N. Patra, 2012) concludes that evaluating combinations of genes when looking for differential expression between experiment classes reveal interesting information that will not be discovered otherwise. As a result, the simple method of selecting just the best individual features may fail dramatically. Further selection has to be done by more advanced methods that take feature dependencies into account. These operate either by evaluating growing feature sets (forward selection) or by evaluating shrinking feature set (backward selection).

Feature selection algorithms with the filter and embedded models may return either a subset of selected features or the weights (measuring features' relevance) of all features. According to the type of the output, feature selection algorithms can be divided into either feature weighting algorithms or subset selection algorithms. Feature selection algorithms of the wrapper model usually return feature subsets, therefore are subset selection algorithms. To the best of our knowledge, currently, most feature selection algorithms are designed to handle learning tasks with single data source. Researchers have started exploring the capability of using multiple auxiliary data and prior knowledge sources for multi-source feature selection (Zhao and Liu, 2008) to effectively enhance the reliability of relevance estimation (Lu et al., 2005; Zhao et al., 2008, 2010a). Given a rich literature exists for feature selection research, a systematically summarization and comparison studies are of necessity to facilitate the research and application of feature selection techniques. Recently, there have been many surveys published to serve this purpose. A comprehensive survey of existing feature selection techniques and a general framework for their unification can be found in (Liu and Yu, 2005). Guyon and Elissee (2003) reviewed feature selection algorithms from statistical learning point of view. In (Saeys et al., 2007; Abeer M. Mohmoud et al., 2013), the authors provided a good survey for applying feature selection techniques in bioinformatics. In (Inza et al., 2004), the authors reviewed and compared the filter with the wrapper model for feature selection. In (Ma and Huang, 2008), the authors explored the representative feature selection approaches based on sparse regularization, which is a branch of embedded feature selection techniques. Representative feature selection algorithms are also empirically evaluated in (Liu et al., 2002; Li et al., 2004; S. Dash et al., 2011; Lai et al., 2006; Ma, 2006; Swartz et al., 2008; Murie et al., 2009) under different problem settings and from different perspectives. We refer readers to these survey works to obtain comprehensive understanding on feature selection research.

4. ESTIMATING CLASSIFIER PERFORMANCE: PREDICTION ERROR

The issue of assessment of prediction error of a classifier also deserves much attention (Braga-Neto et al, 2004, S Dash et al., 2011). For parametric classifiers, given the class conditional densities, the probability of misclassification or Bayes error rate can also be used to quantify classifier performance; however, obtaining the analytic expression for this error rate is difficult in general. Therefore, empirical prediction/classification error remains to be the popular and practical performance measure. The empirical classification error is the ratio of wrong decisions to the total number of cases studied. The true error rate is statistically defined as the error rate of a classifier on an asymptotically large number of new cases that converge in the limit to the actual population distribution. During training, underlying parameters of a classifier are adjusted/estimated using the information contained in the training samples. The prediction accuracy can initially be evaluated by testing the classifier back on the training set and noting the resultant *training error*. This type of assessment of classifier performance, based on training error, is instrumental during the design phase. However, it may not be an accurate indicator of the final or overall performance of the classifier.

Raudys and Jain, 1991, state that "the estimate of the classification error depends on the particular training and test samples used, so it is a random variable. One should, therefore, investigate the bias and the variance of the error rates estimates. In particular, one should ask whether enough test samples were used to evaluate the classifier; or the test samples different from training samples? If the training set contains too many samples with characteristics different from the population they represent (i.e., outliers), or excessive training is done so that the classifier learns even the inherent noise in the samples, the *generalizability* performance of the classifier will be poor. Therefore, while evaluating prediction accuracy of classification methods, it is important not to use the training error only. In general, the training error rates tend to be biased optimistically, i.e., the true error rate is almost invariably higher than the training error rate. If there are plenty of training samples available, one can partition the overall training set into two sets and use one for training and the other for testing. If we design the classifier based on a small training set, the generalizability performance of the classifier will be poor again.

A common technique to assess classifier performance in such situations is to use m-fold cross-validation (CV). In this technique, the overall set of n training samples is randomly divided into m approximately equal size and balanced set of subsets. Then, each time one of these subsets is excluded from the overall training set and used as a test set. This is repeated over the m sub-samples and the resultant test error rates are averaged to obtain the so-called m-fold CV error rate. However, m can also be set equal to n ize of the training set in the case in which we have the Leave One-Out Cross-Validation (LOOCV). The case of $m = 2$ is also known as the *holdout* method.

5. UNSUPERVISED CLASSIFICATION METHODS APPLIED TO GENE EXPRESSION DATA

Clustering, also known as unsupervised classification, looks for the natural groupings in a multidimensional dataset (e.g., gene expression profiles) based on a similarity or dissimilarity measure. Unlike class prediction, in clustering, classes are unknown and explored from the data itself. While clustering divides the data into similar groups, the classification assigns an observation to one of the already known groups. Clustering can be divided into two main categories; namely, *partitional and hierarchical clustering*.

Given n samples with p genes each, the aim of the *partitional clustering* method is to partition the samples into K clusters so that the gene profiles in a sample group are more similar to each other than to gene profiles in different sample groups. A similar definition can be made if the aim is to cluster genes instead. The value of K is either pre-specified or can be estimated from gene expression profile dataset (M. Dash and H. Liu, 2000).

There are two popular *partitional clustering* strategies: *square-error* and *mixture modelling*. The sum of the squared Euclidian distances between the genes in a cluster and the cluster centre is called within-cluster variation. The sum of the within-cluster variations in a clustering scheme is used as a criterion in K-means clustering (Z. Zhao and H. Liu, 2007). This clustering is also known as minimum variance partition. K-means clustering is computationally efficient and gives satisfactory results if the clusters are compact and well separated in the feature space. Incorporating fuzzy criterion into K-means clustering results in fuzzy K-means clustering (also known as fuzzy C-means, FCM) in which each data point has a degree of membership to each class (H. Liu and L. Yu, 2005). The concept of degree of membership in fuzzy clustering is similar to the *posterior probability in a mixture modelling setting*.

K-Means Algorithm

Mixture modelling based clustering assumes that each measurement comes from a distribution characterized by a probability density function that is a *mixture* of several components. It is generally assumed that all the density components have the same functional form. Finite *mixture modelling* is a widely used technique for probability density function estimation (M. Dash and H. Liu, 2000) and found significant applications in various biological problems. The mixture com-

Algorithm 3. k-means(k,D)

```
1.choose k data points as the initial centroids (cluster centers)
2.repeat
3.          for each data point x ∈ D do
4.                  compute the distance from x to each centroids;
5.                  assign x to the closest centroid // a centroid represents a cluster
6.          endfor
7.re-compute the centroids using the current cluster memberships
8.until the stopping criterion is met
```

ponents i.e., their underlying parameters such as mean and variance for the case of normal mixtures and their weights can be estimated using the EM algorithm (K. Nigam et al, 2000; Jennifer G., et al., 2004), which is an iterative method for optimizing the likelihood function in situations where there is some missing information e.g., the class memberships of the data points. Typically, the *K- means algorithm* is used to initialize the EM to ensure that it will find a "good" local maximum. This is often considered sufficient in practical applications. *Mixture modelling* based algorithms perform superior compared to other methods such as K-means, when the data is coming from overlapping densities.

Mixture Model-Based Clustering

1. Each cluster is mathematically represented by a parametric distribution. Examples: Gaussian (continuous), Poisson (discrete)
2. The entire data set is modelled by a mixture of these distributions.
3. An individual distribution used to model a specific cluster is often referred to as a component distribution.
4. Each component is a Gaussian distribution parameterized by μk, Σk. Denote the data by x, $x \in Rd$. The density of component k is

$$f_k(x) = \phi(x \mid \mu_k, \Sigma_k)$$
$$= \frac{1}{\sqrt{(2\pi)^d |\Sigma_k|}} \exp\left(\frac{-(x - \mu_k)^t \Sigma_k^{-1}(x - \mu k)}{2}\right)$$

5. The prior probability (weight) of component k is ak . The mixture density is

$$f(x) = \sum_{k=1}^{K} a_k f_k(x) = \sum_{k=1}^{K} a_k \phi(x \mid \mu_k \cdot \Sigma_k)$$

In the context of gene expression, Hierarchical clustering (HC) was first used by (Eisen et al., 1998) to visualize multidimensional cDNA microarray data. HC starts with each object as a singleton cluster, and then at every level, the dissimilarity matrix, a matrix representing the pair-wise dissimilarity between clusters, is updated using a distance metric to form the next layer.

The average-linkage method, which uses the average of the pair-wise distances between the members of two clusters, is a common one. (Alizadeh et al., 2000), used HC with centroid linkage and Pearson correlation based distance metrics on both gene and sample axes. The end product of the HC is a tree or dendogram.

Dendograms can be built in two different ways; bottom-up (agglomerative) or top-down (divisive).

Table 2 shows the classical clustering methods applied to gene expression data along with their important properties, pros, and cons.

6. FUTURE SCOPE

The current development in scientific research will lead to the prevalence of ultrahigh dimensional data generated from the high-throughput techniques (Fan et al., 2009) and the availability of many useful knowledge sources resulting from collective work of cutting-edge research. Hence one important research topic in feature selection is:

- To develop computational theories that help scientists to keep up with the rapid advance of new technologies on data collection and processing. We also notice that there is a chasm between symbolic learning and statistical learning that prevents scientists from taking advantage of data and knowledge in a seamless way. Symbolic learning works well with knowledge and statistical learning works with data.

- Explanation-based learning is one such example that would provide an efficient way to bridge this gap. The technique of explanation-based feature selection will enable us to use the accumulated domain knowledge to help narrow down the search space and explain the learning results by providing reasons why certain features are relevant.

- As high-throughput techniques keep evolving, many contemporary research projects in scientific discovery generate data with ultrahigh dimensionality. For instance, the next-generation sequencing techniques in genetics analysis can generate data with several giga features on one run. Computation inherent in existing methods makes them hard to directly handle data of such high dimensionality, which raises the simultaneous challenges of computational power, statistical accuracy, and algorithmic stability. To address these challenges, researchers need to develop efficient approaches for fast relevance estimation and dimension reduction. Prior knowledge can

Table 2. Classical clustering methods applied to gene expression data

Method	Properties	Pros	Cons
K-means	Identifies clusters by minimizing the overall within-cluster variance.	Computationally very efficient. It can find hyper-spherical or hyper-ellipsoidal clusters. Due its practicality and reasonable results, is frequently used to initialize other more complicated clustering methods to speed up convergence.	*K* and initial cluster centers need to be specified. Clusters have to be compact and well separated.
Fuzzy *K*-means (Fuzzy *C*-means)	Similar to *K*-means but every object has a degree of membership to the *K* clusters.	The degree of membership information is helpful in identifying new clusters.	Computationally inefficient and may require additional parameters.
Mixture modeling	Objects are assumed to be drawn from the mixture of *K* distributions. Distribution parameters are estimated using the well-known EM algorithm.	Always converges to local minimum. Better than *K*-means when the classes are overlapping distributions. It has probabilistic measure of membership.	*K* and initialization is required.
Hierarchical clustering	Clusters using agglomerative or divisive approach. Uses a dissimilarity matrix to form the tree or dendogram.	Computationally efficient.	Output is a dendogram, not clusters per se. Different clusters can be found by cutting the dendogram at different levels.

play an important role in this study, for example, by providing effective ways to partition original feature space to subspaces, which leads to significant reduction on search space and allows the application of highly efficient parallel techniques.

- Knowledge oriented sparse learning: fitting sparse learning models via utilizing multiple types of knowledge. This direction extends multi-source feature selection (Zhao and Liu, 2008). Sparse learning allows joint model fitting and features selection. Given multiple types of knowledge, researchers need to study how to use knowledge to guide inference for improving learning performance, such as the prediction accuracy, and model interpretability. For instance, in microarray analysis, given gene regulatory network and gene ontology annotation, it is interesting to study how to simultaneously infer with both types of knowledge, for example, via network dynamic analysis or function concordance analysis, to build accurate prediction models based on a compact set of genes. One direct benefit of utilizing existing knowledge in inference is that it can significantly increase the reliability of the relevance estimation (Zhao et al., 2010). Another benefit of using knowledge is that it may reduce cost by requiring fewer samples for model fitting.

- Explanation-based feature selection (EBFS): feature selection via explaining training samples using concepts generalized from existing features and knowledge. EBFS is related to the research of explanation-based learning (EBL) and relational learning. EBFS (Liu et al., 2011) can generate sensible explanations to show why the selected features are related.

7. CONCLUDING REMARKS

The question of classification "which method is better" does not have a simple answer. There is neither problem-independent "best" learning or pattern recognition system nor feature representation system available. Formal theory and algorithms taken alone are not enough, pattern classification is an empirical subject. In this sense, in gene expression profile classification applications, we are in the middle of a dilemma. In one hand, we are trying to use classification/clustering approaches to get more insight about the underlying mechanisms generating these patterns/profiles, and on the other hand, we need to know about such mechanisms in advance to select the most-suitable class-predictor or clustering approach.

An interesting finding of years of pattern classification research is that there is no single approach that will entirely solve complex classification problems and some methods may perform better than others in some parts of the feature space (Raudys SJ, et al., 1991). Motivated by these facts, classifier combination has become a major topic of research recently.

In this chapter, we have given an overview of pattern classification or recognition methods and discussed important issues such as pre-processing of gene expression data, curse of dimensionality, feature extraction/selection, and measuring or estimating classifier performance. We discussed and summarized important properties such as generalizability (sensitivity to overtraining), built-in feature selection, ability to report prediction strength, and transparency (ease of understanding of the operation) of different class-predictor design approaches to provide a quick and concise reference.

REFERENCES

Aber, M. M., et al. (2013). Analysis of machine learning techniques for gene selection and classification of microarray data. In *Proceedings of the 6th International Conference on Information Technology*. ICIT.

Alizadeh, A. A., Eisen, M. B., & Davis, R. E. et al. (2000). Distinct types of diffuse large B-cell lymphoma identified by gene expression profiling. *Nature*, *403*, 503–511. doi:10.1038/35000501 PMID:10676951

Alizadeh, A. A., Ross, D. T., Perou, C. M., & Rijn, M. (2001). Towards a novel classification of human malignancies based on gene expression patterns. *The Journal of Pathology*, *195*, 41–52. doi:10.1002/path.889 PMID:11568890

Braga-Neto, & Dougherty. (2004). Is cross-validation valid for small sample microarray classification? *Bioinformatics (Oxford, England)*, *20*, 374–380. doi:10.1093/bioinformatics/btg419 PMID:14960464

Cawley, G. C., Talbot, N. L. C., & Girolami, M. (2007). Sparse multinomial logistic regression via Bayesian l1 regularisation. In *Proceedings of NIPS*. NIPS.

Chawla, S. (2010). Feature selection, association rules network and theory building. In *Proceedings of the 4th Workshop on Feature Selection in Data Mining*. IEEE.

Daelemans, W., Hoste, V., De Meulder, F., & Naudts, B. (2003). Combined optimization of feature selection and algorithm parameter interaction in machine learning of language. In *Proceedings of the 14th European Conference on Machine Learning (ECML-2003)* (pp. 84–95). ECML.

Das, S. (2001). Filters, wrappers and a boosting-based hybrid for feature selection. In *Proceedings of the 18th Int'l Conf. Machine Learning* (pp. 74- 81). IEEE.

Dash, M., Choi, K., Scheuermann, P., & Liu, H. (2002). Feature selection for clustering- A filter solution. In *Proceedings of the Second Int'l Conf. Data Mining* (pp. 115-122). IEEE.

Dash, M., & Liu, H. (1997). Feature selection for classification. *Intelligent Data Analysis*, *1*(3), 131–156. doi:10.1016/S1088-467X(97)00008-5

Dash, S., & Patra, B. N. (2012). Rough set aided gene selection for cancer classification. In *Proceedings of the 7th International Conference on Computer Sciences and Convergence Information Technology*. IEEE.

Dash, S., & Patra, B. N. (2012). Study of classification accuracy of microarray data for cancer classification using hybrid, wrapper and filter feature selection method. In *Proceedings of the 2012 International Conference on Bioinformatics & Computational Biology, WORLDCOMP'12*. WORLDCOMP.

Dash, S., & Patra, B.N. (2013). Redundant gene selection based on genetic and quick-reduct algorithms. *International Journal on Data Mining and Intelligent Information Technology Application*.

Ding, J. et al. (2012). Feature based classifiers for somatic mutation detection in tumour-normal paired sequencing data. *Bioinformatics (Oxford, England)*, *28*(2), 167–175. doi:10.1093/bioinformatics/btr629 PMID:22084253

Dobbin, K., & Simon, R. (2005). Sample size determination in microarray experiments for class comparison and prognostic classification. *Biostatistics (Oxford, England)*, *6*, 27–38. doi:10.1093/biostatistics/kxh015 PMID:15618525

Duda, R., Hart, P., & Stork, D. (2001). *Pattern classification* (2nd ed.). New York: Wiley.

Dy, J. G., & Brodley, C. E. (2004). Feature selection for unsupervised learning. *Journal of Machine Learning Research*, *5*, 845–889.

Efron, B., Hastie, T., Johnstone, I., & Tibshirani, R. (2004). Least angle regression. *Annals of Statistics*, *32*, 407–449. doi:10.1214/009053604000000067

Esseghir, M. A. (2010). Effective wrapper-filter hybridization through grasp schemata. In *Proceedings of the 4th Workshop on Feature Selection in Data Mining*. IEEE.

Fan, J., Samworth, R., & Wu, Y. (2009). Ultrahigh dimensional feature selection: Beyond the linear model. *Journal of Machine Learning Research*, *10*, 2013–2038. PMID:21603590

Freudenberg, J., Boriss, H., & Hasenclever, D. (2004). Comparison of pre processing procedures for oligo-nucleotide micro-arrays by parametric bootstrap simulation of spike-in experiments. *Methods of Information in Medicine*, *43*, 434–438. PMID:15702196

Getz, G., & Domany, E. (2003). Coupled two-way clustering server. *Bioinformatics (Oxford, England)*, *19*, 1153–1154. doi:10.1093/bioinformatics/btg143 PMID:12801877

Gorodetsky, V., & Samoylov, V. (2010). Feature extraction for machine learning: Logic probabilistic approach. In *Proceedings of the 4th Workshop on Feature Selection in Data Mining*. IEEE.

Hall, M. A. (2000). Correlation-based feature selection for discrete and numeric class machine learning. In *Proceedings of the 17th Int'l Conf. Machine Learning* (pp. 359-366). IEEE.

Halvorsen, O. J., Oyan, A. M., & Bo, T. H. et al. (2005). Gene expression profiles in prostate cancer: Association with patient subgroups and tumour differentiation. *International Journal of Oncology*, *26*, 329–336. PMID:15645116

Han, J., & Kamber, M. (2001). *Data mining: Concepts and techniques*. San Francisco: Morgan Kaufman.

Inza, I., Larranaga, P., Blanco, R., & Cerrolaza, A. (2004). Filter versus wrapper gene selection approaches in DNA microarray domains. *Artificial Intelligence in Medicine*, *31*, 91–103. doi:10.1016/j.artmed.2004.01.007 PMID:15219288

Irizarry, R. A., Bolstad, B. M., Collin, F., Cope, L. M., Hobbs, B., & Speed, T. P. (2003). Summaries of affymetrix GeneChip probe level data. *Nucleic Acids Research*, *31*, e15. doi:10.1093/nar/gng015 PMID:12582260

Jaeger, J., Weichenhan, D., Ivandic, B., & Spang, R. (2005). Early diagnostic marker panel determination for microarray based clinical studies. *Statistical Applications in Genetics and Molecular Biology*, *4*(9). PMID:16646862

Jiang, D., Pei, J., & Zhang, A. (2003). DHC: A density-based hierarchical clustering method for time-series gene expression data. In *Proceedings of the BIBE 2003: Third IEEE Intl Symp Bioinformatics and Bioeng* (pp. 393-400). IEEE.

John, G. H., Kohavi, R., & Pfleger, K. (1994). Irrelevant feature and the subset selection problem. In *Proceedings of the 11th Int'l Conference on Machine Learning* (pp. 121-129). IEEE.

Kim, Y., Street, W., & Menczer, F. (2000). Feature selection for unsupervised learning via evolutionary search. In *Proceedings of the Sixth ACM SIGKDD Int'l Conf. Knowledge Discovery and Data Mining* (pp. 365-369). ACM.

Lee, H., Hong, S., & Kim, E. (2009). Neural network ensemble with probabilistic fusion and its application to gait recognition. *Neurocomputing, 72*, 1557–1564. doi:10.1016/j.neucom.2008.09.009

Lee, J. W., Lee, J. B., Park, M., & Song, S. H. (2005). An extensive comparison of recent classification tools applied to microarray data. *Computational Statistics & Data Analysis, 48*, 869–885. doi:10.1016/j.csda.2004.03.017

Lee, W., Stolfo, S. J., & Mok, K. W. (2000). Adaptive intrusion detection: A data mining approach. *AI Rev., 14*(6), 533–567.

Leopold, E., & Kindermann, J. (2002). Text categorization with support vector machines: How to represent texts in input space? *Machine Learning, 46*, 423–444. doi:10.1023/A:1012491419635

Li, T., Zhang, C., & Ogihara, M. (2004). A comparative study of feature selection and multiclass classification methods for tissue classification based on gene expression. *Bioinformatics (Oxford, England), 20*(15), 2429–2437. doi:10.1093/bioinformatics/bth267 PMID:15087314

Liu, H., Li, J., & Wong, L. (2002). A comparative study on feature selection and classification methods using gene expression profiles and proteomic patterns. *Genome Inform, 13*, 51–60. PMID:14571374

Liu, H., & Motoda, H. (1998). *Feature selection for knowledge discovery and data mining*. Boston: Kluwer Academic. doi:10.1007/978-1-4615-5689-3

Liu, H., & Motoda, H. (1998). *Feature selection for knowledge discovery and data mining*. Boston: Kluwer Academic Publishers. doi:10.1007/978-1-4615-5689-3

Liu, H., & Motoda, H. (Eds.). (2007). *Computational methods of feature selection*. New York: Chapman and Hall/CRC Press.

Liu, H., & Yu, L. (2005). Toward integrating feature selection algorithms for classification and clustering. *IEEE Transactions on Knowledge and Data Engineering, 17*(4), 491–502. doi:10.1109/TKDE.2005.66

Liu, J., Ji, S., & Ye, J. (2009). Multi-task feature learning via efficient l2,1-norm minimization. In *Proceedings of the Twenty-Fifth Conference on Uncertainty in Artificial Intelligence*. IEEE.

Liu, M. Setiono, & Zhao. (2011). Feature selection: An ever evolving frontier in data mining. In *Proceedings of JMLR: Workshop and Conference The Fourth Workshop on Feature Selection in Data Mining*. JMLR.

Ma, S. (2006). Empirical study of supervised gene screening. *BMC Bioinformatics, 7*, 537. doi:10.1186/1471-2105-7-537 PMID:17176468

Mitra, P., Murthy, C. A., & Pal, S. K. (2002). Unsupervised feature selection using feature similarity. *IEEE Transactions on Pattern Analysis and Machine Intelligence, 24*(3), 301–312. doi:10.1109/34.990133

Moorthy, K., Mohamad, M. S. B., & Deris, S. (2013). Multiple gene sets for cancer classification using gene range selection based on random forest. In *Proceedings of ACIIDS 2013* (LNAI), (vol. 7802, pp. 385–393). Berlin: Springer.

Murie, C., Woody, O., Lee, A., & Nadon, R. (2009). Comparison of small n statistical tests of differential expression applied to microarrays. *BMC Bioinformatics, 10*, 45. doi:10.1186/1471-2105-10-45 PMID:19192265

Ng, k.s., & Liu, H. (2000). Customer retention via data mining. *AI Rev., 14*(6), 569-590.

Nguyen, H. V., & Gopalkrishnan, V. (2010). Feature extraction for outlier detection in high-dimensional spaces. In *Proceedings of the 4th Workshop on Feature Selection in Data Mining*. IEEE.

Nigam, K., Mccallum, A. K., Thrun, S., & Mitchell, T. (2000). Text classification from labeled and unlabeled documents using EM. *Machine Learning*, *39*, 103–134. doi:10.1023/A:1007692713085

Quinlan, J. R. (1993). *C4.5: Programs for machine learning*. San Francisco: Morgan Kaufmann.

Raudys, S. J., & Jain, A. K. (1991). Small sample size effects in statistical pattern recognition: Recommendations for practitioners. *IEEE Transactions on Pattern Analysis and Machine Intelligence*, *13*, 252–264. doi:10.1109/34.75512

Saeys, Y., Inza, I., & Larraaga, P. (2007). A review of feature selection techniques in bioinformatics. *Bioinformatics (Oxford, England)*, *23*(19), 2507–2517. doi:10.1093/bioinformatics/btm344 PMID:17720704

Simon, R. (2003). Diagnostic and prognostic prediction using gene expression profiles in high-dimensional microarray data. *British Journal of Cancer*, *89*, 1599–1604. doi:10.1038/sj.bjc.6601326 PMID:14583755

Song, L., Smola, A., Gretton, A., Borgwardt, K., & Bedo, J. (2007). Supervised feature selection via dependence estimation. In *Proceedings of the International Conference on Machine Learning*. IEEE.

Sun, Y., Babbs, C. F., & Delp, E. J. (2005). A comparison of feature selection methods for the detection of breast cancers in mammograms: Adaptive sequential floating search vs. genetic algorithm. *IEEE Eng Med Biol Soc*, *6*, 6532–6535. PMID:17281766

Swartz, M. D., Yu, R. K., & Shete, S. (2008). Finding factors influencing risk: Comparing Bayesian stochastic search and standard variable selection methods applied to logistic regression models of cases and controls. *Statistics in Medicine*, *27*(29), 6158–6174. doi:10.1002/sim.3434 PMID:18937224

Taskar, B., Obozinski, G., & Jordan, M. I. (2006). *Multi-task feature selection*. Berkeley, CA: UC Berkeley.

Wang, J., Bo, T. H., Jonassen, I., Myklebost, O., & Hovig, E. (2003). Tumor classification and marker gene prediction by feature selection and fuzzy c-means clustering using microarray data. *BMC Bioinformatics*, *4*, 60. doi:10.1186/1471-2105-4-60 PMID:14651757

Weston, J., Elisse, A., Schoelkopf, B., & Tipping, M. (2003). Use of the zero norm with linear models and kernel methods. *Journal of Machine Learning Research*, *3*, 1439–1461.

Xing, E., Jordan, M., & Karp, R. (2001). Feature selection for high-dimensional genomic microarray data. In *Proceedings of the 15th Int'l Conf. Machine Learning* (pp. 601-608). IEEE.

Xu, Z., Jin, R., Ye, J., Michael, J., Lyu, R., & King, I. (2009). Discriminative semi-supervised feature selection via manifold regularization. In *Proceedings of the 21st International Joint Conference on Artificial Intelligence IJCAI' 09*. IEEE.

Yang, J., Wang, H., Wang, W., & Yu, P. (2003). Enhanced bi-clustering on expression data. In *Proceedings of the Third IEEE Symposium on Bioinformatics and Bioengineering* (pp. 321-327). IEEE.

Yang, J., Wang, W., Wang, H., & Yu, P. (2002). Delta-clusters: Capturing subspace correlation in a large data set. In *Proceedings of the 18th International Conference on Data Engineering* (pp. 517-528). IEEE.

Zhang, Y., Ding, C., & Li, T. (2008). Gene selection algorithm by combining relief and mrmr. *BMC Genomics*, *9*, S27. doi:10.1186/1471-2164-9-S2-S27 PMID:18831793

Zhao, Z., & Liu, H. (2007). Spectral feature selection for supervised and unsupervised learning. In *Proceedings of the International Conference on Machine Learning (ICML)*. ICML.

Zhao, Z., Wang, L., & Liu, H. (2010). Efficient spectral feature selection with minimum redundancy. In *Proceedings of the 24th AAAI Conference on Artificial Intelligence*. AAAI.

Zhu, J., Rosset, S., Hastie, T., & Tibshirani, R. (2003). 1-norm support vector machines. In *Advances in Neural Information Processing Systems*. Academic Press.

KEY TERMS AND DEFINITIONS

Clustering: It's task of grouping a set of objects in such a way that objects in the same group are called cluster that are more similar to each other than to those in other groups. It is a main task of exploratory data mining, and a popular technique for statistical data analysis used in many fields such as machine learning, pattern recognition, image analysis, information retrieval, and bioinformatics.

Cross-Validation: This technique is used to assess the results of a statistical analysis mainly used in predicting the goal. It involves partitioning a sample of data into complementary subsets, performing the analysis on e training set and validating the analysis on the validation set or testing set.

Curse of Dimensionality: Many phenomena are referred to by this name in areas such as numerical analysis, sampling, combinatorics, machine learning and data mining. The common theme of these problems is that when the dimensionality increases, the volume of the space increases so fast that the available data becomes sparse. This sparsity becomes a problem for finding significant result.

Ensemble Technique: In statistics and machine learning, ensemble methods use multiple models to obtain better predictive performance. It requires more computation time to evaluate the prediction than of a single model. Therefore, ensembles may be thought of as a way to compensate poor learning algorithms by performing a lot of extra computation.

Gene Expression Profile: Measurement of the expressions of thousands of genes at once to show a global picture of cellular function. These profiles distinguish between cells that react to a particular treatment.

Heuristic Criterion: Provides a quick solution that is good enough for solving the problem at hand. This solution may not be the best of all the actual solutions to this problem, or it may simply approximate the exact solution. But it is still valuable because finding it does not require a prohibitively long time.

Microarray Technology: Collection of DNA spots impinged to a solid surface and this is used to measure the expression levels of large numbers of genes simultaneously.

Overfitting: It occurs when a model describes random error or noise instead of the underlying relationship in statistics and machine learning problems. Generally, it occurs when a model has too many parameters relative to the number of observations. An over fitting model will generally have poor predictive performance, as it can exaggerate minor fluctuations in the data.

Chapter 6
Soft Subspace Clustering for Cancer Microarray Data Analysis:
A Survey

Natthakan Iam-On
Mae Fah Luang University, Thailand

Tossapon Boongoen
Royal Thai Air Force Academy, Thailand

ABSTRACT

A need has long been identified for a more effective methodology to understand, prevent, and cure cancer. Microarray technology provides a basis of achieving this goal, with cluster analysis of gene expression data leading to the discrimination of patients, identification of possible tumor subtypes, and individualized treatment. Recently, soft subspace clustering was introduced as an accurate alternative to conventional techniques. This practice has proven effective for high dimensional data, especially for microarray gene expressions. In this review, the basis of weighted dimensional space and different approaches to soft subspace clustering are described. Since most of the models are parameterized, the application of consensus clustering has been identified as a new research direction that is capable of turning the difficulty with parameter selection to an advantage of increasing diversity within an ensemble.

INTRODUCTION

Microarray technology has revolutionized biological and medical research. It becomes a central tool for examining gene expression profiles of a multitude of cells and tissues simultaneously. This innovation provides new opportunities to investigate and understand human disease. Gene expression data obtained from microarray experiments has inspired several novel applications, including the identification of differentially expressed genes for further molecular studies or

DOI: 10.4018/978-1-4666-4936-1.ch006

drug therapy response (Ramaswamy et al, 2003; Tusher et al, 2001; Wallqvist et al, 2002), and the creation of classification systems for improved cancer diagnosis (Cleator and Ashworth, 2004; Spang, 2003). Another typical analysis is to reveal natural structures and identify interesting patterns in the underlying microarray data (Jiang et al, 2004). The cluster analysis of biological samples using microarray data has been widely recognized as a standard practice in biological, clinical and toxicological studies (Carkacioglu et al, 2010; Chen et al, 2011; Golub et al, 1999). In particular to cancer research, it has become almost routine to create gene expression profiles, which can discriminate patients into good and poor prognosis groups, and identify possible tumor subtypes. This analysis offers a useful basis for individualized treatment of disease.

A variety of clustering algorithms and cluster ensemble methods are usually employed for the analysis of gene expression data (Iam-On et al, 2010). Initially, traditional algorithms such as *k*-means (McQueen, 1967) and agglomerative hierarchical clustering (Han and Kamber, 2000) have proven useful for identifying biologically relevant clusters of tissue samples and genes. In response to the challenges of high-dimensional data, especially in microarray gene expression data analysis, the practice of subspace clustering or bi-clustering (Cheng and Church, 2000; Gu and Liu, 2008; Prelic et al, 2006; Tanay et al, 2002; Tseng and Wong, 2005) has recently emerged as a new and effective alternative to any standard technique. Generally, cluster detection is based on a distance or proximity measure between objects of interest. However, with high-dimensional data, meaningful clusters cannot be easily identified as the distances between data objects are increasingly indifferent as dimensionality increases (Boongoen and Shen, 2010). In order to disclose patterns obscured by irrelevant dimensions, a global feature selection or reduction method, e.g., Principle Components Analysis (PCA; Joliffe, 1986), is effective only to a certain extent. Such a technique fails to detect in each dimension, locally varying relevance for distinct object groups. As a result, many different subspace clustering algorithms have been proposed with the common objective of discovering locally relevant dimensions per cluster (Boongoen et al, 2011; Kriegel et al, 2009). With the example in Figure 1 that represents different clusters of n objects $(x_1, x_2, ..., x_n)$ in d dimensions $(f_1, f_2, ...,$

Figure 1. Illustration of three different clusters: Cluster1 in a full dimensional space, Cluster2 and Cluster3 in distinct subspaces or subsets of the original dimensions

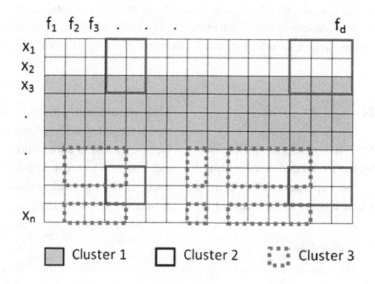

f_d), Cluster1 corresponds to a traditional cluster in a full data space, whilst the others are subspace clusters each of which associates with a specific subset of original dimensions.

Approaches to subspace clustering can be characterized in two categories: crisp and soft. The former finds an exact subspace for each cluster. See the methods of Aggarwal et al (1999), Chakrabarti and Mehrotra (2000) and Kriegel et al (2009) for examples. The latter, a soft subspace clustering method detects clusters in a full data space. For each cluster, different dimensions are assigned with dissimilar weights in accordance with their relevance to the identification of the underlying cluster. In practice, an optimal subspace can be obtained using either wrapper or filter approach (Dy and Brodley, 2004). The former wraps the search around a specific clustering algorithm, whilst the latter selects the dimension subspaces, prior to the actual unsupervised learning process. Most of the existing soft subspace clustering techniques found in the literature (Domeniconi et al, 2007; Gan and Wu, 2008) rely on a specific clustering mechanism, typically k-means to search for the optimal set of weights. This alternative is picked up for its simplicity and efficient clustering process. This survey provides basic concepts of soft subspace clustering and a review of state-of-the-art techniques, which are further categorized into wrapper and filter families. In addition, the practical guidelines for using the consensus clustering or ensemble framework to boost the performance of a soft subspace clustering method are emphasized.

The rest of this chapter is organized as follows. The second section provides the brief background regarding cluster analysis of gene expression data and the concept of soft subspace clustering, from which the present review originates. This includes details of both wrapper and filter categories of soft subspace clustering techniques found in the literature. The empirical study of k-means extensions on several published microarray datasets

is emphasized in the third section. After that, to illustrate the direction of future work, the forth section presents the ensemble methodology that can be used to enhance the quality of soft subspace clustering. The chapter is concluded in the sixth section.

SOFT SUBSPACE CLUSTERINGS

The idea of soft subspace clustering was initially introduced in the study of Friedman and Meulman (2004), with the algorithm called 'Clustering Objects on Subsets of Attributes (COSA)'. This is objectively proposed to determine for each cluster a set of dimensional weights. To illustrate the underlying concept, Figure 2 is given to compare between original and weighted dimensional spaces. As such, the weighting scheme allows the two clusters to be easier to visualized and identified. Specific to Cluster1 in Figure 2(a), the weights w_x and w_y of the dimensions f_x and f_y, respectively, are the same in the original dimensional setting. With respect to the weighted space shown in Figure 2(b), these weights are adjusted such that w_x remains unchanged whilst $w_y = w_x/3$. In other words, dimension f_x is more important than dimension f_y for the first cluster to be structurally dense and clearly identifiable. Likewise, Cluster2 can be obviously recognized and separable from the former in Figure 2(b). This is achieved by setting $w_x = w_y/4$, i.e., for the second cluster, dimension f_x is less important than dimension f_y.

Despite its promising performance, the aforementioned method has been heavily criticized for its inefficiency (Kriegel et al, 2009). This is due to the fact that COSA makes use of hierarchical clustering as the core of its wrapper model. Hence, the resulting time complexity can be as high as $O(n^3)$, where n denotes the number of objects under examination. Following this initial technique, several attempts have been devoted to extend a standard clustering algorithm, mostly

Figure 2. Illustration of two clusters in (a) original dimensional space and (b) weighted dimensional space, where clusters are clearly identified and separable

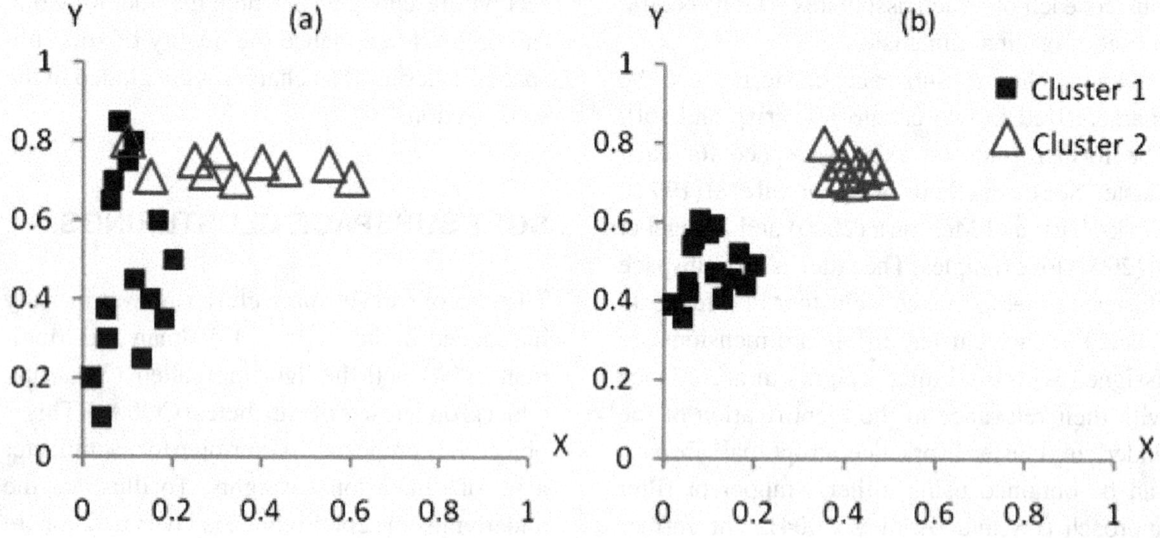

k-mean, such that the resulting analysis model is more efficient than COSA. These include both wrapper-based and filter-based techniques summarized in Table 1.

Wrapper-Based Methods

Most wrapper-based methods to soft subspace clustering, apart from COSA, make use of k-means as the core of their wrapper models. To set the scene for these extensions, basic concepts and terminology are reviewed. k-means is perhaps, the best known clustering technique that partitions objects into clusters. Its name comes from representing each of k clusters by the mean of its members or so-called *centroid*. k-means is an iterative algorithm which constructs a collection of clusters that optimizes a specific criterion or objective function. For k-means, this function is represented as a square-error, i.e., the total distance between each object and its centroid (McQueen, 1967), which is to be minimized.

Table 1. Summarization of wrapper-based and filter-based approaches to soft subspace clustering, where the term 'Complexity' refers to time complexity and n represents the number of examined objects

Category	Method	Reference	Base Algorithm	Complexity
Wrapper	COSA	Friedman and Meulman, 2004	Hierarchical clustering	$O(n^3)$
	LAC	Domeniconi et al, 2007	k-means	$O(n)$
	EWKM	Jing et al, 2007	k-means	$O(n)$
	LWC	Cheng et al, 2008	k-means	$O(n)$
	FSC	Gan and Wu, 2008	k-means	$O(n)$
Filter	R-KM	Boongoen et al, 2011	k-means	$O(n)$
	R-CL	Boongoen et al, 2011	Hierarchical clustering	$O(n^3)$
	R-SPT	Boongoen et al, 2011	Spectral clustering	$O(n^2)$

A general description of the k-means algorithm is given below. Note that the examples of termination criteria are: (i) no changes are made to the cluster centroids (i.e., no reassignment of any object from one cluster to another), (ii) the maximum number of iterations is exceeded, and (iii) there is no improvements in the objective function such as decrease in the square-error. The k-means algorithm is popular largely due to its efficiency, with time complexity of $O(n)$, where n is the number of examined objects.

1. k objects are first randomly selected as initial centroids.
2. Repeat the followings:
    a. Assign each object to the cluster whose centroid is the closest. Note that the Euclidean metric is commonly used to compute the distance between objects and centroids.
    b. The centroid of each cluster is updated as the mean of all current objects in that cluster.
3. Until the termination criterion is met.

LAC (Locally Adaptive Clustering ; Domeniconi et al, 2007) was the first amongst a number of different methods, which extend the aforementioned k-means to accommodate cluster-specific dimensional weights. The term 'weighted cluster' is devised to capture the essence of similarity within a weighted data space. Formally, a weighted cluster is a subset of objects, with cluster-specific dimensional weights, such that the objects in this cluster are closely grouped. To obtain a set of weighted clusters for any given data, LAC follows the basic process specified above, with the following modifications. Unlike k-means, the representative of any discovered cluster is not only the centroid, but also the corresponding dimensional weights. Firstly, with the help of furthest-first heuristics (Hochbaum and Shmoys, 1985), LAC selects an initial collection of k cen-

troid. In addition, all dimensional weights are set to be $1/d$, where d is the number of dimensions. Note that, except for the initialization stage, the summation of all dimension weights per cluster must be equal to 1.

In the iterative process, with respect to the second step of k-means, LAC forms weighted clusters by assigning each object to the nearest centroid. A weighted Euclidean measure together with centroid-specific sets of dimensional weights is used to deliver the underlying distance. Having obtained weighted clusters, k centroids and their associated weights are updated. Intuitively, for any cluster, a high weight is given to a dimension, in which the average of distance between objects and the centroid is small. This is modeled as an exponential relation that has proven to be more sensitive to changes in local dimensional relevance. An additional parameter h is introduced to control the effect of average intra-cluster distance on weight in the aforementioned exponential weighting. According to Domeniconi et al (2007), the value of h is set to 9 for the experiments with DNA microarray datasets. This procedure is repeated until the termination criterion is met.

LWC (Locally Weighted Clustering; Cheng et al, 2008) is developed to overcome limitations with LAC. The constraint of weight summation per cluster to be 1 can lead to a trivial solution. In particular, the dimension with the smallest variation or intra-cluster distance is weighted one, whilst the others are given zero weights. As a result, some dimensions that are informative to the recognition of clusters are entirely overlooked. Also, the algorithmic parameter h that greatly affects the quality of clustering results in practice, is data dependant. There is no simple and effective mechanism to determine its value. To resolve these, LWC modify the weighting constraint such that the product of dimensional weights of any cluster must be equal to one. It is noteworthy that, all dimensional weights are set to 1 initially. This design allows more than a single dimension per cluster to be non-zero, hence avoiding a trivial result. Also, LWC is user-friendly since the coefficient *h* is not required for the LAC-like discrimination of weights.

Following LAC, another technique called EWKM (Entropy Weight k-Means; Jing et al, 2007) has been invented for soft subspace clustering of high-dimensional sparse data. Like previous methods, a dimensional weight per cluster specifies the probability of contribution of that dimension in forming the cluster. More specifically, the entropy of dimensional weights is exploited to represent the certainty of dimensions in the cluster identification. With EWKM, the objective function of *k*-means is modified by adding the weight entropy term. To optimize this is to simultaneously minimize the within cluster dispersion and maximize the negative weight entropy to stimulate more dimensions to contribute to the identification of clusters. As such, the problem of disclosing clusters by few dimensions can be avoided. In fact, a positive parameter g is used to control by the strength of the incentive for clustering on more dimensions. According to the empirical study of Jing et al (2007), EWKM is reported to perform well with g being set to 0.5.

In line with the creation of LAC and EWKM, FSC (Fuzzy Subspace Clustering; Gan and Wu, 2008) also aims for determining cluster-specific dimensional weights, using the concept and terminology inherited from a typical fuzzy clustering such as c-means (Bezdek and Hathaway, 1988). The weight component of its core objective function is fuzzified via the parameter a $\hat{I}$ (1, ¥), i.e., fuzzy index. This is usually set to be around 1.1 for any general application. However, with FSC, it is desirable that dimensions relevant to the cluster identification obtain large weights, while the resulting weights of non-relevant dimensions are small or close to zero. As a result, the value around 2 is recommended by Gan and Wu (2008) for this differentiation.

Filter-Based Methods

With those wrapper-based methods, dimensional weights are repeatedly updated, along the iterative minimization of intra-cluster variances. The quality control is based on the distances between object members to the disclosed cluster centers, which can be sub-optimal at times. As such, the accuracy of weights cannot always be maintained. To address this shortcoming, a filter-based technique, called R-KM (Reliability-based *k*-means; Boongoen et al, 2011; Iam-On and Boongoen, 2012), has been developed such that the search for weighted clusters becomes less dependent to intermediate centroids. This enables the update of cluster-specific weights to be more accurate. The new method exploits data reliability measure of Boongoen and Shen (2010) to preliminarily construct an object-dimension association matrix that represents locally relevance degree of each dimension for every data object. Each matrix entry represents the strength that an object is similar to (or associates with) a set β *{1... n-1}* of its nearest-neighboring objects in a particular dimension.

This so-called reliability measure has an intuitive interpretation towards the problem of subspace clustering. When it approaches 1, the dimension is highly relevant to the local cluster which an examined object is an element in. If however, the underlying measure is close to nil, the dimension is irrelevant to the clustering of that object. Note that estimation of the aforementioned metric relies on the search for β nearest neighbors of any object in question. According to Boongoen and Shen (2010), the time complexity of $O(n^2)$ with a brute-force search can be substantially reduced to $O(n)$ using a sorting mechanism, e.g., the pancake sort (Cohen and Blum, 1995), prior the actual search process.

Specific to R-KM, the object-dimension association matrix can be naturally employed in the weight determination. Given any cluster, each of its dimensional weights is summarized from the matrix entries corresponding to those objects that belong to the cluster. After empirical evaluation with a number of aggregation operators, a minimum is suggested for this fusion. Unlike those wrapper-based extensions of k-means whose weighting depends totally on the centroids, R-KM approximates the weights using both centroids and the association matrix that remains unchanged during the iterative refinement procedure. In addition to k-means, the underlying matrix can be coupled with any standard clustering to form a filter-based model. To generalize this intuition, another two methods, R-CL (Reliability-based hierarchical clustering) and R-SPT (Reliability-based spectral clustering), have also been proposed and reported to be better than their original counterparts (Boongoen et al, 2011).

R-CL extends the complete linkage (CL) approach (King, 1967) of the well-known agglomerative hierarchical clustering technique (Jain and Dubes, 1988). In principle, it generates a tree, called dendogram, as nested groups of data organized hierarchically. The algorithm begins by considering each data sample as a cluster, and then gradually merges similar clusters until all the clusters are combined into one big group, i.e., the top node of the resulting dendogram. The CL technique requires an adjacency matrix that represents pairwise-proximity measures amongst objects as an input. The original matrix is based on a uniform dimensional weight setting, which is improved by R-CL using the information of locally relevance encoded in the object-dimension association matrix. With this view in mind, the new adjacency matrix now presents the weighted distance amongst each object pair. The minimum operator is used again here to homogenize dimensional weights of any two objects under question. As an improvement of the spectral clustering technique of Ng et al (2001), R-SPT first generates a square matrix, which represents the pairwise similarity between objects. With the original

model, this is estimated from an unweighted adjacency matrix. On the other hand, R-SPT makes use of the weighted variation that is identical to that of R-CL, to derive the resulting similarity matrix. Having done this, the k largest eigenvectors of this matrix (chosen to be orthogonal to each other in the case of repeated Eigen values) are retrieved, and form the transformed matrix by stacking the eigenvectors in columns. Then, each row of the new matrix is normalized to have a unit length. To create the final data partition, k-means is used to divide objects (i.e., rows of the transformed matrix) into a partition of k clusters. It is noteworthy that R-KM is the most efficient among these filter-based models with time complexity converging to $O(n)$, while R-SPT and R-CL are more computational demanding as their complexity are $O(n^2)$ and $O(n^3)$, respectively.

EMPIRICAL STUDY ON MICROARRAY DATA

To provide an empirical perspective, the performance of several soft subspace clustering algorithms that have been developed as extensions of k-means, are assessed on the published microarray data collection summarized in Table 2. This is taken from the study of de Souto et al (2008), in which a large set of gene expression datasets have been collected from original microarray experiments. This collection provides significant differences in types of cancer, microarray chips, numbers of tissue samples and gold-standard classes. Following the evaluation framework exploited by Iam-On et al (2010) in the study of cluster ensembles, classes revealed in the corresponding microarray experiments are used as a reference partition, to which a clustering can be compared to judge its quality, using Normalized Mutual Information (*NMI [0, 1]*) validity index introduced by Strehl and Ghosh (2002). The present evaluation study compares the quality of data partitions generated by the selected soft subspace

Table 2. Details of investigated microarray datasets: number of samples (n), number of genes (d), and number of known sample classes (K)

Dataset	n	d	K
Brain-Tumor	50	1,377	4
Bladder-Carcinoma	40	1,203	3
CNS	42	1,379	5
CRC	37	2,202	2
DLBCL1	62	2,093	4
DLBCL2	77	798	2
Leukemia1	72	2,194	3
Leukemia2	72	1,877	2
Lung-Tumor1	66	4,553	4
Lung-Tumor2	181	1,626	2

clustering methods and relevant techniques. These include the baseline model of k-means (KM) and three other standard hierarchical clusterings: single-linkage (SL), complete-linkage (CL), and average-linkage (AL). Specific to the category of soft subspace clustering, both wrapper-based and filter-based algorithms are examined: R-KM, EWKM, LAC and FSC.

Based on the quality measure of NMI, Table 3 compares the performance of four soft subspace clustering techniques, against four other compared standard methods. Note that the reported NMI measures of each non-deterministic method, whose different runs may generate dissimilar results, is generalized as the average of 50 trials. The size of nearest neighbor set β is set to 3 for R-KM. For each trial, the parameter g of EWKM is randomly selected from [0.5, 1] and the parameter h of LAC is randomly selected from [5, 9]. Similarly, the parameter α of FSC is configured to 2. It is clearly shown in the table that R-KM consistently improves the quality of its baseline model, i.e. KM. In addition, it has the best NMI

Table3. NMI measures with known number of clusters (K). The highest two measures for each dataset are highlighted in boldface, and corresponding standard deviations are given in parentheses.

Dataset	Method							
	R-KM	LAC	EWKM	FSC	KM	SL	CL	AL
Brain-Tumor	**0.493** (0.074)	0.353 (0.090)	0.238 (0.110)	0.349 (0.107)	**0.435** (0.122)	0.148 (0.000)	0.349 (0.000)	0.133 (0.000)
Bladder-Carcinoma	**0.380** (0.113)	**0.362** (0.118)	0.255 (0.130)	0.292 (0.137)	0.312 (0.125)	0.161 (0.000)	0.288 (0.000)	0.144 (0.000)
CNS	**0.423** (0.093)	**0.491** (0.086)	0.334 (0.095)	0.356 (0.094)	0.285 (0.113)	0.210 (0.000)	0.380 (0.000)	0.210 (0.000)
CRC	**0.125** (0.090)	0.075 (0.076)	0.076 (0.081)	0.117 (0.098)	0.075 (0.078)	0.026 (0.000)	**0.168** (0.000)	**0.168** (0.000)
DLBCL1	**0.524** (0.084)	0.502 (0.068)	0.398 (0.151)	0.496 (0.056)	0.505 (0.088)	0.093 (0.000)	0.465 (0.000)	**0.642** (0.000)
DLBCL2	**0.126** (0.061)	**0.128** (0.068)	0.053 (0.042)	0.066 (0.055)	0.103 (0.066)	0.094 (0.000)	0.094 (0.000)	0.094 (0.000)
Leukemia1	**0.574** (0.099)	0.359 (0.123)	0.278 (0.150)	**0.484** (0.136)	0.447 (0.160)	0.078 (0.000)	0.213 (0.000)	0.078 (0.000)
Leukemia2	**0.204** (0.125)	0.154 (0.209)	0.064 (0.096)	**0.222** (0.184)	0.092 (0.098)	0.068 (0.000)	0.042 (0.000)	0.027 (0.000)
Lung-Tumor1	**0.165** (0.046)	**0.158** (0.056)	0.110 (0.056)	0.153 (0.052)	0.142 (0.064)	0.073 (0.000)	0.048 (0.000)	0.073 (0.000)
Lung-Tumor2	**0.793** (0.137)	**0.684** (0.162)	0.230 (0.307)	0.378 (0.252)	0.553 (0.329)	0.078 (0.000)	0.008 (0.000)	0.078 (0.000)

scores in five out of ten microarray datasets investigated herein. Specific to LAC, it provides the best clustering results across eight clustering methods on CNS and DLBCL2 datasets. However, it fails to outperform KM on several datasets: Brain-Tumor, CRC, DLBCL1, and Leukemia1. EWKM is comparatively less effective than R-KM and LAC. It also performs worse than KM on eight microarray datasets. Despite its promising results on Leukemia1 and Leukemia2, FSC often fails to beat its baseline and other soft subspace counterparts.

Among four standard clustering method included in this experiment, KM is likely to the preferred alternative, with exceptional performance on Brain-Tumor. In contrary to this generalization, CL and AL have the best NMI measures on CRC dataset. Figure 3 confirms the aforementioned findings, with SL being the worst between four basic methods. This figure that represents the average NMI scores across all datasets, suggests R-KM and LAC to be the most effective, as compared to the base line and two other soft subspace models.

DISCUSSION AND FUTURE RESEARCH

In the literature, these soft subspace clustering techniques have proven effective to identifying clusters in a number of domain problems, especially microarray gene expression data analysis. However, it is pointed out by Kriegel et al (2009) that most methods are subjected to algorithmic parameters, which can greatly influence their performance. See Table 4 for the summarization of these parameters. Different parameter settings result in distinct clustering models with dissimilar behavior (Iam-On et al, 2010). The No Free Lunch theorem (Wolpert and Macready, 1995) also suggests[1] there is no single clustering model that performs best for all datasets (Kuncheva and Hadjitodorov, 2004), i.e., no single model is able to discover all types of cluster shapes and structures presented in data (Duda et al, 2000; Fred and Jain, 2005; Xue et al, 2009). This problem of selecting parameters, or alternative algorithms, has been a troublesome issue, especially with a new set of data. In such

Figure 3. NMI scores of eight examined clustering methods, as the average across all datasets

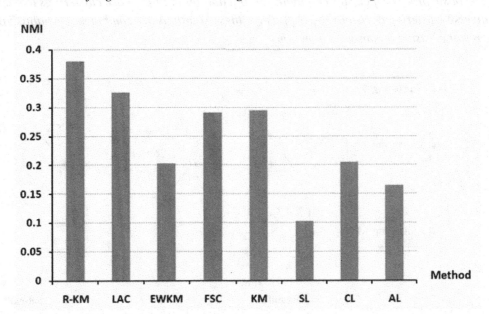

Table 4. Summarization of parameters for soft subspace clustering methods included in this survey. Note that the user-defined number of clusters k is commonly required in addition to those specified below.

Method	Parameter	Description	General Setting
COSA	$l \geq 0$	Incentive for more dimensions per cluster	0.2-0.4
LAC	$h \geq 0$	Coefficient for the effect of intra-cluster distance to weight	9
EWKM	$g \geq 0$	Incentive for more dimensions per cluster	0.5
LWC	-	-	-
FSC	$\alpha \hat{I} (1, ¥)$	Fuzzifier of weight component	2
R-KM	$\beta \{1, n-1\}$	Size of nearest neighbor set	2-4
R-CL	$\beta \{1, n-1\}$	Size of nearest neighbor set	2-4
R-SPT	$\beta \{1, n-1\}$	Size of nearest neighbor set	2-4

a case where prior knowledge is generally minimal, the performance of any particular method is inherently uncertain.

An initial attempt that uses the cluster ensemble methodology to obtain a more robust and accurate outcome from a soft subspace clustering method has been reported by Domeniconi et al (2007). The general framework of cluster ensembles is illustrated in Figure 4. Solutions achieved from different base clusterings, also called *ensemble members*, are aggregated to form the final partition. This meta-level method involves two major tasks of generating a cluster ensemble and producing the final partition, which is normally referred to as a consensus function (Iam-On et al, 2011).

Specific to LAC, the setting of parameter h is data dependant with an optimal value being normally achieved through multiple trials. This drawback has turned to be useful for generating diversity within a cluster ensemble, where ensemble members represent LAC with different h

Figure 4. The basic process of cluster ensembles. It first applies multiple base clusterings to a dataset X to obtain diverse clustering decisions ($p_1...p_M$). Then, these solutions are combined to establish the final clustering result p* using a consensus function.

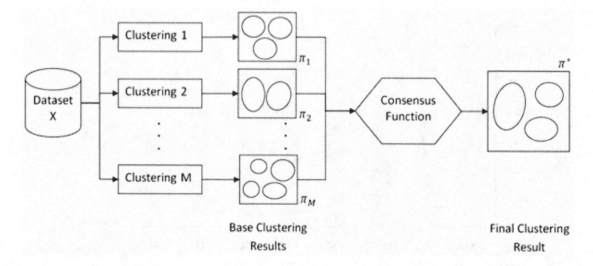

values. It has been shown that ensembles are most effective when built from a set of predictive models whose errors are dissimilar (Kittler et al, 1998; Kuncheva and Vetrov, 2006). The level of diversity can be further enhanced with the joint use of the aforementioned random parameter setting and other heuristics such as applying manifold subsets of initial data to base clusterings. In practice, these can be obtained by projecting data onto different subspaces (Fern and Brodley, 2003) or using data sampling techniques (Fischer and Buhmann, 2003).

Having obtained the ensemble, a rich collection of consensus functions are made available for creating the final result. Examples of well-known functions are: (i) the feature-based approach that treats the problem of cluster ensembles as the clustering of categorical data (Nguyen and Caruana, 2007; Topchy et al, 2005), (ii) the direct approach that finds the final partition through relabeling the base clustering results (Fischer and Buhmann, 2003; Gionis et al, 2005), (iii) the graph-based approach that employs the graph representation and partitioning technique (Fern and Brodley, 2004; Iam-On et al, 2010; Strehl and Ghosh, 2002), and (iv) the pairwise similarity approach that makes use of co-occurrence relationships between all pairs of data points (Fred and Jain, 2005; Iam-On and Garrett; Monti et al, 2003). This prescribed ensemble approach is not limited only to LAC, but applicable to other soft subspace clustering methods. And for microarray data analysis, the resulting clustering models are sought to provide more accurate data exploration, whilst being user friendly to general practitioners.

CONCLUSION

While the dimensional space is usually complex, it is observed that the intrinsic dimensionality of a data cluster is commonly much smaller than the original. In other words, each dimension may not necessarily be uniformly significant for different regions of the data space. This encourages and results in a variety of research that aims to search for a meaningful space over a given set of data. Initial attempts to achieve that goal have been realized as global dimension reduction techniques and dimension selection criteria. While the former works on the derivation of new axes in the reduced space onto which the original data space is projected, the latter search for a subset of original dimensions that is highly correlated with object groups. Specific to cluster analysis, these lead to a the idea of adaptive distance metrics, which are later on implemented as hard and soft subspace clustering methods. Both categories produce good results with microarray gene expression data, using different strategies. While a hard subspace model relies on the search for a definite subset of dimensions per cluster, the soft counterpart configures dimensional weights based on local relevance. This review describes several state-of-the-art approaches to soft subspace clustering, which can be further categorized as wrapper-based or filter-based method. In general, a standard clustering algorithm like k-means is used as the core of a wrapper, in which cluster-specific weights are normally updated along the search for cluster members. With this framework, the resulting wrapper model cannot be extended beyond the algorithm used as its main component. In contrary, with a filter-based approach, information used to derive weighted is constructed before the actual clustering process. Hence, it can be coupled with several clustering algorithms to form a customized soft subspace model. Almost all the revised techniques are parameterized such that their performance depends highly on user input and data in question. As such, the application of ensembles is recently introduced to resolve this dilemma, where random parameter settings can raise diversity, hence accuracy of the ensemble. A number of different cluster ensembles are made available in the literature, and their combinations with soft subspace clusterings are sought to be a new challenge to improving the accuracy of data analysis, especially for microarray gene expression data.

REFERENCE

Aggarwal, C., Procopiuc, C., Wolf, J. L., Yu, P. S., & Park, J. S. (1999). Fast algorithms for projected clustering. In *Proceedings of ACM SIGMOD International Conference on Management of Data* (pp. 61-72). ACM.

Bezdek, J., & Hathaway, R. (1988). Recent convergence results for the fuzzy c-means clustering algorithms. *Journal of Classification, 5*(2), 237–247. doi:10.1007/BF01897166

Boongoen, T., Shang, C., Iam-On, N., & Shen, Q. (2011). Extending data reliability measure to a filter approach for soft subspace clustering. *IEEE Transactions on Systems, Man and Cybernetics. Part B, 41*(6), 1705–1714.

Boongoen, T., & Shen, Q. (2010). Nearest-neighbor guided evaluation of data reliability and its applications. *IEEE Transactions on Systems, Man and Cybernetics. Part B, 40*(6), 1622–1633.

Carkacioglu, L., Atalay, R. C., Konu, O., Atalay, V., & Can, T. (2010). Bi-k-bi clustering: Mining large scale gene expression data using two-level biclustering. *International Journal of Data Mining and Bioinformatics, 4*(6), 701–721. doi:10.1504/IJDMB.2010.037548 PMID:21355502

Chakrabarti, K., & Mehrotra, S. (2000). Local dimensionality reduction: A new approach to indexing high dimensional spaces. In *Proceedings of International Conference on VLDB* (pp. 89-100). VLDB.

Chen, L. C., Yu, P. S., & Tseng, V. S. (2011). WF-MSB: A weighted fuzzy-based biclustering method for gene expression data. *International Journal of Data Mining and Bioinformatics, 5*(1), 89–109. doi:10.1504/IJDMB.2011.038579 PMID:21491846

Cheng, H., Hua, K. A., & Vu, K. (2008). Constrained locally weighted clustering. In *Proceedings of International Conference on VLDB* (pp. 90-101). VLDB.

Cheng, Y., & Church, G. M. (2000). Biclustering of expression data. In *Proceedings of International Conference on Intelligent Systems for Molecular Biology* (pp. 93-103). IEEE.

Cleator, S., & Ashworth, A. (2004). Molecular profiling of breast cancer: Clinical implications. *British Journal of Cancer, 90*, 1120–1124. doi:10.1038/sj.bjc.6601667 PMID:15026788

Cohen, D. S., & Blum, M. (1995). On the problem of sorting burnt pancakes. *Discrete Applied Mathematics, 61*, 105–120. doi:10.1016/0166-218X(94)00009-3

de Souto, M., Costa, I., de Araujo, D., Ludermir, T., & Schliep, A. (2008). Clustering cancer gene expression data: A comparative study. *BMC Bioinformatics, 9*, 497. doi:10.1186/1471-2105-9-497 PMID:19038021

Domeniconi, C., Gunopulos, D., Ma, S., Yan, B., Al-Razgan, M., & Papadopoulos, D. (2007). Locally adaptive metrics for clustering high dimensional data. *Data Mining and Knowledge Discovery, 14*(1), 63–97. doi:10.1007/s10618-006-0060-8

Duda, R. O., Hart, P. E., & Stork, D. G. (2000). *Pattern classification*. Hoboken, NJ: Wiley-Interscience.

Dy, J. G., & Brodley, C. E. (2004). Feature selection for unsupervised learning. *Journal of Machine Learning Research*, 5, 845–889.

Fern, X. Z., & Brodley, C. E. (2003). Random projection for high dimensional data clustering: A cluster ensemble approach. In *Proceedings of International Conference on Machine Learning* (pp. 186-193). IEEE.

Fern, X. Z., & Brodley, C. E. (2004). Solving cluster ensemble problems by bipartite graph partitioning. In *Proceedings of International Conference on Machine Learning* (pp. 36-43). IEEE.

Fischer, B., & Buhmann, J. M. (2003). Bagging for path-based clustering. *IEEE Transactions on Pattern Analysis and Machine Intelligence*, 25(11), 1411–1415. doi:10.1109/TPAMI.2003.1240115

Fred, A. L. N., & Jain, A. K. (2005). Combining multiple clusterings using evidence accumulation. *IEEE Transactions on Pattern Analysis and Machine Intelligence*, 27(6), 835–850. doi:10.1109/TPAMI.2005.113 PMID:15943417

Friedman, J. H., & Meulman, J. J. (2004). Clustering objects on subsets of attributes. *Journal of the Royal Statistical Society. Series B. Methodological*, 66(4), 825–849. doi:10.1111/j.1467-9868.2004.02059.x

Gan, G. J., & Wu, J. H. (2008). A convergence theorem for the fuzzy subspace clustering (FSC) algorithm. *Pattern Recognition*, 41, 1939–1947. doi:10.1016/j.patcog.2007.11.011

Gionis, A., Mannila, H., & Tsaparas, P. (2005). Clustering aggregation. In *Proceedings of International Conference on Data Engineering* (pp. 341-352). IEEE.

Golub, T., Slonim, D., Tamayo, P., Huard, C., Gaasenbeek, M., & Mesirov, J. et al. (1999). Molecular classification of cancer: Class discovery and class prediction by gene expression monitoring. *Science*, 286, 531–537. doi:10.1126/science.286.5439.531 PMID:10521349

Gu, J., & Liu, J. S. (2008). Bayesian biclustering of gene expression data. *BMC Genomics*, 9(Suppl 1), S4. doi:10.1186/1471-2164-9-S1-S4 PMID:18366617

Han, J., & Kamber, M. (2000). *Data mining: Concepts and techniques*. San Francisco: Morgan Kaufmann.

Hochbaum, D. S., & Shmoys, D. B. (1985). A best possible heuristic for the k-center problem. *Mathematics of Operations Research*, 10(2), 180–184. doi:10.1287/moor.10.2.180

Iam-On, N., & Boongoen, T. (2012). New soft subspace method to gene expression data clustering. In *Proceedings of IEEE-EMBS International Conference on Biomedical and Health Informatics* (pp. 984-987). IEEE.

Iam-On, N., Boongoen, T., & Garrett, S. (2010). LCE: A link-based cluster ensemble method for improved gene expression data analysis. *Bioinformatics (Oxford, England)*, 26(12), 1513–1519. doi:10.1093/bioinformatics/btq226 PMID:20444838

Iam-On, N., Boongoen, T., Garrett, S., & Price, C. (2011). A link-based approach to the cluster ensemble problem. *IEEE Transactions on Pattern Analysis and Machine Intelligence*, 33(12), 2396–2409. doi:10.1109/TPAMI.2011.84 PMID:21576752

Iam-On, N., & Garrett, S. (2010). LinkCluE: A MATLAB package for link-based cluster ensembles. *Journal of Statistical Software, 36*(9).

Jain, A. K., & Dubes, R. C. (1988). *Algorithms for clustering data.* Upper Saddle River, NJ: Prentice Hall.

Jiang, D., Tang, C., & Zhang, A. (2004). Cluster analysis for gene expression data: A survey. *IEEE Transactions on Knowledge and Data Engineering, 16*(11), 1370–1386. doi:10.1109/TKDE.2004.68

Jing, L., Ng, M. K., & Huang, J. Z. (2007). An entropy weighting k-means algorithm for subspace clustering of high-dimensional sparse data. *IEEE Transactions on Knowledge and Data Engineering, 19*(8), 1026–1041. doi:10.1109/TKDE.2007.1048

Joliffe, I. (1986). *Principal component analysis.* New York: Springer. doi:10.1007/978-1-4757-1904-8

King, B. (1967). Step-wise clustering procedures. *Journal of the American Statistical Association, 69*, 86–101. doi:10.1080/01621459.1967.10482890

Kittler, J., Hatef, M., Duin, R., & Matas, J. (1998). On combining classifiers. *IEEE Transactions on Pattern Analysis and Machine Intelligence, 20*(3), 226–239. doi:10.1109/34.667881

Kriegel, H. P., Kroger, P., & Zimek, A. (2009). Clustering high-dimensional data: A survey on subspace clustering, pattern-based clustering, and correlation clustering. [-ex.]. *ACM Transactions on KDD, 3*(1), 1.

Kuncheva, L. I., & Hadjitodorov, S. T. (2004). Using diversity in cluster ensembles. In *Proceedings of the IEEE International Conference on Systems, Man & Cybernetics* (pp. 1214-1219). IEEE.

Kuncheva, L. I., & Vetrov, D. (2006). Evaluation of stability of k-means cluster ensembles with respect to random initialization. *IEEE Transactions on Pattern Analysis and Machine Intelligence, 28*(11), 1798–1808. doi:10.1109/TPAMI.2006.226 PMID:17063684

McQueen, J. (1967). Some methods for classification and analysis of multivariate observations. In *Proceedings of the Fifth Berkeley Symposium on Mathematical Statistics and Probability* (pp. 281-297). IEEE.

Monti, S., Tamayo, P., Mesirov, J. P., & Golub, T. R. (2003). Consensus clustering: A resampling-based method for class discovery and visualization of gene expression microarray data. *Machine Learning, 52*(1-2), 91–118. doi:10.1023/A:1023949509487

Ng, A., Jordan, M., & Weiss, Y. (2001). On spectral clustering: Analysis and an algorithm. *Advances in NIPS, 14.*

Nguyen, N., & Caruana, R. (2007). Consensus clusterings. In *Proceedings of IEEE International Conference on Data Mining* (pp. 607-612). IEEE.

Prelic, A., Bleuler, S., Zimmermann, P., Wille, A., Buhlmann, P., & Gruissem, W. et al. (2006). A systematic comparison and evaluation of biclustering methods for gene expression data. *Bioinformatics (Oxford, England), 22*(9), 1122–1129. doi:10.1093/bioinformatics/btl060 PMID:16500941

Ramaswamy, S., Ross, K., Lander, E., & Golub, T. (2003). A molecular signature of metastasis in primary solid tumours. *Nature Genetics, 33*, 49–54. doi:10.1038/ng1060 PMID:12469122

Spang, R. (2003). Diagnostic signatures from microarrays: A bioinformatics concept for personalized medicine. *BIOSILICO, 1*, 264–268. doi:10.1016/S1478-5382(03)02329-1

Strehl, A., & Ghosh, J. (2002). Cluster ensembles: A knowledge reuse framework for combining multiple partitions. *Journal of Machine Learning Research*, *3*, 583–617.

Tanay, A., Sharan, R., & Shamir, R. (2002). Discovering statistically significant biclusters in gene expression data. *Bioinformatics (Oxford, England)*, *18*(1), 136–144. doi:10.1093/bioinformatics/18.suppl_1.S136 PMID:12169541

Topchy, A. P., Jain, A. K., & Punch, W. F. (2005). Clustering ensembles: Models of consensus and weak partitions. *IEEE Transactions on Pattern Analysis and Machine Intelligence*, *27*(12), 1866–1881. doi:10.1109/TPAMI.2005.237 PMID:16355656

Tseng, G., & Wong, W. (2005). Tight clustering: A resampling-based approach for identifying stable and tight patterns in data. *Biometrics*, *61*, 10–16. doi:10.1111/j.0006-341X.2005.031032.x PMID:15737073

Tusher, V., Tibshirani, R., & Chu, G. (2001). Significance analysis of microarrays applied to the ionizing radiation response. *Proceedings of the National Academy of Sciences of the United States of America*, *98*(9), 5116–5121. doi:10.1073/pnas.091062498 PMID:11309499

Wallqvist, A., Rabow, A., Shoemaker, R., Sausville, E., & Covell, D. (2002). Establishing connections between microarray expression data and chemotherapeutic cancer pharmacology. *Molecular Cancer Therapeutics*, *1*, 311–320. PMID:12489847

Wolpert, D. H., & Macready, W. G. (1995). *No free lunch theorems for search* (Technical Report SFI-TR-95-02-010). Santa Fe, NM: Santa Fe Institute.

Xue, H., Chen, S., & Yang, Q. (2009). Discriminatively regularized least-squares classification. *Pattern Recognition*, *42*(1), 93–104. doi:10.1016/j.patcog.2008.07.010

KEY TERMS AND DEFINITIONS

Base Clustering: Also called 'ensemble member'.

Cluster Ensemble: A meta-learning model, where a group of data clustering results are aggregated and used to generate the final result, that is usually better than that of each initial clustering.

Data Clustering: The process/mechanism of dividing data instances under examination into distinct groups. It is normally used for data preprocessing and visualization.

Data Subspace: A subset of original data, i.e. a compact set of data samples captured in a definite group of attributes/features.

DNA Microarray: This denotes a collection of microscopic DNA spots attached to a solid surface. It is used to measure the expression levels of large numbers of genes simultaneously or to genotype multiple regions of a genome.

Hard Clustering: This is used to define a data clustering whose results are precise, i.e. each data instance belongs to only one cluster/group.

Soft Clustering: Unlike hard clustering, a soft clustering process allows every data instance to associate with more than one cluster, each with a definite strength level called 'membership degree'.

ENDNOTES

[1]   The No Free Lunch theorem seems to apply here because the problem of clustering can be reduced to an optimization problem - we are seeking to find the optimal set of clusters for a given dataset via an algorithm.

Section 2
Foundations of Knowledge Representation

Chapter 7
Multi–Objective Genetic and Fuzzy Approaches in Rule Mining Problem of Knowledge Discovery in Databases

Harihar Kalia
Seemanta Engineering College, India

Satchidananda Dehuri
Ajou University, Korea

Ashish Ghosh
Indian Statistical Institute, India

ABSTRACT

Knowledge Discovery in Databases (KDD) is the process of automatically searching patterns from large volumes of data by using specific data mining techniques. Classification, association, and associative classification (integration of classification and association) rule mining are popularly used rule mining techniques in KDD for harvesting knowledge in the form of rule. The classical rule mining techniques based on crisp sets have bad experience of "sharp boundary problems" while mining rule from numerical data. Fuzzy rule mining approaches eliminate these problems and generate more human understandable rules. Several quality measures are used in order to quantify the quality of these discovered rules. However, most of these objectives/criteria are conflicting to each other. Thus, fuzzy rule mining problems are modeled as multi-objective optimization problems rather than single objective. Due to the ability of finding diverse trade-off solutions for several objectives in a single run, multi-objective genetic algorithms are popularly employed in rule mining. In this chapter, the authors discuss the multi-objective genetic-fuzzy approaches used in rule mining along with their advantages and disadvantages. In addition, some of the popular applications of these approaches are discussed.

DOI: 10.4018/978-1-4666-4936-1.ch007

INTRODUCTION

Knowledge Discovery in Databases (KDD) (Fayyad, Piatetsky-Shapiro, & Smyth, 1996) refers to the non-trivial, iterative, and interactive process of discovering high-level/abstract knowledge from love level/raw datasets in the form of patterns, models, and rules etc., which are convincing, narrative, potentially useful, and comprehensible.

Data mining (Cios, Pedrycz, Swiniarski, & Kurgan, 2012) is used as a central step of KDD process, performed either through semi-automatic, or automatic methods. In particular, it involves inferring algorithms for tasks like classification, association rule mining, associative classification, clustering, data visualization, and sequential pattern analysis (Han & Kamber, 2006) for exploring the data and discovering previously unknown patterns.

Fuzzy logic/fuzzy sets (Zadeh, 1988) used in knowledge discovery process, make them more flexible in comparison to classical hard computing techniques and make the system tolerant to vagueness, uncertainty, biased, and approximation. Furthermore, it makes use of this tolerance in achieving tractability, robustness and low cost solution to real-world problems. Use of linguistic variables and linguistic terms used in knowledge mining/rule mining process enhance the knowledge representation and facilitates the interpretation of knowledge/rules in linguistic terms as well as successfully evades unnatural boundaries arise in the partitioning of the attribute domains.

Rule mining (Fayyad, Piatetsky-Shapiro, & Smyth, 1996) is an emerging approach in data mining employed to handle and analyze the huge amount of data in order to extract the wealth of knowledge. It is a process of discovering knowledge in the form of IF-THEN rules from large datasets. These knowledge representation schemes in IF-THEN rule format are popular as the discovered knowledge is represented at a high level of abstraction using few logical conditions, which make knowledge representation more comprehensible.

The IF-THEN rule is an expression of the form:

IF (A given set of conditions are satisfied)
THEN Conclusion(s) (1)

The "IF" part of the rule is called antecedent or precondition, which consists of one or more attribute tests that are logically connected and "THEN" part is called consequent.

Basing on the types of set utilized in attribute representation the IF-THEN are classified as: crisp rules which uses crisp set and fuzzy rules which uses fuzzy sets.

Crisp rules are best suited for categorical/Boolean data. In case of quantitative/continuous data, these rules use a sharp cutoff in selecting attributes, which is a major drawback.

As an example, let us consider a rule used for a job selection;

IF (Age ≥ 18) AND (Height ≥ 165) AND
(Weight ≥ 55) THEN Selected (2)

In this rule, the candidate either with one day less than age 18 or having height 164.9cm or having weight 54.95kg is not selected, which is very unsympathetic.

On the contrary fuzzy rules uses linguistic variables and linguistic values that are defined by context-dependent fuzzy sets whose meanings are spell out by membership functions. In particular very-young, young, middle-aged, old and very-old for age attribute, short, medium and tall for height attribute and low-weight, medium-weight and high-weight for weight attribute and determine the membership degree in [0,1] of the attribute using fuzzy set. Hence the height of 164 is regarded as tall with membership degree less than 165 as tall.

Hence using fuzzy set the above crisp rule towards job selection may look like;

IF (Age is Young) AND (Height is Tall) (Weight is Medium) THEN Selected (3)

In this rule the candidate with one day less than age 18 or having height 164.9cm or having weight 54.95kg may be selected.

Hence fuzzy rules are popular over comparison to crisp rules. Moreover, the features like: capability to handle data with non-linearity, vagueness, and impreciseness enhance the popularity of fuzzy rules.

Interpretability and accuracy of the rules are two basic properties/objectives of fuzzy rule mining, which are generally contradicts to each other. In single objective optimization approach, we can find a best solution corresponding to the minimum or maximum value of a single objective function, which knobs all these objectives into one. Hence it cannot provide a set of different solutions that trade the objectives against each other. However, in multi-objective optimization approach we are able to find a set of compromised solutions, known as the trade-off, non-dominated, non-inferior or Pareto-optimal solutions. So a single solution cannot obtain which optimizes both objectives. Hence fuzzy rule mining problem is solved by modeled as a multi-objective optimization problem in order to find good solutions.

Finding Pareto-optimal solutions via conventional methods like weighting method (Cohen, 1978), constraint method (Cohen, 1978), etc., may incur the limitations like: (i) all solution points cannot be identified because the appropriate weights are not known in advance in case of weighted method and appropriate constraint levels are not known in advance for constraint method, (ii) both methods have high computational complexity. As opposed to these methods genetic algorithms (GAs) can find many non-dominated

solutions at a time, in a single run, by maintaining and continually improving a population of solutions, for which used as a popular tool in solving multi-objective optimization problem.

In solving multi-objective problem by GAs, multiple objectives cause problems within GAs, as the separate objectives have unequal effective ranges. If the used multi-objective ranking method is not range-independent, then one or more objectives in the problem can dominate the others; give rise to poor solutions, which prompts to use multi-objective genetic algorithms in solving these problems.

In data mining, both crisp rule mining and fuzzy rule mining are categorized as: classification, association, and associative classification/classification based on association. Classification finds small set of rules with training data and builds a classifier aiming at classifying the unseen data. Association spawns certain association link between the data items. There is no fixed target for association rule mining, where as the target is fixed for classification rule mining, which is the "class". Classification based on association is an integration of classification and association, which utilize association rule in classification rule mining.

Moreover, the tasks of discovering IF-THEN rules from large data are growing. Some of the areas, where the process of discovering IF-THEN rules is tremendously accepted are: engineering (Pham, 1999), medical diagnosis (Kaur, 2006), manufacturing (Yu, Xi, & Zhou, 2008), network intrusion detection (Zainal, Maarof, & Shamsuddin, 2009), agriculture (Shaffer, & Brodahl, 1998), recommender system (Garcia, Ramero, Ventura, & De Castro, 2009), financial forecasting (Tsang, Yung, & Li, 2004), stock prediction (Tang, Xu, Wan, & Zhang, 2002), fault detection (Ruiz, Coton, Maria, Espuna, & Puigjaner, 2001), geographical information systems (GISs) (Stockwell, 1999) and Robotics control (Maeda1995), etc.

MULTI-OBJECTIVE OPTIMIZATION PROBLEM

Finding best result under the given conditions is known as optimization. An optimization problem with more than one objective function, locating one or more optimum solutions is referred as multi-objective optimization.

Single objective optimization method finds a best solution to the multi-objective problem, corresponding to the minimum or maximum value of a single objective function, by combining all objectives using some weights. Hence it cannot provide a set of different solutions that trade different objectives against each other. However, multi-objective optimization methods simultaneously optimize two or more conflicting objectives subject to certain constraints and find a set of equally good solutions.

According to Osyczka (Osyczka, 1985), multi-objective optimization problem (MOP) can be defined as: "A vector of decision variables which satisfies constraints and optimizes a vector function whose elements represent the objective functions. These functions form a mathematical description of performance criteria which are usually in conflict with each other. Hence the term "optimizes" means finding such a solution, which would give the values of all the objective functions acceptable to the decision maker."

Mathematically this can be stated and visualized as follows:

Find the vector

$$\vec{x} = \left\langle x_1, x_2, \ldots\ldots, x_d \right\rangle$$

which can optimize the vector function

$$\overrightarrow{f\left(\vec{x}\right)} = \left\langle f_1\left(\vec{x}\right), f_2\left(\vec{x}\right), \ldots\ldots, f_n\left(\vec{x}\right) \right\rangle$$

simultaneously and satisfy m inequality constraints

$$g_i\left(\vec{x}\right) \geq 0, i = 1, 2, \ldots\ldots, m ,$$

and p equality constraints

$$h_j\left(\vec{x}\right) = 0, j = 1, 2, \ldots., p.$$

In practice there exist no single optimal solution for MOP; instead there exists a set of optimal solutions, each one judging a certain trade-off among the objectives.

This concept is termed as Pareto optimality, originally proposed by Francis Ysidrimal Edge Worth (Edge worth, 1881) and generalized by Vilfredo Pareto (Pareto, 1896). A vector of solutions $\vec{x}$ is called Pareto optimal, if there exists no feasible vector $\vec{x}$, which would increase some criterion without causing a simultaneous decrease in at least one other criterion, in case of a maximization problem. This is accepted as the Pareto optimum solution. Pareto optimum set is generally called an efficient solution set or a non-dominated solution set.

Hence the design goal of all multi-objective algorithms are (Deb, 2001): (i) how to find solutions close/converge to the Pareto optimal front, which is a stochastic process, and (ii) how to keep diversity among the solutions in the solution set so obtained.

There are three approaches used to cope up with the MOPs, namely (i) the conventional weighted-sum-approach; (ii) the lexicographical approach; and (iii) the Pareto approach.

Weighted sum approach is the most commonly approach used in rule mining literature, to handle MOP, where the multi-objective problem is transformed into a single objective problem by using a weighted sum objective function (Osyczka, 1985).

That is the fitness value f of a given candidate rule R is typically measured by the following formula:

$$f(R) = w_1 * f_1(R) + w_2 * f_2(R) \\ +\ldots\ldots + w_n * f_n(R) \tag{4}$$

where, $w_i \in [0,1]$ denotes the weight assigned to criteria , $\sum w_i = 1$ and n is the number of evaluation criteria.

In practice the weight assigned to each of the criteria is never zero. Simplicity and ease of use are the main strength of this method. However the main drawback is the proper assignment of weight values. The weight assignment in this formula is ad-hoc, either based on somewhat unclear intuition of the user about the relative importance of different quality criteria or in trial. The error experimentation with different weight values is another drawback, which is in fact the most difficult aspect in rule mining. Hence the values of these weights can be determined empirically. Another problem with these weights is that, once a formula with precise values of weights has been defined and given to a rule mining algorithm, the rule mining algorithm try to find the best rule for that set of weights, missing the opportunity of finding other rules that might be actually more interesting to the user, representing a better trade-off quality criteria. In particular, weighted formulas involving a linear combination of different quality criteria have the limitation that they cannot find solutions in a concave region of the Pareto front.

In Lexicographic approach priorities are set to different objectives and then optimize the objectives in their order of priority. Hence, when two or more candidate rules are compared with each other to choose the best one, the first thing to do is to compare their performance measure for the highest priority objective. If one candidate rule is significantly better than the other with respect to that objective, the former is chosen. Otherwise the performance measure of the two candidate rules is compared with respect to the next priority objective. The process is repeated until a clear winner is obtained or until all the criteria are used. In the latter case, if there is no clear winner, one can simply select the rule optimizing the highest priority objective. The lexicographic approach has an advantage over the weighted sum approach: the former avoids the mixing of non-commensurable criteria in the same formula. Indeed, the lexicographic approach treats each of the criteria separately, recognizing that each criterion measures a different aspect of quality of a candidate solution. As a result, the lexicographic approach avoids the drawbacks associated with the weighted-sum approach such as the problem of fixing weights. The lexicographic approach usually requires one to specify a tolerance threshold for each criterion. It is not trivial to specify these thresholds in an unbiased way.

In Pareto approach instead of transforming a multi-objective problem into a single objective problem before solving it, one can use multi-objective problem solving techniques directly. This concept states that when many objectives are simultaneously optimized, there is no single optimal solution; instead there is a set of optimal solutions called Pareto optimal set, each one considering a certain trade-off among the objectives.

In complex search spaces, wherein exhaustive search is infeasible, it is very difficult to guarantee Pareto optimality. Therefore instead of the true set of optimal solutions (Pareto set), one usually aims to derive a set of non-dominated solutions with objective values (Pareto front) as close as possible to the objective values of the Pareto set. We say that a vector of decision variables is a Pareto optimal or strong Pareto optimal if there does not exist another one, such that for all $i = 1, 2, \ldots, n$ and for at least one j.

Mathematically a vector $\vec{x}^* \in \Omega$, the search space is Pareto optimal or strong Pareto optimal iff there is no vector $\vec{x} \in \Omega$, with characteristics

$$f_i\left(\vec{x}^{\,*}\right) \le f_i\left(\vec{x}\right), \ \forall i$$

and

$$f_j\left(\vec{x}^{\,*}\right) < f_j\left(\vec{x}\right)$$

for at least one *j*. If only the second conditions hold, then $\vec{x}^{\,*}$ is said to be weakly Pareto optimal. The vector corresponding to the solutions included in the Pareto optimal set is called non-dominated.

RULE MINING PROBLEM OF KDD

This section discusses the preliminaries concepts associated with rule mining problem of KDD by segregating in different subsections.

Knowledge Discovery in Databases

In real world, the volume of data warehouse is increased almost doubled in every year. In these complex data repositories, a lot of interesting knowledge/information is stored in hidden form, which will be beneficial for users. Manual mining of these needful informations are quite infeasible and hence necessitates some automatic/semi-automatic process. Knowledge discovery (Weiss, & Indurkhya, 1998) solve this purpose, which is an interdisciplinary field that merges together databases, statistics, machine learning and related areas in order to extract valuable information and knowledge in large volumes of data.

Knowledge Discovery in Databases (KDD) is a repeated, investigative and modeling of huge data repositories. It can be defined as a systematized process of discovering legitimate novel, valuable, interesting, comprehensible patterns from large

and complex data sets. KDD process discovered valuable knowledge from raw data using the functions narrated below:

1. **Goal Identification:** Identifying the goal of KDD process from the end-user's prospective.
2. **Application Domain Recognition:** The application domain for the problem should be visualized.
3. **Data Set Selection:** The target dataset or subset of samples on which discovery is performed must be chosen properly.
4. **Data Cleaning:** The filtration of selected data set is done in order to eliminate/alter the missing values/noise.
5. **Feature Selection:** Unnecessary variables are eliminated and data are formatted to be fitted for goal determination.
6. **Goal Mapping:** KDD goals are matched with appropriate data mining task.
7. **Process Identification:** Choosing the appropriate models and parameters suitable for KDD process.
8. **Data Mining:** Required patterns are searched and expressed in desirable format such as: classification, regression, clustering, association etc.
9. **Interpretation:** Requisite knowledge is deduced from the mined patterns.
10. **Supplementary Work:** The mined knowledge is utilized and may fit into any step for further action.
11. **Documentation:** The resulted knowledge is properly documented and reported to interested or target audience.

The discovered knowledge becomes unnecessary if it just like a black box, which makes predictions without explaining them. In such cases the user may not trust it. Hence discovered knowledge must be comprehensible, which can be achieved by using a high-level knowledge representation scheme. A set of IF-THEN prediction rules are suitable choice in context of data mining, where each rule is of the form:

$$IF \left\langle a\ set\ of\ conditions\ are\ satisfied \right\rangle THEN \left\langle forecast\ some\ value\ for\ an\ attribute \right\rangle \quad (5)$$

Crisp rules and fuzzy rules are two categories of IF-THEN rules, based on the types of set used to express the conditions of the rule, which are discussed below.

Crisp Rule Mining

Crisp rule mining expresses the knowledge in IF-THEN format as in equation (1) using the crisp sets. In other words the antecedent conditions of the rule are based on crisp sets. The predictive accuracy, comprehensibility and interestingness are the three common measures used in judging the goodness of rules. The predictive accuracy measure the accuracy of the extracted rules. That is the how accurately it classifies the data. Comprehensibility refers to simplicity of the rule, measured by number of rules and number of conditions involved in the rule and tries to quantify the understandability of the rule. Interestingness based on factors like: novelty, surprisingness, coverage, conciseness, coverage, peculiarity, diversity, actionability and usefulness of the generated rule.

As the said objectives are conflicting to each other, in order to find a good trade-off between these objectives crisp rule mining can be visualized as multi-objective optimization problem.

Classification, association and associative classification are three forms of IF-THEN rules. These classical rule mining techniques, based on crisp set are very efficiently deal the Boolean data/categorical data, which are illustrated below.

Crisp Classification Rule

Classification aims at predicting the value, i.e., the class of a user-specified goal attribute based on the values of other attributes, called the predicting attributes.

The (crisp) classification problem can be defined as: Given a set of predefined and disjoint classes

$$\left\{ C_1, C_2, \ldots\ldots, C_n \right\}$$

a set of features

$$\left\{ f_1, f_2, \ldots f_n \right\}$$

and a set of training data T with predefined class label, the task is to build a set of IF-THEN rules, which are able to assign a class label to each unseen/future object/record/instance.

The general format of classification rule is:

$$IF \left\langle Set\ of\ Conditions \right\rangle THEN \left\langle Class \right\rangle (6)$$

where each condition is a triplet

$$\left\langle attribute, operator, value \right\rangle$$

where value is any value from the domain of attribute, the operator is any relational operator from

$$\left\{ =, <, >, \leq, \geq \right\}$$

such as < *Salary* $\geq$ *25,000*>.

For example: IF (< *Age>18>* and *<Aggregate PCM mark>45%>* and *< Qualified-*

AIEEE/OJEE=yes) THEN (Engg-Admimission-Eligibility=OK) is a typical classification rule.

Classification rule mining process accomplishes using two steps. First step term as training phase, build a classifier by analyzing the training dataset and in second step test data are verified using the generated rules in training phase.

The classification rules in rules set must satisfy the mutually exclusiveness and exhaustiveness. Mutually exclusiveness refers to the independence of rules from each other and every record is covered by at most one rule refers to mutually exclusive. Exhaustiveness means that every possible combination of values is taken into account and each record is covered by at least one rule.

The discovered classification rules should have high classification accuracy, comprehensible and more interesting (Dehuri, & Mall, 2004). These objectives are conflicting to each other. So in order to find a good balance between these objectives classification rule mining problem modeled as a multi-objective optimization problem.

Crisp Association Rule

Association rule mining is a procedure of discovering a number of relationships among the attributes or attribute values in a large database. The association rule mining problem originates in market basket analysis which aims at identify the buying behavior of the retail customers or the associations among the items purchased together at super market/store. Subsequently association rule discovery applied in various research areas due to their practical expediency.

Frequent item sets searching are the basic element in association rule mining. An item may be product in a supermarket example and the set of items is called item sets. For example, {bread} is an item and {bread, butter, milk} is an item set. The occurrences of an item/item sets in the dataset are called support.

The support of an item/item set Y is defined as:

$$Supp(Y) = \frac{Number \ of \ Transaction \ contain \ Y}{Total \ number \ of \ Transactions} \quad (7)$$

An item or the item set is said to be frequent item if its support is higher than the user defined minimum support value.

For a dataset, all possible association rules can be generated from the searched frequent items. *Apriori* is the primitive algorithm used for searching frequent item sets.

Association rules can be expressed as:

$$IF \langle Some \ conditions \ are \ satisfied \rangle \ THEN \langle Predict \ some \ value \ of \ other \ attribute(s) \rangle \quad (8)$$

In particular the rule looks like:

$$IF \quad X \quad THEN \quad Y \quad (9)$$

or

$$X \Rightarrow Y, \ where \ X \cap Y = \varphi \quad (10)$$

For example, in market-basket data a typical association rule may be:

$$\{Bread, Butter\} \Rightarrow \{Jam\} \quad (11)$$

The support of the rule is support of the item set $\{X,Y\}$.

The confidence measure of a rule is computed using the formula:

$$Conf(X \Rightarrow Y) = \frac{Supp(X \cap Y)}{Supp(X)} \quad (12)$$

The rule is said to be a strong rule if its *support* and *confidence* are higher than the user specified minimum *support* and *confidence* value.

In its basic form association rule mining problem aims at finding all the association rules with support and confidence higher than the user-specified thresholds called minimum support and minimum confidence. Particularly, low minimum support increases the number of rules. In fact this single minimum support value is a control parameter for the number of extracted association rules. Apriori (Agrawal, & Srikant, 1994) and Frequent Pattern-Growth (Han, Pei, & Yin 2000) are two most used classical association rule mining algorithms based on single minimum support threshold value. As a drawback, "Rare item problem" is caused by this single minimum support value in rule mining, which are: frequent itemsets that contain rare items are missed when minimum support is set too high and large numbers of frequent itemsets are produced when minimum support is set to a very low value, i.e. a very low *minsupp* value leads to the generation of all possible combinations (combinatorial explosion). Multiple support models called Multiple Support Apriori (Liu, Hsu, & Ma 1999) is proposed in order to solve this problem, using the idea of setting minimum item support for each item in the database.

Besides support and confidence, the qualities of association rules are measured using different metric, viz. comprehensibility, rule interestingness, lift, correlation, all-confidence, collective strength, conviction, leverage, etc. and hence association rule mining problem viewed as a multi-objective optimization problem (Ghosh, & Nath, 2004; Dehuri, Jagadev, Ghosh & Mall, 2006) with one or more objectives beyond support and confidence.

Crisp Associative Classification Rule

Associative classification mining is a classification approach which assimilates association rule mining and classification rule mining into a single system (Liu, Hsu, & Ma, 1998). These are special form association rules whose consequent contain only one attribute, which is a class label.

In associative classification approach, classifiers are constructed using association rules (Liu, Hsu, & Ma, 1998) in training phase. The extracted class association rules are of the form:

$$IF \left\langle A \quad set \quad of \quad attributes \right\rangle THEN \quad Class \quad C \tag{13}$$

or

$$A \Rightarrow C \tag{14}$$

Where A is the set of attributes and C is the class label.

The basic interesting measures support and confidence, used in association rule mining, also used as the common interesting measure for associative classification rule.

For an associative classification rule $A \Rightarrow C$, the support rule is defined as the numbers of objects in dataset are match with the rule condition having a class label C. The confidence of the rule is the number of object match with rule condition having class label C over the number of object matching with rule conditions.

Basically rule mining process comprise of three steps:

1. Generation of candidate association rules from the training set with pre specified support and confidence threshold.
2. Reduction of rule sets, if possible.
3. Predicting the class of test data.

The support-confidence framework used in association rule mining is inherited and used by the associative classification approach.

All the measures are used for classification approaches are used in associative classification such as accuracy, comprehensibility, lift, J-measure, kappa, etc. A list of interesting measures can be found in (Heravi, & Zaiane, 2010).

Fuzzy Rule Mining

The classical/conventional rule mining techniques are very efficiently the Boolean/categorical data. But in case quantitative data, these methods encounter problem like "sharp boundary problem" and "partial belongings" problems, by following the discrete interval method. In particular, followed discrete interval method in transforming/partitioning quantitative data to categorical/Boolean form, will either discard or overemphasizes the data points which are close to the boundary of the interval. Adaption of fuzzy sets/fuzzy logic resolves these problems by using linguistic variables.

More specifically, the kinship with human knowledge representation, the adaptability and transparency of fuzzy sets/fuzzy logic make the rules more understandable to the expert as well as to the wider addressees. They are also capable in solving complex, nonlinear and/or ill-defined problems by integrating a priori qualitative knowledge and expertise about system behavior and dynamics

Fuzzy rules express the IF-THEN rules using linguistic variables/expressions. Linguistic variables define the value of a variable both qualitatively and quantitatively by defining a symbol for a fuzzy set and defining a meaning of the fuzzy set respectively. For example, the linguistic variables may be high, low, small, old, very old etc.

Fuzzy rules are also expressed as "*IF Antecedent(s) THEN Conclusion(s)*", where antecedents and conclusions are propositions/set of propositions containing linguistic variables. These linguistic variables along with fuzzy IF-THEN-rules develop the acceptance for indistinctness and improbability and hence able to mimics the human behavior in decision making.

More specifically, a fuzzy rule with k premises is of the form:

$$IF \ X_1 \ is \ A_{i_1} \ \theta \ X_2 \ is \ A_{i_2} \ ... \ \theta \ X_k \ is \ A_{i_k} \ THEN \ B_i \tag{15}$$

where $X_1, X_2, ..., X_k$ are crisp inputs to the rule and $A_{i_1}, A_{i_2}, ..., A_{i_k}$ and B_i are linguistic variables. The operator θ may be logical AND or logical OR or XOR operator.

The result of fuzzy rule mining process is powered by membership functions. .In practice it is very difficult to assign appropriate membership functions to the items. So majority of the algorithms based on predefined membership functions, generally supplied by the expert. But it is quite infeasible to set/supply appropriate membership functions for an item. Hence this process of assigning membership functions is subsequently automated by the fuzzy rule mining algorithms. Genetic algorithms are utilized in many approaches for this purpose.

Commonly used membership functions (Zimmermann, 1996) used in fuzzy system modeling is the following:

- **Triangular Membership Function:** A triangular membership function defined as:

$$triangle\left(x; a, b, c\right) = \\ \max\left(\min\left(\frac{x-a}{b-a}, \frac{c-x}{c-b}\right), 0\right) \tag{16}$$

- **Trapezoidal Membership Function:** A trapezoidal membership function is defined as:

$$trapezoid\left(x; a, b, c, d\right) =$$
$$\max\left[\min\left(\frac{x-a}{b-a}, 1, \frac{d-x}{d-c}\right), 0\right] \qquad (17)$$

- **Sigmoid Membership Function:** A Sigmoid membership function is defined as:

$$sigmoid(x; k, c) = \frac{1}{1 + e^{-k(x-c)}} \qquad (18)$$

where sharpness of the function is influenced by the parameter k. If $k > 0$, the function is open on right site, on the other hand, if $k < 0$ the function is open on left site.

- **Gaussian Membership Function:** A Gaussian membership function is a defined by:

$$gaussian(x; \sigma, c) = e^{-\left(\frac{x-c}{\sigma}\right)^2} \qquad (19)$$

where c is the center and σ is the width of the membership function.

Interpretability and accuracy are two basic criteria needed for a fuzzy rule, where accuracy concerns about the ability of proper classification of unseen data and interpretability concerns about the clarity of rules. Although there is no single definition for interpretability but it is related to the following factors.

- **Dimensionality of the Data:** In handling high-dimensional problems by fuzzy-rule based systems, the difficulty is the increase in number of rules and number of condi- tions in antecedent part of the rule. Feature selection is the best remedy for this prob- lem, which select only a few variables for designing fuzzy systems.

- **Membership Function Generation:** The membership function corresponds to each linguistic variable should be consistent with human's knowledge and intuition. Ballini and Gomide (Ballini, & Gomide, 2002) suggest that, triangular membership function is the best choice, when we have no complete knowledge about the problem.

- **Fuzzy Reasoning:** The reasoning method used in the rule mining process should be easy such that conclusion drawing proce- dure must be human understandable.

In fuzzy rule mining utilization of all existing attributes may generate the "course of dimension- ality" problem with respect to rule number and augment the computational cost. Feature selection is incorporated as a remedial measure to this issue, in order to filter out the irrelevant and unnecessary features. Feature selection, in fuzzy rule mining may provide the following benefits.

- **Enhancement of Accuracy and Reliability:** Exclusion/filtration of irrel- evant features which have no influences on outcome can improve the accuracy and re- liability of rules.

- **Reduction of Problem Space:** The lesser number features reduces the problem space of rule mining problem as well as the com- plexity of the generated rules.

- **Fewer Training Data:** Training data size is reduced with the decrease in input di- mension, which in turns avoid the risk of over-fitting.

Similar to the case of crisp rule mining, there are three types of fuzzy rules: fuzzy classification rule, fuzzy association rule and fuzzy associative classification rules, which are explained below.

Fuzzy Classification Rule Mining

In practice, majority of the classification problems (probably problems either with quantitative attributes or with both quantitative and categorical) does not have well defined class boundary according to the definition of crisp classes, which creates fuzziness and hence incurred errors. Fuzzy logic alternatively reduces this error and popularly used in the said task.

Fuzzy classification rules are of the form (Kuncheva, 2000):

$$IF\ x_1\ is\ A_1\ AND\ x_2\ is\ A_2\ AND\ \dots\quad x_n\ is\ A_n\ THEN\ Class\ C \tag{20}$$

where $x_1, x_2, \dots, x_n$ are the attributes of the patterns, $A_1, A_2, \dots, A_n$ are linguistic terms defined by fuzzy sets used in representing the attributes and *Class C* is the class assigned to the pattern.

Following basic steps are adapted in fuzzy classification rule generation from the real dataset.

Step 1: (Normalization) The attributes of data sets are normalized in to real numbers in the unit interval [0, 1] (if they are not in [0, 1]) using the formula:

$$x_{nor} = \frac{x - x_{min}}{x_{max} - x_{min}} \tag{21}$$

where x_{nor} is the normalized value, x is the original value and x_{min} and x_{max} are the minimum and maximum value of the attributes respectively.

Step 2: (Fuzzification) The data are partitioned using fuzzy sets either supplied by the expert or generated automatically.

Step 3: (Candidate Rule Set Generation) A set of candidate fuzzy rules is generated heuristically using the training data set, which can be performed as follows:

a. Create antecedent part of the rules using all combination of fuzzy sets.

b. For each rule, calculate the compatibility degree of each training patterns.

c. The consequent/class label of a rule is the class label of the pattern with highest compatibility grade with respect to the rule.

Fuzzy Association Rule

A typical fuzzy association rule is of the form (Kouk, Fu, & Wong, 1998):

$$IF\ P\ is\ F\ THEN\ Q\ is\ G \tag{22}$$

where

$$F = \left\{ f_1, f_2, \dots, f_m \right\}$$

and

$$G = \left\{ g_1, g_2, \dots, g_n \right\}$$

are set of fuzzy sets used in describing set of items

$$P = \left\{ p_1, p_2, \dots, p_m \right\}$$

and

$$Q = \left\{ q_1, q_2, \dots, q_n \right\}$$

respectively with $P \cap Q = \varphi$, and $P, Q \subset I$.

The pair $\langle P, F \rangle$ is defined as a fuzzy item set, in which $P \subseteq I$ is an item set and F is a set of fuzzy sets associated with attributes in P.

The support of a fuzzy item set $\langle P, F \rangle$, denoted as $FS(\langle P, F \rangle)$ is calculated using following equation.

$$FS(\langle P, F \rangle) = \frac{\sum_{v=1}^{m} \left[\begin{array}{c} \alpha_{p_1}\left(t_v[p_1]\right) \otimes \alpha_{p_2}\left(t_v[p_2]\right) \otimes \\ \ldots\ldots \otimes \alpha_{p_l}\left(t_v[p_l]\right) \end{array} \right]}{|D|} \quad (23)$$

where

- $P = \{p_1, p_2, \ldots, p_l\}$ and t_v is the vth record in D.
- $\otimes$ is the T-norm operator of fuzzy logic, similar to AND in traditional logic.
- $\alpha_{p_k}\left(t_v[p_k]\right)$ is calculated using the formula:

$$\alpha_{p_k}\left(t_v[p_k]\right) = \begin{cases} m_{p_k}\left(t_v[p_k]\right) & if \quad m_{p_k}\left(t_v[p_k]\right) \geq \theta \\ 0 & otherwise \end{cases}$$

where m_{p_k} is the membership function of fuzzy set f_{p_k} associated with p_k and θ is the threshold for membership value specified by users.

- $|D|$, denotes the total number of transactions in the database D.

A fuzzy item set $\langle P, F \rangle$ may be a frequent item set if its support is greater or equal to a fuzzy minimum support (denoted as fminsupp) supplied by the user. That is,

$$FS(\langle P, F \rangle) \geq f\min\sup p \quad (24)$$

The support of a fuzzy association rule

$$P \quad is \quad F \quad \Rightarrow \quad Q \quad is \quad G$$

is calculated as:

$$FS\left(P \quad is \quad F \quad \Rightarrow \quad Q \quad is \quad G\right) = FS\left(\langle P \cup Q, F \cup G \rangle\right) \quad (25)$$

The confidence of a fuzzy association rule

$$P \quad is \quad F \quad \Rightarrow \quad Q \quad is \quad G$$

is calculated as:

$$FC\left(P \quad is \quad F \quad \Rightarrow \quad Q \quad is \quad G\right) = \frac{FS\left(\langle P \cup Q, F \cup G \rangle\right)}{FS\left(\langle P, F \rangle\right)} \quad (26)$$

A fuzzy association rule is accepted, if support and confidence value is greater than the predefined minimum support and minimum confidence value. That is fuzzy support and fuzzy confidences are primary quality measures of fuzzy association rules. Comprehensibility, interpretability, number of fuzzy sets used etc. are some other quality measures. Many other quality measures for fuzzy association rule mining can be found in (Gyenesei, & Teuhola, 2010).

Like crisp ARM, fuzzy association rules are discovered via two phases. In first phase all possible frequent item set are obtained from the input database. In second phase all possible confident fuzzy association rules are mined from the frequent item sets obtained in first phase.

Fuzzy Associative Classification Rule

A fuzzy associative classification rule is defined as:

$$IF \quad P \quad is \quad F \quad THEN \quad Class \quad C \qquad (27)$$

where

$$P = \left\{ p_1, p_2, ..., p_k \right\}$$

represents set of attributes/item sets and

$$F = \left\{ f_1, f_2, ..., f_k \right\}$$

is the associated fuzzy sets and C is the class label.

Associative classification rules are generated in two stages similar to crisp case:

- Extraction of fuzzy association rule.
- Generation of fuzzy associative classification rule from the extracted fuzzy association rule.

MULTI-OBJECTIVE GENETIC ALGORITHMS

The evolutionary algorithms/genetic algorithms (Holland, 1975) are optimized a set of solutions in a single run instead of a single solution and

hence create a new solution by combining several good solutions. In particular, genetic algorithms are optimization methods based on probabilistic operators, inspired by the "survival of the fittest" principle and mimic the behaviors from the processes of natural evolution and natural genetics. Mathematically it can be modeled as:

$$P\left(t+1\right) = S\left(V\left(P\left(t\right)\right)\right) \qquad (28)$$

where $P\left(t\right)$ denotes the population at time t, which is came across by a random variation V and successively give $P\left(t+1\right)$, a new population by a selection operator S.

Genetic algorithms are operates on the encoding of the problem instead of the problem itself. Encoding is a mapping mechanism between the solution space and chromosomes. A chromosome is a solution vector of the problem, called an individual, which is made up of discrete units called genes. A set of coded chromosomes is called a population. With the basic operators: selection and variation, a genetic algorithm executed iteratively on the population, where variation is a combination of two probabilistic operators: crossover and mutation. Genetic algorithms make use of the objective function and probabilistic transition rule respectively for selection and for crossover and mutation.

Basic genetic operators used in genetic algorithm are:

- **Selection Operator:** Selection operator select good solutions from a population retaining the population size unchanged and proceeds one generation to next generation with a better solutions. Tournament selection, proportionate selection and ranking selection are popular selection methods.
- **Crossover Operator:** Genetic algorithm creates new stings by interchanging some parts of randomly chosen strings from

mating pool. Generally the strings are selected for crossover based on a priori probability called crossover probability. Single point crossover, two-point crossover and uniform crossover are popular crossover techniques.

- **Mutation Operator:** Genetic algorithm changes some changes in the strings from mating pool to maintain diversity among in the population. Numbers of stings selected for mutation are also selected by a priori probability called crossover probability. Mutation operator follows crossover operator.

A typical Genetic algorithm work as follows:

Step 1: Generate a random population of *n* chromosomes, which represent a suitable solution for the problem.

Step 2: For each chromosome *y* in the population, evaluate the fitness function.

Step 3: Building new population by the carrying out the following steps:

    a.   Select n parent chromosome from the population based on the fitness value. That is, select the chromosome with better fitness.

    b.   Create new offspring by crossover in parent chromosomes with certain crossover probability.

    c.   Mutate the genes, at each position of new offspring with certain mutation probability.

Step 4: Replace the current population with the newly generated population.

Step 5: If the termination condition is satisfied, stop and return the best chromosome found, otherwise go to Step-II.

Multi-objective genetic algorithms are modified version of a simple genetic algorithm, designed to solve multi-objective optimization problem. In particular, multi-objective genetic algorithms are stochastic optimization techniques, capable of handling very large, complex and high dimensional search space and multiple objectives and able to generate whole Pareto-optimal solutions in a single run. These algorithms followed almost alike optimization mechanism followed by genetic algorithms but use the dominance relation as new concept. Additionally these algorithms are also applying some compassionate methods like niching. Multi-objective genetic algorithms extend a traditional genetic algorithm in two aspects: selection mechanism and diversity maintenance scheme. The fitness assignment scheme adopted by MOGA is also different from simple GA. Elitism is also a new constituent in MOGA.

Multi-objective genetic algorithms are based on three approaches such as: aggregation based approach, population based approach and Pareto based approach based.

Broadly, multi-objective genetic algorithms can be divided into two groups such as: algorithms treating Pareto-optimal solutions explicitly and algorithms treating Pareto-optimal solutions explicitly. Most the current algorithms like NSGA-II (Deb, Pratap, Agrawal, & Meyarivan, 2002), SEPA2 (Zitler, Laumanns, & Thiele, 2001), NCGA (Wantanabe, Hiroyassu, & Miki, 2003) and NRSGA (Ghosh, & Das, 2008) are coming under second category.

Based on the use of elitism multi-objective genetic algorithms are divided in to two categories, such as elitism multi-objective GA and non-elitism multi-objective GA (Coello, 2006). Vector Evaluated Genetic Algorithm (VEGA), Multiple objectives GA (MOGA), Non-dominated sorting GA (NSGA) and Niched Pareto GA (NPGA) are non-elitists multi-objective GAs, where as Non-dominated sorting GA-II(NSGA-II), Non-dominated Rank based Sorting Genetic Algorithm (NRSGA), Multi-objective Messy GA are popular elitists multi-objective GAs.

The practices followed for genetic learning in rule mining process can be divided into three different categories based on their chromosome coding procedure (Fernandez, Garcia, Luengo, Bernado-Mansilla, & Herrera, 2010), such as: Chromosome = Rule, Chromosome = Rule Set and Chromosome = Decision Tree or Tree Rule.

In "Chromosome = Rule" scheme each rule is encoded in a single chromosome and the whole population evolves to the final rule-set. This is again sub-divided into three types: Michigan approach (Holland, & Reitman, 1978), Iterative Rule Learning approach and Genetic Cooperative Competitive Learning approach.

Michigan approach (Booker, Goldberg, & Holland, 1989) otherwise called as learning classifier system. Here the rule set is successively updated via the one-by-one examination of training samples. It uses reinforcement learning and the GA, to learn rules which guide its performance in a given environment. It requires less memory and fewer evaluations.

The Iterative Rule Learning(IRL) approach (Venturini, 1993) consider the best individual as the solution and the global solutions is figured by the best individuals obtained in multiple running of the algorithm. In fact, the genetic algorithm/ EA learns rule by rule iteratively and discards the samples from training data which is covered by each newly generated rule, following a divide-and-conquer approach. A typical multi-objective genetic algorithm may look like as illustrated in Figure 1.

The Genetic Cooperative Competitive Learning (GCCL) approach (Greene, & Smith, 1993) codifies the rule base using the whole population or a part of it. A specified mechanism for maintaining diversity among the population is followed, which prevent the individuals for converging to same area of search space. The best fitted rules faced a competition to be in the final population.

Figure 1. Simple multi-objective genetic algorithm

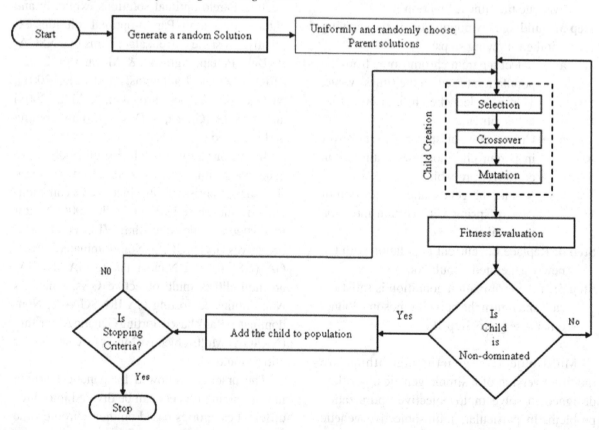

In "Chromosome = Rule set" scheme each individual represents a whole rule set. This approach is known as Pittsburg approach (Smith, 1980). This approach maintains a population of candidate rule sets whose quality is evaluated with a fitness function which consider different aspects of rule sets.

In "Chromosome = Decision Tree or Tree Rule" scheme decision trees are combine with GAs (Carvalho, & Freitas, 2004). The search potential of GA is used for finding highly accurate final tree. The tree is interpreted as a rule set, formed by the disjunction of the rules resulted in each branch of the tree. Hence the chromosome can encode the full tree or a just a tree node.

Genetic algorithms have the demerits like: (i) it takes long run-time in achieving optimal solution and (ii) the population may converge towards a limited region of the Pareto front, and hence ignore the interesting solution. As opposed to this, multi-objective genetic algorithms are able to exploit and explore multiple solutions in parallel and also able to find an extensive set of non-dominated solutions in a single run. Hence MOGA are good choice for solving multi-objective optimization problem.

MULTI-OBJECTIVE GENETIC FUZZY RULE MINING

Fuzzy models are popular over other nonlinear models such as neural networks due to their interpretability. The design of fuzzy systems involves two conflicting objectives: accuracy maximization and complexity minimization (i.e., interpretability maximization).

Interpretability literally means understandability, which is a subjective property having no concrete definition but govern by several factors such as model structure, the number of fuzzy rules, number of linguistic variables, the shape of mem-

bership functions, etc. Basically as pointed out by Jin et al., (Jin, 2000), interpretability depends on the following essential factors.

- **The Number of Linguistic Variables/Simplicity of Rules:** The rules should have less number of linguistic variables, as short rules are more human understandable then long rules.
- **The Number of Rules:** The classifiers should contain fewer rules, as it will be easy to verify. Intellectual human being suggested that the number of fuzzy rules should not be more than ten.
- **Completeness of Rules:** Rules under consideration must cover the whole input space. That is for each effective input variable combination there must be at least one fuzzy rule.
- **Consistency:** There should be good correspondence between the rules.
- **Compactness:** Every included rule must be unique. Even if the antecedent of one rule may not contained in any other rule. Compactness may be achieved, if rule generation step in any process, an optimization step is applied for excluding unnecessary and redundant rules.
- **Membership Functions:** The membership functions used in the system should satisfy the convexity and normality principle.

To resolve the long rule problem "don't care" condition is used in the antecedent part/partition of feature space. Interpretability, accuracy and improvement of generalization capability are also upheld by the use of "don't care" condition.

Beyond the optimization of above objectives, there exists various associated tasks in fuzzy classification rule generation process, that are: fuzzy partitioning, identification of fuzzy sets, selection of membership functions, automatic rule generation, tuning of membership functions, tuning of rule base etc. As a whole fuzzy classification rule mining process is modeled as an optimization problem and solved using genetic algorithms. This hybridization of genetic algorithm and fuzzy system is known as Genetic Fuzzy Systems (GFS) (Herrera, 2008). It has been proven that genetic algorithms to produce transparent and compact fuzzy rules, with high accuracy.

Genetic algorithms solves these multi-objective models of fuzzy classification rule mining problem efficiently, but take a longer time in finding the solutions as well as produce only a single solutions at a time. The generated solutions also converge to a limited region of the Pareto front, disregarding the solutions which may be interesting. Moreover it solves these problems by aggregating all the objectives into a single one. These prompt the researchers to employ multi-objective genetic algorithm for the purpose.

Multi-objective genetic algorithms are able to generate a family of valid solutions where each solution has an affinity to gratify a definite measure to a superior level than another. Hence they are employed in solving fuzzy classification rule mining problems, which generate as many as non-dominated solutions with better trade-off between the objectives, as opposed to genetic fuzzy system or using scalarized objective function. This integration/hybridization termed as multi-objective genetic-fuzzy system (Ishibuchi, &Nojima, 2007).

Multi-Objective Genetic-Fuzzy Approaches in Classification

In data mining and machine learning, classification is one of the major problems (Han, & Kamber, 2006). Classification aims at framing a mapping that can determine the class of a new pattern from the data sets, using a set of correctly classified pattern as training set. Classification rules operated by fuzzy logic/fuzzy sets are called fuzzy rule based classification rules.

As describes above, the primary goals of fuzzy rule/fuzzy classification rule-based system are: accuracy maximization and complexity minimization/ interpretability maximization, which are contradicts each other. Due to this conflict, an ideal fuzzy system is not possible which optimize both goals simultaneously. Hence the primary motivation of fuzzy classification rule mining problems is to find rules with a good trade-off / compromise between these objectives.

Ishibuchi and Murata (Ishibuchi, Murata, & Turksen, 1997) modeled this problem as a two-objective problem using: maximization of number of correctly classified training patterns and minimization of number selected rules, where a large number of candidate rules are generated using heuristic criteria and then an multi-objective genetic algorithm (NSGA-II, SEPA or SEPA2) is used to search non-dominated rules using the two criteria. Authors extend this algorithm to a three objective problem (Ishibuchi, Nakashima, & Murata, 2001) using total number of antecedent conditions/total rule length as third objective.

Ishibuchi et al., (Ishibuchi, & Yamamoto, 2004) proposed an approach for multi-objective fuzzy classification rule mining, which works in two phases. In first phase, first candidate fuzzy if-then rules are generated from numerical data and prescreened using confidence and support as two rule evaluation measures. Then a small number of fuzzy if-then rules are selected from the prescreened candidate rules using multi-objective evolutionary algorithms using three objectives: maximization of the classification accuracy, minimization of the number of selected rules, and minimization of the total rule length. Authors extend a multi-objective genetic algorithm to a multi-objective genetic local search (MOGLS) algorithm where a local search procedure adjusts the selection of each candidate rule. A learning algorithm of rule weights called certainty factors is combined with MOGLS algorithm.

Jin et al., (Ji-lin, Yuan-long, Zong-yi, Li-min, & Zhong-zhi, 2006) proposed multi-objective genetic algorithm based approach for constructing an interpretable and precision fuzzy classification system from data. Authors approached this problem in two stages, applying multi-objective genetic algorithm in each stage. First stage comprise of two tasks: feature selection and partitioning. For feature selection, a dynamic grid partitioning method (Wong, & Chen, 2000) is performed using a multi-objective genetic algorithm with three objectives: maximization of precision, minimization of number of features and minimization of number of fuzzy rules, in order to resolve the course of dimensionality issue. Then to obtain an interpretable fuzzy system, a neighboring overlapping method is used for determining parameters of the membership functions and a "don't care" function (Ishibuchi, Nakashima, & Murata, 2001), a special membership function is used. In second stage, a compact fuzzy classification system is build using a multi-objective genetic algorithm with three objectives such as: maximization of accuracy, minimization of the number of features and minimization of average length of fuzzy rules. Finally a constraint genetic algorithm is employed for optimization of resulted fuzzy classification system to enhance the interpretability and accuracy. A two-objective genetic algorithm is applied in finding multiple non-dominated solutions, from which final solution is chosen.

Nojima and Ishibuchi (Ishibuchi, & Nojima, 2009) incorporate the user preference, represented by a preference function, into multi-objective genetic fuzzy rule selection for pattern classification problems. This function can be changed during evolution directly by user, which is considered as an objective function. This approach finds non-dominated solutions i.e. fuzzy-rule-based classifiers considering three objectives: accuracy maximization, complexity minimization, and preference maximization.

Ishibuchi et al., (Ishibuchi, Kuwajima, & Nojima, 2007) use the idea of using Pareto-optimal and near Pareto-optimal rules with respect to support and confidence as candidate rules in genetic fuzzy rule selection. Authors modify Pareto dominance by introducing a dominance margin ε in the same manner as in (Laumanns, Thiele, & Zitler, 2002) to extract not only Pareto-optimal rules but also near Pareto optimal rules. A similar modification method was also used to improve the performance of MOGAs under the name of ε-dominance (Deb, Mohan, & Mishra, 2005).

Zong-Yi et al. proposed an approach based on multi-objective genetic algorithm based approach (Zong-Yi, Yong, Yuan-Long, & Guo-Qiang, 2008) to construct multiple Pareto-optimal fuzzy classification rules, considering accuracy as well as interpretability. Antecedents and consequents of the rules are identified separately for reducing computational burden. A modified Gath-Geva fuzzy clustering algorithm is employed for the purpose. Intially, this operation yield a rational fuzzy rule based system. In second stage NSGA-II, a Pareto multi-objective genetic algorithm and the interpretability-driven simplification techniques are applied to optimize the structure of initial fuzzy system and the parameters iteratively.

Pulkkinen (Pulkkinen, 2009) uses a 3-parameter membership function tuning with dynamic constraints in multi-objective fuzzy classification rule mining problem, which improves the accuracy without deteriorating the transparency of fuzzy system. Authors also used a special method in creating initial population, which reduces the search space by eliminating the extraneous features.

Cannone et al., (Cannone, Alonso, & Magdalena, 2011) use a novel index for evaluating comprehensibility in the context of a three-objective evolutionary framework for designing highly interpretable fuzzy rule-based classifiers, which is named as logical view index (LVI) and it is based on a semantic cointension approach. The proposed evolutionary algorithm consists of embedding the HILK (Highly Interpretable Linguistic Knowledge) fuzzy modeling methodology into the classical NSGA-II with the aim of maximizing accuracy, readability, and comprehensibility of the generated fuzzy rule-based classifiers.

Nojima and Ishibuchi (Nojima, & Ishibuchi, 2006) proposed a multi-classifier coding scheme and an entropy-based diversity criterion in evolutionary multi-objective optimization algorithms for the design of fuzzy ensemble classifiers. In a multi-classifier coding scheme, an ensemble classifier is coded as an integer string. Each string is evaluated by using its accuracy and diversity. Authors use two accuracy criteria: the overall classification rate of the string as an ensemble classifier and the average classification rate of component classifiers in the ensemble classifier. They use the entropy of outputs from component classifiers in the ensemble classifier as a diversity criterion.

Nojima et al., (Nojima, Kaisho, & Ishibuchi, 2010) extended the multi-objective genetic fuzzy rule selection approach in different ways which are based on Pareto-optimal and near Pareto-optimal rule, and able to determine an accurate and simple rule set by considering the accuracy maximization and the complexity minimization as two objectives. One extension is to add compatible rules with misclassified patterns into candidate rules for genetic fuzzy rule selection. The other is to tune membership functions after genetic fuzzy rule selection.

Di Nuovo and Catania (Di Nuovo, & Catania, 2009), proposed a multi-objective genetic algorithm (MOGA) based approach in designing deep-tuned Fuzzy Rule Based Classifier Systems (FRBCSs) from examples, considering both rule learning and fuzzy memberships tuning. This technique generates a FRBCS which includes certain operators, known as linguistic hedges or modifiers, which are able to improve accuracy without losses in interpretability. In this method the MOGA is used to learn the FRBCS and to set the operators in order to optimize both model accuracy and metrics of interpretability, compactness and transparency in a single algorithm.

Gacto et al., (Gacto, Alcala, & Herrera, 2012) proposed a multi-objective evolutionary algorithm

SEPA2 $_{SI}$ (SEPA2 with Semantic interpretability) based on SEPA2 for tuning fuzzy rule based systems by considering accuracy and interpretability as two objectives. In order to preserve the interpretability of the system, authors define a new objective called semantic interpretability index, which is combination three metrics: membership function's displacement, membership function's symmetry and membership function's area similarity. These metrics helpful preserve the original shapes of the membership functions in tuning the membership functions parameters.

Antonelli et al., adopt partition integrity as an objective of the evolutionary process in (Antonelli, Ducange, Lazzerini, & Marcelloni, 2011). Partition integrity can be measured by using a purposely defined index based on the similarity between the partitions learned during the evolutionary process and the initial interpretable partitions defined by an expert. Then, a three-objective evolutionary algorithm is used which generates a set of multi-objective fuzzy rule based systems with different trade-offs between complexity, accuracy and partition integrity by concurrently learning the rule base and the membership parameters of the linguistic variables. Accuracy is assessed in terms of mean squared error between the actual and the predicted values, complexity is calculated as the total number of conditions in the antecedents of the rules and integrity is measured by using the purposely defined index.

Antonelli et al., proposed a framework of multi-objective evolutionary fuzzy systems (Antonelli, Ducange, & Marcelloni, 2011), in which the search space grows as the number of features of the dataset increases, leading to a slow and possibly difficult convergence of the evolutionary algorithm. As for fitness evaluation, datasets with a large number of instances require very high computational costs, authors propose a co-evolutionary approach to generate sets of Mamdani fuzzy rule-based systems with different trade-offs between accuracy and interpretability.

Authors handle high dimensional and large datasets together and from these learn the rule base and the membership function parameters simultaneously. To reduce the search space, they perform the multi-objective evolutionary learning of the rule base by selecting reduced sets of rules and conditions from a previously generated rule base. Again to reduce the computational costs, during the multi-objective evolutionary learning process, periodically, a single-objective genetic algorithm evolves a population of reduced training sets.

Zhang et al., (Zhang, Wu, Xing, & Hu, 2011) proposed an approach to construct a set of interpretable and precise fuzzy systems based on the Pareto multi-objective cooperative co-evolutionary algorithm (PMOCCA). For improving the performance and reducing the computational burden authors used feature selection in first step. In second step, a fuzzy clustering algorithm is applied to identify the initial fuzzy system. Finally, the PMOCCA is utilized in evolving the initial fuzzy system to optimize the number of rules, the antecedents of the rules and the parameters of the antecedents simultaneously. Additionally the interpretability-driven simplification techniques are used iteratively to reduce the fuzzy systems, which improve the interpretability of the fuzzy systems.

Alcala et al. proposed a multi-objective fuzzy classification rule mining approach (Alcalá, Nojima, Herrera, & Ishibuchi, 2009) which is based on the generation of a set of candidate fuzzy classification rules considering a priori fixed granularity or multiple fuzzy partitions with different granularities for each attribute. Subsequently, a multi-objective evolutionary optimization algorithm is applied to perform fuzzy rule selection. Authors provide a mechanism to generate single granularity-based fuzzy classification rules for multi-objective genetic fuzzy rule selection, which can specify appropriate single granularities for fuzzy rule extraction before performing multi-objective genetic fuzzy rule selection.

Multi-Objective Genetic-Fuzzy Approaches in Association Rule Mining

The objectives of fuzzy association rule mining are based on the quality of extracted rules. These qualities are preciseness, generality/specificity, interestingness etc. Multi-objective genetic algorithms are used for mining fuzzy association rules as large amount of metrics are used for quality measure.

Beyond the basic metrics: support and confidence, there exists a lot of measures used in judging quality of fuzzy association rules. Some of them are:

- **Comprehensibility:** It refers to the measure of number of attributes present in the rule, which is defined as follows[63]:

$$Comprehensibility = \frac{\log\left(1 + |A|\right)}{\log\left(1 + |A \cup C|\right)} \quad (29)$$

- **Correlation:** It is measure of dependence, based on the co-occurrence between the antecedent and conclusion of the rule. That is:

$$Corr = \frac{Co\,var iance\ of\ Antecedent\ and\ Conclusion}{\sqrt{\begin{array}{l} Variance\ of\ Antecedent \\ \times\ Variance\ of\ Conclusion \end{array}}} \quad (30)$$

where,

$$Co\,var iance = FuzzySupport\left(Antecedent \cap Conclusion\right) - FuzzySupport\left(Antecedent\right) \times FuzzySupport(Conclusion) \quad (31)$$

Mehmet Kaya proposed a multi-objective genetic algorithm based approach (Kaya, 2006) for mining optimized fuzzy association rules using strongness, interestingness and comprehensibility as three objectives. Author modeled each of these individual objectives as a multi-objective problem considering different objectives. The strongness is modeled using three objectives: support, confidence and average number of fuzzy sets in the rule or maximum number of fuzzy sets. Support, average number of fuzzy sets in the rule or maximum number of fuzzy sets and correlations are considered for modeling interestingness. For comprehensibility support, confidence and comprehensibility are considered as three objectives. Authors used a Pareto based genetic algorithm for the specified task.

Kaya and Alhaji designed a clustering method (Kaya, & Alhaji, 2004), which uses multi-objective genetic algorithm in deciding number of fuzzy sets and discover both membership function and fuzzy association rules automatically. This process automatically adjusts the fuzzy sets and finds many large item sets in small time, by tuning jointly the number of fuzzy sets and the base values of membership functions for each quantitative attributes. The number of large item sets and the time required for determining fuzzy sets (inverse of time required to find large item sets) are regarded as two objectives in modeling the problem as multi-objective. The Pareto GA (Zitzler, & Thiele, 1999), a multi-objective algorithm is used for the purpose.

Kaya et al., (Kaya, & Alhajj, 2004a) designed a multi-objective genetic algorithm based method for finding optimized fuzzy association rules including instantiated and uninstantiated attributes, considering support, confidence and number of fuzzy sets as objectives.

Kaya and Alhaji use a clustering method (Kaya, & Alhajj, 2004), which employs multi-objective GA for the automatic discovery of membership functions used in determining fuzzy quantitative association rules. Proposed approach optimizes the number of fuzzy sets and their ranges according to multi-objective criteria in a way to maximize the number of large item sets with respect to a given minimum support value. Hence two objective parameters in terms of large item sets and the time required to determine fuzzy sets are used in the approach, which are conflicting with each other. A Pareto GA, (Zitler, & Thiele, 1999) with multiple objective optimization capabilities used by authors.

Chen et al., (Chen, Hong, & Tseng, 2010) proposed a SPEA2 based multi-objective fuzzy association rule mining approach, which adopted a fine-grained fitness assignment strategy, a density estimation technique, and an enhanced archive truncation method to derive better Pareto solutions (Zitler, Laumanns, & Thiele, 2001). A sophisticated multi-objective approach is employed to find the appropriate sets of membership functions for fuzzy data mining. Minimizing the suitability of membership functions, which based on two factors, coverage factor and overlap factor, to avoid two bad types of membership functions and maximizing the total number of large 1-itemsets are used as objectives in finding the Pareto front.

Santhi Thilagam and Ananthanarayana (Santhi Thilagam, & Ananthanarayana, 2008), proposed an approach for mining optimized fuzzy association rules of different orders. Authors also used an approach to define membership functions for all the continuous attributes in a database by using clustering techniques. Proposed approach, extract and optimize fuzzy association rules together using multi-objective genetic algorithm by considering the objectives such as fuzzy support, fuzzy confidence and rule length.

Alcala-Fdez et al., (Alcala-Fdez, Alcala, Gacto, & Herrera, 2009) designed a new fuzzy data-mining algorithm for extracting both fuzzy association rules and membership functions by means of a genetic learning of the membership functions and a basic method for mining fuzzy association rules. The 2-tuples linguistic representation model is used, which allow user to adjust the context associated to the linguistic term membership functions.

Multi-Objective Genetic-Fuzzy Approaches in Associative Classification

Fuzzy associative classification rules can also be model as a multi-objective optimization problem using the objectives like support, confidence, comprehensibility, interpretability, accuracy and many other objectives.

Weigang et al., (Weigang, & Xiuli, 2011) proposed a multi-objective evolutionary fuzzy associative classification method (MOEA-FACM), based on a variant apriori algorithm and a multi-objective GA, NSGA-II. In determining gene rate good quality rule set, a fuzzy confirmation measure based on probabilistic dependence is used. A set of candidate fuzzy association rules are generated using a modified apriori algorithm. Then using NSGA-II a small number of fuzzy associative rules are selected from these rules. In rule selection maximization of classification accuracy, minimization of the number of selected rules and minimization of the total fuzzy items in antecedent of an association rules are used as three objectives.

APPLICATION AREAS OF MULTI-OBJECTIVE FUZZY-GENETIC APPROACHES

Some of the application areas of multi-objective fuzzy genetic approaches are summarized as follows.

Robotics

Munoz-Salinas et al., (Munoz-Salinas, Aguirre, Cordon, & Garcia-Silvente, 2008) applied a fuzzy logic multi-objective genetic algorithm to a fuzzy visual system for door detection in an autonomous robot. Fuzzy visual system is based on a hierarchical structure of three different fuzzy classifiers, which are collectively permits the robot to detect the presence of doors in the images captured by its camera. The system accuracy is measured by two conflicting criteria: the positive and negative rates of door detection and hence modeled as a multi-objective optimization problem. Castillo et al., (Castillo, Trujillo, & Melin, 2007) apply fuzzy logic and multi-objective genetic algorithm in an offline point-to-point automouns mobile robot path planning problem, which aims at generating valid paths or trajectories for an Holonomic robot to use, to move from a starting point to a destination point across a flat map of a terrain represented by a two dimensional grid with obstacles and dangerous ground that robot should prevaricate. This problem is solved by modeling as a multi-objective problem with two objectives: minimization of length and minimization of difficulty.

Finance and Marketing

Casillas et al., (Casillas, & Martínez-López, 2009), proposed a multi-objective genetic fuzzy approach in consumer behavior modeling. In marketing, the information about consumer variables of interest is generally obtained in form of question, which contains diverse items. Marketing modelers necessitate some abstract variables/unobserved variables to build consumer models. In these cases, we can't assign a number to the value of certain unobserved variables; rather a scattered set of numbers can be assigned. Conventional data mining techniques are failed for these cases. So a multi-objective genetic algorithm based on fuzzy rules is solved the purpose. Khalili-Damghari et al., (Khalili-Damghari, Sadi-Nezhad, Lotfi, & Tavana, 2013) proposed a multi-objective fuzzy rule based framework for sustainable project portfolio selection problems in a real-world financial services institution. The selection of a subset of projects from a high number of projects makes the port folio selection problem complex. The proposed framework integrates and synthesizes from a data mining model with results from a Data Envelope Analysis model and an evolutionary algorithm to design the structure of the fuzzy rule based system. Accuracy maximization and complexity minimization are two objectives considered in the model. Ghandar and Michalewicz (Ghandar, & Michalewicz, 2011) examine the advantages of simple models over more complex ones for financial prediction, by a genetic fuzzy framework. Authors investigate how model interpretability can offer additional benefits by realizing useful properties in computationally intelligent systems for financial modeling. They proposed and test an approach for learning momentum based strategies that predict price movements of the Bombay Stock Exchange (BSE). Finally evaluate the relationship between the predictive capability and interpretability of fuzzy rule based systems obtained using Multi-Objective Evolutionary Algorithms (MOEA).

Intrusion Detection

Tsang et al., apply a multi-objective genetic fuzzy system in anomaly intrusion detection system (Tsang, Kwong, & Wang, 2005), by modeling as MOP with two objectives: maximizing detection rate in intrusion attacks and minimizing false positive rate in network traffic. The proposed system find accurate and interpretable fuzzy rule from network data (KDD-Cup99) using an agent-based evolutionary computation framework. Mahajan and Reshamwala (Mahajan, & Reshamwala, 2011) proposed a multi-objective genetic algorithm for Fuzzy Time Interval (FTI) sequential pattern mining applied to discover optimized sequences in the network traffic data to classify and detect intrusion. Fuzzy solves the sharp boundary problem and the refinement ability of GA helps to find the global optimum FTI sequential patterns. Confidence and Coverage are two objectives used to prune the traditional Apriori algorithm.

The basic objective is to achieve find maximum confidence and maximum coverage in the FTI sequential patterns. Authors define the confidence of the FTI sequences for first time.

Systems Engineering

Gacto et al. (Gacto, Alcala, & Herrera, 2012), proposed a specific multi-objective evolutionary algorithm, for finding more compact fuzzy logic controllers as a means for best combination of rules and hence to improve the system performance, in solving the Heating, Ventilating and Air Conditioning (HVAC) system control problems. Authors combine lateral tuning of linguistic variables with rule selection. Two objectives: maximizing the system performance and minimizing the number of generated rules are considered in the system. This algorithm is based on SEPA2 but adopt a different mechanism for guiding the search towards the desired Pareto Zone. An advance concept such as incest prevention is incorporated in the system which helps in improving the exploration/exploitation trade-off as well as the convergence ability.

Pulkkinen et al., (Pulkkinen, Hytonen, & Koivisto, 2008) applied a fuzzy logic based multi-objective genetic algorithm approach in developing a model, which works as a reasoning mechanism in a bioaerosol detector, which necessitates the ability to distinguish between safe and harmful aerosols. True positive (TP) and false positive (FP) rates are used as the metrics due to the uneven misclassification costs and class distributions of the collected data. This model requires interpretability as another requirement which builds up the confidence for the developed model. These objectives are contradicting and hence a multi-objective evolutionary algorithm is applied to find trade-off in the models. Fuzzy classifiers (FCs) are selected as a model type and are identified by hybrid genetic fuzzy system (GFS) which initializes the population adequately using decision trees (DTs) and simplification operations. The interpretability (transparency of fuzzy partition) and accuracy (TP and FP rates) are used as objectives in multi-objective optimization. In maintaining consistency in rule base a heuristic rule and rule condition removal is applied to offspring population.

Milasi et al., (Milasi, Jamali, & Lucas, 2007) proposed an intelligent method called BELBIC (Brain Emotional Learning Based Intelligent Controller), which is used to control the Locally Linear Neuro-Fuzzy Model (LOLIMOT) of Washing Machine. The Locally Linear Neuro-Fuzzy Model of Washing Machine is obtained based on previously extracted data. Two contradictory objectives, energy consumption and effectiveness of washing process are used as two objectives in modeling this problem. A Multi Objective Genetic Algorithm is used for tuning the BELBIC parameters, which provides a set of non-dominated set of points. This proposed controller results the desired outcome and gives the reasonable and smooth control signals which are very important in control problems.

Classification and Forecasting

Feng and Liu (Feng, & Liu, 2006), proposed a fuzzy rule-based classifier for electrical load pattern classification by using multi-objective genetic algorithm and fuzzy association rule mining. Multi-objective genetic algorithm is used to automatically select the rules with better classification accuracy and interpretability, and the key concepts of fuzzy association rule mining are the bases of heuristic rule selection for improving the performance of genetic algorithm searching. Similarly, Li and Jiaju (Li, & Jiaju, 2005) designed a fuzzy rule-based classifier for electrical load pattern classification based on the knowledge of historical data sets. A multi-objective genetic algorithm is applied to choose the Pareto rules with two criteria, the classification accuracy and interpretability of fuzzy rules in classifying the electrical load.

Social Network and Management

Kilic and Casillas (Kilic, & Casillas, 2012) proposed a new hybrid genetic-fuzzy system modeling methodology based on multi-objective genetic fuzzy systems and applied to a strategic level decision making problem called innovation management in order to generate knowledge, which are beneficial for the senior managers. Carmona et al., (Carmona, Gonzalez, Del Jesus, & Herrera, 2009) apply a multi-objective genetic fuzzy approach for subgroup discovery, called NMEF-SD. Subgroup discovery (SD) is a descriptive induction task whose goal is to discover interesting individual patterns in relation to a specific property of interest for the user.

FUTURE RESEARCH DIRECTION

The idea of combing association and classification rule mining for generating a new set of algorithms under the umbrella of associative classification rule mining is outlined as a new research area. Authors of this chapter are also in the process of developing semi-supervised and active learning schemes for rule mining problems.

CONCLUSION

This chapter has discussed some basic concepts, definitions, and overview of certain techniques to uncover rules with certain characteristics. The process of uncovering these rules is based on the best attributes and combined effort of genetic algorithms, fuzzy theory, and multi-criteria optimization. The rule discovery process is task dependent i.e., classification task rule discovery process is different from association rule discovery process. With a goal of measuring and enhancing the understandability, accuracy, and interestingness of a rule, many metrics and methods have been developed. It has been observed that, multi-objective fuzzy-genetic classification algorithms are providing many alternative solutions to the decision makers in contrast to classical algorithms with single objective optimization.

REFERENCES

Agrawal, R., Imieliński, T., & Swami, A. (1993). Mining association rules between sets of items in large databases. *SIGMOD Record*, *22*(2), 207–216. doi:10.1145/170036.170072

Agrawal, R., & Srikant, R. (1994). Fast algorithms for mining association rules. In *Proceedings of the 20th Int. Conf. Very Large Data Bases,* (Vol. 1215, pp. 487-499). VLDB.

Alcalá, R., Alcalá-Fdez, J., Gacto, M. J., & Herrera, F. (2007). A multi-objective evolutionary algorithm for rule selection and tuning on fuzzy rule-based systems. In *Proceedings of Fuzzy Systems Conference,* (pp. 1-6). IEEE.

Alcalá, R., Nojima, Y., Herrera, F., & Ishibuchi, H. (2009). Generating single granularity-based fuzzy classification rules for multi-objective genetic fuzzy rule selection. In *Proceedings of Fuzzy Systems* (pp. 1718–1723). IEEE.

Alcala-Fdez, J., Alcalá, R., Gacto, M. J., & Herrera, F. (2009). Learning the membership function contexts for mining fuzzy association rules by using genetic algorithms. *Fuzzy Sets and Systems*, *160*(7), 905–921. doi:10.1016/j.fss.2008.05.012

Antonelli, M., Ducange, P., Lazzerini, B., & Marcelloni, F. (2011). Learning knowledge bases of multi-objective evolutionary fuzzy systems by simultaneously optimizing accuracy, complexity and partition integrity. *Soft Computing*, *15*(12), 2335–2354. doi:10.1007/s00500-010-0665-0

Antonelli, M., Ducange, P., & Marcelloni, F. (2011). A new approach to handle high dimensional and large datasets in multi-objective evolutionary fuzzy systems. In Proceedings of Fuzzy Systems (FUZZ), (pp. 1286-1293). IEEE.

Ballini, R., & Gomide, F. (2002). Learning in recurrent, hybrid neuro-fuzzy networks. [). IEEE.]. *Proceedings of Fuzzy Systems*, *1*, 785–790.

Booker, L. B., Goldberg, D. E., & Holland, J. H. (1989). Classifier systems and genetic algorithms. *Artificial Intelligence*, *40*(1-3), 235–282. doi:10.1016/0004-3702(89)90050-7

Cannone, R., Alonso, J. M., & Magdalena, L. (2011). Multi-objective design of highly interpretable fuzzy rule-based classifiers with semantic cointension. In Proceedings of Genetic and Evolutionary Fuzzy Systems (GEFS), (pp. 1-8). IEEE.

Carmona, C. J., González, P., Del Jesús, M. J., & Herrera, F. (2009). Non-dominated multi-objective evolutionary algorithm based on fuzzy rules extraction for subgroup discovery. In *Hybrid artificial intelligence systems* (pp. 573–580). Berlin: Springer. doi:10.1007/978-3-642-02319-4_69

Carvalho, D. R., & Freitas, A. A. (2004). A hybrid decision tree/ genetic algorithm method for data mining. *Information Science*, *163*(1-3), 13–35. doi:10.1016/j.ins.2003.03.013

Casillas, J., & Martínez-López, F. J. (2009). Mining uncertain data with multi-objective genetic fuzzy systems to be applied in consumer behavior modeling. *Expert Systems with Applications*, *36*, 1645–1659. doi:10.1016/j.eswa.2007.11.035

Castillo, O., Trujillo, L., & Melin, P. (2007). Multiple objective genetic algorithms for path-planning optimization in autonomous mobile robots. *Soft Computing*, *11*(3), 269–279. doi:10.1007/s00500-006-0068-4

Chen, C. H., Hong, T. P., & Tseng, V. S. (2010). A SPEA2-based genetic-fuzzy mining algorithm. In Proceedings of Fuzzy Systems (FUZZ), (pp. 1-5). IEEE.

Cios, K. J., Pedrycz, W., Swiniarski, R. W., & Kurgan, L. A. (2012). *Data mining: A knowledge discovery approach*. New York: Springer-Verlag.

Coello, C. A. C. (2006). Evolutionary multi-objective optimization: A historical view of the field. *IEEE Computational Intelligence Magazine*, *1*(1), 28–36. doi:10.1109/MCI.2006.1597059

Cohen, J. L. (1978). *Multi-objective programming and planning*. New York: Academic Press.

Cvetković, D., Parmee, I., & Webb, E. (1998). Multi-objective optimization and preliminary air-frame design. In *Adaptive computing in design and manufacture* (pp. 255–267). London: Springer. doi:10.1007/978-1-4471-1589-2_20

Deb, K. (2001). *Multi-objective optimization using evolutionary algorithms*. New York: John Wiley and Sons.

Deb, K., Mohan, M., & Mishra, S. (2005). Evaluating the ε-domination based multi-objective evolutionary algorithm for a quick computation of Pareto-optimal solutions. *Evolutionary Computation*, *13*(4), 501–525. doi:10.1162/106365605774666895 PMID:16297281

Deb, K., Pratap, A., Agarwal, S., & Meyarivan, T. (2002). A fast and elitist multi-objective genetic algorithm: NSGA-II. *IEEE Transactions on Evolutionary Computation*, *6*(2), 182–197. doi:10.1109/4235.996017

Dehuri, S., Ghosh, A., & Mall, R. (2006). Genetic algorithms for multi-criterion classification and clustering in data mining. *International Journal of Computing & Information Sciences*, *4*(3), 143–154.

Dehuri, S., Jagadev, A. K., Ghosh, A., & Mall, R. (2006). Multi-objective genetic algorithm for association rule mining using a homogeneous dedicated cluster of workstations. *American Journal of Applied Sciences*, *3*(11), 2086–2095. doi:10.3844/ajassp.2006.2086.2095

Dehuri, S., & Mall, R. (2004). Mining predictive and comprehensible classification rules using multi-objective genetic algorithm. In *Proceedings of the ADCOM*, (pp. 99-104). ADCOM.

Di Nuovo, A. G., & Catania, V. (2009). Linguistic modifiers to improve the accuracy-interpretability trade-off in multi-objective genetic design of fuzzy rule based classifier systems. In *Proceedings of Intelligent Systems Design and Applications* (pp. 128–133). IEEE. doi:10.1109/ISDA.2009.97

Edgeworth, F. Y. (1881). *Mathematical physics*. London: P. Keagan.

Fayyad, U. M., Piatetsky-Shapiro, G., & Smyth, P. (1996). From data mining to knowledge discovery: An overview. In *Advances in knowledge discovery and data mining* (pp. 1–34). Cambridge, MA: MIT Press.

Feng, L., & Liu, Z. (2006). Effects of multi-objective genetic rule selection on short-term load forecasting for anomalous days. In *Proceedings of Power Engineering Society General Meeting*. IEEE.

Fernandez, A., Garcia, S., Luengo, J., Bernado-Mansilla, E., & Francisco, H. (2010). Genetic-based machine learning for rule induction: State of art, taxonomy and comparative study. *IEEE Transactions on Evolutionary Computation*, *14*(6), 913–943. doi:10.1109/TEVC.2009.2039140

Fonseca, C. M., & Fleming, P. L. (1995). An overview of evolutionary algorithms in multi-objective optimization. *Evolutionary Computation*, *3*, 1–16. doi:10.1162/evco.1995.3.1.1

Freitas, A. A. (2003). A survey of evolutionary algorithms for data mining and knowledge discovery. In *Advances in evolutionary computing* (pp. 819–845). Academic Press. doi:10.1007/978-3-642-18965-4_33

Gacto, M. J., Alcalá, R., & Herrera, F. (2009). A multi-objective evolutionary algorithm for tuning fuzzy rule based systems with measures for preserving interpretability. In *Proceedings of IFSA/EUSFLAT Conf.* (pp. 1146-1151). IFSA.

Gacto, M. J., Alcalá, R., & Herrera, F. (2010). Integration of an index to preserve the semantic interpretability in the multi-objective evolutionary rule selection and tuning of linguistic fuzzy systems. *IEEE Transactions on Fuzzy Systems, 18*(3), 515–531. doi:10.1109/TFUZZ.2010.2041008

Gacto, M. J., Alcala, R., & Herrera, F. (2012). A multi-objective evolutionary algorithms for an effective tuning of fuzzy logic controllers in heating, ventilating and air conditioning systems. *Applied Intelligence, 36*(2), 330–347. doi:10.1007/s10489-010-0264-x

Garcia, E., Romero, C., Ventura, S., & De Castro, C. (2009). An architecture for making recommendations to courseware authors using association rule mining and collaborative filtering. *User Modeling and User-Adapted Interaction, 19*(1-2), 99–132. doi:10.1007/s11257-008-9047-z

Ghandar, A., & Michalewicz, Z. (2011). An experimental study of multi-objective evolutionary algorithms for balancing interpretability and accuracy in fuzzy rule base classifiers for financial prediction. In *Proceedings of Computational Intelligence for Financial Engineering and Economics (CIFEr)* (pp. 1–6). IEEE.

Ghosh, A., & Das, M. K. (2008). Non-dominated rank based sorting genetic algorithms. *Fundamenta Informaticae, 83*(3), 231–252.

Ghosh, A., & Nath, B. (2004). Multi-objective rule mining using genetic algorithms. *Information Sciences, 163*, 123–133. doi:10.1016/j.ins.2003.03.021

Greene, D. P., & Smith, S. F. (1993). Competition-based induction of decision models from examples. *Machine Learning, 13*(23), 229–257. doi:10.1023/A:1022622013558

Gyenesei, A., & Teuhola, J. (2001). Interestingness measures for fuzzy association rules. In *Principles of data mining and knowledge discovery* (pp. 152–164). Berlin: Springer. doi:10.1007/3-540-44794-6_13

Han, J., & Kamber, M. (2006). *Data mining concepts and techniques* (2nd ed.). San Francisco: Morgan Kaufmann.

Han, J., Pei, J., & Yin, Y. (2000). Mining frequent patterns without candidate generation. *SIGMOD Record, 29*(2), 1–12. doi:10.1145/335191.335372

Herrera, F. (2008). Genetic fuzzy systems: taxonomy, current research trends and prospects. *Evolutionary Intelligence, 1*, 27–46. doi:10.1007/s12065-007-0001-5

Holland, J. H. (1975). *Adaptation in natural and artificial systems*. Ann Arbor, MI: University of Michigan Press.

Holland, J. H., & Reitman, J. S. (1978). Cognitive systems based on adaptive algorithms. In *Pattern-directed inference systems*. Academic Press.

Ishibuchi, H., Kuwajima, I., & Nojima, Y. (2007). Use of Pareto-optimal and near Pareto-optimal candidate rules in genetic fuzzy rule selection. In *Analysis and design of intelligent systems using soft computing techniques* (pp. 387–396). Berlin: Springer. doi:10.1007/978-3-540-72432-2_39

Ishibuchi, H., Murata, T., & Turksen, I. B. (1997). Single-objective and two-objective genetic algorithms for selecting linguistic rules for pattern classification problems. *Fuzzy Sets and Systems*, *89*(2), 135–150. doi:10.1016/S0165-0114(96)00098-X

Ishibuchi, H., Nakashima, T., & Murata, T. (2001). Three objective genetic-based machine learning for linguistic rule extraction. *Information Science*, *136*, 109–133. doi:10.1016/S0020-0255(01)00144-X

Ishibuchi, H., & Yamamoto, T. (2004). Fuzzy rule selection by multi-objective genetic local search algorithms and rule evaluation measures in data mining. *Fuzzy Sets and Systems*, *141*(1), 59–88. doi:10.1016/S0165-0114(03)00114-3

Isibuchi, H., & Nojima, Y. (2007). Analysis of interpretability-accuracy tradeoff of fuzzy systems by multi-objective genetic-based machine learning. *International Journal of Approximate Reasoning*, *44*, 4–31. doi:10.1016/j.ijar.2006.01.004

Jalali-Heravi, M., & Zaïane, O. R. (2010). A study on interestingness measures for associative classifiers. In *Proceedings of the 2010 ACM Symposium on Applied Computing* (pp. 1039-1046). ACM.

Ji-Lin, C., Yuan-Long, H., Zong-Yi, X., Li-Min, J., & Zhong-Zhi, T. (2006). A multi-objective genetic-based method for designing fuzzy classification systems. *International Journal of Computer Science and Network Security*, *6*(8A), 110–117.

Jin, Y. (2000). Fuzzy modeling of high-dimensional systems: complexity reduction and interpretability improvement. *IEEE Transactions on Fuzzy Systems*, *8*, 212–222. doi:10.1109/91.842154

Kaur, H., & Wasan, S. K. (2006). Empirical study on applications of data mining techniques in healthcare. *Journal of Computer Science*, *2*(2), 194–200. doi:10.3844/jcssp.2006.194.200

Kaya, M. (2006). Multi-objective genetic algorithm based approaches for mining optimized fuzzy association rules. *Soft Computing*, *10*, 578–586. doi:10.1007/s00500-005-0509-5

Kaya, M., & Alhajj, R. (2004). Integrating multi-objective genetic algorithms into clustering for fuzzy association rules mining. In *Proceedings of Data Mining* (pp. 431–434). IEEE. doi:10.1109/ICDM.2004.10050

Kaya, M., & Alhajj, R. (2004a). Multi-objective genetic algorithm based method for mining optimized fuzzy association rules. In *Proceedings of Intelligent Data Engineering and Automated Learning* (pp. 758–764). Berlin: Springer. doi:10.1007/978-3-540-28651-6_113

Khalili-Damghari, K., Sadi-Nezhad, S., Lotfi, F. H., & Tavana, M. (2013). A hybrid fuzzy rule-based multi-criteria framework for sustainable project portfolio selection. *Journal of Information Science*, *220*, 442–462. doi:10.1016/j.ins.2012.07.024

Kilic, K., & Casillas, J. (2012). Hybrid genetic-fuzzy system modeling application in innovation management. In J. Casillas et al. (Eds.), *Management intelligent systems* (pp. 25–34). Berlin: Springer-Verlag. doi:10.1007/978-3-642-30864-2_3

Kouk, C. M., Fu, A., & Wong, M. H. (1998). Fuzzy association rules in databases. *SIGMOD*, *27*(1), 41–46. doi:10.1145/273244.273257

Kuncheva, L. I. (2000). *Fuzzy classifier design*. Berlin: Springer. doi:10.1007/978-3-7908-1850-5

Laumanns, M., Thiele, L., Deb, K., & Zitzler, E. (2002). Combining convergence and diversity in evolutionary multi-objective optimization. *Evolutionary Computation*, *10*(3), 263–282. doi:10.1162/106365602760234108 PMID:12227996

Li, F., & Jiaju, Q. (2005). Electrical load forecasting based on load patterns. *Power System Technology, 29*(4), 23–26.

Liu, B., Hsu, W., & Ma, Y. (1998). Integrating classification and association rule mining. In *Proceedings of 4th ACM SIGKDD International Conference on Knowledge Discovery and Data Mining* (pp. 80-86). New York, NY: ACM.

Liu, B., Hsu, W., & Ma, Y. (1999). Mining association rules with multiple minimum supports. In *Proceedings of the Fifth ACM SIGKDD International Conference on Knowledge Discovery and Data Mining* (pp. 337-341). ACM.

Maeda, M., Shimakawa, M., & Murakami, S. (1995). Predictive fuzzy control of an autonomous mobile robot with forecast learning function. *Fuzzy Sets and Systems, 72*(1), 51–60. doi:10.1016/0165-0114(94)00271-8

Mahajan, S., & Reshamwala, A. (2011). An approach to optimize fuzzy time-interval sequential patterns using multi-objective genetic algorithm. In *Technology systems and management* (pp. 115–120). Berlin: Springer. doi:10.1007/978-3-642-20209-4_16

Milasi, R. M., Jamali, M. R., & Lucas, C. (2007). Intelligent washing machine: A bio-inspired and multi-objective approach. *International Journal Control. Automation and Systems, 5*(4), 436–443.

Munoz-Salinas, R., Aguirre, E., Cordon, O., & Garcia-Silvente, M. (2008). Automatic tuning of a fuzzy visual system using evolutionary algorithms: Single-objective vs. multi-objective approaches. *IEEE Transactions on Fuzzy Systems, 16*(2), 485–501. doi:10.1109/TFUZZ.2006.889954

Nojima, Y., & Ishibuchi, H. (2006). Designing fuzzy ensemble classifiers by evolutionary multi-objective optimization with an entropy-based diversity criterion. In *Proceedings of Hybrid Intelligent Systems* (pp. 59–59). IEEE.

Nojima, Y., & Ishibuchi, H. (2006). Designing fuzzy ensemble classifiers by evolutionary multi-objective optimization with an entropy-based diversity criterion. In *Proceedings of Hybrid Intelligent Systems* (pp. 59–59). IEEE.

Nojima, Y., & Ishibuchi, H. (2009). Incorporation of user preference into multi-objective genetic fuzzy rule selection for pattern classification problems. *Artificial Life and Robotics, 14*(3), 418–421. doi:10.1007/s10015-009-0700-3

Nojima, Y., Kaisho, Y., & Ishibuchi, H. (2010). Accuracy improvement of genetic fuzzy rule selection with candidate rule addition and membership tuning. In Proceedings of Fuzzy Systems (FUZZ), (pp. 1-8). IEEE.

Osyczka, A. (1985). Multi-criteria optimization for engineering design. In J. S. Gero (Ed.), *Design optimization* (pp. 193–227). Academic Press.

Pareto, V. (1896). *Cours d'economie politique.* Lausanne: F. Rouge.

Pham, D. T., & Pham, P. T. N. (1999). Artificial intelligence in engineering. *International Journal of Machine Tools & Manufacture, 39*(6), 937–949. doi:10.1016/S0890-6955(98)00076-5

Pulkkinen, P. (2009). A multi-objective genetic fuzzy system for obtaining compact and accurate fuzzy classifiers with transparent fuzzy partitions. In *Proceedings of Machine Learning and Applications* (pp. 89–94). IEEE.

Pulkkinen, P., Hytonen, J., & Koivisto, H. (2008). Developing a bioaerosol detector using hybrid genetic fuzzy systems. *Engineering Applications of Artificial Intelligence, 21*(8), 1330–1346. doi:10.1016/j.engappai.2008.01.006

Ruiz, D., Cantón, J., María Nougués, J., Espuña, A., & Puigjaner, L. (2001). On-line fault diagnosis system support for reactive scheduling in multipurpose batch chemical plants. *Computers & Chemical Engineering, 25*(4), 829–837. doi:10.1016/S0098-1354(01)00657-3

Shaffer, M. J., & Brodahl, M. K. (1998). Rule-based management for simulation in agricultural decision support systems. *Computers and Electronics in Agriculture*, *21*(2), 135–152. doi:10.1016/S0168-1699(98)00031-3

Smith, S. F. (1980). *A learning system based on genetic algorithms*. (Ph. D. Dissertation). University of Pittsburgh, Pittsburgh, PA.

Srikant, R., & Agrawal, R. (1996). Mining quantitative association rules in large relational tables. *SIGMOD Record*, *25*(2), 1–12. doi:10.1145/235968.233311

Stockwell, D. (1999). The GARP modeling system: Problems and solutions to automated spatial prediction. *International Journal of Geographical Information Science*, *13*(2), 143–158. doi:10.1080/136588199241391

Tang, Y., Xu, F., Wan, X., & Zhang, Y. Q. (2002). Web-based fuzzy neural networks for stock prediction. In *Proceedings of Second International Workshop on Intelligent Systems Design and Application,* (pp. 169-174). IEEE.

Thilagam, P. S., & Ananthanarayana, V. S. (2008). Extraction and optimization of fuzzy association rules using multi-objective genetic algorithm. *Pattern Analysis & Applications*, *11*(2), 159–168. doi:10.1007/s10044-007-0090-x

Tran, K. D. (2009). An improved multi-objective evolutionary algorithm with adaptable parameters. *International Journal of Intelligent Systems Technologies and Application Archive*, *7*(4), 347–369. doi:10.1504/IJISTA.2009.028052

Tsang, C. H., Kwong, S., & Wang, H. (2005). Anomaly intrusion detection using multi-objective genetic fuzzy system and agent-based evolutionary computation framework. In *Proceedings of Data Mining* (pp. 789–792). IEEE.

Tsang, E., Yung, P., & Li, J. (2004). EDDIE-automation, a decision support tool for financial forecasting. *Decision Support Systems*, *37*(4), 559–565. doi:10.1016/S0167-9236(03)00087-3

Venturini, G. (1993). SIA: A supervised inductive algorithm with genetic search for learning attributes based concepts. [Berlin: Springer.]. *Proceedings of Machine Learning, ECML-93*, 280–296.

Watanabe, S., Hiroyasu, T., & Miki, M. (2003). Multi-objective rectangular packing problem and its applications. In *Evolutionary multi-criterion optimization* (pp. 565–577). Berlin: Springer. doi:10.1007/3-540-36970-8_40

Weigang, H., & Xiuli, S. (2011). A fuzzy associative classification method based on multi-objective evolutionary algorithm. *Journal of Computer Research and Development*, *48*(4), 567–575.

Weiss, S. M., & Indurkhya, N. (1998). *Predictive data mining: A practical guide*. San Francisco: Morgan Kaufmann.

Wong, C.-C., & Chen, C.-C. (2000). A GA-based method for constructing fuzzy systems directly from numerical data. *IEEE Transactions on Systems, Man and Cybernetics. Part B*, *30*, 904–911.

Yu, J., Xi, L., & Zhou, X. (2008). Intelligent monitoring and diagnosis of manufacturing processes using an integrated approach of KBANN and GA. *Computers in Industry*, *59*(5), 489–501. doi:10.1016/j.compind.2007.12.005

Zadeh, L. A. (1988). Fuzzy logic. *IEEE Computer*, *21*(4), 88–91. doi:10.1109/2.53

Zainal, A., Maarof, M. A., & Shamsuddin, S. M. (2009). Ensemble classifiers for network intrusion detection system. *Journal of Information Assurance and Security*, *4*, 217–225.

Zhang, Y., Wu, X. B., Xing, Z. Y., & Hu, W. L. (2011). On generating interpretable and precise fuzzy systems based on Pareto multi-objective cooperative co-evolutionary algorithm. *Applied Soft Computing*, *11*(1), 1284–1294. doi:10.1016/j.asoc.2010.03.005

Zimmermann, H. J. (1996). *Fuzzy set theory and its applications* (3rd ed.). Dordrecht, The Netherlands: Kluwer. doi:10.1007/978-94-015-8702-0

Zitzler, E., Laumanns, M., & Thiele, L. (2001). *SEPA2: Improving the performance of the strength of pareto evolutionary algorithm*. Zurich, Switzerland: Swiss Federal Institute of Technology.

Zitzler, E., & Thiele, L. (1999). Multi-objective evolutionary algorithms: A comparative case study and the strength Pareto approach. *IEEE Transactions on Evolutionary Computation*, *3*(4), 257–271. doi:10.1109/4235.797969

Zong-Yi, X., Yong, Z., Yuan-Long, H., & Guo-Qiang, C. (2008). Multi-objective fuzzy modeling using NSGA-II. In *Proceedings of Cybernetics and Intelligent Systems* (pp. 119–124). IEEE.

ADDITIONAL READING

Casillas, J. (Ed.). (2003). *Interpretability issues in fuzzy modeling* (Vol. 128). Springer. doi:10.1007/978-3-540-37057-4

Dehuri, S., & Mall, R. (2006). Predictive and comprehensible rule discovery using multi-objective genetic algorithm. *Knowledge-Based Systems*, *19*, 413–421. doi:10.1016/j.knosys.2006.03.004

Dubois, D., & Prade, H. (1980). *Fuzzy sets and systems: theory and applications*. New York: Academic.

Duda, R. O., Hart, P. E., & Stork, D. G. (2001). *Pattern classification* (2nd ed.). New York: Wiley.

Duncange, P., & Marcelloni, F. (2011). *Multi-objective evolutionary fuzzy systems*. Berlin/Heidelberg, Germany: Springer-Verlag.

Frawley, W., Piatasky-Sapiro, G., & Mathews, C. (1991). *Knowledge discovery in databases: an overview*. AAAI/MIT Press.

Freitas, A. A. (2002). *Data mining and knowledge discovery with evolutionary algorithms*. Springer. doi:10.1007/978-3-662-04923-5

Ghosh, A., Dehuri, S., & Ghosh, S. (Eds.). (2008). *Multi-objective evolutionary algorithms for knowledge discovery from databases* (Vol. 98). Springer. doi:10.1007/978-3-540-77467-9

Ghosh, A., & Jain, L. C. (Eds.). (2005). *Evolutionary computation in data mining* (Vol. 163). Springer. doi:10.1007/3-540-32358-9

Ishibuchi, H., Kuwajima, I., & Nojima, Y. (2006, September). Multi-objective association rule mining. In *PPSN Workshop on Multiobjective Problem Solving from Nature* (Vol. 12).

Ishibuchi, H., Kuwajima, I., & Nojima, Y. (2008). Multi-objective classification rule mining. In *Multiobjective Problem Solving from Nature* (pp. 219–240). Springer Berlin Heidelberg. doi:10.1007/978-3-540-72964-8_11

Ishibuchi, H., Nakashima, T., & Nii, M. (2005). *Classification and modeling with linguistic information granules: advanced approaches advanced approaches to linguistic data mining*. Springer.

Ishibuchi, H., Nozaki, K., Yamamoto, N., & Tanaka, H. (1995). Selecting fuzzy if-then rules for classification problem using genetic algorithm. *IEEE Transactions on Fuzzy Systems*, *3*(3), 260–270. doi:10.1109/91.413232

Jin, Y. (Ed.). (2006). *Multi-objective machine learning* (Vol. 16). Springer. doi:10.1007/3-540-33019-4

Jozwiak, L., & Postula, A. (2002). Genetic engineering versus natural evolution: genetic algorithm with deterministic operators. *Journal of Systems Architecture*, *48*(1-3), 99–112. doi:10.1016/S1383-7621(02)00094-2

Maimon, O. Z., & Rokach, L. (Eds.). (2005). *Data mining and knowledge discovery handbook*. Springer. doi:10.1007/b107408

Michie, D., Spiegelhalter, D. J., & Taylor, C. C. (1994). *Machine learning, neural and statistical classification*. New York: Ellis Horwood.

Mitchell, T. M. (1997). *Machine Learning*. McGraw-Hill.

Setzkorn, C., & Paton, R. C. (2005). On the use of multi-objective evolutionary algorithms for the induction of fuzzy classification rule systems. *Bio Systems*, *81*(2), 101–112. doi:10.1016/j.biosystems.2005.02.003 PMID:15939532

Xiong, X., & Funk, P. (2006). Construction of fuzzy knowledge bases incorporating feature selection. *Soft Computing*, *10*, 796–804. doi:10.1007/s00500-005-0009-7

Zadeh, L. A. (1975). Fuzzy Sets. *Information and Control*, *8*, 338–353. doi:10.1016/S0019-9958(65)90241-X

Zhou, E., & Khotanzad, A. (2007). Fuzzy classifier design using genetic algorithm. *Pattern Recognition*, *40*, 3401–3414. doi:10.1016/j.patcog.2007.03.028

KEY TERMS AND DEFINITIONS

Association: Association refers to the procedure of discovering a number of relationships among the attributes or attribute values in a large database.

Associative Classification: Associative classification refers to process of discovering classification rules using association rule. In other word, associative classification rules are special type association rules whose consequents are class label.

Classification: Classification is the process of finding a model or function, which provides a modularized, neatly explained format for decision, compatible with a human being's reasoning procedure. With respect to machine learning, classification refers to establishment of rules by which we can classify the new sample into the existing classes that are known in advance.

Data Mining: Data mining is an iterative process used as a central step of KDD process, performed either through semi-automatic, or automatic methods.

Fuzzy Logic: Fuzzy logic is a computing approach based on "degrees of truth" instead of traditional "true or false" (1 or 0) Boolean logic.

Genetic Algorithm: Genetic algorithms are optimization methods based on probabilistic operators, inspired by the "survival of the fittest" principle and mimic the behaviors from the processes of natural evolution and natural genetics.

KDD: Knowledge Discovery in Databases (KDD) refers to the non-trivial, iterative, and interactive process of discovering high-level/abstract knowledge in form of patterns, models, and rules etc., which are convincing, narrative, potentially useful, and comprehensible from low level/raw datasets.

Multi-Objective Optimization: Multi-objective optimization is a task of finding one or more optimum solutions for an optimization problem involving more than one objective.

Chapter 8
Rough Sets and Approximate Reasoning

B. K. Tripathy
VIT University, India

ABSTRACT

Several models have been introduced to capture impreciseness in data. Fuzzy sets introduced by Zadeh and Rough sets introduced by Pawlak are two of the most popular such models. In addition, the notion of intuitionistic fuzzy sets introduced by Atanassov and the hybrid models obtained thereof have been very fruitful from the application point of view. The introduction of fuzzy logic and the approximate reasoning obtained through it are more realistic as they are closer to human reasoning. Equality of sets in crisp mathematics is too restricted from the application point of view. Therefore, extending these concepts, three types of approximate equalities were introduced by Novotny and Pawlak using rough sets. These notions were found to be restrictive in the sense that they again boil down to equality of sets and also the lower approximate equality is artificial. Keeping these points in view, three other types of approximate equalities were introduced by Tripathy in several papers. These approximate equalities were further generalised to cover the approximate equalities of fuzzy sets and intuitionistic fuzzy sets by him. In addition, considering the generalisations of basic rough sets like the covering-based rough sets and multigranular rough sets, the study has been carried out further. In this chapter, the authors provide a comprehensive study of all these forms of approximate equalities and illustrate their applicability through several examples. In addition, they provide some problems for future work.

INTRODUCTION

Almost all concepts we use in natural languages are vague. So, the theories based on crisp notions like the crisp set theory (Set theory based upon Cantor's notion of sets (Cantor, 1983) have low utility in real life situations. Uncertainty is usually associated with the boundary region approach, which is based upon the observation that existence of objects which cannot be uniquely classified relative to a set or its complement. This was first formulated in 1893 by the father of modern logic,

DOI: 10.4018/978-1-4666-4936-1.ch008

German logician, Gottlob Frege (Dummet, 1967). Vagueness is not allowed in classical mathematics based on set theory; interesting for philosophy and is a nettlesome problem for natural language, cognitive science, artificial intelligence, machine learning, philosophy and computer science. The exploit of the tolerance for imprecision, uncertainty and partial truth is essential to achieve tractability, robustness and low solution cost.

This has led to the development of several imprecise models extending the crisp set model so far. One of the foremost of such models is the notion of fuzzy sets introduced by L.A.Zadeh (Zadeh, 1965) in 1965. Fuzzy sets capture impreciseness in data through the notion of graded membership of elements instead of the binary membership defined through the characteristic functions for crisp sets. Later on this basic model has been extended to several other general models like the notion of intuitionistic fuzzy sets by K.T.Attanasov (Atanassov, 1986) in 1982 and the notion of interval valued fuzzy sets. Approximate reasoning uses fuzzy sets and fuzzy logic to model human reasoning. It lacks the precision of the exact reasoning in classical logic but it is more effective dealing with complex and ill-defined systems.

Another such important model is the notion of rough sets introduced by (Pawlak, 1982). In the beginning it was supposed to be a competing model to fuzzy sets. But, later on it was shown in (Dubois and Prade, 1990) in 1990 that far from being competitive these models complement each other and they introduced the hybrid models by combining these two models. Imprecision in this approach is expressed by the boundary region of a set. In fact, the idea of rough set is based upon approximation of a set by a pair of sets, called the lower and upper approximation of the set.

Comparison of sets plays a major role in classical set theory. Two sets are said to be equal in crisp set theory iff they have the same elements. This notion is independent of the user or more precisely the user knowledge about the universe dealt with. When we move to the representation of approximate knowledge through rough sets the usual comparisons lose their meaning and in a sense or of no use. To bring about more meaning into such comparisons of rough sets which translate into approximate comparison of knowledge bases,(Novotny and Pawlak, 1985a,1985b,1985c) introduced three notions of rough equalities (bottom, top and total) in 1985 and established several of their properties. This is an important feature from the application point of view. The reason being that, in certain cases it might not be possible for us to conclude about the equality of two sets from the available knowledge in the mathematical sense. But, we can only say that, according to our state of knowledge, they have close features which are enough to assume that they are approximately equal. That is, basing upon our knowledge and requirement we can assume that the two sets are indistinguishable. These concepts are used to achieve approximate reasoning using rough sets which is in the same lines as approximate reasoning using fuzzy sets and fuzzy logic.

It was observed by (Tripathy, Mitra and Ojha, 2008) that even these notions of approximate equalities are restricted in the sense that they boil down to equality of sets. So, the notions of rough equivalences were introduced and were found to be more realistic. Carrying out his study further (Tripathy, 2011) introduced two other types of approximate equalities, namely approximate rough equalities and approximate rough equivalences. A comparative analysis of these four sets of approximate equalities has shown that the notion of approximate rough equivalence is the best and most applicable in real life situations.

The above notions have been extended to incorporate the approximate equalities of fuzzy sets in (Tripathy, Jhawar and Vats, 2012). The notions introduced are leveled approximate equalities for fuzzy sets, which generalize the basic approximate equalities for basic sets. In a recent paper (Tripathy and Panda, 2012) extended all these notions further to the setting of intuitionistic fuzzy sets. The number of equivalence relations (Pawlak, 1982, 1991), which was used as the mathematical notion in his definition of rough sets is relatively small in comparison to the number of relations available in real life situations or otherwise. So, by relaxing the requirements of an equivalence relation, using the general notion of a cover, several types of covering based rough sets have been introduced in recent past (Bonikowski, Bryniarski and Wybraniec, 1998; Zhu, 2007a, 2007b, 2007c; Zhu and Wang, 2003 and Zhu and Wang, 2006). The concepts of four types of approximate equalities introduced above were generalised to the context of covering based rough sets in (Tripathy, Panda and Mitra, 2012; Tripathy and Tripathy, 2009). In this chapter we introduce the results for the first three types of covering based rough sets. The other cases are under future studies. The definition of basic rough sets of Pawlak depends upon single granulation from the granular computing point of view. Extending this, two types of multigranular rough sets was introduced by Qian et al, called the optimistic multigranular rough sets (Qian and Liang, 2006) and the pessimistic multigranular rough sets (Qian, Liang and Dang, 2010). All the four types of approximate equalities have been defined and their properties have been studied by Tripathy et al (Tripathy and Mitra, 2013a, 2013b; Tripathy, Rawat, Divya and Parida, 2013; Tripathy and Saraf, 2013). We discuss these studies in brief. Finally we propose some problems for further studies. The chapter ends with an exhaustive bibliography of source materials consulted during the compilation of this piece of work.

BASIC NOTIONS AND DEFINITIONS

In this section, we introduce some concepts and notations to be used throughout this chapter.

Rough Sets

Let U be a universe of discourse and R be an equivalence relation over U. By U/R we denote the family of all equivalence classes of R, referred to as categories or concepts of R. The basic philosophy of rough sets is that knowledge is deep-seated in the classificatory abilities of human beings and other species. Knowledge is connected with the variety of classification patterns related to specific parts of real or abstract worlds called the universe. Knowledge consists of a family of various classification patterns of a domain of interest, which provide explicit facts about reality together with the reasoning capacity able to deliver implicit facts derivable from explicit knowledge.

Usually we do not deal with a single classification but a family of classifications over a universe. By a knowledge base we mean a relational system K = (U, R), where R is a family of equivalence relations over U.

For any subset P of R the intersection of all equivalence relations in P is denoted by IND(P) and is called the indiscernibility relation over P.

Definition 1: Given any subset X of U and R in IND(K), we associate two subsets

$$\underline{R}X = \bigcup\{Y \in U \ / \ R : Y \subseteq X\}$$

and

$$\overline{R}X = \bigcup\{Y \in U \ / \ R : Y \cap X \neq \phi\}$$

called the R-lower and R-upper approximations of X respectively.

The R-boundary of X is denoted by $BN_R(X)$ and is given by

$$BN_R(X) = \overline{R}X - \underline{R}X$$

The elements of $\underline{R}X$ are those elements of U which can be certainly classified as elements of X and elements of $\overline{R}X$ are those elements of U which can possibly be classified as elements of X with the knowledge of R.

Definition 2: We say that X is rough (Pawlak, 1982 and Pawlak, 1991) with respect to Riff

$$\underline{R}X \neq \overline{R}X$$

or equivalently

$$BN_R(X) \neq \phi$$

and R-definable otherwise.

Approximate Equalities of Sets

As described in the introduction, sometimes exact equality (equality in the mathematical sense) is too stringent to apply in day to day life. We often talk about equality of sets or domains, which can be considered to be equal for the purpose or under the circumstances in real life situations. So, approximate equalities play a significant role in our reasoning. Also, it is dependent upon the knowledge the assessors have about the domain under consideration as a whole but mostly not the knowledge about individuals. The question now arises so as to find metrics to measure the equality. This is provided by the equivalence relations defined over the domain. Of course, this can be extended to other types of relations also (see for instance (Bonikowski, 1998; Degang, Changzhong and Qinghua, 2007; Degang, Wenxiu, Yeung and Tsang, 2006; Tripathy and Tripathy, 2009; Tripathy and Panda, 2012).

The Kinds of Approximate Equalities

In order to define the approximate equalities we take the following conditions on the lower and upper approximations of sets X and Y:

- (L1) $\underline{R}X = \underline{R}Y$
- (L2) Both $\underline{R}X$ and $\underline{R}Y$ are ϕ or not ϕ together
- (U1) $\overline{R}X = \overline{R}Y$
- (U2) Both $\overline{R}X$ and $\overline{R}Y$ are U or not-U together

Taking different combinations of the two types of conditions on lower approximations and the two types of conditions on upper approximations we get four kinds of approximate equalities of sets. This is summarized in the following table:

Let T(i, j) ; i = 1, 2 and j = 1, 2 denote the (i, j)th position in the above table. Then

1. Three different types approximate equalities called rough equalities were introduced in (Novotny and Pawlak, 1985a, 1985b, 1985c) by taking T(1,1) into consideration.
2. Three different types of approximate equalities called rough equivalences were introduced in (Tripathy, Mitra and Ojha, 2008) by taking T(2, 2) into consideration.
3. Three different types of approximate equalities called approximate rough equivalences were introduced by (Tripathy, 2011) by taking T(2, 1) into consideration.
4. Three different types of approximate equalities called approximate rough equalities were introduced in (Tripathy, 2011) by taking T(1, 2) into consideration.

Rough Equalities of Sets

As mentioned above, (Novotny and Pawlak 1985a, 1985b, 1985c) introduced three types of approximate equalities, extending the idea of mathematical equality of two sets. We state these definitions below.

Definition 3: Let $K = (U, \mathcal{R})$ be a knowledge base, X, Y $\subset$ U and R $\in$ IND(K) . We say that

1. Two sets X and Y are bottom R-equal (X br_eq Y) if and only if L1 holds true.
2. Two sets X and Y are top R-equal (X tr_eq Y) if and only if U1 holds true.
3. Two sets X and Y are R-equal (X r_eq Y) iff (X br_eq Y) and (X tr_eq Y); equivalently, L1 and U1 both hold true.

It can be easily verified that the relations bottom R-equal, top R-equal and R-equal are equivalence relations over P(U), the power set of U. The concept of approximate equality of sets refers to the topological structure of the compared sets but not the elements they consist of. Thus sets having significantly different elements may be rough equal.

In fact, if X br_eq Y then $\underline{R}X = \underline{R}Y$ and as

$$X \supseteq \underline{R}X, Y \supseteq \underline{R}Y$$

X and *Y* can differ in elements of $X - \underline{R}X$ and $Y - \underline{R}Y$. However, it is easy to check that two sets X and Y may be R-equal in spite of $X \cap Y = \phi$.

As noted by Pawlak ([12], p.26), rough equality of sets is of relative character, that is things are equal or not equal from our point of view depending on what we know about them. So, in a sense the definition of rough equality refers to our knowledge about the universe.

Basic Properties of Rough Equalities

The following properties of rough equalities are well known (see for instance (Pawlak, 1991)):

Property 1: X br_eq Y if and only if $X \cap Y$ br_eq X and $X \cap Y$ br_eq Y.
Property 2: X tr_eq Y if and only if $X \cup Y$ tr_eq X and $X \cup Y$ tr_eq Y.

Property 3: If X tr_eq X' and Y tr_eq Y' then $X \cup Y$ tr_eq $X' \cup Y'$.
Property 4: If X br_eq X' and Y br_eq Y' then $X \cap Y$ br_eq $X' \cap Y'$.
Property 5: If X tr_eq Y then $X \cup -Y$ is tr_eq U.
Property 6: If X br_eq Y then $X \cap -Y$ is br_eq ϕ.
Property 7: If $X \subseteq Y$ and Y tr_eq ϕ then X tr_eq ϕ.
Property 8: If $X \subseteq Y$ and X tr_eq U then Y tr_eq U.
Property 9: X tr_eq Y if and only if $-X$ br_eq $-Y$.
Property 10: If X br_eq ϕ or Y br_eq ϕ then $X \cap Y$ br_eq ϕ.
Property 11: If X tr_eq U or Y tr_eq U then $X \cup Y$ tr_eq U .

It is noted in (Pawlak, 1991) that the properties (4) to (14) fail to hold if tr_eq is replaced by br_eq or vice versa. However, it was shown in (Tripathy, Mitra and Ojha, 2008) that

1. The properties (10) to (14) hold true under the interchange.
2. The properties (8) and (9) holds true under interchange if $BN_R(Y) = \phi$.
3. Also suitable conditions have been provided for the properties (4), (5), (6) and (7) to hold under interchange.

Rough Equivalences of Sets

Definition 4: For any two subsets *X* and Y, we say that X is bottom rough equivalent to Y (X br_eqv Y) if and only if L2 holds. We put the restriction here that for bottom R equivalence of X and Y either both $\underline{R}X$ and $\underline{R}Y$ are equal to *U* or none of them is equal to *U*.

Definition 5: For any two subsets *X* and Y, we say that X is top rough equivalent to Y (X tr_eqv Y) if and only if U2 holds. We put the restriction here that for top R-equivalence of X and Y either both $\overline{R}X$ and $\overline{R}Y$ are equal to ϕ or none of them is equal to ϕ.

Definition 6: For any two subsets X and Y, we say that X is rough equivalent to Y (X r_eq Y) if and only if both L2 and U2 hold simultaneously.

We would like to note here that when two sets X and Y are rough equivalent, the restrictions in Definition 4 and Definition 5 become redundant.

Basic Properties of Rough Equivalence

It may be noted that many of the algebraic properties for crisp set equalities have been studied to establish their validity (Tripathy, Mitra and Ojha, 2008). In this section we state some of the properties of rough equivalences of sets obtained in (Tripathy, Mitra and Ojha, 2008; Tripathy, 2009). These properties are similar to those of rough equalities. Some of these properties which do not hold in full force, sufficient conditions have been obtained. Also, the necessity of such conditions is verified. To state these properties, we need the concepts of different rough inclusions (Pawlak, 1991) and rough comparisons (Tripathy, Mitra and Ojha, 2008; Tripathy, 2009 and Tripathy, Mitra and Ojha, 2009).

Definition 7: Let $K = (U, \mathcal{R})$ be a knowledge base, X, Y $\subseteq$ U and R $\in$ IND(K). Then

1. We say that X is bottom rough included in Y (X br_included Y) if and only if $\underline{R}X \subseteq \underline{R}Y$.
2. We say that X is top rough included in Y (X tr_included Y) if and only if $\overline{R}X \subseteq \overline{R}Y$.

3. We say that X is rough *included* in Y (X r_included Y) if and only if X br_included Y and X tr_included Y.

Definition 8:

1. We say X, Y $\subseteq$ U are bottom rough comparable if and only if X br_included Y or Y br_included X holds.
2. We say X, Y $\subseteq$ U are top rough comparable if and only if X tr_included Y or Y tr_included X holds.
3. We say X, Y $\subseteq$ U are rough comparable if and only if X and Y are both top and bottom rough comparable.

Property 12:

1. If X $\cap$ Y br_eqv X and Y (both) then X is br_eqv Y.
2. The converse of (i) is not true in general and an additional condition that is sufficient but not necessary for the converse to be true is that X and Y are bottom rough comparable.

Property 13:

1. If $X \cup Y$ tr_eqv X and Y (both) then X is tr_eqv Y.
2. The converse of (i) is not true in general and an additional condition that is sufficient but not necessary for the converse to be true is that X and Y are top rough comparable.

Property 14:

1. If X is tr_eqv X' and Y is tr_eqv Y' then it may or may not be true that $X \cup Y$ is tr_eqv $X' \cup Y'$.

2. A sufficient but not necessary condition for the result in (i) to be true is that X and Y are top rough comparable and X' and Y' are top rough comparable.

Property 15:

1. X br_eqv X' and Y br_eqv Y' may or may not imply that $X \cap Y$ br_eqv $X' \cap Y'$.
2. A sufficient but not necessary condition for the result in (i) to be true is that X and Y are bottom rough comparable and X' and Y' are bottom rough comparable.

Property 16:

1. X tr_eqv Y may or may not imply that $X \cup -Y$) tr_eqv U.
2. A sufficient but not necessary condition for result in (i) to hold is that X br_eq Y.

Property 17:

1. X br_eqv Y may not imply that $X \cap -Y$) is br_eqv ϕ.
2. A sufficient but not necessary condition for the result in (i) to hold true is that X tr_eqv Y.

Property 18: If $X \subseteq Y$ and Y br_eqv ϕ then X br_eqv ϕ.

Property 19: If $X \subseteq Y$ and X is tr_eqv U then Y tr_eqv U.

Property 20: X tr_eqv Y if and only if $-X$ br_eqv $-Y$.

Property 21: X br_eqv ϕ, Y br_eqv to ϕ $\Rightarrow X \cap Y$ br_eqv ϕ.

Property 22: If X tr_eqv U or Y tr_eqv U then $X \cup Y$ tr_eqv U.

Replacement Properties for Rough Equivalence

In parallel to the properties of interchange for rough equalities, replacement properties for rough equivalences were established in (Pawlak, 1991). Some of the replacement properties hold directly. Some hold partially and sufficient but not necessary conditions have been provided in this article.

Examples

In this section, we shall produce the two examples considered in (Tripathy, Mitra and Ojha, 2008; Tripathy, Mitra and Ojha, 2009) to illustrate the superiority of the concepts of rough equivalence over rough equalities.

Example 1: Universe of Cattle

Let us consider the cattle in a locality as our universal set C. We define a relation R over C by x R y if and only if x and y are cattle of the same kind. This is an equivalence relation decomposes the universe into disjoint equivalence classes. Suppose for example, C = {Cow, Buffalo, Goat, Sheep, Bullock}. Let X and Y be the set of cattle owned by two persons P1 and P2 in the locality. We cannot talk about the equality of X and Y in the usual sense as the cattle cannot be owned by two different people. Similarly, we cannot talk about the rough equality of X and Y except the trivial case when both the persons do not own any cattle.

There different possibilities for approximate equality or otherwise of X and Y to hold have been discussed in ([15],[16]) and are categorized under six cases as follows:

Case 1: $\overline{RX}, \overline{RY}$ are not U and $\underline{RX}, \underline{RY}$ are ϕ. That is P1 and P2 both have some kind of cattle but do not have all cattle of any kind in the locality. So, they are equivalent.

Case 2: $\overline{RX}, \overline{RY}$ are not U and $\underline{RX}, \underline{RY}$ are not ϕ. That is P1 and P2 both have some kind of cattle and have all cattle of some kind in the locality. So, they are equivalent.

Case 3: $\overline{RX}, \overline{RY}$ are U and $\underline{RX}, \underline{RY}$ are ϕ. That is P1 and P2 both cattle of all kinds but do not have all cattle of any kind in the locality. So, they are equivalent.

Case 4: $\overline{RX}, \overline{RY}$ are U and $\underline{RX}, \underline{RY}$ are not ϕ. That is P1 and P2 both have all kinds of cattle and also have all cattle of some kind in the locality. So, they are equivalent.

There are two different cases under which we can talk about the non- equivalence of P1 and P2.

Case 5: one of $\overline{RX}, \overline{RY}$ is U and the other one is not. Then, out of P1 and P2 one has cattle of all kinds and the other one does not have so. So, they are not equivalent.

Case 6: Out of $\underline{RX}, \underline{RY}$, one is ϕ and the other one is not. Then, out of P1 and P2 one does not have all cattle of any particular kind, where as the other has all cattle of at least one kind. So, they are not equivalent.

Example 2: Universe of Shares

Let us consider the example of a stock exchange dealing with shares of different companies. The shares of different companies are of different denomination and are related to branches of the companies at different locations.

We take S as the set of shares of different companies under the control of the stock exchange. We define three relations R_1, R_2 and R_3 on S as follows:

1. For $x, y \in S$, we say $x R_1 y$ if and only if x and y are of the same denomination.

2. For $x, y \in S$, we say $x R_2 y$ if and only if x and y are from branches with the same location.

3. For $x, y \in S$, we say $x R_3 y$ if and only if x and y belong to the same company.

It is easy to check that each R_1, R_2 and R_3 is an equivalence relation on S. Let P_1 and P_2 be two persons having shares in the stock exchange. S_1 and S_2 be the set of shares owned by them respectively. Ordinary set equality and rough equality notions cannot be applied to the sets S_1 and S_2 to compare the two persons from the ownership of shares point of view as the same share cannot be owned by more than one person in any stock exchange. However, from our common sense point of view and real life experience we know that two persons can be considered equivalent (or indistinguishable). For example, persons having shares from the same companies are equivalent to each other. Similarly, persons having shares of same denomination are equivalent. Also, persons having shares of branches of same location of different companies can be considered as equivalent.

Moving further, persons having shares of same company and same denominations can be considered as equivalent and persons having shares of same companies of same denominations and from branches of same location can also be considered as equivalent to each other. Mathematically, we are considering the intersections of

$$R_1, R_2 \ and \ R_3$$

pair wise or all of them taken at a time, which are known to be equivalence relations as intersection of any number of equivalence relations is an equivalence relation.

Let S be a stock exchange having the set of shares:

$$S = \{s_1, s_2, s_3, \ldots s_{50}\}$$

Suppose these shares are of three denominations of values Rs.10, Rs.15 and Rs.20 (we mention as V_1, V_2 and V_3). Then we define:

$$R_1 = \{V_1 = \{s_1, s_4, s_7, s_{10}, s_{13}, s_{16}, s_{19}, s_{22}, s_{25},$$
$$s_{28}, s_{31}, s_{34}, s_{37}, s_{40}, s_{43}, s_{46}, s_{49}\},$$
$$V_2 = \{s_2, s_5, s_8, s_{11}, s_{14}, s_{17}, s_{20}, s_{23}, s_{26},$$
$$s_{29}, s_{32}, s_{35}, s_{38}, s_{41}, s_{44}, s_{47}, s_{50}\},$$
$$V_3 = \{s_3, s_6, s_9, s_{12}, s_{15}, s_{18}, s_{21}, s_{24}, s_{27},$$
$$s_{30}, s_{33}, s_{36}, s_{39}, s_{42}, s_{45}, s_{48}\}\}.$$

The shares belong to branches of different companies at four locations L_1, L_2, L_3 and L_4.

So, we define:

$$R_2 = \{L_1 = \{s_1, s_5, s_9, s_{13}, s_{17}, s_{21}, s_{25}, s_{29}, s_{33},$$
$$s_{37}, s_{41}, s_{45}, s_{49}\},$$
$$L_2 = \{s_2, s_6, s_{10}, s_{14}, s_{18}, s_{22}, s_{26}, s_{30},$$
$$s_{34}, s_{38}, s_{42}, s_{46}, s_{50}\},$$
$$L_3 = \{s_3, s_7, s_{11}, s_{15}, s_{19}, s_{23}, s_{27}, s_{31},$$
$$s_{35}, s_{39}, s_{43}, s_{47}\},$$
$$L_4 = \{s_4, s_8, s_{12}, s_{16}, s_{20}, s_{24}, s_{28}, s_{32},$$
$$s_{36}, s_{40}, s_{44}, s_{48}\}\}.$$

The exchange contains shares of five different companies C_1, C_2, C_3, C_4 and C_5. We define

$$R_3 =$$
$$\{C_1 = \{s_1, s_6, s_{11}, s_{16}, s_{21}, s_{26}, s_{31}, s_{36}, s_{41}, s_{46}\},$$
$$C_2 = \{s_2, s_7, s_{12}, s_{17}, s_{22}, s_{27}, s_{32}, s_{37}, s_{42}, s_{47}\},$$
$$C_3 = \{s_3, s_8, s_{13}, s_{18}, s_{23}, s_{28}, s_{33}, s_{38}, s_{43}, s_{48}\},$$
$$C_4 = \{s_4, s_9, s_{14}, s_{19}, s_{24}, s_{29}, s_{34}, s_{39}, s_{44}, s_{49}\},$$
$$C_5 = \{s_5, s_{10}, s_{15}, s_{20}, s_{25}, s_{30}, s_{35}, s_{40}, s_{45}, s_{50}\}\}.$$

Let

$$P_1, P_2, S_1 \text{ and } S_2$$

be as above.

Case 1: Let

$$S_1 = \{s_1, s_5, s_{10}\} \text{ and } S_2 = \{s_2, s_4, s_{16}, s_{23}\}.$$

Then

$$\underline{R_1}S_1 = \underline{R_1}S_2 = \phi \text{ and } \overline{R_1}S_1 =$$
$$V_1 \bigcup V_2 \neq U \text{ and } \overline{R_1}S_2 = V_1 \bigcup V_2 \neq U.$$

From the point of view of holding shares of similar denominations, both P_1 and P_2 do not hold all shares of any particular denomination and they do not hold shares of all denominations. So they are rough equivalent.

Case 2: Let

$$S_1 = \{s_1, s_5, s_6, s_9, s_{10}\}$$
$$\text{and } S_2 = \{s_4, s_8, s_{11}, s_{13}\}.$$

Then

$$\underline{R_1}S_1 = \underline{R_1}S_2 = \phi$$
$$\text{and } \overline{R_1}S_1 = U \text{ and } \overline{R_1}S_2 \neq U.$$

So, P_1 and P_2 are bottom equivalent as none of them has all the shares of any particular denomination. But they are not totally rough equivalent as P_1 has shares of denomination Rs.20 where as P_2 does not hold any such share.

Case 3: Let

$S_1 = \{s_1, s_4, s_7, s_{10}, s_{13}, s_{16}, s_{19}, s_{22},$
$s_{25}, s_{28}, s_{31}, s_{34}, s_{37}, s_{40}, s_{43}, s_{46}, s_{49}\}$ and

$S_2 = \{s_3, s_6, s_9, s_{12}, s_{15}, s_{18}, s_{21}, s_{24},$
$s_{27}, s_{30}, s_{33}, s_{36}, s_{39}, s_{42}, s_{45}, s_{48}\}.$

Then

$\underline{R_1}S_1 \neq \phi \text{ and } \underline{R_1}S_1 \neq \phi.$

Again

$\overline{R_1}S_1 \neq U \text{ and } \overline{R_1}S_2 \neq U.$

From the point of view of holding shares of similar denominations, both P_1 and P_2 hold all the shares of a particular denomination and they do not hold shares of all denominations. So they are rough equivalent.

Case 4: Let

$S_1 = \{s_1, s_2, s_3, s_4, s_{51}, s_6\}$
and $S_2 = \{s_7, s_8, s_9, s_{10}, s_{11}, s_{12}\}.$

Then

$\underline{R_1}S_1 = \phi \text{ and } \underline{R_1}S_1 = \phi.$

Again

$\overline{R_1}S_1 = U \text{ and } \overline{R_1}S_2 = U.$

From the point of view of holding shares of similar denominations, both P_1 and P_2 do not holds all the shares of a particular denomination but they do hold at least one share of all denominations. So they are rough equivalent.

Case 5: Let

$S_1 = \{s_2, s_5, s_8, s_{11}, s_{14}, s_{17}, s_{20}, s_{23}, s_{26},$
$s_{29}, s_{32}, s_{35}, s_{38}, s_{41}, s_{44}, s_{47}, s_{48}, s_{49}, s_{50}\}$

and

$S_2 = \{s_1, s_4, s_7, s_{10}, s_{13}, s_{16}, s_{19}, s_{22},$
$s_{25}, s_{28}, s_{31}, s_{34}, s_{37}, s_{40}, s_{43}, s_{46}\}$

Then $\underline{R_1}S_1 \neq \phi$ and $\underline{R_1}S_2 = \phi$. Again $\overline{R_1}S_1 = U$ and $\overline{R_1}S_2 \neq U$. So, P_1 holds all the shares of the denomination Rs.10 whereas P_2 does not have this property and P_1 holds some share of each denominations whereas P_2 has shares of denomination R.10 only. So P_1 and P_2 are not rough equivalent.

Similarly, we can show different rough equivalence for holding shares of different branches and different companies, that is with respect to the relations R_2 and R_3 respectively.

Let us consider two relations at a time, say R_1 and R_2, that is shares of same denomination and of same branches. By direct calculation, we have

$R_1 \cap R_2 = \{\{s_1, s_{13}, s_{25}, s_{37}, s_{49}\},$
$\{s_{10}, s_{22}, s_{34}, s_{46}\}, \{s_7, s_{19}, s_{31}, s_{43}\},$
$\{s_{16}, s_{28}, s_{40}\}, \{s_5, s_{17}, s_{29}, s_{41}\},$

$\{s_2, s_{14}, s_{26}, s_{28}, s_{50}\}, \{s_{11}, s_{23}, s_{35}, s_{47}\},$
$\{s_8, s_{20}, s_{32}, s_{44}\}, \{s_9, s_{21}, s_{33}, s_{45}\},$

$\{s_6, s_{18}, s_{30}, s_{42}\}, \{s_3, s_{15}, s_{27}, s_{39}\},$
$\{s_{12}, s_{24}, s_{36}, s_{48}\}\}.$

Case 6: Let

$$S_1 = \{s_1, s_{11}, s_{21}, s_{31}, s_{41}\}$$

and

$$S_2 = \{s_2, s_{12}, s_{22}, s_{32}, s_{42}\}$$

Then

$$(\underline{R_1 \cap R_2})S_1 = \phi = (\underline{R_1 \cap R_2})S_2$$

and

$$\overline{(R_1 \cap R_2)}S_1 \neq U$$

and

$$\overline{(R_1 \cap R_2)}S_2 \neq U.$$

So, P_1 and P_2 do not hold all shares of any particular branch and same denomination. Also, they do not have such share across all the branches and of same denomination. So they are rough equivalent.

Case 7: Let

$$S_1 = \{s_1, s_{13}, s_{25}, s_{37}, s_{49}, s_{50}\}$$

and

$$S_2 = \{s_{11}, s_{12}, s_{24}, s_{36}, s_{48}\}$$

Then

$$(\underline{R_1 \cap R_2})S_1 \neq \phi$$

and

$$(\underline{R_1 \cap R_2})S_2 \neq \phi$$

Again

$$\overline{(R_1 \cap R_2)}S_1 \neq U$$

and

$$\overline{(R_1 \cap R_2)}S_2 \neq U.$$

So, P_1 and P_2 hold all shares of same particular branch which are of same denomination. But, they do not have such share across all the branches and of same denomination. So they are rough equivalent.

Case 8: Let

$$S_1 = \{s_1, s_2, s_3, s_5, s_6, s_7, s_8, s_9, s_{10}, s_{11}, s_{12}, s_{16}\}$$

and

$$S_2 = \{s_{13}, s_{14}, s_{15}, s_{17}, s_{18}, s_{19},$$
$$s_{20}, s_{21}, s_{22}, s_{23}, s_{24}, s_{28}, s_{36}, s_{48}\}$$

Then

$$(\underline{R_1 \cap R_2})S_1 = \phi$$

and

$$\overline{(R_1 \cap R_2)}S_2 = \phi$$

Again

$$\overline{(R_1 \cap R_2)}S_1 = U$$

and

$$\overline{(R_1 \cap R_2)}S_2 = U.$$

From the point of view of same denomination and same branch office shares of the stock exchange P_1 and P_2 does not hold all shares of any particular branch and same denomination. But, they have such share across all the branches and of same denomination. So they are rough equivalent.

Case 9: Let

$$S_1 = \{s_{18}, s_{30}, s_{39}, s_{40}, s_{41}, s_{42},$$
$$s_{43}, s_{44}, s_{45}, s_{46}, s_{47}, s_{48}, s_{49}, s_{50}\}$$

and

$$S_2 = \{s_{13}, s_{14}, s_{15}, s_{17}, s_{19},$$
$$s_{20}, s_{21}, s_{22}, s_{23}, s_{24}, s_{28}, s_{36}\}.$$

Then

$$\underline{(R_1 \cap R_2)}S_1 = \phi$$

and

$$\underline{(R_1 \cap R_2)}S_2 = \phi$$

Again

$$\overline{(R_1 \cap R_2)}S_1 = U$$

and

$$\overline{(R_1 \cap R_2)}S_2 \neq U.$$

So, P_1 and P_2 are bottom equivalent as none of them has all the shares of any particular branch and same denomination. But they are not totally rough equivalent as P_1 has at least one share across all the branches and of same denomination where as P_2 does not hold at least one share across all the branches and of same denomination.

Case 10: Let

$$S_1 = \{s_6, s_{18}, s_{30}, s_{42}, s_{39}, s_{40}, s_{41},$$
$$s_{43}, s_{44}, s_{45}, s_{46}, s_{47}, s_{48}, s_{49}, s_{50}\}$$

and

$$S_2 = \{s_{13}, s_{14}, s_{15}, s_{17}, s_{19},$$
$$s_{20}, s_{21}, s_{22}, s_{23}, s_{24}, s_{28}, s_{36}\}$$

Then

$$\underline{(R_1 \cap R_2)}S_1 \neq \phi$$

and

$$\underline{(R_1 \cap R_2)}S_2 = \phi$$

Again

$$\overline{(R_1 \cap R_2)}S_1 = U$$

and

191

$$\overline{(R_1 \cap R_2)}S_2 \neq U.$$

Here, P_1 has all the shares of a particular branch of same denominations; whereas P_2 does not have this property. So, they are not bottom rough equivalent as far as holding shares of same branch and same denomination is concerned. Similarly, P_1 has shares of every branches of every denomination; whereas P_2 does not have this property. So, they are not top rough equivalent also.

Finally, we consider all three relations at a time. Then

$$R_1 \cap R_2 \cap R_3 = \{\{s_1\}, \{s_2\}, \{s_3\}, ..., \{s_{49}\}, \{s_{50}\}\}.$$

We see that any two share holders are rough equivalent with respect to holding of shares of same denomination, same branch and same company is concerned. As, a share holder must have at least one share and when more than one share holders are there, none can have all shares, we see that for P_1 and P_2 we have only one case

$$\underline{(R_1 \cap R_2 \cap R_3)}S_1 \neq \phi,$$

$$\underline{(R_1 \cap R_2 \cap R_3)}S_2 \neq \phi$$

and

$$\overline{(R_1 \cap R_2 \cap R_3)}S_1 \neq U,$$

$$\overline{(R_1 \cap R_2 \cap R_3)}S_2 \neq U.$$

Approximate Rough Equivalence and Approximate Rough Equality of Sets

As mentioned in the table in section 2.1, there are two other types of approximate equalities; which we call as approximately rough equivalent and approximately rough equal, out of which approximately rough equivalent is more general than the concept of rough equality and restricted than the concept of rough equivalence and also seems to be more novel than the two types of approximate equalities. We reproduce below the definitions of the two types of approximate equalities below.

Definition 9: We say that two sets X and Y are approximately rough equivalent if and only if L2 and U1 hold true, that is when both

$\underline{R}X$ and $\underline{R}Y$ are ϕ or not ϕ together.

and $\overline{R}X = \overline{R}Y$.

Definition 10: We say that two sets X and Y are approximately rough equal if and only if L1 and U2 hold true, that is when $\underline{R}X = \underline{R}Y$ and both $\overline{R}X$ and $\overline{R}Y$ are U or not U together.

Comparisons

In this section we shall provide a comparative study of the four different types of approximate equalities.

1. The condition L1, on interpretation states that two sets are lower approximately equal if and only if the two sets have the same

lower approximation; that is both the sets must include exactly the same equivalence classes. This sounds alright in numerical examples. But, when we move to practicalities, it is found that the condition requires some elements of the universe to belong to both the sets; which seems to be unnatural. For example, taking the example of cattle into consideration, we cannot have cases where the same set of cattle belonging to two different persons. In the example of shares, any share belonging to two different people is not feasible. The examples show that in only rare and restricted cases, this property may be satisfied. Since we are using this property in case of both rough equal and approximately rough equal definitions, these two cases of rough equalities seem to have lesser utility than the other two.

2. No doubt the condition U2 provides freedom to define equality in a very approximate sense and is quite general than U1. But, sometimes it seems to be unconvincing. For example, let us take the cattle example into consideration. When P1 and P2 both are not equal to U, we say that they are top rough equivalent. Suppose a person has a cow and a buffalo in the locality and another has most of the other animals in the locality. Then they are top rough equivalent, by using this definition, which does not seem to be convincing. On the other hand, if we take U1 into consideration then the above two persons are not top rough equal. However, P1 and P2 shall be top rough equal if and only if they contain cattle of same kind, irrespective of their number and it satisfies common sense reasoning although it is approximate.

3. Let us now analyse the concept of approximate rough equivalence. It is neither unconvincing nor unnatural. Two persons can be said to be equal in this sense only when

they have nonempty intersections with same equivalence classes and either include all or none of the elements of the equivalence classes separately. Since it is impossible for two persons to have the same set of cattle of any kind this is the best possible type of approximate equality from all angles.

4. The fourth type of approximate equality defined above has both the problems mentioned in 1 and 2. So this happens to be the worst type of approximate equality which we can talk about.

General Properties

In this section we shall consider the general properties of the two new types of approximate equalities introduced by us in this paper.

Approximate Rough Equivalence Properties

Since the definition of approximate rough equivalence is a combination of L2 and U1, the general properties are just to be picked up from those of the other types of approximate equalities. We mention them below.

The properties (2), (3), (5), (7), (8), (11), (12), (15), (17), (18) and (21) hold true.

Approximate Rough Equality Properties

Since the definition of approximate rough equivalence is a combination of L1 and U2, the general properties are just to be picked up from those of the other types of approximate equalities. We mention them below.

The properties (1), (4), (6), (10), (13), (14), (16), (19), (21), and (22) hold true.

It may be noted that the property (20) does not hold for any of the above two types of approximate equalities.

Properties with Replacements

In this section we shall consider the properties with lower approximate rough equivalence replaced with upper approximate rough equivalence and vice versa for the two new types of approximate equalities introduced by us in this paper.

Approximate Rough Equivalence Properties

Since the definition of approximate rough equivalence is a combination of L2 and U1, the general properties are just to be picked up from those of the other types of approximate equalities. We mention them below.

1. The properties (7), (8), (11) hold under the interchange. Also, the properties (13), (14), (16), (19) and (22) hold true.
2. The property (5) holds true under interchange $BN_R(Y) = \phi$.
3. The properties (2) and (3) hold under suitable conditions.

Approximate Rough Equality Properties

Since the definition of approximate rough equivalence is a combination of L1 and U2, the general properties are just to be picked up from those of the other types of approximate equalities. We mention them below.

1. The property (10) hold true under the interchange. Also, the properties (15), (16), (17) and (21) hold true.
2. The property (6) holds true under interchange if $BN_R(Y) = \phi$.
3. The properties (1) and (4) hold under interchange under suitable conditions.

Approximate Equalities Using Rough Fuzzy sets

The notion of fuzzy sets was introduced in (Zadeh, 1965) as a model to capture uncertainty in data much before the notion of rough sets being introduced by Pawlak. We provide below a formal definition of this notion.

Definition 11: Let U be a universal set . Then a fuzzy set X defined over U is associated with a

membership function μ_X

defined as follows.

$$\mu_X : U \to [0,1], \tag{4}$$

such that for every $x \in U, \mu_X(x) \in [0,1]$.

That is every x is associated with a membership value, which is a real number in the interval [0, 1].

In the beginning, when rough set was introduced in (Pawlak. 1982), it was supposed to be a rival theory to that of fuzzy sets. However, it was pointed out in (Dubois and Prade, 1990) that far from the apprehension, these two theories are complementary to each other. In fact, they introduced the hybrid models of rough fuzzy sets and fuzzy rough sets. In the next section we shall define rough fuzzy sets and use it to define various types of approximate equalities of fuzzy sets using rough sets.

Rough Fuzzy Sets

It was established in (Dubois and Prade, 1990) that instead of being rival theories, the two theories of fuzzy sets and rough sets complement each other. In fact they combined these two concepts to develop the hybrid models of fuzzy rough sets and rough fuzzy sets. Rough fuzzy sets are defined as follows.

Definition 12: Let (U, R) be an approximation space and U/R = { $X_1, X_2, ... X_n$ }. Then for any X ∈ F(U), $\underline{R}X$ and $\overline{R}X$, the lower and upper approximations of X with respect to R are fuzzy sets in U/R. That is,

$$\underline{R}X, \overline{R}X : U / R \rightarrow [0,1],$$

such that:

$$\underline{R}X(X_j) = \inf_{y \in X_j} X(y)$$

$$\overline{R}X(X_j) = \sup_{y \in X_j} X(y)$$

for all j = 1, 2,... n. The pair $(\underline{R}X, \overline{R}X)$ is called a rough fuzzy set associated with X.

Definition 13: Let (U, R) be an approximation space and U/R = { $X_1, X_2, ... X_n$ }. Then for any X ∈ F(U), we define

$$(\underline{R}X)_F, (\overline{R}X)_F : U \rightarrow [0,1]$$

such that for any

$$x \in X_i, i = 1, 2, ... n$$

we have

$$(\underline{R}X)_F(x) = (\underline{R}X)(X_i)$$

$$(\overline{R}X)_F(x) = (\overline{R}X)(X_i)$$

These fuzzy sets, associated with the lower and upper approximations of a fuzzy set are such that they have constant membership value over each granule X_i induced by R on U.

Approximate Equalities Using Rough Fuzzy Sets

Following the four types of approximate equalities, we can define four types of generalised approximate equalities depending upon rough approximation of fuzzy sets as follows.

Here, we take X and Y to be fuzzy sets. $\underline{R}X$ and $\underline{R}Y$ are the lower approximations of X and Y. $\overline{R}X$ and $\overline{R}Y$ are the upper approximations of X and Y respectively. For any fuzzy set A, we denote the $\alpha - cut$ of A by A_α and it consists of elements of U having membership value greater than α. When $\alpha = 0$, we obtain the support set of A, denoted by $A_{>0}$. Since the $\alpha - cut$ of a fuzzy set is a crisp set, the equalities in the table below are crisp set equalities.

Let T(i, j) ; i = 1, 2 and j = 1,2 denote the (i, j)th position in the above table. When X and Y are crisp sets, the concepts in Table 2 reduce to the corresponding concepts in Table 1. Since α is a real number lying in [0, 1], we get infinitely many levels of equalities under each of the four categories in Table 1.

Table 1. Approximate rough equalities

Lower Approximation	Upper Approximation	
	U1	**U2**
L1	Rough Equalities	Approximate Rough Equalities
L2	Approximate Rough Equivalence	Rough Equivalence

Table 2. Approximate rough fuzzy equalities

Lower Approximation	Upper Approximation	
	$(\overline{RX})_\alpha = (\overline{RY})_\alpha$	$(\overline{RX})_\alpha$ and $(\overline{RY})_\alpha$ are U or not U together
$(\underline{RX})_\alpha = (\underline{RY})_\alpha$	α − Rough Fuzzy Equality	α − Approximate Rough Fuzzy Equality
$(\underline{RX})_\alpha$ and $(\underline{RY})_\alpha$ are ϕ or not ϕ together	α − Approximate Rough Fuzzy Equivalence	α − Rough Fuzzy Equivalence

Examples

In this section we provide examples to illustrate the relative efficiencies of the four types of approximate equalities of fuzzy sets introduced in the above section.

Example3

We illustrate here with one example, the applicability and relative efficiency of the four approximate equalities of fuzzy sets. Let U =

$\{x_1, x_2, x_3, x_4, x_5, x_6, x_7, x_8\}$

R be an equivalence relation on U such that U/R =

$\{\{x_1, x_2\}, \{x_3, x_4, x_5, x_6\}, \{x_7, x_8\}\}$,

$X = \{(x_1, 0.2), (x_2, 0.8), (x_3, 0.7),$
$(x_4, 0.4), (x_5, 0.6), (x_6, 0), (x_7, 1), (x_8, 0)\}$ *and*
$Y = \{(x_1, 0), (x_2, 0.7), (x_3, 0.9), (x_4, 0.6),$
$(x_5, 0.4), (x_6, 0.2), (x_7, 0.8), (x_8, 0.8)\}$

be two fuzzy sets defined over U. Then we have,

$\underline{RX} = \{(x_1, 0.2), (x_2, 0.2), (x_3, 0),$
$(x_4, 0), (x_5, 0), (x_6, 0), (x_7, 0), (x_8, 0)\}$

So,

$(\underline{RX})_{>0} = \{x_1, x_2\} \neq \phi.$

$\underline{RY} = \{(x_1, 0), (x_2, 0), (x_3, 0.2), (x_4, 0.2),$
$(x_5, 0.2), (x_6, 0.2), (x_7, 0.3), (x_8, 0.3)\}. So,$

$(\underline{RY})_{>0} = \{x_3, x_4, x_5, x_6, x_7, x_8\} \neq \phi.$

$X^C = \{(x_1, 0.8), (x_2, 0.2), (x_3, 0.3),$
$(x_4, 0.6), (x_5, 0.4), (x_6, 1), (x_7, 0), (x_8, 1)\}$

$\underline{RX}^C = \{(x_1, 0.2), (x_2, 0.2), (x_3, 0.3),$
$(x_4, 0.3), (x_5, 0.3), (x_6, 0.3), (x_7, 0), (x_8, 0)\}$
$\overline{RX} = \{(x_1, 0.8), (x_2, 0.8), (x_3, 0.7),$
$(x_4, 0.7), (x_5, 0.7), (x_6, 0.7), (x_7, 1), (x_8, 1)\}$
$(\overline{RX})_{>0} = \{x_1, x_2, x_3, x_4, x_5, x_6, x_7, x_8\} = U.$

$Y^C = \{(x_1, 1), (x_2, 0.3), (x_3, 0.1), (x_4, 0.4),$
$(x_5, 0.6), (x_6, 0.8), (x_7, 0.2), (x_8, 0.7)\}$
$\underline{RY}^C = \{(x_1, 0.3), (x_2, 0.3), (x_3, 0.1), (x_4, 0.1),$
$(x_5, 0.1), (x_6, 0.1), (x_7, 0.2), (x_8, 0.2)\}$
$\overline{RY} = \{(x_1, 0.7), (x_2, 0.7), (x_3, 0.9), (x_4, 0.9),$
$(x_5, 0.9), (x_6, 0.9), (x_7, 0.8), (x_8, 0.8)\}$
$(\overline{RY})_{>0} = \{x_1, x_2, x_3, x_4, x_5, x_6, x_7, x_8\} = U.$

We find that the two fuzzy sets are similar to each other in the sense that the membership values of the elements in the two sets differ by very small numbers. Still these are neither rough fuzzy equal nor approximately rough fuzzy equal. But these two are approximately rough fuzzy equivalent and rough fuzzy equivalent. So, the last two notions are more realistic than the earlier two.

Example 4

Let us modify example 4.3.1 slightly by taking

$$X = \{(x_1, 0), (x_2, 0), (x_3, 0.7), (x_4, 0.4),$$
$$(x_5, 0.6), (x_6, 0.2), (x_7, 1), (x_8, 0)\} and$$
$$Y = \{(x_1, 0.2), (x_2, 0.2), (x_3, 0.9), (x_4, 0.6),$$
$$(x_5, 0.2), (x_6, 1), (x_7, 0), (x_8, 0)\}$$

Then we have,

$$\underline{R}X = \{(x_1, 0), (x_2, 0), (x_3, 0.2), (x_4, 0.2),$$
$$(x_5, 0.2), (x_6, 0.2), (x_7, 0), (x_8, 0)\}$$

So,

$$(\underline{R}X)_{>0} = \{x_3, x_4, x_5, x_6\} \neq \phi.$$

$$\underline{R}Y = \{(x_1, 0.2), (x_2, 0.2), (x_3, 0.2), (x_4, 0.2),$$
$$(x_5, 0.2), (x_6, 0.2), (x_7, 0), (x_8, 0)\}.$$

$$So, (\underline{R}Y)_{>0} = \{x_1, x_2, x_3, x_4, x_5, x_6\} \neq \phi.$$

$$X^C = \{(x_1, 1), (x_2, 1), (x_3, 0.3), (x_4, 0.6),$$
$$(x_5, 0.4), (x_6, 0.8), (x_7, 0), (x_8, 1)\}$$

$$\underline{R}X^C = \{(x_1, 1), (x_2, 1), (x_3, 0.3), (x_4, 0.3),$$
$$(x_5, 0.3), (x_6, 0.3), (x_7, 0), (x_8, 0)\}$$
$$\overline{R}X = \{(x_1, 0), (x_2, 0), (x_3, 0.7), (x_4, 0.7),$$
$$(x_5, 0.7), (x_6, 0.7), (x_7, 1), (x_8, 1)\}$$
$$(\overline{R}X)_{>0} = \{x_3, x_4, x_5, x_6, x_7, x_8\} \neq U.$$

$$Y^C = \{(x_1, 0.8), (x_2, 0.8), (x_3, 0.1),$$
$$(x_4, 0.4), (x_5, 0.2), (x_6, 0), (x_7, 1), (x_8, 1)\}$$
$$\underline{R}Y^C = \{(x_1, 0.8), (x_2, 0.8), (x_3, 0), (x_4, 0),$$
$$(x_5, 0), (x_6, 0), (x_7, 1), (x_8, 1)\}$$
$$\overline{R}Y = \{(x_1, 0.2), (x_2, 0.2), (x_3, 1), (x_4, 1),$$
$$(x_5, 1), (x_6, 1), (x_7, 0), (x_8, 0)\}$$
$$(\overline{R}Y)_{>0} = \{x_1, x_2, x_3, x_4, x_5, x_6\} \neq U.$$

We find that the two fuzzy sets differ much in the membership values of their elements, particularly for the elements x_6 and x_7. Still the two sets are rough fuzzy equivalent as per definition. This is the flexibility provided by this characterization in the upper approximation. But, as $\overline{R}X \neq \overline{R}Y$, the two fuzzy sets are not approximately rough fuzzy equivalent. So, once again we conclude that approximate rough fuzzy equivalence is more realistic than the other three types of approximate equivalences.

Comparison of Approximate Rough Fuzzy Equalities

1. The condition that two fuzzy sets are lower approximately equal if and only if the two sets have the same $\alpha -$ support set of lower approximation is satisfied in only those rare and restricted cases where the members have

same membership values from and after α. Since we are using this property in case of both rough fuzzy equal and approximately rough fuzzy equal definitions, these two cases of rough fuzzy equalities seem to have lesser utility than the corresponding rough fuzzy equivalences

2. The condition that the two upper approximations be equal provides freedom to define equality in a very approximate sense and is quite general than these two being equal to U or not simultaneously. As illustrated in the above examples, the later restriction sometimes seems to be less unconvincing.

3. The concept of approximate rough fuzzy equivalence is neither unconvincing nor unnatural. This is the most natural and best among the four types as provided through examples 4.1 and 4.2 above.

4. The fourth type of approximate rough fuzzy equality happens to be the worst among the four types of approximate equalities considered.

Properties of Approximate Equalities of Fuzzy Sets

Properties similar to the basic properties rough sets hold true for fuzzy rough sets. The following four of these properties are to be used by us in establishing the properties of approximate equalities of fuzzy sets.

Let R be an equivalence relation defined over U and X, Y ∈ F(U). Then

$$\underline{R}(X \cap Y) = \underline{R}(X) \cap \underline{R}(Y) \tag{5}$$

$$\underline{R}(X \cup Y) \supseteq \underline{R}(X) \cup \underline{R}(Y) \tag{6}$$

$$\overline{R}(X \cap Y) \subseteq \overline{R}(X) \cap \overline{R}(Y) \tag{7}$$

$$\overline{R}(X \cup Y) = \overline{R}(X) \cup \overline{R}(Y) \tag{8}$$

General Properties

The definitions of bottom-inclusion, top R-inclusion and R-inclusion for crisp sets can be extended in a natural way to fuzzy sets as follows.

Definition 14: Let R be an equivalence relation defined on U and X, Y ∈ F(U). Then

1. We say that X is bottom (R, α)-included in Y ($X \subseteqq_{R,\alpha} Y$) if and only if

$$(\underline{R}X)_\alpha \subseteq (\underline{R}Y)_\alpha$$

2. We say that X is top (R, α)-included in Y $\left(X \tilde{\subset}_{R,\alpha} Y \right)$ if and only if

$$(\overline{R}X)_\alpha \subseteq (\overline{R}Y)_\alpha.$$

3. We say that X is (R, α)-included in Y $\left(X \tilde{\subseteqq}_{R,\alpha} Y \right)$ if and only if $X \subseteqq_{R,\alpha} Y$ and $X \tilde{\subset}_{R,\alpha} Y$

Definition 15:

1. We say X, Y ∈ F(U) are α − bottom rough comparable if and only if $X \subseteqq_{R,\alpha} Y$ or $Y \subseteqq_{R,\alpha} X$ holds.

2. We say X, Y ∈ F(U) are α − top rough comparable if and only if $X \tilde{\subset}_{R,\alpha} Y$ or $Y \tilde{\subset}_{R,\alpha} X$ holds.

3. We say X, Y $\in$ F(U) are α – rough comparable if and only if X and Y are both top and bottom rough α – comparable.

Definition 16: We say that two fuzzy sets X and Y are α – bottom (rough equal/approximately rough equal, rough equivalent/approximately rough equivalent) if and only if:

$$(\underline{R}X)_\alpha = (\underline{R}Y)_\alpha$$

$(\underline{R}X)_\pm$ and $(\underline{R}Y)_\pm$

are equal to Æor not equal to Ætogether

Definition 17: We say that two fuzzy sets X and Y are α – top (rough equal/approximately rough equal, rough equivalent/approximately rough equivalent) if and only if:

$$(\overline{RX})_\alpha = (\overline{RY})_\alpha,$$

$(\underline{R}X)_\pm$ and $(\underline{R}Y)_\pm$

are equal to U or not equal to U together

We state below the properties of some of the four types of approximate α – rough fuzzy equalities below without proof. The proofs are similar to the approximate rough equality cases (Tripathy, 2011).

Property 23:

1. If $X \cap Y$ is α – b_eqv. to both X and Y then X is α – b_eqv. to Y
2. The converse of 1 is not true in general and an additional condition that is sufficient but not necessary for the converse to be true is that X and Y are α – bottom rough comparable.

Property 24:

1. If $X \cup Y$ is α – t_eqv. to both X and Y then X is α – t_eqv. to Y.
3. The converse of 1 is not true in general and an additional condition that is sufficient but not necessary for the converse to be true is that X and Y are top α – rough comparable.

Property 25:

1. If X is α – t_eqv. to X' and Y is α – t_eqv. to Y' then it may or may not be true that $X \cup Y$ is α – t_eqv. to $X' \cup Y'$.
2. A sufficient but not necessary condition for the result in 1 to be true is that X and Y are α – top rough comparable and X' and Y' are α – top rough comparable.

Property 26:

1. X is α – b_eqv. to X' and Y is α – b_eqv. to Y' may or may not imply that $X \cap Y$ is α – b_eqv. to $X' \cap Y'$
2. A sufficient but not necessary condition for the result in (i) to be true is that X and Y are α – bottom rough comparable and X' and Y' are α – bottom rough comparable.

Property 27:

1. X is α – t_eqv. to Y may or may not imply that $X \cup (-Y)$ is α – t_eqv. to U.
2. A sufficient but not necessary condition for result in (i) to hold is that $X = Y$.

Property 28:

1. X is α – b_eqv. to Y may not imply that $X \cap (-Y)$ is α – b_eqv. to ϕ.
2. A sufficient but not necessary condition for the result in (i) to hold true is that $X \simeq Y$.

Property 29: If $X \subseteq Y$ and Y is $\alpha - $b_eqv. to ϕ then X is $\alpha - $ b_eqv. to ϕ.

Property 30: If $X \subseteq Y$ and X is t_eqv. to U then Y is t_eqv. to U.

Property 31: X is $\alpha - $t_eqv. to Y if and only if $-X$ is $\alpha - $b_eqv. to $-Y$.

Property 32: X is $\alpha - $b_eqv. to ϕ, Y is b_eqv. to $\phi \Rightarrow X \cap Y$ is $\alpha - $b_eqv. to ϕ.

Property 33: If X is $\alpha - $t_eqv. to U or Y is t_eqv. to U then $X \cup Y$ is $\alpha - $t_eqv. to U.

Replacement Properties for Rough Fuzzy Equivalence

In parallel to the properties of interchange for rough equalities, the following properties were proved in (Tripathy, Jhawar and Vats, 2012).

Property 34:

1. If $X \cap Y$ is $\alpha - $t_eqv. to both X and Y then X is $\alpha - $t_eqv. Y.
2. The converse of 1 is not true in general and an additional condition that is sufficient but not necessary for the converse to be true is that equality holds in (3.2.3).

Property 35:

1. $X \cup Y$ is $\alpha - $b_eqv. to X and $X \cup Y$ is $\alpha - $b_eqv. to Y then X is $\alpha - $b_eqv. to Y
2. The converse of 1 is not true in general and an additional condition that is sufficient but not necessary for the converse to be true is that equality holds in (3.2.2).

Property 36:

1. X is $\alpha - $b_eqv. to X' and Y is $\alpha - $b_eqv. to Y' may not imply $X \cup Y$ is $\alpha - $b_eqv. to $X' \cup Y'$.

2. A sufficient but not necessary condition for the conclusion of 1 to hold is that equality holds in (6).

Property 37:

1. X is $\alpha - $t_eqv. to X' and Y is $\alpha - $t_eqv. to Y' may not necessarily imply that $X \cap Y$ is $\alpha - $t_eqv. to $X' \cap Y'$.
2. A sufficient but not necessary condition for the conclusion in (i) to hold is that equality holds in (7).

Property 38: X is $\alpha - $b_eqv. to Y may or may not imply $X \cup -Y$ is $\alpha - $b_eqv. to U.

Property 39: X is $\alpha - $t_eqv. to Y may or may not imply $X \cap -Y$ is $\alpha - $t_eqv. to ϕ.

Properties (29) to (33) hold true under replacements.

Case Studies

In this section we provide two real world examples to illustrate the rough fuzzy approximate equalities.

Example 5: Let us take the universe U as the set of people in a town. We define a relation R over U as two people x and y are R-related to each other iff they belong to the same ward. This relation is clearly an equivalence relation over U and obviously decomposes U into equivalence classes, which are people in individual wards. Based on their literacy status, we define some fuzzy sets over U as "Very Poor", "Poor", "Below Average", "Average", "Above Average", "Good" and "Very Good". Let us consider the uniformity of the distribution of any two strata of people from the above over the wards. Consider for example "Good" and "Average", if the upper approximations of these two fuzzy sets with respect to R are same then they are equally distributed over all the wards containing them. On the other hand if both their upper approximations are U, then these two classes of people are equally distributed over all the wards in the town.

Example 6: Let us consider the financial status of students in undergraduate courses in a state. We define a relation R over U and two students are R-related to each other iff they belong to the same college. This relation is an equivalence relation over the set U and decomposes it into equivalence classes, which are students in individual colleges. Based on their financial status we define some fuzzy sets over U as "Very Bad", "Bad", "Average", "Good" and "Very Good" in the state. These financial statuses can be represented by fuzzy sets using the income of their parents in a year. Here we would like to find the uniform distribution of a particular category of students over different colleges of the state. Suppose we want to find the distribution of students having their financial statuses "Average" and "Good", then we take the upper approximation of these two sets. If these are equal and not equal to U then the distribution is equally uniform over these colleges. If both are equal and each is equal to U then the distribution is equally uniform over all the colleges in the state. If these are not equal then we can say that the distribution is not equally uniform. We can have similar analysis over any pair of these fuzzy sets.

Approximate Equalities Using Rough Intuitionistic Fuzzy Sets

Following the patterns for approximate equalities we can define four types of approximate equalities for intuitionistic fuzzy sets as follows (Tripathy and Panda, 2012).

Here, we take X and Y to be intuitionistic fuzzy sets.

$$\underline{R}X = (M\underline{R}X, N\underline{R}X)$$

and

$$\underline{R}Y = (M\underline{R}Y, N\underline{R}Y)$$

are the lower approximations of X and Y

$$\overline{R}X = (M\overline{R}X, N\overline{R}X)$$

and

$$\overline{R}Y = (M\overline{R}Y, N\overline{R}Y)$$

are the upper approximations of X and Y respectively. Following definition 2.5.2, let the corresponding intuitionistic fuzzy sets on U be

$$(\underline{R}X)_{IF}, (\underline{R}Y)_{IF}, (\overline{R}X)_{IF} \, and \, (\overline{R}Y)_{IF}$$

respectively. For any intuitionistic fuzzy set A, we denote the $(\alpha, \beta) - cut$ of A by

$$A_{\alpha,\beta} = \{x : MA(x) > \alpha \text{ and } NA(x) < \beta\}$$

Note 1: When A is a fuzzy set, we have $NA(x) = 1 - MA(x)$. So, taking $^2 = 1 - \alpha$ we see that $(A)_{\alpha,\beta} = A_{\pm}$. Hence, Table 3 reduces to Table 2. In general, we have two control parameters α and β with the user. Since $(\alpha, \beta) \in J$, we have infinite number of ways to talk about the approximate equalities of two intuitionistic fuzzy sets under four major categories in Table 3. Further, when $\pm = 0$ we get the rough equalities for crisp sets. Since the $(\alpha, \beta) - cut$ of an intuitionistic fuzzy set is a crisp set, the equalities in the table below are crisp set equalities.

Table 3. Approximate rough intuitionistic fuzzy equalities

Lower Approximation	Upper Approximation	
	$((\overline{R}X)_{IF})_{\alpha,\beta} = ((\overline{R}\,Y)_{IF})_{\alpha,\beta}$	$((\overline{R}X)_{IF})_{\alpha,\beta}$ and $((\overline{R}\,Y)_{IF})_{\alpha,\beta}$ Are U or not U together
$((\underline{R}X)_{IF})_{\alpha,\beta} = ((\underline{R}\,Y)_{IF})_{\alpha,\beta}$	(α,β) - Rough Intuitionistic Fuzzy Equality	(α,β) - Approximate Rough Intuitionistic Fuzzy equality
$((\underline{R}X)_{IF})_{\alpha,\beta}$ and $((\underline{R}\,Y)_{IF})_{\alpha,\beta}$ Are ϕ or not ϕ together	(α,β) - Approximate Rough Intuitionistic Fuzzy Equivalence	(α,β) - Rough Intuitionistic Fuzzy Equivalence

A General Analysis of Rough Equalities

In this section we provide a comparative analysis of the four types of rough equalities of intuitionistic fuzzy sets. However, the same analysis is applicable for rough equalities for fuzzy sets as well as rough equalities for crisp sets.

If

$$((\underline{R}X)_{IF})_{\alpha,\beta} = ((\underline{R}Y)_{IF})_{\alpha,\beta}$$

then either both $((\underline{R}X)_{IF})_{\alpha,\beta}$ and $((\underline{R}Y)_{IF})_{\alpha,\beta}$ are equal to ϕ or both are not equal to ϕ. So, (α,β) – Rough Fuzzy Equality is a special case of (α,β) – Approximate Rough Fuzzy Equivalence and (α,β) – Approximate Rough Fuzzy Equality is a special case of (α,β) – Rough Fuzzy Equivalence. Similarly, if

$$((\overline{R}X)_{IF})_{\alpha,\beta} = ((\overline{R}Y)_{IF})_{\alpha,\beta}$$

then either $((\overline{R}X)_{IF})_{\alpha,\beta}$ and $((\overline{R}Y)_{IF})_{\alpha,\beta}$ are both equal to U or both not equal to U. So, (α,β) –

Rough Fuzzy Equality is a special case of (α,β) – Approximate Rough Fuzzy Equality and (α,β) – Approximate Rough Fuzzy Equivalence is a special case of (α,β) – Rough Fuzzy Equivalence.

2.   So, it is very clear that (α,β) – Rough Fuzzy Equality is a special case of all the other three types of rough intuitionistic fuzzy approximate equalities and (α,β) – Rough Fuzzy Equivalence is a generalization of all the other three types of rough intuitionistic fuzzy approximate equalities.

3.   However, we cannot have a scale of the four types of rough intuitionistic fuzzy approximate equalities as the two types (α,β) – Approximate Rough Fuzzy Equality and (α,β) – Approximate Rough Fuzzy Equivalence have no comparison in general.

4.   The analysis in the above three cases is applicable to all the special cases, that is for rough fuzzy approximate equality and rough approximate equality.

We can represent the above analysis in the diagram shown in Figure 1 (Here the arrows represent implication).

Figure 1. Relationship among approximate rough fuzzy equalities

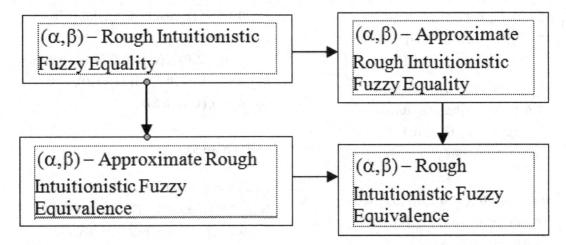

Examples

We illustrate here with one example, the applicability and relative efficiency of the four approximate equalities of intuitionistic fuzzy sets.

Example 7: Let U =

$$\{x_1, x_2, x_3, x_4, x_5, x_6, x_7, x_8\}$$

R be an equivalence relation on U such that U/R =

$$\{\{x_1, x_2\}, \{x_3, x_4, x_5, x_6\}, \{x_7, x_8\}\},$$

$X = \{(x_1, 0.2, 0.7), (x_2, 0.8, 0.1),$
$(x_3, 0.7, 0.2), (x_4, 0.4, 0.4), (x_5, 0.6, 0.3),$
$(x_6, 0, 0.8), (x_7, 1, 0), (x_8, 0.7, 0.2)\}$ *and*
$Y = \{(x_1, 0, 0.8), (x_2, 0.7, 0.2), (x_3, 0.9, 0),$
$(x_4, 0.6, 0.2), (x_5, 0.4, 0.4), (x_6, 0.2, 0.7),$
$(x_7, 0.8, 0.1), (x_8, 0.8, 0.1)\}$

be two fuzzy sets defined over U. Then we have,

$(\underline{R}X)_{IF} = \{(x_1, 0.2, 0.7), (x_2, 0.2, 0.7),$
$(x_3, 0, 0.8), (x_4, 0, 0.8), (x_5, 0, 0.8), (x_6, 0, 0.8),$
$(x_7, 0.7, 0.2), (x_8, 0.7, 0.2)\}$

So, taking

$\alpha = 0.1, \beta = 0.8,$

we find that

$((\underline{R}X)_{IF})_{\alpha,\beta} = \{x_1, x_2\} \neq \phi.$

$(\underline{R}Y)_{IF} = \{(x_1, 0, 0.8), (x_2, 0, 0.8),$
$(x_3, 0.2, 0.7), (x_4, 0.2), (x_5, 0.2, 0.7),$
$(x_6, 0.2, 0.7), (x_7, 0.8, 0.1), (x_8, 0.8, 0.1)\}.$

So, $((\underline{R}Y)_{IF})_{\alpha,\beta} =$
$\{x_3, x_4, x_5, x_6, x_7, x_8\} \neq \phi$

$X^C = \{(x_1, 0.7, 0.2), (x_2, 0.1, 0.8),$
$(x_3, 0.2, 0.7), (x_4, 0.4, 0.4), (x_5, 0.3, 0.6),$
$(x_6, 0.8, 0), (x_7, 0, 1), (x_8, 0.2, 0.7)\}$

$(\underline{R}X^C)_{IF} = \{(x_1, 0.1, 0.8), (x_2, 0.1, 0.8),$
$(x_3, 0.2, 0.7), (x_4, 0.2, 0.7), (x_5, 0.2, 0.7),$
$(x_6, 0.2, 0.7), (x_7, 0, 1), (x_8, 0, 1)\}$

$((\overline{RX})_{IF} = \{(x_1, 0.8, 0.1), (x_2, 0.8, 0.1),$
$(x_3, 0.7, 0.2), (x_4, 0.7, 0.2), (x_5, 0.7, 0.2),$
$(x_6, 0.7, 0.2), (x_7, 1, 0), (x_8, 1, 0)\}$
$((RX)_{IF})_{\alpha,\beta} = \{x_1, x_2, x_3, x_4, x_5, x_6, x_7, x_8\} = U.$

$Y^C = \{(x_1, 0.8, 0), (x_2, 0.2, 0.7), (x_3, 0, 0.9),$
$(x_4, 0.2, 0.6), (x_5, 0.4, 0.4), (x_6, 0.7, 0.2),$
$(x_7, 0.1, 0.8), (x_8, 0.1, 0.8)\}$
$(\underline{R}Y^C)_{IF} = \{(x_1, 0.2, 0.7), (x_2, 0.2, 0.7),$
$(x_3, 0, 0.9), (x_4, 0, 0.9), (x_5, 0, 0.9),$
$(x_6, 0, 0.9), (x_7, 0.1, 0.8), (x_8, 0.1, 0.8)\}$
$(\overline{RY})_{IF} = \{(x_1, 0.7, 0.2), (x_2, 0.7, 0.2),$
$(x_3, 0.9, 0), (x_4, 0.9, 0), (x_5, 0.9, 0),$
$(x_6, 0.9, 0), (x_7, 0.8, 0.1), (x_8, 0.8, 0.1)\}$
$((RY)_{IF})_{\alpha,\beta} = \{x_1, x_2, x_3, x_4, x_5, x_6, x_7, x_8\} = U.$

Analysis 1: The two intuitionistic fuzzy sets are similar to each other in the sense of membership and non-membership values and we see that with the levels 0.1 and 0.8. These two intuitionistic fuzzy sets are neither rough intuitionistic fuzzy equal nor approximately rough intuitionistic fuzzy equal. But they are approximate rough intuitionistic fuzzy equivalent and rough intuitionistic fuzzy equivalent. So, the last two notions are more realistic than the other two.

Example 8:

Let us modify example 3.1 slightly by taking

$X = \{(x_1, 0, 0.8), (x_2, 0, 0.8), (x_3, 0.7, 0.2),$
$(x_4, 0.4, 0.4), (x_5, 0.6, 0.3), (x_6, 0.2, 0.7),$
$(x_7, 1, 0), (x_8, 0, 0.8)\}$ and
$Y = \{(x_1, 0.2, 0.6), (x_2, 0.2, 0.6), (x_3, 0.9, 0),$
$(x_4, 0.6, 0.2), (x_5, 0.2, 0.6), (x_6, 1, 0),$
$(x_7, 0, 0.9), (x_8, 0, 0.8)\}$

Then we have,

$(\underline{R}X)_{IF} = \{(x_1, 0, 0.8), (x_2, 0, 0.8),$
$(x_3, 0.2, 0.7), (x_4, 0.2, 0.7), (x_5, 0.2, 0.7),$
$(x_6, 0.2, 0.7), (x_7, 0, 0.8), (x_8, 0, 0.8)\}$

So, taking $\alpha = 0.1$ and $\beta = 0.8$,

we have $((\underline{R}X)_{IF})_{\alpha,\beta} =$
$\{x_3, x_4, x_5, x_6\} \neq \phi.$

$(\underline{R}Y)_{IF} = \{(x_1, 0.2, 0.6), (x_2, 0.2, 0.6),$
$(x_3, 0.2, 0.6), (x_4, 0.2, 0.6), (x_5, 0.2, 0.6),$
$(x_6, 0.2, 0.6), (x_7, 0, 0.9), (x_8, 0, 0.9)\}.$
So, $((\underline{R}Y)_{IF})_{\alpha,\beta} = \{x_1, x_2, x_3, x_4, x_5, x_6\} \neq \phi.$

$X^C = \{(x_1, 0.8, 0), (x_2, 0.8, 0), (x_3, 0.2, 0.7),$
$(x_4, 0.4, 0.4), (x_5, 0.3, 0.6), (x_6, 0.7, 0.2),$
$(x_7, 0, 1), (x_8, 0.8, 0)\}$

$(\underline{R}X^C)_{IF} = \{(x_1, 0.8, 0), (x_2, 0.8, 0),$
$(x_3, 0.2. 0.7), (x_4, 0.2, 0.7), (x_5, 0.2, 0.7),$
$(x_6, 0.2, 0.7), (x_7, 0, 1), (x_8, 0, 1)\}$
$(\overline{RX})_{IF} = \{(x_1, 0, 0.8), (x_2, 0, 0.8),$
$(x_3, 0.7, 0.2), (x_4, 0.7, 0.2), (x_5, 0.7, 0.2),$
$(x_6, 0.7, 0.2), (x_7, 1, 0), (x_8, 1, 0)\}$
$((RX)_{IF})_{\alpha,\beta} = \{x_3, x_4, x_5, x_6, x_7, x_8\} \neq U.$

$Y^C = \{(x_1, 0.6, 0.2), (x_2, 0.6, 0.2), (x_3, 0, 0.9),$

$(x_4, 0.2, 0.6), (x_5, 0.6, 0.2), (x_6, 0, 1),$

$(x_7, 0.9, 0), (x_8, 0.8, 0)\}$

$(\underline{R}Y^C)_{IF} = \{(x_1, 0.6, 0.2), (x_2, 0.6, 0.2),$
$(x_3, 0, 1), (x_4, 0, 1), (x_5, 0, 1), (x_6, 0, 1),$
$(x_7, 0.8, 0), (x_8, 0.8, 0)\}$

$(\overline{R}Y)_{IF} = \{(x_1, 0.2, 0.6), (x_2, 0.2, 0.6),$
$(x_3, 1, 0), (x_4, 1, 0), (x_5, 1, 0), (x_6, 1, 0),$
$(x_7, 0, 0.8), (x_8, 0, 0.8)\}$

$((\overline{R}Y)_{IF})_{\alpha,\beta} = \{x_1, x_2, x_3, x_4, x_5, x_6\} \neq U.$

Also,

$N(\underline{R}(X \cap Y))_{IF}(u) =$
$\underset{y \in [u]_R}{\sup}\ N(X \cap Y)(y) =$
$\underset{y \in [u]_R}{\sup}\ \max\{NX(y), NY(y)\}$
$= \max\{\underset{y \in [u]_R}{\sup}\ NX(y),$
$\underset{y \in [u]_R}{\sup}\ NY(y)\} =$
$\max\{N(\underline{R}X)_{IF}(u), N(\underline{R}Y)_{IF}(u)\} =$
$N(\underline{R}X \cap \underline{R}Y)_{IF}(u).$
So, $(N(\underline{R}(X \cap Y))_{IF}(u))_{\alpha,\beta} =$
$(N(\underline{R}X \cap \underline{R}Y)_{IF}(u))_{\alpha,\beta}$

Analysis 2: We find that the two intuitionistic fuzzy sets differ much in the membership values of their elements, particularly for the elements x_6 and x_7. Still the two sets are rough intuitionistic fuzzy equivalent as per definition. This is the flexibility provided by this characterization in the upper approximation. But, as

$$(\overline{R}X)_{\alpha,\beta} \neq (\overline{R}Y)_{\alpha,\beta}$$

the two fuzzy sets are not approximately rough intuitionistic fuzzy equivalent. So, once again we conclude that approximate rough intuitionistic fuzzy equivalence is more realistic than the other three types of intuitionistic fuzzy approximate equalities.

Properties of Approximate Equalities of Rough Intuitionistic Fuzzy Sets

Properties similar to the basic properties of rough sets hold true for rough intuitionistic fuzzy sets. The following four properties are to be used by us in establishing the properties of approximate equalities of intuitionistic fuzzy sets.

Let R be an equivalence relation defined over U and $X, Y \in IF(U)$. Then for any $(\pm, ^2) \in J$, we have

$$((\underline{R}(X \cap Y))_{IF})_{\alpha,\beta} = ((\underline{R}(X))_{IF} \cap (\underline{R}(Y))_{IF})_{\alpha,\beta} \tag{9}$$

$$((\underline{R}(X \cup Y))_{IF})_{\alpha,\beta} \supseteq ((\underline{R}(X))_{IF} \cup (\underline{R}(Y))_{IF})_{\alpha,\beta} \tag{10}$$

$$((\overline{R}(X \cap Y))_{IF})_{\alpha,\beta} \subseteq ((\overline{R}(X))_{IF} \cap (\overline{R}(Y))_{IF})_{\alpha,\beta} \tag{11}$$

$$((\overline{R}(X \cup Y))_{IF})_{\alpha,\beta} = ((\overline{R}(X))_{IF} \cup (\overline{R}(Y))_{IF})_{\alpha,\beta} \tag{12}$$

We provide the proofs of (5.3.1) and (5.3.2) only. The other two proofs are similar.

Proof of (9):

For any $u \in U$, we have
$M(\underline{R}(X \cap Y))_{IF}(u) =$
$\underset{y \in [u]_R}{\inf}\ M(X \cap Y)(y) =$
$\underset{y \in [u]_R}{\inf}\ \min\{MX(y), MY(y)\} =$
$\min\{\underset{y \in [u]_R}{\inf}\ MX(y), \underset{y \in [u]_R}{\inf}\ MY(y)\} =$
$\min\{M\underline{R}X(u), M\underline{R}Y(u)\} =$
$M((\underline{R}X \cap \underline{R}Y))_{IF}(u).$
So, $(M(\underline{R}(X \cap Y))_{IF}(u))_{\alpha,\beta} =$
$((M(\underline{R}X \cap \underline{R}Y))_{IF}(u))_{\alpha,\beta}$

Hence (9) holds true.
Proof of (10):

Since $X \subseteq XUY$ and $Y \subseteq$
XUY it follows that $(\underline{R}X)_{IF} \subseteq$
$(\underline{R}(XUY))_{IF}$ and $(\underline{R}Y)_{IF} \subseteq (\underline{R}(XUY))_{IF}$.
Hence, $(\underline{R}X)_{IF} \cup (\underline{R}Y)_{IF} \subseteq (\underline{R}(XUY))_{IF}$.
So, $((\underline{R}X)_{IF} \cup (\underline{R}Y)_{IF})_{\alpha,\beta} \subseteq ((\underline{R}(XUY))_{IF})_{\alpha,\beta}$.

To show that the inclusion can actually be strict we provide one simple example. Here, we are taking

$\beta = 1 - \alpha$ and $\alpha = 0$,

which is enough to establish our claim.

Let $U = \{x_1, x_2, x_3, x_4, x_5\}$
and R be such that $U / R =$
$\{\{x_1, x_2, x_4\}, \{x_3, x_5\}\}$
$X = \{(x_1, 0.1, 0.8), (x_2, 0.5, 0.4), (x_3, 0.4, 0.4),$
$(x_4, 0.2, 0.7), (x_5, 0.6, 0.3)\}$ and
$Y = \{(x_1, 0.3, 0.6), (x_2, 0.2, 0.6), (x_3, 0.6, 0.3),$
$(x_4, 0.7, 0.2), (x_5, 0.9, 0.1)\}$.

$M(\underline{R}(XUY))_{IF}(x_4) =$
$M(\underline{R}(XUY))_{IF}(x_2) =$
$M(\underline{R}(XUY))_{IF}(x_1) =$
$\inf\limits_{y \in [x_1]_R} Max\{MX(y), MY(y)\}$
$= \inf\{\max(0.1, 0.3), \max(0.5, 0.2),$
$\max(0.2, 0.7)\} = \inf\{0.3, 0.5, 0.7\} = 0.3$.

Similarly,

$M(\underline{R}(XUY))_{IF}(x_3) =$
$M(\underline{R}(XUY))_{IF}(x_5) = 0.6$

$N(\underline{R}(XUY))_{IF}(x_4) = N(\underline{R}(XUY))_{IF}(x_2) =$
$N(\underline{R}(XUY))_{IF}(x_1) = \sup\limits_{y \in [x_1]_R} Min\{NX(y), NY(y)\} =$
$\sup\{\min(0.8, 0.6), \min(0.4, 0.6), \min(0.7, 0.2)\} =$
$\sup\{0.6, 0.4, 0.2\} = 0.6$.

Similarly, $N(\underline{R}(XUY))_{IF}(x_3) =$
$N(\underline{R}(XUY))_{IF}(x_5) = 0.3$. So, $(\underline{R}(XUY))_{IF} =$
$\{(x_1, 0.3, 0.6), (x_2, 0.3, 0.6), (x_3, 0.6, 0.3),$
$(x_4, 0.3, 0.6), (x_5, 0.6, 0.3)\}$.

General Properties

The definitions of bottom R-inclusion, top R-inclusion and R-inclusion for crisp sets and fuzzy sets can be extended in a natural way to intuitionistic fuzzy sets as follows.

Definition 18: Let R be an equivalence relation defined on U and X, Y $\in$ IF(U). Then

1. We say that X is bottom (R, α, β)-included in Y

$$\left(X \subseteq_{(R,\alpha,\beta)} Y\right)$$

if and only if

$$((\underline{R}X)_{IF})_{\alpha,\beta} \subseteq ((\underline{R}Y)_{IF})_{\alpha,\beta}$$

2. We say that X is top (R, α, β)-included in Y

$$\left(X \tilde{\subseteq}_{(R,\alpha,\beta)} Y\right)$$

if and only if

$$\left((\overline{R}X)_{IF}\right)_{\alpha,\beta} \subseteq \left((\overline{R}Y)_{IF}\right)_{\alpha,\beta}.$$

3. We say that X is (R, α, β)-included in Y

$$\left(X \; \tilde{\subseteq}_{(R,\alpha,\beta)} \; Y\right)$$

if and only if $X \subsetneq_{R,\alpha,\beta} Y$ and $X \; \tilde{\subset}_{R,\alpha,\beta} \; Y$

Definition 19:

1. We say $X, Y \in IF(U)$ are (α, β) − bottom rough comparable if and only if $X \subsetneq_{R,\alpha,\beta} Y$ or $Y \subsetneq_{R,\alpha,\beta} X$ holds.

2. We say $X, Y \in IF(U)$ are (α, β) − top rough comparable if and only if $X \; \tilde{\subset}_{R,\alpha,\beta} \; Y$ or $Y \; \tilde{\subset}_{R,\alpha,\beta} \; X$ holds.

3. We say $X, Y \in IF(U)$ are (α, β) − rough comparable if and only if X and Y are both top and bottom rough (α, β) − comparable.

4. We say $X, Y \in IF(U)$ are (α, β) − rough comparable if and only if X and Y are both top and bottom rough (α, β) − comparable.

Definition 20: We say that two intuitionistic fuzzy sets X and Y are (α, β) − bottom (rough equal/approximately rough equal, rough equivalent / approximately rough equivalent) if and only if

$$\left((\underline{R}X)_{IF}\right)_{\alpha,\beta} = \left((\underline{R}Y)_{IF}\right)_{\alpha,\beta},$$

$$\left((\underline{R}X)_{IF}\right)_{\alpha,\beta} \text{ and } \left((\underline{R}Y)_{IF}\right)_{\alpha,\beta}$$

are equal to φ or not equal to φ together.

Definition 21: We say that two intuitionistic fuzzy sets X and Y are (α, β) − top (rough equal/ approximately rough equal, rough equivalent/approximately rough equivalent) if and only if

$$\left((\overline{R}X)_{IF}\right)_{\alpha,\beta} = \left((\overline{R}Y)_{IF}\right)_{\alpha,\beta},$$

$$\left((\underline{R}X)_{IF}\right)_{\alpha,\beta} \text{ and } \left((\underline{R}Y)_{IF}\right)_{\alpha,\beta}$$

are equal to U or not equal to U together). We state below the properties of some of the four types of approximate (α, β) − rough fuzzy equalities below without proof. The proofs are similar to the approximate rough equality cases [20].

In the properties below, we use A is (α, β) - bottom related to B to mean either

$$\left((\underline{R}A)_{IF}\right)_{\alpha,\beta} = \left((\underline{R}B)_{IF}\right)_{\alpha,\beta}$$

or

$$\left((\underline{R}A)_{IF}\right)_{\alpha,\beta} \text{ and } \left((\underline{R}B)_{IF}\right)_{\alpha,\beta}$$

are ϕ or not ϕ together.

Also, we use A is (α, β) - top related to B to mean that either

$$\left((\overline{R}A)_{IF}\right)_{\alpha,\beta} = \left((\overline{R}B)_{IF}\right)_{\alpha,\beta}$$

or $\left((\overline{R}A)_{IF}\right)_{\alpha,\beta}$ and $\left((\overline{R}B)_{IF}\right)_{\alpha,\beta}$

are U or not U together.

Property 40:

If $X \cap Y$ is

(α, β) - bottom related

to both X and Y then X is

(α, β) - bottom related to Y.

2. The converse of (1) is not true in general and an additional condition that is sufficient but not necessary for the converse to be true is that X and Y are (α, β) – bottom rough comparable.

Proof

There are two cases.

Case 1:

If $(\underline{R}(X \cap Y)_{IF})_{\alpha,\beta} = ((\underline{R}X)_{IF})_{\alpha,\beta}$
and $(\underline{R}(X \cap Y)_{IF})_{\alpha,\beta} = ((\underline{R}Y)_{IF})_{\alpha,\beta}$
then $((\underline{R}X)_{IF})_{\alpha,\beta} = ((\underline{R}Y)_{IF})_{\alpha,\beta}$.
Then the proof follows.

Case 2:

If $(\underline{R}(X \cap Y)_{IF})_{\alpha,\beta}$ and $((\underline{R}X)_{IF})_{\alpha,\beta}$
are ϕ or ($\neq \phi$) together then and
$(\underline{R}(X \cap Y)_{IF})_{\alpha,\beta}$ and $((\underline{R}Y)_{IF})_{\alpha,\beta}$ are ϕ or ($\neq \phi$)
together respectively. So that $((\underline{R}X)_{IF})_{\alpha,\beta}$
and $((\underline{R}Y)_{IF})_{\alpha,\beta}$ are ϕ or ($\neq \phi$) together.
Hence the proof follows.

Conversely,

If $((\underline{R}X)_{IF})_{\alpha,\beta} = ((\underline{R}Y)_{IF})_{\alpha,\beta}$ then by
(9) $((\underline{R}(X \cap Y))_{IF})_{\alpha,\beta} =$
$((\underline{R}X)_{IF})_{\alpha,\beta} \cap ((\underline{R}Y)_{IF})_{\alpha,\beta}$
$= ((\underline{R}X)_{IF})_{\alpha,\beta} = ((\underline{R}Y)_{IF})_{\alpha,\beta}$.
So, the proof follows.

Next, if $(\underline{R}X)_{\alpha,\beta}$ and $(\underline{R}Y)_{\alpha,\beta}$ are both ϕ
then $(\underline{R}(X \cap Y))_{\alpha,\beta} = (\underline{R}X)_{\alpha,\beta} \cap (\underline{R}Y)_{\alpha,\beta} =$
ϕ. So, the converse is true. However, if
both $(\underline{R}X)_{\alpha,\beta}$ and $(\underline{R}Y)_{\alpha,\beta}$ are not equal to ϕ
then $(\underline{R}(X \cap Y))_{\alpha,\beta}$ may be ϕ. So that the
result may not be true. In addition, if
$(\underline{R}X)_{\alpha,\beta}$ and $(\underline{R}Y)_{\alpha,\beta}$ are bottom (α, β)
- comparable then $(\underline{R}(X \cap Y))_{\alpha,\beta} =$
$(\underline{R}X)_{\alpha,\beta}$ or $(\underline{R}Y)_{\alpha,\beta}$ as the case may be.
So, it is also not ϕ and the proof follows.

Property 41:

1. If $X \cup Y$ is (α, β) - top related to both X and Y then X is (α, β) - top related to Y.

2. The converse of 1 is not true in general and an additional condition that is sufficient but not necessary for the converse to be true is that X and Y are top (α, β) – rough comparable.

●   **Proof:** Similar to that of property 40.

Property 42:

1, If X is

(α, β) - top related

to X' and Y is

(α, β) - top related

to Y' then it may or may not be true that $X \cup Y$ is

(α, β) - top related $X' \cup Y'$.

2. A sufficient but not necessary condition for the result in 1 to be true is that X and Y are

(α, β) – top rough comparable and X' and Y' are (α, β) – top rough comparable.

Proof

Proof of 1: There are two cases

Case 1:

Suppose $((\overline{RX})_{IF})_{\alpha,\beta} = ((\overline{RX}')_{IF})_{\alpha,\beta}$ and $((\overline{RY})_{IF})_{\alpha,\beta} = ((\overline{RY}')_{IF})_{\alpha,\beta}$. Then using (12), it follows that $((R(X \cup Y))_{IF})_{\alpha,\beta} = ((R(X' \cup Y'))_{IF})_{\alpha,\beta}$.

Case 2:

Suppose both $((\overline{RX})_{IF})_{\alpha,\beta}, ((\overline{RX}')_{IF})_{\alpha,\beta}$ and $((\overline{RY})_{IF})_{\alpha,\beta}, ((\overline{RY}')_{IF})_{\alpha,\beta}$ are U or not U together then

it may happen that one of $((\overline{R(XUY)})_{IF})_{\alpha,\beta}$ and $((\overline{R(X'UY')})_{IF})_{\alpha,\beta}$ is U and the other one is not U.

So that the equality does not hold.
Proof of 2:

But, if X and Y are (α, β) - top rough comparable and X' and Y' are also (α, β) - top rough comparable then $((R(X \cup Y))_{IF})_{\alpha,\beta}$ is equal to one of $((R(X))_{IF\_\alpha,\beta}$ and $(R(Y))_{\alpha,\beta}$ and so is the case for $((R(X UY'))_{IF})_{\alpha,\beta}$.
So, the equality follows.

The claim that the condition is not necessary follows from the fact that it is not necessary in the base case.

The proofs of the following properties can be carried out similarly. We only state them.

Property 43:

X is

(α, β) - bottom related X'

and Y is

(α, β) - bottom related to Y'

may or may not imply that $X \cap Y$ is

(α, β) - bottom related

to $X' \cap Y'$

2. A sufficient but not necessary condition for the result in 1 to be true is that X and Y are (α, β) – bottom rough comparable and X' and Y' are (α, β) – bottom rough comparable.

Property 44:

1. X is (α, β) - top related to Y may or may not imply that $X \cup (-Y)$ is (α, β) - top related to U.
2. A sufficient but not necessary condition for result in 1 to hold is that

X and Y are (α, β) - bottom rough equal.

Property 45:

1.   X is

(α, β) - bottom related

to Y may not imply that $X \cap (-Y)$ is

(α, β) - bottom related

to ϕ.

2.   A sufficient but not necessary condition for the result in 1 to hold true is that

X and Y are (α, β) - top rough equal.

Property 46: If $X \subseteq Y$ and Y is

(α, β) - bottom related

to ϕ then X

(α, β) - bottom related

to ϕ.

Property 47: If $X \subseteq Y$ and X is

(α, β) - top related

to U then Y is

(α, β) - top related

to U.

Property 48: X is

(α, β) - top related

to Y if and only if –X is

(α, β) - bottom related

to –Y.

Property 49: If X is

(α, β) - bottom related

to ϕ and Y is

(α, β) - bottom related

to ϕ then $X \cap Y$ is (α, β) - bottom related to ϕ.

Property 50: If X is

(α, β) - top related

to U or Y is

(α, β) - top related

to U then $X \cup Y$ is

(α, β) - top related

to U.

Replacement Properties for Rough Intuitionistic Fuzzy Equivalence

We state below the properties which are obtained by interchanging bottom rough intuitionistic fuzzy equalities with top rough intuitionistic fuzzy equalities. The proofs are similar to the properties in section 5.4. So, we omit them.

Property 51:

1. *If $X \cap Y$ is (α, β)
—top related to both X and Y
then X is (α, β) — top related to Y.*

2. The converse of 1 is not true in general and an additional condition that is sufficient but not necessary for the converse to be true is that equality holds in (3.2.3).

Property 52:

1. *If $X \bigcup Y$ is $(\alpha, \beta) - bottom\ related$ to both X and Y then X is (α, β) $-top\ related\ to\ Y$.*

2. The converse of 1 is not true in general and an additional condition that is sufficient but not necessary for the converse to be true is that equality holds in (3.2.2).

Property 53:

1. *If X is $(\alpha, \beta) - bottom\ related$ to X and Y is $(\alpha, \beta) - bottom\ related\ to Y'$ may not imply $X \bigcup Y$ is (α, β) $-bottom\ related\ to\ X'\bigcup Y'$.*

2. A sufficient but not necessary condition for the conclusion of 1 to hold is that equality holds in (6).

Property 54:

1. *If X is $(\alpha, \beta) - top\ related$ to X and Y is $(\alpha, \beta) - top\ related\ to Y'$ may not imply $X \bigcap Y$ is (α, β) $-top\ related\ to\ X'\bigcap Y'$.*

2. A sufficient but not necessary condition for the conclusion in 1 to hold is that equality holds in (7).

Property 55:

X is $(\alpha, \beta) - bottom\ related\ to\ Y$ may or may not imply $X \bigcup -Y$ is (α, β) $-bottom\ related\ to\ U$.

Property 56:

X is $(\alpha, \beta) - top\ related\ to\ Y$ may or may not imply $X \bigcap -Y$ is (α, β) $-top\ related\ to\ U$.

Properties (46) to (50) hold true under replacements.

Real Life Examples

Example 9: Let us consider the universal set of all faculties in colleges in a state. We define x R y if and only if x and y belong to the same college. This is an equivalence relation and decomposes the set of faculties into equivalence classes, which are colleges in the state. We define two intuitionistic fuzzy sets G and Y over the universe as comprising of "good" faculty and "young" faculty. These two concepts can be defined through intuitionistic fuzzy membership values. For example a faculty x can be considered as a member of G as (x, 0.6, 0.2) and the same faculty can be defined as a member of Y as (x, 0.7, 0.1).

Case 1: Suppose

$$(\underline{R}G)_{IF} = (\underline{R}Y)_{IF}$$

It implies that the colleges for which all the faculties are good also have all the faculties young.

Case 2: Suppose

$(\underline{R}G)_{IF}$ and $(\underline{R}Y)_{IF}$ are ϕ or not ϕ together

This implies that either there is no college which contains all good faculty or young faculty or there are some colleges which contain all good faculties or all young faculties. Unlike case-I, here the set of colleges may not be same.

Case 3: Suppose

$$\left(\overline{RG}\right)_{IF} = \left(\overline{RY}\right)_{IF}$$

It implies that the set of colleges which have at least one good faculty is same as the set of colleges which have at least one young faculty.

Case 4: Suppose

$\left(\overline{RG}\right)_{IF}$ and $\left(\overline{RY}\right)_{IF}$

are U or not U together.

If both are U then it implies that all the colleges have at least one good faculty as well as at least one young faculty. If both are not U it implies there are some colleges which do not have any young faculty and there some colleges which do not have any good faculty. Unlike case-III, here the same colleges may not have this feature.

Note 2: We can have combinations of the above four cases to get the four types of approximate equalities provided in table 5.1. For example,

if we have both case I and case III are true then we can conclude that the colleges for which all the faculties are good also have all the faculties young and those colleges have some faculties young also have some faculties who are good.

Note 3: It may be noted that we can add control values α and β to discuss the above cases and make them refined. For example, if we want a goodness factor of 0, 5 and also a youth factor of also 0.5 we can do so by taking $\alpha = 0.5$ and also we may like to take $\beta = 0.1$. This will enable us to consider only those faculties who are having high goodness factor as well as high youth factor for comparison. Also, we can reduce the factor of not being good or not being young to filter out faculties having high negative values.

Covering Based Rough Sets

As mentioned in the introduction, there are four types of covering based rough sets introduced in the literature. This is basically due to the four different types of upper approximations introduced. In the next few sections we shall introduce the covering based rough sets (Zhu, 2007c). However, we shall provide the definitions of three types of covering based rough sets here for the sake of completeness. There are three more types of covering based rough sets in the literature (see for example, Zhu, 2007b).

Covering Based Rough Sets of First Type

We first introduce the concepts necessary for defining the covering based rough sets of first type and define it.

Definition 22: Let U be a universe of discourse and C be a family of subsets of U. C is called a *cover* of U if no subset in C is empty and UC = U. We call (U, C) the covering approximation space and the covering C is called the family of approximation sets.

Definition 23: Let (U, C) be an approximation space and x be any element of U. Then the family $Md(x) = \{K \in C : x \in K \wedge \forall S \in C, (x \in S \wedge S \subseteq K \Rightarrow K = S)\}$ is called the minimal description of the object x.

Definition 24: For any set $X \subseteq U$, the family of sets $C_*(X) = \{K \in C : K \subseteq X\}$ is called the family of sets bottom approximating the set X.

Definition 25: The set $X_* = \cup C_*(X)$ is called the lower approximation of the set X.

Definition 26: The set $X_*^* = X \setminus X_*$ is called the boundary of the set X.

Definition 27: The family of sets Bn(X) = $U\{Md(x): x \in X_*^*\}$ is called the family of sets approximating the boundary of the set X.

Definition 28: The family of sets

$$C^*(X) = C_*(X) \cup Bn(X)$$

is called the family of sets top approximating the set X.

Definition 29: The set

$$X_1^* = \cup C^*(X)$$

is called the CB-upper approximation of the first type of the set X.

Definition 30: A set X is called exact when

$$C^*(X) = C_*(X)$$

Equivalently, X is exact when $X_1^* = X_*$. Otherwise, X is said to be a covering based rough set of the first type.

Covering Based Rough Sets of Other Types

We would like to note here that for all the four types of covering based rough sets, the definition of lower approximation is same.

Definition 31: Let (U, C) be a covering approximation space. For a set $X \subseteq U$, the set X_2^* = $U\{K / K \in C, K \cap X \neq \phi\}$ is called the covering upper approximation of second type of X.

If $X_* = X_2^*$ is said to exact. Otherwise, X is called a covering based rough set of the second type.

Definition 32: Let (U, C) be a covering approximation space. For a set $X \subseteq U$, the set X_3^* = $U\{Md(x) | x \in X\}$ is called the covering based upper approximation of the third type of X. If $X_* = X_3^*$, X is said to be exact. Otherwise, X is called a covering based rough set of the third type.

Covering Based Rough Approximate Equalities

Definition 33: Let (U, C) be an approximation space and $X, Y \subseteq U$. We say that

- (13) Two sets X and Y are bottom C-equal (X bC_eq Y) iff $X_* = Y_*$.
- (14) Two sets X and Y are top C-equal of type-i (X tC_eq(i) Y) iff $X_i^* = Y_i^*$, where X_i^*, Y_i^* denote the covering based upper approximations of X and Y respectively of type-i, I =1,2,3.

- (15) Two sets X and Y are C-equal of type-i, i= 1, 2, 3 (X C_eq(i) Y) iff $X_* = Y_*$ and $X_i^* = Y_i^*$.

Several properties were established for approximate equalities of basic rough sets. We shall try to establish these properties for the four types of covering based rough sets below. We would like to note that since the definition of lower approximation for all the four types are same the differences will occur for properties involving upper approximations only.

To establish the properties of approximate equalities, we require the following theorems:

Theorem 1: Let $X, Y \subseteq U$. Then the following properties hold for the lower and upper approximations of covering based rough sets: For all types of covering based rough sets X and Y

$$X_* \cup Y_* \subseteq (X \cup Y)_* \tag{17}$$

For X and Y being covering based rough sets of any type, we have

$$X_* \cap Y_* \supseteq (X \cap Y)_* \tag{18}$$

For covering based rough sets of type i, we have

$$(X \cap Y)_i^* \subseteq X_i^* \cap Y_i^*, i = 1, 2, 3. \tag{19}$$

For X and Y being covering based rough sets of type I, we have

$$(X \cup Y)_i^* \subseteq X_i^* \cup Y_i^*, i = 1, 2, 3. \tag{20}$$

Theorem 2: (Zhu, 2007, Theorem 1) For $X, Y \subseteq U$,

$$(X \cap Y)_* = X_* \cap Y_* \tag{21}$$

if C satisfies the following:
For every

$$K_1, K_2 \in C, K_1 \cap K_2 \tag{22}$$

is a union of finite elements in C.

Theorem 3: (Zhu, 2007, Theorem 3) For $X, Y \subseteq U$,

$$(X \cup Y)_1^* = X_1^* \cup Y_1^* \tag{23}$$

if and only if (22) is satisfied.

Theorem 4: (Zhu, 2007, Proposition 10) For covering based rough sets of type 2, for $X, Y \subseteq U$,

$$(X \cup Y)_2^* = X_2^* \cup Y_2^* \tag{24}$$

Theorem 5: (Zhu, 2007, Proposition 21) For covering based rough sets of type 3, for $X, Y \subseteq U$,

$$(X \cup Y)_3^* = X_3^* \cup Y_3^* \tag{25}$$

Theorem 6: (Zhu, 2007, Lemma 1) For $X, Y \subseteq U$,

$$X \subseteq Y \Rightarrow X_1^* \subseteq Y_1^* \tag{26}$$

Theorem 7: (Zhu, 2007, Proposition 10) For second type of covering upper approximation, for $X, Y \subseteq U$,

$$X \subseteq Y \Rightarrow X_2^* \subseteq Y_2^* \tag{27}$$

Theorem 8: (Zhu, 2007, Theorem 15) For $X, Y \subseteq U$,

$$\neg X_* = (\neg X)_2^* \tag{28}$$

if C is a partition.

Theorem 9: (Zhu, 2007, Proposition 21) For the third type of covering based upper approximation for $X, Y \subseteq U$,

$$X \subseteq Y \Rightarrow X_3^* \subseteq Y_3^* \tag{29}$$

Properties of Covering Based Rough Equalities of Type 1

Property 57: X bC_eq Y if $X \cap Y$ bC_eq X and $X \cap Y$ bC_eq Y.

The converse is not true in general. It is true when (22) holds true.

- **Proof:** If $X \cap Y$ bC_eq X and $X \cap Y$ bC_eq Y then clearly X bC_eq Y. Conversely, under the additional hypothesis, and Theorem 2, we have

$$(X \cap Y)_* = X_* \cap Y_*,$$

we get the conclusion.

Property 58: X tC_eq(1) Y if $X \cup Y$ tC_eq(1) Y and $X \cup Y$ is tC_eq(1) Y.

The converse is not true in general. It is true if (22) holds true.

- **Proof:** The first part follows directly. Conversely, under the additional hypothesis using Theorem 1, we have

$$(X \cup Y)_1^* = X_1^* \cup Y_1^*$$

So, as $X_1^* = Y_1^*$, we get the conclusion.

Property 59: X tC_eq(1) X' and Y tC_eq(1) Y' $\Rightarrow X \cup Y$ tC_eq(1) $X' \cup Y'$ is not true in general and it is true if in addition (22) holds true.

- **Proof:** Using Theorem 3, under the additional hypothesis we have

$$(X \cup Y)_1^* = X_1^* \cup Y_1^* =$$
$$X_1'^* \cup Y_1'^* = (X' \cup Y')_1^*$$

So, the conclusion follows.

Property 60: X bC_eq(1) X' and Y bC_eq(1) Y' $\Rightarrow X \cap Y$ tC_eq(1) $X' \cap Y'$ is not true in general and it is true if in addition (22) holds true.

- **Proof:** The proof is similar to property 59. We only use Theorem 2 instead of Theorem 3.

Property 61: X tC_eq(1) Y $\Rightarrow X \cup \neg Y$ tC_eq(1) U is not true in general.

- **Proof:** This property does not in general, as we do not have the equality,

$$C^*(\neg Y) = \neg C_*(Y)$$

for every $Y \subseteq U$. No sufficient condition exists in literature for this property to hold.

Property 62: If (22) is satisfied then X bC_eq(1) Y

$$\Rightarrow X \cap \neg Y \, bC\_eq \, \phi$$

- **Proof:** Similar to that of property 61.

Property 63: If (22) is satisfied then $X \subseteq Y$ and $Y\ tC\_eq(1)\ \phi \Rightarrow X\ tC\_eq(1)\ \phi$.

- **Proof:** We have $Y\ tC\_eq\ \phi \Rightarrow Y^* = \phi$. Also, by theorem 3, $X_1^* \subseteq Y_1^*$. So, $X_1^* = \phi$. Hence $X\ tC\_eq(1)\ \phi$.

Property 64: If (22) is satisfied then $X \subseteq Y$ and $X\ tC\_eq(1)\ U \Rightarrow X\ tC\_eq(1)\ U$.

- **Proof:** Similar to that of property 63.

Property 65: It is not true in general that $X\ tC\_eq(1)\ Y$ if and only if

$$\neg X\ bC\_eq\ \neg Y.$$

- **Proof:** The reason is similar to the proof of (61).

Property 66: Suppose (22) is satisfied. Then, if $X\ bC\_eq\ \phi$ or $Y bC\_eq(1)\ \phi$ then $X \cap Y\ bC\_eq\ \phi$.

- **Proof:** Using theorem 2 above, under the hypothesis, we have

$$(X \cap Y)_* = X_* \cap Y_*$$

So, if any one of

$X_*\ or\ Y_*\ is\ equal\ to\ \phi,$

we get

$$(X \cap Y)_* = \phi$$

and the proof follows.

Property 67: If (22) is satisfied then $X\ tC\_eq(1)$ U or $Y\ tC\_eq(1)$ U implies $X \cup Y\ tC\_eq(1)$ U.

- **Proof:** Using theorem 3 above, under the hypothesis, we have

$$(X \cup Y)_1^* = X_1^* \cup Y_1^*$$

So, if any one of $X_1^*\ or\ Y_1^*$ is equal to U, we get $(X \cup Y)_1^* = U$ and the proof follows.

Properties of Covering Based Rough Equalities of Type 2

As noted above the properties (57), (60), (62) and (66) also hold true for covering based rough sets of type 2. The other properties are as follows.

Property 68: $X\ tC\_eq(2)\ Y$ iff $X \cup Y\ tC\_eq(2)$ X and $X \cup Y\ tC\_eq(2)$ Y.

- **Proof:** The proof is similar to that of (58). We only note that by Theorem 4, (24) holds directly in this case. So, no additional condition is necessary for the converse to be true.

Property 69: $X\ tC\_eq(2)$ X' and $Y\ tC\_eq(2)$ Y' if and only if

$$X \cap Y\ tC\_eq(2)\ X' \cap Y'$$

is not true in general.

- **Proof:** The proof is similar to (59). However, there is no direct condition available so far so that it can hold.

Property 70: $X tC\_eq(2)\ Y \Rightarrow X \cup \neg Y\ tC\_eq(2)$ U is not true in general. This is true if C is a partition.

- **Proof:** The proof is similar to property (61). We only note that by Theorem 8 and (20), we have

$$(X \cup \neg Y)^*_2 = X^*_2 \cup (\neg Y)^*_2 = X^*_2 \cup \neg Y_* = Y^*_2 \cup (\neg Y)^*_2 = (Y \cup \neg Y)^*_2 = U^* = U.$$

Property 71: $X \subseteq Y$ and X tC_eq(2) ϕ $\Rightarrow$ Y tC_eq(2) ϕ.

- **Proof:** The proof is similar to property (63). We only note that by Theorem 7, (27) directly holds and no other condition is necessary.

Property 72: $X \subseteq Y$ and X tC_eq(2) U Y tC_eq(2) U.

- **Proof:** The proof is same as for (64).

Property 73: X tC_eq(2) Y if and only if $\neg X$ tC_eq(2) $\neg Y$.

- **Proof:** The proof follows from Theorem 8.

Property 74: If X tC_eq(2) U or Y tC_eq(2) U then $X \cup Y$ tC_eq(2) U.

- **Proof:** The proof is similar to property (67). We note that by Theorem 4, (24) holds directly in this case and so no additional condition is necessary.

Properties of Covering Based Rough Equalities of Type 3

As mentioned above, properties (57), (60), (62) and (66) hold for covering based rough sets of type 3 also. As regards the other properties we have the following:

Property 75: X tC_eq(3) Y if and only if $X \cup Y$ tC_eq(3) X and $X \cup Y$ tC_eq(3) Y.

- **Proof:** The proof is similar to (58). We only note that by Theorem 5, (25) holds directly in this case. So, no additional condition is necessary for the converse to be true.

Property 76: X tC_eq(3) X' and Y tC_eq(3) Y' if and only if $X \cap Y$ tC_eq(3) $X' \cap Y'$. Is not true in general.

- **Proof:** The proof is similar to (59). In this case, there is no direct condition is available so far.

Property 77: X tC_eq(3) Y $\Rightarrow$ $X \cup \neg Y$ tC_eq(3) U is not true in general.

- **Proof:** The proof is similar to (60). However, there is no result so far to establish the validity of it.

Property 78: $X \subseteq Y$ and Y tC_eq(3) ϕ $\Rightarrow$ X tC_eq(3) ϕ

- **Proof:** Proof is similar to (63). We only note that by Theorem 9, (29) holds directly and no other condition is necessary.

Property 79: $X \subseteq Y$ and X tC_eq(3) U $\Rightarrow$ Y tC_eq(3) U.

- **Proof:** Similar to (64).

Property 80: X tC_eq(3) Y if and only if $\neg X$ tC_eq(3) $\neg Y$ is not true in general.

- **Proof:** The proof is similar to (65). However, there is no parallel result to Theorem 8 for type 2 covering based rough sets in this case.

Property 81: X tC_eq(3) U or Y tC_eq(3) U then $X \cup Y$ tC_eq(3) U.

- **Proof:** The proof is similar to (63). We note that by Theorem 5, (25) holds directly in this case and so no additional condition is necessary.

Note 4: We note that several other covering based rough sets other than the above three types are available. The above properties can be extended to these types of covering based rough sets also.

Approximate Equalities Using Multigranular Rough Sets

The basic rough set defined by Pawlak is single granular from the granular computing point of view. So, recently (Qian and Liang, 2006 and Qian, Liang and Dang, 2010) have extended its definition in two ways to define multigranular computing using rough sets. The first extension is called the optimistic multigranular rough sets and the second one is called the pessimistic multigranular rough sets. We provide below the definitions of the two types. However, instead of using the notation for the pessimistic multigranular rough sets taken by Qian we use the more intuitive notation used by (Tripathy and Mitra, 2013a).

Definition 34: Let K= (U, **R**) be knowledge base, **R** be a family of equivalence relations, $X \subseteq U$ and $R, S \in \mathbf{R}$. We define the optimistic multigranular (Qian and Liang, 2006) lower approximation and optimistic multigranular upper approximation of X with respect to R and S in U as

$$\underline{R+S}\, X = \{\, x \mid [x]_R \subseteq X \text{ or } [x]_S \subseteq X\} \quad (30)$$

and

$$\overline{R+S}\, X = \;\sim (\underline{R+S}(\sim X)). \quad (31)$$

Definition 35: Let K= (U, **R**) be a knowledge base, **R** be a family of equivalence relations, $X \subseteq U$ and $R, S \in \mathbf{R}$. We define the pessimistic multigranular (Qian, Liang and Deng, 2010) lower approximation and pessimistic multigranular upper approximation of X with respect to R and S in U as

$$\underline{R*S}\, X = \{\, x \mid [x]_R \subseteq X \text{ and } [x]_S \subseteq X\} \quad (32)$$

and

$$\overline{R*S}\, X = \;\sim (\underline{R*S}(\sim X)). \quad (33)$$

The following properties are satisfied for multigranular rough sets with respect to their union and intersection (Qian and Liang, 2006; Qian, Liang and Dang, 2009; Tripathy and Mitra, 2013a, 2013b),

$$\underline{(R+S)}(X \cap Y) \subseteq \underline{(R+S)}X \cap \underline{(R+S)}Y \quad (34)$$

$$\overline{(R+S)}(X \cup Y) \supseteq \overline{(R+S)}X \cup \overline{(R+S)}Y \quad (35)$$

$$\underline{(R+S)}(X \cup Y) \supseteq \underline{(R+S)}X \cup \underline{(R+S)}Y \quad (36)$$

$$\overline{(R+S)}(X \cap Y) \subseteq \overline{(R+S)}X \cap \overline{(R+S)}Y \quad (37)$$

$$\underline{(R * S)(X \cap Y)} = \underline{(R * S)X} \cap \underline{(R * S)Y} \tag{38}$$

$$\overline{(R * S)(X \cup Y)} = \overline{(R * S)X} \cup \overline{(R * S)Y} \tag{39}$$

$$\underline{(R * S)(X \cup Y)} \supseteq \underline{(R * S)X} \cup \underline{(R * S)Y} \tag{40}$$

$$\overline{(R * S)(X \cap Y)} \subseteq \overline{(R * S)X} \cap \overline{(R * S)Y} \tag{41}$$

The approximate equalities defined above for single granulations have been extended to multigranulations in (Tripathy and Mitra 2013a, 2013b, Tripathy, Rawat, Divya and Parida,2013, Tripathy and Saraf, 2013). We introduce these definitions below.

Definition 36: Let R and S be two equivalence relations on U and $X, Y \subseteq U$. Then

1. X and Y are optimistic bottom rough equal to each other with respect to R and S (X Ob_R+S_eq Y) if and only if

$$\underline{R + SX} = \underline{R + SY}$$

2. X and Y are optimistic top rough equal to each other with respect to R and S (X Ot_R+S_eq Y) if and only if

$$\overline{R + SX} = \overline{R + SY}$$

3. X and Y are optimistic rough equal to each other with respect to R and S (X O_R+S Y) if and only if

$$\underline{R + SX} = \underline{R + SY}$$

and

$$\overline{R + SX} = \overline{R + SY} +$$

Definition 37: Let R and S be two equivalence relations on U and $X, Y \subseteq U$. Then

1. X and Y are pessimistic bottom rough equal to each other with respect to R and S (X Pb_R*S_eq Y) if and only if

$$\underline{R * SX} = \underline{R * SY}$$

2. X and Y are pessimistic top rough equal to each other with respect to R and S (X Pt_R*S_eq Y) if

and only if

$$\overline{R * SX} = \overline{R * SY}$$

3. X and Y are pessimistic rough equal to each other with respect to R and S (X P_R*S Y) if and only if

$$\underline{R * SX} = \underline{R * SY}$$

and

$$\overline{R * SX} = \overline{R * SY}.$$

Definition 38: Let R and S be two equivalence relations on U and $X, Y \subseteq U$. Then

1. X and Y are Optimistic bottom rough equivalent to each other with respect to R and S (X Ob_R+S_eqv Y) if and only if

$$\underline{R + SX} \; and \; \underline{R + SY}$$

are ϕ or not ϕ together.

2. X and Y are optimistic top rough equivalent to each other with respect to R and S (X Ot_R+S_eqv Y) if and only if

$$\overline{R+S}X \text{ and } \overline{R+S}Y$$

are equal to U or not U together.

3. X and Y are optimistic rough equivalent to each other with respect to R and S (X O_R+S_eqv Y) if and only if

$$\underline{R+S}X \text{ and } \underline{R+S}Y$$

are ϕ *or not* ϕ together and

$$\overline{R+S}X \text{ and } \overline{R+S}Y$$

are equal to U or not U together.

Definition 39: Let R and S be two equivalence relations on U and $X, Y \subseteq U$. Then

1 . X and Y are pessimistic bottom rough equivalent to each other with respect to R and S (X Pb_R*S_eqv Y) if and only if

$$\underline{R*S}X \text{ and } \underline{R*S}Y$$

are ϕ *or not* ϕ together.

2 . X and Y are pessimistic top rough equivalent to each other with respect to R and S (X Pt_R*S_eqv Y) if and only if

$$\overline{R*S}X \text{ and } \overline{R*S}Y$$

are equal to U or not U together.

3. X and Y are pessimistic rough equivalent to each other with respect to R and S (X P_R*S_eqv Y) if and only if

$$\underline{R*S}X \text{ and } \underline{R*S}Y$$

are ϕ *or not* ϕ together and

$$\overline{R*S}X \text{ and } \overline{R*S}Y$$

are equal to U or not U together.

Definition 40: Let R and S be two equivalence relations on U and $X, Y \subseteq U$. Then

1. X and Y are optimistic bottom multigranular approximate rough equal with respect to R and S (X Ob_R+S aeq Y) if and only if

$$\underline{R+S}X = \underline{R+S}Y$$

2. X and Y are optimistic top multigranular approximate rough equal with respect to R and S (X Ot_R+S aeq Y) if and only if $\overline{R+S}X \text{ and } \overline{R+S}Y$ are equal to U or not U together.

3. X and Y are optimistic multigranular approximate rough equal to each other with respect to R and S (X O_R+S_eq Y) if and only if

$$\underline{R+S}X = \underline{R+S}Y$$

and $\overline{R+S}X \text{ and } \overline{R+S}Y$ are equal to U or not U together.

Definition 41: Let R and S be two equivalence relations on U and $X, Y \subseteq U$. Then

1. X and Y are pessimistic bottom multigranular approximate rough equal with respect to R and S (X Pb_R*S aeq Y) if and only if $\underline{R*S}X = \underline{R*S}Y$.

2. X and Y are pessimistic top multigranular approximate rough equal with respect to R and S (X Pt_R*S_aeq Y) if and only if $\overline{R*S}X$ *and* $\overline{R*S}Y$ are equal to U or not U together.

3. X and Y are pessimistic multigranular approximate rough equal to each other with respect to R and S (X P_R*S_aeq Y) if and only if

$$\underline{R*S}X = \underline{R*S}Y$$

and $\overline{R*S}X$ *and* $\overline{R*S}Y$ are equal to U or not U together.

Definition 42: Let R and S be two equivalence relations on U and $X, Y \subseteq U$. Then

1. X and Y are optimistic bottom multigranular approximate rough equivalent with respect to R and S (X Pb_R+S aeqv Y) if and only if

$$\underline{R+S}X \ and \ \underline{R+S}Y$$

are ϕ or not ϕ together

2. X and Y are optimistic top multigranular approximate rough equivalent with respect to R and S (X Pt_R+S aeqv Y) if and only if $\overline{R+S}X = \overline{R+S}Y$.

3. X and Y are optimistic multigranular approximate rough equivalent to each other with respect to R and S (X P_R+S_aeqv Y) if and only if

$$\underline{R+S}X \ and \ \underline{R+S}Y$$

are ϕ or not ϕ together and $\overline{R+S}X = \overline{R+S}Y$

Definition 43: Let R and S be two equivalence relations on U and $X, Y \subseteq U$. Then

1. X and Y are pessimistic bottom multigranular approximate rough equivalent with respect to R and S (X Pb_R*S aeqv Y) if and only if

$$\underline{R*S}X \ and \ \underline{R*S}Y$$

are ϕ or not ϕ together

2. X and Y are pessimistic top multigranular approximate rough equivalent with respect to R and S (X Pt_R*S aeqv Y) if and only if $\overline{R*S}X = \overline{R*S}Y$.

3. X and Y are pessimistic multigranular approximate rough equivalent to each other with respect to R and S (X P_R*S_aeqv Y) if and only if

$$\underline{R*S}X \ and \ \underline{R*S}Y$$

are ϕ or not ϕ together and $\overline{R*S}X = \overline{R*S}Y$.

Properties of Multigranular Approximate Equalities

The establishment of the pessimistic properties of approximate equalities with respect to multigranular rough sets and the corresponding replacement properties depend upon the properties (7.9) to (7.12), which are similar to the single granulation case; all the general and replacement properties discussed for single granulation remain true.

However, the corresponding properties for optimistic multigranular rough approximation equalities and the replacement properties change as the properties (34) to (37) are different from the corresponding properties in the single granulation case. So, we only present the properties for the optimistic cases below. Out of the 11 properties in the base case, properties 7-11 are similar. So, we mention only the properties 1-6 for both general and replacement cases.

General Properties for Optimistic Multigranular Rough Equality

X is Ob_R+S_eq Y if $X \cap Y$ is Ob_R+S_eq X and Y both. The converse is not necessarily true. (77)

X is Ot_R+S_eq Y if $X \cup Y$ is Ot_R+S_eq X and Y both. The converse is not necessarily true. (78)

X is Ot_R+S_eq X' and Y is Ot_R+S_eq Y' may not imply that $X \cup Y$ is Ot_R+S_eq $X' \cup Y'$. (79)

X is Ob_R+S_eq X' and Y is Ob_R+S_eq Y' may not imply that $X \cap Y$ is Ob_R+S_eq $X' \cap Y'$. (80)

X is Ot_R+S_eq Y $\Rightarrow X \cup \neg Y$ Ot_R+S_eq U (81)

X is Ob_R+S_eq Y $\Rightarrow X \cap \neg Y$ Ob_R+S_eq ϕ (82)

Replacement Properties for Optimistic Multigranular Rough Equality

X is Ot_R+S_eq Y if $X \cap Y$ is Ot_R+S_eq X and Y both. The converse may not be true. (83)

X is Ob_R+S_eq Y if $X \cup Y$ is Ob_R+S_eq X and Y both. The converse may not be true (84)

X is Ob_R+S_eq X' and Y is Ob_R+S_eq Y' may not imply that $X \cup Y$ is Ob_R+S_eq $X' \cup Y'$. (85)

X is Ot_R+S_eq X' and Y is Ot_R+S_eq Y' may not imply that $X \cap Y$ is Ob_R+S_eq $X' \cap Y'$. (86)

X is Ob_R+S_eq Y may not imply that $X \cup \neg Y$ is Ob_R+S_eq U. (87)

General Properties for Optimistic Multigranular Rough Equivalence

If $X \cap Y$ is b_R+S_eqv to X and
1. $X \cap Y$ is b_R+S_eqv to Y then (88) X is b_R+S_eqv to Y.

2. The converse of 1 is not necessarily true.
3. The converse cannot be true even if X and Y are bottom R+S comparable.

The converse is true in 3
4. *if* $\underline{R}X \cup \underline{S}Y = U$ and $\underline{R}Y \cup \underline{S}X = U$

5. The conditions in 3 are not necessary.

1. *If $X \cup Y$ is t_R+S_eqv to X and $X \cup Y$ is t_R+S_eqv to Y then X is t_R+S_eqv to Y.*   (89)

2. The converse of 1 is not necessarily true.
3. The converse cannot be true even if X and Y are top R+S comparable.

4. *The converse is true in 3 if $[\overline{RX} \cap \overline{SY}] = \phi$ and $[\overline{RY} \cap \overline{SX}] = \phi$*

5. The conditions in 3 are not necessary.

1. *If X is t_R+S_eqv to X' and Y is t_R+S_eqv to Y' then it may or may not be true that $X \cup Y$ is t_R+S_eqv to $X' \cup Y'$.*

2. *The result is true if X, Y and X', Y' are top rough comparable and $[\overline{RX} \cap \overline{SY}] = \phi$ and $[\overline{RY} \cap \overline{SX}] = \phi$, $[\overline{RX'} \cap \overline{SY'}] = \phi$ and $[\overline{RY'} \cap \overline{SX'}] = \phi$*

3. The conditions in 2 are not necessary.

1. *If X is b_R+S_eqv to X' and Y is b_R+S_eqv to Y' then it may or may not be true that $X \cap Y$ is t_R+S_eqv to $X' \cap Y'$.*   (91)

2. *If X, Y and X', Y' are top rough comparable and $\underline{R}X \cup \underline{S}Y = U$ and $\underline{R}Y \cup \underline{S}X = U$, $\underline{R}X' \cup \underline{S}Y' = U$ and $\underline{R}Y' \cup \underline{S}X' = U$.*

3. The conditions in 2 are not necessary

1. *X is t_R+S_eqv to Y may or may not imply that $X \cup \neg Y$ is t_R+S_eqv to U.*   (92)

2. X is b_R+S_eqv to Y is not a sufficient condition for 1 to be true.

3. *However, if $[\overline{RX} \cap \overline{SY}] = \phi$ and $[\overline{RY} \cap \overline{SX}] = \phi$ then (ii) is true*

4. The conditions in 3 are not necessary.

1. *X is b_R+S_eqv to Y may or may not imply that $X \cap \neg Y$ is t_R+S_eqv to ϕ.*   (93)

2. X is t_R+S_eqv to Y is not a sufficient condition for (i) to be true.

3. *However, if $\underline{R}X \cup \underline{S}Y = U$ and $\underline{R}Y \cup \underline{S}X = U$ then (ii) is true*.

4. The conditions in 3 are not necessary.

Replacement Properties for Optimistic Multigranular Rough Equivalence

If $X \cap Y$ is t_R+S_eqv to X and $X \cap Y$ is t_R+S_eqv to Y then (94) *X is t_R+S_eqv to Y.*

The converse of 1 is not necessarily true.

If $X \cup Y$ is b_R+S_eqv to X and $X \cup Y$ is b_R+S_eqv to Y then X (95) *is b_R+S_eqv to Y.*

The converse of 1 is not necessarily true.

X is b_R+S_eqv to X' and Y is b_R+S_eqv to Y'
may not necessarily imply that (96)
$X \cup Y$ is b_R+S_eqv to $X' \cup Y'$.

X is t_R+S_eqv to X' and Y is t_R+S_eqv to Y' may not necessarily imply that $X \cap Y$ is t_R+S_eqv to $X' \cap Y'$. (97)

X is b_R+S_eqv to Y may or may not imply that $X \cup \neg Y$ is (98) *b_R+S_eqv to U.*

X is t_R+S_eqv to Y may or may not imply that $X \cap \neg Y$ is (99) *t_R+S_eqv to ϕ.*

General Properties for Optimistic Multigranular Approximate Rough Equality

X Ob_R+S_aeq Y if $X \cap Y$ Ob_R+S_aeq Y and $X \cap Y$ Ob_R+S_aeq Y . The converse may not be true (100)

X Ot_R+S_aeq Y if $X \cup Y$ Ot_R+S_aeq Y and $X \cup Y$ Ot_R+S_aeq Y . The converse may not be true (101)

X Ot_R+S_aeq X' and Y Ot_R+S_aeq Y' may not imply that $X \cup Y$ Ot_R+S_aeq $X' \cup Y'$ (102)

X Ob_R+S_aeq X' and Y Ob_R+S_aeq Y' may not imply that $X \cap Y$ Ob_R+S_aeq $X' \cap Y'$. (103)

If X Ot_R+S_aeq Y then $X \cup -Y$ Ot_R+S_ aeq U. (104)

If X Ob_R+S_aeq Y then $X \cap -Y$ Ob_R+S_ aeq ϕ. (105)

Replacement Properties for Optimistic Multigranular Approximate Rough Equality

X Ot_R+S_aeq Y if $X \cap Y$ Ot_R+S_aeq Y and $X \cap Y$ Ot_R+S_aeq Y . The converse may not be true. (106)

X Ob_R+S_aeq Y if $X \cup Y$ Ob_R+S_aeq Y and $X \cup Y$ Ob_R+S_aeq Y . The converse may not be true. (107)

X Ob_R+S_aeq X' and Y Ob_R+S_aeq Y'
may not imply that $X \cup Y$ Ob_R+S_aeq
$X' \cup Y'$. (108)

X Ot_R+S_aeq X' and Y Ot_R+S_aeq Y' may
not imply that $X \cap Y$ Ot_R+S_aeq $X' \cap Y'$. (109)

If X Ob_R+S_aeq Y then it may not be true
that $X \cup -Y$ Ob_R+S_aeq U. (110)

If X Ot_R+S_aeq Y then it may not be true that
$X \cap -Y$ Ot_R+S_aeq ϕ. (111)

The properties for the optimistic multigranular approximate rough equivalence are similar to the above three sets of properties. The reader may consult (Tripathy and Saraf, 2013) for reference.

SOME PROPOSALS FOR FUTURE WORK

In this section we state some problems in the lines of the work presented in this paper, which can be tackled for advancement of this field of research. These are

1. Algebraic properties of rough sets for only one case of approximate equalities, that is rough equivalence has been handled so far. It would be interesting to try the validity of these results in case of other approximate equalities discussed here. In particular, the verification for covering based approximate equalities and multigranular equalities will be very interesting.
2. The properties for covering based rough sets of only three types of such extensions have been discussed. However, at least three more types of such extensions exist in literature. It will be interesting to develop approximate equalities of such sets. In particular, the case of the fifth type of covering based rough sets,

called the topological type, which is perhaps the most natural type will be interesting.
3. The basic concept of rough sets has been generalised in many directions. It would be interesting to work the approximate equalities for all such extensions and discuss real life applications.

CONCLUSION

Equality of sets in the mathematical sense is very stringent and has very limited applications. One of the drawbacks of this definition is that the users have no role and hence their knowledge is not used in deciding the equality of the concerned sets. In order to incorporate user knowledge Novotny and Pawlak introduced rough equalities of sets, which were later extended to define three more types of approximate equalities using rough sets by Tripathy et al. A comparative analysis of these four types of approximate equalities of sets using rough sets shows their relative applicability and efficiency.

In the same lines as done for crisp sets, the equality of fuzzy sets in the fuzzy mathematical sense does not use the user knowledge. So, it is natural to extend this notion using rough sets to define the approximate equalities of fuzzy sets. Tripathy et al have done so and introduced all the four types of rough equalities of fuzzy sets. Also, this has been done by introducing the concepts of graded equalities. Intuitionistic fuzzy sets extend to make them more applicable in real life situations. Tripathy et al have extended the four types of equalities to the context of intuitionistic fuzzy sets. Several real life examples have been provided for each of the cases of crisp sets, fuzzy sets and intuitionistic fuzzy sets to illustrate the ideas introduced. An extension of basic rough sets is the several types of covering based rough sets. Tripathy and Tripathy have defined the approximate equalities for three of these types and established their properties. The basic rough sets introduced by Pawlak is single granular from the granular computing point of view. Two types of multigranular rough sets have been introduced called the optimistic multigranular and pessimistic multigranular rough sets. We discussed the four types of approximate equalities using rough sets in the last section of this chapter.

Most importantly, the equalities discussed above induce approximate reasoning. The reasoning process results in making the outcome more realistic and matches with the reasoning we do in day to day lives. The examples taken from the real life situations derive very interesting conclusions in terms of equalities of sets. Also, we have proposed some problems for further study.

REFERENCES

Atanassov, K. T. (1986). Intuitionistic fuzzy sets. *Fuzzy Sets and Systems*, *20*, 87–96. doi:10.1016/S0165-0114(86)80034-3

Bonikowski, Z., Bryniarski, E., & Wybraniec, U. (1998). Extensions and intensions in the rough set theory. *Journal of Information Science*, *107*, 149–167. doi:10.1016/S0020-0255(97)10046-9

Cantor, G. (1883). *Grundlagen einer allgemeinen mannigfaltig-keitslehre*. Leipzig, Germany: B.G. Teubner.

Degang, C., Changzhong, W., & Qinghua, H. (2007). A new approach to attribute reduction of consistent and inconsistent covering decision systems with covering rough sets. *Journal of Information Science*, *177*, 3500–3518. doi:10.1016/j.ins.2007.02.041

Degang, C., Wenxiu, Z., Yeung, D., & Tsang, E. C. C. (2006). Rough approximations on a complete completely distributive lattice with applications to generalized rough sets. *Journal of Information Science*, *176*, 1829–1848. doi:10.1016/j.ins.2005.05.009

Dubois, D., & Prade, H. (1990). Rough fuzzy sets and Fuzzy rough sets. *International Journal of General Systems*, *17*(1), 191–209. doi:10.1080/03081079008935107

Dummett, M. (1967). Gottlob Frege (1848-1925). In P. Edwards (Ed.), *The encyclopedia of philosophy* (Vol. 3, pp. 225–237). New York: Academic Press.

Novotny, M., & Pawlak, Z. (1985a). Characterization of rough top equalities and rough bottom equalities. *Bull. Polish Acad. Sci. Math.*, *33*, 91–97.

Novotny, M., & Pawlak, Z. (1985b). On rough equalities. *Bull. Polish Acad. Sci. Math.*, *33*, 99–104.

Novotny, M., & Pawlak, Z. (1985c). Black box analysis and rough top equality. *Bull. Polish Acad. Sci. Math.*, *33*, 105–113.

Pawlak, Z. (1982). Rough sets. *Int. Jour. of Computer and Information Sciences*, *11*, 341–356. doi:10.1007/BF01001956

Pawlak, Z. (1991). *Rough sets: Theoretical aspects of reasoning about data*. London: Kluwer Academic Publishers.

Qian, Y. H., & Liang, J. Y. (2006). Rough set method based on multi-granulations. In *Proceedings of the 5th IEEE Conference on Cognitive Informatics*, (vol. 1, pp. 297 – 304). IEEE.

Qian, Y. H., Liang, J. Y., & Dang, C. Y. (2010). Pessimistic rough decision. In *Proceedings of RST 2010*. Zhoushan, China: RST.

Tripathy, B. K. (2009). On approximation of classifications, rough equalities and rough equivalences. *Springer International Studies in Computational Intelligence, 174*, 85–133. doi:10.1007/978-3-540-89921-1_4

Tripathy, B.K. (2011). An analysis of approximate equalities based on rough set theory. *International Journal of Advanced Science and Technology, 31*.

Tripathy, B. K., Jhawar, A., & Vats, E. (2012). An analysis of generalised approximate equalities based on rough fuzzy sets. In *Proceedings of the International Conf. on SocPros 2011*. SocPros.

Tripathy, B. K., & Mitra, A. (2013a). On the approximate equalities of multigranular rough sets and approximate reasoning. In *Proceedings, 4th IEEE International Conference on Computing, Communication and Networking Technologies* (ICCCNT 2013). IEEE.

Tripathy, B. K., & Mitra, A. (2013b). On approximate equivalences of multigranular rough sets and approximate reasoning. *International Journal of Information Technology and Computer Science, 10*, 103–113. doi:10.5815/ijitcs.2013.10.11

Tripathy, B. K., Mitra, A., & Ojha, J. (2008). On rough equalities and rough equivalences of sets. In *RSCTC 2008 (LNAI)* (Vol. 5306, pp. 92–102). Akron, OH: Springer-Verlag. doi:10.1007/978-3-540-88425-5_10

Tripathy, B.K., Mitra, A., & Ojha, J. (2009). Rough equivalence and algebraic properties of rough sets. *International Journal of Artificial Intelligence and Soft Computing, 1*(2/3/4), 271 – 289.

Tripathy, B. K., & Panda, G. K. (2012). Approximate equalities on rough intuitionistic fuzzy sets and an analysis of approximate equalities. *International Journal of Computer Science Issues, 9*(2), 371–380.

Tripathy, B. K., Panda, G. K., & Mitra, A. (2009). Covering based rough equality of sets and comparison of knowledge. In *Proceedings of the Inter. Conf. in Mathematics and Computer Science* (ICMCS 2009). ICMCS.

Tripathy, B. K., Rawat, R., Divya, V., & Parida, S. C. (2013). *On multigranular approximate rough equalities and approximate reasoning*. VIT University.

Tripathy, B. K., & Saraf, P. (2013). *On multigranular approximate rough equivalences and approximate reasoning*. IJISA. doi:10.5815/ijitcs.2013.10.11

Tripathy, B. K., & Tripathy, H. K. (2009). Covering based rough equivalence of sets and comparison of knowledge. In *Proceedings of the IACSIT Spring Conference 2009*. IACSIT.

Zadeh, L. A. (1965). Fuzzy sets. *Information and Control, 8*(11), 338–353. doi:10.1016/S0019-9958(65)90241-X

Zakowski, W. (1983). Approximation in space. *Demonstratio Mathematica, 16*, 761–769.

Zhu, W. (2007a). Basic concepts in covering-based rough sets. In *Proceedings of 3rd IEEE International Conference on Natural Computation*. IEEE Computer Society.

Zhu, W. (2007b). Topological approaches to covering rough sets. *Journal of Information Science, 177*, 1499–1508. doi:10.1016/j.ins.2006.06.009

Zhu, W. (2007c). On three types of covering-based rough sets. *IEEE Transactions on Knowledge and Data Engineering, 19*(8), 1131–1143. doi:10.1109/TKDE.2007.1044

Zhu, W., & Wang, F. Y. (2003). Reduction and axiomization of covering generalized rough sets. *Journal of Information Science, 152*, 217–230. doi:10.1016/S0020-0255(03)00056-2

Zhu, W., & Wang, F. Y. (2006). Relationships among three types of covering rough Sets. In *Proceedings of IEEE GrC*, (pp. 43-48). IEEE.

KEY TERMS AND DEFINITIONS

Approximate Equality: The equalities of sets which are not exactly equal in the mathematical sense.

Approximate Reasoning: Reasoning which deals with partially true statements instead of binary valued Aristotelian logic statements.

Cover: A decomposition of a universe into components which may not be disjoint but their union is equal to the whole universe.

Fuzzy Set: A model to handle imprecision in data, introduced by L.A.Zadeh, uses graded membership of elements in a set instead of binary membership as for crisp sets.

Granule: The smallest addressable unit of knowledge in a knowledge base.

Hybrid Models: Models which are combinations of two or more elementary models.

Intuitionistic Fuzzy Set: A model to handle imprecision in data, introduced by K.T.Attanasov, uses the concept of non-membership of elements as being not one's complement to membership as in fuzzy sets.

Partition: A decomposition of a universe into disjoint components whose union is the whole universe.

Rough Set: A model to handle imprecision in data, introduced by Z.Pawlak, handles imprecision through the boundary approach proposed by G.Frege, the father of modern logic.

Chapter 9
Case–Based Reasoning and Some Typical Applications

Durga Prasad Roy
National Institute of Technology, India

Baisakhi Chakraborty
National Institute of Technology, India

ABSTRACT

Case-Based Reasoning (CBR) arose out of research into cognitive science, most prominently that of Roger Schank and his students at Yale University, during the period 1977–1993. CBR may be defined as a model of reasoning that incorporates problem solving, understanding, and learning, and integrates all of them with memory processes. It focuses on the human problem solving approach such as how people learn new skills and generates solutions about new situations based on their past experience. Similar mechanisms to humans who intelligently adapt their experience for learning, CBR replicates the processes by considering experiences as a set of old cases and problems to be solved as new cases. To arrive at the conclusions, it uses four types of processes, which are retrieve, reuse, revise, and retain. These processes involve some basic tasks such as clustering and classification of cases, case selection and generation, case indexing and learning, measuring case similarity, case retrieval and inference, reasoning, rule adaptation, and mining to generate the solutions. This chapter provides the basic idea of case-based reasoning and a few typical applications. The chapter, which is unique in character, will be useful to researchers in computer science, electrical engineering, system science, and information technology. Researchers and practitioners in industry and R&D laboratories working in such fields as system design, control, pattern recognition, data mining, vision, and machine intelligence will benefit.

INTRODUCTION

Case-based Reasoning (CBR) is a recent approach to problem solving and learning that has got a lot of attention over the last few years. The basic idea had been first introduced in the US and then underlying theories have spread to other countries. It is a recent approach of Artificial Intelligence (AI) to solve problem and learning. In CBR, new problems are often similar to previously encountered problems and the current solution is mostly based on past solution.

DOI: 10.4018/978-1-4666-4936-1.ch009

Sometime it called a methodology which can solve a new problem remembering previous experience. It consists of four stages; Case Retrieve, Case reuse, Case revise and Case retain. It is a problem solving paradigm which is different from other AI approaches. CBR is able to utilize the specific knowledge of previously experience and contain problem as cases. A new problem is solved by finding a similar past case and reusing it in the new problem situations. Now-a-days CBR field is developing rapidly. It is used in many areas like diagnoses, pattern recognition, planning and troubles shooting.

BACKGROUND AND MOTIVATION

What is case-based reasoning? Basically: To solve a new problem by remembering a previous similar situation and by reusing information and knowledge of that situation. Let us illustrate this by looking at some typical problem solving situations which is described in A. Aamodt, E. Plaza (1994).

- A physician - after having examined a particular patient in his office - gets a reminding to a Patient that he treated two weeks ago. Assuming that the reminding was caused by a similarity of important symptoms (and not the patient's hair-color, say), the physician uses the diagnosis and treatment of the previous patient to determine the disease and treatment for the patient in front of him.
- A drilling engineer, who have experienced two dramatic blow out situations, is quickly reminded of one of these situations (or both) when the combination of critical measurements matches those of a blow out case. In particular, he may get a reminding to a mistake he made during a previous blow-out, and use this to avoid repeating the error once again.

- A financial consultant working on a difficult credit decision task uses a reminding to a previous case, which involved a company in similar trouble as the current one, to recommend that the loan application should be refused.

The first CBR workshops were organized in 1988, 1989, and 1991 by the U.S. Defence Advanced Research Projects Agency (DARPA). Which is formally marked the birth of the discipline of case-based reasoning. In 1993, the first European workshop on case-based reasoning (EWCBR, 1993) was held in Kaiserslautern, Germany. That was a great success, and that attracted more than 120 delegates and over 80 papers. Since then, many international workshops and conferences on CBR have been held in different parts of the world.

Now a day some of the Organizations such as IBM, VISA International, Volkswagen, British Airways, and NASA have already made use of CBR in applications such as customer support, quality assurance, aircraft maintenance, process planning, and decision support, and many more applications.

SOME INTERESTING APPLICATIONS OF CBR

- **Case-Based Problem Solving:** The case based on previous experience is that it can be used for future problems solving, and can be referred to as a past case, stored case or retained case. Case-Based Reasoning terminology usually presents case on the problem situation. Case-Based reasoning is most successful techniques for software development. This technique is rapidly making practical usage outside AI community.
- **Learning in CBR:** Learning in CBR happens as a natural sequel to problem solving. When a new problem is successfully

solved, then the experience with the solution is retained in order to reuse it in solving future similar problems. If an attempt to solve a problem fails, then the reason of failure is identified and stored. This experience of failure also helps in the learning process so that the experience can be referred in solving future problems. Each time a Problem is handled, it gives a new learning experience. A Problem may or may not be solved. System learns from application of solved problem as well as from failed experiences.

- **Help-Desk System:** Help Desk support system is an important part of any organization. Due to increasing demand of users and rising complexity of systems, different methods of building help desk systems require more attention. Case-Based Reasoning is one of the best approaches which uses knowledge discovery to make help desk systems. For example, the retrieval of related cases can be improved by using designs of CBR and genetic algorithms. Case bases are used for design of best variety of common help desk systems. There are many Case Bases available in the market that can be bought and used to enhance efficiency of help desk systems.

- **Technical Diagnosis Support System:** CBR is widely applicable to the diagnosis of problems and the identification of solutions to them. Not only for troubleshooting, CBR is used as strategic tool for decision making. Experts systems are built for diagnosis and for serving as diagnostic assistant

- **Experience Feedback Support Systems:** In Case-Based reasoning, this follows the Diagnosis Support System. The learning of past experience is used as feedback support by exploring the possibilities to collect this sort of information from experiences.

- **Advanced Planning and Design Support system:** Design Support system is used to

support human designers in architectural and industrial design. This is also good implementation and support of Case-Based Reasoning techniques.

HISTORY OF CBR

The roots of case-based reasoning in AI is found in the works of Roger Schank on dynamic memory and the central role that a reminding of earlier situations (episodes, cases) and situation patterns (scripts, MOPs) has in problem solving and learning (Schank, 1982). Other trails into the CBR field has come from the study of analogical reasoning (Gentner, 1983), and - further back – from theories of concept formation, problem solving and experiential learning within philosophy and psychology (e.g. Wittgenstein (1953), Tulving (1972), Smith (1981)).

The first system that might be called a case-based reasoner was the CYRUS system, developed by Janet Kolodner (Kolodner, 1983), at Yale University (Schank's group). CYRUS was based on Schank's dynamic memory model and MOP theory of problem solving and learning (Schank, 1982). It was basically a question-answering system with knowledge of the various travels and meetings of former US Secretary of State Cyrus Vance. The case memory model developed for this system has later served as basis for several other case-based reasoning systems (including MEDIATOR (Simpson, 1985), PERSUADER (Sycara, 1988), CHEF (Hammond, 1989), JULIA (Hinrichs, 1992), CASEY (Koton, 1989)).

Another basis for CBR, and another set of models, was developed by Bruce Porter and his group (Porter, 1986) at the University of Texas, Austin. They initially addressed the machine learning problem of concept learning for classification tasks. This lead to the development of the PROTOS system (Bareiss, 1989), which emphasized on integrating general domain knowledge and specific case knowledge into a unified representation structure. The combination of cases with general domain knowledge was pushed further in GREBE (Branting, 1991), an application in the domain of law. Another early significant contribution to CBR was the work by Edwina Rissland and her group at the University of Massachusetts, Amhearst. With several law scientists in the group, they were interested in the role of precedence reasoning in legal judgements (Rissland, 1983). Cases 5 (precedents) are here not used to produce a single answer, but to interpret a situation in court, and to produce and assess arguments for both parties. This resulted in the HYPO system (Ashley, 1990), and later the combined case-based and rule-based system CABARET (Skalak, 1992). Phyllis Koton at MIT studied the use of case-based reasoning to optimize performance in an existing knowledge based system, where the domain (heart failure) was described by a deep, causal model. This resulted in the CASEY system (Koton, 1989), in which case-based and deep model-based reasoning was combined.

In Europe, research on CBR was taken up a little later than in the US. The CBR work seems to have been stronger coupled to expert systems development and knowledge acquisition research than in the US. Among the earliest results was the work on CBR for complex technical diagnosis within the MOLTKE system, done by Michael Richter together with Klaus Dieter Althoff and others at the University of Kaiserslautern (Althoff, 1989). This lead to the PATDEX system (Richter, 1991), with Stefan Wess as the main developer, and later to several other systems and methods (Althoff, 1991). At IIIA in Blanes, Enric Plaza and Ramon Lopez de Mantaras developed a case-based learning apprentice system for medical diagnosis (Plaza, 1990), and Beatrice Lopez investigated the use of case based methods for strategy-level reasoning (Lopez, 1990). In Aberdeen, Derek Sleeman's group studied the use of cases for knowledge base refinement. An early result was the REFINER system, developed by Sunil Sharma (Sharma, 1988).

Another result is the IULIAN system for theory revision (Oehlmann, 1992). At the University of Trondheim, Agnar Aamodt and colleagues at Sintef studied the learning aspect of CBR in the context of knowledge acquisition in general, and knowledge maintenance in particular. For problem solving, the combined use of cases and general domain knowledge was focused (Aamodt, 1989). This lead to the development of the CREEK system and integration framework (Aamodt, 1991), and to continued work on knowledge-intensive case-based reasoning. On the cognitive science side, early work was done on analogical reasoning by Mark Keane, at Trinity College, Dublin, (Keane, 1988), a group that has developed into a strong environment for this type of CBR. In Gerhard Strube's group at the University of Freiburg, the role of episodic knowledge in cognitive models was investigated in the EVENTS project (Strube, 1990),that lead to the group's current research profile of cognitive science and CBR.

Currently, the CBR activities in the United States as well as in Europe are spreading out (see, e.g. DARPA (1991), IEEE (1992), EWCBR (1993), Allemagne (1993), and the rapidly growing number of papers on CBR in almost any AI journal). Germany seems to have taken a leading position in terms of number of active researchers, and several groups of significant size and activity level have been established recently. From Japan and other Asian countries, there are also activity points, for example in India (Venkatamaran, 1993). In Japan, the interest is to a large extent focused towards the parallel computation approach to CBR (Kitano, 1993).

FUNDAMENTALS OF CBR METHODS

All case based reasoning methods have same thing common: to identify problem and purpose solution for it and also update from learning of past experience. Some time these are based on the specified area of problem which is very important to make new method. But we can classify CBR methods according to their properties.

Main Types of CBR Methods

CBR method cases used for different purpose like organizing, retrieving, utilizing and indexing the knowledge. All CBR methods may be make purely self dependent and automatic. Each CBR method can be modified and updated according to the differences between two cases. The matching of cases, adaptation of solutions, and learning from an Experience. CBR methods may be purely self-contained and automatic. We discuss some CBR methods type below

- **Exemplar-Based Reasoning:** This approach is used for problem solving classification task, to find the right for the unclassified exemplar.
- **Instance Based Reasoning:** This approach is especially dedicated of exemplar based reasoning into Syntactic CBR approach. Basically representation of instance is very easy. This is non generalization approach due to the concept learning problem addressed and machine learning method.
- **Memory-Based Reasoning:** The main focus of case base methods is memory organization and access. This method consists on some cases as large memory, accessing and searching in this memory. The main characteristic of this method is parallel processing technique.
- **Case-Based Reasoning:** This term has some special typical CBR method that makes it different from other terms. Firstly typically case is considered to have a certain degree of richness of information contained on it. This term also have property

of methods may be modify a retrieved solution when applied in a different problem solving context.

- **Analogy-Based Reasoning:** This term is often used as characterize methods that solve the new problem based on past cases from a different domain. Some time it is used as a synonym to case based reasoning to describe the typical case based approach. The main focus of approach is mapping problem like finding a way to transfer and map to present problem.
- **Analogy-Based Reasoning:** This term is often used as characterize methods that solve the new problem based on past cases from a different domain. Some time it is used as a synonym to case based reasoning to describe the typical case based approach. The main focus of approach is mapping problem like finding a way to transfer and map to present problem.

CBR Methods and System

CBR methods and systems has two main parts

- A process model of the CBR cycle.
- A task-method structure for case-based reasoning.

The first is a dynamic model that identifies the main sub processes of a CBR cycle, their interdependencies and products. The second is a task-oriented view, where a task decomposition and related problem solving methods are described.

The CBR Cycle

At the highest level of generality, a general CBR cycle may be described by the following four processes

1. RETRIEVE the most similar case or cases.
2. REUSE the information and knowledge in that case to solve the problem.
3. REVISE the proposed solution.
4. RETAIN the parts of this experience likely to be useful for future problem solving.

A new problem is solved by retrieving one or more previously experienced cases, reusing the case in one way or another, revising the solution based on reusing a previous case, and retaining the new experience by incorporating it into the existing case base.

New case is used to RETRIEVE a case from the collection of previous cases. The retrieved case is combined with the new case - through REUSE - into a solved case. During RETAIN, useful experience is retained for future reuse, and the case base is updated by a new learned case, or by modification of some existing cases. As indicated in the figure, general knowledge usually plays a part in this cycle, by supporting the CBR processes.

A Task-Method Structure for Case-Based Reasoning

Tasks are set up depending on the goals of the system, and a Particular task is performed by applying one or more methods. A task-method decomposition of CBR defines in Figure 2.

Figure 1. CBR Cycle (Aamodt and Plaza)

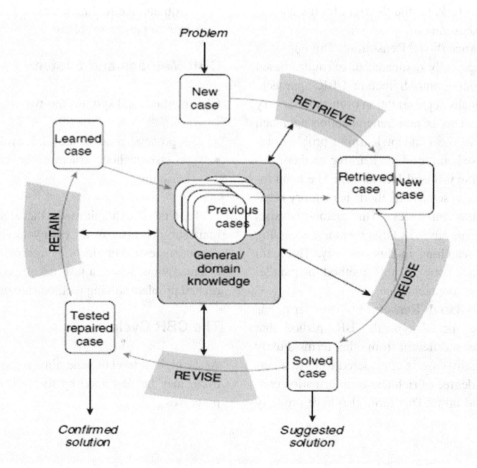

Figure 2. A task-method decomposition of CBR

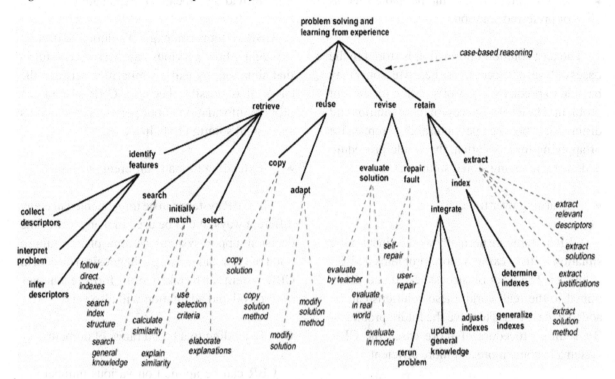

Advantages of CBR

CBR has many advantages as compare to other sub fields of AI.

• Reducing the knowledge acquisition task.

The knowledge acquisition task of CBR consists of collection of relative past cases, and their representation and storage. In the rule based systems, knowledge acquisition is necessary by extracting a set of rules.

• Avoiding repeating mistakes made in the past.

In CBR system failure and success record, as well as reason to failure record kept. This information about cause of the failure is used in the future for reducing the failure outputs.

• Providing flexibility in knowledge modelling.

CBR systems used past experience as domain knowledge and can provide reasonable solution, appropriate solution through adaptation. But, model based system cannot solve problem due to fixed modelling and formulation that is on the boundary of their knowledge.

• Reasoning in domains that have not been fully understood, defined or modelled.

CBR system can still be developed by only adding small set of causes from the domain, in situation where too insufficient knowledge exists to build a causal model. The addition of new cases is caused of expanded knowledge of CBR System. These are used in this direction that is determined by the cases encountered in its problem solving.

- Making prediction of the probable success of preferred solution.

The past solution information is stored in the bases of level of success; case based reasoner may be able to predict success of solution for current problem. The level of success of these solution and differentiate between pervious and current cause of applying these solution, the whole procedure is done by referring stored solution.

- Learning over time.

CBR systems are normally worked in learning situation as they express more problems and get solutions. The level of success tested and determined in the real world, these solutions can be added to case bases to solve the future problems. By adding procedure of more cases the CBR systems become more and more efficient.

- Reasoning with incomplete or imprecise data of concepts.

The retrieved cases are not may be very similar solution to the current case. When they are within some defined potential of similarity to the present case, any drought and incompleteness can be dealt by Case-Based reasoner. These factors have a little impact on performance, because the increasing lack of similarity between the current and retrieved cases.

- Avoiding repeating all the steps that need to be taken to arrive at a solution.

Reusing a pervious solution also allow the actual steps to taken to reach that solution to be reused for solving other problems. Because in problem domain that requires a well defined process to create solution of new problem, but alternative approach of modifying an earlier solution can reduce this process.

- Providing a means of explanation.

CBR systems can explain solution to user by explaining how pervious case was successful in that situation, by using similarities between the cases. It is possible because, CBR system can provide information about pervious case and its successful solution to help a user.

- Extending to many different purpose.

The CBR system can be implemented in many different ways. It can be used in many forms like decision support systems, creating plan, arguing a point of view and making a diagnosis. The data in CBR system can be taken in any form, techniques of retrieval and adaptation will also vary.

- Extending to a broad range of domains.

CBR can be applied on various numbers of application domains. This is due to the appearing of unlimited number of ways representing, indexing, adapting and retrieving cases.

- Reflecting human reasoning.

As we used CBR methodology in real life at many places it is not difficult to convince the developers, user and managers of the validity of the paradigm. So, human can understand a CBR system reasoning and explanation and are able to convince of the validity of the solution they receive from the systems.

Drawback of CBR

- Critics of CBR argue that it is an approach that accepts anecdotal evidence as its main operating principle. Without statistically relevant data for backing and implicit generalization, there is no guarantee that the generalization is correct.

- If Domains is not novel or exceptional, cases may be modelled better with rules base system.

Some Prominent CBR Systems

Some Prominent CBR system has build in this following area.

- **SMART:** Support management automated reasoning technology for Compaq customer service.
- **Appliance Call Center:** Automation at General Electric.
- **CLAVIER:** Applying case-based reasoning on to composite part fabrication.
- **Form Tool:** Plastics Color Matching.
- **CoolAir:** HVAC specification and pricing system.
- **Vidur:** A CBR based intelligent advisory system, by C-DAC Mumbai, for farmers of North-East India.
- **jCOLIBRI:** A CBR framework that can be used to build other custom user-defined CBR systems.
- **CAKE:** Collaborative Agile Knowledge Engine.
- **Edge Platform:** Applies CBR to the healthcare, oil & gas and financial services Sectors.
- **KATE:** It developed by AcknoSoft. It mainly used for Technical support and e-commerce with a focus on web-based solutions.
- **SpotLight:** It developed by Atlantis Aerospace Corporation, it is a computer-based job aid that helps maintenance technicians or machine operators solve problems more efficiently by letting them know whether a similar problem has occurred before, and how it was solved. The

tools are specifically designed to support complex diagnosis and trouble shooting of machines.

- **ART*Enterprise:** It developed by Brightware Inc., it is the latest incarnation of Brightware's flagship development product. Brightware, based in California, were formerly a division of Inference Corporation, one of the oldest established vendors of AI tools and the major player in the Case-Based Reasoning tool market. Brightware market ART*Enterprise as an integrated, object-oriented, applications development tool, designed for MIS developers offering a variety of representational paradigms including: a procedural programming language; objects supporting multiple inheritance, encapsulation and polymorphism; rules; and Case-Based Reasoning. This is all packaged with a GUI builder, sophisticated version Control facilities, and an impressive ability to link to data repositories in most proprietary DBMS formats for developing client-server applications. Moreover, ART*Enterprise offers cross-platform support for most operating systems, windowing systems and hardware platforms (i.e., you can develop on one platform and deliver to others).
- **Spotlight:** It developed by Case Bank Support Systems Inc. It used for faster fault resolution and throughput.
- **ReMind:** It developed by Cognitive Systems Inc. by support from the US DARPA programme. It was originally developed for the Macintosh and has since been ported to MS Windows and UNIX platforms. It is available as a C library for embedding in other applications, and as an interactive development environment. Unfortunately, Cognitive Systems ceased

trading in 1996. However, ReMind Version 2.0 is under development at the Navy Centre for Applied Research in Artificial Intelligence at the Naval Research Laboratory in Washington DC. It is not clear though when the new version will be released or who may retail it. Information on ReMind 1.1 has been included because it is still widely used and has been a very influential tool and will continue to influence the functionality and look and feel of CBR tools. ReMind supports nearest neighbor, inductive, knowledge guided inductive and template retrieval. It provides adaptation through a adaptation formulae, can import data from database records and has a modest interface builder.

- **ESTEEM:** It developed by Esteem Software Inc. It is written in Intellicorp's Kappa-PC and is now in version 1.4. ESTEEM can Kappa's inference engine, thus enabling developers to create adaptation rules. It supports applications that access multiple case-bases and nested cases. This means that one can reference another case-base through an attribute slot in a case. ESTEEM supports various similarity assessment methods including feature counting, weighted feature computation, inferred feature computation. It also can automatically generate feature weights, either using an ID3 weight generation method, or a gradient descent weight generation method. Moreover, users can incorporate their own similarity functions into ESTEEM if they wish. ESTEEM is very reasonably priced and is well suited as a teaching tool or an entry level CBR product.

- **CasePower:** It developed by Inductive Solutions Inc. It builds its cases within the spreadsheet environment of Microsoft Excel. CasePower is a specialised tool for constructing Excel spreadsheets that can be analysed using CBR. Within the limited confines of Excel, it provides basic CBR functionality, mainly suitable for numeric applications. Symbolic data can be represented as ordered hierarchies that are mapped to numerical ranges.

- **k-Commerce (formerly called CBR3 or CBR Express, CasePoint, Generator & WebServer):** It developed by Inference Corporation. It is most successful and mature CBR products to date, with end users in 22 countries. k-Commerce is specifically tailored to the vertical market of customer support, including both product selection and troubleshooting, and dominates this sector. The product range includes support for: k-Commerce from Inference, telephone call centres, self-help web server access,automatic provision of support via email, interactive voice responce systems, and Internet Chat room support, Inference can provide consultancy support in most countries and their products support many major languages. They can also provide shrink wrapped case-bases for trouble shooting MS Office and Lotus applications, Novell Netware and other IT major domains.

- **TechMate:** It developed by IET-Intelligent Electronics. IET - Intelligent Electronics' TechMate 5.2 is a problem resolution tool for complex equipment production, service and maintenance environments. It combines model-based reasoning with case-based reasoning. TechMate 5.2 combines advanced algorithms with the outcome of extensive research. Diagnostic assessments are based on hierarchical probabilistic inference networks, adapted for testing and diagnosis. This adaptation extends to TechMate 5.2's knowledge base, which uses universal knowledge about testing, service and maintenance to dramatically reduces the time required to model a sytem compared to conventional methods. Its Dynamic Test Selection is based on information theory techniques, combined with real-life considerations through which test sequences are actually possible and effective, regardless of their theoretical information content. TechMate 5.2's learning tool combines statistical methods with manipulation of the probabilistic inference network, as well as model-based learning.

- **KnowMan:** It developed by Intellix. It used as a unique self generalizing learning algorithm. Historically AI has been divided into several major areas of research, one being Neural Nets and another being classical (or symbolic) AI. Neural Networks have mainly been concerned with learning and generalization while classical AI is concerned with reasoning. These are major aspects of what constitutes intelligence. Intellix A/S has incorporated both of these elements into a software framework called S.O.U.L. (Self-Optimising Universal Learner). The core-technology behind S.O.U.L. is a combination of the best from Neural Networks, expert systems and their own inventions in the field of artificial intelligence.

- **ReCall:** It developed by Isoft. It works in multidisciplinary teams of professionals, with expertise in mathematics, physics, computer science, logistics, engineering, systems and management science, using technologies that range from statistical analysis to neural nets and stochastic modeling. In this manner, they help clients interpret data, model cause and effect relationships, and link strategies together to form concrete, achievable plans. In order to

enable their clients to remain ahead of their competition, the Knowledge Technologies Group creates solutions which are driven by the real-world application of a number of techniques which have typically emerged from the artificial intelligence, machine learning and operations research fields. These ever-evolving technology areas include case-based reasoning.

- **CASE Advisor & Case Advisor Webserver:** It is developed by Sententia Software Inc. It used to intelligent problem diagnosis and resolution system which allows an organization to efficiently author and retrieve solutions from a "knowledge database" to solve customer problems. Marketed by Sententia Software Inc. of Simon Fraser University in Canada it is similar in look and feel to Inference's CBR products. There are three components to the software; Case Advisor Authoring, the case authoring environment, Case Advisor Problem Resolution, the runtime case retrieval engine, and Case Advisor WebServer. Case Advisor Webserver is an intelligent customer support application for organizations wishing to provide customer support on the internet. Case Advisor Authoring is a very simple tool, similar in look to the Inference's CBR Express Versions 1 and 2. The case author is presented with a syntax free environment for entering the details of a case's name, description, solution and confirming questions.

- **CBR-Works and Inference's k-Commerce:** It developed by tecInno GmbH. It used to fast way to produce a customer support knowledge base containing a company's solutions and expertise. Knowledge Builder, with Expert Reasoning™, allows you to easily capture and organize the support advice of technicians by simply recording problems, causes, solutions, and questions (i.e., cases).. Web Advisor delivers the intelligent advice to customers and employees over the Internet or a corporate intranet. The interactive problem resolution offered by Web Advisor is an effective way for all users, regardless of how sophisticated they are, to solve their own problems and answer their own questions.

- **HELPDESK-3:** It developed by TreeTools. It used designed to automated help desk. It uses heuristic search to retrieve cases and can handle natural language problem descriptions.
- **The Easy Reasoner, CPR & Help!CPR:** It developed by The Haley Enterprise Inc. It offers several CBR products: The Easy Reasoner is a CBR product that includes both associative memory and decision tree technologies in addition to the rule-based capabilities required for reasoning and case adaptation.CPR (Case-based Problem Resolution) is a C++ class library that provides embeddable problem resolution based on case-retrieval and diagnosis. Help!CPR is an application program for problem resolution and knowledge publishing based on CPR ActivFiX -- CPR encapsulated in an embeddable Active X control for COM integration and Visual Basic applications.CPR Server delivers Help!CPR to LAN or web clients and Java applications over the web.
- **The RapidReasoner:** It developed by Webpresence Technology. It is a Malaysian company that provides support and services to enable corporations to understand, master and exploit Internet-related technologies. The RapidReasoner is a Java Case-Based Reasoning system that can provide simple diagnostic advice or product selection on the Web.

SOME TYPICAL CBR APPLICATIONS: KNOWLEDGE MANAGEMENT WITH CASE BASED REASONING APPLIED ON FIRE EMERGENCY HANDLING

Case-Based Reasoning is a Knowledge Management mechanism that allows knowledge acquisition through learning and experience undergone in the process of problem solving applying similarity-based reasoning. Problem representation is by means of metadata representation of certain knowledge items stored in a repository termed Case-Base. Here we discusses on a Fire Emergency Handling System where fire cases have ontological representation implemented in Object-oriented Java platform that assists fire fighters or administrators to take a decision on the resources required to handle or control fire.

Use of CBR as KM Tool for Emergency Services

Whenever there is an emergency, there is neither much time nor much data for the services team to sit, analyze and decide on the course of action by the Emergency Handling/Management team. Hence, instead of a complex simulation model, simple empirical methods are used to determine the course of action.

1. Classify the situation based on the limited data available,
2. Retrieve a predetermined solution for this class of situation from some archive of such solutions.

To improve on this simple principle, the size of the archive can be increased and the dimensionality of the classification mechanism can also be increased to enhance the flexibility of the available set of responses. Here, we can make use of case library to store several cases or experiences related to different situational inputs and employ CBR to classify and retrieve the cases. CBR combines problem solving with sustained learning through the experience in problem solving. It can learn both from successful solutions as well as from the failed ones. Hence, CBR helps in improvement of knowledge through experience in handling cases and offering solutions. Fire Emergency is one of the key areas where CBR may be employed for effective solution to a fire case problem to assist decision in fire handling to fire fighters.

Application of CBR in Fire Emergency

It has been found that fire fighters gain experience and knowledge through attendance at different fire incidents and through study of certain procedures and archetypal incidents. Though identical recurrence of situations is rare, fire fighters try to handle a fire situation from experience gathered from similar situations by comparing the similarity of the situations with respect to certain factors representing the situation. They base their decisions on their experiences. Similarly, CBR may be used as a decision support tool through reference to a "problem case" with a similar case in the case base of case library. Though no two cases are identical, if CBR is able to identify similar cases, the decisions for the earlier cases may assist the Fire Emergency Handling team to take correct decision on the solution of the earlier incidents through similarity measurement tools. Routine decisions may benefit from CBR. Non-routine cases those are unfamiliar and not too repeated may also benefit from such CBR tools. Similarity-based situation recognition and decision according to the decision of the past situation helps automate decision process, thus making the services quick, responsive, effective and efficient. This is mentioned a Gary Klein's study concluded that 80% of non-routine decisions were taken by Incident commanders (ICs) of fire incidents using recognition-primed decision (RPD) model and routine incidents showed still higher percentage of decisions through similarity-based models. Thus, CBR tools may be used to provide solutions for critical incidents and would prove to be a very strong decision support tool.

CBR applications can cater to highly complex, incompletely understood non-specific domains as it only records cases as experiences. Both solved and failed solutions to problem cases may be recorded for the CBR to learn through experience of old and new cases. It also provides solutions where there is no specific algorithm to solve it. However, a case library needs to be built before the system can prove its usefulness. Moreover, in order to revise a solution or retain it for future problem solving, CBR system needs a human interface to determine what is right or wrong for offering a solution. The CBR provides suggestive solutions matching the Query, not necessarily absolutely "correct" solution. There should be human interface to determine the same. However, CBR is proposed in this chapter to assist decision making and problem solving, not to provide a singular correct solution.

Framework of Emergency Handling Services

The framework of jCOLIBRI version 2 has been chosen for realization of Fire Emergency Handling Recommender (FEHR). It is a Java based framework used to develop knowledge intensive CBR applications and helps in integration of ontology in them. Integration of ontology in the CBR applications facilitates case representations. For determining similarity between the cases for similarity based retrieval of a query case, content-based reasoning methods are used. It is an open source framework that has been one of the main reasons for adopting it for our application development. The ontology support of jCOLIBRI is built around Onto Bridge library developed by GAIA research group to easily manage ontologies with Description Logic Reasoners for use in Semantic

Webs. This new design is a complete white box framework open to java developers to include the features of jCOLIBRI in their CBR applications.

In this application, the case base is composed of several fire cases. The system receives a current fire emergency condition as a query, compares the query with the previous fire cases in the case base using a similarity function, and returns the most similar ones. After the retrieval, these most similar cases can be adapted according with the restrictions of the query. Each case is represented by several attributes: fire location, fire cause, area under fire, number of fire exits, wind velocity, neighbor in wind direction, presence of water bodies, assets at risk, population, humidity, height, flammability, the extinguisher used, number of fire engines required, the remedial actions taken and manpower required to put off the fire and save the citizens. In our application, the extinguisher used, number of fire engines required, the remedial actions taken and man power required will be considered as the solution of the case meanwhile the remaining attributes will be the fire case description. A typical CBR Query for Fire Emergency Handling would look like Table 1.

Table 1. Typical CBR query for fire emergency handling

Attribute	Value
Fire location	Night club
Fire cause	Man-made
Area under fire	700 sq. m
Number of fire exits	Single
Wind velocity	Not Applicable
Neighbour in-wind direction	Not Applicable
Presence of water bodies	Nil
Assets at risk	0.5 million dollars
Population	120
Humidity	0.8
Height	20 m
Flammability	Medium

The application in this chapter is to allow Fire Emergency service providers a framework to take a decision on how many fire engines, type of extinguisher, remedial action and manpower to be used in action when there is a fire emergency call based on the solution to the query depending on the fire case description. The solution to the "problem" of "fire case description" measured in terms of similarity between past occurred fire's cases would assist the fire administrator in taking a quick decision to act on the problem devoid of bureaucratic administrative hierarchy. Here the problem solving case is of "Fire description". Since it is an Emergency Service, an automated solution to the problem would certainly assist in taking quick action on the problem (the fire emergency call) saving time rather than involving bureaucratic administrative hierarchy. Saving time necessarily means faster response to emergency calls thus increasing the efficiency of performance of the service provider.

Methodology

'The Fire Emergency Handling Recommender' (FEH Recommender) has been implemented using jCOLIBRI2. Following sections describe the development process of this application in an incremental way. Before starting with the implementation, this section describes the features and behavior of the FEH Recommender application. In this application, the Case Base is composed of several fire cases. The system receives a current fire emergency condition as a Query, compares the Query with the previous fire cases in the Case Base using a similarity function, and returns the most similar Cases. After the retrieval, these most similar cases can be adapted according with the restrictions of the Query.

Each Case is represented by several attributes that relate to fire like: fire location, fire cause, area under fire, number of fire exits, wind velocity, neighbour in-wind direction, presence of water bodies, assets at risk, population, humidity, height, flammability, type of fire extinguishers used to handle fire, number of fire engines required, the remedial actions taken and man power required to put off the fire and save the citizens.

In our application, the type of extinguisher used, number of fire engines required, the remedial actions taken and man power required will be considered as the solution of the case meanwhile the remaining attributes will be the fire case description. Hence, our cases are divided into: a description used to retrieve similar cases given a query, and a solution that is adapted depending on the values of the query.

Steps of CBR Application for FEHR

- **Define/Configure Queries:** In this step the user defines the Query to the system. He/She has to define the values of the differ-

ent attributes of the current fire emergency situation: fire location, cause, area, number of safety exits etc.

- **Configure Similarity:** Here the user configures the similarity measure used to retrieve the Cases most similar to the given Query. JCOLIBRI2 implements several similarity functions that can be used depending on the type of the attribute (integers, strings, etc.).

Weights can be assigned to each attribute of the query that will be taken into account when computing the average of all attributes. Also, some similarity functions can have parameters used to configure the similarity measure.

Finally, the k value indicates how many cases must be retrieved. We are using an algorithm named K Nearest Neighbor (k-NN) that computes

Figure 3. Applet for define/configure query step

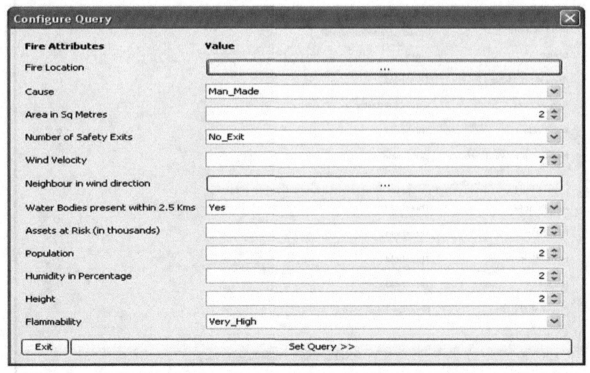

the similarity of the Query with all the cases and then orders the result depending on that similarity value. Then the first k most similar cases are returned.

- **Retrieved Cases:** This step shows the documents retrieved by the k-NN method. It shows each Case and its percentage of similarity to the Query.
- **Adaptation:** In this step the system adapts the retrieved Cases to the requirements of the user depending on the values defined in the Query. This stage use to be very domain dependent. In our FEH Recommender application we adapt the number of fire engines required depending on the area under fire, assets at risk and population defined in

the query. We also adapt the man power required depending on the population of the region. In our system, we use simple direct proportions to perform the adaptation.

After adapting the solution of the Cases, their description can be substituted by the description of the Query. At this point, the system will manage a list of working Cases that are different from the Cases in the Case Base. These working Cases represent possible solutions to the problem described in the Query.

- **Revise Cases:** Once cases have been adapted, the user (or a domain expert, in this case the fire handling agent) would adjust the values of the working cases in a manual way.

Figure 4. Applet for configure similarity

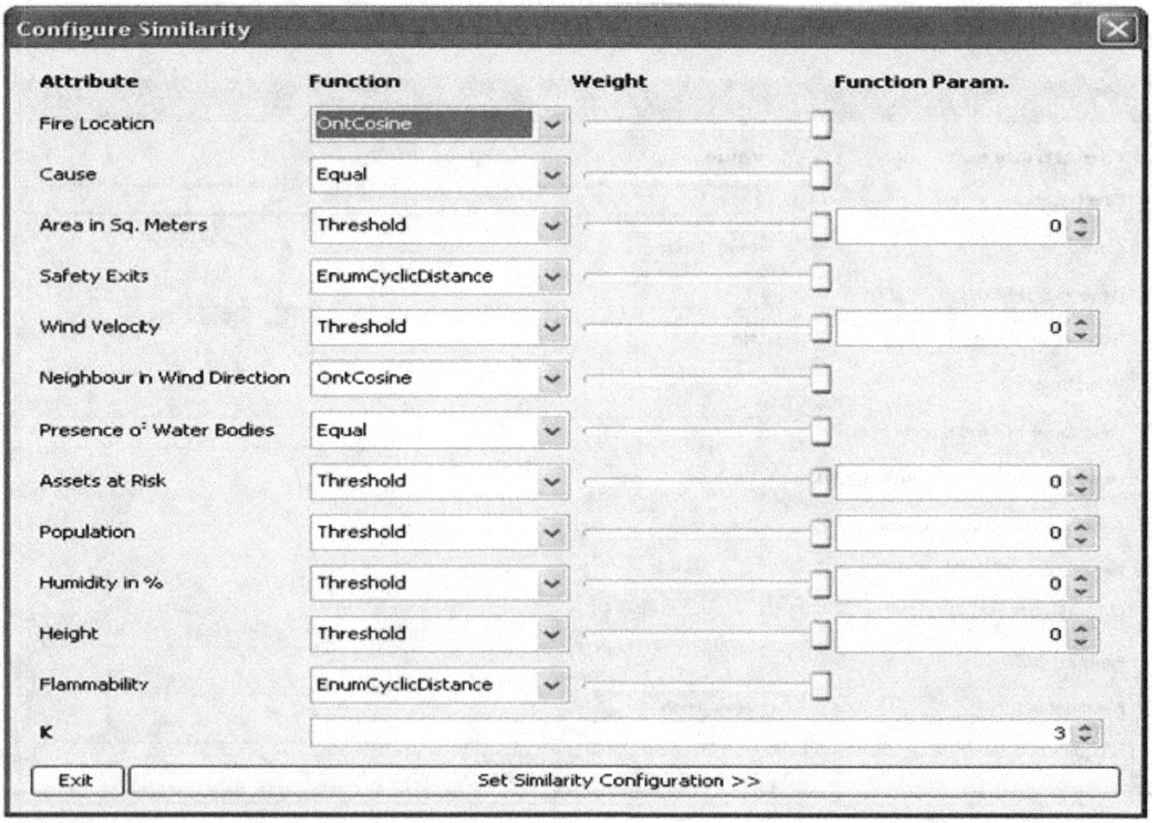

Figure 5. Adaptation step

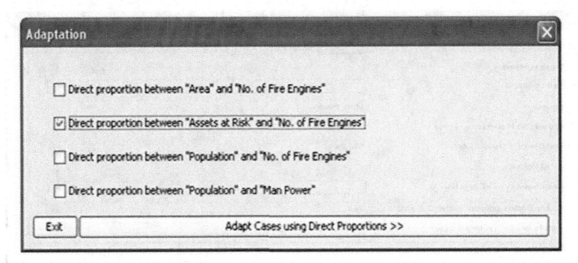

For example, if the fire cause is such that water cannot be used to extinguish the fire, then the type of extinguisher (say foam) has to be explicitly mentioned by the expert. Another situation may be that retrieved cases are not similar enough to the requirements of the Query and the fire handling agent has to define manually the solution of the Case.

- **Retain Cases:** Finally, the fire handling agent would save the new emergency case into the case base for being used in future queries. If it is done, a new Id must be assigned to the fire case.

The Ontology structure followed for Case base is as Figure 7.

The FEHR framework shows that CBR may be used as an effective tool of decision making. Depending on the similarity function, the retrieved cases may be used to automate the decision regarding solution of the "problem" that is placed as "Query".

FEVER-TYPE DETECTION SYSTEM: A COMBINATION OF CBR AND BOTTOM-UP APPROACH

In this chapter application of knowledge-based fever detection based on the combination of methodology of case-based reasoning (CBR) and bottom up approach has been proposed. CBR is an approach for solving problems based on solutions of similar past case. Cases are stored in a database of cases called a case base (CB). To solve an actual problem a notation of similarities between problems is used to retrieve similar cases from the case base. The solutions of these similar cases are then used as starting points for solving the actual problem. Bottom up approach is needed when there are multiple solutions and among these, only one solution needs to be identified. This chapter discusses on a fever detection system which helps the hospitals to detect the type of fever the patient is suffering from using symptoms of patients.

Figure 6. Applet for revise cases

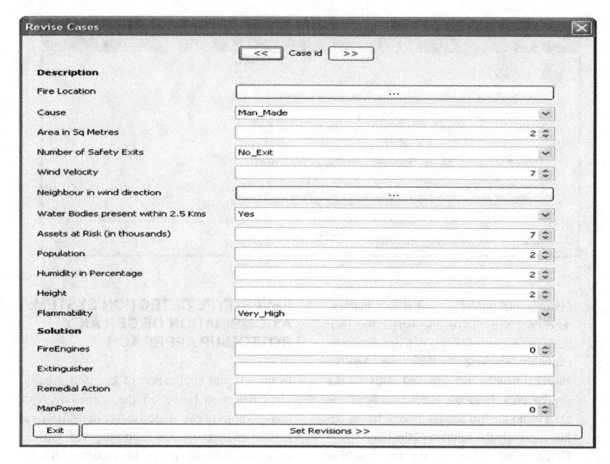

System Concept Development

Fever detection system is a combination of two approaches: (i) CBR Approach (ii) Bottom up approach.

1. CBR Approach: In CBR approach, working principle of a CBR (Retrieve, Reuse, revise and Retain) is included.
2. Bottom up approach: Bottom-up parsing is a strategy for analyzing unknown information that attempts to identify the most fundamental units first, and then to infer higher-order structures from them. The name comes from the concept of a parse tree, in which the most fundamental units are at the bottom, and structures composed of them are in successively higher layers, until at the top of the tree a single unit, or start symbol, comprises all of the information being analyzed.

Here in Figure 8 a block diagram of Bottom up approach has been shown where input units are at the bottom. Here inputs units are four type of fever; F1, F2, F3 and F4. The System compares the fever type according to the algorithm implemented in the system and the output or resultant is the fever type F3 which is a fever from the input set of probable fever types. The output is indicated on the top of the diagram, Figure 8.

Fever Classification

According to variation in temperature behaviour, fever can be divided into basically four categories. Categories are stated below:

Figure 7. Ontology structure for Case Base of FEHR

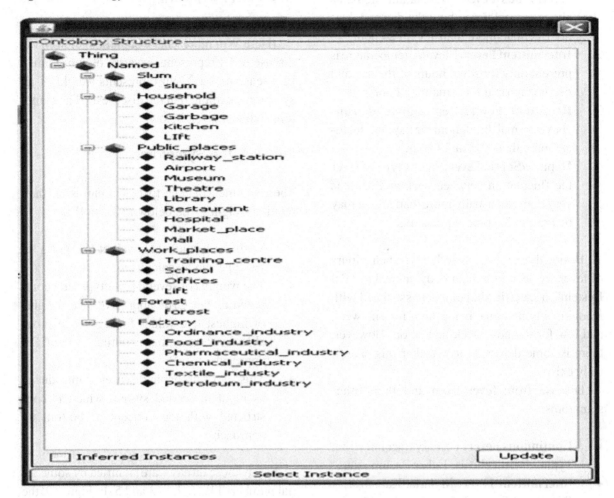

Figure 8. Bottom up approach diagram

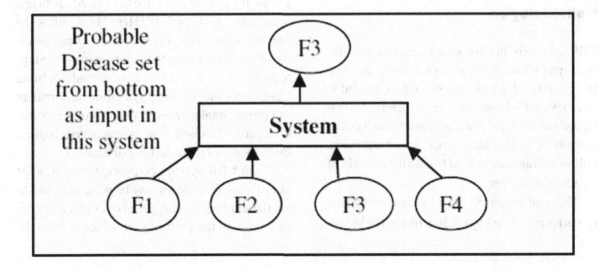

1. **Continuous Fever:** Temperature remains above normal throughout the day and does not fluctuate more than 1°C in 24 hour.
2. **Intermittent Fever:** Elevated temperature is present only for some hours of the day and become normal for remaining hours.
3. **Remittent Fever:** Temperature remains above normal throughout the day and fluctuate more than 1°C in 24 hour.
4. **Hepatic/Septic Fever:** In this type of fever the fluctuation between peak and nadir is very high and usually more than 5°C. It may be present in some septicaemia.

Beside those types, one other type behaviours of fever are seen in human body, named as "Pal Epstein", a specific kind of fever associated with Hodgkin's lymphoma, being high for one week and low for the next week and so on. However, there is some debate as to whether this pattern truly exists.

Disease from fever from and their other symptoms:

- **Continuous Fever:** Urinary tract infection, Typhoid, Brucellosis, Lobar Pneumonia,
- **Intermittent Fever:** Malaria, Kala-azar,
- **Remittent Fever:** Infective endocarditic,
- **Hepatic/Septic Fever:** Diseased liver.

Methodologies

CBR approach: In CBR system, patient will give their symptoms and the severity of the symptoms. In this system basically the severity is divided in three levels: high (assigned value 7), medium (assigned value 5) and low (assigned value 3). And every symptom has an assigned weight and index. Following function is used to calculate weight of a particular disease.

The final weigh S_u (Total weight for disease type u) is calculated by the function given below,

$$S_u = \sum (Wtu * Ut) / \sum Wu \qquad (1)$$

(Here Wtu represents weight of symptom t in disease u, Ut represents severity of symptoms t in disease u and $\sum Wu$ represents weight of all symptoms exhibited in the disease u). The symptoms table is given below:

Indexing the Symptoms

The assignment of index to the symptoms and their relative weight given below in Table II:

- With the formula (1), weight (SU) of a fever type can be calculated.
- The weights of several fever types are compared as per CBR approach. The weights of highest five values form a set of probable fever types that is output of the CBR approach.
- This set of probable diseases is introduced as input in second system which is constructed with the concept of bottom up approach

Firstly those diseases are signified by some serial numbers like 1, 2, 3, 4 and 5. In Figure 9, the process of comparison is shown by a table where every fever has an array corresponding to required symptoms that needs a value to be filled up. In this array there is '1' and '0'. Here '1' signifies the presence of a particular symptom and '0' represents the absence of a symptom. Here, patient's symptoms mean the symptoms a patient suffers from. Comparing the required symptoms and patient symptoms, total number of matches of symptoms for a particular disease can be calculated. Highest match is declared as the final disease.

From CBR system, comparing weight, a set of probable fever types may be achieved. And to get the ultimate fever type, a bottom up theory is applied onto the probable set achieved from the

Figure 9. Comparison of required symptoms of probable disease and patient symptoms

Disease	Required symptoms	Patient symptoms	Total match
1	1 0 1 1 0 0	1 0 1 1 1 0	3
2	1 0 1 1 1 0	1 0 1 1 1 0	4
3	1 0 0 0 1 0	1 0 1 1 1 0	2
4	1 0 1 0 1 0	1 0 1 1 1 0	3
5	1 0 1 1 0 0	1 0 1 1 1 0	3

CBR approach. In this methodology, symptoms of every probable disease are compared with patient input and highest match is decided as a resultant disease as shown in Figure 9.

To show how bottom up approach works here total process is stated with an example below:

Example

In the first stage of system when there is a large set of fever types, with the help of CBR system that large is minimize to a small set of disease . This small set of probable disease is numbered as 1,2,3,4,5 and every disease has a set of symptoms. After comparing with these symptoms with patient symptoms, highest matching disease will be the particular disease that a patient has.

Architecture of Fever Detection System

The total system is divided into two main part, first is CBR system and second one is Bottom up theory.

In CBR system, at front end there is Fever recommender environment, from this environment there is two modules:

1. Administrator module
2. Query and output module

At Administrator Module, cases can be updated, deleted or modified in presence of a Medical officer. In Query and output Module Query is processed and output graph and resultant table is shown. The query is processed by computational Module and data is fetched from CBR Module where cases are stored at following Case base. A new case can be insert to Casebase with an expert opinion by Medical officer. From CBR system a set of probable disease is extracted and after that using Bottom up theory this set is minimized to a particular disease.

Result

After comparing the graph shown at Figure 12, it can be stated that only CBR approach gives the result which is 70% same like original result. But, when the Bottom up approach is used the system result gets more accurate with original result. After using bottom up approach on CBR technology the result becomes 95% same as original result which is shown in Figure 13.

Centralized Database for Smarter Result

A Case Based system becomes smarter with the increment of database size or cases. This is one of the interesting features a case based system

Figure 10. Total architecture of fever detection system

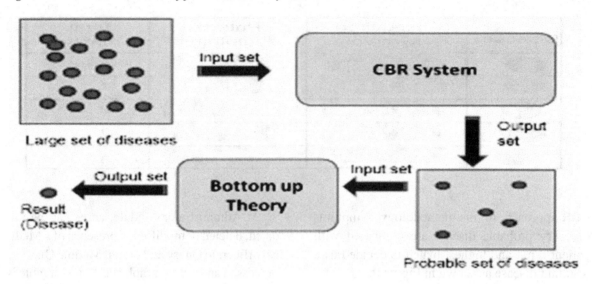

Figure 11. Architecture of the CBR part of fever detection system

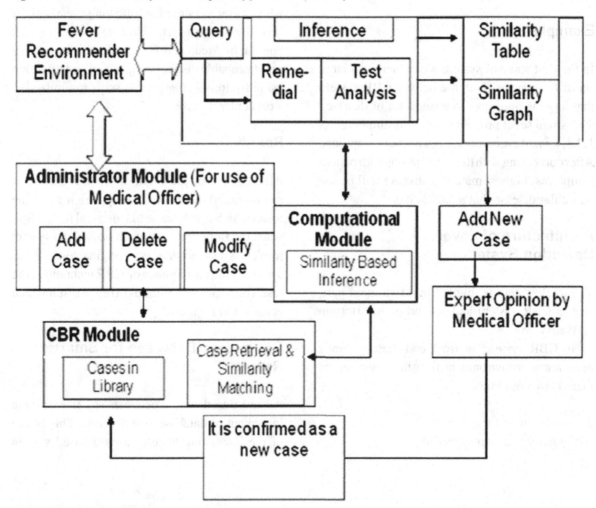

Figure 12. Comparison graph of the original vs. CBR result

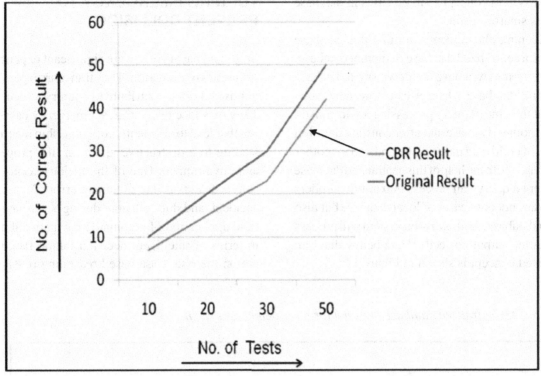

Figure 13. Comparison graph of the system vs. original result

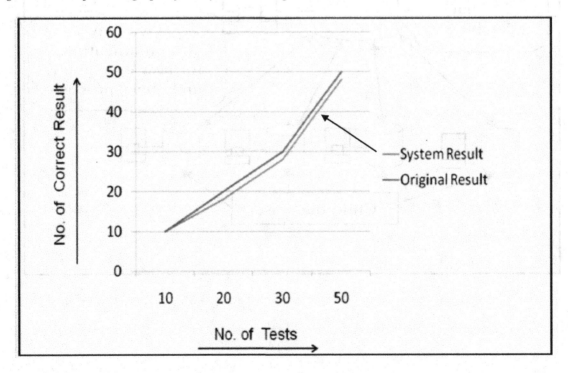

has. This fever detection system is based on Case based system concept so more cases in database makes smarter result.

Keeping above theory in mind this database can be a centralized database or mother database. Every system will have their own small database or child database where it can store new cases and at the time of query processing it will consult with mother database and after constant duration cases of child data base will be updated to mother database. With the help of this centralized database concept a query can process maximum numbers of cases, not only cases of local database but also other database. And as a result system will process a smarter output correctly. Here below diagram of stated concept is shown in Figure 14:

APPLICATION OF CBR FOR SHIP TURNING EMERGENCY TO PREVENT COLLISION

Ships and naval vessels are significant expensive properties of the nation. They transport expensive goods and often contribute to country's security. They may face many critical emergency cases in sea that lead to accidents, collision, ship overturn leading to a destructive effect on life, property and environment. One of the major reasons for ship accidents is due to human error. To reduce accidents and ship collisions during ocean navigation, application of automated navigational aids in terms of intelligent decision taking facilities are on the rise. Case-based reasoning (CBR) is

Figure 14. Centralized database diagram for fever detection system

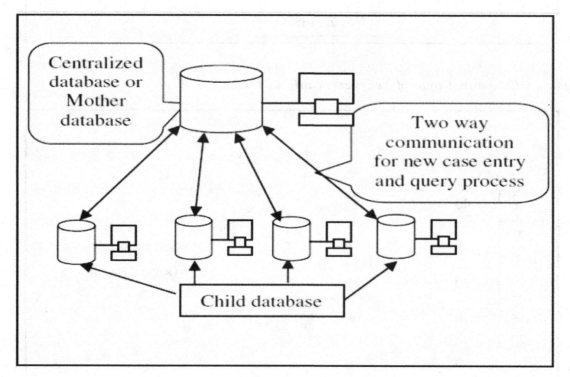

a problem solving technique that solves present problem taking reference from variety of similar problem situations. It can render decision-making easier by retrieving past solutions from situations that are similar to the one at hand and make necessary adjustments in order to adapt them. Here a Case-based reasoning system for handling ship turning problem has been proposed. The system's accuracy depends on the efficient retrieval of possible solutions, and the proposed algorithm improves the effectiveness of solving the similarity to a new case at the other hand.

Ship Turning Problem

The changing characteristic of the ship course and motion track is called ship turning. The turning of moving object in stable surface is much easier to track and measure than an object moving on unstable surface. A ship at sea moves on unstable surface. If ship at sea faces a sudden obstacle in front, for example, a low bridge or iceberg, it my suffer collision and damage and loss of property and lives. To avoid the collision it requires to turn the ship at an turn angle sufficient to avoid collision within an allowable turn time so that the obstacle may be avoided by changing the track or path of the ship from the original course of movement within a time limit. The turn angle and turn time are dependent on several natural factors, difficult to estimate and determine making the job of the captain of the ship difficult to manage collision. An effort has been made to list the factors determining the turning angle and the turn time of the ship and finding relation among the input factors and the output required factors, i.e. turning angle and turn-time. Then, a case base of previous incidents of navigating the ship away from normal course to avoid collision may be kept in the Case Base which may assist the captain of the ship to take a correct decision on the turning angle within manageable turn time.

Turning angle (β) of a ship is depends upon several factors. Some may be following factors:

1. Wind velocity (Vw).
2. Wind direction (Dw).
3. Initial Ship speed (Vs).
4. Final Ship Speed (Us).
5. Wave making resistance (Rw)
6. Turning Direction (Tdirection)
7. Water blowing (Current speed)

Turn time (Ttime) depends upon several factors, following factors.

1. Length of ship (Ls)
2. Sea density:ρ
3. Ship load (weight) Sw

A. Description of Factors

The wind velocity V_w, affects the speed of the ship. The speed of ship depends upon wind direction D_w.

If the wind is blowing in the direction of the movement of the ship, then final ship speed increases:

$$U_s = \text{Vs} + (V_w/900) \tag{1}$$

If the wind is blowing against of the direction of the ship in this case ship speed Vs decreased.

$$\text{Us} = \text{Vs} - (V_w/900) \tag{2}$$

The final or Resultant ship speed U_s is the important factor to turn ship. the turn angle β is inversely proportional to Resultant ship speed

$$\text{Cos } \beta \propto U_s^{-1} / \beta \alpha \cos^{-1}(U_s^{-1}) \tag{3}$$

The wind direction affects the turning angle β of ship.

Case 1: If the range of wind direction D_w between 0° to 180°, $0° < D_w < 180°$ and ship turn Right direction OR

If the range of wind direction D_w between 180° to 360°, $1800 < D_w < 360°$ and ship turn Left direction

$$U_s = Vs - (V_w/900) \tag{4}$$

From Equation 3:

$$\beta \propto \cos^{-1}((Vs - (V_w/900))-1) \tag{5}$$

Case 2: If wind direction Dw between 0° to 180°, $0° < D_w < 180°$ and ship turn Left direction or If wind direction Dw between 180° to 360°, $180° < D_w < 360°$ and ship turn Right direction.

$$U_s = Vs + (V_w/900)$$

From Equation 3:

$$\beta \propto . (Vs + (V_w/900))-1) \tag{6}$$

Wave making resistance Rw is simple in concept but difficult to quantify. As it moves through the water, the ship makes waves, which cost energy.

$$U_s^2 \propto R_w$$

$$SU_s \propto \sqrt{R_w}$$

From Equation 3:

$$\beta \propto Cos^{-1}(\sqrt{} \tag{7}$$

Ship speed is inversely proportional to $^{-\frac{1}{2}}$

$$V_s \propto \left(\sqrt{}\right)^{-1} \tag{8}$$

Current water velocity Vs inversely proportional to $\rho-1/2$.

$$V_s \propto \left(\sqrt{} p\right)^{-1} \tag{9}$$

Compare Equation 8 and Equation 9:

Us $\propto$ Vs

From Equation 3:

$$\beta \propto cos^{-1}\left(V_s^{-1}\right) \tag{10}$$

Finally proposed a equation:

$$\beta \propto Cos^{-1}\left(U_s^{-1}\right) * Cos^{-1}\left(\sqrt{} R_w^{-1}\right) * Cos^{-1}(V_s^{-1})$$

If wind is blowing in ship direction:

$$\beta \propto cos^{-1}((Vs + (Vw/900))^{-1}) * Cos^{-1}(\sqrt{} R_w^{-1}) *$$

$$Cos^{-1}(V_c^{-1}) * Cos^{-1}((Vs + (Vw/900))^{-1}) *$$

$$Cos^{-1}(R_w^{-1}) * Cos^{-1}(V_c^{-1}) \tag{11}$$

If wind is blowing in ship's opposite direction:

$$\beta \propto Cos^{-1}\left(Vs - \left(Vw / 900\right)\right)^{-1} * Cos^{-1}$$

$$(\sqrt{R_w^{-1}})*$$

$$Cos^{-1}(-V_c^{-1})\beta$$

$$\propto X_2 Cos^{-1}\left(Vs - \left(Vw / 900\right)\right)^{-1} *$$

$$Cos^{-1}(\sqrt{R_w^{-1}}) * Cos^{-1}(-V_c^{-1}) \qquad (12)$$

x1, x2 are proportionally constants.

The Turning time is proportional to ship length Ls, ship load and water density.

$$Ttime \propto Ls$$

$$Ttime \propto Sload$$

$$Ttime \propto .$$

The proposed equation

$$Ttime \propto . * \rho * Sw$$

$$Ttime = x3 *Ls * \rho * Sw \qquad (13)$$

x3 is a constant

If the constants x1, x2 and x3 are worked out statistically from similar situations, then, it is not difficult to analytically determine the turning angle and the turn time of a ship. If cases are stored in a Case base for turning angles and turn time, then for emergency situations, when it is necessary to divert the ship from its original course to avoid collision in event of iceberg or any other obstacle, the CBR system may be able to guide the captain as to how muck to deviate the ship from the original course and the time needed to complete the operation. However, the final decision lies on the captain or the navigator of the ship, the system may just provide guidance to him as an assistant for taking a fast decision on the turning angle and turn time.

Algorithm of Ship Turning Problem

1. Describe input parameters for current case.
   a. Input parameters: wind velocity, wind direction, ship, speed, Propeller speed, Wave making resistance, Turning direction, current velocity.
   b. output parameter: turning angle, Turn time.
2. Declare variables for input parameter:
   a. Vw = wind velocity, Vs = ship speed, Rw = Wave making Resistance, Dw = wind direction, $T_{direction}$ = Turning direction, Vc = Current velocity, ρ= Sea density, Ls =Length of ship, Sw = weight of ship.
3. Declare variables for output parameters
   a. β = Turning angle, Ttime = Turning time.
4. Assign input values to input parameters.
5. Set the similarity function for each input variables.
   a. "EQUAL" //EQUAL describes the value which is equal to input value.
   b. "THRESHOLD" // THRESHOLD denoted the values that are larger than input value.
   c. "INTERVAL" //INTERVAL denoted the values that are lower than input value.
6. For each input parameter declare the similarity functions:
   a. For each input parameter, User select anyone similarity function among: EQUAL, THRESHOLD, INTERVAL.
7. After the storing similarity functions, declare the proportionality factors (x1, x2, x3).
8. Define x1, x2 as function of wind velocity, ship velocity, Current velocity and Wave resistance.
9. Define x3 as function of ship length, ship weight (load) and sea-density.
10. For each input parameter, declare the weight function for each parameter.

11. Assign and store the value for each weight function corresponding to each parameter.
12. Enter the Query to be compared to the cases in the case base.
13. State as to how many closest neighbor comparisons to be made in the k-NN algorithm use for similarity comparison (i.e. declare the value of k).
14. Display the result value for output parameters turning angle, turn time.
15. Generate graph of similar cases corresponding to the declared value of k.
16. Perform adaptation of the query case after comparison in Step (xii).
17. Revise the case with manual, expert intervention.
18. Retain the case as a new Case with new Case Id.

Application of CBR to Ship Turning in Order to Prevent Collision

CBR applications can cater to highly complex, incompletely understood non-specific domains as it only records cases as experiences. Both solved and failed solutions to problem cases may be recorded for the CBR to learn through experience of old and new cases. It also provides solutions where there is no specific algorithm to solve it. However, a case library needs to be built before the system can prove its usefulness. Moreover, in order to revise a solution or retain it for future problem solving, CBR system needs a human interface to determine what is right or wrong for offering a solution. The CBR provides suggestive solutions matching the Query, not necessarily absolutely "correct" solution.

There should be human interface to determine the same. However, CBR is proposed in this chapter to assist decision making and problem solving, not to provide a singular correct solution. For CBR to actually provide accurate guidance to the Captain regarding turning problem, the effectiveness of the system depends on how well the case library is built up based on the correctness of the cases. Our proposed work is based on hypothetical cases and not on real cases as it is an empirical example to establish the fact that CBR may be applied to automate decisions on ship turning to avoid collision. Moreover as ships and naval vessels correspond to national property and security, not all facts and figures are freely available on media or internet. So, the effort in this chapter has more emphasis on the CBR methodology applied to solve the ship turning problem rather than to build real-time cases of ships avoiding collision.

Framework for Ship Turning Problem

NetBeans IDE6.7 has been used as the front-end tool for the development of this application. IDE is an open-source integrated development environment. It provides an interface between user and backend database (Mysql server). NetBeans IDE supports development of all Java application and all the functions of the IDE are provided by modules. Each module provides a well defined function, and NetBeans contains all the modules needed for Java development in a single download, allowing the user to start working immediately. MySQL server 4.0 used as backend of the projects. It stores the cases. The java code retrieves and retains the information from MySQL Server Database. The MySQL development project has made its source code available under the terms of the GNU General Public License, as well as under a variety of proprietary agreements. MySQL is owned and sponsored by a single for-profit firm, the Swedish company MySQL AB, now owned by Sun Microsystems, a subsidiary of Oracle Corporation. In this application, the case base is composed of several ship turning cases that have been arbitrarily assumed just for experimentation purpose. It is not taken from any real-time sources. The system receives a current ship emergency condition as a query, compares the query with the previous Ship emergency case in the case base using a similarity function, and returns the most similar ones. After the retrieval, these most similar cases can be adapted according with the restrictions of the query. Each case is represented by several attributes that represent the ship emergency factors in Table 2.

The application in this chapter is to allow an experimental framework to the Captain of a Ship to take a decision on the turn angle and turn time. The solution to the "problem" of "ship turning problem" measured in terms of similarity between past occurred cases would assist the Captain in taking a quick decision to act on the problem situation as only experience or manual decision

Table 2. Symptoms-index table

Symptoms	Index	Weight
Headache	A	3
Body pain	B	5
Joint pain	C	7
Vomiting	D	7
Chills	E	7
Poor appetite	F	3
Loose bowels	G	5
Nausea	H	5
Urine problem	I	7
Abdominal pain	J	3
Diarrhea	K	7
Nose bleeds	L	5
Cough	M	5
Skin problem	N	5
Sweating	O	5
Chest Pain	P	7
Depression	Q	3
Coated tongue	R	7
Dark Urine	S	7
Pale stool	T	7
Breathing problem	U	7
Anemia	V	5

Table 3. Typical CBR query for ship turning problem handling

Attribute	Value
Wind direction	Input parameter
Wind velocity	Input parameter
Initial ship speed	Input parameter
Final ship speed	Input parameter
Wave making resistance	Input parameter
Turning direction	Input parameter
Current velocity	Input parameter
Ship length	Output parameter
Sea density	Output parameter
Ship weight	Output parameter

may not be enough to guide him. Since it is an Emergency Service, an automated solution to the problem would certainly assist in taking quick action on the problem saving time thus saving time, life, and property.

Steps of CBR Application for Ship turning

- **Define/Configure Queries:** In this step the user defines the Query to the system. He/She has to define the values of the different attributes of the current ship problem situation.
- **Configure Similarity:** Here the user configures the similarity measure used to retrieve the Cases most similar to the given Query. Weights may be assigned to each attribute of the query that will be taken into account when computing the average of all attributes. Also, some similarity functions can have parameters used to configure the similarity measure. Finally, the k value indicates how many cases must be retrieved. We are using an algorithm named K Nearest Neighbor (k-NN) that computes the similarity of the Query with all the cas-

es and then orders the result depending on that similarity value. Then the first k most similar cases are returned.

- **Retrieved Cases:** This step shows the documents retrieved by the k-NN method. It shows each Case and its percentage of similarity to the Query. The system also generates a graph to show the similarity between the best match cases. In the snapshot, we have used k=2.
- **Adaptation:** In this step the system adapts the retrieved Cases to the requirements of the user depending on the values defined in the Query.

After adapting the solution of the Cases, their description can be substituted by the description of the Query. At this point, the system will manage a list of working Cases that are different from the Cases in the Case Base. These working Cases represent possible solutions to the problem described in the Query.

- **Revise Cases:** Once cases have been adapted, the user (or a domain expert, in this case the Captain of the ship) would adjust the values of the working cases in a manual way.

Figure 15. Applet for define/configure query step

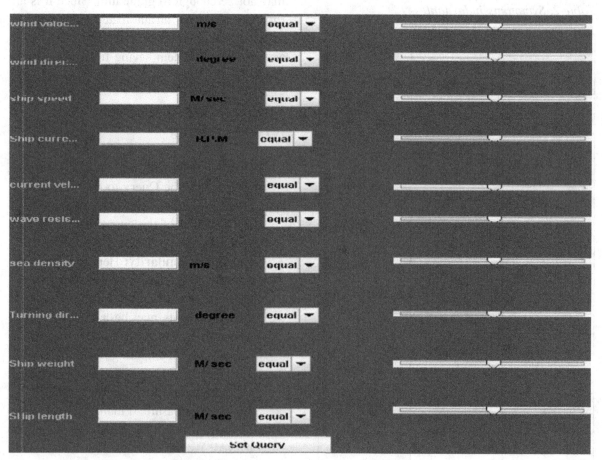

Figure 16. (a) Graph for problem case. Closest case match, Turn angle: 38% similarity (b) Graph for problem case. Closest case match, Turn time: 96.9% similarity

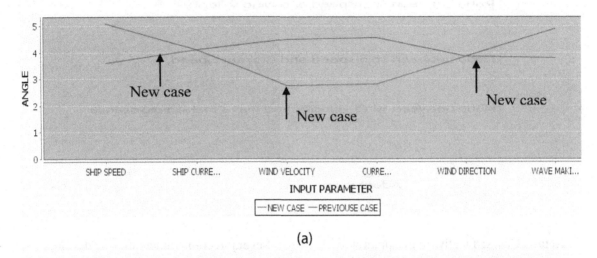

(a)

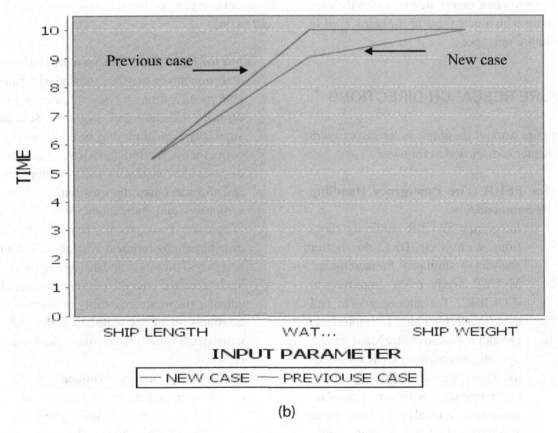

(b)

Figure 17. Adaptation step

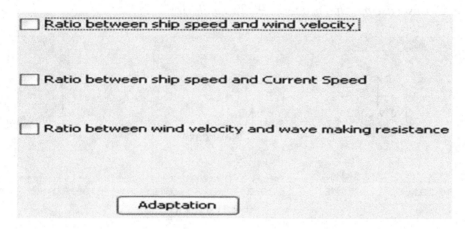

- **Retain Cases:** Finally, the Captain would save the new emergency case into the case base with a new Case Id for being used in future references.

FUTURE RESEARCH DIRECTIONS

The future work of the applications discussed in this chapter is discussed as follows:

1. **For FEHR (Fire Emergency Handling Recommender):**
   a. Integrating myCBR similarity functions with jCOLIBRI2 for better analysis of similarity measurements. MyCBR needs to be imported to jCOLIBRI2 for understandable and user-friendly Graphical User Interface.
   b. Developing a Knowledge Management System incorporating CBR for effective Query-Retrieval allowing human expert interface for decision control on non-routine critical cases. This should also allow adding cases not quite similar to other cases.

Several recommenders may be developed for disaster management, flood and tsunami hadling, and so on.

2. **For the Fever Detection System:** The fever detection model may be extended with suitable modifications for several disease and disorder detection and diagnosis. Several similarity algorithms may be developed for correct and accurate diagnosis techniques for diseases like cancer with multiple symptoms and disorders like diabetes with multiple symptoms and indications. Several such Diagnostic Assistants may be used across a distributed environment with provision to access real time case updates through XML feeds at regular intervals of time. This would enhance the usage and utility of diagnostic assistants on a large scale across the globe which shall benefit the medical community on whole.

3. **For the Ship Turning Problem:**
   a. Proper and accurate Case Representations with the following attributes: Case Id, Ship_Name, Date and Time of emergency/accident situation, loca-

tion, navigational aids, Property and life at Stake, all the factors listed in Table no. 1 as well as visibility, time of occurrence of the incident, that is day/night, presence of ice, wave height, temperature and humidity along with other weather conditions.

b. Developing a Knowledge Management System incorporating CBR for effective Query-Retrieval allowing human expert interface for decision control on non-routine critical cases. This should also allow adding cases not quite similar to other cases.

c. Data collection (in the form of textual data) from various web pages (serving as repositories to gather knowledge going through specific cases at a time, and finding the solution), to increase the case base, from varied examples. This gives the system more intelligence to analyze the query solution (on knowledge worker intervention or through intelligent agents).

CONCLUSION

This Chapter focuses on basic case based reasoning and its applications so that the reader gains some insight into the scope of these application areas. The Fire Emergency Handling Recommender discussed is a CBR application of handling fire cases based on jCOLIBRI 2. It provides decision making assistance to fire handlers/ administrators/ fighters in the event of a fire breakout. However, CBR needs to be incorporated into a Knowledge Management System for effective Query-Retrieval of Case-Based Queries. On the other hand, Fever Detection System is a simple prototype developed for detecting fever cases for theoretical study. This model may be largely extended to cater to

diagnosis of various categories of fever and other diseases like cancer, diabetes etc. The Ship Turning Problem Handling may provide decision making assistance to Pilot/Captain/local steer person on board. However, CBR needs to be incorporated into a Knowledge Management System for effective Query-Retrieval of Case-Based Queries.

REFERENCES

Aamodt, A., & Plaza, E. (1994). Case-based reasoning: Foundational issues, methodological variations, and system approaches. *AI Communications, 7*(1), 39–59.

Adomavicius, G., & Kwon, Y. O. (2007). New recommendation techniques for multi criteria rating systems. *IEEE Intelligent Systems, 22*(3), 48–55. doi:10.1109/MIS.2007.58

Adomavicius, G., & Tuzhilin, A. (2005). Toward the next generation of recommender systems: A survey of the state-of-the-art and possible extensions. *IEEE Transactions on Knowledge and Data Engineering, 17*(6), 734–749. doi:10.1109/TKDE.2005.99

Alexandrini, F., & Krechel, D. (2003). Integrating CBR into health care organization. In *Proceedings of the 16th IEEE Symposium on Computer-Based Medical Systems,* (pp. 130-135). IEEE.

Belecheanu, R., Pawar, K. S., Barson, R. J., Bredehorst, B., & Weber, F. (2003). The application of case based reasoning to decision support in new product development. *Integrated Manufacturing Systems, 14*(1), 36–45. doi:10.1108/09576060310453335

Bonzano, A., Cunningham, P., & Meckiff, C. (1996). ISAC: A CBR system for decision support in air traffic control. In *Advances in case-based reasoning (LNCS)* (Vol. 1168, pp. 44–57). Berlin: Springer. doi:10.1007/BFb0020601

Bryant, S. M. (1997). A case-based reasoning approach to bankruptcy prediction modeling. *International Journal of Intelligent Systems in Accounting Finance & Management*, *6*(3), 195–214. doi:10.1002/(SICI)1099-1174(199709)6:3<195::AID-ISAF132>3.0.CO;2-F

Buta, P. (1994). Mining for financial knowledge with CBR. *AI Expert*, *9*(2), 34–41.

Cao, L., & Zhang, C. (2007). Domain-driven data mining: A framework. *IEEE Intelligent Systems*, *22*(4), 78–79. doi:10.1109/MIS.2007.67

Chakraborty, B., Ghosh, D., & Ranjan, R. (2010). Knowledge management with case-based reasoning applied on fire emer handling. In *Proceedings of 8th IEEE International Conference on Industrial Informatics* (INDIN 2010) (pp. 708-713). IEEE.

Chang, C. L. (2005). Using case-based reasoning to diagnostic screening of children with developmental delay. *Expert Systems with Applications*, *28*, 237–240. doi:10.1016/j.eswa.2004.09.002

Chang, P. C., & Lai, C. Y. (2005). A hybrid system combining self-organizing maps with case-based reasoning in wholesaler's new-release book for forecasting. *Expert Systems with Applications*, *29*, 183–192. doi:10.1016/j.eswa.2005.01.018

Chen, Y. K., Wang, C.-Y., & Feng, Y.-Y. (2010). Application of a 3NN+1 based CBR system to segmentation of the notebook computers market. *Expert Systems with Applications*, *37*(1), 276–281. doi:10.1016/j.eswa.2009.05.002

Chiu, C. (2002). A case-based customer classification approach for direct marketing. *Expert Systems with Applications*, *22*(2), 163–168. doi:10.1016/S0957-4174(01)00052-5

Chiu, C., Chang, P. C., & Chiu, N. H. (2003). A case-based expert support system for due-date assignment in a water fabrication factory. *Journal of Intelligent Manufacturing*, *14*(3–4), 287–296. doi:10.1023/A:1024693524603

Cirovic, G., & Cekic, Z. (2002). Case-based reasoning model applied as a decision support for construction projects. *Kybernete*, *31*(5/6), 896–908. doi:10.1108/03684920210432844

Coello, C. A. (2000). An updated survey of GA-based multi objective optimization techniques. *ACM Computing Surveys*, *32*(2), 109–143. doi:10.1145/358923.358929

Dempster, R. T. (1974). The measurement and modelling of iceberg drift. *IEEE Ocean*, *74*(1), 125–129.

Deyashi, S., Banerjee, D., & Chakraborty, B. (2012). Fever-type detection system: A combination of CBR and bottom up approach. In *Proceedings of 10th IEEE International Conference on Industrial Informatics (INDIN)*, (pp. 962 – 967). IEEE.

Deyashi, S., Banerjee, D., Chakraborty, B., Ghosh, D., & Debnath, J. (2011). Application of CBR on viral fever detection system (VFDS). In *Proceedings of IEEE INDIN 2011*. Lisbon, Portugal: IEEE.

Dixena, D., Chakraborty, B., & Debnath, N. (2011). Application of case-based reasoning for ship turning emergency to prevent collision. In *Proceedings of 9th IEEE International Conference on Industrial Informatics (INDIN)*, (pp. 654 – 659). IEEE.

Ebada, A., & Maksoud, M. A. (2005). Applying neural networks to predict ship turning track manoeuvring. In *Proceedings of 8th Numerical Towing Tank Symposium*. Academic Press.

Firestone, J. M., & Elroy, M. (2003). *Key issues in the future of knowledge management*. London: Butterworth – Heinemann.

Fu, Y., & Shen, R. (2004). GA based CBR approach in Q&A system. *Expert Systems with Applications*, *26*(2), 167–170. doi:10.1016/S0957-4174(03)00117-9

Garrell, J. M., Golobardes, E., Bernado, E., & Llora, X. (1999). Automatic diagnosis with genetic algorithms and case-based reasoning. *Artificial Intelligence in Engineering*, *13*(4), 367–372. doi:10.1016/S0954-1810(99)00009-6

Golobardes, E., Llora, X., Salamo, M., & Marti, J. (2002). Computer aided diagnosis with case-based reasoning and genetic algorithms. *Knowledge-Based Systems*, *15*, 45–52. doi:10.1016/S0950-7051(01)00120-4

Goodchild, A. V., & Daganzo, C. F. (2004). *Reducing ship turn-around time using double-cycling, research reports*. Berkeley, CA: UC Berkeley.

Govedarova, N., Stoyanov, S., & Popchev, I. (2003). An ontology based CBR architecture for knowledge management in BULCHINO catalogue. In *Proceedings of International Conference on Computer Systems and Technologies*. CompSysTech.

Gronau, N., & Laskowski, F. (2003). Using case-based reasoning to improve. In *Spring Information Retrieval in Knowledge Management Systems (LNCS)* (Vol. 2663, p. 954). Berlin: Springer.

Hsu, C. I., Chiu, C., & Hsu, P. L. (2004). Predicting information systems outsourcing success using a hierarchical design of case-based reasoning. *Expert Systems with Applications*, *26*(3), 435–441. doi:10.1016/j.eswa.2003.10.002

Jo, H., & Han, I. (1996). Integration of case-based forecasting, neural network, and discriminate analysis for bankruptcy prediction. *Expert Systems with Applications*, *11*(4), 415–422. doi:10.1016/S0957-4174(96)00056-5

Juan, Y. K., Shin, S. G., & Perng, Y. H. (2006). Decision support for housing customization: A hybrid approach using case-based reasoning and genetic algorithm. *Expert Systems with Applications*, *31*(1), 83–93. doi:10.1016/j.eswa.2005.09.010

Kilama, W., & Ntoumi, F. (2009). Malaria: A research agenda for the eradication era. *Lancet*, *374*(9700), 1480–1482. doi:10.1016/S0140-6736(09)61884-5 PMID:19880004

Kim, K. (2004). Toward global optimization of case-based reasoning systems for financial forecasting. *Applied Intelligence*, *21*(3), 239–249. doi:10.1023/B:APIN.0000043557.93085.72

Kim, K., & Han, I. (2001). Maintaining case-based reasoning systems using a genetic algorithms approach. *Expert Systems with Applications*, *21*(3), 139–145. doi:10.1016/S0957-4174(01)00035-5

Kolodner, J. (1983). Reconstructive memory: A computer model. *Cognitive Science*, *7*, 281–328. doi:10.1207/s15516709cog0704_2

Kolodner, J. L. (1993). *Case-based reasoning: Techniques for enterprise systems*. San Mateo, CA: Morgan Kaufman.

Krupka, J., Kasparova, M., & Jirava, P. (2009). Case-based reasoning model in process of emergency management. *Advances in Soft. Computing*, *59*, 77–84.

Kumar, P., Gopalan, S., & Sridhar, V. (2005). Context enabled multi-CBR based recommendation engine for e-commerce. In *Proceedings of the IEEE international conference on e-business engineering (ICEBE)* (pp. 237–244). IEEE Press.

Lebowitz, M. (1983). Memory-based parsing. *Artificial Intelligence*, *21*, 363–404. doi:10.1016/S0004-3702(83)80019-8

Lee, T., & Chen, I. (2005). A two-stage hybrid credit scoring model using artificial neural networks and multivariate adaptive regression splines. *Expert Systems with Applications*, *28*(4), 743–752. doi:10.1016/j.eswa.2004.12.031

Lenz, M., Bartsch-Sporl, B., Burkhard, H., & Wess, S. (1998). Case-based reasoning technology – From foundation to applications. *Lecture Notes in Artificial Intelligence*, *1400*, 273–297.

Leung, K., Cheong, F., & Cheong, C. (2007). Consumer credit scoring using an artificial immune system algorithm. In *Proceedings of the IEEE International Conference on Evolutionary Computation (CEC 2007)* (pp. 3377–3384). IEEE Press.

Li, H., & Sun, J. (2010). Business failure prediction using hybrid2 case-based reasoning (H2CBR). *Computers & Operations Research, 37*(1), 137–151. doi:10.1016/j.cor.2009.04.003

Li, H., Sun, J., & Sun, B. L. (2009). Financial distress prediction based on OR-CBR in the principle of k-nearest neighbors. *Expert Systems with Applications, 36*(1), 643–659. doi:10.1016/j.eswa.2007.09.038

Liao, T. W., Zhang, Z., & Mount, C. R. (1998). Similarity measures for retrieval in case based reasoning systems. *Applied Artificial Intelligence, 12*, 267–288. doi:10.1080/088395198117730

Liu, Y. C., Yang, Y. Y., Lin, F., & Du, X. (2009). Case learning in CBR based agent systems for ship collision avoidance. In *Principles of Practice in Multi-Agent Systems (LNCS)* (Vol. 5925, pp. 542–551). Berlin: Springer. doi:10.1007/978-3-642-11161-7_40

Lopez, M., McSherry, R., Bridge, D. D., Leake, D., Smyth, B., & Craw, S. (2005). Retrieval, reuse, revision, and retention in case-based reasoning. *The Knowledge Engineering Review, 20*(3), 215–240. doi:10.1017/S0269888906000646

Montazemi, A. R., & Gupta, K. M. (1997). A framework for retrieval in case-based reasoning systems. *Annals of Operations Research, 72*, 51–73. doi:10.1023/A:1018960607821

Pal, S. K., & Shiu, S. C. K. (2004). Foundations of soft case-based reasoning. CH-1, ISBN 0-471-08635-5

Roger, S. (1982). *Dynamic memory: A theory of learning in computers and people*. New York: Cambridge University Press.

Schmidt, R., & Gierl, L. (2001). Case-based reasoning for medical knowledge-based systems. *International Journal of Medical Informatics, 64*(2-3), 355–367. doi:10.1016/S1386-5056(01)00221-0 PMID:11734397

Shen, Z., Guo, C., & Yan, Y. (2008). Mathematical modelling and simulation of ultra large container ship motion. In *Proceedings of 7th International Conference on System Simulation and Scientific Computing, ICSC 2008*, (pp. 693-696). ICSC.

Shimazu, H. (2002). ExpertClerk: A conversational case-based reasoning tool for developing salesclerk agents in e-commerce webshops. *Artificial Intelligence Review, 18*(3/4), 223–244. doi:10.1023/A:1020757023711

Shimazu, H., Shibata, A., & Nihei, K. (2001). Expert guide: A conversational case based reasoning tool for developing mentor in knowledge space. *Applied Intelligence, 14*(1), 33–48. doi:10.1023/A:1008350923935

Shin, K. S., & Han, I. (1999). Case-based reasoning supported by genetic algorithms for corporate bond rating. *Expert Systems with Applications, 16*, 85–95. doi:10.1016/S0957-4174(98)00063-3

Shin, K.-S., & Han, I. (1999). Case-based reasoning supported by genetic algorithms for corporate bond rating. *Expert Systems with Applications, 16*(2), 85–95. doi:10.1016/S0957-4174(98)00063-3

Shin, K. S., & Han, I. (2001). A case-based approach using inductive indexing for corporate bond rating. *Decision Support Systems, 32*(1), 41–52. doi:10.1016/S0167-9236(01)00099-9

Shiu, C. K., & Pal, S. K. (2001). Case-based reasoning: concepts, features and soft computing. *Applied Intelligence, 21*(3), 233–238. doi:10.1023/B:APIN.0000043556.29968.81

Smyth, B., Keane, M., & Cunningham, P. (2001). Hierarchical case-based reasoning integrating case-based and decomposition problem-solving techniques for plant-control software design. *IEEE Transactions on Knowledge and Data Engineering, 13*(5), 793–812. doi:10.1109/69.956101

Sycara, K. (1988). Using case-based reasoning for plan adaptation and repair. In *Proceedings Case-Based Reasoning Workshop*. Morgan Kaufmann.

Tseng, H. E., Chang, C. C., & Chang, S. H. (2005). Applying case-based reasoning for product configuration in mass customization environments. *Expert Systems with Applications, 29*(4), 913–925. doi:10.1016/j.eswa.2005.06.026

Veloso, M. M., & Carbonell, J. (1993). Derivational analogy in prodigy. *Machine Learning, 10*(3), 249–278. doi:10.1023/A:1022686910523

Venkatamaran, S., Krishnan, R., & Rao, K. K. (1993). A rule-rule-case based system for image analysis. In *Proceedings of First European Workshop on Case-Based Reasoning*. University of Kaiserslautern.

Wasto, I. (1997). *Applying case-based reasoning: Techniques for enterprise systems*. San Francisco, CA: Morgan Kaufmann.

Watson, I. (2011). Knowledge management and case based reasoning: A perfect match? In *Proceedings of the Fourteenth International Florida Artificial Intelligence Research Society Conference*, (pp. 118-122). Academic Press.

Yang, H. L., & Wang, C. S. (2008). Two stages of case-based reasoning – Integrating genetic algorithm with data mining mechanisms. *Expert Systems with Applications, 35*(1–2), 262–272. doi:10.1016/j.eswa.2007.06.027

Yang, H. L., & Wang, C. S. (2009). Recommender system for software project planning – One application of revised CBR algorithm. *Expert Systems with Applications, 36*(5), 8938–8945. doi:10.1016/j.eswa.2008.11.050

Yang, H. L., & Wang, C. S. (2009). Personalized recommendation for IT certification test in e-learning environment. *Journal of Research and Practice in Information Technology, 41*(4), 295–306.

Yang, Q. (2007). Learning actions from data mining models. *IEEE Intelligent Systems, 22*(4), 79–81.

ADDITIONAL READING

Aktas, M., Pierce, M., Fox, G., & Leake, D. (2004). A web based conversational case-based recommender system for ontology aided metadata discovery. *In Proceedings of the Fifth IEEE/ACM International Workshop on Grid Computing (GRID 2004)*. IEEE Computer Society Press.

Bridge, D., Göker, M. H., McGinty, L., & Smyth, B. (2006). Case-based recommender systems. *The Knowledge Engineering Review, 20*(3), 315–320. doi:10.1017/S0269888906000567

Brigitte, B.-S., Althoff, K.-D., & Meissonnier, A. (1997). Learning From and Reasoning About Case-based Reasoning Systems. In *proceeding of the fourth German conference on Knowledge-Based Systems*, BSR Consulting GMBH, Munchen, Center of learning system and Application.

Brüninghaus, S., & Ashley, K. D. (2001). The role of information extraction for textual CBR. *In Proceedings of the 4th International Conference on Case-Based Reasoning, ICCBR '01*, pages 74–89. Springer-Verlag.

Delany, S. J., & Bridge, D. (2006). Feature-based and feature-free textual CBR: A comparison in spam filtering. *In Procs. of the 17th Irish Conference on Artificial Intelligence and Cognitive Science*, pages 244–253, Belfast, Northern Ireland.

Delany, S. J., & Bridge, D. (2007). Catching the drift: Using feature-free case-based reasoning for spam filtering. *In Procs. of the 7th International Conference on Case Based Reasoning*, Belfast, Northern Ireland.

Díaz-Agudo, B., & González-Calero, P. A. (2001). Knowledge intensive CBR through ontologies. *In Procs of the UK CBR Workshop.*

Díaz-Agudo, B., & González-Calero, P. A. (2002). CBROnto: a task/method ontology for CBR. In S. Haller, & G. Simmons (Eds.), *Procs. of the 15th International FLAIRS'02 Conference. AAAI Press.*

Díaz-Agud,o B., & González-Calero P. A. (2006). Ontologies in the Context of Information Systems, *chapter An ontological approach to develop Knowledge Intensive CBR systems*, page 45. Springer-Verlag.

Funk, P., & González-Calero, P. A. (2004). Advances in Case-Based Reasoning, *7th European Conference, ECCBR 2004*, Madrid, Spain, August 30 - September 2, 2004, Proceedings, volume 3155 of Lecture Notes in Computer Science. Springer.

Gomez-Gauchia, H., Díaz-Agudo, B., Gomez-Martin, P. P., & González- Calero, P. A. (2005) Supporting conversation variability in cobber using causal loops. *In Case-Based Reasoning Research and Development- Proc. of the ICCBR'05.* Springer Verlag LNCS/LNAI.

González-Calero, P. A., Gómez-Albarrán, M., & Díaz-Agudo, B. (1999). Applying dls for retrieval in case-based reasoning. *In Procs. of the 1999 Description Logics Workshop (Dl '99).* Linkopings universitet, Sweden.

Leake, D. (1997). *Case Based Reasoning. Experiences, Lessons and Future Directions. AAAI Press.* USA: MIT Press.

Lenz, M. (1998).Defining knowledge layers for textual case-based reasoning. In Proceedings of the 4th *European Workshop on Advances in Case-Based Reasoning, EWCBR-98*, pages 298–309. Springer-Verlag.

Mantaras, R. L. de and Plaza E. (1997). Case-based reasoning: An overview. *AI Communications, 10*(1).

McGinty, L., & Smyth, B. (2002). Comparison-based recommendation. In *ECCBR '02: Proceedings of the 6th European Conference on Advances in Case-Based Reasoning*, pages 575–589, London, UK. Springer-Verlag.

McSherry, D. (2002). Diversity-conscious retrieval. *In ECCBR '02: Proceedings of the 6th European Conference on Advances in Case-Based Reasoning, pages 219–233*, London, UK. Springer-Verlag.

McSherry, D. (2003). Similarity and compromise. In Case-Based Reasoning Research and Development, *5th International Conference on Case-Based Reasoning, ICCBR,* pages 291–305.

Napoli, A., Lieber, J., & Courien, R. (1996). Classification-based problem solving in cbr. In I. Smith and B. Faltings, editors, *Advances in Case-Based Reasoning–(EWCBR'96).* Springer-Verlag, Berlin Heidelberg New York.

Recio-García, J. A., Díaz-Agudo, B., Gómez-Martín, M. A., & Wiratunga, N. (2005). Extending jCOLIBRI for textual CBR. In H. Muñoz-Avila and F. Ricci, editors, Proceedings of Case-Based Reasoning Research and Development, *6th International Conference on Case-Based Reasoning, ICCBR 2005*, volume 3620 of Lecture Notes in Artificial Intelligence, subseries of LNCS, pages 421–435, Chicago, IL, US. Springer.

Recio-García, J. A., Díaz-Agudo, B., González-Calero P. A., & Sánchez-Ruiz- Granados, A. (2006). Ontology based cbr with jcolibri. In R. Ellis, T. Allen, and A. Tuson, editors, Applications and Innovations in Intelligent Systems XIV. Proceedings of AI-2006, the Twenty-sixth SGAI *International Conference on Innovative Techniques and Applications of Artificial Intelligence,* pages 149–162, Cambridge, United Kingdom, December. Springer.

Recio-García, J. A., Díaz-Agudo, B., & González-Calero, P. A. (2007). Textual CBR in jCOLIBRI: From Retrieval to Reuse. In D. C. Wilson and D. Khemani, editors, Workshop Proceedings of the 7th *International Conference on Case-Based Reasoning (ICCBR'07),* pages 217–226, Belfast, Northen Ireland, August 13-16.

Salotti, S., & Ventos, V. (1998). Study and formalization of a case-based reasoning system using a description logic. In B. Smyth and P. Cunningham, editors, *Advances in Case-Based Reasoning – (EWCBR'98).* Springer-Verlag.

Shimazu, H. (2002). ExpertClerk: A Conversational Case-Based Reasoning Tool for Developing Salesclerk Agents in E-Commerce Webshops. *Artif. Intell. Rev.,* 18(3- 4),223–244.

Stahl, A., Wess, S., & Wilke, W. (1998). Collecting experience on the systematic development of CBR applications using the INRECA methodology. *Lecture Notes in Computer Science, 1488,* 460–470. doi:10.1007/BFb0056356

KEY TERMS AND DEFINITIONS

Case Based Reasoning (CBR): It is a process of solving new problems based on the solutions of similar past problems using a database of cases.

Case Representation: It is Case presentation in terms of features and attributes.

Classification: It is the process of arrangement of objects according to common qualities or attributes.

Emergency: It is an accident or incident requiring immediate attention.

Knowledge Management Mechanism: It comprises of a range of strategies and practices used in an organization to identify, create, represent, distribute, and enable adoption of insights and experiences. Such insights and experiences comprise knowledge, either embodied in individuals or embedded in organizations as processes or practices.

Query: It is a form of questioning the database to retrieve some data.

Similarity-Based Reasoning: An approach to intelligent system opposite to deductive reasoning, this reasoning approach draws conclusions by similarity rather than by chaining generalized rules.

Chapter 10
Hybrid Genetic Algorithm:
An Optimization Tool

Kedar Nath Das
NIT Silchar, India

ABSTRACT

Real coded Genetic Algorithms (GAs) are the most effective and popular techniques for solving continuous optimization problems. In the recent past, researchers used the Laplace Crossover (LX) and Power Mutation (PM) in the GA cycle (namely LX-PM) efficiently for solving both constrained and unconstrained optimization problems. In this chapter, a local search technique, namely Quadratic Approximation (QA) is discussed. QA is hybridized with LX-PM in order to improve its efficiency and efficacy. The generated hybrid system is named H-LX-PM. The supremacy of H-LX-PM over LX-PM is validated through a test bed of 22 unconstrained and 15 constrained typical benchmark problems. In the later part of this chapter, a few applications of GA in networking optimization are highlighted as the scope for future research.

INTRODUCTION

Optimization is an art of selecting the best alternative amongst a given set of options. It is central to any problem involving decision making in many disciplines such as engineering, mathematics, statistics, economics, and computer science. Now, more than ever, it is increasingly vital to have a firm grasp of the topic due to the rapid progress in computer technology, including the development and availability of user-friendly software,

high-speed and parallel processors, and networks. Secondly, the problems, in general, arising in real life situations are highly complex and non-linear in nature. Some of them are unconstrained and some involve constraints. For such problems, it is a great challenge for the researchers to find the global optimal solution over many local optimal solutions. For example, a view of many local and single global minimum, is presented in Figure 1 for Ackley function (for n=2), which is a typical benchmark problem defined as

DOI: 10.4018/978-1-4666-4936-1.ch010

Figure 1. Ackley Function: A 3D view for n=2

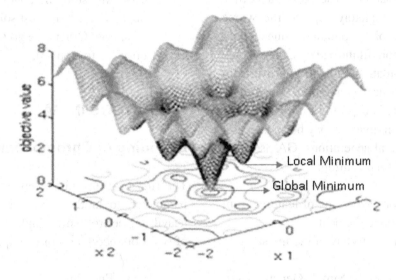

$$-20 * exp(-0.02\sqrt{\frac{1}{n}\sum_{i=1}^{n} x_i^2})$$

$$-exp(\frac{1}{n}\sum_{i=1}^{n} \cos\left(2\pi x_i\right)) + 20 + e \qquad (1)$$

To handle such highly nonlinear problems with high complexity, the traditional methods become handicaped as it is a difficult task to check the auxiliary conditions like differentiability and continuity of the function in hand. Therefore, the evolutionary methods achieved enough popularity in recent years as they do not require any auxiliary conditions to be satisfied.

Genetic Algorithm (GA) (introduced by J. Holand in 1975) is one of such evolutionary methods, which is discussed briefly in section 2. GA operators are discussed in section 3. However, using simple GA sometimes puts the simulation suffering from getting trapped in local minima and sometimes results in premature convergence. To avoid such situations, researchers frequently use the hybrid versions of the GA. A case study on quadratic approximation based hybridization is described in section 4. In the same section, the effect of hybridization to simple GA is realized

through a set of benchmark functions. Moreover, some real life applications are also presented. In section 5, some probable application areas in *'Networking optimization'* are highlighted for researchers' interest. Lastly, the conclusion of the chapter is drawn in section 6.

GENETIC ALGORITHM

This section discusses the basics of Genetic Algorithm (GA). Holland is considered to be the father of GA. Later works on GA can be found in Goldberg (1989), Michalewicz (1992), Deb (1995, 2001), Mitchell (1996), Back (1996), Gen and Cheng (1997), Rajasekaran and Pai (2003) etc.

GA is based on the Darwin's principle - 'The survival of the fittest'. It works by evolving a population of individuals over a number of generations. A fitness value is assigned to each individual in the population, where the fitness computation depends upon the application. At each generation for the reproduction, individuals are selected from population according to their fitness values. Then the individuals are crossed to generate new individuals with some high crossover probability, and the new individuals are mutated with some low mutation probability. The individuals thus generated may completely replace the worse individuals in the old population. Since selection is based on more fit individuals, the average fitness of the population tends to improve from one generation to next generation. The fitness of best individuals is expected to improve over time, and the best individual may be chosen as a solution after several generations. GA uses two basic processes from evolution:

- Inheritance or the passing of features from one generation to the next.
- Competition or survival of the fittest.

The pseudo code of the Simple Genetic Algorithm comprises the following steps.

1. **Start:** Generate random population of *n* chromosomes or strings (suitable solutions for the problem).
2. **Fitness:** Evaluate the fitness $F(x)$ of each chromosome *x* in the population.
3. **New Population:** Create a new population by repeating following steps until the new population is complete. i. e. The satisfactory result is achieved or the stopping criterion is fulfilled.
4. **Selection:** Select two parent chromosomes from a population according to their fitness (better the fitness, higher the chance for being selected for the next population).
5. **Crossover:** With a probability (Pc) the parents go for mating to form new offspring (children).
6. **Mutation:** With a probability (Pm), mutate new offspring at each locus (position in chromosome).
7. **Accepting:** Place new offspring in the new population.
8. **Replace:** Use newly generated population for a further run of the algorithm.

9. **Test:** If the stopping condition is satisfied, stop, and return the best solution in current population. Otherwise go to step X.
10. **Loop:** Go to step (ii).

OPERATORS IN GA

Encoding of Chromosomes

The first task in a GA is encoding of decision parameters to another space. Encoding depends heavily on the problem at hand. There are a number of types of encoding. For example:

- Binary Encoding
- Real Encoding
- Permutation Encoding
- Tree Encoding

Usually binary and real encoding are popular and are discussed below.

A. Binary Encoding

In binary encoding the chromosomes are encoded as strings of binary alphabets '0' and '1'. Binary encoding is the most common one, used in the initial research on GA for its simplicity. In binary encoding, every chromosome is a string of bits 0 or 1.

Binary encoding gives many possible chromosomes even with a small number of alleles. On the other hand, this encoding is often not natural for many problems and sometimes corrections must be made after crossover and/or mutation.

B. Real Encoding

The real encoding uses the real value of the parameters directly in generating the initial population. It is made to generate randomly in between the allowed range of each decision variable. This type of encoding system is much useful as it is very easy to handle and efficient to apply, as compared with the binary encoding. Henceforth the discussion in this chapter is based only on real coded GA. Therefore, some useful operators frequently used in the literature for the real coded GA are only explained below.

Selection Operator

Basically the selection operator is a preference provider for better individuals, to allow them to pass on their genes to the next generation. But, the goodness of each individual depends on the fitness. So the fitness may be determined by an objective function or by a subjective judgment.

Inspired by the role of natural selection in evolution, Genetic Algorithm performs a selection process in which the more fit members of the population survive, and the least fit members are die off. In a constrained optimization problem, the notion of fitness depends partly on whether a solution is feasible (i.e. whether it satisfies all of the constraints), and partly on its objective function value. Moreover, it guides the evolutionary algorithm towards ever-better solutions. A value for fitness is assigned to each solution (chromo-

some) depending on how close it actually is to solving the problem. Thus it enables the GA to approach the optimal solution.

To select better chromosomes from a population, many selection operators like Tournament selection, Roulette wheel selection, Rank selection etc exist in literature. Two types of popular selection operators are discussed below.

A. Tournament Selection

In the tournament selection, tournaments are played between two solutions and the better solution is chosen and placed in the mating pool. This is explained in Figure 2, where the values indicate the fitness values of the chromosomes. To start with, 1st and 2nd solution are picked and the best fit one is placed at the 1st slot of the mating pool. Next, to fill the 2nd slot, better from the 2nd and 3rd solutions are picked. The same process continues till all the slots are filled. This way, each solution is dragged to participate in exactly two tournaments. The best solution in a population will win both times, thereby making two copies of it in the new population. Using a similar argument, the worst solution will lose in both tournaments and will be eliminated from the population. In this way, any solution in the population will have

Figure 2. Pictorial representation of tournament selection

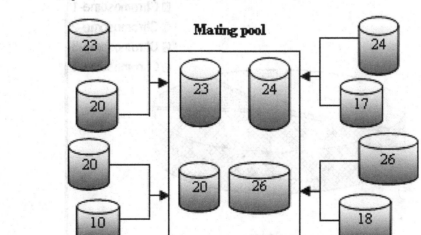

either zero, one or two copies in the new population. This is all about the tournament selection of size 2. In general, the tournament selection of size 'n' means that for the selection mechanism, 'n' individuals participate at a time.

B. Roulette Wheel Selection

Parents are selected according to their fitness. Imagine a *Roulette Wheel* where all the chromosomes in the population are placed as shown in Figure 3. The probability of selecting a chromosome is proportional to the value of its (comparative) fitness values of each chromosome. The bigger the value is (e.g. Chromosome-3 in Figure 3), the larger the probability to get it selected for the mating pool. This mimics the nature of the Roulette Wheel game where a marble is thrown in the wheel and the players having maximum share has the better chance to win.

Crossover Operator

By crossover operator, parents from the mating pool go for mating. As a result two new individuals are generated, called 'children'. The position of the participated parents, are now filled/replaced

with those newly generated children. In this section an efficient crossover operator called 'Laplace Crossover' [introduced by Deep and Thakur (2007a)] is being reconsidered in the GA cycle for hybridization.

Laplace Crossover

The Laplace Crossover Operator (LX) is a parent centric operator that uses Laplace Distribution. The Density Function of Laplace distribution is given by

$$f(x) = \frac{1}{2b} \exp\left(-\frac{|x-a|}{b}\right), -\infty < x < \infty \quad (2)$$

and Distribution function of Laplace distribution is given by

$$F(x) = \begin{cases} \frac{1}{2} \exp\left(\frac{|x-a|}{b}\right), & x \leq a \\ 1 - \frac{1}{2} \exp\left(-\frac{|x-a|}{b}\right), & x > a \end{cases} \quad (3)$$

Figure 3. Roulette wheel

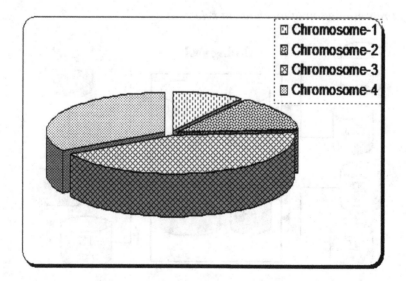

where, $a \in R$ is called the location parameter and $b > 0$ is termed as scale parameter. Lower the value of b, higher is the probability of creating offsprings near the parents. For example, if $b = 0.5$ the probability of creating offsprings near the parents is higher and for $b = 1$, distant points are likely to be created as offsprings.

Using LX, two offsprings

$$y^{(1)} = (y_1^{(1)}, y_2^{(1)}, ..., y_n^{(1)})$$

and

$$y^{(2)} = (y_1^{(2)}, y_2^{(2)}, ..., y_n^{(2)})$$

are generated from a pair of parents

$$x^{(1)} = (x_1^{(1)}, x_2^{(1)}, ..., x_n^{(1)})$$

and

$$x^{(2)} = (x_1^{(2)}, x_2^{(2)}, ..., x_n^{(2)})$$

in the following way.

First, two uniformly distributed random numbers $u_i, u_i^{'} \in \left[0, 1\right]$ are generated. Then a random number β_i is generated that follows the Laplace distribution just by inverting the distribution function of Laplace distribution as follows

$$\beta_i = \begin{cases} a - b \log_e(u_i), & u_i^{'} \leq \dfrac{1}{2} \\ a + b \log_e(u_i), & u_i^{'} > \dfrac{1}{2} \end{cases} \quad (4)$$

The offsprings are given by the equation

$$y_i^{(1)} = x_i^{(1)} + \beta_i \left| x_i^{(1)} - x_i^{(2)} \right| \quad (5)$$

$$y_i^{(2)} = x_i^{(2)} + \beta_i \left| x_i^{(1)} - x_i^{(2)} \right| \quad (6)$$

Mutation Operator

Mutation operator mutates very few of the genes in a population to modify some individuals with a new look. Thus it helps in maintaining the diversity in the population. Deep and Thakur (2007b) introduced a new mutation operator called 'power mutation' which is being reconsidered for the further study of hybridization.

Power Mutation

The Power Mutation (PM) by is based on Power Distribution. Its distribution function is given by

$$f(x) = px^{p-1} \quad 0 \leq x \leq 1 \quad (7)$$

and the density function is given by

$$F(x) = x^p \quad 0 \leq x \leq 1 \quad (8)$$

where $p > 0$ is the index of the distribution. PM is used to create a solution y in the vicinity of a parent solution $\bar{x}$ in the following manner. First a uniform random number t between 0 and 1 is created and a random number s is created which follows the above mentioned distribution. Then following formula is used to create the muted solution

$$y = \begin{cases} \bar{x} - s(\bar{x} - x^l) & if\ t < r \\ \bar{x} + s(x^u - \bar{x}) & if\ t \geq r \end{cases} \quad (9)$$

where

$$t = \dfrac{\bar{x} - x_i^l}{x_i^u - x_i^l}$$

and x^l and x^u are lower and upper bounds of the decision variable and r is a uniformly distributed random number between 0 and 1. The strength of mutation is governed by the index of the mutation (p). For small values of p less perturbance in the solution is expected and for large values of p more diversity is achieved. The probability of producing a mutated solution y on left (right) side of $\bar{x}$ is proportional to distance of $\bar{x}$ from x^l (x^u) and the muted solution is always feasible.

Elitism

Elitism means the advocacy of leadership. The mechanism of complete elitism is as follows:

1. Store the fitness values of the population before and after the GA cycle.
2. Combine these two to get a population of double size.
3. Arrange them in descending order of their fitness values.
4. Preserve the first half to reinitialize the population for the next GA cycle.

Many a time, 'Elitism' is useful to apply at the end of GA cycle as an additional operator, just not to lose the better individuals obtained so far. In this present study elitism is used effectively.

HYBRID GA

In spite of bearing much ability, GA gets trapped in local optima most of the time while solving optimization problems. Sometimes, the premature convergence is unavoidable. Therefore in order:

1. To overcome the above mentioned lacuna.
2. To accelerate the speed of convergence.
3. To improve the solution quality in terms of objective function value.

One such local search called "Quadratic Approximation" is considered for hybridization in GA cycle, which is discussed below.

Quadratic Approximation

Quadratic approximation (QA) is first introduced by Mohan and Shankar (1994) and later used by Deep and Das (2008). QA consists of two major steps as follows.

1. Select the individuals R1 bearing the best fitness value in the population. Choose two random distinct individuals, R2 and R3.
2. Find the point of minima (child) of the quadratic surface passing through R1, R2 and R3 defined as:

Child= 0.5*

$$\left[\frac{(R_2^2 - R_3^2)f(R_1) + (R_3^2 - R_1^2)f(R_2) + (R_1^2 - R_2^2)f(R_3)}{(R_2 - R_3)f(R_1) + (R_3 - R_1)f(R_2) + (R_1 - R_2)f(R_3)} \right] \quad (10)$$

where $f(R1)$, $f(R2)$ and $f(R3)$ are the fitness function values at R1, R2 and R3, respectively. The above formula produces the minima of the quadratic surface passing through R1, R2 and R3. A typical diagram of 3D quadratic approximation is observed in the following Figure 4. In this figure, the evaluation of a child by Equation (10) is located at the bottom of the quadratic surface for a fixed set of R1, R2 and R3, in a minimization function. Sometimes it is expected that the child does not obey the allowable range for a particular variable. In that instance, the lower (upper) range of that variable is to be treated as child, according to the closeness of the obtained child to the bounds. The mechanism (flow chart) of QA is reflected in Figure 5.

To deal with the processes of QA, the tournament selection method seems to be more effective method while solving nonlinear optimization

Figure 4. Location of Child in QA

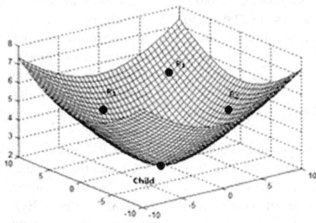

Figure 5. Flow Diagram of QA

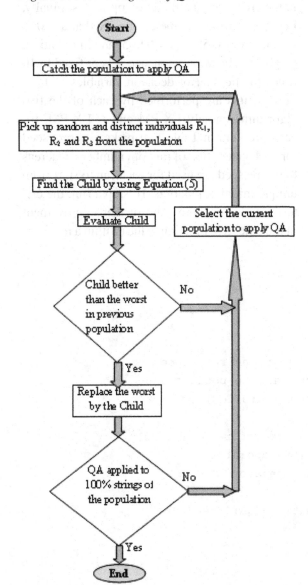

problems. This selection picks up the better solution between two different individuals, in terms of function fitness and constraint violation. Thus this selection does not depend on the nature of the problem under consideration.

It is worth here to note that the next two subsections deal with the realization of GA-QA hybridization for unconstrained and constrained optimization problems, respectively.

Hybrid GA for Unconstrained Optimization

In Deep and Thakur [2007b] a new real coded genetic algorithm called LX-PM is presented. LX-PM uses the Laplace Crossover and Power Mutation. Its performance is evaluated by Deep and Thakur on a number of unconstrained test problems taken from literature by comparing with similar crossover (Heuristic Crossover) and similar mutation (Non-Uniform or Makinen, Periaux and Toivanen Mutation) operators. However, there is a scope of improvement still, in the methodology of LX-PM to improve the solution quality and the convergence speed. In this section an attempt is made to incorporate the Quadratic Approximation (QA) (discussed in the previous subsection) as an additional operator in the GA cycle in order to investigate few better individuals further. This hybrid version thus generated is now abbreviated as H-LX-PM. The performance of LX-PM and H-LX-PM (introduced by Deep and Das, 2008) is evaluated and compared over a set of 22 standard benchmark problems of varying difficulty levels.

Hybrid GA

The pseudo code of H-LX-PM becomes as shown in Algorithm 1.

In the above, if QA step is eliminated, then it will become the pseudo code for LX-PM. It is also worth here to note that the QA is introduced at the end of each GA cycle just after completion of the complete elitism. Hence it helps in replacing few individuals in the population obtained after selection, crossover, mutation and elitism by probably few improved individuals. Here 'improved' in the sense of having better objective function values closer towards the minima.

Results and Discussion

In order to demonstrate the effectiveness of the hybridization of the Real Coded Genetic Algorithm, H-LX-PM, a set of 22 benchmark scalable test problems is selected from literature. These problems are of varying difficulty levels. The problems include unimodal and multimodal functions which are scalable (the problem size can be varied as per the user's choice). Here problem size for all problems is kept fixed to 10 for simulation. However, more or less the parallel results are found to be obtained by varying the size of the problems (showing all results is not in the scope of this chapter). The test bed of the problems is listed in Table 1.

LX-PM and H-LX-PM are implemented in C++ and the experiments are carried out on a P-IV, 2.8 GHz machine with 512 MB RAM under WINXP platform. Extensive experiments have been exhibited to fine tune the parameters present in the crossover and mutation operators. Finally, in crossover the parameters are fixed at a = 0, b = 0.35, Pc = 0.55, Pm = 0.005, and in mutation, p = 0.25. The population size is kept fixed to 10 times the number of decision variables. A total of 100 runs are performed by each of the two algorithms namely LX-PM and H-LX-PM, for each problem in Table 1. It picks different seed for each generation of random numbers, whereas the same seed are used for each run to start from unique initial population. To stop a run, the criterion is either there is no further improvement in the objective function value (within a radius of

Algorithm 1.

```
begin
        Generation = 0
        Generate initial population randomly using real encoding
        Evaluate fitness of each individual in the population
        While (termination criterion is not satisfied) do
                Generation = Generation + 1
                Apply tournament selection operator (of size 3)
                Apply Laplace crossover (LX) operator
                Apply power mutation (PM) operator
                Apply complete elitism
                Apply quadratic approximation (QA) operator
        end do
end begin
```

Table 1. $Benchmark functions used as test bed

Sl.	Name	Function	Bounds
1	Ackley	$-20\exp\left(-0.02\sqrt{\frac{1}{n}\sum_{i=1}^{n}x_i^2}\right)-\exp\left(\frac{1}{n}\sum_{i=1}^{n}\cos\left(2\pi x_i\right)\right)+20+e$	[-30,30]
2	Cosine Mixture	$0.1n+\sum_{i=1}^{n}x_i^2-0.1\sum_{i=1}^{n}\cos(5\pi x_i)$	[-1,1]
3	Exponential	$1-\left(\exp\left(-0.5\sum_{i=1}^{n}x_i^2\right)\right)$	[-1,1]
4	Griewank	$1+\frac{1}{4000}\sum_{i=1}^{n}x_i^2-\prod_{i=1}^{n}\cos\left(\frac{x_i}{\sqrt{i}}\right)$	[-600, 600]
5	Levy and Montalvo-1	$\frac{\pi}{n}\left(10\sin^2\left(\pi y_1\right)+\sum_{i=1}^{n-1}\left(y_i-1\right)^2\left[1+10\sin^2\left(\pi y_{i+1}\right)\right]+\left(y_n-1\right)^2\right), y_i=1+\frac{1}{4}\left(x_i+1\right)$	[-10,10]
6	Levy and Montalvo-2	$0.1\left(\left(\sin^2\left(3\pi x_1\right)+\sum_{i=1}^{n-1}\left(x_i-1\right)^2\left[1+\sin^2\left(3\pi x_{i+1}\right)\right]+\left(x_n-1\right)^2\left[1+\sin^2\left(2\pi x_n\right)\right]\right)\right)$	[-5,5]
7	Paviani	$45.778+\sum_{i=1}^{10}\left[(\ln(x_i-2))^2+(\ln(10-x_i))^2\right]-\left(\prod_{i=1}^{10}x_i\right)^{0.2}$	[2,10]
8	Rastrigin	$10n+\sum_{i=1}^{n}\left[x_i^2-10\cos\left(2\pi x_i\right)\right]$	[-5.12, 5.12]
9	Rosenbrock	$\sum_{i=1}^{n-1}\left[100\left(x_{i+1}-x_i^2\right)^2+\left(x_i-1\right)^2\right]$	[-30,30]
10	Schwefel	$418.9829n-\sum_{i=1}^{n}x_i\sin\left(\sqrt{|x_i|}\right)$	[-500, 500]
11	Sinusoidal	$3.5-\left[2.5\prod_{i=1}^{n}\sin\left(x_i-\frac{\pi}{6}\right)+\prod_{i=1}^{n}\sin\left(5\left(x_i-\frac{\pi}{6}\right)\right)\right]$	[0, π]
12	Zakharov's	$\sum_{i=1}^{n}x_i^2+\left(\sum_{i=1}^{n}\frac{i}{2}x_i\right)^2+\left(\sum_{i=1}^{n}\frac{i}{2}x_i\right)^4$	[-5.12, 5.12]
13	Sphere	$\sum_{i=1}^{n}x_i^2$	[-5.12, 5.12]

continued on following page

Table 1. Continued

Sl.	Name	Function	Bounds
14	Axis Parallel Hyper Ellipsoid	$$\sum_{i=1}^{n} i x_i^2$$	[-5.12, 5.12]
15	Schewefel-3	$$\sum_{i=1}^{n} \lvert x_i \rvert + \prod_{i=1}^{n} \lvert x_i \rvert$$	[-10,10]
16	Neumaier 3	$$\frac{n(n+4)(n-1)}{6} + \sum_{i=1}^{n} \left(x_i - 1 \right)^2 - \sum_{i=2}^{n} x_i x_{i-1}$$	$\left[-n^2, n^2 \right]$
17	Salomon	$$1 - \cos\left(2\pi \lVert x \rVert \right) + 0.1 \lVert x \rVert, \ \lVert x \rVert = \sqrt{\sum_{i=1}^{n} x_i^2}$$	[-100, 100]
18	Ellipsoidal	$$\sum_{i=1}^{n} (x_i - i)^2$$	$\left[-n, n \right]$
19	Schaffer 1	$$0.5 + \left. \left(\left(\sin \sqrt{\sum_{i=1}^{n} x_i^2} \right)^2 - 0.5 \right) \middle/ \left(1 + 0.001 \left(\sum_{i=1}^{n} x_i^2 \right) \right)^2 \right.$$	[-100, 100]
20	Brown3	$$\sum_{i-1}^{n-1} \left[\left(x_i^2 \right)^{\left(x_{i+1}^2 + 1 \right)} + \left(x_{i+1}^2 \right)^{\left(x_i^2 + 1 \right)} \right]$$	[-1,4]
21	New function	$$\sum_{i=1}^{n} \left(0.2 x_i^2 + 0.1 x_i^2 \sin 2x_i \right)$$	[-10,10]
22	Cigar	$$x_1^2 + 100000 \sum_{i=2}^{n} x_i^2$$	[-10,10]

$All are minimization problems having minimum value as 0

0.01) for 100 consecutive generations or a maximum of 2000 generations is attained. A run is considered to be a success if the objective function value obtained by the algorithm is within 1% accuracy of the known optimal value.

Out of a total of 100 independent runs, the success rate comparison for each problem is recorded in the 1st part of Table 2. Of the successful runs, the average number of function evaluations (2nd part of Table 2), the computational time (Table 3), the mean and the standard deviation of the optimal fitness (objective function) value (Table 4) using LX-PM and H-LX-PM are reported. For all the tables in this chapter, the bold face values indicate the superior value for that particular problem. The method of the corresponding column is treated as the better method over the other for that particular problem.

Table 2. Comparative Success Rate and Average number of function evaluations using LX-PM and H-LX-PM

Prob. No.	Success Rate		Average Function Evaluations	
	LX-PM	H-LX-PM	LX-PM	H-LX-PM
1	0	1	*	35700
2	35	100	18505	22526
3	97	100	14047	21214
4	0	24	*	32833
5	19	100	16847	22242
6	53	92	14286	21593
7	65	100	19433	26936
8	0	7	*	34557
9	8	100	43800	370352
10	0	87	*	61831
11	59	98	18530	23640
12	19	100	22021	23690
13	68	100	18216	22618
14	60	100	18028	22492
15	38	100	20913	26272
16	2	100	39550	162066
17	0	0	*	*
18	42	100	18930	24058
19	0	2	*	25600
20	78	100	18343	23286
21	64	100	18756	22470
22	5	100	28920	27404

First Method of Analysis

The brief view of comparative performance from Tables 2-4 is presented in Table 5. Now from Table 5 it is clear that only one problem (no. 17) couldn't be solved by either of the methods. Out of the rest 21 problems, the number of function evaluations and hence the computational time required to solve by H-LX-PM is bit higher than that of LX-PM. However, the success rate is much higher, the average objective function value is much better and the standard deviation is much smaller in H-LX-PM than the corresponding LX-PM. It is worthy here to note that by H-LX-PM,

14 problems could be solved by 100% success, whereas no problem with 100% could be solved by LX-PM. Further, with the availability of more and more high-speed computing facilities, the issue of computational time difference in seconds is not of much concern. Still it is wise to record them. Thus, it can roughly be said that H-LX-PM outperforms LX-PM in most of the cases.

Second Method of Analysis

In view of these conflicting conclusions based on different criteria, it is difficult to judge the better algorithm between LX-PM and H-LX-PM.

Table 3. Comparative computational time (in seconds) using LX-PM and H-LX-PM

Prob. No.	LX-PM	H-LX-PM	Prob. No.	LX-PM	H-LX-PM
1	*	**0.531**	12	**0.372**	0.492
2	**0.281**	0.343	13	**0.224**	0.347
3	**0.189**	0.270	14	**0.222**	0.346
4	*	**0.517**	15	**0.230**	0.375
5	**0.257**	0.460	16	**0.477**	2.356
6	**0.285**	0.546	17	*	*
7	**0.322**	0.490	18	**0.235**	0.362
8	*	**0.462**	19	*	**0.399**
9	**0.770**	7.301	20	**0.404**	0.575
10	*	**0.875**	21	**0.286**	0.481
11	**0.246**	0.401	22	**0.363**	0.395

Table 4. Comparative mean and standard deviation of the optimal objective function value using LX-PM and H-LX-PM

Prob.	Mean		Standard Deviation	
	LX-PM	H-LX-PM	LX-PM	H-LX-PM
1	*	**6.10E-14**	*	**0.00E+00**
2	9.72E-04	**1.57E-15**	1.40E-03	**1.50E-15**
3	9.54E-04	**1.32E-15**	1.97E-03	**2.68E-15**
4	*	**4.01E-03**	*	**4.43E-03**
5	1.33E-03	**1.18E-12**	2.41E-03	**3.07E-18**
6	4.78E-04	**1.89E-13**	1.25E-03	**2.64E-18**
7	1.87E-03	**4.70E-04**	2.54E-03	**7.23E-14**
8	*	**1.65E-14**	*	**1.67E-14**
9	9.55E+00	**1.29E+00**	3.37E+00	**1.81E+00**
10	*	**1.27E-04**	*	**6.82E-13**
11	1.46E-03	**3.46E-15**	2.34E-03	**1.39E-15**
12	1.65E-03	**7.41E-21**	1.91E-03	**6.04E-20**
13	1.75E-03	**1.94E-22**	2.30E-03	**5.32E-22**
14	1.54E-03	**1.73E-21**	2.48E-03	**1.17E-20**
15	2.08E-03	**1.43E-13**	2.58E-03	**2.79E-13**
16	3.40E-01	**2.98E-03**	2.14E-01	**1.05E-03**
17	*	*	*	*
18	1.50E-03	**1.78E-15**	2.39E-03	**1.19E-15**
19	*	**9.72E-03**	*	**2.78E-17**
20	1.63E-03	**3.81E-21**	2.29E-03	**2.25E-20**
21	1.54E-03	**1.76E-21**	2.29E-03	**1.01E-20**
22	3.08E-03	**3.93E-21**	3.19E-03	**2.76E-20**

Table 5. Comparison of LX-PM with H-LX-PM in analyzing Tables 2-4

Quality of H-LX-PM over LX-PM	Success Rate (Ref. Table 2)	Average no. of function evaluations (Ref. Table 2)	Time (in sec.) (Ref. Table 3)	Mean Obj. function value (of successful runs) (Ref. Table 4)	Mean SD (of successful runs) (Ref. Table 4)
Better	**21**	5	5	21	21
Equal	1*	1*	1*	1*	1*
Worse	0	**16**	**16**	0	0
* It is only problem (no. 17) which couldn't be solved by both LX-PM and H-LX-PM.					

Hence to measure the winner, a Performance Index (Mohan and Nguyen, 2004) in its extended form is used and is discussed below.

Consider three criteria, namely: (i) success rate to measure the *reliability*, (ii) average number of function evaluations to measure the *efficiency* and (iii) the mean of the optimal objective function value attained to measure the *accuracy* of the algorithms. A Performance Index (PI), is designed as follows:

$$PI = \frac{1}{N_p} \sum_{i=1}^{N_p} \left(k_1 \alpha_1^i + k_2 \alpha_2^i + k_3 \alpha_3^i \right) \qquad (11)$$

where

$$\alpha_1^i = \frac{Sr^i}{Tr^i}$$

$$\alpha_2^i = \begin{cases} \dfrac{Mo^i}{Ao^i}, & if\ Sr^i > 0 \\ 0, & if\ Sr^i = 0 \end{cases}$$

and

$$\alpha_3^i = \begin{cases} \dfrac{Mf^i}{Af^i}, & if\ Sr^i > 0 \\ 0, & if\ Sr^i = 0 \end{cases}, \text{ for } i = 1, 2, ..., N_p$$

- Sr^i: Number of successful runs of *ith* problem.
- Tr^i: Total number of runs of *ith* problem
- Ao^i: Mean optimal objective function value obtained by an algorithm of *ith* problem
- Mo^i: Minimum of mean optimal objective function value obtained by all the algorithms of *ith* problem
- Af^i: Average number of function evaluations of successful runs required by an algorithm in obtaining the solution of *ith* problem
- Mf^i: Minimum of average number of function evaluations of successful runs required by all algorithms in obtaining the solution of *ith* problem
- N_p: Total number of problems analyzed.

Note that k_1, k_2 and k_3 ($k_1 + k_2 + k_3 = 1$ and $0 \le k_1,\ k_2,\ k_3 \le 1$) are the weights assigned to percentage of success, mean optimal objective function value and average number of function evaluations of successful runs, respectively. From this definition it is seen that PI is a function of k_1, k_2 and k_3. However, since $k_1 + k_2 + k_3 = 1$, one of k_i, $i = 1, 2, 3$ can be eliminated to reduce the number of dependent variables from the expression of PI. But it is still difficult to analyze the behaviour of PI, because the surface plots of PI for all three algorithms are overlapping and it is difficult to visualize them. Therefore, if equal weights are assigned to two terms at a time in the PI expression, then PI becomes a function of one variable only. The resultant cases are as follows.

$$k_1 = w, \ k_2 = k_3 = \frac{1-w}{2}, \ where \ 0 \le w \le 1$$

$$k_2 = w, \ k_1 = k_3 = \frac{1-w}{2}, where \ 0 \le w \le 1$$

$$k_3 = w, \ k_1 = k_2 = \frac{1-w}{2}, \ where \ 0 \le w \le 1$$

In each of the Figures 6, 7 and 8, the horizontal axis represents the weights corresponding to the first, second and third term of the expression of PI, namely percentage of success, mean optimal objective function value and average number of function evaluations of successful runs, respectively. This weight is varied from 0 to 1. The vertical axis represents the value of PI, also lying between 0 and 1. The graphs corresponding to LX-PM and H-LX-PM are superimposed and the one that has higher PI is taken to be the better than the other.

From Figure 6 it is clear that with respect to percentage of success, H-LX-PM is always better than LX-PM. From Figure 7 it is observed that with respect to mean optimal objective function value, although H-LX-PM is always better than LX-PM the difference between PI is very large if this weight assigned a value 0, and is very marginal if this weight is assigned a value 1. From Figure 8 it is seen that with respect to average number of function evaluations of successful runs, although H-LX-PM is always better than LX-PM the difference between PI is small if this weight has a value 0, and is very large if this weight has a value 1. Therefore, H-LX-PM is more reliable, more efficient and more accurate than LX-PM. However, depending upon the priority that the user might like to give to the three factors a suitable choice between the two algorithms can be made. Hence clearly, H-LX-PM outperforms LX-PM.

Figure 6. Performance Index of LX-PM and H-LX-PM, when percentage of success is varied between 0 and 1

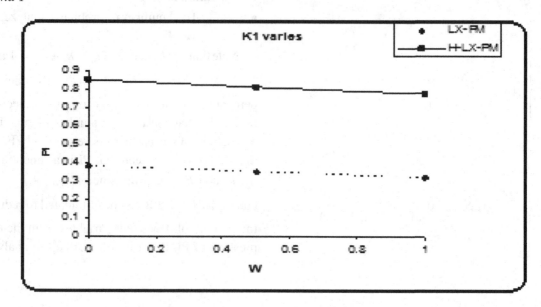

Figure 7. PI of LX-PM and H-LX-PM, when mean optimal objective function value is varied between 0 and 1

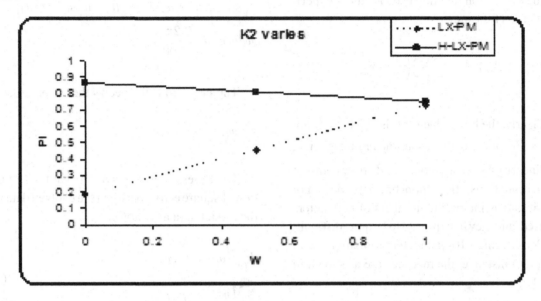

Figure 8. Performance Index of LX-PM and H-LX-PM, when average number of function evaluations of successful runs is varied between 0 and 1

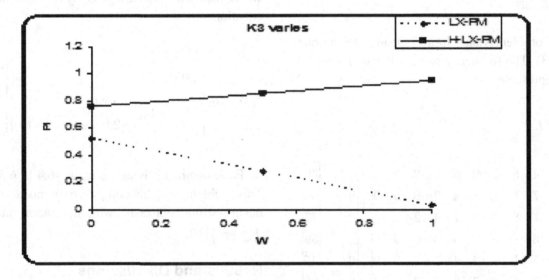

Applications

In this section we present two popular real life nonlinear optimization problems and use the LX-PM and H-LX-PM to solve these problems.

Problem 1: System of Linear Equations

This problem is taken from Eshelman, Mathias and Schaeffer (1997). The problem may be stated as solving for the elements of a vector, X, given the matrix A and vector B in the expression: A.X = B. The evaluation function used for these experiments is as follows:

$$P_{sle}\left(x_1, x_2, \ldots, x_n\right) = \sum_{i=1}^{n}\sum_{j=1}^{n}\left(a_{ij} - x_j\right) - b_i \quad (12)$$

Clearly, the best value for this objective function is $P_{sle}\left(x^*\right) = 0$. Inter-parameter linkage (i.e., nonlinearity) is easily controlled in systems of linear equations, their non-linearity does not deteriorate as increasing numbers of parameters are used, and they have proven to be quite difficult.

Considering a 10-parameter problem (Lozano et al, [5]) instance, the matrices are as shown in Box 1.

Problem 2: Frequency Modulation Sounds Parameter Identification Problem

This problem is taken from (Tsutsui and Fujimoto, 1993). The frequency modulation sound model is represented by

Box 1.

$$
\begin{vmatrix}
5 & 4 & 5 & 2 & 9 & 5 & 4 & 2 & 3 & 1 \\
9 & 7 & 1 & 1 & 7 & 2 & 2 & 6 & 6 & 9 \\
3 & 1 & 8 & 6 & 9 & 7 & 4 & 2 & 1 & 6 \\
8 & 3 & 7 & 3 & 7 & 5 & 3 & 9 & 9 & 5 \\
9 & 5 & 1 & 6 & 3 & 4 & 2 & 3 & 3 & 9 \\
1 & 2 & 3 & 1 & 7 & 6 & 6 & 3 & 3 & 3 \\
1 & 5 & 7 & 8 & 1 & 4 & 7 & 8 & 4 & 8 \\
9 & 3 & 8 & 6 & 3 & 4 & 7 & 1 & 8 & 1 \\
8 & 2 & 8 & 5 & 3 & 8 & 7 & 2 & 7 & 5 \\
2 & 1 & 2 & 2 & 9 & 8 & 7 & 4 & 4 & 1
\end{vmatrix}
\begin{vmatrix}
1 \\ 1 \\ 1 \\ 1 \\ 1 \\ 1 \\ 1 \\ 1 \\ 1 \\ 1
\end{vmatrix}
=
\begin{vmatrix}
40 \\ 50 \\ 47 \\ 59 \\ 45 \\ 35 \\ 53 \\ 50 \\ 55 \\ 40
\end{vmatrix}
$$

$$y(t) = a_1\sin\left(w_1 t\theta + a_2\sin\left(w_2 t\theta + a_3\sin\left(w_3 t\theta\right)\right)\right),$$

$$where \quad \theta = \frac{2\pi}{100}$$

The problem is to specify the six parameters:

$$a_1, w_1, a_2, w_2, a_3, w_3$$

The fitness function is defined as the summation of square errors between the evolved data and the model data as follows:

$$P_{fms}\left(a_1, w_1, a_2, w_2, a_3, w_3\right) = \sum_{t=0}^{100}\left(y(t) - y_0(t)\right)^2 \quad (13)$$

where the model data are given by the following equation:

$$y_0(t) = 1.0\times\sin\left(5.0\times t\theta - 1.5\times\sin\left(4.5\times t\theta + 2.0\times\sin\left(4.9\times t\theta\right)\right)\right).$$

Each parameter is in the range -6.4 to 6.35. This problem is highly complex multimodal one having strong epistasis, with minimum value $P_{fms}\left(x^*\right) = 0$.

Results and Discussions

Each of the two real world problems 1 and 2 are run 100 times. The parameter setting and the stopping criteria are as discussed in Section 4. A run is considered to be a success if, the obtained objective value is with in 0.5 and 20 for the real life problems 1 and 2, respectively. The mean of the optimal objective function values and the standard deviations are reported for the successful runs only. Both the real world problems are solved by both LX-PM and H-LX-PM. The comparative results for problem 1 and 2 are reported in Tables 6 and 7 respectively.

From Tables 6 and 7, it is observed that although H-LX-PM takes more time to solve the problems with a higher number of function evaluations the H-LX-PM yields a better solution with a higher success rate. Further, since the standard deviations are also lower in case of H-LX-PM, it is more stable than LX-PM.

In order to visualize the effect of the hybridization in finding the objective function value (fitness function value), the convergence graphs for LX-PM and H-LX-PM are plotted in Figures 9 and 10 for problems 1 and 2 respectively. The horizontal axis shows the generation number and the vertical axis shows the optimal objective function for a typical run. It is observed that although both LX-PM and H-LX-PM started from the same starting point the fitness function value improved more rapidly while using H-LX-PM, particularly during the initial generations of a run.

Hence it is observed that although H-LX-PM is less efficient it is more reliable, more accurate and more stable than LX-PM. Thus, in totality H-LX-PM is recommended to solve these two typical real life problems to get improved success rates with better optimum values.

Hybrid GA for Constrained Optimization

Constrained Handling Techniques

GA performs well in solving unconstrained optimization problem. However, it faces difficulties in solving highly constrained optimization problems. This is because the traditional search operators of GA (viz. crossover and mutation) are blind to constraints. In such circumstances, it is very likely that the candidate solutions generated by these operators during the search process would violate certain constraints. A special and proper treatment is often required to maintain the applicability of GAs and to prevent the genetic search from leaving the feasible region. Quite a large number of methods have been developed to handle constraints when evolutionary algorithms are used (Kim and Myung (1996 & 1997), Mi-

Table 6. Performance comparison of LX-PM and H-LX-PM to solve the system of linear equations

Methods	Success Rate	Average No. of Function Evaluations	Time (in sec.)	Mean Obj. Function Value (of Successful Runs)	Mean SD (of Successful Runs)
LX-PM	39%	**19294**	**0.201**	0.336352	0.105848
H-LX-PM	**100%**	31500	0.477	**0.115572**	**0.061183**

Table 7. Performance comparison of LX-PM and H-LX-PM to solve frequency modulation sounds parameter identification problem

Methods	Success Rate	Average No. of Function Evaluations	Time (in sec.)	Mean Obj. Function Value (of Successful Runs)	Mean SD (of Successful Runs)
LX-PM	16%	**23250**	**2.26**	15.3688	5.17363
H-LX-PM	24%	45036	4.52	**14.5191**	**4.37356**

Figure 9. Generation wise convergence for System of linear equations

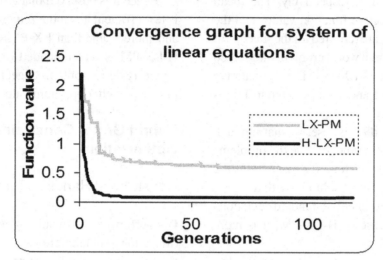

Figure 10. Generation wise convergence for Frequency modulation sounds parameter identification problem

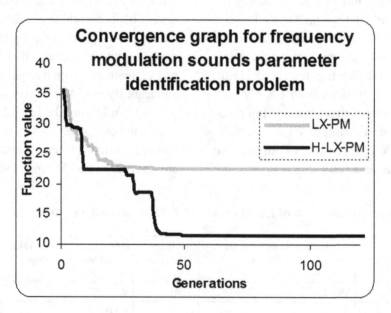

chalewicz (1996), Myung and Kim(1996), Orvosh and Devis (1995)). The major strategies used in literature can be classified as Rejecting strategy, Repairing strategy, Modifying genetic operator strategy, Penalty function strategy. Among these, penalty function strategy is most commonly used. The main drawback of this approach is that penalty parameter needs to be fine tuned. If this parameter is not handled properly then there are more chances of getting infeasible solutions.

Deb and Agarwal (1999) proposed a Niched-Penalty approach for constraint handling in GAs which does not require any penalty parameter. Coello and Mezura (2002) proposed a constraint handling approach for GAs which uses a dominance-based selection scheme that does not require the fine tuning of a penalty function to maintain diversity. Akhtar et al. (2002) proposed a Socio-Behavioral simulation based approach to solve engineering optimization problems. They simulate societies in this approach. Each society has a leader which is followed by other members of that society. Besides this they also form a leader's society which is formed by the leader of each society. They are called "general leaders". Constraints are handled by ranking the solutions based on non-dominance checking inside their corresponding society. The main advantage of this approach is that it requires low number of function evaluations to obtain the near optimal solution, if not the optimum. Its main drawback is that the implementation is not easy. To improve the solution quality further a new multi-parent crossover and a local search technique is introduced (Saber et. al., 2011) for constrained optimization problem.

To handle the constraints the dynamic penalty is used in the penalty function which is regulated by the generation number (Crossley and Williams, 1997). This mechanism to make the penalty dynamic is being used in this paper.

Two selection criteria are implemented in this present work. First, in order to select best individuals from a given population (size = 10*N) to form a mating pool (size = 10*N), a selection strategy is needed (see subsection 2.1). Second, in order to find the best individual in a certain population in the sense of better objective function value and lesser constraint violation, another selection strategy is used (see subsection 2.2).

Tournament Selection Strategy

For the constrained optimization, the tournament selection method is less sensitive to the choice of the penalty function. In most cases the constant penalty method with a great value of the penalty coefficient will produce good results. Kundu and

Osyczka (1996) showed that tournament selection gives better results while solving multi-criteria constrained optimization problems using the distance method. Deb (1997) used tournament selection in his genetic adaptive search method and applied it to solve several mechanical design constrained problems (Kundu, 1996). The selection strategy is used in this chapter. It is verified that this distance method is very effective while solving highly constrained single criterion optimization problems as well as the problems with computationally expensive objective function. It is based on three different scenarios.

1. If both chromosomes are not in the feasible region the one which is closer to the feasible region is taken to the next generation. The values of the objective function are not calculated for either of chromosomes.
2. If one chromosome is in the feasible region and the other one is out of the feasible region the one which is in the feasible region is taken to the next generation. The values of the objective function are not calculated for either chromosome.
3. If both chromosomes are in the feasible region, the values of the objective function are calculated for both chromosomes and the one, which has a better value of the objective function, is taken to the next generation.

All the above three situations are well placed in Figure 11.

Adaptive Penalty

Researchers use the penalty parameter to forcefully drag the infeasible points to the feasible reason. It is observed that when simulation runs, after few iterations, the objective value get stagnant and they come closer to each other in the population. Hence there is a need of heavy penalty if the value gets trapped in a particular value. In this section

Figure 11. The idea of the constraint tournament method

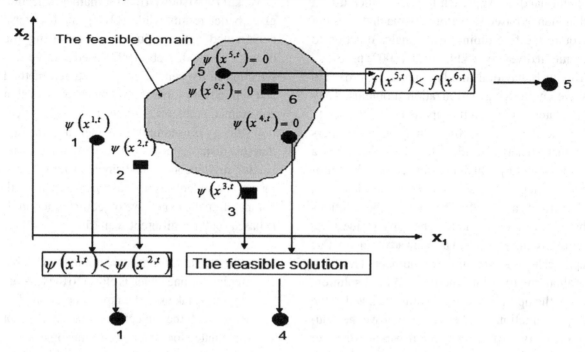

an adaptive penalty is therefore presented that will be a function of iteration number "t". The adaptive penalty follows as following steps.

Step 1: For a fixed generation 't', choose a penalty parameter $R^{(t)}$, which is defined as

$$R^{(t)} = 10^{\left\lfloor \frac{t}{300} \right\rfloor} \tag{14}$$

where $\lfloor . \rfloor$ indicates the floor function.

The change of penalty parameter $R^{(t)}$ occurs in successive sequences of the penalty function method. For the constraint handling technique, an exterior penalty term is used, where the bracket operator assigns a positive value to the infeasible points. With a small initial value of $R^{(t)}$ the GA cycle starts. As $R^{(t)}$ increases in successive sequences, the solution improves by forcing the infeasible points towards the feasibility and finally approaches the optimal point, which is close to the true solution.

Step 2: Find the fitness function of each individuals in the population by using the bracket operator penalty. This penalty is mostly useful in handling inequality constraints (Deb, 1995). The fitness function is

$$F\left(x^{(t)}, R^{(t)}\right) = f\left(x^{(t)}\right) + \Omega\left(R^{(t)}, g^{(t)}, h^{(t)}\right) \tag{15}$$

where f stands for the objective function and Ω stands for penalty term which is given by

$$\Omega = R\left\langle g\left(x\right) \right\rangle^2 \tag{16}$$

where

$$\langle \alpha \rangle = \begin{cases} 0, & \text{if } \alpha \geq 0 \\ \alpha, & \text{if } \alpha < 0 \end{cases} \tag{17}$$

Step 3: The tournament selection is used to select more fit individuals.

In this section, the LX-PM-C and H-LX-PM-C (introduced by K. Deep and K. N. Das, 2013) is designed from LX-PM and H-LX-PM respectively, just by developing the algorithm for solving constrained optimization problems.

Results and Discussion

A set of 15 constrained benchmark problems of different dimensions have been considered in order to compare the performance of LX-PM-C and H-LX-PM-C. They are listed in an Appendix at the last of this chapter. The fine tune of the scaling parameter b1 used in the Laplace crossover (Holland, J. 1975), probability of crossover Pc and probability of Pm are made by hand out computation. The finally recommended parameter setting is recoded in Table 8.

Under the same experimental setup and by keeping the recommended parameters fixed, each problem is run 100 times. The stopping criterion is either a maximum of 2000 generations is attained or no notable improvement is observed in

the objective function value of the best individual in consecutive 100 generations. Here notable improvement means, if BP is the prior best point and OP is the obtained best point of the current generation, then |BP − OP| > 0.001. A run is considered to be success if the objective function obtained by the algorithm is within 1% accuracy of the known optimal value. The success rates are reported in Table 9. For the successful runs the average number of function calls (Table 10), the computational time (Table 11), the mean and S. D. (Table 12) of the objective function values are reported.

Analysis of results

Analyzing the result from Table 2 in terms of success rate, out of 100 independents runs for 15 problems under consideration, H-LX-PM-C performs better in 9 problems, equally in 5 problems and worse in only 1 problem than LX-PM-C. Similarly, from Table 10 it is verified that H-LX-PM-C takes less number of function evaluations in 12 problems, where as only in 3 problems it takes more. It is worth to note here from Table 11 that this hybrid version takes more time in all the problems to solve. However looking at Table 12, H-LX-PM-C is worse in only 2 problems in terms of objective function value, where as better in 5 and equally performs in 8 numbers of problems.

Table 8. Final fine tuned parameter values

Algorithms	b1	Pc	Pm
LX-PM-C	0.5	0.9	0.025
H-LX-PM-C	0.95	0.7	0.0125

Table 9. Percentage of success for 100 runs

Pb. No.	LX- PM-C	H-LX-PM-C	Pb. No.	LX-PM-C	H-LX-PM-C
1	100	100	9	100	100
2	99	98	10	0	2
3	3	5	11	100	100
4	98	100	12	52	100
5	5	5	13	37	38
6	11	12	14	13	29
7	15	22	15	2	4
8	34	52			

Table 10. Average number of function evaluations

Pb. No.	LX-PM-C	H-LX-PM-C	Pb. No.	LX-PM-C	H-LX-PM-C
1	25649	**25439**	9	10055	**10038**
2	30768	**30472**	10	*	**10800**
3	10586	**10204**	11	10190	**10060**
4	52504	**49209**	12	**10105**	10295
5	32520	**31428**	13	**10269**	10344
6	10405	**10273**	14	13766	**12524**
7	10246	**10153**	15	10560	**10120**
8	**30829**	31259			

Table 11. Average computational time (in sec.)

Pb. No.	LX-PM-C	H-LX-PM-C	Pb. No.	LX-PM-C	H-LX-PM-C
1	**0.1203**	0.5116	9	**0.2845**	0.3574
2	**0.2195**	0.7176	10	*	**0.4060**
3	**0.0620**	0.1904	11	**0.2900**	0.3611
4	**0.7026**	1.4472	12	**0.0706**	0.2222
5	**0.3188**	0.7908	13	**0.0740**	0.2057
6	**0.0712**	0.2163	14	**0.0961**	0.3571
7	**0.0627**	0.1945	15	**0.0748**	0.2110
8	**0.2983**	0.6169			

H-LX-PM-C also attains less standard deviation in finding optimal solution in most of the problems as compared with LX-PM-C.

GA IN NETWORKING OPTIMIZATION

Many often in science and engineering, it becomes a challenge to solve 'network optimization problems' which are NP hard. Such areas include prediction of secondary structure in RNA, VLSI design, information/coding theory, map labelling, scheduling, computer vision, pattern recognition etc. Four graph theoretic situations related to networking optimization are discussed below.

1. Maximum Independent Set Problem (MISP)
2. Minimum Vertex Cover (MVC)
3. Maximum Clique Problem (MCP)
4. Minimum Labelling Spanning Tree (MLST)

In spite of the availability of many traditional methods to solve them, many a times they fail to provide a solution, especially when the problem is associated with high. Hence the alternate paradigms like GA / hybrid GA are unavoidable at least to provide a near optimal solution, if not the optimal one. In the other hand, the hybrid versions help not only to reduce the computational time but also to provide more accurate results.

Table 12. Mean objective function value and S. D.

Problem Number	Mean function values		S. D.	
	LX-PM-C	H-LX-PM-C	LX-PM-C	H-LX-PM-C
1	-320.000	-320.000	0.0000	0.0000
2	-313.000	-313.000	0.0000	0.0000
3	13.644	13.641	0.0223	0.0451
4	682.433	682.282	1.3023	0.8681
5	-11.976	-11.951	0.0726	0.0693
6	-5.475	-5.475	0.0125	0.0125
7	-16.742	-16.745	0.0999	0.1072
8	5139.564	5134.106	16.0353	18.7828
9	-1.000	-1.000	0.0000	0.0000
10	*	-0.993	*	0.0006
11	-1.000	-1.000	0.0000	0.0000
12	0.250	0.250	0.0004	0.0000
13	0.502	0.501	0.0015	0.0014
14	-0.096	-0.096	0.0006	0.0003
15	-6955.844	-6937.021	35.4933	19.2784

The next subsections include the definitions of above four graphical scenarios. Later, the procedure to handle such problems by Genetic algorithm is demonstrated in only one of the aspects namely MVC.

Maximum Independent Set Problem (MISP)

A graph G consists of a vertex set V and an edge set E. Two vertices are said to be adjacent vertices in G if there exists an edge connecting them. Independent set of G is a subset S of V where no two vertices are adjacent. Maximal Independent Set of G is that independent set S where the addition of any vertex to S from (G-S) breaks the independence property of S. Maximum Independent Set Problem (MISP) is to find that maximal independent set of G that contains maximum number of vertices. Let us consider an example of the graph G shown in Figure 12. For G, {1,4} is

Figure 12. Example of MISP

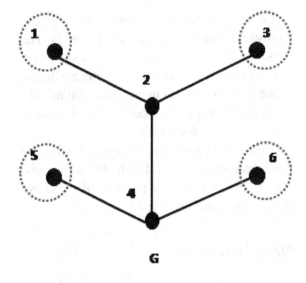

an independent set, {1,4,3} is a maximal independent set and {1,3,5,6} is a maximum independent set, which is the maximal independent set with maximum number of vertices.

Minimum Vertex Covering (MVC)

Given a graph G = (V, E). Minimum vertex covering (MVC) is to find the smallest subset V' of V such that:

$$\forall \langle i, j \rangle \in E, i \in V' \lor j \in V'$$

For the graph G in Figure 13, {1, 3} is an example of MVC.

Maximum Clique Problem (MCP)

A graph is said to be complete if there exist an edge between each pair of vertices in G. Finding the largest complete sub-graph of a given a graph G is known as maximum clique problem (MCP). Mathematically, for a given graph G=(V,E), MCP is to find the largest subset $V' \subseteq V$ such that:

$$\forall \langle i, j \rangle \in E, i \in V' \lor j \in V$$

Let us consider an example of the graph G consists of 10 vertices as shown in Figure 14. The set S = {1,2,3,4} constitutes the largest sub-graph of G (shown in bold lines) and is the maximum clique of G. It is worth to note here that no sub-graph of G that contains more number of vertices than S, is a complete graph.

Now it is interesting to observe that all above three problems are equivalent by following theorem. Hence, solving one problem of the above implies the solutions of rest two.

Figure 13. Ex. of MVC

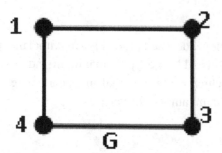

Figure 14. Ex. of MCP

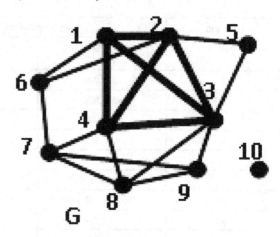

Theorem: (Equivalent Statements)

The following statements are equivalent.

1. V' is the maximum independent set in G
2. V-V' is the minimum vertex cover of G.
3. V' is the maximum clique in $G^c = \left(V, E^c \right)$

where

$$E^c = \left\{ (i, j) : i, j \in V \land (i, j) \notin E \right\}.$$

The following Figure 15 clarify the concept of above theorem, where V' indicates the vertices circled in red.

Minimum Labelling Spanning Tree (MLST)

An acyclic connected graph is called Tree. For any graph G, Spanning tree is a tree (sub-graph of G) that contains all the vertices of G. Minimum Spanning Tree (MST) of G is that spanning tree of G contains minimum number of edges. Minimum labelling spanning tree is a new concept arises in the networking optimization. Let G is a weighted graph where each edge is assigned with some weights. Then, Minimum Label Spanning Tree (MLST) of G is the spanning tree with least number of different labels (or weights).

Figure 15. Equivalency in graphs

MISP Vs. MCV

A. **V' is the maximum independent set in G**

B. **V-V' is the minimum vertex cover of G.**

MISP Vs. Maximum Clique

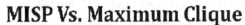
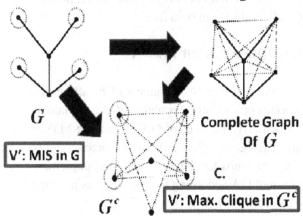

Mathematically, given a graph $G = (V, E)$ with a labeling function $L(e) \forall e \in E$, then the MLST is a spanning tree such that $|L_{ST}|$ is minimized. L_{ST} refers to the labels in the spanning tree. The minimum label spanning tree (MLST) problem arises when it is required to design an 'uniform' network that uses different communications media, or links owned by as few particles as possible. An example is shown in Figure 16, where differ-

Figure 16. Ex. of MLST

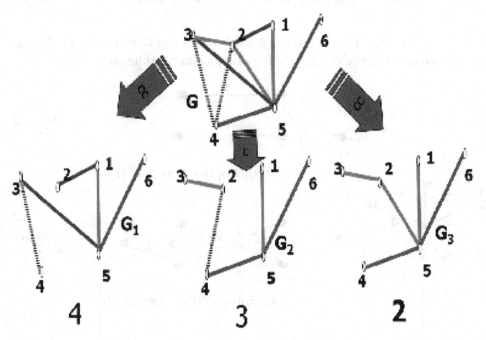

ent colors refer to different labels. In this figure, each of G1, G1, G3 is an MST of G, but G3 is the MLST of G that uses only 2 (minimum) number of labels shown in bold face.

GA approach for MVCA

In this section, a basic concept of handling networking optimization problem by GA is explained. Particularly, the steps of GA for solving MVCA are highlighted. Researchers are encouraged to use such steps for the computational implementation of GA according to their need as per their concerned problems.

The GA parameters can be treated as follows:

Encoding

Let L represents the set of different labels exist in a given graph G. An individual (or a chromosome) in a population is a feasible solution, which is defined as a subset L' of L' such that all the edges with labels in L' construct a connected subgraph of G and span all the nodes of G. To create an initial population, it is required to code

each individual. New individuals can be generated simply by adding new labels to an empty set restricted to V, just upto getting a connected Graph. Each label in L' is viewed as a gene here. Two observations have been defined to identify a feasible solution and an optimal solution respectively, with which it requires to seek a feasible solution with the least number of labels. For a chromosome number of labels is treated as its fitness value. An example of encoding for the feasible solutions for a given graph G is explained in Figure 17. Clearly, G contains 3 labels {1, 2, 4} as shown in Figure 17 (a). The subgraph of G induced by {1, 4}, having fitness value 2, is given in Figure 17(b) and induced by {2}, having fitness value 1, is given in Figure 17(c). Both induced figures represent encoding of two different feasible solutions of the graph G.

Crossover

This operator generates one new offspring from two parents. First take the union of the labels of two parents and sort them in the decreasing order of their frequencies. To the empty offspring, go

Figure 17. (a) The given graph G, (b) Encoding feasible solution of G induced by {1, 4} and (c) Encoding feasible solution of G induced by {2}, which is also an optimal solution

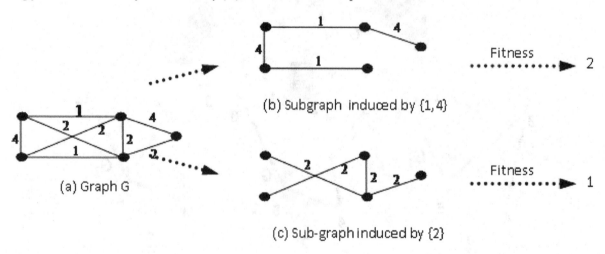

on adding labels in their sorted order until the offspring represents a feasible solution. For example, let us consider parent 1 with labels P[1] = {1,2,3} and parent 2 with label P[2] = {1,3,4} as given in Figure 18. P[1] and P[2] undergo crossover to generate the offspring O. First, the labels of P[1] and P[2] are combined to get I[1] = {1,2,3,4}, in which labels are already sorted in the decreasing order of their frequencies. Label 1, 2, 3 and 4 occur with frequencies 4, 3, 2 and 2 respectively. Let us consider a null graph restricted to the vertices of the I[1]. First add the label {1}, which is the label with the largest frequency. As the graph obtained is induced by {1} and is not connected, so label {2} with the second largest frequency is added. Still the graph induced by {1,2} is disconnected. So just add the next label {3}. Now a connected graph O = {1,2,3} is obtained, which is the required offspring. Here I[1],

I[2] and I[3] are treated as the intermediate states during crossover in generating the offspring 'O' after crossover between the parents P[1] and P[2].

Mutation

Let G be some graph and S be its candidate solution obtained after crossover. Consider a label α $\in$ (G – S), and add it to S to form S1. Keep on removing the labels with the least to most frequently occurring labels, until the S1 remains feasible. An example is shown in the Figure 19. In this figure a solution S is induced by the labels {1,3,4} and consider a label {2} which is not there in S and add it to get S1 = {1,2,3,4}, which already contains the labels with the descending order of their frequencies. Keep on removing labels from right to left with keeping the feasibility in mind. So, first try to remove {4}. Still the remaining

Figure 18. Crossover between two parents P[1] and P[2] to produce the offspring O

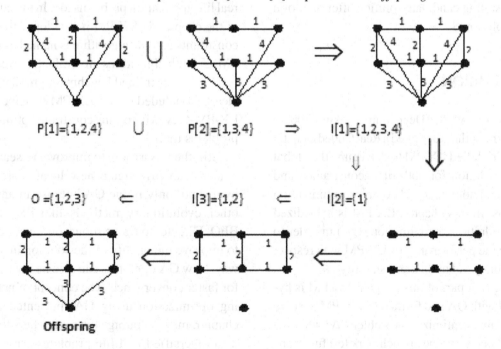

Figure 19. Mutation of the solution [S]

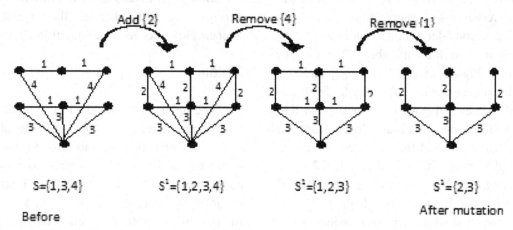

graph is connected. Now when we try to remove the next label {3}, it is found that the graph becomes infeasible. So without removing the label {3}, go for the next label 2, where we will face the same problem. So remove the next and the last label {1}. After removing this, still the graph S1 remains feasible. Hence the obtained graph S1 is the resulting candidate solution after mutation of the solution S.

CONCLUSION

In an earlier work (Deep and Thakur, 2007a, 2007b), the authors designed a Real Coded Genetic Algorithm called LX-PM to determine the global optimal solution for both of unconstrained and constrained nonlinear and complex optimization problems. In this chapter, LX-PM is hybridized with Quadratic Approximation (QA) in order to improve the performance of LX-PM with respect to efficiency, reliability and stability.

In the first part of this chapter, LX-PM is hybridized with QA and formed H-LX-PM to solve unconstrained optimization problem. A wide variety of 22 unconstrained benchmark test functions are considered from literature. In addition to it,

two popular real world application problems are solved both by LX-PM and H-LX-PM. From the results and discussions it is concluded that H-LX-PM takes bit more time and function evaluations to solve a problem in general, but at the same time, it is more reliable, more accurate and more stable than LX-PM, not only for test problems but also for real life application problems too. In the later part of the chapter, H-LX-PM is developed to handle constraints and the algorithm is named as H-LX-PM-C. Both algorithms are evaluated over a test bed of 15 constrained benchmark problems. It is clearly concluded that H-LX-PM-C outperforms LX-PM-C even in solving constraint optimization problems too.

Still there is a room to improve. Researchers/readers can investigate new local searches to hybrid not only in the GA but also in any such other evolutionary methods like PSO, ACO, BFO, DE, etc; to frame robust optimization tool to improve the quality of the solution in a better way. New GA operators can also be investigated for faster convergence. The concept of networking optimization using GA, presented in this chapter, may encourage the researchers to apply it in diversified real life problems arise across engineering design.

REFERENCES

Akhtar, S., Tai, K., & Ray, T. (2002). A socio-behavioral simulation model for engineering design optimization. *Journal of Engineering Optimization, Taylor & Francis, 34*(4), 341–354. doi:10.1080/03052150212723

Back, T. (1996). *Evolutionary algorithms in theory and practice*. New York: Oxford University Press.

Chootinan, P., & Chen, A. (2006). Constraint handling in genetic algorithms using a gradient-based repair method. *Computers & Operations Research, 33*, 2263–2281. doi:10.1016/j.cor.2005.02.002

Coello, C. A., & Mezura, M. E. (2002). Constraint-handling in genetic algorithms through the use of dominance-based tournament selection. *Advanced Engineering Informatics, 16*, 193–203. doi:10.1016/S1474-0346(02)00011-3

Deb, K. (1995). *Optimization for engineering design: Algorithms and examples*. New Delhi: Prentice-Hall of India.

Deb, K. (1997). A robust optimal design technique for mechanical component design. In *Evolutionary algorithms in engineering applications*. Berlin: Springer Verlag. doi:10.1007/978-3-662-03423-1_27

Deb, K. (2001). *Multi-objective optimization using evolutionary algorithms*. London: John Wiley and Sons.

Deb, K., & Agarwal, S. (1999). A niched-penalty approach for constraint handling in genetic algorithms. In *Proceedings of the ICANNGA*. Portoroz, Slovenia: ICANNGA.

Deep, K., & Das, K. N. (2008). Quadratic approximation based hybrid genetic algorithm for function optimization. *AMC, 203*, 86–98.

Deep, K., & Das, K. N. (2013). A novel hybrid genetic algorithm for constrained optimization. *International Journal of System Assurance Engineering and Management, 4*(1).

Deep, K., & Thakur, M. (2007a). A new crossover operator for real coded genetic algorithms. *Applied Mathematics and Computation, 188*(1), 895–911. doi:10.1016/j.amc.2006.10.047

Deep, K., & Thakur, M. (2007b). A new mutation operator for real coded genetic algorithms. *Applied Mathematics and Computation, 193*(1), 211–230. doi:10.1016/j.amc.2007.03.046

Eshelman, L. J., Mathias, K. E., & Schaffer, J. D. (1997). Convergence controlled variation. In R. Belew, & M. Vose (Eds.), *Foundations of genetic algorithms* (Vol. 4, pp. 203–224). San Francisco: Morgan Kaufmann.

Floudas, C. A., & Pardalos, P. M. (1990). *A collection of test problems for constrained global optimization algorithms. Belin*. Springer Verlag. doi:10.1007/3-540-53032-0

Gen, M., & Cheng, R. (1997). *Genetic algorithms and engineering design*. New York: Wiley.

Goldberg, D. E. (1989). *Genetic algorithms in search, optimization and machine learning*. New York: Addison-Wesley.

Himmelblau, D. M. (1997). *Applied nonlinear programming*. New York: McGraw-Hill.

Holland, J. (1975). *Adaptation in natural and artificial systems*. Ann Arbor, MI: University of Michigan Press.

Kim, J. H., & Myung, H. (1996). A two phase evolutionary programming for general constrained optimization problem. In *Proceedings of the Fifth Annual Conference on Evolutionary Programming*. San Diego, CA: Academic Press.

Kim, J. H., & Myung, H. (1997). Evolutionary programming techniques for constrained optimization problems. *IEEE Transactions on Evolutionary Computation, 1*(2), 129–140. doi:10.1109/4235.687880

Kundu, S., & Osyczka, A. (1996). Genetic multicriteria optimization of structural systems. In *Proceedings of the 19th International Congress on Theoretical and Applied Mechanics (ICTAM)*. Kyoto, Japan: IUTAM.

Levy, A. V., & Montalvo, A. (1985). The tunneling algorithm for the global minimization of functions. *Society for Industrial and Applied Mathematics, 6*, 15–29.

Michalewicz, Z. (1992). *Genetic algorithms + data structures = evolution programs*. New York: Springer-Verlag. doi:10.1007/978-3-662-02830-8

Michalewicz, Z. (1996). *Genetic algorithms + data structures = evolution programs*. Berlin: Springer-Verlag. doi:10.1007/978-3-662-03315-9

Michalewicz, Z., & Naguib, F. A. (1994). Evolutionary optimization of constrained problems. In *Proceedings of the 3rd Annual Conference on Evolutionary Programming*, (pp. 98–108). World Scientific.

Michalewicz, Z., & Schoenauer, M. (1996). Evolutionary algorithms for constrained parameter optimization problems. *Evolutionary Computation, 4*(1), 1–32. doi:10.1162/evco.1996.4.1.1

Mitchell, M. (1996). *An introduction to genetic algorithms*. Cambridge, MA: MIT Press.

Mohan, C., & Nguyen, H. T. (2004). A controlled random search technique incorporating the simulating annealing concept for solving integer and mixed integer global optimization problems. *Int. Jr. of Computational Optimization and Applications, 14*, 103–132. doi:10.1023/A:1008761113491

Mohan, C., & Shanker, K. (1994). A random search technique for global optimization based on quadratic approximation. *Asia Pacific Journal of Operation Research, 11*, 93–101.

Morgan Kaufmman. Crossley, W. A., & Williams, E. A. (1997). A study of adaptive penalty functions for constrained genetic algorithm based optimization. In *Proceedings of AIAA 35th Aerospace Sciences Meeting and Exhibit*. Reno, NV: AIAA.

Myung, H., & Kim, J. H. (1996). Hybrid evolutionary programming for heavily constrained problems. *Bio Systems, 38*, 29–43. doi:10.1016/0303-2647(95)01564-7 PMID:8833746

Orvosh, D., & Davis, L. (1995). Using a genetic algorithm to optimize problems with feasibility constraints. In *Proceedings of the Sixth International Conference on Genetic Algorithms* (pp. 548-552). Echelman.

Rajasekaran, S., & Pai, G. A. V (2003). *Neural networks, fuzzy logic, and genetic algorithms: Synthesis and applications*. New Delhi: Prentice-Hall of India Pvt. Ltd.

Saber, M. E., Ruhul, A. S., & Daryl, L. E. (2011). Improved genetic algorithm for constrained optimization. In *Proceeding of International Conference on Computer Engineering & Systems (ICCES)* (pp. 111-115). ICCES.

Salkin, H. M. (1975). *Integer programming*. Amsterdam: Edison Wesley Publishing Com.

Schittkowski, K. (1987). More examples for mathematical programming codes. *Lecture Notes in Economics and Mathematical Systems, 282*.

Tsutsui, S., & Fujimoto, Y. (1993). Forking genetic algorithm with blocking and shrinking modes. In *Proceedings of the Fifth Int. Conf. on Genetic Algorithms* (pp. 206-213).

KEY TERMS AND DEFINITIONS

Benchmark Problems: These are the standard problems which are being used by researchers for testing the efficiency of their designed/proposed techniques for both unconstrained and constrained optimization problems. These are readily available in the internet.

Chromosomes: Chromosomes are the probable candidates generated to form a population while undergoes any evolutionary method for optimization.

Crossover: It is an operator to recombine tow different chromosomes (or parents) in the GA cycle to produce two new offsprings (or children).

Mutation: It is an operator being used in the GA cycle to mutate very few of the positions in the population of chromosomes to produce new chromosomes.

Real Coded Genetic Algorithm: The genetic algorithm that uses the real encoding system, i.e. to directly assume the parameters for decision variables within the provided range, is called a real coded genetic algorithm.

APPENDIX

Problem 1: (Salkin, 1975)

$$\underset{x}{Max}\, f\left(x\right) = 3x_1 + x_2 + 2x_3 + x_4 - x_5$$

Subject to:

$$25x_1 - 40x_2 + 16x_3 + 21x_4 + x_5 \leq 300$$
$$x_1 + 20x_2 - 50x_3 + x_4 - x_5 \leq 200$$
$$60x_1 + x_2 - x_3 + 2x_4 + x_5 \leq 600$$
$$-7x_1 + 4x_2 + 15x_3 - x_4 + 65x_5 \leq 700$$
$$1 \leq x_1 \leq 4; 80 \leq x_2 \leq 88; 30 \leq x_3 \leq 35; 145$$
$$\leq x_4 \leq 150; 0 \leq x_5 \leq 2$$

Solution: x = (4, 88, 35, 150, 0)T, $f^*\left(x\right) = 320$

Problem 2: (Himmelblau,1972)

$$\underset{x}{Max}\, f\left(x\right) = 25\left(x_1 - 2\right)^2 + \left(x_2 - 2\right)^2 + \left(x_3 - 1\right)^2$$
$$+ \left(x_4 - 4\right)^2 + \left(x_5 - 1\right)^2 + \left(x_6 - 4\right)^2$$

Subject to:

$$x_1 + x_2 - 2 \geq 0$$
$$6 - x_1 + x_2 \geq 0$$
$$2 + x_1 - x_2 \geq 0$$
$$2 - x_1 + 3x_2 \geq 0$$
$$\left(x_3 - 3\right)^2 + x_4 - 4 \geq 0$$
$$\left(x_5 - 3\right)^2 + x_6 - 4 \geq 0$$

$$0 \leq x_1 \leq 5; 0 \leq x_2 \leq 1; 1 \leq x_3 \leq 5; 0 \leq x_4 \leq 6;$$
$$0 \leq x_5 \leq 5; 0 \leq x_6 \leq 10;$$

Solution: x = (5, 1, 5, 0, 5, 10) T, $f^*\left(x\right) = 310$

Problem 3: (Schittkowski, 1987)

$$Min_x f\left(x\right) = \left(x_1^2 + x_2 - 11\right)^2 + \left(x_1 + x_2^2 - 7\right)^2$$

Subject to:

$$4.84 - \left(x_1 - 0.05\right)^2 - \left(x_2 - 2.5\right)^2 \geq 0$$
$$x_1^2 + \left(x_2 - 2.5\right)^2 - 4.84 \geq 0$$

$$0 \leq x_1 \leq 6; 0 \leq x_2 \leq 6$$

Solution: x = (2.246826, 2.381865) T, $f^*\left(x\right) = 13.59085$

Problem 4: (Michalewicz et al.,1996)

$$Min_x f\left(x\right) = \left(x_1 - 10\right)^2 + 5\left(x_2 - 12\right)^2 + x_3^4$$
$$+ 3\left(x_4 - 11\right)^2 + 10x_5^6 + 7x_6^2$$
$$+ x_7^4 - 4x_6 x_7 - 10x_6 - 8x_7$$

Subject to:

$$127 - 2x_1^2 - 3x_2^4 - x_3 - 4x_4^2 - 5x_5 \geq 0$$
$$282 - 7x_1 - 3x_2 - 10x_3^2 - x_4 + x_5 \geq 0$$
$$196 - 23x_1 - x_2^2 - 6x_6^2 + 8x_7 \geq 0$$
$$-4x_1^2 - x_2^2 + 3x_1 x_2 - 2x_3^2 - 5x_6 + 11x_7 \geq 0$$
$$-10 \leq x_i \leq 10, i = 1, 2..., 7.$$

Solution: x = (2.330499, 1.951372, -0.4775414, 4.365726, -0.6244870, 1.038131, 1.594227) T $f^*\left(x\right) = $ 680.6300573

Problem 5: (Floudas and Pardalos, 1990)

$$Min_x f\left(x\right) = x_1^{0.6} + x_2^{0.6} + x_3^{0.4}$$
$$+2x_4 + 5x_5 - 4x_3 - x_6$$

Subject to:

$$x_2 - 3x_1 - 3x_4 = 0$$
$$x_3 - 2x_2 - 3x_5 = 0$$
$$4x_4 - x_6 = 0$$
$$x_1 + 2x_4 - 4 \leq 0$$
$$x_2 + x_5 - 4 \leq 0$$
$$x_3 + x_6 - 6 \leq 0$$

$$0 \leq x_1 \leq 3; 0 \leq x_2 \leq 4; 1 \leq x_3 \leq 4; 0 \leq x_4 \leq 2;$$
$$0 \leq x_5 \leq 2; 0 \leq x_6 \leq 6;$$

Solution: x = (0.67, 2, 4, 0, 0, 0) T, $f^*(x)$ = -11.96

Problem 6: (Levy and Montalvo, 1985)

$$\underset{x}{Min}\, f(x) = -x_1 - x_2$$

Subject to:

$$x_2 \leq 2 + 2x_1^4 - 8x_1^3 + 8x_1^2$$
$$x_2 \leq 4x_1^4 - 32x_1^3 + 88x_1^2 - 96x_1 + 36$$

$$0 \leq x_1 \leq 3; 0 \leq x_2 \leq 4$$

Solution:: x = (2.3295, 3.1783) T, $f^*(x)$ = -5.5078

Problem 7: (Floudas and Pardalos, 1990)

$$\underset{x}{Min}\, f(x) = -12x_1 - 7x_2 + x_2^2$$

Subject to:

$$-2x_1^4 - x_2 + 2 = 0$$

$$0 \leq x_1 \leq 2; 0 \leq x_2 \leq 3$$

Solution: x = (0.7175, 1.47)T, $f^*\left(x\right)$ = -16.7391

Problem 8: (Michalewicz and Schoenauer.,1996)

$$Min_{x} f\left(x\right) = 3x_1 + 0.000001\, x_1^3 + 2\, x_2$$
$$+\left(0.000002\,/\,3\right)x_2^3$$

Subject to:

$x_4 - x_3 + 0.55 \geq 0$

$x_3 - x_4 + 0.55 \geq 0$

$1000\sin(-x_3 - 0.25) + 1000\sin(-x_4 - 0.25)$

$+894.8 - x_1 = 0$

$1000\sin(x_3 - 0.25) + 1000\sin(x_3 - x_4 - 0.25)$

$+894.8 - x_2 = 0$

$1000\sin(x_4 - 0.25) + 1000\sin(x_4 - x_3 - 0.25)$

$+1294.8 = 0$

$0 \leq x_i \leq 1200,\ i = 1,2;$

$-0.55 \leq x_i \leq 0.55,\ i = 3,4$

Solution: x = (679.9453, 1026.067, 0.1188764, -0.3962336)T, $f^*\left(x\right) = 5126.4981$

Problem 9, 10, 11: (Michalewichz et al.,1994)

$$Min_{x} f\left(x\right) =$$

$$\begin{cases} f_1 = x_2 + 10^{-5}(x_2 - x_1)^2 - 1 & if\ 0 \leq x_1 < 2 \\[2mm] f_2 = \dfrac{1}{27\sqrt{3}}\left(\left(x_1 - 3\right)^2 - 9\right)x_2^3 & if\ 2 \leq x_1 < 4 \\[2mm] f_3 = \dfrac{1}{3}\left(x_1 - 2\right)^3 + x_2 - \dfrac{11}{3} & if\ 4 \leq x_1 \leq 6 \end{cases}$$

Subject to:

$$\frac{x_1}{\sqrt{3}} - x_2 \geq 0$$
$$-x_1 - \sqrt{3}x_2 + 6 \geq 0$$

$$0 \leq x_2 \leq 5$$

Solution: x = (0, 0) T, (3, $\sqrt{3}$) T, (4, 0) T, $f^*\left(x\right) = -1$

Problem 12: (Kim and Myung,1996)

$$\underset{x}{Min}\, f\left(x\right) = 100\left(x_2 - x_1^2\right)^2 + \left(1 - x_1\right)^2$$

Subject to:

$$-x_1 - x_2^2 \leq 0$$
$$-x_1^2 - x_2 \leq 0$$

$$-0.5 \leq x_1 \leq 0.5; 0 \leq x_2 \leq 1$$

Solution: x = (0.5, 0.25) T, $f^*\left(x\right) = 0.25$

Problem 13: (Kim and Myung,1996)

$$\underset{x}{Min}\, f\left(x\right) = 0.01 \times \left(x_1^2 + x_2^2\right)$$

Subject to:

$$-x_1 x_2 + 25 \leq 0$$
$$-x_1^2 - x_2^2 + 25 \leq 0$$

$$2 \leq x_1 \leq 50; 0 \leq x_2 \leq 50$$

Solution: x = $\left(\sqrt{250}, \sqrt{250}\right)^T$, $f^*\left(x\right) = 0.5$

Problem 14: (Chootinan and Chen,2006)

$$Max_x f(x) = \frac{\sin^3(2\pi x_1)\sin(2\pi x_2)}{x_1^3(x_1 + x_2)}$$

Subject to:

$$x_1^2 - x_2 + 1 \leq 0$$
$$1 - x_1 + (x_2 - 4)^2 \leq 0$$

$$0 \leq x_1 \leq 10; 0 \leq x_2 \leq 10$$

Solution: x = (1.2279713, 4.2453733) T, $f^*(x) = 0.095825$

Problem 15: (Michalewicz and Schoenauer, 1996)

$$Min_x f(x) = (x_1 - 10)^3 + (x_2 - 20)^3$$

Subject to:

$$(x_1 - 5)^2 + (x_2 - 5) - 100 \geq 0$$
$$-(x_1 - 6)^2 - (x_2 - 5) + 82..82 \geq 0$$

$$13 \leq x_1 \leq 100; 0 \leq x_2 \leq 100$$

Solution: x = (14.095, 0.84296)T,

$$f^*(x) = -6961.81381$$

Chapter 11
Knowledge Representation Using Formal Concept Analysis:
A study on Concept Generation

Ch. Aswani Kumar
VIT University – Vellore-632014, India

Prem Kumar Singh
VIT University – Vellore-632014, India

ABSTRACT

Introduced by Rudolf Wille in the mid-80s, Formal Concept Analysis (FCA) is a mathematical framework that offers conceptual data analysis and knowledge discovery. FCA analyzes the data, which is represented in the form of a formal context, that describe the relationship between a particular set of objects and a particular set of attributes. From the formal context, FCA produces hierarchically ordered clusters called formal concepts and the basis of attribute dependencies, called attribute implications. All the concepts of a formal context form a hierarchical complete lattice structure called concept lattice that reflects the relationship of generalization and specialization among concepts. Several algorithms are proposed in the literature to extract the formal concepts from a given context. The objective of this chapter is to analyze, demonstrate, and compare a few standard algorithms that extract the formal concepts. For each algorithm, the analysis considers the functionality, output, complexity, delay time, exploration type, and data structures involved.

INTRODUCTION

Formal Concept Analysis (FCA) is a mathematical framework based on mathematical order and lattice theory which supports knowledge discovery in databases. The unique aspect of FCA is the integration of several components of conceptual data and knowledge processing. These components include discovery and reasoning with concepts and dependencies in data, visualization of concepts and dependencies. With such integration, FCA has been successfully applied in different domains

DOI: 10.4018/978-1-4666-4936-1.ch011

including gene expression data analysis, ontology design, software code analysis, psychology etc (Kaytoue et al. 2011, Krohn et al. 1999, Mephu & Ngiwoua, 1998, Priss 2006, Priss & Old 2004, Priss et al., 2007). Knowledge representation in FCA is shown in the form of formal concepts (Boulicaut & Besson 2008, Ganter & Wille 1999, Jurekevicius & Vasilecas 2009, Stumme 2009, Stumme et al. 2002), concept lattices(Stumme et al. 1998, Valtchev et al. 2002, Wille 1982) and association rules(Agrawaal & Srikant, 1994, Aswani Kumar, 2011, Aswani Kumar & Srinivas, 2010, Stumme et al. 2001, Zhang and Wu 2011). FCA starts the analysis on a data matrix, known as formal context, specifying a set of objects, a set of attributes and the relation between them (Wille, 1982). FCA has been successfully extended into fuzzy settings(Ghosh et al, 2010, Prem Kumar and Aswani Kumar, 2012a, 2012b, Maio et al., 2012), however this study is focused on FCA in crisp setting. From the formal context, FCA finds the natural clusters of objects that share a common subset of attributes and natural clusters of attributes that are shared by natural object clusters (Shi et al., 2007). A formal concept is a pair containing object cluster and corresponding attribute cluster. Concept lattice structure visualizes all the concepts (Belohlavek and Vychodil, 2009). The notion "formal" emphasizes that concepts are mathematical objects. The sets of objects and attributes in a formal concept mutually relate each other through a Galois connection which induces closure operator. The set of all the concepts of a given context is partially ordered and form a complete lattice. Main features of FCA include mathematical background, algorithmic methods that can perform conceptual clustering through concept lattice, rule mining through attribute implications, data apposition and concatenation makes FCA a suitable paradigm for KDD (Maddouri, 2005, Stumme, 1995, Zhang & Wu, 2011). Due to the closure properties and mathematical order theory that FCA follows, only the patterns of maximal size are extracted which reduces the

exploration and increases the efficiency while mining the data. Through attribute implications, FCA provides a compact representation of knowledge. These attribute implications are closely associated with functional dependencies in the database field (Poelmans et al. 2010, Stumme 2002a, Wu et al. 2009).

Unlike other data mining techniques where highly iterative approaches are used, FCA organizes knowledge as a conceptual hierarchy. The basic notions of FCA are formal context, formal concept and concept lattice. Among the tasks of FCA, computing the formal concepts from the large binary matrices is a complex one. Several algorithms have been designed that compute all the concepts from a given context (Carpineto & Romano 2004, Hermann & Sertkaya, 2008, Kuznetsov & Obiedkov 2000, Kuznetsov & Obiedkov 2002). In this study we concentrate on Bordat, Next Neighbor, Object intersection, Next Closure algorithm. Generally the formal contexts are of four types: Average density, Small and Sparse, Large and dense and linearly incremental. It has been established in literature that these algorithms works better on these contexts(Carpineto & Romano 2004, Kuznetsov & Obiedkov 2000). Hence our analysis is focused on concept generation from these algorithms. The study is concentrated on the step by step demonstration of each algorithm, procedure for generating the concepts, and building the line diagrams. In the next section we present the brief background about FCA and its issues.

BACKGROUND

Analysis of concepts, concept formation and conceptual learning are central to cognitive informatics. Key notions of FCA are formal context, formal concept and concept lattice. A formal context represents data in the form of triplet such as $\mathbf{K} = (\mathbf{G}, \mathbf{M}, I)$, where $\mathbf{G}$ is a finite set of objects and $\mathbf{M}$ is a finite set of attributes, and $I (I \subseteq \mathbf{G} \times \mathbf{M})$ is a relation between the objects and its attributes.

A relationship $(O, A) \in I$ exists iff object $O \in \mathbf{G}$ has attribute $A \in \mathbf{M}$. For a formal context $\mathbf{K}$, operators $\uparrow$: $2^{\mathbf{G}} \rightarrow 2^{\mathbf{M}}$ and $\downarrow$: $2^{\mathbf{M}} \rightarrow 2^{\mathbf{G}}$ are defined for every $O \subseteq \mathbf{G}$ and $A \subseteq \mathbf{M}$ by (Ganter & Wille 1999),

$$f(O) = O^{\uparrow} = \{a \in A | (o, a) \in I, \, \forall \, o \in O\}$$

$$g(A) = A^{\downarrow} = \{o \in O | (o, a) \in I, \, \forall \, a \in A\}$$

The operators $\uparrow$ and $\downarrow$ are known as concept forming operators (Belohlavek et al., 2004). The ordered pair (f, g) defines a Galois connection between $\mathbf{G}$ and $\mathbf{M}$ iff $\forall \, O \subseteq \mathbf{G}$ and $A \subseteq \mathbf{M}$: $O \subseteq g(A) \leftrightarrow A \subseteq f(O)$, and it satisfy the following properties:-

$$O_1 \subseteq O_2 \Rightarrow f(O_2) \subseteq f(O_1)$$

$$A_1 \subseteq A_2 \Rightarrow g(A_2) \subseteq g(A_1)$$

$$O \subseteq g(f(O))$$

$$A \subseteq f(g(A))$$

The operator f applied on a set of objects, provides a set of attributes which are covered by these objects and vice versa using the operator g. The ordered pair (O, A) is called as formal concept if

$O = g(A)$, and $A = f(O)$ (Ganter, 1984, Ganter et al.,2005)

A formal concept is an ordered pair of two sets (O, A), where $O \subseteq \mathbf{G}$ is called as extent and $A \subseteq \mathbf{M}$ is called as intent and they form the Galois connection. If (f, g) be a Galois connection between $\mathbf{G}$ and $\mathbf{M}$ then $\phi = f$ o g is a closure operator on $\mathbf{G}$, and $\psi = g$ o f is a closure operator on $\mathbf{M}$. Through the closure property one can neither enlarge the extent or intent of formal concept. If (O_1, A_1) and (O_2, A_2) are formal concepts, then

(O_1, A_1) is super-concept of (O_2, A_2) and (O_2, A_2) is sub-concept of (O_1, A_1) if $(O_2, A_2) \leq (O_1, A_1)$: $\Leftrightarrow O_2 \subseteq O_1$ ($\Leftrightarrow A_2 \supseteq A_1$)(Valtchev et al. 2002, Deogun & Saquer, 2004). The relation $\leq$ is called the hierarchical order of the concept (Aho et al., 1983). Then the ordered set $\mathbf{C} = (O, A; \leq)$ is called concept lattice (Burgmann & Wille, 2006), if $\forall$ (O_1, A_1), $(O_2, A_2) \in \mathbf{C}$, there exists a greatest common sub-concept and a least common super-concept (Davey & Priestley, 2002, Karl, 1994). The process of concept formation is considered as knowledge discovery where by construction of concept set constitutes to mining phase (Venter et al. 1997). While navigating the lattice in downward, the attribute set size increases and the objects that share these attributes decreases and vice versa (Birkhoff, 1940). Hence, navigating the lattice in the downward is called specialization and while upward navigation is called generalization.

Intent of concept is a closed item set when it satisfies the Galois operator defined on $\mathbf{M}$. In data mining for two item sets A_1 and A_2, if $A_1 \leq A_2$ then $A_1 \subset A_2$. This notion is similar to the super and sub concept hierarchies in FCA. Also if $A_1 \leq A_2$, then the order relation $A_1 \subset A_3 \subset A_2$ does not satisfy by any $A_3 \in \mathbf{M}$. FCA provides Duquenne-Guigues (DG) basis and the Luxenburger basis for finding the exact and partial association rules. The DG basis handles rules with 100% confidence. These are minimal and non redundant set of rules from which all other rules can be derived. The Luxenburger basis contains the rules with confidence less than 100% representing the approximate association rules. This is in similar to the representation of frequent closed patterns in frequent itemset mining. Readers can refer: for introductory information for the concept generation and line diagram algorithms (Birkhoff, 1940, Baixeries et al., 2009, Belohlavek & Vychodil, 2006, Berry et al., 2000, Berry et al. 2007, Bordat, 1986, Carpineto &

Romano, 1996, Ganter, 2002, Godin & Missaoui, 1994, Iordache, 2011, Kuznetsov & Obiedkov, 2002, Lee et al, 2011, Lindig, 2000, Norris, 1974, No-urine & Reynaud,1999, Strok & Neznanov, 2010, Vander et al., 2004a, Vander et al. 2004b, Yun et al. 2008,), for applications of FCA (Aswani Kumar 2011a, 2011b, 2013, Aswani Kumar et al, 2012, Aswani Kumar & Srinivas, 2010a, Kaytoue et al. 2011, Krajca et al. 2010, Krohn et al. 1999, Mephu et al., 1998, Priss 2006, Priss & Old 2004, Priss et al., 2007, Stumme et al., 2002, Valtchev et al., 2004, Wille, 2009, 2008, Zhang & Wu, 2011), for reducing the number of formal concepts and size of concept lattice in FCA (Aswani Kumar, 2011b, Aswani Kumar & Srinivas, 2010b, Belohlavek & Vychodil, 2009, Ganter & Wille, 1999, Li et al. 2011, 2012a, 2012b, 2013a, 2013b, Rouane et al., 2010, Stumme, 2002b, Stumme et al. 2002, Shoumei & Chengming, 2008, Wu et al., 2009, Dias & Viera, 2013, Zhang et al. 2013) and FCA in the fuzzy setting (Aswani Kumar, 2012, Ghosh et al., 2010, Prem Kumar & Aswani Kumar 2012a, 2012b, 2012c). Very recently, Prem Kumar and Aswani Kumar (2012c) provided another way of representation of concept lattice through interval-valued fuzzy graph for reducing the size of concept lattice, which is another concern. In the next section we describe the concept generation algorithms.

MAIN FOCUS OF THE CHAPTER

Concept Generation

Computing the formal concepts and their visualization in lattice structure is an important concern for practical applications. For this purpose several algorithms have been proposed. These algorithms include Bordat, Next Neighbor, Object Intersection, Next closure, Close By One (CBO), FCbo, Titanic, L-Nourine, L-Norris, Godin, Chein, Dowling, Valtchev, Addintent, Border and iPred

algorithm. These algorithms are categorized with several properties like generating concepts, building line diagram, top down Depth First Search (DFS) or Breadth First Search (BFS), bottom up, and lexical order. The performance of these algorithms depends on the size of context. Hence on these aspects we analyze first four algorithms.

Bordat algorithm is introduced by Bordat (1986). It is a first top-down concept generation algorithm, which uses tree structure for fast storing and retrieval of concepts. This algorithm used external neighborhoods, which are denoted by N^+: if $x \in$ **M**, $N^+(x) = \{y \in O \mid (y, x) \notin I\}$, and if $x \in$ **G**, $N^+(x) = \{y \in A \mid (x, y) \notin I\}$. Then we find Non-Dominating (ND) maxmods. A vertex x is called dominating if $N^+(y) \subseteq N^+(x)$ otherwise the vertex is Non-Dominating (Berry et al., 2000, 2007). If each vertex of $x \in$ **X** dominates every other vertex of **X**, then we call **X** as maxmods. These maxmods are used to generate concepts containing **X**, by DFS method. The generated concepts from Bordat algorithm are stored in a queue. From the queue, we explore each concept, calling it as marked concept, for generating the next concepts. This process works repeatedly for next marked concepts in queue. This algorithm processes any concept only once for generating next concepts. Hence, for generating next concept it takes at most min ($|$**M**$|$, $|$**G**$|$) closures. Next Neighbor algorithm is proposed by Lindig (2000) and finds concepts with the help of lower neighbors as given in Carpineto & Romano (2004). Starting from top element of concept lattice, the algorithm generates concepts by top down BFS method and builds the line diagram. DFS method also works equally for Next Neighbor algorithm. The order of generating the concepts at each level by the Next Neighbor algorithm may not coincide with the order used to build the lattice. It is batch type algorithm, related to Chein algorithm (Kuznetsov & Obiedkov 2002). The Chein algorithm takes O ($|$**G**$|^3|$**M**$||$**C**$|$) time complexity where as Next Neighbor algorithm takes O ($|$**G**$|^2|$**M**$||$**C**$|$). The polynomial delay time for Chein algorithm is O ($|G|^3|M|$) where as for Next Neighbor algorithm is O ($|G||M|^2$). Object Intersection algorithm is introduced by Carpineto and Romano (2004). This algorithm is an incremental type algorithm; original version of this algorithm is Norris algorithm (Norris, 1974). Norris algorithm uses no structure for generating the concepts where as object intersection algorithm follows the finding intersection between intent for generating the concepts. The time complexity of the Norris algorithm is O ($|G|^2 |M||C|$) where as time complexity of object intersection algorithm is O ($|C||G||M|$) (Carpineto & Romano, 2004, Kuznetsov & Obiedkov 2002). In this algorithm, we find the intersection of all the object intents. Then we calculate the extents for these intents, to derive the new concepts. This algorithm finds all possible intersections between the set of objects associated with each attributes and vice versa for generating the concepts. For generating the concepts it considers one attribute (object) at a time and generates the extents (intents). Hence it generates the concepts linearly. Object intersection algorithm store and retrieve the concepts in O ($|M|$) time. Next Closure algorithm is proposed by Ganter (Ganter 1984, Ganter,2002). The algorithm works in bottom up manner for generating the concepts in batchwise. The earlier generated concepts are placed into the stack. This algorithm finds closures for each object (attribute) and lexical order between them. For deciding the next closure, the algorithm searches in the stack. Next closure uses lexicographical order for drawing the lattice diagram. Extensions or improvements of these algorithms are available in the literature(Baixeries et al., 2009, Vander el al., 2004a, 2004b, Krajca et al., 2010). AddIntent is an incremental type algorithm (Vander at al., 2004a, 2004b). It takes first objects of the context and inserts the next objects to generate the new concepts and lattice. This algorithm builds lattice in bottom up fashion. The algorithm has the time complexity of O ($|C||G|^2|M|$) and worst case O ($|C||G|^3|M|$) where $|C|$ is number of concepts. For average and dense contexts AddIntent algorithm works slower than Bordat algorithm. Recently, Baixeries *et al.*, (2009) presented iPred algorithm for building the lattices. This algorithm finds immediate predecessor from calculated candidate set. In the next section we describe the analysis of algorithms with an example.

Analysis

We analyze the algorithms based on properties like exploring type, time complexity, polynomial delay time and the data structures. Also, we discuss upon which algorithm is preferred when we have small, average, large contexts and also to draw line diagrams for each steps. We have considered a context, shown in Table 1 (Carpineto & Romano, 2004).

Table 1. Context of Vertebrates Animal

	Breathes in Water (a)	Can Fly (b)	Has Beak (c)	Has Hands (d)	Has Skeleton (e)	Has Wings (f)	Lives in Water (g)	Is Viviparous (h)	Produces Light (i)
Bat (1)		X			X	X		X	
Eagle (2)		X	X		X	X			
Monkey (3)				X	X			X	
Parrotfish(4)	X		X		X		X		
Penguin (5)			X		X	X	X		
Shark (6)	X				X		X		
Lantern fish (7)	X				X		X		X

BORDAT ALGORITHM

The Bordat algorithm steps are defined in Table 2. We illustrate the algorithm for the context as given below:

Step 1: First we find ND maxmods (1234567, e) from Table 1. From step 2 of algorithm, the external neighbors are N^+(a)={1,2,3,5}, N^+(b)={3,4,5,6,7}, N^+(c)={ 1,3,6,7}, N^+(d)={1,2,4,5,6,7}, N^+(e)={0}, N^+(f)={3,4,6,7}, N^+(g)={1,2,3}, N^+(h)={2,4,5,6,7}, N^+(i)={1,2,3,4,5,6}. All the external neighbors dominate {e}, {a} dominates {g}, {b} dominates {f}, {d} dominates {h}, {i} dominates {a}. Hence, ND maxmods are {a}, {c}, {e}, {f}, {g}, and {h}. When we explore them for finding concepts, we get {1234567,e}, {467,aeg}, {4567, eg}, {245,ce}, {125,ef}, {13,eh}. From this list the maxmod concept is (1234567, e).

Step 2: The top concept (1234567, e) becomes a marked concept in the queue. Since all the objects are available in this concept, hence we can find ND maxmods with help of Table 1. From step 2 of the algorithm, the external neighbors are N^+(a)={1,2,3,5}, N^+(b)={3,4,5,6,7}, N^+(c)={1,3,6,7}, N^+(d)={1,2,4,5,6,7}, N^+(e)={0}, N^+(f)={3,4,6,7}, N^+(g)={1,2,3}, N^+(h)={2,4,5,6,7}, N^+(i)={1,2,3,4,5,6}. Here {a} dominates {g}, {b} dominates {f}, {d} dominates {h}, {i} dominates {a}. So ND maxmods are {a}, {c}, {f}, {g}, and {h}. They generate concepts {467,ag}, {245, c}, {125, f}, {4567, g}, {13, h}. From step 2 of the algorithm, we get $O^\uparrow \leftarrow$ {e} + {g} become {g}+{e}={g, e} (or c, f, h) and $A^\downarrow \leftarrow$ {1234567} - N^+ {X}={1234567}-{123}={4567}. Similarly for all ND maxmods, attributes are {aeg}, {c, e}, {e, g},

Table 2. Bordat algorithm

Sl No	Instructions
	Input: A concept (O, A) and a set of marked concept of P
1	$G \leftarrow I((P\text{-}O) \cup A)$; Compute the partition of P-O in **G** into maxmods;

2	For x in marked do marked $\leftarrow$ marked $\cup$ M(x); compute the set of ND (non- dominating)
	 ND $\leftarrow$ 0;
	 For $x \in$ P-O do
	 If D[x]=|M(x)| then ND $\leftarrow$ ND $\cup$ M(x);
	 If desirable, generate the cover of (O,A)
	 For $X \in$ ND do
	 $O^\uparrow \leftarrow O + X$; $A^\downarrow \leftarrow O - N^+(X)$
	 Print($O^\uparrow, A^\downarrow$)

3	For $X \in$ (ND- marked) //generate unprocessed descendant of (O, A)
	 $O^\uparrow \leftarrow O + X$; $A^\downarrow \leftarrow O - N^+(X)$
	 Print ($O^\uparrow, A^\downarrow$);
	   Update (pre);
	 Concept (($O^\uparrow, A^\downarrow$), marked);
	   Update (Post);
	 marked $\leftarrow$ marked $\cup$ X;
	 Update Algorithm:-
	   Input: A variable V set to pre or to post;
	 Output: Tables T and D are modified using current values of X and ($O^\uparrow, A^\downarrow$);
	 a. Begin choose a representative $x \in X$
	 // Update Table D by deletion of property set X;
	 b. For $y \in$ (P-O)-X do
	 If T(y, x) =0 then
	 If V= pre then D[y] $\leftarrow$ D[y] – |X| ;
	 Else D[y] $\leftarrow$ D[y]+|X|;
	 // Update table by simulation deletion of objects $\in$ $N^+(x)$;
	 c. For j $\in N^+($ x) do
	 Z$\leftarrow$ $N^+(j)$ –X ; U$\leftarrow$ (P-O) –Z –X ;
	 d. For (u, z) $\in$ (U, Z) do
	 If V=pre then
	 T(u,z) $\leftarrow$ T(u,z) -1;
	 If T(u,z) 0 then D[u] $\leftarrow$ D[u]+1
	 Else //V=post
	 T(u,z)) $\leftarrow$ T(u,z) + 1;
	 If T(u,z) =1 then D[u] $\leftarrow$ D[u]-1;
	 e. End

4	End
	Output: Direct successors of (O, A), which are not encountered.

{e, f} and {e, h}. Then generated concepts are (467, aeg), (4567, eg), (245, ce), (125, ef), (13, eh). The line diagram of these concepts is shown in Figure 1.

Step 3: The next marked concept is {4567, eg}. From steps 2 and 4 of the algorithm, attributes of set X and objects of set $N^+(x)$ disappear. Hence the objects {123} and, attributes {e, g} disappear in Table 3. With help of the attributes shown in Table 3 and external neighbors $N^+(a)=\{5\}, N^+(b)=\{4,5,6,7\}$, $N^+(c)=\{6,7\}$, $N^+(d)=\{4,5,6,7\}$, $N^+(f)=\{4,6,7\}$, $N^+(h)=\{4,5,6,7\}$, $N^+(i)=\{4,5,6\}$ we find ND maxmods. Clearly {b}, {d} and {h} are dominating, and {i} is dominating {a}, {f} is dominating {c}, then ND maxmods are {a} and {c}. Then the generated concepts are (467, aeg) and (45, ceg). The line diagram of these concepts is shown in Figure 2.

Step 4: The next marked concept is (245, ce). Applying the step 2 and 3 as demonstrated above, using objects {2, 4, 5}, attributes {a,

Table 3. Context for objects (4567)

	a	b	c	d	f	h	i
4	X		X				
5			X		X		
6	X						
7	X						X

b, d, f, g, h, i} and external neighbors $N^+(a) = \{2,5\}$, $N^+(b) = \{4,5\}$, $N^+(d) = \{2,4,5\} = N^+(h) = N^+(i)$, $N^+(g) = \{2\}$, $N^+(f) = \{4\}$ from Table 4, we find the ND maxmods. Clearly we can observe that {d}, {h}, {i}, are dominating, and {a} is dominating {g}, {b} is dominating {f}, then ND maxmods are {g} and {f}. They generate the concepts (45, ceg), (25, cef). The line diagram of these concepts is shown in Figure 3.

Step 5: The next marked concept is (125, ef). Using the objects {1, 2, 5}, attributes {a, b, c, d, g, h, i} and external neighbors from Table 5, $N^+(a) = \{1,2,5\}$, $N^+(b) = \{5\}$, $N^+(c) = \{1\}$, $N^+(d) = \{1,2,5\}$, $N^+(g) = \{1,2\}$, $N^+(h)$

Figure 1. Line diagram for step 2 in section 4.1

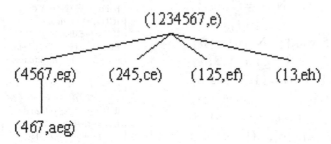

Figure 2. Line diagram for context of Table 3

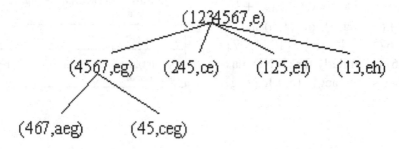

Figure 3. Line diagram for context of Table 4

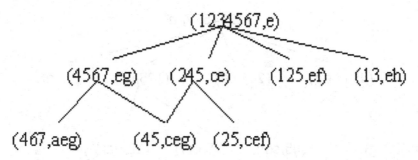

Table 4. Context for objects (245)

	a	b	d	f	g	h	i
2		X		X			
4	X				X		
5				X	X		

Table 5. Context for objects (125)

	a	b	c	d	g	h	i
1		X				X	
2		X	X				
5			X		X		

$= \{2,5\}$, $N^+(i) = \{1,2,5\}$, we find ND maxmods for the marked concept. Clearly we can observe that $\{a\}$, $\{d\}$, and $\{i\}$ are dominating, and $\{h\}$ is dominating $\{b\}$, $\{g\}$ is dominating $\{c\}$, then ND maxmods are $\{b\}$ and $\{c\}$. They generate the concepts (12, bef) and (25, cef). The line diagram of these concepts is shown in Figure 4.

Step 6: The next marked concept is (13, eh). Using objects $\{13\}$, attributes (a, b, c, d, f, g, i) and external neighbors from Table 6, $N^+(a) = \{1,3\}$, $N^+(b) = \{3\}$, $N^+(c) = \{1,3\}$, $N^+(d) = \{1\}$, $N^+(f) = \{3\}$, $N^+(g) = \{1,3\}$, $N^+(i) = \{1,3\}$, we find ND maxmods. We can observe that $\{a\}$, $\{c\}$, $\{g\}$, $\{i\}$ are dominat-

ing, and $N^+(b) = N^+(f) = \{3\}$. Hence we combine $\{b\}$ and $\{f\}$ by step 2 of algorithm shown in Table 2 that, if $D(x) = |M(x)|$ then $ND \leftarrow ND \cup M(x)$ which means $N^+(bf) = \{3\}$. Then $\{bf\}$ and $\{d\}$ are ND maxmods. They generate the concepts (1, befh), (3, deh). The line diagram of these concepts is shown in Figure 5.

Step 7: The next marked concept is (467, aeg). Using objects $\{4, 6, 7\}$, attributes $\{b, c, d, f, h, i\}$ and external neighbors from Table 7, $N^+(b) = \{4, 6, 7\}$, $N^+(c) = \{6, 7\}$, $N^+\{d\} = \{4, 6, 7\}$, $N^+(f) = \{4, 6, 7\}$, $N^+(h) = \{4, 6, 7\}$, $N^+(i) = \{4, 6\}$, we find ND maxmods. Clearly $\{b\}$, $\{d\}$, $\{f\}$, $\{h\}$ are dominating

Figure 4. Line diagram for context of Table 5

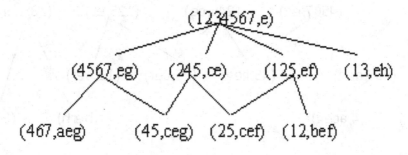

Figure 5. Line diagram for context of Table 6

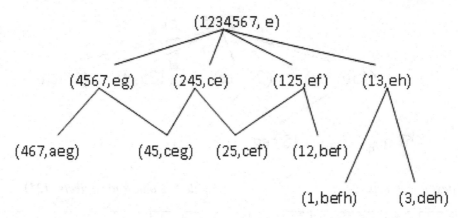

Table 6. Context for objects (13)

	a	b	c	d	f	g	i
1		X			X		
3				X			

Table 7. Context for objects (467)

	b	c	d	f	h	I
4		X				
6						
7						X

{c} and {i}. Then {c} and {i} are ND maxmods. They generate the concepts (4, aceg), (7, aegi). The line diagram of these concepts is shown in Figure 6.

Step 8: The next marked concept is {45, ceg}. Using the attributes {a, b, d, f, h, i}, objects {4, 5} and external neighbors from Table 8, $N^+(a)$={5}, $N^+(b)$=$N^+(d)$=$N^+(h)$=$N^+(i)$={4,5}, $N^+(f)$={4}, we find ND maxmods. Clearly,

{b}, {d}, {h}, {i} are dominating {a} and {f}. Then {a} and {f} are ND maxmods. They generate the concepts (4, aceg) and (5, cefg). The line diagram of these concepts is shown in Figure 7.

Step 9: The next marked concept is (25, cef). Using attributes {a, b, d, g, h, i}, objects {2, 5} and external neighbors from Table 9, $N^+(a)$ = {2, 5}, N^+{b} = {5}, N^+{d} = {2,

Figure 6. Line diagram for context of Table 7

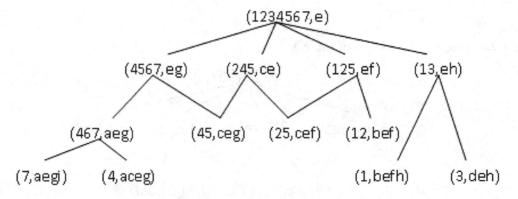

Figure 7. Line diagram for context of Table 8

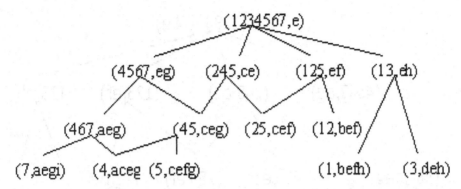

Table 8. Context for objects (45)

	a	b	d	f	h	i
4	X					
5				X		

Table 9. Context for objects (25)

	a	b	d	g	h	i
2		X				
5				X		

5}, $N^+(g) = \{2\}$, $N^+(h) = \{2, 5\}$, $N^+\{i\} = \{2, 5\}$ we find ND maxmods. Clearly, {a}, {d}, {h}, {i} are dominating {b} and {g}. Then ND maxmods are {b} and {g}. They generate the concepts {2, bcef}, {5, cefg}. The line diagram of these concepts is shown in Figure 8.

Step 10: The next marked concept is (12, bef). To find the ND maxmods we can use the

attributes {a, c, d, g, h, i}, objects {1, 2} and external neighbors from Table 10 $N^+\{a\} = N^+\{d\} = N^+\{g\} = N^+\{i\} = \{1, 2\}$, $N^+\{c\} = \{1\}$, $N^+\{h\} = \{2\}$. Clearly, {a}, {d}, {g}, {i} are dominating {c} and {h}. Then ND maxmods are {c} and {h}. They generate the concepts {1, befh} and {2, bcef}. The line diagram of these concepts is shown in Figure 9.

Figure 8. Line diagram for context of Table 9

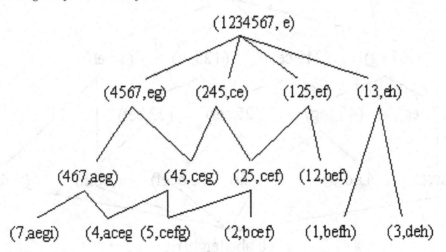

Figure 9. Line diagram for context of Table 10

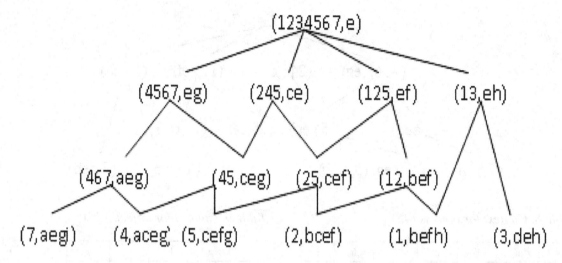

Table10. Context for objects (12)

	a	c	d	g	h	i
1					X	
2		X				

Step 11: Now, no marked concept is in the queue. Then from algorithm step 3, we consider all the attributes, A= {a, b, c, d, e, f, g, h, i} and find A^{ι}. We can conclude, from Table1 that there is no object which covers all the attributes. The finally generated concept is {0, abcdefghi}, where {0} is used for representing null. The line diagram is shown in the Figure 10.

From the above steps, we can understand that Bordat algorithm finds ND maxmods for each concept in DFS fashion and builds the line diagram.

Figure 10. Line diagram for step 11 in section 4.1

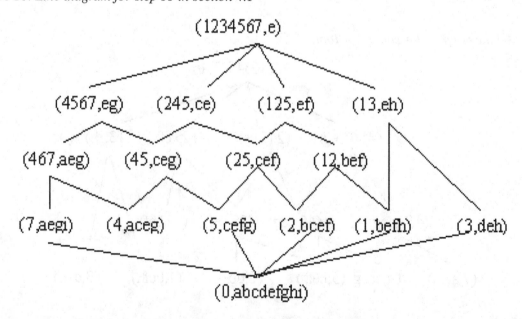

Complexity of this computation increases when the size of the context is too large. For a small context, the algorithm finds ND maxmods, update and build the line diagram at each step. We can conclude that Bordat algorithm performs well for context of average size. The comparison with other algorithms is given in Table 22.

NEXT NEIGHBOR ALGORITHM

The Next Neighbor algorithm steps are defined in Table 11. We illustrate the algorithm for the given context as follows.

Table 11. Next Neighbor Algorithm

Input: Context(G, M, I)	
Sl No	Instructions
1	$C = (G, G^\uparrow)$
2	E=0;

3	while currentlevel $\neq 0$
	 nextlevel=0;
	 for each $(O, A) \in$ currentlevel
	 lowerNeighbors = Find lowerNeighbors (O, A);
	
	 for each $(O_1, A_1) \in$ lowerNeighbors
	
	 if$(O_1, A_1) \notin$ **c**
	
	 c=c $\cup$ (O_1, A_1)
	
	 nextlevel= nextlevel $\cup$ (O_1, A_1)
	
	 Add edge$(O, A) \leftarrow (O_1, A_1)$ to **E**
	 Find lowerNeighbors (O, A)
	 a. candidates =0;
	 b. **for each** $a \in$ **M** but $a \notin A$.
	 c. $O_1 = (A \cup \{a\})^\uparrow$
	 d. $A_1 = \{O_1\}^\uparrow$
	 e. **if** $(O_1, A_1) \notin$ candidates then
	 f. candidates = candidates $\cup$ (O_1, A_1)
	 g. **return** maximally general candidates

4	currentlevel = nextlevel
Output: The concept lattice L= (**C, E**) of (**G, M,** I).	

Step 1: First we find maximally generated candidates which cover all the objects {1234567} of given context. Then we can check whether it is covered by any attribute. To verify it, we apply concept forming operators "↑" and "↓" as shown in step 1 of the algorithm. We get,

$$\{1234567\}^\uparrow = \{e\}$$

and

$$\{e\}^\downarrow = \{1234567\}$$

This means (1234567, e) is a concept and is the top element of lattice.

Step 2: The current level is (1234567, e). We explore remaining attributes with combination of intent {e} for finding next neighbors. The candidates for this concept are:-

$$\{\{ae\}^\downarrow, \{ae\}^{\downarrow\uparrow}\} = (467, aeg)$$

$$\{\{be\}^\downarrow, \{be\}^{\downarrow\uparrow}\} = (12, bef)$$

$$\{\{ce\}^\downarrow, \{ce\}^{\downarrow\uparrow}\} = (245, ce)$$

$$\{\{de\}^\downarrow, \{de\}^{\downarrow\uparrow}\} = (3, deh)$$

$$\{\{ef\}^\downarrow, \{ef\}^{\downarrow\uparrow}\} = (125, ef)$$

$$\{\{eg\}^\downarrow, \{eg\}^{\downarrow\uparrow}\} = (4567, eg)$$

$$\{\{eh\}^\downarrow, \{eh\}^{\downarrow\uparrow}\} = (13, eh)$$

$$\{\{ei\}^\downarrow, \{ei\}^{\downarrow\uparrow}\} = (7, aegi)$$

We find lower neighbors for the concept of attribute {e}, which can be derived from step 3 of the algorithm. From the above candidates, (245, ce), (4567, eg), (13, eh), (125, ef) are lower neighbors for the concept (1234567, e). The line diagram for this level is shown in Figure 11.

Step 3: The current level is (4567, eg). We find next neighbors using Table 12.

The candidates for this concept are:

$$\{\{aeg\}^{\downarrow}, \{aeg\}^{\downarrow\uparrow}\} = (467, aeg)$$

$$\{\{beg\}^{\downarrow}, \{beg\}^{\downarrow\uparrow}\} = (0, bdegh)$$

$$\{\{ceg\}^{\downarrow}, \{ceg\}^{\downarrow\uparrow}\} = (45, ceg)$$

$$\{\{deg\}^{\downarrow}, \{deg\}^{\downarrow\uparrow}\} = (0, bdegh)$$

$$\{\{efg\}^{\downarrow}, \{efg\}^{\downarrow\uparrow}\} = (5, cefg)$$

$$\{\{egh\}^{\downarrow}, \{egh\}^{\downarrow\uparrow}\} = (0, bdegh)$$

$$\{\{egi\}^{\downarrow}, \{egi\}^{\downarrow\uparrow}\} = (7, aegi)$$

The lower neighbors are (467, aeg), (45, ceg) and the line diagram is shown in Figure 12.

Step 4: Then current level is (245, ce). We find next neighbor of this concept using Table 13.

The candidates for this concept are: -

$$\{\{ace\}^{\downarrow}, \{ace\}^{\downarrow\uparrow}\} = (4, aceg)$$

$$\{\{bce\}^{\downarrow}, \{bce\}^{\downarrow\uparrow}\} = (2, bcef)$$

$$\{\{dce\}^{\downarrow}, \{dce\}^{\downarrow\uparrow}\} = (0, cdehi)$$

$$\{\{cef\}^{\downarrow}, \{cef\}^{\downarrow\uparrow}\} = (25, cef)$$

Figure 11. Line diagram for step 2 in section 4.2

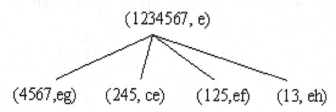

Table 12. Context for objects (4567)

	Breathe In water (a)	Can Fly (b)	Has Beak (c)	Has Hands (d)	Has Skeleton (e)	Has Wings (f)	Lives in Water (g)	Is Viviparous (h)	Produces Light (i)
Parrotfish(4)	X		X		X		X		
Penguin (5)			X		X	X	X		
Shark (6)	X				X		X		
Lantern fish (7)	X				X		X		X

Figure 12. Line diagram for context of Table 12

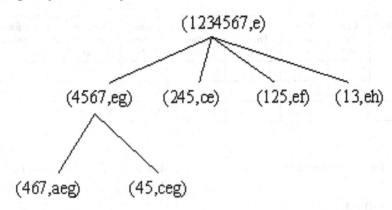

Table 13. Context for objects (245)

	Breathe in Water (a)	Can Fly (b)	Has Beak (c)	Has Hands (d)	Has Skeleton (e)	Has Wings (f)	Lives in Water (g)	Is Viviparous (h)	Produces Light (i)
Eagle (2)		X	X		X	X			
Parrotfish(4)	X		X		X		X		
Penguin (5)			X		X	X	X		

$$\{\{ceg\}^{\downarrow}, \{ceg\}^{\downarrow\uparrow}\} = (45, ceg)$$

$$\{\{ceh\}^{\downarrow}, \{ceh\}^{\downarrow\uparrow}\} = (0, cdehi)$$

$$\{\{cei\}^{\downarrow}, \{cei\}^{\downarrow\uparrow}\} = (0, cdehi)$$

The lower neighbors are (45, ceg), (25, cef) and the line diagram is shown in Figure 13.

Step 5: Then current level is (125, ef). We find next neighbor of this concept using Table 14.

Figure 13. Line diagram for context of Table 13

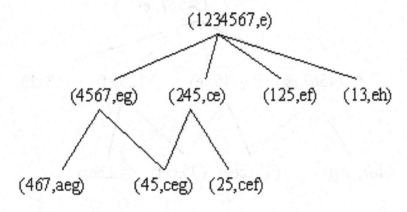

Table 14. Context for objects (125)

	Breathe in Water (a)	Can Fly (b)	Has Beak (c)	Has Hands (d)	Has Skeleton (e)	Has Wings (f)	Lives in Water (g)	Is Viviparous (h)	Produces Light (i)
Bat (1)		X			X	X		X	
Eagle (2)		X	X		X	X			
Penguin(5)			X		X	X	X		

The candidates for this concept are:

$$\{\{aef\}^{\downarrow}, \{aef\}^{\downarrow\uparrow}\} = (0, adefi)$$

$$\{\{bef\}^{\downarrow}, \{bef\}^{\downarrow\uparrow}\} = (12, bef)$$

$$\{\{cef\}^{\downarrow}, \{cef\}^{\downarrow\uparrow}\} = (25, cef)$$

$$\{\{def\}^{\downarrow}, \{def\}^{\downarrow\uparrow}\} = (0, adefi)$$

$$\{\{gef\}^{\downarrow}, \{gef\}^{\downarrow\uparrow}\} = (5, cefg)$$

$$\{\{efh\}^{\downarrow}, \{efh\}^{\downarrow\uparrow}\} = (1, befh)$$

$$\{\{efi\}^{\downarrow}, \{efi\}^{\downarrow\uparrow}\} = (0, adefi)$$

The lower neighbors are (12, bef), (25, cef) and the line diagram is shown in Figure 14.

Step 6: Then current level is (13, eh). We find the next neighbor for this concept using Table 15.

The candidates for this concept are:

$$\{\{aeh\}^{\downarrow}, \{aeh\}^{\downarrow\uparrow}\} = (0, aceghi)$$

$$\{\{beh\}^{\downarrow}, \{beh\}^{\downarrow\uparrow}\} = (1, befh)$$

$$\{\{ceh\}^{\downarrow}, \{ceh\}^{\downarrow\uparrow}\} = (0, aceghi)$$

$$\{\{deh\}^{\downarrow}, \{deh\}^{\downarrow\uparrow}\} = (3, deh)$$

Figure 14. Line diagram for context of Table 14

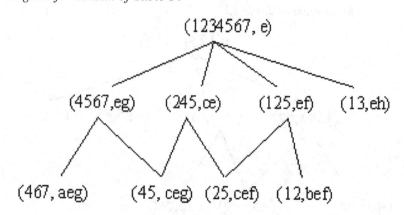

Table 15. Context for objects (13)

	Breathe in Water (a)	Can Fly (b)	Has Beak (c)	Has Hands (d)	Has Skeleton (e)	Has Wings (f)	Lives in Water (g)	Is Viviparous (h)	Produces Light (i)
Bat (1)		X			X	X		X	
Monkey(3)				X	X			X	

$$\{\{efh\}^{\downarrow}, \{efh\}^{\downarrow\uparrow}\} = (1, befh)$$

$$\{\{egh\}^{\downarrow}, \{egh\}^{\downarrow\uparrow}\} = (0, aceghi)$$

$$\{\{ehi\}^{\downarrow}, \{ehi\}^{\downarrow\uparrow}\} = (0, aceghi)$$

The lower neighbors are (1, befh), (3, deh) and the line diagram is shown in Figure 15.

Step 7: Then current level is (467, aeg). We find the next neighbor for this concept using Table 16.

The candidates for this concept are:

$$\{\{abeg\}^{\downarrow}, \{abeg\}^{\downarrow\uparrow}\} = (0, abdefgh)$$

$$\{\{aceg\}^{\downarrow}, \{aceg\}^{\downarrow\uparrow}\} = (4, aceg)$$

Figure 15. Line diagram for context of Table 15

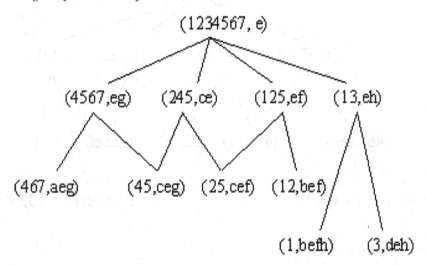

Table 16. Context for objects (467)

	Breathe in Water (a)	Can Fly (b)	Has Beak (c)	Has Hands (d)	Has Skeleton (e)	Has Wings (f)	Lives in Water (g)	Is Viviparous (h)	Produces Light (i)
Parrotfish(4)	X		X		X		X		
Shark (6)	X				X		X		
Lantern fish (7)	X				X		X		X

$$\{\{adeg\}^{\downarrow}, \{adeg\}^{\downarrow\uparrow}\} = (0, abdefgh)$$

$$\{\{aefg\}^{\downarrow}, \{aefg\}^{\downarrow\uparrow}\} = (0, abdefgh)$$

$$\{\{aegh\}^{\downarrow}, \{aegh\}^{\downarrow\uparrow}\} = (0, abdefgh)$$

$$\{\{aegi\}^{\downarrow}, \{aegi\}^{\downarrow\uparrow}\} = (7, aegi)$$

The lower neighbors are (4, aceg) and (7, aegi) and the line diagram is shown in Figure 16.

Step 8: Then current level is (45, ceg). We find next neighbor for this concept using Table 17.

The candidates for this concept are:

$$\{\{aceg\}^{\downarrow}, \{aceg\}^{\downarrow\uparrow}\} = (4, aceg)$$

$$\{\{bceg\}^{\downarrow}, \{bceg\}^{\downarrow\uparrow}\} = (0, bcdeghi)$$

$$\{\{cdeg\}^{\downarrow}, \{cdeg\}^{\downarrow\uparrow}\} = (0, bcdeghi)$$

$$\{\{cefg\}^{\downarrow}, \{cefg\}^{\downarrow\uparrow}\} = (5, cefg)$$

$$\{\{cefh\}^{\downarrow}, \{cefh\}^{\downarrow\uparrow}\} = (0, bcdeghi)$$

$$\{\{cegi\}^{\downarrow}, \{cegi\}^{\downarrow\uparrow}\} = (0, bcdeghi)$$

Figure 16. Line diagram for context of Table 16

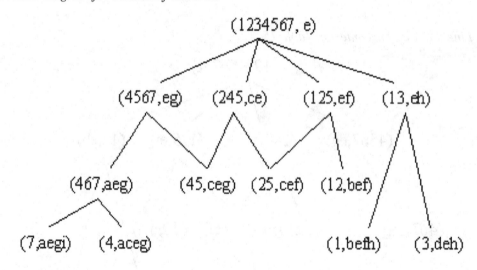

Table 17. Context for objects (45)

	Breathe in Water (a)	Can Fly (b)	Has Beak (c)	Has Hands (d)	Has Skeleton (e)	Has Wings (f)	Lives in Water (g)	Is Viviparous (h)	Produces Light (i)
Parrotfish(4)	X		X		X		X		
Penguin (5)			X		X	X	X		

The lower neighbors are (4, aceg) and (5, cefg) and the line diagram is shown in Figure 17.

Step 9: Then current level is (25, cef). We find next neighbor for this concept using Table 18.

The candidates for this concept are:

$$\{\{acef\}^{\downarrow}, \{acef\}^{\downarrow\uparrow}\} = (0, acdefhi)$$

$$\{\{bcef\}^{\downarrow}, \{bcef\}^{\downarrow\uparrow}\} = (2, bcef)$$

$$\{\{cdef\}^{\downarrow}, \{cdef\}^{\downarrow\uparrow}\} = (0, acdefhi)$$

$$\{\{cefg\}^{\downarrow}, \{cefg\}^{\downarrow\uparrow}\} = (5, cefg)$$

$$\{\{cefh\}^{\downarrow}, \{cefh\}^{\downarrow\uparrow}\} = (0, acdefhi)$$

$$\{\{cefi\}^{\downarrow}, \{cefi\}^{\downarrow\uparrow}\} = (0, acdefhi)$$

The lower neighbors are (2, bcef), (5, cefg) and the line diagram is shown in Figure 18.

Step 10: The current level is (12, bef). We find next neighbor for this concept using Table 19.

The candidates for this concept are:

$$\{\{abef\}^{\downarrow}, \{abef\}^{\downarrow\uparrow}\} = (0, abdefgi)$$

$$\{\{bcef\}^{\downarrow}, \{bcef\}^{\downarrow\uparrow}\} = (2, bcef)$$

Figure 17. Line diagram for context of Table 17

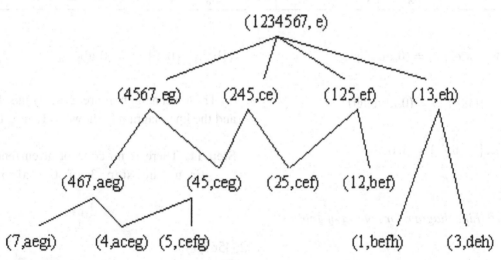

Table 18. Context for objects (25)

	Breathe in Water (a)	Can Fly (b)	Has Beak (c)	Has Hands (d)	Has Skeleton (e)	Has Wings (f)	Lives in Water (g)	Is Viviparous (h)	Produces Light (i)
Eagle (2)		X	X		X	X			
Penguin(5)			X		X	X	X		

Figure 18. Line diagram for context of Table 18

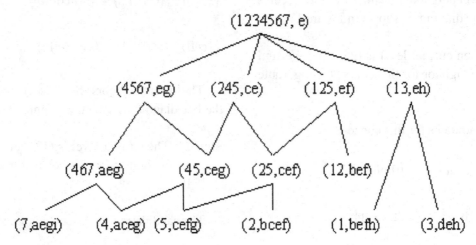

Table 19. Context for objects (12)

	Breathe in Water (a)	Can Fly (b)	Has Beak (c)	Has Hands (d)	Has Skeleton (e)	Has Wings (f)	Lives in Water (g)	Is Viviparous (h)	Produces Light (i)
Bat (1)		X			X	X		X	
Eagle(2)		X	X		X	X			

$$\{\{bdef\}^{\downarrow}, \{bdef\}^{\downarrow\uparrow}\} = (0, abdefgi)$$

$$\{\{befi\}^{\downarrow}, \{befi\}^{\downarrow\uparrow}\} = (0, abdefgi)$$

$$\{\{befg\}^{\downarrow}, \{befg\}^{\downarrow\uparrow}\} = (0, abdefgi)$$

The lower neighbors are (2, bcef) and (1, befh) and the line diagram is shown in Figure 19.

$$\{\{befh\}^{\downarrow}, \{befh\}^{\downarrow\uparrow}\} = (1, befh)$$

Step 11: There is no concept at current level. From the step 3 of the algorithm,

Figure 19. Line diagram for context of Table 19

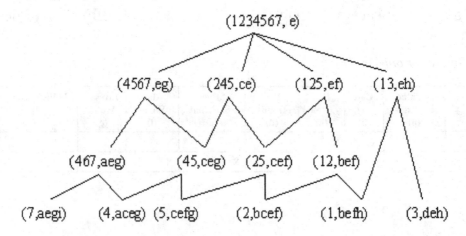

$O_1 = (abcdefghi)^{\downarrow} = \{0\}$, so $A_1 = \{O_1\}^{\uparrow} = \{abcdefghi\}$. Since (O_1, A_1) is not a candidate and from algorithm, (0, abcdefghi) is last next neighbor. The final lattice structure is shown in Figure 20. This concept lattice diagram is similar to the lattice generated by Carpineto and Romano (2004).

From the above steps we can understand that, the Next Neighbor finds all the lower neighbors by the combination of each and every attributes (objects) of given context, with attributes (objects) of generated concepts. This algorithm computes more candidates for finding the lower neighbors in top down BFS manner. DFS method also works equally for this algorithm. We can observe that the above steps are computed in top down BFS manner. Due to these reasons for a large context, algorithm takes more time for computing the concepts and line diagram. But, due to the same reasons, for a small context the algorithm requires few combinations of attributes (objects) and hence requires less time.

OBJECT INTERSCETION ALGORITHM

The Object Intersection algorithm steps are shown in Table 20. We demonstrate the algorithm as follows.

Step 1: $\{1\}^{\uparrow} = \{befh\}$, $\{befh\}^{\downarrow} = \{1\}$. The generated concept is (1, befh).

Step 2: $\{2\}^{\uparrow} = \{bcef\}$, $\{bcef\}^{\downarrow} = \{2\}$. The generated concept is (2, bcef).

Step 3: $\{3\}^{\uparrow} = \{deh\}$, $\{deh\}^{\downarrow} = \{3\}$. The generated concept is (3, deh).

Step 4: $\{4\}^{\uparrow} = \{aceg\}$, $\{aceg\}^{\downarrow} = \{4\}$. The generated concept is (4, aceg).

Figure 20. Line diagram for step 11 in section 4.2

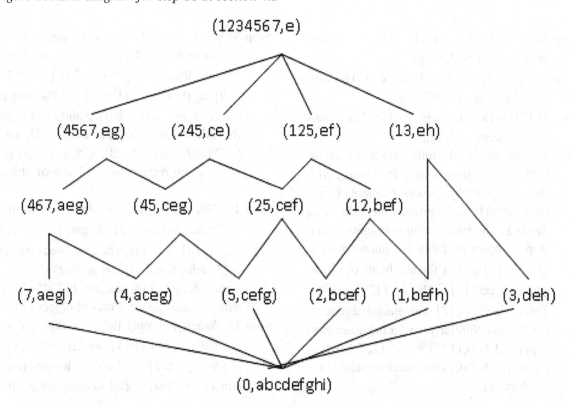

Table 20. Object intersection algorithm

Input: Context (G, M, *I*)	
Sl No	**Instructions**
1	$C = (M^{\downarrow}, M)$
2	**for** each $O \in G$ for each $(O, A) \in C$ intersection$= A \cap \{O\}^{\downarrow}$; if intersection is different from any concept intent in **C** then $C = C \bigcup \{ \{\text{intersection}\}^{\downarrow}, (\text{intersection})\}$

3	Covering edges(**C**, (**G, M,** *I*))
	for each(O, A) , set count of any concept in **C** to 0
	for each $a \in M\backslash A$;
	
	intersection $= O \cap \{a\}^{\downarrow}$;
	
	find $(O_1, A_1) \in C$ such that O_1 =intersection
	
	count(O_1, A_1) =count(O_1, A_1))+1;
	
	if ($| A_1 |$-|A|)=count(O_1, A_1) +1;
	
	Add edge $(O_1, A_1) \rightarrow (O, A)$ to **E**.

4	Stop.
Output: The concept lattice L= (**C, E**) of (**G, M,** *I*) with covering edges.	

Step 5: $\{5\}^{\uparrow} = \{cefg\}$, $\{cefg\}^{\downarrow} = \{5\}$. The generated concept is (5, cefg).

Step 6: $\{6\}^{\uparrow} = \{aeg\}$, $\{aeg\}^{\downarrow} = \{467\}$. The generated concept is (467, aeg).

Step 7: $\{7\}^{\uparrow} = \{aegi\}$, $\{aegi\}^{\downarrow} = \{7\}$. The generated concept is (7, aegi).

Step 8: Now we take the intersection of each attribute (object) of objects (attribute), with the attributes (objects) of remaining objects (attributes) from the given context shown in Table 1. The intersection is obtained from step 3 shown in Table 20, intersection = $\{O \cap \{a\}^{\downarrow}\}$. For the attributes of object $\{1\}$, we get $\{1\} \cap \{b\}^{\downarrow} = \{12\}$, $\{12\}^{\uparrow} = \{bef\}$, $\{bef\}^{\downarrow} = \{12\}$. The generated concept is (12, bef). Similarly we get the other concepts, (12, bef), (1234567, e), (125, ef), (13, eh) and (1, befh), using remaining attributes of object $\{1\}$.

Step 9: When we apply step 3 of algorithm, for the attributes of object $\{2\}$, with attributes of other objects, we get $\{2\} \cap \{b\}^{\downarrow} = \{12\}$, $\{12\}^{\uparrow} = \{bef\}$, $\{bef\}^{\downarrow} = \{12\}$. The generated concept is (12, bef). Similarly we get the other concepts, (12, bef), (245, ce), (1234567, e), (125, ef), (25, cef) and (2, bcef), using remaining attributes of object $\{2\}$.

Step 10: When we apply the algorithm, for the attributes of object $\{3\}$, we get, $\{3\} \cap \{d\}^{\downarrow} = \{3\}$, $\{3\}^{\uparrow} = \{deh\}$. The generated concept is (3, deh). Similarly, we get the other concepts, (3, deh), (13, eh), and $\{1234567, e\}$, using remaining attributes of object $\{3\}$.

Step 11: When we apply the algorithm, for the attributes of object $\{4\}$, we get $\{4\} \cap \{a\}^{\downarrow} = \{467\}$, $\{467\}^{\uparrow} = \{aeg\}$. The generated concept is (467, aeg). Similarly we get the other concepts, (467, aeg), (245, ce), (1234567, e), (4567, eg), (45, ceg) and (4, aceg), using remaining attributes of object {4}.

Step 12: When we apply the algorithm for the attributes of object {5}, we get $\{5\} \cap \{c\}^{\downarrow}$ = {245}, $\{245\}^{\uparrow}$ = {ce}. The generated concept is (245, ce). Similarly, we get other concepts, (245, ce}, (1234567, e), (125, ef), (4567, eg), (45, ceg) and (5, cefg), using remaining attributes of the object {5}.

Step 13: When we apply the algorithm for the attributes of objects {6}, we get $\{6\} \cap \{a\}^{\downarrow}$ = {467}, $\{467\}^{\uparrow}$ = {aeg}. The generated concept is (467, aeg). Similarly, we get the other concepts, (467, aeg}, (1234567, e) and (4567, eg), using remaining attributes of the object {6}. .

Step 14: When we apply the algorithm for the attributes of object {7}, we get $\{7\} \cap \{a\}^{\downarrow}$ = {467}, $\{467\}^{\uparrow}$ = {aeg}. The generated concept is (467, aeg). Similarly, we get other concepts (467, aeg}, (1234567, e), (4567, eg) and (7, aegi), using remaining attributes of the object {7}.

Step 15: Now we take intersection of all attributes {abcdefghi} and explore them by the operator " $\downarrow$ "and " $\uparrow$ " get $\{abcdefghi\}^{\downarrow}$ = {0}, $O^{\uparrow}$ = {abcdefghi}. The last generated concept is (0, abcdefghi), where {0} is used for representing null.

Object Intersection does not support the construction of the line diagram, because there is no relationship between lexicographic order and the order defined over the concepts in the lattice. Literature used concept covering algorithm further for generating the line diagram of the concepts generated by Object Intersection algorithm. The time complexity of concept covering algorithm is O (|C||M| (|G|+|M|) (Carpineto & Romano, 2004, Kuznetsov & Obiedkov 2002). If the given context is of incremental type with respect to intersection

of attributes (objects) and then the algorithm performs well. Hence, if we require concepts as well as line diagram, then the Object Intersection algorithm complexity increases. One of the main drawbacks of this algorithm is that, it generates similar concepts repeatedly.

NEXT CLOSURE ALGORITHM

The Next Closure algorithm steps are shown in Table 21. We demonstrate the algorithm as given below.

Step 1: The smallest object which covers all attributes in the context shown in Table 1 is {0}. From the step 5 of algorithm, we find that, $O^{\uparrow}$ = {abcdefghi} and

Table 21. Ganter next closure algorithm

Input:-(G,M,I)	
Sl No	**Instructions**
1	if $A \subseteq$ **M**$= \{a_1, a_2, ..., a_{m-1}, a_m\}$ Then find $A \otimes a_i = \{(A \cap (a_1, a_2, ..., a_{i-1})) \cup (a_i)\}$ $A^{\downarrow\uparrow} \leftarrow A$ is closure operator and $\quad O^{\uparrow\downarrow} \leftarrow o$.
2	if it is first time then it is concept $(O^{\uparrow}, \{A \cap \{(A \cap (a_1, a_2, ..., a_{i-1})) \cup (a_i)\}^{\downarrow\uparrow})$ else $(a_i) = \max\{a_i / a_i \in M \setminus A\}$ $A = A \cup \{a_i\}$
3	Then again repeat step 1 and 2 for generating other next closure concepts.
4	The smallest common attribute subset is $\quad O^{\uparrow\downarrow}$.
5	Above properties are dual so we can also apply on object at the place of Attributes for generating Next closure concepts.
Output: - The set of Lexicographical order concepts ($O^{\uparrow\downarrow}$, $A^{\downarrow\uparrow}$).	

$\{abcdefghi\}^{\downarrow} = \{0\}$

so (0, abcdefghi) is a concept, where {0} is used for representing null.

Step 2: Now we find next batch of concepts from a given context where the objects are subset of {1234567}. We find the lexicographic order for each object and verify the order by the closure operator defined in step 1 of algorithm. The order we find is {1, befh}, {2, bcef}, {3, deh}, {4, aceg}, {5, cefg}, {6, aeg}, {7, aegi}. We push them into a stack and apply the step 1 and 2 of algorithm on the popped concepts. The generated concepts are, (1, befh) (2, bcef), (3, deh), (4, aceg), (5, cefg), (7, aegi). We can observe that (6, aeg) is not a concept, since $\{6\}^{\uparrow\downarrow} = \{467\}$, $\{aeg\}^{\downarrow\uparrow} = \{aeg\}$. The lexical order between these concepts is shown in Figure 21.

Step 3: When we apply step 2 of algorithm on earlier generated concepts we get $a(1) = \max$ (aegi, aceg) = {aeg} $\in$ **M**. Similarly for other generated concepts of above step 2, we get, $a(2) = \max$ (aceg, cefg) = {ceg}, a

(3) = max (cefg, bcef) = {cef}, $a(4)$ = max (bcef, befh) = {bef}, $a(5)$ = max (befh, deh) = {eh}. Then, these attributes are pushed into the stack. For finding lexicographical order we apply closure operator on the popped attributes, using step 1 of algorithm. We get the concepts, (467, aeg), (45, ceg), (25, cef), (12, bef), (13, eh). The lexical order between these concepts is shown in Figure 22.

Step 4: When we apply the steps 1 and 2 of algorithm, on the concepts generated in the above steps, we get, $a(1)$=max(aeg, ceg)={eg}, $a(2)$=max(ceg, cef)={ce}, $a(3)$=max(cef, bef)={ef}, $a(4)$=max(bef, eh)={e}. Then applying step 2 of algorithm, the generated concepts are, (4567, eg), (245, ce), (125, ef), (1234567, e). The lexicographical order of these concepts is shown in Figure 23.

Step 5: We again apply the steps 1 and 2 of algorithm, on the concepts generated in the above steps, we get, $a(1)$ =max {e g, c e} = max {c e, e f} = max {e f, e} = {e}. This generates the same concept (1234567, e), which is generated in the above step. Then the algorithm stops the execution since stack

Figure 21. Lexical order for step 2 in section 4.4

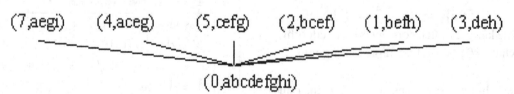

Figure 22. Lexical order for step 3 in section 4.4

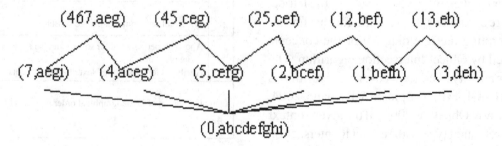

Figure 23. Lexical order for step 4 in section 4.4

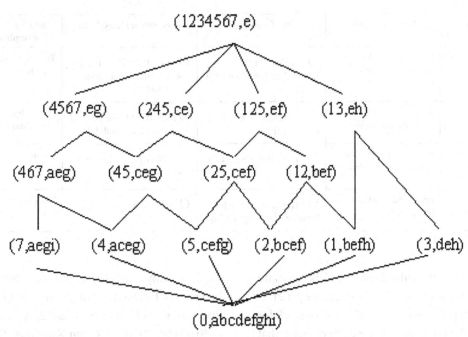

is empty. The final lattice diagram is shown in Figure 23, which is similar to generated by Carpineto and Romano (2004).

From the above steps we can observe that, Next Closure algorithm finds lexical order and build the lattice using binary search, which takes minimum time than sequential search. Also, this algorithm generates concepts in batch and store them in a stack. Ganter's algorithm requires less space due to the fact that it does not use the generated concepts to generate next concepts. Due to these properties, Ganter's algorithm is preferred when a given context is large. However if the context is small and sparse, then it takes more time as generating the concepts and lexical order requires already generated concepts.

DISCUSSIONS AND CONCLUSION

Computing the formal concepts and their visualization in concept lattice structure is an important concern for practical applications. For this purpose several algorithms have been proposed.

However, in this chapter, we have analyzed Bordat, Next Neighbor, Object Intersection and Next Closure algorithms and the summary is shown in Table 22.

The study concludes that, Object Intersection algorithm works faster, when context is linear with respect to number of input objects (attributes). However, this algorithm generates similar concepts repeatedly and will not generate the concept lattice. Also Object Intersection algorithm generates new concept by taking intersection of objects (attributes) of given context. Next Neighbor algorithm is preferred for small or sparse context. But for large and dense contexts this algorithm works slowly (Carpineto & Romano, 2004, Kuznetsov & Obiedkov 2002).

Bordat algorithm is more suitable for average context, especially when it is necessary to build the line diagram. It generates concepts in batch using generated concepts in top down DFS fashion. For generating the line diagram, Bordat algorithm requires more space than other algorithms (Kuznetsov & Obiedkov 2002). When the number of objects is small, algorithm works slowly when compared with other algorithms.

Table 22. Comparison of algorithms

Algorithm	Exploring Type	Time Complexity	Polynomial Delay Time	Data Structures Used for Implementation
Bordat Algorithm	Descending order in batch with earlier concept	$O(|G||M|*|M||L|)$ Where, L is size of concept lattice	$O(|G||M|*|M|)$ for finding non dominating maxmods and update.	Trie, depth first search and Queue
Next Neighbor Algorithm	Ascending order With attribute/object	$O(|C||G||M|*|M|)$ where C is concept.	$O(|G||M|*|M|)$ for removal of non maximal candidate	Queue, breadth first search and RB-Tree.
Object Intersection Algorithm	Incremental type with intersection of object	$O(|C||G||M|)$ where C is concept.	$O(|G||M|)$ to retrieve and store the concept.	Queue
Ganter Next Closure Algorithm	Enumeration with lexical order	$O(|G|*|G||M||L|)$ where L is size of concept lattice.	$O(|G|*|G||M|)$	Stack and binary search.

Next Closure algorithm is preferred for large and dense data. It uses less memory space for generating the concepts. Ganter's algorithm uses stack for generating the concepts, so we can conclude that the size of stack at one level does not exceed total number of objects in the context (Ganter, 2002, Ganter & Reuter, 1991). Ganter's algorithm also builds the lexicographical order between the generated concepts using the binary search. Our study concludes that, the choice of using an algorithm for generating concepts and line diagram should be based on the properties of input data, size of context and application. The practical limits of these algorithms are as follows. The Bordat algorithm does not suit for the less memory environment. For small and sparse formal contexts, Ganters' Next Closure algorithm and Bordat algorithm works slower when compared with other algorithms. Since Next Neighbor algorithm requires more time to select the lower neighbors, it cannot be applied on large formal contexts. Object intersection algorithm uses concept covering algorithm separately to build the lattice structure from the obtained formal concepts. Hence, it is not suitable for large and dense contexts.

This study is helpful for the application of FCA in various fields(Aswani Kumar 2011a, 2011b, 2013, Aswani Kumar et al, 2012, Aswani Kumar & Srinivas, 2010a, Aswani Kumar & Sumangali 2012, Kaytoue et al. 2011, Krajca et al. 2010, Krohn et al. 1999, Li et al. 2011, 2012a, 2012b, 2013a, 2013b, Mephu et al., 1998, Priss 2006, Priss & Old 2004, Priss et al., 2007, Stumme et al., 2002, Valtchev et al., 2004, Wille, 2002, Zhang & Wu, 2011, Zhang et al. 2013) . In the process of concept generation a major problem is how to reduce the number of formal concept and size of concept lattice. Hence, in future our research work will concentrate on reducing the number of (fuzzy) formal concepts and size of concept lattice structure.

ACKNOWLEDGMENT

Authors acknowledge the financial support from National Board of Higher Mathematics, Dept. of Atomic Energy, Govt. of India under the grant 2/48(11)/2010-R&D II/10806.

REFERENCES

Agrawal, R., & Srikant, R. (1994). Fast algorithm for mining association rules. In *Proceedings of 20ᵗʰ International Conference on Very Large Databases* (pp. 487-99). VLDB.

Aho, A. V., Hopcroft, J. E., & Ullman, J. D. (1983). *Data structures and algorithms*. Amsterdam: Addison Wesley.

Baixeries, J., Szathmary, L., Vatchel, P., & Godibn, R. (2009). Yet a faster algorithm for building the hasse diagram of concept lattice. In *International Conference on Formal Concept Analysis* (LNAI), (vol. 5548, pp. 162-177). Berlin: Springer-Verlag.

Belohlavek, R., Sklenar, V., & Zacpal, J. (2004). Formal concept analysis with hierarchically ordered attributes. *International Journal of General Systems, 33*, 383–394. doi:10.1080/0308107041 0001679715

Belohlavek, R., & Vychodil, V. (2006). Replacing full rectangles by dense rectangles: Concepts lattices and attribute implications. In *Proceedings of IEEE International Conference Information Reuse & Integration* (pp. 117-22). IEEE.

Belohlavek, R., & Vychodil, V. (2009). Formal concept analysis with background knowledge: Attribute priorities. *IEEE Transactions on Systems, Man, and Cybernetics, 39*(4), 399–409. doi:10.1109/TSMCC.2008.2012168 PMID:19109092

Berry, A., Bordat, J. P., & Cogis, O. (2000). Generating all minimal separator of a graph. *International Journal of Foundations of Computer Science, 11*, 397–404. doi:10.1142/S0129054100000211

Berry, A., Bordat, J. P., & Sigayret, A. (2007). A local approach to concept generation. *Annals of Mathematics and Artificial Intelligence, 49*(1/4), 117–136. doi:10.1007/s10472-007-9063-4

Birkhoff, G. (1940). *Lattice theory*. Washington, DC: American Mathematical Society, Colloquium Publication.

Bordat, J. P. (1986). Calcul pratique du trellis de galois d'une correspondance. *Mathematiques et Sciences Humaines, 96*, 31–47.

Boulicaut, J. F., & Besson, J. (2008). Actionability and formal concepts: A data mining perspective. In *International Conference on Formal Concept Analysis* (LNAI), (vol. 4933, pp. 14-31). Berlin: Springer-Verlag.

Burgmann, C., & Wille, R. (2006). The basic theorem in preconcept lattices. In *International Conference on Formal Concept Analysis* (LNCS), (vol. 3874, pp. 80-88). Berlin: Springer—Verlag.

Carpineto, C., & Romano, G. (1996). A lattice conceptual clustering system and its application to browsing retrieval. *Machine Learning, 24*, 95–122. doi:10.1007/BF00058654

Carpineto, C., & Romano, G. (2004). *Concept data analysis: Theory and applications*. Hoboken, NJ: John Wiley & Sons. doi:10.1002/0470011297

Davey, B. A., & Priestley, M. A. (2002). *Introduction of lattices and order*. Cambridge, UK: Cambridge University Press. doi:10.1017/CBO9780511809088

Deogun, J. S., & Saquer, J. (2004). Monotone concept for formal concept analysis. *Discrete Applied Mathematics, 144*, 70–78. doi:10.1016/j.dam.2004.05.001

Dias, S. M., & Viera, J. (2013). Applying the JBOS reduction method for relevant knowledge extraction. *Expert Systems with Applications, 40*(5), 1880–1887. doi:10.1016/j.eswa.2012.10.010

Ganter, B. (1984). *Two basic algorithms in concept analysis (Technical Report No-831)*. Technishe Hoschule Darmstadt.

Ganter, B. (2002). *Formal concept analysis: Algorithmic aspects (Technical Report)*. Technical University Dresden.

Ganter, B., Stumme, G., & Wille, R. (2005). *Formal concept analysis: Foundations and applications*. Berlin: Springer Verlag.

Ganter, B., & Wille, R. (1999). *Formal concept analysis: Mathematical foundations*. Berlin: Springer Verlag. doi:10.1007/978-3-642-59830-2

Ghosh, P., Kundu, K., & Sarkar, D. (2010). Fuzzy graph representation of fuzzy concept lattice. *Fuzzy Sets and Systems, 161*, 1669–1675. doi:10.1016/j.fss.2009.10.027

Godin, R., & Missaoui, R. (1994). An incremental concept formation approach for learning from databases. *Theoretical Computer Science, 133*, 387–419. doi:10.1016/0304-3975(94)90195-3

Hermann, M., & Sertkaya, B. (2008). On the complexity of computing generators of closed sets. In *International Conference on Formal Concept Analysis* (LNAI), (vol. 4933, pp. 158-168). Berlin: Springer-Verlag.

Iordache, O. (2011). Formal concept analysis. *Modelling Multilevel Systems, 9*, 143–162. doi:10.1007/978-3-642-17946-4_9

Jurekevicius, D., & Vasilecas, O. (2009). Formal concept analysis for concept collecting and their analysis. *Scientific Paper, 751*, 22–39.

Karl, E. W. (1994). A first course in formal concept analysis: How to understand line diagram. In Soft Stat'93 Advances in Statistical Software, (vol. 4, pp. 429-438). Gustav Fisher Verlag.

Kaytoue, M., Kuznetsov, S. O., Napoli, A., & Duplessis, S. (2011). Mining gene expression data with pattern structures in formal concept analysis. *Information Sciences, 181*, 1989–2001. doi:10.1016/j.ins.2010.07.007

Krajca, P., Outrata, J., & Vychodil, V. (2010). Advances in algorithms based on CBO. In *Proceedings of CLA* (pp. 325-337). CLA.

Krohn, U., Davies, N. J., & Weeks, R. (1999). Concept lattices for knowledge management. *BT Technology Journal, 17*(4), 108–116. doi:10.1023/A:1009607427957

Kumar, C. A. (2011a). Mining association rules using non-negative matrix factorization and formal concept analysis. In *5th International Conference on Information Processing*, (vol. 157, pp. 31-39). Berlin: Springer --Verlag.

Kumar, C. A. (2011b). Knowledge discovery in data using formal concept analysis and random projections. *International Journal of Applied Mathematics and Computer Science, 21*(4), 745–756. doi:10.2478/v10006-011-0059-1

Kumar, C. A. (2012). Fuzzy clustering based formal concept analysis for associaton rules mining. *Applied Artificial Intelligence, 26*(3), 274–301. doi:10.1080/08839514.2012.648457

Kumar, C. A. (2013). Designing role-based access model using formal concept analysis. *Security and Communication Networks, 6*, 373–383. doi:10.1002/sec.589

Kumar, C. A., Radvansky, M., & Annapurna, J. (2012). Analysis of vector space model, latent semantic indexing and formal concept analysis for information retrieval. *Cybernetics and Information Technologies, 12*(1), 34–48.

Kumar, C. A., & Srinivas, S. (2010a). Mining associations in health care data using formal concept analysis and singular value decomposition. *Journal of Biological System, 18*(4), 787–807. doi:10.1142/S0218339010003512

Kumar, C. A., & Srinivas, S. (2010b). Concept lattice reduction using fuzzy k-means clustering. *Expert Systems with Applications, 37*, 2696–2704. doi:10.1016/j.eswa.2009.09.026

Kumar, C. A., & Sumangali, K. (2012). A performance of evaluation of employees of an organization using formal concept analysis. In *Proceedings of International Conference on Pattern Recognition, Informatics & Medical Engineering* (pp. 94-98). IEEE.

Kuznetsov, S. O. (2004). Machine learning and formal concept analysis. In *Proceedings of International Conference on Formal Concept Analysis* (pp. 287-312). IEEE.

Kuznetsov, S. O., & Obiedkov, S. A. (2000). *Algorithm for construction of the set of all concepts and their line diagram (Preprint MATH-AI-05)*. Dresden, Germany: TU-Dresden.

Kuznetsov, S. O., & Obiedkov, S. A. (2002). Comparing performance of algorithms for generating concept lattices. *Journal of Experimental & Theoretical Artificial Intelligence, 14*(2/3), 189–216. doi:10.1080/09528130210164170

Lee, M. C., Chen, H. H., & Li, S. Y. (2011). FCA based concept constructing and similarity measurement algorithms. *International Journal of Advancements in computing. Technology (Elmsford, N.Y.), 3*(1).

Li, J., Mei, C., Kumar, C.A., & Zhang, X. (2013a). On rule acquisition in decision formal context. *International Journal of Machine Learning and Cybernetics.*

Li, J., Mei, C., & Lv, Y. (2011). A heuristic knowledge reduction method for decision formal contexts. *Computers & Mathematics with Applications (Oxford, England), 61*(4), 1096–1106. doi:10.1016/j.camwa.2010.12.060

Li, J., Mei, C., & Lv, Y. (2012a). Knowledge reduction in formal decision contexts based on an order preserving mapping. *International Journal of General Systems, 41*(2), 143–161. doi:10.1080/03081079.2011.634410

Li, J., Mei, C., & Lv, Y. (2012b). Knowledge reduction in real decision formal contexts. *Information Sciences, 189*, 191–207. doi:10.1016/j.ins.2011.11.041

Li, J., Mei, C., & Lv, Y. (2013b). Incomplete decision contexts: Approximate construction, rule acquisition and knowledge reduction. *International Journal of Approximate Reasoning, 54*(1), 149–165. doi:10.1016/j.ijar.2012.07.005

Lindig, C. (2000). Fast concept analysis. In *ICCS (LNCS)* (Vol. 1867, pp. 152–161). Berlin: Springer.

Maddouri, M. (2005). A formal concept analysis approach to discover association rules from data. In *Concept lattices and their applications* (pp. 10–21). Academic Press.

Maio, C. D., Fenza, G., Loia, V., & Senatore, S. (2012). Hierarchical web resources retrieval by exploiting fuzzy formal concept analysis. *Information Processing & Management, 48*(3), 399–418. doi:10.1016/j.ipm.2011.04.003

Mephu, N. E., & Njiwoua, P. (1998). Using lattice – based framework as a tool for feature extraction. In *Feature extraction construction and selection: A data mining perspective* (pp. 205–216). Boston: Kluwer Academic Publishers.

No-urine, L., & Reynaud, O. (1999). A fast algorithm for building lattices. *Information Processing Letters, 71*, 199–204. doi:10.1016/S0020-0190(99)00108-8

Norris, E. M. (1974). An algorithm for computing the maximal rectangle in a binary relation. *Journal of the ACM, 21*, 356–366.

Poelmans, J., Elzinga, P., Viaene, S., & Dedene, G. (2010). Formal concept analysis in knowledge discovery: A survey. In *Proceedings of 18ᵗʰ International Conference on Conceptual Structures* (pp. 139-53). IEEE.

Priss, U. (2006). Formal concept analysis in information science. *Annual Review of Information Science & Technology, 40*, 521–543. doi:10.1002/aris.1440400120

Priss, U., & Old, L. J. (2004). Modelling lexical databases with formal concept analysis. *Journal of Universal Computer, 10*(8), 967–984.

Priss, U., Polovina, S., & Hill, R. (2007). Conceptual structures: Knowledge architectures for smart applications. In *Proceeding of 15 International Conferences on Conceptual Structures* (LNAI), (Vol. 4604). Sheffield, UK: Springer Verlag.

Rouane, H. M., Huchard, M., Napoli, A., & Valtchev, P. (2010). Using formal concept analysis for discovering knowledge patterns. In *Proceedings of 7th International Conference of Concept Lattices & Their Applications* (pp. 223-34). IEEE.

Shi, H. F., Hua, Q., & Zhang, P. (2007). The formal concept analysis of the document clusters. In *Proceedings of 6th International Conference on Machine Learning and Cybernetic* (pp. 3381-3385). IEEE.

Shoumei, C., & Chengming, Q. (2008). Incremental formation algorithm based on concept semilattice. In *Proceedings of International Symposium on Computational Intelligence and Design* (pp. 148-151). IEEE.

Singh, P. K., & Kumar, C. A. (2012a). A method for reduction of fuzzy relation in fuzzy formal context. In *Proceedings of International Conference on Mathematical Modelling and Scientific Computation*, (vol. 283, pp. 343-350). Berlin: Springer-Verlag.

Singh, P. K., & Kumar, C. A. (2012b). A method for decomposition of fuzzy formal context. *Procedia Engineering, 38*, 1852–1857. doi:10.1016/j.proeng.2012.06.228

Singh, P. K., & Kumar, C. A. (2012c). Interval-valued fuzzy graph representation of concept lattice. In *Proceedings of 12th International Conference on Intelligent Systems Design and Applications* (pp. 604-609). IEEE.

Strok, F., & Neznanov, A. (2010). Comparing and analyzing the computational complexity of FCA algorithms. In *Proceedings of Annual Research Conference of the South African Institute of Computer Scientists and Information Technologists* (pp. 417-420). IEEE.

Stumme, G. (1995). Attribute exploration with background implications and exceptions. In *Data analysis and information system* (pp. 457–466). New York: Springer.

Stumme, G. (2002a). Efficient data mining based on formal concept analysis. In *Proceedings of 13th International Conference on Database and Expert System Applications* (LNCS), (vol. 2453, pp. 534-546). Berlin: Springer-Verlag.

Stumme, G. (2002b). Formal concept analysis on its way from mathematics to computer science. In *Conceptual Structures Integration & Interfaces, 10 th International Conferences on Conceptual Structures* (LNAI), (vol. 2393, pp. 2-19). Berlin: Springer Verlag.

Stumme, G. (2009). Formal concept analysis. In *Handbook on ontologies* (pp. 177–200). Academic Press. doi:10.1007/978-3-540-92673-3_8

Stumme, G., Taouil, R., Bastide, Y., Pasquier, N., & Lakhal, L. (2001). Intelligent structuring and reducing of association rules with formal concept analysis. [LNAI]. *Advances in Artificial Intelligence, 2174*, 335–350.

Stumme, G., Taouil, R., Bastide, Y., Pasquier, N., & Lakhal, L. (2002). Computing iceberg concept lattice with titanic. *Data & Knowledge Engineering, 42*, 189–222. doi:10.1016/S0169-023X(02)00057-5

Stumme, G., Wille, R., & Wille, U. (1998). Conceptual knowledge discovery in databases using formal concept analysis methods. In *Principles of data mining and knowledge discovery (LNAI)* (Vol. 1510, pp. 450–458). Berlin: Springer-Verlag. doi:10.1007/BFb0094849

Valtchev, P., Missaoui, R., Godin, R., & Meridji, M. (2002). A framework for incremental generation of frequent closed item sets using Galois (concept) lattices. *Journal of Experimental & Theoretical Artificial Intelligence, 14*(2/3), 115–142. doi:10.1080/09528130210164198

Valtchev, P., Missaoui, R., & Lebrun, P. (2002). A partition based approach towards constructing Galois (concept) lattices. *Discrete Mathematics, 256*(3), 801–829. doi:10.1016/S0012-365X(02)00349-7

Valtchev, P., Missaousi, R., & Godin, R. (2004). Formal concept analysis for knowledge discovery and data mining: The new challenges. In *Proceedings of 2nd International Conference on Formal Concept Analysis* (LNAI), (vol. 2961, pp. 352-371). Berlin: Springer.

Van Der, M. F., Obiedkov, S., & Kourie, D. (2004a). Add intent: A new incremental algorithm for constructing concept lattices. In *ICFCA (LNAI)* (Vol. 2961, pp. 342–385). Berlin: Springer-Verlag.

Van der, M. F., Obiedkov. S., & Kourie, D. (2004b). Add intent: A new incremental algorithm for conctructing concept lattices. In *Proceedings of ICFCA 2004* (pp. 372-385). ICFCA.

Venter, F. J., Oosthuizen, G. D., & Ross, J. D. (1997). Knowledge discovery in databases using concept lattices. *Expert Systems with Applications, 13*(4), 259–264. doi:10.1016/S0957-4174(97)00047-X

Wille, R. (1982). Restructuring lattice theory: An approach based on hierarchy of concepts. In I. Rival (Ed.), *Ordered sets* (pp. 445–470). Boston: Reidel. doi:10.1007/978-94-009-7798-3_15

Wille, R. (2002). Why can concept lattice support knowledge discovery in databases. *Journal of Experimental & Theoretical Artificial Intelligence, 14*(2/3), 81–92. doi:10.1080/09528130210164161

Wille, R. (2008). Formal concept analysis as applied lattice theory. In *Proceedings of 4th International Conferences on Concept Lattices and Their Applications* (pp. 42-67). Berlin: Springer-Verlag.

Wu, W. Z., Leung, Y., & Mi, J. S. (2009). Granular computing and knowledge reduction in formal contexts. *IEEE Transactions on Knowledge and Data Engineering, 21*(10), 1461–1474. doi:10.1109/TKDE.2008.223

Yun, L., Yunhao, Y., Xin, G., Yen, S., & Ling, C. (2008). A fast algorithm for generating concepts. In *Proceedings of International Conference on Information and Automation* (pp. 1728-1733). IEEE.

Zhang, S., & Wu, X. (2011). Fundamentals of associations rules in data mining and knowledge discovery. *Wiley Interdisciplinary Reviews: Data Mining & Knowledge Discovery, 1*(2), 97–116. doi:10.1002/widm.10

Zhang, X., Mei, C., Ched, D., & Li, J. (2013). Multi-confidence rule acquisition oriented attribute reduction of covering decision systems via combinatorial optimization. *Knowledge-Based Systems*. doi:10.1016/j.knosys.2013.06.012

KEY TERMS AND DEFINITIONS

Complete Lattice: A hasse diagram of lattice structure in which there exist an infimum and a supremum for the elements together with the partial ordering in given elements called as complete lattice.

Concept Lattice: A complete lattice which represents the hierarchical ordering between the generated formal concepts from a given formal context which reflects specialization and Generalization between the concepts called as concept lattice.

Formal Concept Analysis: Formal Concept Analysis(FCA) is a mathematical order based on lattice theory which provides formal concept, concept lattice and attribute implication for knowledge discovery and representation task.

Formal Concept: Formal concept is a basic unit of thought for deriving the knowledge. Formal concept is a pair of set of objects and set of their properties closed with Galois connection called as extent and intent respectively.

Formal Context: Formal context is basic notion of FCA which represents set of objects, set of attributes and relation between them.

Galois Connection: Galois connection is a pair of mapping between two partial ordered sets satisfying monotone, antitone and idempotent conditions.

Knowledge Representation: Knowledge representation is an area of artificial intelligence which discuss the integration of knowledge, their consistency and efficient representation for their understandability by humans.

Section 3
Foundations of Computational Intelligence

Chapter 12
Heterogeneous Data Structure "r–Atrain"

Ranjit Biswas
Jamia Hamdard University, India

ABSTRACT

The data structure "r-Train" ("Train" in short) where r is a natural number is a new kind of powerful robust data structure that can store homogeneous data dynamically in a flexible way, in particular for large amounts of data. But a train cannot store heterogeneous data (by the term heterogeneous data, the authors mean data of various datatypes). In fact, the classical data structures (e.g., array, linked list, etc.) can store and handle homogeneous data only, not heterogeneous data. The advanced data structure "r-Atrain" ("Atrain" in short) is logically almost analogous to the data structure r-train (train) but with an advanced level of construction to accommodate heterogeneous data of large volumes. The data structure train can be viewed as a special case of the data structure atrain. It is important to note that none of these two new data structures is a competitor of the other. By default, any heterogeneous data structure can work as a homogeneous data structure too. However, for working with a huge volume of homogeneous data, train is more suitable than atrain. For working with heterogeneous data, atrain is suitable while train cannot be applicable. The natural number r is suitably predecided and fixed by the programmer depending upon the problem under consideration and also upon the organization/industry for which the problem is posed.

INTRODUCTION

Data structures are generally based on the ability of a computer to fetch and store data efficiently at any place in its memory. The data structures record and array are based on computing the addresses of data items with arithmetic operations; while the linked data structures are based on storing addresses of data items within the structure itself. Data structures can be classified in several ways, viz. Primitive/Non-primitive, Homogeneous/Heterogeneous, Static/Dynamic,

DOI: 10.4018/978-1-4666-4936-1.ch012

Linear/Non-linear, etc. The cost of memory space to store data using the data structure array is least. At the same time a basic demerit of using array is that it needs contiguous free bytes of memory which may not be always available if the array size is large, even if huge amount of free bytes be available in the memory at different locations. For example, at some point of time it may happen that 2^{20} number of free bytes available in the memory whereas 2^7 free contiguous bytes are not available. Consequently, an array of 65 positive integers can not be accommodated in the memory at this point of time, whereas a linked list of a large number of integers can be accommodated easily here. This is one of the basic advantages of using linked list. However, linked lists require more memory space compared to arrays because of an extra field in each node where address of the next node is stored. There are a number of useful data structures viz. Splay Trees and Dynamic Trees (Sleator & Tarjan, 1983; Sleator & Tarjan, 1985), hash table, AVL Trees (Velskii & Landis, 1962), B-Trees (Bayer & McCreight, 1972), Red-black trees (Bayer, 1972), Treaps (Seidel & Aragon, 1996), HAT (Sitarski, 1996), Graphs, Multigraphs (Biswas, Alam, & Doja, 2012; Biswas, Alam, & Doja, 2013), etc. developed by different authors for various purposes with different philosophy for different kind of requirements (one could see any good book for details viz. Aho, Hopcroft, & Ullman, 1983; Shaffer, 2001; Knuth, 1968; Lynch, 1996; Cormen, Leiserson, Rivest, & Stein, 2001). *There are some situations where we need to create an entirely new type of data structure of generalized nature, and creating such a new but simple data structure is not always a straightforward task.*

In this chapter we discuss about two new powerful data structures "r-Train" (or 'Train' in short) and "r-Atrain" (or "Atrain" in short) which are very suitable for storing huge volume of data. The natural number r is suitably pre-decided and fixed by the programmer depending upon the problem under consideration and also upon the organization/ industry for which the problem is posed.

While train stores homogeneous data, atrain is suitable for the purpose of storing heterogeneous data. The term "Atrain" is an abbreviation for "Advanced train". The two data structures r-train and r-atrain do not have any conflict of interest at all, although both are potential enough to accommodate huge volume of data. There is no competition between r-atrain and r-train in application areas, because r-train can not be applicable for heterogeneous data and r-atrain is not more suitable data structure than r-train if the data are homogeneous.

HOMOGENEOUS DATA STRUCTURE "r-TRAIN" (TRAIN)

The data structure 'r-train' (train, in short) is a new and a robust kind of dynamic homogeneous data structure which encapsulates the merits of the arrays and of the linked lists, and at the same time inherits a reduced amount of their characteristic demerits. By the nature 'dynamic' we mean that it changes over time, it is not like static. Apparently it may seem that the homogeneous data structure r-train is of hybrid nature, hybrid of linked list and array; but construction-wise (by virtue of its architecture) it is more. Using the data structure 'r-train', a large number of homogeneous data elements can be stored and basic operations like insertion/deletion/search can be executed very easily. In particular parallel programming can be done very easily in many situations with improved time complexities and performance efficiency. The notion of r-train is not a direct generalization of that of the linked lists. It is not just a linked list of arrays as it looks so, but something more. However, every linked list is an example of 1-train (i.e. r-train with r = 1). The main aim of introducing the data structure 'r-train' is how to store a large or very large array in memory in an alternative way successfully, and how to perform the fundamental operations of data structures efficiently while the data are huge in count. For small size arrays it is obvious that the data structure train should not be used as an alternative to array. One basic demerit of train inherited from the properties of array is that new data can not be inserted in between two existing consecutive data, because we preserve the unique index of each and every data which remains unaltered althrough the time. The data structure train dominates the data structures array, linked list, etc., in particular while dealing with huge volume of homogeneous data. It is neither a dynamic array (Goodrich, Kloss, & John, 1999) nor a HAT (Sitarski, 1996). To know about train, few useful terms and objects are to be understood as preliminaries first of all.

Larray

Larray is not a valid word in dictionary. Larray stands for "Like ARRAY". A larray is like an array of elements of identical datatype, where zero or more number of elements may be null element (i.e. no element, empty). Denote the null element by ε. Assuming that ε is of the same datatype, the memory space reserved for it will be same as that required by any other element of the larray. The number of elements (including ε) in a larray is called the length of the larray.

Example of larrays :-

1. $a = < 5, 2, \varepsilon, 13, 25, \varepsilon, 2, >$
2. $b = < 6, 9, 8>$
3. $c = <\varepsilon>$
4. $d = <\varepsilon, \varepsilon, \varepsilon, \varepsilon>$
5. $e = < 2.8, \varepsilon, \varepsilon, \varepsilon, \varepsilon >$
6. $f = < >$, which is called empty larray.

If all the elements of a larray are ε, then it is called a null larray. Any null larray is denoted by θ. Clearly θ could be of any length (any non-negative integer) and hence null larray is not unique. As a special instance, the empty larray f above is also a null larray of length 0(zero), i.e. with 0(zero) number of ε elements. But empty larray and null larray are not the same concept in our work here. Empty larray is a unique object unlike null larray. In our theory, an object like k $= < , , , >$ is an undefined object and hence should not be confused with empty larray or null larray .

In the above examples, the larrays c and d are null larrays, but e is not. The larray f is empty larray but c, d are not. It is obvious that two distinct larrays may contain ε elements of different datatypes, because ε elements of a larray are of the same datatype analogous to that of the non-ε elements of that larray (by virtue of its construction). For example, each ε element in the larray a above requires 2 bytes in memory, whereas each ε element in the larray e above requires 4 bytes in memory. Similarly, each ε element in the larray d above requires as many bytes as defined at the time of creation of d. But for the case of larray d, we can not extract any idea about the datatype of the ε elements of d just by looking at it. In such case we must have information from outside. By using the name z of a larray z, we do also mean the address of the larray z in the memory, analogous to the case in arrays.

Coach of a r-Train

By a coach C we mean a pair (A,**e**) where A is a non-empty larray (could be a null larray) and **e** is an address in the memory. Here **e** is basically a kind of link address. Its significance is that it says the address of the next coach, and thus it links two coaches. If the coach C is a single coach or the last coach then the address field **e** will be put equal to an invalid address, otherwise **e** will be the address of the next coach. There is no confusion in differentiating the two objects **e** and ε. *In fact, a possible value of* **e** *can never be* ε *for any* coach.

A coach can be easily stored in memory where the data **e** resides next to the last element of the larray A in the memory. Logical diagram of a coach of r-train is available at subsequent pages in Figures 1, 2, 3, 4, 5, and 6.

Figure 1. A 3-train with 3 coaches

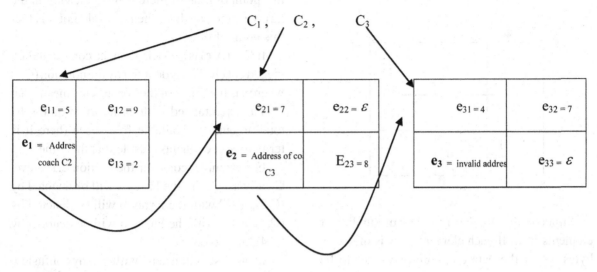

Figure 2. A r-train with 50 coaches

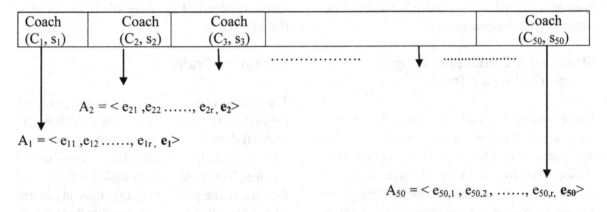

Figure 3. A coach C_i of a 11-train

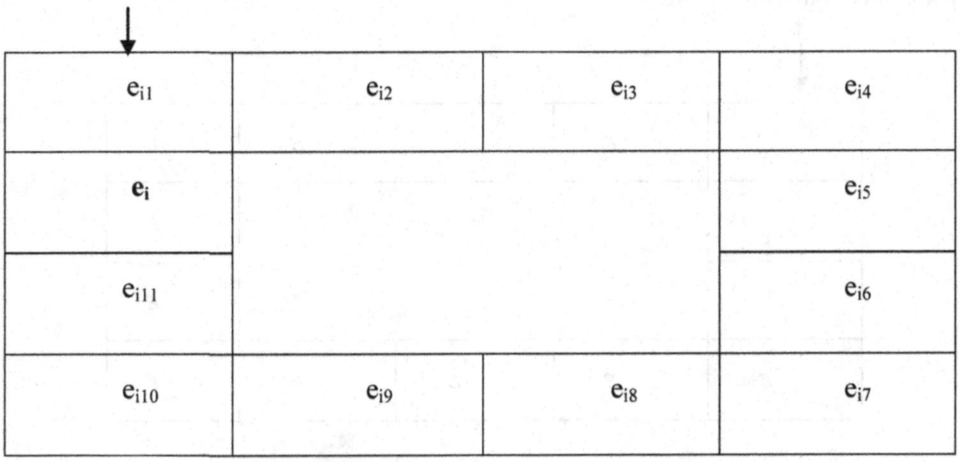

e_{i1}	e_{i2}	e_{i3}	e_{i4}
e_i			e_{i5}
e_{i11}			e_{i6}
e_{i10}	e_{i9}	e_{i8}	e_{i7}

Figure 4. A full coach of a 7-train

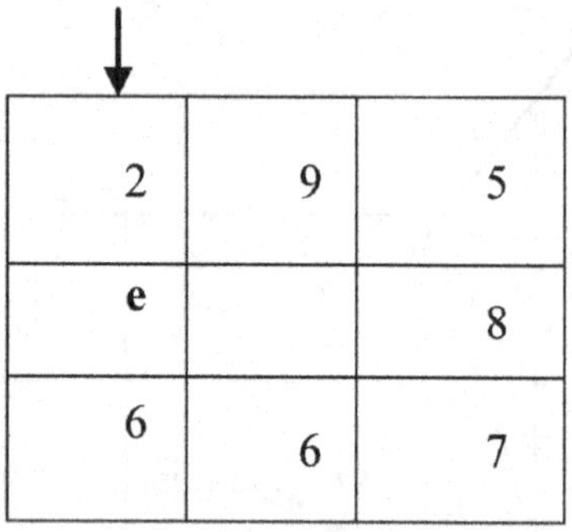

2	9	5
e		8
6	6	7

Suppose that the larray A has m number of elements in it. If each element of A is of size x bytes and if the data **e** require two bytes to be stored in memory, then to store the coach C in memory, exactly $(m.x + 2)$ number of consecutive bytes are required, and accordingly the coach be created by the programmer.

Status of a Coach and Tagged Coach (TC) of a r-Train

The status s of a coach is a non-negative integer variable which is equal to the number of ε elements present in it (i.e. in its larray) at this point of time. Therefore, $0 \leq s \leq r$. The significance of the variable s is that it informs us about the exact number of free spaces available in the coach at this point of time. If there is no ε element in the larray of the coach C, then the value of s is 0 at this point of time.

If $C = (A,\mathbf{e})$ is a coach, then the corresponding tagged coach (TC) is denoted by the notation (C,s) where s is the status of the coach. This means that C is a coach tagged with an information on the total amount of available free space (here it is termed as ε elements) inside it at this time.

For example, consider the section 2.1 above. Clearly a TC with the larray a will be denoted by $(C,2)$, a TC with the larray b will be denoted by $(C,0)$, a TC with the larray d will be denoted by $(C,4)$, and so on.

In our discussion here, without any confusion, the two statements "there is no ε element in the larray" and "there is no ε element in the coach" will have identical meaning where the larray is that of the coach.

r-Train (or Train)

The data structure 'r-train' is a new powerful, robust, and flexible homogeneous which is very useful if there are large number of homogeneous data. A r-train is basically a linked list of tagged coaches. This linked list is called the 'pilot' of the r-train. The pilot of a train is thus, in general, a linked list. But, if we are sure that there will be

Figure 5. An empty coach of a 13-train

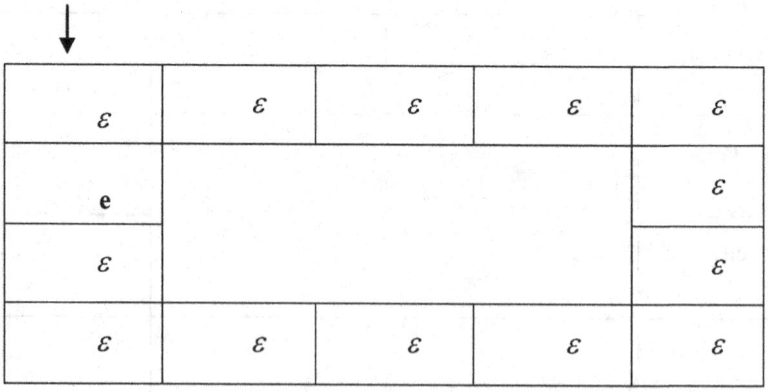

ε	ε	ε	ε	ε
e				ε
ε				ε
ε	ε	ε	ε	ε

Figure 6. A coach of a 7-train which is neither empty nor full

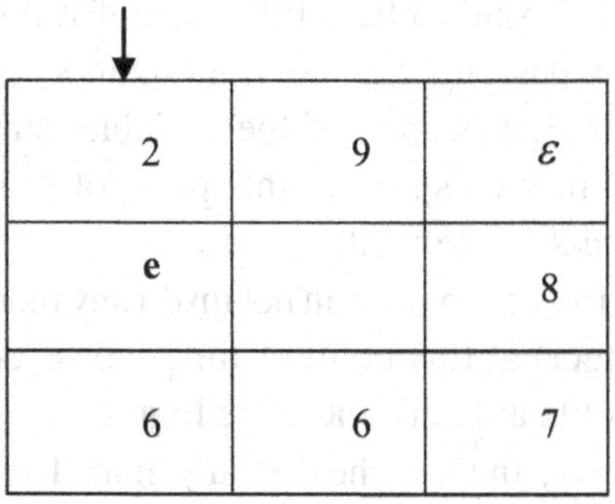

2	9	ε
e		8
6	6	7

no requirement of any extra coach in future, then it is better to implement pilot as an array.

The number of coaches in a r-train is called the 'length' of the r-train which may increase or decrease time to time. A 'r-train' may also be called by the name 'train' if there is no confusion.

A r-train T of length l (> 0) will be denoted by the following notation:

$$T = <(C_1, s_{C1}), (C_2, s_{C2}), (C_3, s_{C3}), \ldots \ldots, (C_l, s_{Cl}) >,$$

where the coach C_i is (A_i, e_i) with A_i being a larray of length r, e_i being the address of the next coach C_{i+1} (or an invalid address in case C_i is the last coach) and s_{Ci} being the status of the coach C_i, for i = 1, 2, 3, ..., l.

For a r-train, START is the address of the pilot (viewing its implementation in memory as a linked list). Thus START points at the data C_1 in memory. The length l of the pilot could be any natural number, but the larrays of the TCs are each of fixed length r which store data elements (including ε elements) of common datatype where r is a natural number. Thus, by name, 1-train, 60-train, 75-train, 100-train, etc. are few instances of r-train, where the term 0-train is undefined.

The notion of the data structure r-train is a new but very simple data structure, a type of 2-tier data structure, having very convenient methods of executing various fundamental operations like insertion, deletion, searching etc., for huge number of data, in particular for parallel computing. The most important characteristic of the data structure r-train is that it is likely that it can store x number of elements of identical datatype even if an array of size x of same elements can not be stored in memory, at some moment of time. And also, the data can be well accessed by using the indices.

In a r-train, the coach names $C_1, C_2, C_3, \ldots \ldots,$ C_l do also mean the addresses (pointers) serially numbered like in case of arrays, for example: the array z = (5, 9, 3, 2) can be easily accessed by calling its name z only.

Status of a coach in the data structure r-train reflects the availability of a seat (i.e. whether a data element can be stored in this coach now or not). Status may vary with time. Each coach of a r-train can accommodate exactly r number of data elements serially numbered, each data element being called a passenger. Thus each coach of a r-train points at a larray of r number of passengers. *By definition, the data e_i is not a passenger for any i.*

Consider a coach $C_i = (A_i, e_i)$. In the larray $A_i = <e_{i1}, e_{i2}, e_{i3}, \ldots \ldots \ldots, e_{i(r-1)}, e_{ir}>$, the data element e_{ij} is called the "j th passenger" or "j th data element" for j = 1, 2, 3, 4,..., r. Thus we can view a r-train as a linked list of larrays. Starting from any coach, one can visit the inside of all the next coaches but not any of the previous coaches. The r-train is a forward linear object, not a type of circular one. It is neither a dynamic array nor a HAT. It has an added advantage over HAT that starting from one data element, all the next data elements can be read well without referring to any hash table or the pilot.

Example

Any linked list is a 1-train where each coach is having a common status equal to zero (as each coach accommodates one and only one passenger).

However the converse is not necessarily true, i.e. if each coach of a train is having status 0, it does not necessarily mean that the train is a 1-train (linked list). The notion of 1-train is not a generalization of 'linked list'.

Example

Consider a 3-train T of length 3 given by

$$T = < (C_1, 0), (C_2, 1), (C_3, 1) >,$$

where $C_1 = < 5, 9, 2, e_1 >$, and $C_2 = < 7, \varepsilon, 8, e_2 >$, and

$$C_3 = < 4, 7, \varepsilon,$$

an invalid-address $>$.

Here e_1 is the address of coach C_2 (i.e. address of larray A_2), and e_2 is the address of coach C_3 (i.e. address of larray A_3). Since it is a 3-train, each coach C_i can accommodate exactly three passenger (including ε element, if any).

In coach C_1, the larray is $A_1 = <5, 9, 2>$ which means that the first passenger is the integer 5, second passenger is the integer 9, and the last/third passenger is the integer 2; the data e_1 being the address of the next coach C_2. Thus, T is a larray of three TCs which are $(C_1, 0)$, $(C_2, 1)$, and $(C_3, 1)$.

The logical diagram of the above mentioned 3-train T is shown in Figure 1 where data in coaches are to be read clockwise starting from e_{11} for the coach C_1, from e_{21} for the coach C_2, from e_{31} for the coach C_3.

Figure 2 shows a r-train with 50 coaches.

Figure 3 shows one coach (ith coach) of a 11-train, where data are to be read clockwise starting from e_{i1}.

Full Coach in a r-Train

A coach is said to be a full coach if it does not have any passenger ε, i.e. if its status s is 0. The physical significance of the variable 'status' is "availability of space at this point of time" for storing a data element.

In a full coach, we can not insert any more data (passenger) at this point of time (however, may be possible at later time). See Figure 4.

Clearly, the coaches of any linked list (i.e. 1-train) are all full, and always full.

Empty Coach in a r-Train

A coach is said to be an empty coach if every passenger of it is ε, i.e. if the corresponding larray is a null larray.

Thus for an empty coach of a r-train, the status is equal to r. A coach may be sometimes neither empty nor full (see Figure 6).

A r-Train in Memory

Consider the data : 9.2, 2.4, 5.8, 1.4, 7.8, 6.5, 7.8, 4.3, 2.9, 6.8, 7.1 which are stored in the Data Segment of the 8086 memory using the data structure 3-train, as shown below, starting from START = 0A02h :-

The above 3-train is $T = < (10A5h, 0), (BA98h, 0), (00ADh, 0), (E49Bh, 1) >$ which is of length 4 where the coach C_1 begins from the address 10A5h, the coach C_2 begins from the address BA98h, the coach C_3 begins from the address 00ADh, the coach C_4 begins from the address E49Bh. Here START = 0A02h, i.e. the pilot of this 3-train is stored at the address 0A02h. Also in this example, the pilot is implemented as an array, not using linked list.

Table 1. A r-Train in 8086 memory

Address	Memory Content	Size
	X (an invalid Address)	2 bytes
	ε	4 bytes
	7.1	4 bytes
E49Bh	6.8	4 bytes
	00AD h	2 bytes
	6.5	4 bytes
	7.8	4 bytes
BA98h	1.4	4 bytes
	BA98 h	2 bytes
	5.8	4 bytes
	2.4	4 bytes
10A5h	9.2	4 bytes
	1	2 bytes
0A0Dh	C_4 = E49b h	2 bytes
	0	2 bytes
C_3 = 0A0Ah	C_3 = 00AD h	2 bytes
	0	2 bytes
0A06h	C_2 = BA98 h	2 bytes
	0	2 bytes
START = 0A02h	C_1 = 10A5 h	2 bytes
	E49B h	2 bytes
	2.9	4 bytes
	4.3	4 bytes
00ADh	7.8	4 bytes

FUNDAMENTAL OPERATIONS ON THE DATA STRUCTURE 'R-TRAIN'

The two fundamental operations on the data structure r-train are 'insertion' and 'deletion' which are defined below:

Insertion

There are two types of insertion operation in the data structure r-train: -

1. Insertion (addition) of a new coach in a r-train.
2. Insertion of a data element (passenger) in a coach of a r-train.

1. Insertion of a New Coach in a r-Train

Insertion of a new coach can be done at the end of the pilot, nowhere else. Consider the r-train T = < (C_1, s_{C1}), (C_2, s_{C2}), (C_3, s_{C3}), ..., (C_k, s_{Ck}) >, with k number of coaches, where the coach C_i = (A_i, e_i) for i = 1, 2, 3, ..., k.

After insertion of a new coach, the updated r-train immediately becomes the following r-train:

$$T = <(C_1, s_{C1}), (C_2, s_{C2}), (C_3, s_{C3}), ..., (C_k, s_{Ck}), (C_{k+1}, r)>.$$

Initially at the time of insertion, we create C_{K+1} as an empty coach (i.e. with status = r) which is likely to get filled-up with non-ε passengers (data) later on with time.

For insertion of a new coach C_{K+1} in a r-train, we need to do the following: -

1. Update the pilot (linked list)
2. e_k in C_k is to be updated and to be made equal to the address C_{K+1}
3. Set $e_{k+1, j} = \varepsilon$ for j = 1, 2, ..., r
4. Set e_{k+1} = an invalid address.
5. Set s_{Ck+1} = r.

2. Insertion of an Element X Inside the Coach Ci = (A_i, e_i) of a r-Train

Insertion of an element (a new passenger) x inside the coach C_i is feasible if x is of same datatype (like other passengers of the coach) and if there is an empty space available inside the coach C_i. *If status of C_j is greater than 0 then data can be stored successfully in the coach, otherwise insertion operation fails here. After each successful insertion, the status s of the coach is to be updated by doing $s = s – 1$.*

For insertion of x, we can replace the lowest indexed passenger ε of C_i with x.

Deletion

There are two types of deletion operation in the data structure r-train: -

1.   Deletion of a data element ($\neq \varepsilon$) from any coach of the r-train.
2.   Deletion of the last coach C_i, if it is an empty coach, from a r-train.

1. Deletion of a Data e_{ij} ($\neq \varepsilon$) from the Coach C_i of a r-Train

Deletion of e_i from the coach C_i is not allowed as it is the link. But we can delete a data element e_{ij} from the coach C_i. Deletion of a data (passenger) from a coach means replacement of the data by an ε element (of same datatype). Consequently, if $e_{ij} = \varepsilon$, then the question of deletion does not arise. Here it is pre-assumed that e_{ij} is a non-ε member element of the coach C_i .

For $j = 1, 2, ……, r$, deletion of e_{ij} is done by replacing it by the null element ε , and updating the status s by doing $s = s+1$. Deletion of a data element (passenger) does not effect the size r of the coach.

For example, consider the tagged coach (C_i, m) where

$$C_i = < e_{i1}, e_{i2}, e_{i3}, e_{i4,................}, e_{ir} > .$$

If we delete e_{i3} from the coach C_i then the updated tagged coach will be $(C_i, m+1)$ where

$$C_i = < e_{i1}, e_{i2}, \varepsilon, e_{i4},......, e_{ir} >$$

2. Deletion of the Last Coach C_i from a r-Train

Deletion of coaches from a r-train is allowed from the last coach only and in backward direction, one after another. An interim coach can not be deleted.

The last coach C_i can be deleted if it is an empty coach (as shown in Figure 7).

If the last coach is not empty, it can not be deleted unless its all the passengers are deleted to make it empty.

To delete the empty last coach C_i of a r-train, we have to do the following actions: -

1.   Update e_{i-1} of the coach C_{i-1} by storing an invalid address in it.
2.   Delete (C_i, r) from the r-train

$$T = < (C_1, s_{C1}), (C_2, s_{C2}), (C_3, s_{C3}), ..., (C_{i-1}, s_{Ci-1}), (C_i, r) >,$$

and get the updated r-train

$$T = < (C_1, s_{C1}), (C_2, s_{C2}), (C_3, s_{C3}), ..., (C_{i-1}, s_{Ci-1}) > .$$

3.   Update the pilot.

Searching for a Passenger (Data) in a r-Train of Length k

Searching a data x in a r-train T is very easy.

Figure 7. An empty last coach of a 9-train which can be deleted

ε	ε	ε	ε
invalid address			ε
ε	ε	ε	ε

1. If we know in advance the coach number Ci of the passenger x, then visiting the pilot we can enter into the coach Ci of the r-train directly and then can read the data-elements ei1, ei2, …….., eir of the larray Ai for a match with x.

2. If we do not know the coach, then we start searching from the coach C1 onwards till the last coach. We need not go back to the pilot for any help. Here lies an important dominance of the data structure r-train over the data structure HAT introduced by Sitarski (1996).

In case of multi processor system the searching can be done in parallel very fast, which is obvious from the physiology of the data structure r-train.

In the next section, the notion of the heterogeneous data structure 'r-Atrain' (Atrain) is introduced.

r-ATRAIN (ATRAIN): A POWERFUL HETEROGENEOUS DATA STRUCTURE

In a homogeneous data structure the data elements considered are all of the same datatype, like in array, linked list, r-train, etc. In a heterogeneous data structure data elements are of various datatypes as in a 'structure'. In this section an upgradation of the homogeneous data structure r-Train is introduced which is a new but heterogeneous data structure 'r-Atrain'. The term "Atrain" stands for the phrase 'Advanced train', because in the construction of r-Atrain we incorporate few advanced features (not available in r-train) which make it suitable to deal with heterogeneous data, in particular while there are a large volume of heterogeneous data. The data structure r-Atrain is not a substitute or a competitor of the data structure r-train to the programmers or developers. For working with homogeneous data, r-train is suitable while r-atrain is not. But for working with heterogeneous data, r-atrain is

suitable while r-train can not be applicable. The term "train" has been coined from the usual railways transportation systems because of a lot of similarities in nature of the object r-train with the actual train of railways systems; and analogously the terms coach, passenger, availability of seats, etc. were used in the way of constructing the data structure r-train.

Now, let us think of more reality here. In railways transport system we see that in most of the trains one or more coaches are created for pantry, one or more coaches are for accommodating postal mails, one or more are for accommodating booked luggage, one or more are for accommodating goods, one or more exclusively for ladies, etc. and most of the coaches are for accommodating passengers. Different coaches are there for accommodating different types of contents, i.e. for accommodating heterogeneous types of contents. With this real example, it is encouraged to develop a new data structure 'r-Atrain' where coaches may accommodate data of various datatypes, but no coach is allowed to accommodate data of different datatypes. The datatype in a r-atrain may vary from coach to coach (unlike in r-train), but in a coach all data must be homogeneous i.e. of identical datatype. Thus each coach is homogeneous although the atrain is heterogeneous.

Before proceeding to introduce 'r-atrain', few terminologies needs to be defined:

Code of a Datatype and CD-Table

A table is to be created by the concerned organization to fix integer code for each datatype under use in the organization. This is not an absolute set of codes to be followed universally by every organization, but it is a local document for the concerned organization. For different organizations, this table could be different. But once it is fixed by an organization it should not be altered by this organization, except that addition of new datatypes and corresponding codes may be decided and be incorporated in the table at any stages later retaining the existing records. This table is called Code of Datatype Table or CD-Table (in short).

A sample CD-Table of a hypothetical organization is shown below for the sake of understanding:-

It may be noted that for the datatypes character, integer, boolean, etc. the space requirement is known to us as it is absolutely fixed, whereas for the datatype string (appearing twice in this case) the space requirement has been fixed at 20 bytes for one kind and 12 bytes for another kind, fixed by the choice of the concerned organization (developers).

Coach of a r-Atrain

By a coach C of a r-atrain we mean a pair (A,e) where A is a non-empty larray (could be a null larray) and e is an address in the memory. Here e is basically a kind of link address. Its significance is that it says the address of the next coach, and thus it links two coaches in the r-atrain. If the coach C is a single coach or the last coach then the address field e will be put equal to an invalid address, otherwise e will be the address of the next coach.

A coach can be easily stored in memory where the data e resides next to the last element

Table 2. An example of a CD Table of an organization

Sr. No.	Datatype	Space Required in Bytes (n)	Code of Datatype (c)
1	Character	1	0
2	Integer	2	1
3	Real	4	2
4	String	20	3
5	String	12	4
6	String	8	5
7	....	....	....
8	....	....	....
9	....	....	....

of the larray A in the memory. Logical diagram of a coach in a r-atrain is available at subsequent pages in Figures 8, 9, 10, 11, 12, and 13 (few instances only). A coach in a r-atrain can store homogeneous data only, not heterogeneous data. But different coaches of a r-atrain store data elements of different datatypes, and thus the data structure r-atrain is a kind of heterogeneous data structure. For constructing a coach for a r-atrain in an organization, we must know in advance the datatype of the data to be stored in it. For this we have to look at the CD-Table of the organization, and reserve space accordingly for r number of data.

Suppose that the larray A has r number of elements in it of a given datatype. If each element of A is of size x bytes (refer to CD-Table) and if the data e requires two bytes to be stored in memory, then to store the coach C in memory exactly (r.x + 2) number of consecutive bytes are required, and accordingly the coach be created by the programmer (concerned organization). In our discussion henceforth, by the phrase "datatype of a coach" we shall always mean the datatype of the data elements of the coach. A coach stores and can store only homogeneous data (i.e. data of identical datatype), but datatype may be different for different coaches in a r-atrain. And in this way a r-atrain can accommodate heterogeneous data of large volume.

Status of a Coach and Tagged Coach (TC) in a r-Atrain

The status s of a coach in a r-atrain is a pair of information (c, n), where c is a non-negative integer variable which is the code of datatype (with reference to the concerned CD-Table) of the data to be stored in this coach and n is a non-negative integer variable which is equal to the number of ε elements present in it (i.e. in its larray) at this point of time. Therefore, $0 \leq n \leq r$. In the status s = (c, n) of a coach, the information c is called the "code-status" of the coach and the information n is called the "availability-status" of the coach

Figure 8. A 3-atrain with 3 coaches

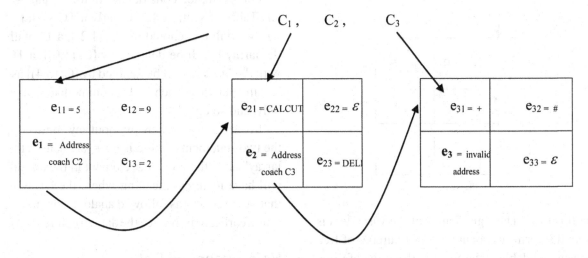

Figure 9. A r-atrain with 50 coaches

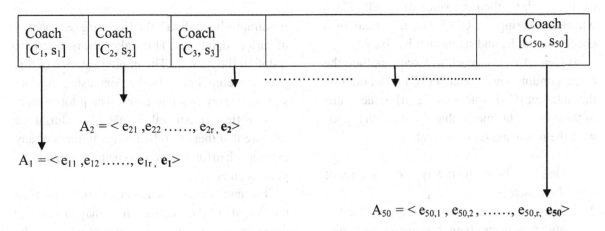

Figure 10. A coach C_i of a 11-atrain

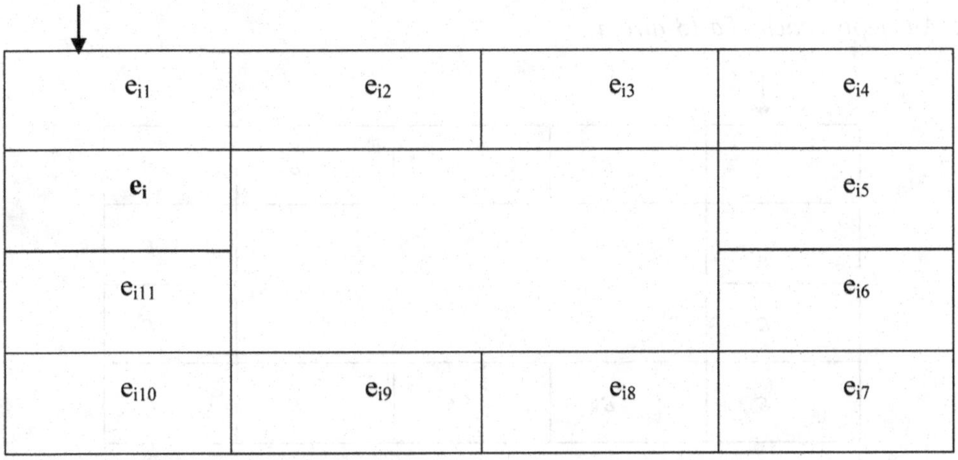

e_{i1}	e_{i2}	e_{i3}	e_{i4}
e_i			e_{i5}
e_{i11}			e_{i6}
e_{i10}	e_{i9}	e_{i8}	e_{i7}

Figure 11. A full coach of a 7-atrain

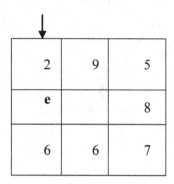

2	9	5
e		8
6	6	7

at this time. The significance of the variable n is that it informs us about the exact number of free spaces available in the coach at this point of time. If there is no ε element at this time in the larray of the coach C, then the value of n is 0. Thus, without referring the CD-Table, the status of a coach can not be and should not be fixed.

If C = (A,**e**) is a coach in a r-atrain, then the corresponding tagged coach (TC) is denoted by the notation [C,s], where s = (c, n) is the status of the coach. This means that C is a coach tagged with the following two information:

1. One signifying the datatype of the data of the coach.
2. The other reflects the total amount of available free spaces (here it is termed as ε elements) inside the coach at this time.

For example, consider section-2.1 and the CD-Table of section-4.1. Clearly a TC with the larray a will be denoted by [C, (1,2)], a TC with the larray b will be denoted by [C, (1,0)], a TC with the larray d will be denoted by [C, (3,4)] assuming that this coach will accommodate strings only, and so on.

In our discussion here, without any confusion, the two statements "there is no ε element in the larray" and "there is no ε element in the coach" will have identical meaning where the larray is that of the coach (as followed analogously in section-2 earlier to introduce the data structure train).

Heterogeneous Data Structure r-Atrain

A r-atrain is basically a linked list of tagged coaches of various datatypes. This linked list is called the 'pilot' of the r-atrain. The implementation of this pilot in memory can also be done using the data structure array in some cases. The pilot of an r-atrain is thus, in general, a linked list. But, if we are sure that there will be no requirement of any extra coach in future, then it is better to implement pilot as an array.

The number of coaches in a r-atrain is called the 'length' of the r-atrain which may increase or decrease time to time. A 'r-atrain' may also be called by the name 'atrain', if there is no confusion.

Figure 12. An empty coach of a 13-atrain

ε	ε	ε	ε	ε
e				ε
ε				ε
ε	ε	ε	ε	ε

Figure 13. A coach of a 7-atrain which is neither empty nor full

CALCUTTA	BOMBAY	ε
e		MADRAS
PUNE	BANGALORE	DELHI

An r-atrain T of length l (> 0) will be denoted by the following notation

$$T = <[C_1, s_{C1}], [C_2, s_{C2}], [C_3, s_{C3}], \ldots, [C_l, s_{Cl}]>,$$

where the coach C_i is (A_i, e_i) with A_i being a larray of length r, e_i being the address of the next coach C_{i+1} (or an invalid address in case C_i is the last coach) and s_{Ci} being the status (c_i, n_i) of the coach C_i, for i = 1, 2, 3, ..., l.

For a r-atrain, START is the address of the pilot (viewing its implementation in memory as a linked list). Thus START points at the coach C_1 in memory. The length l of the pilot could be any natural number, but the larrays of the TCs are each of fixed length r which store data elements (including ε elements) of heterogeneous datatype, although each coach itself can accommodate homogeneous data only, not heterogeneous data, where r is a natural number. Thus, by name, 1-atrain, 40-atrain, 64-atrain, 150-atrain, etc. are few instances of r-atrain, where the term 0-atrain is undefined.

The notion of the heterogeneous data structure r-atrain is a new but very simple data structure, a type of 2-tier data structure, having very convenient methods of executing various fundamental operations like insertion, deletion, searching etc. for huge number of heterogeneous data, in particular for parallel computing. The most important characteristic of the data structure r-atrain is that it is likely that it can store x number of elements of identical datatype (besides storing data elements of other datatypes) even if an array of size x of same data elements can not be stored in memory, at some moment of time.

In a r-atrain, the data can be well accessed by using the indices. The coach names C_1, C_2, C_3, ..., C_l do also mean the addresses (pointers) serially numbered as in case of arrays, for example:- the array z = (5, 9, 3, 2) can be easily accessed calling by its name z only.

The second information in the status of a coach is a dynamic information which reflects the availability of a seat (i.e. whether a valid data element can be stored now in this coach or not) while the first information is always static but can be different for different coaches. The first information 'code-status' of a coach does never alter by virtue of the construction principle of a coach, but the status of this coach may vary with time as the second information 'availability-status' may vary with time dynamically. Every coach of a r-atrain can accommodate exactly r number of homogeneous data elements serially numbered, each data element being called a passenger. Thus each coach of a r-atrain points at a larray of r number of passengers. *By definition, the data e_i is not a passenger for any i.*

Consider a coach $C_i = (A_i, e_i)$ of a r-atrain. In the larray $A_i = <e_{i1}, e_{i2}, e_{i3}, \ldots, e_{i(r-1)}, e_{ir}>$, the data element e_{ij} is called the "j th passenger" or "j th data element" for j = 1, 2, 3, 4,..., r. Thus we can view a r-atrain as a linked list of heterogeneous larrays. Starting from any coach, one can visit the inside of all the next coaches but not any of the previous coaches. The r-atrain is a forward linear object, not a type of circular one. It is neither a dynamic array nor a HAT. It has an added advantage over HAT that starting from one data element, all the next data elements can be read well without referring to any hash table or the pilot.

Example

Any linked list is a 1-atrain where the coaches are having a common status (c, 0), c being the code of the datatype. But the notion of 1-atrain is not a generalization of 'linked list'. It may be mentioned here that, by default, any heterogeneous data structure can be used as a homogeneous data structure, although not preferred in general.

Example

Refer to the CD-Table of section-4.1. Consider a 3-atrain T of length 3 given by

$$T = < [C_1, (1,0)], [C_2, (3,1)], [C_3, (0,1)] >,$$

where

$$C_1 = < 5, 9, 2, \mathbf{e}_1 >,$$

and

$$C_2 = < CALCUTTA, \varepsilon, DELHI, \mathbf{e}_2 >,$$

and

$$C_3 = < +, \#, \varepsilon,$$

an invalid-address >.

Here $\mathbf{e}_1$ is the address of the coach C_2 (i.e. address of larray A_2) in this 3-atrain, and $\mathbf{e}_2$ is the address of the coach C_3 (i.e. address of larray A_3). Since it is a 3-atrain, each coach C_i can accommodate exactly three passenger (including ε elements, if any).

In coach C_1, the status is (1, 0) which means that this coach can accommodate data of integer datatype (with reference to the CD-Table) and there is no free space in this coach at this point of time. The larray is A_1 = <5, 9, 2> which means that the first passenger is the integer 5, second passenger is the integer 9, and the last/ third passenger is the integer 2; the data $\mathbf{e}_1$ be-

ing the address of the next coach C_2. Thus, T is a larray of three TCs which are $[C_1, (1,0)]$, $[C_2, (3,1)]$ and $[C_3, (0,1)]$. The logical diagram of this 3-atrain T is shown in Figure 8 where data in coaches are to be read clockwise starting from e_{11} for the coach C_1, from e_{21} for the coach C_2, from e_{31} for the coach C_3.

Figure 9 shows a r-atrain with 50 number of coaches.

Figure 10 shows one coach (ith coach) of a 11-atrain, where data are to be read clockwise starting from e_{i1}

Full Coach in a r-Atrain

A coach in a r-atrain is said to be a full coach if it does not have any passenger ε, i.e. if its status s is (c, 0) where c is the code of its datatype.

In a full coach, we can not insert (insertion operation is explained in later section here) any more data (passenger) at this point of time (however, may be possible at later point of time). See Figure 11.

It is a full coach of a 7-atrain with status (1,0) as per CD-Table of section-4.1. Clearly, the coaches of any linked list (which is a 1-atrain) are all full, and always full.

Empty Coach in a r-Atrain

A coach in a r-atrain is said to be an empty coach if every passenger of it is ε, i.e. if the corresponding larray is a null larray.

Thus for an empty coach of a r-atrain, the status is equal to (c,r). A coach may be sometimes neither empty nor full (see Figure 13).

A r-Atrain in Memory

Refer to the CD-Table of section-4.1. Consider the data : 9.2, 2.4, 5.8, CALCUTTA, DELHI, BOMBAY, t, +, *, 6, 7 which are stored in the Data Segment of the 8086 memory using the data structure 3-atrain, as shown below starting from START = 0A02h. This is a 3-atrain T = < [10A5h, (2,0)], [BA98h, (3,0)], [00ADh, (0,0)], [E49Bh, (1,1)] > which is of length 4 where the coach C_1 begins from the address 10A5h, the coach C_2 begins from the address BA98h, the coach C_3 begins from the address 00ADh, the coach C_4 begins from the address E49Bh. Here START = 0A02h, i.e. the pilot of this 3-atrain is stored at the address 0A02h. Also in this example, the pilot is implemented as an array, not using linked list. However, for a big size pilot linked list representation may be preferred.

FUNDAMENTAL OPERATIONS ON THE DATA STRUCTURE 'r-ATRAIN'

The two fundamental operations on the data structure r-atrain (atrain) are 'insertion' and 'deletion' which are defined below:

Insertion

There are three types of insertion operation in the data structure r-atrain: -

1. Insertion (addition) of a new coach in a r-atrain.
2. Insertion of a data element (passenger) in a given coach of a r-atrain.
3. Insertion of a data element (passenger) in a r-atrain.

1. Insertion of a New Coach in a r-Atrain

Insertion of a new coach can be done at the end of the pilot, nowhere else. The first job is to decide about the datatype of the coach which is required now to be inserted.

Table 3. A r-atrain in 8086 memory

Address	Memory Content	Size
	X (an invalid Address)	2 bytes
	ε	2 bytes
	7	2 bytes
E49Bh	6	2 bytes
	00AD h	2 bytes
	BOMBAY	20 bytes
	DELHI	20 bytes
BA98h	CALCUTTA	20 bytes
	BA98 h	2 bytes
	5.8	4 bytes
	2.4	4 bytes
10A5h	9.2	4 bytes
	1	2 bytes
	1	2 bytes
0A0Dh	C_4 = E49b h	2 bytes
	0	2 bytes
	0	2 bytes
C_3 = 0A0Ah	C_3 = 00AD h	2 bytes
	0	2 bytes
	3	2 bytes
0A06h	C_2 = BA98 h	2 bytes
	0	2 bytes
	2	2 bytes
START = 0A02h	C_1 = 10A5 h	2 bytes
	E49B h	2 bytes
	*	1 byte
	+	1 byte
00ADh	T	1 byte

353

Consider the r-atrain $T = < [C_1, s_{C1}], [C_2, s_{C2}], [C_3, s_{C3}], ..., [C_k, s_{Ck}] >$, with k number of coaches, where the coach $C_i = (A_i, e_i)$ for i = 1, 2, 3, ..., k.

After insertion of a new additional coach, the updated r-atrain immediately becomes the following r-atrain:

$T = < [C_1, s_{C1}], [C_2, s_{C2}], [C_3, s_{C3}], ..., [C_k, s_{Ck}], [C_{k+1}, r] >$.

Initially at the time of insertion, we create C_{K+1} as an empty coach with status = (c,r) where c is the code of the intended datatype of the coach and since the new coach is empty therefore the number of available space is r at this time, but the coach is likely to get filled-up with non-ε passengers (data) later on with time.

For insertion of a new coach C_{K+1} in a r-atrain, we need to do the following steps: -

1. Read the CD-Table for the code c of the datatype of the new coach intended for insertion. If the code c is not available in the CD-Table, expand CD-Table accordingly.
2. Update the pilot (linked list).
3. e_k in C_k is to be updated and to be made equal to the address C_{K+1}.
4. Set $e_{k+1,j} = \varepsilon$ for j = 1, 2, ..., r
5. Set e_{k+1} = an invalid address.
6. Set $s_{Ck+1} = (c,r)$.

2. Insertion of an Element X Inside the Coach Ci = (A_i, e_i) of a r-Atrain

Insertion of an element (a new passenger) x inside the coach C_i is feasible if x is of same datatype (like other passengers of the coach C_i) and if there is an empty space available inside the coach C_i. If the availability-status n of C_i is greater than 0 then data can be stored successfully in this coach, otherwise insertion operation fails here at this

moment of time. For insertion of x, we can replace the lowest indexed passenger ε of C_i with x.

After each successful insertion, the availability-status n of the coach is to be updated by doing n = n − 1, and thus by updating the status $S_{Ci} = (c,n)$ by its new value given by $S_{Ci} = (c,n-1)$.

3. Insertion of an Element X in a r-Atrain

In this case too, the code c (with reference to the CD-Table) corresponding to the datatype of the data x plays an important role in the process of insertion. An initial search is done for the coaches (starting from C_1 onwards) which are having the same code c in their status. Suppose that, the array of the code-matched coaches so extracted from the pilot is

$Z = (\varsigma_1, \varsigma_2, \varsigma_3, ... \varsigma_t)$.

If the array Z is a null array or if the availability-status is zero for each and every member of Z, then the insertion operation is to be done by inserting a new coach C_μ, first of all, as per steps mentioned above in sub-section 5.1.1 and then by performing the insertion operation as per steps mentioned above in sub-section 5.1.2.

Otherwise we find out the coach ς_k in Z with lowest index k for which the availability-status n is > 0, and then perform the insertion operation as per steps mentioned in sub-section 5.1.2 above.

Deletion

There are two types of deletion operation in the data structure r-atrain: -

1. Deletion of a data element ($\neq \varepsilon$) from any coach of the r-atrain.
2. Deletion of the last coach C_i, if it is an empty coach, from a r-atrain.

1. Deletion of a Data e_{ij} ($\neq \varepsilon$) from the Coach C_i of a r-Atrain

Deletion of e_i from the coach C_i is not allowed as it is the link. But we can delete a data element e_{ij} from the coach C_i. Deletion of a data (passenger) from a coach means replacement of the data by an ε element (of same datatype). Consequently, if $e_{ij} = \varepsilon$, then the question of deletion does not arise. Here it is pre-assumed that e_{ij} is a non-ε member element of the coach C_i.

For $j = 1, 2, \ldots, r$, deletion of e_{ij} is done by replacing it by the null element ε, and updating the availability-status n by doing n = n+1. Deletion of a data element (passenger) does not effect the size r of the coach.

For example, consider the tagged coach $[C_i, (c_i,m)]$ where

$$C_i = \langle e_{i1}, e_{i2}, e_{i3}, e_{i4}, \ldots\ldots\ldots, e_{ir} \rangle$$

If we delete e_{i3} from the coach C_i, then the updated tagged coach will be

$$[C_i, (c_i, m+1)]$$

where

$$C_i = \langle e_{i1}, e_{i2}, \varepsilon, e_{i4}, \ldots\ldots, e_{ir} \rangle$$

2. Deletion of the Last Coach C_i from a r-Atrain

Deletion of coaches from a r-atrain is allowed from the last coach only and in backward direction, one after another. An interim coach can not be deleted. Advertently, we avoid here any kind of deletion of interim coach. The last coach C_i can be deleted if it is an empty coach (as shown in Figure 14).

If the last coach is not empty, it can not be deleted unless its all the passengers are deleted to make it empty.

Figure 14. An empty last coach of a 9-atrain which can be deleted

ε	ε	ε	ε
invalid address			ε
ε	ε	ε	ε

To delete the empty last coach C_i of a r-atrain, we have to do the following actions:

1. Update e_{i-1} of the coach C_{i-1} by storing an invalid address in it.

2. Delete $[C_i, (c_i,r)]$ from the r-atrain

$$T = \langle [C_1, s_{C1}], [C_2, s_{C2}], [C_3, s_{C3}], \ldots,$$

$$[C_{i-1}, s_{Ci-1}], [C_i, (c_i,r)] \rangle,$$

and get the updated r- atrain

$$T = \langle [C_1, s_{C1}], [C_2, s_{C2}],$$

$$[C_3, s_{C3}], \ldots\ldots, [C_{i-1}, s_{Ci-1}] \rangle.$$

3. Update the pilot.

Searching for a Data X in a r-Atrain T of Length K

Searching for a data x in a r-atrain T is very easy. If we know in advance the coach number Ci of the passenger x, then by visiting the pilot we can enter into the coach Ci of the r-atrain directly and then can read the data-elements e_{i1}, e_{i2}, $\ldots\ldots$, e_{ir} of the larray Ai for a match with x. Otherwise, the code c (with reference to the CD-Table) of the datatype of the data x plays an important role in the process of searching. The initial search is done for the coaches (starting from C_1 onwards) which are having the same code c in their status. Suppose that the array of the code-matched coaches so extracted is $Z = (Ç_1, Ç_2, Ç_3, \ldots\ldots, Ç_{t-1}, Ç_t)$. If the array Z is a null array, the search fails. Otherwise we start searching inside, beginning from the coach $Ç_1$ onwards till the last coach $Ç_t$ of Z. The search may lead to either success or failure. We need not go back to the pilot for any help during the tenure of our searching process. Here lies an important dominance of the data structure r-atrain over the data structure HAT introduced by Sitarski (1996).

In case of multi-processor system the searching can be done in parallel very fast, which is obvious from the architecture of the data structure r-atrain.

EMPIRICAL ANALYSIS

Today's supercomputer or multiprocessor system which can provide huge parallelism has become the dominant computing platform (through the proliferation of multi-core processors), and the term has come to stand for highly flexible advanced level of data structures that can be accessed by multiple threads which may actually access heterogeneous data simultaneously, that can run on different processors simultaneously. In most of the giant business organizations, the system has to deal with a large volume of heterogeneous data for which the data structures of the existing literature can not always lead to the desired optimal satisfaction. The very common and frequent operations like Insertion, deletion, searching, etc. are required to be much faster even if the data are huge in number, even if the data are of heterogeneous types. Such situations require some way or some method which work more efficiently than the simple rudimentary data structures such as arrays, linked lists, hash tables, binary search trees, dictionary, etc. Obviously, there is a need of a dash of creativity of a new or better performed heterogeneous data structure which at the same time must be of rudimentary in nature.

The data structure r-atrain (atrain) is neither a dynamic array nor a HAT. It is reasonably space efficient as well. Parallel processing will be easier for huge amount of heterogeneous data if stored using the data structure r-atrain. The pilot of a atrain is, in general, a linked list. But, if we are sure that there will be no requirement of any extra coach in future, then it is better to implement pilot as an array. Although the notion of r-atrain is closely analogous to that of r-train, but none conflicts the interest of other in application areas. Coaches in a r-train can store homogeneous data only, not heterogeneous data. But in a r-atrain the coaches accommodate heterogeneous data (although the data of a coach are always homogeneous and can not be heterogeneous). In r-train, all coaches are of common datatype. For working with homogeneous data train is suitable, not atrain. However, for working with heterogeneous data, atrain is suitable while train can not be applicable. The introduction of CD-Table is a pre-requisite to create any r-atrain for an organization. But addition of new datatypes and corresponding codes can be decided and incorporated at any later stages on retaining all the existing records in the table. The CD-Table is a kind of local document which may vary from organization to organization. The 'status' of a coach at any moment of time in a train reveals only one information which is about the availability of seat inside this coach at that time, whereas the 'status' of a coach in a r-train reveals two information about the coach one of which is same as in the case of a train i.e. about the availability of seat inside this coach at that time, and the other is about the Code of the datatype (as per CD-Table) of the valid contents of the coach.

The natural number r is suitably predecided and fixed by the programmer depending upon the problem under consideration and also upon the organization/industry for which the problem is posed. We do not feel it appropriate to propose r in a r-train or in a r-atrain as a variable. Both the notion of r-train and r-atrain can be made much more flexible if r is made to vary from coach to coach. But, if we do so, the overhead cost/complexity over the totality of the implementation task may dominate the extra benefit of flexibility expected to be exploited. Making r a variable is in fact not required because it is alternatively equivalent to opening new empty coaches whenever required; and opening a new coach is an easy task here in a r-train or in a r-atrain. An undesirable situation apparently seems to happen if we have to open a new empty coach just for storing one or two or very less number of data elements, in particular while r is not a small integer. But in giant organizations of todays fast and very dynamic business trends around the world, such situations in general will surely remain for temporary tenure only, and hence of minor concern or of no concern at all to those organizations. Nowadays memory space is not costly, but faster execution of operations contribute a lot to the growth of the organizations, especially of those who are giants.

CONCLUSION

In this chapter we study mainly two new data structures for storing data while they are huge in volume. The data structure 'r-train' (or 'train' in short) is a homogeneous data structure which can deal with a large volume of homogeneous data very efficiently. The data structure r-atrain (or, atrain) is a robust kind of dynamic heterogeneous data structure which encapsulates the merits of the arrays and of the linked lists, but are different from them and can deal with huge volume of heterogeneous data. The term 'Atrain' stands for "Advanced train". Codes in C or in any higher level language for the operations viz. Create_larray, Create_r-atrain, Insert_Coach, Insert_element,

Delete_element, Delete_last_coach, Search_element, etc. are not presented here, and in fact it is a straightforward task for the programmers.

REFERENCES

Aho, A. V., Hopcroft, J. E., & Ullman, J. D. (1983). *Data structures and data structures and algorithms*. Reading, MA: Addison Wesley.

Bayer, R. (1972). Symmetric binary B-trees, data structures and maintenance algorithms. *Acta Informatica, 1*, 290–306. doi:10.1007/BF00289509

Bayer, R., & McCreight, E. M. (1972). Organization and maintenance of large ordered indexes. *Acta Informatica, 1*(3), 173–189. doi:10.1007/BF00288683

Biswas, R. (2011). r-Train (train): A new flexible dynamic data structure. *Information: An International Journal, 14*(4), 1231–1246.

Biswas, R. (2012). Heterogeneous data structure r-Atrain. *Information: An International Journal, 15*(2), 879–902.

Biswas, S. S., Alam, B., & Doja, M. N. (2012). A theoretical characterization of the data structure 'multigraph'. *Journal of Contemporary Applied Mathematics, 2*(2).

Biswas, S. S., Alam, B., & Doja, M. N. (2013). Generalization of Dijkstra's algorithm for extraction of shortest paths in directed multigraphs. *Journal of Computer Science, 9*(3), 377–382. doi:10.3844/jcssp.2013.377.382

Biswas, S. S., Alam, B., & Doja, M. N. (2013). Real time multigraphs for communication networks: An intuitionistic fuzzy mathematical model. *Journal of Computer Science, 9*(7), 847–855. doi:10.3844/jcssp.2013.847.855

Cormen, T. H., Leiserson, C. E., Rivest, R. L., & Stein, C. (2001). *Introduction to algorithms* (2nd ed.). Cambridge, MA: MIT Press and McGraw-Hill.

Goodrich, M. T., & Kloss, J. G., II. (1999). Tiered vectors: Efficient dynamic arrays for rank-based sequences. In *Proceedings of the Workshop on Algorithms and Data Structures* (vol. 1663, pp. 205–216). IEEE. doi: 10.1007/3-540-48447-7_21

Knuth, D. E. (1968). *The art of computer programming*. Reading, MA: Addison Wesley.

Lynch, N. A. (1996). *Distributed algorithms*. San Francisco: Morgan Kaufmann Publishers.

Seidel, R., & Aragon, C. R. (1996). Randomized search trees. *Algorithmica, 16*, 464–497. doi:10.1007/BF01940876

Shaffer, C. A. (2001). *A practical introduction to data structures and algorithm analysis*. Upper Saddle River, NJ: Prentice Hall.

Sitarski, E. (1996). Algorithm alley, HATs: Hashed array trees. *Dr. Dobb's Journal, 21*(11).

Sleator, D. D., & Tarjan, R. E. (1983). A data structure for dynamic trees. *Journal of Computer and System Sciences, 26*(3). doi:10.1016/0022-0000(83)90006-5

Sleator, D. D., & Tarjan, R. E. (1985). Self-adjusting binary search trees. *Journal of the ACM, 32*(3), 652–686. doi:10.1145/3828.3835

Velskii, G. M., & Landis, E. M. (1962). An algorithm for the organization of information. *Soviet Mathematics Doklady, 3*, 1259–1263.

KEY TERMS AND DEFINITIONS

Availability-Status: The exact number of free spaces available in the coach at real point of time.

CD-Table: A table created by the concerned organization to fix integer code for each datatype under use in the organization. This is not an absolute set of codes to be followed universally by every organization, but it is a local document for the concerned organization. For different organizations, this table could be different. But once it is fixed by an organization it should not be altered by this organization, except that addition of new datatypes and corresponding codes may be decided and be incorporated in the table at any stages later retaining the existing records.

Coach: A pair (A,**e**) where A is a non-empty larray (could be a null larray) and **e** is an address in the memory.

Code-Status: The code of datatype (with reference to the concerned CD-Table) of the data to be stored in the concerned coach.

Empty Coach: A coach is said to be an empty coach if every passenger of it is ε, i.e. if the corresponding larray is a null larray.

Full Coach: A coach is said to be a full coach if it does not have any passenger ε.

Larray: A larray is like an array of elements of identical datatype, where zero or more number of elements may be null element (i.e. no element, empty).

r-Atrain: A linked list of tagged coaches of heterogeneous datatypes.

r-Train: A linked list of tagged coaches of homogeneous datatype.

Status of a Coach (r-Atrain): The status s of a coach in a r-atrain is a pair of information (c, n), where c is a non-negative integer variable which is the code of datatype (with reference to the concerned CD-Table) of the data to be stored in this coach and n is a non-negative integer variable which is equal to the number of ε elements present in it (i.e. in its larray) at real point of time.

Status of a Coach (r-Train): A non-negative integer variable which is equal to the number of ε elements present in it (i.e. in its larray) at real point of time.

TC: If $C = (A, e)$ is a coach, then the corresponding tagged coach (TC) is denoted by the notation (C,s) where s is the status of the coach.

Chapter 13
Comparative Analysis of Hybrid Soft Set Methods

Debadutta Mohanty
Seemanta Mohavidyalaya, India

ABSTRACT

The whole mathematical scenario has changed with the advent of the Rough Set Theory, a powerful tool to deal with uncertainty and incompleteness of knowledge in information system. With the advancement of research, the Soft Set Theory has emerged as an advanced mathematical tool to deal with data associated with uncertainty. The present chapter endeavors to forge a connection between soft set and rough set and maps a new model rough soft set to address the challenges of vagueness and impreciseness. Although the research contribution of M. Irfan Ali, Dan Meng, et al. and Feng Feng et al. had given distinct definition of rough soft set and soft rough set, the analysis explaining the genesis of these sets is not appropriate. This chapter is a new attempt to construct the relationship between a rough set, soft set, and fuzzy set to form a hybrid soft set giving a concrete comprehensive definition of rough soft set in border perspective.

INTRODUCTION

The introduction and application of theories like probability theory, fuzzy set theory (L.A.Zadeh,1965,1975), Rough set theory (Z.pawlak,1982,1991) as the mathematical tools have strengthened the efficacy of knowledge to deal with uncertainties. However some difficulties crop up when we apply them to solve complicated problems in economics, engineering and environmental sciences. In order to overcome the difficulties in certain extent Molodtsov (D. Molodtsov,1999) introduced the concept of soft set which is considered as new mathematical tool to address uncertainties. Recently research on soft set theory and its application in various field is going on. Several operators of set theory have been introduced, as a result notion of soft groups including algebraic structures of soft sets, notion of soft topological spaces are emerged. Molodtsov in his paper has demonstrated that soft set theory has potential applications in different

DOI: 10.4018/978-1-4666-4936-1.ch013

fields including the smoothness of functions, game theory, operation research, perron integration, probability theory and measurement theory. This paper seeks to explore the basic concepts of fuzzy set, rough set and soft set . Further it introduces the new concept rough soft set, the hybrid model combining rough set with soft set. Rough soft set can be used for many practical application based on rough set or soft set. Based on Pawlak approximation space, the approximation of a soft set is proposed to obtain a hybrid model called rough soft set. Alternatively, a soft set instead of an equivalence relation can be used to granulate the universe. Granulation involves decomposition of whole into parts, organisation involves integration of parts in to whole and causation involves the association of causes and effects.

The paper makes an honest attempt to define fuzzy set, rough set and soft set and then their combinations. The intention of fuzzy set theory introduced by L.A.Zadeh (1965) is to generalize the classical notion of a set and notion of graded membership which represents fuzziness . Zadeh writes "the notion of a fuzzy set provides a convenient point of departure for the construction of a conceptual framework which parallels in many respects and framework used in the case of ordinary sets, but is more general then the later and potentially, may prove to have much wider scope of applicability, particularly in the field of pattern classification and information processing. Essentially, such a framework provides a natural way of dealing with problems in which the sources of imprecision is the absence of sharply defined criteria of class membership rather than the presence of random variables."

LITERARY BACKGROUND

In the present context the theory of fuzzy set is advancing fast in geometrical progression. But difficulty arises to set the membership in each particular case. The nature of the membership function is extremely individual. The fuzzy set operations with membership functions sometimes do not appear natural. To avoid these difficulties, a mathematical tool, called as soft set theory, is developed to deal with uncertainties. In 1999, soft set theory was derived by D.Molodtsov as:

Let U be an initial universe and let E be the set of parameters. A pair (F,E) is called a soft set over U when F is a mapping from E into the set of subsets of U .

Thus a soft set is a parameterized family of subsets of set U .

In 2003 an article "soft set theory" was published by P.K.Maji and others [P.K.Majhi,R. Biswas and A.R.Roy,2003] which strengthened the soft set analysis [P.K.Majhi,R. Biswas and A.R.Roy,2002]. Then the researchers made the research on soft set, soft groups, fuzzy soft set, fuzzy soft group and the combination of soft set, fuzzy set and rough set.

Z.Pawlak introduced Rough set theory a mathematical tool, to deal with uncertainty, vague and imprecise problems. The idea of the rough set consists of the approximation of a set by a pair of sets, called the lower and the upper approximation of their set. The rough set approach is based on knowledge to become agent of some reality and its ability to discern some phenomena, process, object etc.

According to Pawlak , knowledge is based on the ability to classify the objects, and by objects we mean anything.

A knowledge representation system (or an information system) is a pair (U, A) where U is a non empty, finite universe of discourse and A is a set of attributes; each attribute $a \in A$, is a function $a : U \rightarrow V_a$ is the set of values of an attributes a .

In this knowledge century a lot of developments have made combining these three theories by the eminent researchers. It yields soft groups, soft rings, soft topology, vague soft sets, fuzzy soft set, fuzzy soft groups, soft set relations, soft matrix, soft rough set, rough soft set, intuitionistics fuzzy soft set. etc

Definition 1: Fuzzy Set

Consider the classical set A of the universe U ($A \subseteq U$). A fuzzy set B is defined by a set of ordered pairs

$$B = \left\{ \left(x, \mu_A(x) \right) : x \epsilon A, \mu_A(x) \epsilon [0,1] \right\}$$

where $\mu_A(x)$ is a function called membership function, $\mu_A(x)$ specifies the grade or degree to which any element x in A belongs to the fuzzy set B. This definition associates with each element $x \in A$ a real number $\mu_A(x)$ in the interval [0, 1]. Larger values of $\mu_A(x)$ indicates higher degrees of membership.

Definition 2: Intuitionistic Fuzzy Set

Intuitionistic fuzzy set theory was initiated by Atanassov [K.T.Atanassov,1986] which has already been found to have in built potential to deal with vagueness in some special situation. Fuzzy sets are intuitionistic fuzzy set but the converse is not necessarily true. [Z.Liang and P.Shi,2003]

An intuitionistic fuzzy set A of U is an object having the form

$$A = \left\{ \left\langle x, \mu_A(x), \vartheta_A(x) \right\rangle : x \in U \right\}$$

where the function

$$\mu_A : U \to [0,1]$$

and

$$\vartheta_A : U \to [0,1]$$

define the degree of membership and degree of non membership respectively of the element $x \in U$ to the set A and for every $x \in U$,

$$0 \le \mu_A(x), + \vartheta_A(x) \le 1.$$

Here, for $x \in U$, the value $\mu_A(x)$ signifies the membership value of x in A evaluated somehow; where $\vartheta_A(x)$ signifies the non-membership value of x evaluated by identical evaluator and the amount

$$\pi_A(x) = 1 - \mu_A(x) - \vartheta_A(x)$$

is termed as intuitionistic index or hesitation index and is the degree of indeterminacy concerning the membership of x in A.

Definition 3: Rough Set

According to Pawlak, "Knowledge *about a Universe can be considered as one's capability to classify objects of the Universe*". By a classification of a universe U, we mean a set of subsets

$$\{X_1, X_2, \ldots \ldots X_n\}$$

such that

$$X_i \bigcap X_j = \varphi \ \ for \ i \ne \text{j} \ \text{ and } \ \bigcup_{i=1}^{n} X_i = U$$

Let $R \subseteq U \times U$ denote an equivalence relation on U, that is R is a reflexive, symmetric and transitive relation. The equivalence class of an element $x \in U$ with respect to R denoted by $[x]_R$ is the set of all $y \in U$ such that xRy. If two elements x, y in U belong to the same equivalence class then we say that x and y are indistinguishable with respect to relation R. Corresponding to every partition on U there is an equivalence relation, which has these partitions as its equivalence classes. We consider the quotient set U / R consisting of all equivalence classes of R . Here the equivalence class $[x]_R$ containing x plays dual roles. The empty set φ and the equivalence classes are called the elementary sets. The union of one or more elementary sets are called a compound set.

We say an ordered pair $A = (U, R)$, an approximation space and a relational system $\mathcal{K} = (U, \mathcal{R})$ is called a knowledge base, where U is a universe and $\mathcal{R}$ is a family of equivalence relations defined on U where $R \in \mathcal{R}$.

For any set $X \subseteq U$, the lower approximation of X in A under the indiscernibility relation R be defined by

$$\underline{R}(X) = \left\{ x \in U : [x]_R \subseteq X \right\} \qquad (1)$$

And an upper approximation of X under R be defined by

$$\overline{R}(X) = \left\{ x \in U : [x]_R \cap X \neq \varphi \right\} \qquad (2)$$

A set $X \subseteq U$ is called rough with respect to R if and only if

$$\underline{R}(X) \neq \overline{R}(X)$$

and X is called definable with respect to R if and only if

$$\underline{R}(X) = \overline{R}(X)$$

The border line region of X with respect to R be given by

$$BN_R(X) = \overline{R}(X) - \underline{R}(X)$$

For an element $x \in U$, x is certainly in X under the equivalence relation R if and only if $x \in \underline{R}(X)$ and x is possible in X under R if and only if $x \in \overline{R}(X)$. The borderline region under R is the undecidable area of the universe. We say X is rough with respect to R if and only if

$$\underline{R}(X) \neq \overline{R}(X)$$

which is equivalent to $BN_R(X) \neq \varphi$, otherwise X is said to be R-definable if and only if

$$\underline{R}(X) = \overline{R}(X) \qquad .$$

or $BN_R(X) = \varphi$.

Definition 4: Rough Fuzzy Set [D.Dubois,and H.Parade,1990]

Let X be a set and R be an equivalence relation on U . Let F be a fuzzy set in U . The lower and upper approximations $\underline{R}F$ and $\overline{R}F$ of F by R are fuzzy sets on the quotient set X / R with the membership function defined by

$$\mu_{\underline{R}(F)}(x_i) = \inf \left\{ \mu_F(x) : w(x_i) = [x]_R \right\}$$

and

$$\mu_{\overline{R}(F)}(x_i) = \sup \left\{ \mu_F(x) : w(x_i) = [x]_R \right\}$$

where

$$w\left(x_i\right) = \{ x \ / \ x_i \ \text{the name of the}$$

equivalence class $\left[x\right]_R$ }, then the pair ($\underline{R}F$, $\bar{R}F$) is called the rough fuzzy sets of F with respect to R.

SOFT SET AND PROPERTIES

Let U be a initial universe set and E be a set of parameters. Let $P\left(U\right)$ denotes the power set of U and $A \subseteq E$ [P.K.Majhi et al,2003 and M.I.Ali, F.Feng, X.Liu,W.k.Min,M.Shabir, 2009]

Definition 5: A pair $\left(F, A\right)$ is called a soft set over U, where F is a mapping given by $F : A \to P\left(U\right)$. In other words, a soft set over U is a parameterized family of subsets of the universe U. For $e \in A$,$F\left(e\right)$ may be considered as the set of

$e - approximate\,elements\,of\,the\,soft\,set\left(F, A\right).$

Clearly, a soft set is not a set. For illustration, Molodtsov considered several examples in (D.Molodtsov, 1999), one of which we present below.

Example 1: Suppose U is the set of houses under consideration. E is the set of parameters. Each parameter is a word or a sentence.

$E = \{expensive; beautiful; wooden; cheap;$ $in\,the\,green\,surroundings; modern; in\,good$ $repair; in\,bad\,repair\}$

In this case, to define a soft set means to point out expensive houses, beautiful houses, and so on. The soft set $\left(F.E\right)$ describes the "attractiveness of the houses" which Mr. X (say) is going to buy. We consider below the same example in more detail for our next discussion. Suppose that there are six houses in the universe U given by

$$U = \left\{h_1, h_2, h_3, h_4, h_5, h_6\right\}$$

and

$$E = \left\{e_1, e_2, e_3, e_4, e_5\right\}$$

where

- e_1 stands for the parameter 'expensive',
- e_2 stands for the parameter 'beautiful',
- e_3 stands for the parameter 'wooden',
- e_4 stands for the parameter 'cheap',
- e_5 stands for the parameter 'in the green surrounding',

Suppose that

$$F\left(e_1\right) = \{ h_2, h_4\}$$

$$F\left(e_2\right) = \{ h_1, h_3\}$$

$$F\left(e_3\right) = \{ h_3, h_4, h_5\}$$

$$F\left(e_4\right) = \{ h_1, h_3, h_5\}, \ F\left(e_5\right) = \{ h_1\}$$

The soft set $\left(F, E\right)$ is a parameterized family

$$\{F\left(e_i\right), i = 1, 2, 3, \ldots 8\}$$

of subsets of the set U and gives us a collection of approximate descriptions of an object. Considered the mapping F which is "house (.)" where dot (.) is to be filled up by a parameter $e \in E$. Therefore, $F\left(e_1\right)$ means "house (expensive)" whose functional value is the set { $h_{2,}h_{4,}$ }.Thus, we can view the soft set (F,E) as a collections of approximations as below ;

$(F,E) =$ {expensive houses ={ $h_{2,}h_{4,}$ },
Beautiful houses = { $h_{1,}h_{3,}$ },
Wooden houses ={ $h_{3,}h_{4,}h_{5,}$ },
Cheap houses = { $h_{1,}h_{3,}h_{5,}$ },
In the green surrounding = { h_{1} }

where each approximation has two parts

1. A predicate ρ; and
2. An approximate value-set υ (or simply to be called value-set υ

For example, for the approximation "expensive houses = { $h_{2,}h_{4,}$ },we have the following:

1. The predicate name is expensive houses ; and
2. The approximate value set or value set is ={ $h_{2,}h_{4,}$ }

Operations on Soft Set

Now we present the operations defined on soft set theory. [F. Feng, C.Li,V.Davvaz, M.Irfan Ali,2010; D.Mohanty, 2010; D.Mohanty, N.Kalia, L.Pattanayak, B.B.Nayak,2012]

Definition 6: Let (F,A) and (F,B) be two soft sets over a common universe U such that $A\cap B \neq \varnothing$. The restricted intersection of

$(F,A)and(F,B)$

is defined as

$$(F,A)\cap(F,B)=(H,C)$$

where

$$C = A\cap B$$

and

$$H(x) = F(x)\text{for all } x \in C.$$

In addition, we may sometimes adopt a different type of intersection given as follows

Definition 7: Let (F,A) and (G,B) be two soft sets over a common universe U such that

$$A\cap B \neq \varnothing .$$

The extended intersection of

$$(F,A)and(G,B)$$

is defined as

$$(F,A)\cap(G,B)=(H,C)$$

where $C = A\cap B$ and for all $x \in$ C,

$$(x) = F(x)\cap G(x)$$

Definition 8: Let $(F.A)$ and $(G.B)$ be two soft sets over the same universe U such that $A\cap B \neq \varnothing$. The restricted difference of (F,A) and (G,B) is denoted by $(F,A) \sim)$ and is defined as

$$(F,A) \sim (G,B) = H(C)$$

where $C = A \cap B$ and for all $c \in C$,

$$H(c) = F(c) - G(c)$$

the difference of the sets $F(c)$ and $G(c)$.

Definition 9: Let U be an initial universe set, E be the universal set of parameters $A \subset E$.

1. (F, A) is called a relative null soft set (with respect to the parameters set A.) denoted by ϕ_A, if $F(e) = \phi$ for all $e \epsilon A$.

2. (G, A) is called a relative whole soft set (with respect to the parameters A), denoted by U_A, if $F(e) = U$ for all $e \epsilon A$.

The relative whole soft set U_E with respect to the universe set of parameters E is called the absolute soft set over U.

Definition 10: The relative complement of a soft set (F, A) is denoted by $(F, A)^r$ and is defined by

$$(F, A)^r = (F^r, A)$$

where

$$F^r : A \rightarrow P(U)$$

is mapping given by for by

$$F^r(\alpha) = U - F(\alpha)$$

for all $\alpha \in A$.

Clearly,

$$(F, A)^r = U_E \sim (F, A)$$

and

$$((F, A)^r)^r = (F, A)$$

It is worth noting that in the above new definition of complement, the parameter set of the complement $(F, A)^r$ is still the original parameter set instead of as in definition given by P.K.Majhi et al . The complement given by P.K.Majhi et al. may be called neg-complement (or preudo-complement).

Definition 11: Let (F, A) and (G, B) be two soft sets over the same universe U such that $A \cap B \neq \varnothing.$. The restricted union of (F, A) and (G, B) is denoted by

$$(F, A) U_r (G, B)$$

and is defined as

$$(F, A) U_r (G, B) = (H, C)$$

where $C = A \cap B$ and for all

$$c \epsilon C, H(c) = F(c) \cup G(c).$$

Definition 12: The extended union of two soft sets (F, A) and (G, B) over a common universe U is the soft set (H, C), where $C = A \cup B$ and $\forall e \in C$

$$H(e) = \begin{cases} F(e), & if\, e \in A - B \\ G(e), & if\, e \in B - A \\ \quad F(e) \cap G(e), & if\, e \in A \cap B \end{cases}$$

We write $(F, A) \sqcup_g (G, B) = (H, C)$

We note here that every fuzzy set may be considered as soft set and every rough set may be considered as a soft set. And every rough set also be considered as soft set.

Vague Soft Set

Let

$$U = (u_1, u_2, \ldots\ldots, u_n\}$$

an initial universe. A vague set over U is characterized by truth membership function t_v and false membership function f_v where

$$t_v, f_v : U \to [0, 1]$$

and $t_v(u_i)$ is a lower bound on the grade membership of u_i derived from the evidence for u_i and $f_v(u_i)$ is a lower bound on the negation of u_i derived from the evidence against u_i and

$$t_v(u_i) + f_v(u_i) \le 1$$

Definition 13: Let x be a vague value, $x = \left[t_x, 1 - f_x \right]$, where

$$t_x \in [0, 1], f_x \in [0, 1]$$

and

$$0 \le t_x \le 1 - f_x \le 1$$

If $t_x = 1$ and $f_x = 0$ (i.e x $= \left[1, 1 \right]$) then x is called a unit vague value. If $t_x = 0$ and $f_x = 1$ (i.e $x = \left[0, 0 \right]$) then x is called a zero vague value.

Definition 14: Let x and y are two vague values, where

$$x = \left(\left[t_x, 1 - f_x \right] \right)$$

and

$$y = \left(\left[t_y, 1 - f_y \right] \right)$$

$if\, t_x = t_y\, and\, f_x = f_y, then\, vague\, value\, x\, and$
$y\, are\, equal \left(i.e. \left[t_y, 1 - f_y \right] = \left[t_x, 1 - f_x \right] \right)$

Let A and B to be vague sets of the universe

$$U = \left\{ u_1, u_2 \ldots\ldots\ldots u_n \right\}$$

where

$$A = \left[t_A(u_1), 1 - f_A(u_1) \right] / u_1 +$$

$$\left[t_A(u_2), 1 - f_A(u_2) \right] / u_2 + \ldots\ldots +$$

$$\left[t_A(u_n), 1 - f_A(u_n) \right] / u_n,$$

$$B = \left[t_B(u_1), 1 - f_B(u_1) \right] / u_1 +$$

$$\left[t_B(u_2), 1 - f_B(u_2) \right] / u_2 + \ldots\ldots +$$

$$\left[t_B(u_n), 1 - f_B(u_n) \right] / u_n$$

Definition 15: et A be a vague set of the universe U. If

$$\forall u_i \in U, t_A(u_i) = 1 \ and \ f_A(u_i) = 0,$$

then A is called a unit vague set, where $1 \leq i \leq n$,

$$if \forall u_i \in U, t_A(u_i) = 0,$$

and $f_A(u_i) = 1$, then A is called a zero vague set, where $1 \leq i \leq n$.

The complement of a vague set A denoted by A^c and is defined by $t_{A^c} = f_A$ and

$$1 - f_{A^c} = 1 - t_A$$

Definition 16: Let A and B are two vague sets of the universe U. If

$$\forall u_i \in U, [t_A(u_i), 1 - f_A(u_i)] = [t_B(u_i), 1 - f_B(u_i)]$$

then the vague sets $A\,and\,B$ are called equal, where $1 \leq i \leq n$

Definition 17: Let A and B be two vague sets of the universe U if

$$\forall u_i \in U, t_A(u_i) \leq t_B(u_i)$$
$$and\, 1 - f_A(u_i) \leq 1 - f_B(u_i)$$

then the vague set A is included by B, denoted by $A \subseteq B$, where $1 \leq i \leq n$.

Let U be a universe, E be a set of parameters, $V(U)$ the power set of vague set on U and $A \subseteq E$. The concept of vague soft set is given by [W-Xu, J.Ma, S.Wang,G.Hao,2010]

Definition 18: A pair (F, A) is called a vague soft set over universe U, where F is a mapping given by

$$F : A \rightarrow V(U).$$

In other words, a vague soft set over U is a parameterized family of vague set of the universe U. For

$$\varepsilon \in A, \mu_{F(\varepsilon)} : U \rightarrow [0,1]^2$$

is regarded as the set of approximate elements of the vague set, To illustrate the idea, let us reconsider the house example discussed previously.

Example 2: Considered a vague soft set (F, E), where U is of six houses under the consideration of a decision maker to purchase, which is denoted by

$$U = \{h_1, h_2, \ldots\ldots, h_6\}$$

and the parameter set

$$E = \{e_1, e_2, e_3, e_4, e_5\} =$$

{expensive, beautiful, wooden, cheap, in the green surrounding}

The vague soft set (F, E) describes the "attractiveness of the houses" to this decision maker.

Suppose that

$$F(e_1) = ([0.1, 0.2] / h_1, [0.9, 1] / h_2,$$

$[0.3, 0.5] / h_3, [0.8, 0.9] /$

$h_4, [0.2, 0.4] / h_5, [0.4, 0.6] / h_6)$

$F(e_2) = ([0.9, 1] / h_1,$

$[0.2.0.7] / h_2, [0.6, 0.9] / h_3, [0.2, 0.4] /$

$h_4 [0.3, 0.4] / h_5, [0.1, 0.6] / h_6)$

$F(e_3) = ([0.1, 0.2] / h_1,$

$[0.9.1] / h_2, [0.3, 0.5] / h_3, [0.8, 0.9] /$

$h_4, [0.2, 0.4] / h_5, [0.4, 0.6] / h_6)$

$F(e_4) = ([0.8, 0.9\} / h_1, [0., 0.1] /$

$h_2, [0.5, 0.7] / h_3, [0.1, 0.2] /$

$h_4, [0.6, 0.8] / h_5, [0.4, 0.6] / h_6)$

$F(e_5) = ([0.9, 1] / h_1, [0.2, 0.3] /$

$h_2 [0.1, 0.4] / h_3, [0.1, 0.2] /$

$h_4, [0.2, 0.4] / h_5, [0.7, 0.9] / h_6)$

The vague soft set (F, E) is a parameterized family

$$\left\{ \hat{F}(e_i), i = 1, 2, 3, 4, 5 \right\}$$

of vague sets on U and

$(F, E) = \{$expensive houses $=$

$([0.1, 0.2] / h_1, [0.9, 1] / h_2, [0.3, 0.5] /$

$h_3 [0.8, 0.9] / h_4, [0.2, 0.4] / h_5, [0.4, 0.6] / h_6),$

beautiful house $= ([0.9, 1] / h_1, [0.2, 0.7] /$

$h_2, [0.6, 0.9] / h_3 [0.2, 0.4] / h_4, [0.3, 0.4] /$

$h_5, [0.1, 0.6] / h_6), \dots \}.$

Rough Soft Set and Soft Rough Set

Feng Feng [F.Feng,X.Liu, V.L.Fotea,Y.B.Jun, 2011] had defined the soft rough set as follows:

Definition 19: Let (U, R) be a Pawlak approximation space and $\wp = (F, A)$ be soft set over U. The lower and upper rough approximations of $\wp$. th respect to (U, R) are denoted by

$$R_*\left(\wp\right) = F_*, A$$

and

$$R^*\left(\wp\right) = \left(F^*, A\right)$$

which are sub set over U with the set valued mapping given by

$$F_*\left(x\right) = R_*\left(F\left(x\right)\right)$$

and

$$F^*\left(x\right) = R^*\left(F\left(x\right)\right)$$

where $x \in A$.

The operators R_* and R^* are called the lower and upper rough approximation operators on soft set. If

$$R_*\left(\wp\right) \neq R^*\left(\wp\right)$$

then soft set $\wp$. called rough soft set.

Definition 20: Let $S = \left(f, A\right)$ be a soft set over U. Then the pair $P = (U, S)$ is called a soft approximation space. Based on P, we define the following two operations:

$$\underline{apr_p}\left(X\right) = \left\{u \in U : \exists a \in A\left[u \in f\left(a\right) \subseteq X\right]\right\},$$

$$\overline{apr_P}\left(X\right) = \left\{u \in U : \exists a \in A\left[u \in f\left(a\right), f\left(a\right) \cap X \neq \phi\right]\right\},$$

assigning to every subset $X \subseteq U$ two sets $\underline{apr_p}\left(X\right)$ and $\overline{apr_P}\left(X\right)$ called the lower and upper soft rough approximations of X in P, respectively . Moreover,

$$Pos_P\left(X\right) = \underline{apr_p}\left(X\right)$$

$$Neg_P\left(X\right) = U - \overline{apr_P}\left(X\right),$$

$$Bnd_P\left(X\right) = \overline{apr_P}\left(X\right) - \underline{apr_p}\left(X\right)$$

are called the soft positive, soft negative and soft boundary regions of X, respectively.

If $\underline{apr_p}\left(X\right) = \overline{apr_P}\left(X\right)$ is said to be soft definable, otherwise X is called a soft rough set.

By definition, we immediately have that $X \subseteq U$ is a soft definable set if $Bnd_P\left(X\right) = \phi$. Also, it is clear that

$$\underline{apr_p}\left(X\right) \subseteq X$$

and

$$\underline{apr_p}\left(X\right) \subseteq \overline{apr_P}\left(X\right)$$

for all $X \subseteq U$

Nevertheless, it is worth noting that $X \subseteq \overline{apr_P}\left(X\right)$ does not hold in general as illuminated by the following example.

Example 3: [F.Feng, X.Liu, V.L.Fotea, Y.B.Jun, 2011] Suppose that

$$U = \left\{u_1, u_2, u_3, u_4, u_5, u_6\right\}$$

$$E = \{e_1, e_2, e_3, e_4, e_5, e_6\}$$

and

$$A = \{e_1, e_2, e_3, e_4\}$$

Let $S = (f, A)$ be a soft set over U and the soft approximation space $P = (U, S)$.

For

$$X = \{u_3, u_4, u_{5,}\} \subseteq U$$

we have

$$\underline{apr_p}(X) = \{u_3\}$$

and

$$\overline{apr_P}(X) = \{u_1, u_2, u_3, u_5\}$$

Thus

$$\underline{apr_p}(X) \neq \overline{apr_P}(X)$$

and X is soft rough set. Here $X \subsetneq \overline{apr_P}(X)$

But for

$$Y = \{u_3, u_4\} \subseteq U$$

$$\underline{apr_p}(Y) = \{u_3\} = \overline{apr_P}(Y) \subset Y$$

so Y is a soft definable set.

Soft Matrix

[N.Cagman and S. Enginoglu, 2010] produced the definition as

Definition 21: Let U be an initial universe, $P(U)$ be the power set of U, E be the set of all parameters and $A \subseteq E$. A soft set (f_A, E) on the universe U is defined by the set of ordered pairs.

$$(f_A, E) = \{(e, f_A(e)) : e \in E, f_A(e) \in P(U)\}$$

where $f_A : E \to P(U)$ such that $f_A(e) = \phi$ if $e \notin A$.

Here f_A is called approximate function of the soft set (f_A, E). The set $f_A(e)$ is called e-approximate value set or e-approximate set which consists of related objects of the parameter $e \in E$.

Definition 22: Let (f_A, E) be a soft set over U. Then a subset of $U \times E$ is uniquely defined by

$$R_A = \{(u, e) : e \in A, u \in f_A(e)\}$$

Which is called a relation form of (f_A, E), the characteristics functions of R_A is written by

$$\mathcal{X}_{R_A} : U \times E \to [0, 1]$$

where

$$\mathcal{X}_{R_A}(u, e) = \begin{cases} 1 & if (u, e) \in R_A \\ 0 & if (u, e) \notin R_A \end{cases}$$

If

$$U = \left\{ u_1, u_2, u_3, \ldots\ldots\ldots, u_m \right\}$$

$$E = \left\{ e_1, e_2, \ldots\ldots\ldots, e_n \right\}$$

and $A \subseteq E$ then R_A can be represented by, if $a_{ij} = \mathcal{X}_{R_A}\left(u_i, e_j \right)$,

$$R_A = \left(\mathcal{X}_{R_A}\left(u_i, e_j \right) \right)_{m \times n} =$$

$$[a_{ij}]_{m \times n} = \begin{bmatrix} a_{11} & a_{12} \cdots & & a_{1n} \\ a_{21} & a_{22} & \cdots\cdots & a_{2n} \\ a_{m1} & a_{m2} & & \cdots & a_{mn} \end{bmatrix}$$

which is called an $m \times n$ soft matrix of the soft set $\left(f_A, E \right)$ over U.

Accordingly to this definition, a soft set $\left(f_A, E \right)$ is uniquely characterized by the matrix $[a_{ij}]_{m \times n}$. It means that a soft set $\left(f_A, E \right)$ is formally equal to its soft matrix $[a_{ij}]_{m \times n}$. Therefore, we shall identify any soft set with its soft matrix and use these two concepts as interchangeable.

Example 4: Assume that

$$U = \left\{ u_1, u_2, u_3, u_4, u_5 \right\}$$

is a universal set and

$$E = \left\{ e_1, e_2, e_3, e_4 \right\}$$

is set of parameters. If

$$A = \left\{ e_2, e_3, e_4 \right\}$$

and

$$f_A\left(e_2 \right) = \left\{ u_2, u_4 \right\}, f_A\left(e_3 \right) = \phi, f_A\left(e_4 \right) = U$$

then we write a soft set

$$\left(f_A, E \right) = \left\{ \left(e_2, \left\{ u_2, u_4 \right\} \right), \left(e_4, U \right) \right\}$$

and then the relation form of $\left(f_A, E \right)$ is written by

$$R_A = \left\{ \begin{array}{l} \left(u_2, e_2 \right), \left(u_4, e_2 \right), \left(u_1, e_4 \right), \left(u_2, e_4 \right), \\ \left(u_3, e_4 \right), \left(u_4, e_4 \right), \left(u_5, e_4 \right) \end{array} \right\}$$

Hence the soft matrix $[a_{ij}]_{5 \times 4}$ is written by

$$[a_{ij}] =$$

Bijective Soft Set

Definition 23: Let $\left(F, B \right)$ be a soft set over a common universe U, where F is a mapping $F : B \rightarrow P\left(U \right)$ and B is non-empty parameter set. We say that $\left(F, B \right)$ is a bijective soft set if

1 $\bigcup_{e \in B} F\left(e \right) = U$

For any two parameters:

$$e_i, e_j \in B, e_i \neq e_j , F\left(e_i \right) \bigcap F\left(e_j \right) = \varnothing$$

In other words, suppose $Y \subseteq P\left(U \right)$ and

$$Y = \{ F(e_1), F\left(e_2 \right), \ldots\ldots\ldots, F\left(e_n \right) \}, e_i \in B$$

From definition 23, the mapping

$$F : B \rightarrow P(U)$$

can be transformed to the mapping $F : B \rightarrow Y$ which is a bijective function, that is every $y \in Y$ there is exactly one parameter $e \in B$ such that $F(e) = y$ and no un mapped element remains in both $B \, and \, Y$. Simply every element in bijective soft set over U can have one and only one mapping to a parameter.[K.Cong, Z.Xino, X.Zhang, 2010]]

Example 5: Suppose that

$$U = \left\{ x_1, x_2, x_3, x_4, x_5, x_6, x_7 \right\}$$

is a common universe (F, E) is a soft set over U ,

$$E = \left\{ e_1, e_2, e_3, e_4 \right\}$$

The mapping of (F, E) is given below:

$$F(e_1) = \left\{ x_1, x_2, x_3 \right\}$$

$$F(e_2) = \left\{ x_4, x_5, x_6 \right\}$$

$$F(e_3) = \left\{ x_7 \right\}$$

$$F(e_4) = \left\{ x_4, x_5, x_6, x_7 \right\}$$

From definition 23

$$\left(F, \left\{ e_1, e_2, e_3 \right\} \right)$$

and $\left(F, \left\{ e_1, e_4 \right\} \right)$ are bijective soft sets. While

$$\left(F, \left\{ e_1, e_2 \right\} \right)$$

and

$$\left(F, \left\{ e_1, e_3 \right\} \right)$$

are not bijective soft sets.

Instuitionistic Fuzzy Soft Set

Definition 24: Let $IF(U)$ denotes the set of all intuitionistic fuzzy subsets of U .Then a pair $S = (\hat{F}, E)$ is called an instuitionistic fuzzy soft set over U where

$$\hat{F} : E \rightarrow IF(U)$$

be the given mapping.

An intuitionistic fuzzy soft set is parameterized family intuitionistic fuzzy subsets of U . For any $\varepsilon \in E$, $\hat{F}(\varepsilon)$ is referred as the set of ε − approximate elements of the intuitionistic fuzzy subsets $(\hat{F}, E)$. And it is actually an intuitionistic fuzzy set on U . $\hat{F}(\varepsilon)$ can be written as

$$\hat{F}(\varepsilon) = \left\{ x, \mu_{\hat{F}(\varepsilon)}(x), \nu_{\hat{F}(\varepsilon)}(x) : x \in U \right\}$$

Here

$$\mu_{\hat{F}(\varepsilon)}(x) \,,\, \nu_{\hat{F}(\varepsilon)}(x)$$

are respectively the membership degree and non-membership degree that object x holds on the parameter ε .[D.Mohanty,2010 ; A.R.Salleh, 2011]

SOFT SET AND ROUGH SOFT SET

In this section we find some basic definitions for soft set. Throughout this chapter, U denotes an initial Universal set and E is a set of parameters ; the power set of U be denoted by $P(U)$.

Definition 25: A pair (F, A) is called a soft set over U, where $A \subseteq E$ and F is a mapping given by . $F : A \rightarrow P(U)$ .That is, a soft set over U is a parameterized family of subsets of the universe. For $x \in A$, $F(x)$ may be considered as set of x-approximate elements of the soft set (F, A)

Definition 26: Let (F, A) and (G, B) soft sets $A, B \subseteq E$ over a common universe . Then (G, B) is called a subset of (F, A) denoted by $(F, A) \overset{\sim}{\subset} (G, B)$ if

$$B \subseteq A$$

$$G(x) \subseteq F(x) \text{ for all } x \in B,$$

In this case (F, A) is said to be a soft super set of (G, B) .

Definition 27: Two soft sets (F, A) and (G, B), $A, B \subseteq E$ over the common universe U are said to be soft equal if

$$(F, A) \overset{\sim}{\subset} (G, B)$$

and

$$(G, B) \overset{\sim}{\subset} (F, A)$$

This is denoted by

$$(F, A) \overset{\sim}{=} (G, B$$

Definition 28: Let (F, A) and (G, B) be two soft sets over common universe. The union of (F, A) and (G, B) is defined as the soft set (H, C) satisfying the following condition

$$C = (A \cup B)$$

For all $x \in C$

$$H(x) = \begin{cases} F(x), & if \, x \in A - B \\ G(x), & if \, x \in B - A \\ F(x) \cup G(x), if \, , \, x \in A \cap B \end{cases}$$

We use the notation

$$(H, C) = (F, A) \overset{\sim}{\subset} (G, B)$$

Definition 29: Let (F, A) and (G, B) be two soft sets over a common universe . The intersection of (F, A) and (G, B) denoted by

$$(H, C) = (F, A) \overset{\sim}{\cap} (G, B)$$

be defined as the soft set iff $C = (A \cap B)$ and for all $x \in C$,

$$H(x) = F(x) \cap G(x)$$

Definition 30: Let U be an initial universe, E be the set of parameters and $A, B \subseteq E$.

1. (F, A) is called relative null soft set (with respect to the parameter set A) denoted by $\varnothing_A$,if $F(a) = \varnothing$ for all $x \in A$.

The relative soft set with respect to E is called the null soft set over U and is denoted by $\varnothing_E$, if $F(a) = \varnothing$ for all $x \in A$.

2. (G, A) is called a relative whole soft set with respect to the parameter set A, denoted by U_A if $G(e) = U$ for all $e \in A$.

The relative whole soft set with respect to the set of parameter E is called absolute soft set over U and denoted by U_E if $G(x) = U$ for all $x \in E$.

The soft set over U with empty parameter set is called empty soft set over U and is denoted by $\varnothing_\varnothing$. We note here that $\varnothing_\varnothing$ and $\varnothing_A$ are different soft sets over U and

$$\varnothing_\varnothing \tilde{\subset} \varnothing_A \tilde{\subset} (F, A) \tilde{\subset} U_A \tilde{\subset} U_E$$

for all soft set (F, A) over U.

Definition 31: Let

$$E = \{e_1, e_2, e_3, e_4 \ldots \ldots e_n\}$$

be a set of parameter. The not set of E denoted by $-E$, is defined by

$$-E = \{-e_1, -e_2, \ldots \ldots, -e_n\}$$

where

$$-e_k = not\, e_k \quad, 1 \le k \le n$$

The complement of a soft set (F, A) is denoted by $(F, A)^C$ and is defined by

$$(F, A)^C = (F^C, -A)$$

where

$$F^C : -A \to P(U)$$

is a mapping given by

$$F^C(x) = U - F(-x)$$

for all. $x \in -A$

Clearly

$$(U_A)^C = \varnothing_{-A}$$

and

$$(U_E)^C = \varnothing_{-E}.$$

Definition 32: Let (F, A) and (G, B) be two soft sets over the same universe U. and $A, B \subseteq E$. The difference of the soft sets be denoted by

$$(H, C) = (F, A) \tilde{-} (G, B)$$

where $C = (A - B)$ and for all $x \in C$,

$$H(x) = F(x) - G(x)$$

We note here that

$$(F, A)^C \ne U \tilde{-} (F, A)$$

$$\left(F, A\right) \widetilde{\cup} \left(F, A\right)^{C} \neq U_{A}$$

and

$$\left(F, A\right) \widetilde{\cap} \left(F, A\right)^{C} = \varnothing_{\varnothing} \ as \ A \cap - A = \varnothing$$

Examples 6: This example is quoted directly from [D.Molodtsove,1999]

Let the universe

$$U = \left\{h_{1}, h_{2}, h_{3}, h_{4}, h_{5}, h_{6}\right\}$$

be six houses under consideration and let

$$E = \left\{x_{1}, x_{2}, x_{3}, x_{4}, x_{5}\right\}$$

be set of decision parameters. The parameter x_{1} stands for expensive, parameter x_{2} stands for beautiful, x_{3} stands for wooden, x_{4} for cheap and x_{5} for green surroundings. Consider the mapping

$$F : E \to P\left(U\right)$$

given by $F\left(x_{1}\right)$ means house expensive and its functional value is the set $\{h \in U$ is an expensive house$\}$.Suppose it is given that

$$F\left(x_{1}\right) = \text{expensive house} =$$

$$\left\{h_{2}, h_{4}\right\}, \ F\left(x_{2}\right) = \left\{h_{1}, h_{3}\right\}, \ \left(x_{3}\right) = \varnothing,$$

$$F\left(x_{4}\right) = \left\{h_{1}, h_{3}, h_{5}\right\}, \ F\left(x_{5}\right) = \left\{h_{1}\right\}$$

Then the soft set $\left(F, E\right)$ is consisting of the following collection of approximation:

$$\left(F, E\right) = \ \{(expensive \ houses, \ \{h_{2}, h_{4}\}),$$

$$(beautiful \ houses, \left\{h_{1}, h_{3}\right\}),$$

$$(wooden \ houses, \varnothing),$$

$$(\ cheap \ houses, \left\{h_{1}, h_{3}, h_{5}\right\}),$$

$$(in \ green \ surrounding, \left\{h_{1}\right\})\}$$

$$= \ (x_{1}, \{h_{2}, h_{4}\}), \ (\ \{x_{2}, \left\{h_{1}, h_{3}\right\}),$$

$$(x_{3}, \varnothing), \ \left(x_{4}, \left\{h_{1}, h_{3}, h_{5}\right\}\right), \ \left(x_{5}, \left\{h_{1}\right\}\right)\}$$

Example 7: Let

$$U = \left\{h_{1}, h_{2}, h_{3}, h_{4}, h_{5}, h_{6}, h_{7}, h_{8}\right\}$$

be the initial universe and let

$$E = \left\{e_{1}, e_{2}, e_{3}, e_{4}, e_{5}, e_{6}\right\}$$

be set of parameters and let

$$F : E \to P\left(U\right)$$

be a mapping given by

$$F\left(e_{1}\right) = \left\{h_{1}, h_{3}, h_{5}\right\},$$

$$F\left(e_{2}\right) = \varnothing,$$

$$F(e_3) = \{h_1, h_4, h_5, h_6\},$$

$$F(e_4) = \{h_7, h_8\},$$

$$F(e_5) = \{h_8\},$$

$$F(e_6) = \{h_4, h_6, h_8\}$$

Let

$$A = \{e_1, e_2, e_3\},$$

$$B = \{e_1, e_4, e_5, e_6\}$$

Then the soft set

$$(F, A) = \{(e_1, \{h_1, h_3, h_5\}),$$

$$(e_2, \varnothing),$$

$$(e_3, \{h_1, h_4, h_5, h_6\})\}$$

and the soft set

$$(F, B) = \{(e_1, \{h_1, h_3, h_5\}),$$

$$(e_4, \{h_7, h_8\},$$

$$(e_5, \{h_8\}),$$

$$(e_6, \{h_4, h_6, h_8\})\}$$

Then the soft set

$$(F, A)^C = (F^C, -A) =$$
$$\{(-e_1, \{h_2, h_4, h_5 h_6, h_7, h_8\},$$
$$(-e_2, U), (-e_3, \{h_1, h_2, h_7, h_8\}$$

be the complement of the soft set (F, A). Also,

$$(F, A) \widetilde{\cap} (F, B) = (F, C) =$$
$$\{(e_1, \{h_1, h_3, h_5\})$$

and

$$(F, A) \widetilde{\cup} (F, B) =$$
$$(F, \{e_1, e_2, e_3, e_4, e_5, e_6\} = \{(e_1, F(e_1)),$$

$$(e_2, F(e_2)), (e_3, F(e_3)), (e_4, F(e_4)), e_5, F(e_5)), (e_6, F(e_6))\}$$

Also

$$(F, A) \widetilde{-} (F, B) = (F, \{e_2, e_3\}) =$$

$$\{(e_2, \varnothing), (e_3, \{h_1, h_4, h_5, h_6\})\}$$

Example 8: Let

$$U = \{h_1, h_2, h_3, h_4, h_5, h_6, h_7\}$$

be the initial universe of seven houses under consideration, and let

$$E = \{x_1, x_2, x_3, x_4, x_5, x_6\}$$

= {Red, Blue, White, Black, Yellow, Green} be the colour of houses as a set of parameters and

$$F : A \to P(U)$$

and

$$G : B \to P(U)$$

be the mapping given by, for

$$A = \{x_1, x_2, x_3, x_5\},$$

$$B = \{x_1, x_2, x_4, x_6\}$$

it has

$$F(x_1) = \{h_1, h_6\},$$

$$F(x_2) = \{h_1, h_2, h_3\},$$

$$F(x_3) = \varnothing,$$

$$F(x_5) = \{h_1, h_4, h_7\}$$

and as the x – approximate elements differ from person to person, we have

$$G(x_1) = \{h_2, h_3\},$$

$$G(x_2) = \{h_1, h_2, h_6\},$$

$$G(x_4) = \{h_2, h_4, h_6\},$$

$$G(x_6) = \{h_1, h_2, h_6, h_7\}$$

then (F, A) and (G, B) be two soft sets on U.

$$w(F, A) \widetilde{\cap} (G, B) = \{(x_1, \ \varnothing), (x_2, \{h_1, h_2\})\},$$

$$(F, A) \widetilde{\cup} (G, B) =$$
$$\begin{bmatrix} (x_1, \{h_1, h_2 h_3, h_6\}), (x_2, \{h_1, h_2 h_3, h_6\}), \\ (x_3, \varnothing), (x_4, \{h_2, h_4 \ , h_6\}), (x_5, \{h_1, h_4, h_7\}), \\ (x_6, \{h_1, h_2, \ h_6, h_7\}) \end{bmatrix}$$

$$(F, A)^C =$$
$$(F^C, -A) =$$
$$\begin{bmatrix} (not\,x_1, \ \{h_2, h_3 h_4, h_5, h_7\}), \\ (not, blue, (h_4, h_5, h_6 \ , h_7\}), \\ (not\,white, U), \\ (not\,yellow, \{h_2, h_3, h_5, h_6\}) \end{bmatrix} e,,$$

$$(F, A) \widetilde{-} (G, B) =$$
$$\{white, \varnothing), (yellow, \{h_1, h_4, h_7\})\}$$

Example 9: Let

$$U = \{a, b, c, d, e, f\}$$

be the initial universe and

$$E = \{x_1, x_2, x_3, x_4\}$$

be the parameter set. Let the mapping

$$F : E \to P(U)$$

be given by

$$F(x_1) = \{a, b\},$$

$(x_2) = \{c, f\},$

$F(x_3) = \{a, c, f\},$

and

$F(x_1) = \{a, b, c\}$

Here the elements $c, d \in U$ are not approximated any of the parameter of soft set (F, E).

Let

$A = \{x_1, x_2, x_4\}$

and

$B = \{x_1, x_2, x_4\} \subseteq E$

be two subsets of parameters then (F, A) and (F, B) be two soft sets.

Let

$G : E \to P(U)$

be the another mapping given by

$G(x_1) = \{a, b\},$

$(x_2) = \{d\},$

$G(x_3) = \{b, c\}$

and

$G(x_1) = \{c, d, e, f\}$

We note here that $S = (F, A)$ be a soft set over U where $A \subseteq E$ and $F : E \to P(U)$ be a mapping. Then $P = (U, S)$ is a soft approximation space.

Let $P(S)$ be the set of all soft sets over . Then $(U, P(S))$ be called soft knowledge base.

Rough Soft Sets [D.Mohanty, N.Kalia, L.Pattanayak, B.B.Nayak,2012]

Here we introduce rough soft approximations. Let U be the initial universe, the compliment of Y in U is denoted by

$Y^C =\sim Y = U \sim Y$

Let U be the set of all parameters $A \subseteq E$

Definition 33: let $S = (F, A)$ be a soft set over . Then the triplet $P = (U, F.A)$ is called soft approximation space and we define two approximation, for $X \subseteq U$ by

$$\underline{apr}_F(X) = \{u \in U : \exists x \in A, [u \in F(x) \subseteq X]\}$$
$$= \bigcup_{x \in A} \{F(x) : F(x) \subseteq X\}$$

$$\overline{apr}_F(X) = M \ , for \ X \subseteq M$$

and

$$\overline{apr}_F(X) = M \bigcup N \ , for \ X \subsetneq M$$

where

$M = \{u \in U : \exists x \in A,$

$[u \in F(x), F(x) \cap X \neq \varnothing\} =$

$\bigcup_{x \in A} \{F(x) : F(x) \cap X \neq \varnothing\}$

and

$N = \bigcap_{x} \{F^C(x) : x \in (-A)\}.$

are called the soft F-lower approximation and the soft F- upper approximation of X, respectively. That, $\underline{apr}_F(X)$ and $\overline{apr}_F(X)$ are referred to rough soft approximations of X with respect to the parameterized mapping F_A, where,

$$F_A : A \to P(U)$$

be the given mapping. The set $X \subseteq U$ is called F-rough soft set if

$$\overline{apr}_F(X) \neq \underline{apr}_F(X)$$

otherwise X is called F-soft definable set.

We denote the notation F_A to just indicate the parameter set A and the mapping F. That is, F_A and F have the name mapping from A to $P(U)$. In this note we use the notation F instead of F_A everywhere.

The sets

$$POS_F(X) = \underline{apr}_F(X),$$

$$NGX_F(X) = \bigcup_{x \in A} \{F(x) : F(x) \cap X = \varnothing\} =$$
$U \sim M, for\, X \subseteq M$

and

$$BN_F(X) = \overline{apr}_F(X) - \underline{apr}_F(X)$$

are called F – soft positive region, F-soft negative region and F-soft boundary region of X, respectively.

- **Note:** In [F.Feng, X.Liu, V.L.Fotea, Y.B.Jun, 2011] they have given the definition of soft rough set as:

Let $S = (F, A)$ be a soft set over U. Then the pair $P = (S, U)$ is called a soft approximation space. Based on the soft approximation space P, we define the following two operations

$$\underline{apr}_P(X) = \{u \in U : \exists a \in A, [u \in F(a) \subseteq X]\}$$

and

$$\overline{apr}_P(X) = \{u \in U : \exists a \in A, [u \in F(a), F(a) \cap X \neq \varnothing]\}$$

assigning to every subset $X \subseteq U$, two sets $\underline{apr}_P(X)$ and $\overline{apr}_P(X)$ are called the soft P-lower approximation and the soft P-upper approximation of X.

The set $X \subseteq U$ is called soft P-rough set if

$$\overline{apr}_P(X) \neq \underline{apr}_P(X),$$

otherwise X is called soft P-definable.

In an example of Feng Feng et al (2011), it is known that a subset $X \subseteq U$ cannot be approximated by $\overline{apr}_P(X)$, that is, $\overline{apr}_P(X) \not\supseteq X$ and also there exits one $\varnothing \neq X \subseteq U$ for which

$\overline{apr}_P\left(X\right)=\varnothing$ and $\underline{apr}_P\left(X\right)=\varnothing$. So it is not a good definition to define roughness in soft set.

In this note we find the properties by using the definition 33 for F-rough soft set.

Proposition 1: Let $S=\left(F,A\right)$ be a soft set over U and $A\subseteq E$ be a set of parameters and $P=\left(U,F,A\right)$ be the corresponding soft approximation space. The F-rough approximation satisfy the following properties

$$\underline{apr}_F\left(\varnothing\right)=\varnothing\ ,\overline{apr}_F\left(\varnothing\right)=\varnothing$$

$$\underline{apr}_F\left(U\right)=U\ ,\overline{apr}_F\left(U\right)=U$$

$$\underline{apr}_F\left(X\right)\subseteq X\subseteq\overline{apr}_F\left(X\right),X\subseteq U$$

$$\underline{apr}_F\left(X\cap Y\right)=\underline{apr}_F\left(X\right)\cap\underline{apr}_F\left(Y\right)\ ,X,Y\subseteq U$$

$$\underline{apr}_F\left(X\cup Y\right)\supseteq\underline{apr}_F\left(X\right)\cup\underline{apr}_F\left(Y\right)\ ,X,Y\subseteq U$$

$$X\subseteq Y\Rightarrow\underline{apr}_F\left(X\right)\subseteq\underline{apr}_F\left(Y\right)$$

$$X\subseteq Y\Rightarrow\overline{apr}_F\left(X\right)\subseteq\overline{apr}_F\left(Y\right)$$

$$\overline{apr}_F\left(X\cup Y\right)=\overline{apr}_F\left(X\right)\cup\overline{apr}_F\left(Y\right)$$

$$\overline{apr}_F\left(X\cap Y\right)\subseteq\overline{apr}_F\left(X\right)\cap\overline{apr}_F\left(Y\right)$$

Example 10: In the example 4.2 suppose that

$$X=\left\{h_2,h_6\ ,h_7\ ,h_8\right\}\subseteq E$$

and

$$B=\left\{e_1,e_4,e_5,e_6\right\}\subseteq E$$

be the set of parameters, $\left(F,B\right)$ be given soft set, then

$$\underline{apr}_F\left(X\right)=\{h_7\ ,h_8\}$$

and

$$\overline{apr}_F\left(X\right)=M\cup N=\left\{h_4,h_6\ ,h_7\ ,h_8\right\}\cup\left\{h_2\right\}=\left\{h_2,h_4,h_6\ ,h_7\ ,h_8\right\}$$

Thus X is rough soft set with respect to the approximation operator apr_F.

DEPENDENCY

Let U be the non –empty initial universe, and E be the set of all parameters; $A\subseteq E$

Definition 34: Let $S=\left(F,A\right)$ and $T=\left(G,A\right)$ be the two soft sets on . The mapping G (or the approximation operator apr_G depends upon the mapping F (or the approximation operator apr_F) denotes $apr_F\Rightarrow$. if and only if, for any $X\subseteq U$

$F(x) \subseteq G(x)$ *wherever* $X \cap F(x) \neq$ $\varnothing$ *for all* $x \in A$

and

$F(x) \supseteq G(x)$ *wherever* $X \cap F(x) =$ $\varnothing$ *for all* $x \in A$.

It is noted that for $apr_F \Rightarrow$. we have

$$\underline{apr_G}(X) \subseteq \underline{apr_F}$$

(X) for all $X \subseteq U$ from the condition (1). Also from the conditions (1) and (2),

$$\overline{apr_G}(X) \supseteq \overline{apr_F}(X)$$

for all $X \subseteq U$. That is borderline region of any set $X \subset U$ under the approximation operator apr_F is contained in the border line region of X under the approximation operator apr_G .

Definition 35: Let U be a finite initial universe,

$$F, G : A \rightarrow P(U)$$

be two mappings, the approximation operators apr_F and apr_G are equivalent, denoted as apr_F $\Leftrightarrow$. if and only if $apr_F \Rightarrow$. and. $apr_G \Rightarrow$. Also the approximation operators are independent, denoted as $apr_F \nleftrightarrow$. if and only if neither apr_F $\Rightarrow$. nor $apr_G \Rightarrow$. hold.

CONCLUSION

A new concept rough soft set is born out of the challenging situations we face for the imprecise and indefinite nature of information in the event of knowledge explosion in the branches of social sciences, pure sciences and applied sciences. The amalgamation of rough set and soft set gives the Heybridge form of rough soft set. The paper validates the new concept with illustrious examples for application in the required space. A verification of the properties of the rough set strengthens the new concept. To sum up, the dependency of knowledge through rough soft set would empower us to tackle the problems of the information processing.

REFERENCES

Ali, M. I., Feng, F., Liu, W. K., & Shabir, M. (2009). On some new operations in soft set theory. *Computers & Mathematics with Applications (Oxford, England)*, *57*, 1547–1553. doi:10.1016/j.camwa.2008.11.009

Atanassov, K. T. (1986). Intuitionistic fuzzy sets. *Fuzzy Sets and Systems*, *20*(1), 87–96. doi:10.1016/S0165-0114(86)80034-3

Cagman, N., & Enginoglu, S. (2010). Soft matrix theory and its decision making. *Computers & Mathematics with Applications (Oxford, England)*, *59*, 3308–3314. doi:10.1016/j.camwa.2010.03.015

Dubois, D., & Parade, H. (1990). Rough fuzzy set and fuzzy rough set. *International Journal of General Systems*, *17*, 191–209. doi:10.1080/03081079008935107

Feng, F., Li, C., Davvaz, B., & Irfan Ali, M. (2010). Soft sets combined with fuzzy sets and rough sets-A tentative approach. *Soft Computing*, *14*, 899–911. doi:10.1007/s00500-009-0465-6

Feng, F., Liu, X., Fotea, V. L., & Jun, Y. B. (2011). Soft sets and soft rough sets. *Information Sciences*, *181*, 1125–1137. doi:10.1016/j.ins.2010.11.004

Liang, Z., & Shi, P. (2003). Similarity measures on intuitionistic fuzzy sets. *Pattern Recognition Letters*, *24*(15), 2687–2693. doi:10.1016/S0167-8655(03)00111-9

Maji, P. K., & Roy, A. R. (2007). A fuzzy soft set theoretic approach to decision making problems. *Journal of Computational and Applied Mathematics*, *203*(2), 412–418. doi:10.1016/j.cam.2006.04.008

Maji, P. K., Roy, A. R., & Biswas, R. (2002). An application of soft sets in a decision making problem. *Computers & Mathematics with Applications (Oxford, England)*, *44*(8-9), 1077–1083. doi:10.1016/S0898-1221(02)00216-X

Maji, P. K., Roy, A. R., & Biswas, R. (2003). Soft set theory. *Computers & Mathematics with Applications (Oxford, England)*, *45*(4-5), 555–562. doi:10.1016/S0898-1221(03)00016-6

Mohanty, D. (2010). Rough set on generalized covering approximation space. *International Journal of Comp. Science and Research*, *1*(1), 432–449.

Mohanty, D., Kalia, N. R., Pattanayak, L., & Nayak, B. B. (2012). An introduction to rough soft set. *Mathematical Sciences*, *1*(3), 927–936.

Molodtsov, D. (1999). Soft set theory—First results. *Computers & Mathematics with Applications (Oxford, England)*, *37*(4-5), 19–31. doi:10.1016/S0898-1221(99)00056-5

Pawlak, Z. (1982). Rough sets. *Int. Jous. of Comp. Inform. Science*, *2*, 341–356. doi:10.1007/BF01001956

Pawlak, Z. (1991). *Rough sets, theoretical aspects of reasoning about data*. Dordrecht, The Netherlands: Kluwer Academic Publishers.

Salleh, A. R. (2011). From soft sets to intuitionistic fuzzy soft sets: A brief survey. In *Proceedings of the International Seminar on the Current Research Progress in Sciences and Technology (ISSTech '11)*. Universiti Kebangsaan Malaysia—Universitas Indonesia.

Wang, S., Hao, G., Ma, J., & Xu, W. (2010). Vague soft sets & their properties. *Computers & Mathematics with Applications (Oxford, England)*, *59*, 787–794. doi:10.1016/j.camwa.2009.10.015

Yao, Y. Y. (1998). Relational interpretations neighbourhood operators and rough set approximation operators. *Information Science*, *3*, 239–259. doi:10.1016/S0020-0255(98)10006-3

Zadeh, L. A. (1965). Fuzzy sets. *Information and Control*, *8*(3), 338–353. doi:10.1016/S0019-9958(65)90241-X

Zadeh, L. A. (1975). The concept of a linguistic variable and its application to approximate reasoning-I. *Information Sciences*, *8*, 199–249. doi:10.1016/0020-0255(75)90036-5

KEY TERMS AND DEFINITIONS

Fuzzy Set: Let U be a set known as universe. A fuzzy set F in U is characterized by a membership function $f_F(x)$ which associates with each point $x \in U$ a real number in closed interval [0,1].

Rough Set: Let A be any subset of the universe U and R be the knowledge (an equivalence relation) defined on U. If the set A is classified under the knowledge R, then A is called an exact set, otherwise A is rough under R.

Rough Soft Set: A rough Soft set is hybrid set of rough set and soft set where $\underline{apr}_F(X) \neq \overline{apr}_F(X)$ in the approximation space $P = (U, F.A)$.

Soft Set: Soft set is not a set in classical sense. It is a parameterized family of subsets of the universe U. The ordered pair (F, E) is called a soft set where $F : E \to A$ is a mapping and E be a set of parameters, $A \subseteq U$ and $(F, E) = \{(e, F(e)) : e \in E, F(e) \subseteq U\}$.

Chapter 14
Diagram Drawing
Using Braille Text:
A Low Cost Learning Aid for Blind People

Anirban Mukherjee
RCC Institute of Information Technology, India

Utpal Garain
Indian Statistical Institute, India

Arindam Biswas
Bengal Engineering and Science University, India

ABSTRACT

This chapter presents a novel system for drawing geometric diagrams on the Braille medium in order to make the diagrams tactile and accessible by blind people. The computer graphics algorithms for drawing digital shapes have been suitably modified to make them work for the Braille environment. The goodness of the diagrams is measured by quantifying approximation errors in these diagrams. This chapter further demonstrates how computational intelligence can be embedded in the system to develop an intelligent teaching-learning aid for the blind, especially for teaching them figure-based subjects like geometry, physics, engineering, drawing, etc.

INTRODUCTION

In the study of different science and engineering subjects, we often encounter texts or problems that are essentially illustrated by figures or diagrams. To understand (and also solve) a problem, the representative diagrams are not a mere convenience but also an inherent component in a person's cognitive representation of a scientific text or problem. Therefore diagrams are important for the blind people just as much as it is for the sighted people. But generating and communicating graphics for the blind people, in the context of a subject, is not as straightforward as it is for the sighted people.

There has been substantial research work on communicating informational graphics to the blind students. As a result several interfaces, tools, and

DOI: 10.4018/978-1-4666-4936-1.ch014

programs for production of accessible graphics are available in developed countries. But most of these systems are research prototypes and not commercially available. Some systems are available in developed countries but they are prohibitively expensive for wide usage in developing countries. Braille (image) embossers that can generate high resolution tactile images through specialized graphics programs are globally available today, but at high cost. The schools in developing regions cannot afford to have image embossers (for directly printing tactile images) or even image enhancer (for translating any pre-existing image to tactile form). At best the students of these schools can have access to traditional Braille text printers that cannot print tactile image.

So, a genuine problem in mathematics education of the blind people in the developing countries is that they cannot access modern tactile media for sensing geometry drawing. Though manipulatives like nail board or wooden pieces are sometimes used to perceive simple diagrams in lower classes, the lack of frequent access to tactile diagrams of wide varieties in higher classes cause severe compromise with proper science education. Braille text printer is available to them so it would be nice if geometry drawings can be printed on Braille paper. But owing to the irregular dot-grid of the Braille text printing system, standard computer graphics programs or tactile graphics programs cannot be directly used to draw diagrams through such medium.

In the backdrop of the above scenario, one of the two distinct contributions of our research is that we introduce a method by which digital diagrams can be mapped to Braille environment and corresponding tactile diagrams can be produced using traditional Braille text printer. Such printer is the cheapest of its kind and commonly available in most blind schools in countries like India. The proposed method does not make use of any sophisticated interface, rather relies on Braille dot grid with uneven spacing of dots to map elements of a diagram already defined for digital display. Improvisation of such Braille printer (meant to

print text only) to represent geometric diagrams is far more challenging than using image embossers with evenly spaced dots. Here, the size or height of the embossed dots cannot be varied and can only be placed within a 6-dot cell (Braille character). In this chapter, we address a complete set of algorithms for representing point, straight line, and circle using Braille code. We have shown how using these basic shapes, simple geometric figures like triangle, rectangle, parallelogram, etc. and diagrams comprising many shapes and configurations can be generated through Braille text printer.

The other contribution of our research is that we have proposed a simple yet useful method to evaluate line and circle represented in Braille by quantifying the approximation errors. In this chapter we have illustrated the method and shown computation of total error of a Braille geometry diagram. Applying the same method we have compared the diagram errors and accuracy of our system (digital to Braille mapping) with that of the systems produced by other researchers before.

Finally the chapter briefly discusses on how this process for representing diagrams in Braille can be automated by integrating it to an (already developed) automated text-to-diagram conversion system. The objective is to maximize the accessibility benefit to a large section of blind student community in the perspective of providing them low-cost learning aid for science subjects like geometry. The role of computational intelligence in developing such system is highlighted in this section. From literature of tactile graphics and review of NLP-based systems (Mukherjee & Garain, 2008) we hardly find any such approach for automatically producing tactile diagrams from digital diagrams using Braille text printer.

BACKGROUND

Upon examining the technologies used worldwide for communicating informational graphics to the blind students, we observe five different modes of graphic communication: (1) tactile, (2) audio-tactile, (3) audio-haptic, (4) multimodal, and (5) 3D audio.

In tactile mode, tactile images with raised lines or dots are produced on Braille paper by Braille image embossers, tactile image enhancer (Braille Graphics and Tactile Graphics from Repro-Tronics, 2013) and refreshable tactile display (Assistive Technology Products, 2013). Popular and lesser cost models of image embossers cost twice as much as low-cost Braille text printer (which cannot print image) as is evident from Table 1. The embossers come with compatible Braille graphics software, e.g. *IVEO Viewer* (Viewplus, 2013), *PictureBraille* (PictureBraille, 2013), *TGD Pro* (Duxbury Systems Products, 2013), *Tiger Software Suite* (ViewPlus Tiger Software Suite, 2013), *TACTICS* (Way & Barner, 1997), *TeDUB* (Horstmann et al., 2004), and *TGA* (Jayant et al., 2007) for creating and editing tactile graphics. There are some modern tactile toolkits (American Printing House for the Blind, 2013; Braille Geometry Kit, 2013) apart from primitive tools like nail-board-elastic band system and the slate-stylus system to help the blind users get primary idea about geometry shapes. There are several research prototypes in audio-tactile category that provide interactive interfaces to draw and trace the drawing with the help of audio feedback - *IC2D* (Hesham & James, 1999), *TDraw* (Kurze, 1996), *NOMAD* (Parkes, 1991), *Talking Tactile Tablet* (Landau & Gourgey, 2003), and *IVEO touchpad* (Krufka & Barner, 2005) are some examples. Audio-tactile diagrams are also prototyped using tactile pin array device and digitizer (Minagawa & Ohnishi, 1996), (Watanabe et al., 2006). Another prototype *DE-SENVOX* (Borges & Jansen, 1999) uses a specially designed menu system and voice guidance utility to generate simple geometric elements and shapes that is finally embossed on a Braille printer. In the audio-haptic category we find systems that use audio support either with force feedback devices like *Touch Tiles* (Bussel, 2003) or with vibratory touchscreen (with actuators or stylus) (Toennies et al., 2011), to convey graphs and shapes through haptic mode (Lahav & Mioduser, 2008). Guha and Anand (1992) have shown how blind students can trace and perceive diagrams on PC monitors by using an optoelectronic sensor and a haptic device producing vibrotactile output. With advances in 3D audio technology there are research proposals (Roth et al., 2000) which attempt to use 3D immersive auditory cues which are really useful for the blind people to mentally represent the topology

Table 1. Cost and type of Braille embossers (courtesy Rahman et al. (2010) with price updated)

Braille Embosser	Key Features	Cost (US$)
Basic-D by Index Braille	Cannot emboss images; Tractor fed paper; Z-Folding	3,295
Everest by Index Braille	Cannot emboss images; Embosses documents, Braille books, labels, and visiting cards; Can use ink and Braille in same document	4,195
4x4 Pro by Index Braille	Can emboss images with WinBraille; Newspaper format	4,795
Emprint SpotDot by ViewPlus	Print the original ink text together with Braille allowing sighted reader to follow along; embosses images; New easy-to-use operator panel with tactile buttons; Uses the same paper and ink cartridges as an HP Inkjet printer	6,995
Premier 80 by ViewPlus	High-speed Braille along with Tiger super-high-resolution graphics ; Automatic double-sided embossing—no flipping the paper; Production-strength hardware made for running long hours; Compact desktop size—smaller than most production embossers	9,995
4Waves Pro by Index Braille	Can emboss images with WinBraille; High embossing speed; 4 modules + one service module; Low noise level	25,995

of a graphical environment. In the multimodal category there are research prototypes like *SALOME* (Gouy-Pailler et al., 2007), *AudioTact* (Barbieri et al., 2008), *Math Class* (Albert, 2006), etc. which use tactile, haptic, and audio feedback together to give enhanced perception of drawing elements.

With regards to producing tactile diagrams from digital diagrams using ordinary Braille text printer, very limited research can be found in the literature. Rahman et al. (2010) have investigated the potential use of a software solution for converting regular print image into tactile image using low cost Braille text printers. The software is designed for sighted users who are required to select images on a printed page, run the software with the printed image as input, and then print the corresponding tactile image for the blind readers. Using an iterative thresholding technique, the software first obtains a thresholded binary image from an original image after resizing it to fit to

an 84x84 pixel frame. Now, each 3x2 block of pixels in the frame is considered equivalent to a Braille cell (3x2 dots) - there are as many pixel blocks (28x42) in the pixel frame as there are printable Braille cells (28x42) in a Braille sheet. The pattern of the marked pixels in each block is mapped to yield same pattern of raised dots in the corresponding cell of the Braille grid. All the mapped cells (or Braille characters), when printed, reproduce the original image in tactile format. Figure 1 illustrates this method of Braille mapping of a digital line.

This system (Rahman et al., 2010) is somewhat related to our system as it can represent tactile diagrams in terms of embossed Braille dots that usually imply Braille text. But the basic approach taken by this system is linear mapping from an evenly spaced pixel-grid to an unevenly spaced dot-grid which inherently causes some distortion in geometric shape. Moreover, the process does

Figure 1. (a) The pixel frame comprises 42 columns and 28 rows of pixel blocks (shown by red boxes), each containing 3x2 pixels, (b) The Braille grid comprises 42 columns and 28 rows of Braille cells, each containing 3x2 Braille dots. The pixel blocks with black pixels in (a) are mapped to the Braille cells at similar positions in the Braille grid in (b). This ultimately results in a series of raised Braille dots (shown in red) representing the tactile version of the digital line in (a). The pattern of raised dots in a Braille cell represents a character of Braille text.

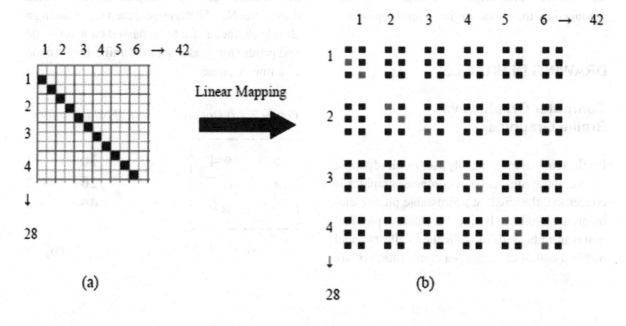

(a)

(b)

not attempt to optimize the number or position of dots to be embossed. Quite expectedly, it causes redundant dots being selected at positions other than the best possible positions with respect to the true entity path. Our system, on the contrary, logically finds the dot nearest to the entity path at any sampling position and further optimizes the number of adjacent dots getting selected to make the best possible outline-representation of an entity.

BrlGraphEditor (Batusic & Urban, 2002) and *Sparsha Chitra* system (Lahiri et al., 2005) are two other software tools (with design similar to the one developed by Rahman et al. (2010)) that convert images into suitable form for printing on a Braille text printer. Both the systems provide a GUI editor that displays graphics in exactly the same resolution as used by the Braille printer. The tactile graphics viewed in the editor can be edited before finally being embossed. In both the systems, no optimization attempt is made to improve the graphics.

The three Braille mapping tools discussed above basically work on existing printed images. Their capability in generating complex geometry diagrams is not readily understood as those were not employed to do so. Moreover, no technique for numerical evaluation of the Braille graphics produced by these systems has been proposed.

DRAWING IN BRAILLE

Computer Graphics vs. Braille Graphics

Braille is a system commonly used by blind people to read and write. As far as computer graphics is concerned, the smallest addressable picture elements are pixels. In Braille, the smallest physical unit is an embossed dot, while the smallest logical unit is a cell or character – a combination of six such dots arranged in a 3 x 2 array. While each pixel can display a color according to the bitmap value, each dot of a Braille cell may be in embossed state depending on the NUMBRL code (Krebs, 1977) of the character to be represented in that cell.

NUMBRL is basically a numeric code that represents the dot patterns in Braille cells. Each dot in a cell has a fixed position value (as shown in Figure 2). The NUMBRL code of a cell is just the sum of the position values of the embossed dots of the cell. For example, consider a cell with embossed dot positions 4-2-6. The NUMBRL code for this cell is $1+20+4 = 25$.

As there are 6 dots in a Braille cell the number of different patterns or NUMBRL codes that can be generated in a cell by embossing a subset of 6 dots at a time is 2^6 or 64. This implies 64 different Braille characters can be printed by a Braille text printer. A given NUMBRL code corresponds to a character of English alphabet or a punctuation symbol or a digit.

In digital graphics (Rogers, 1985) we can algorithmically select and illuminate a set of pixels to generate a line or circle. Similarly, in Braille, the first problem is to identify which dots in which cells are to be embossed for the best possible representation of a line or circle. In the second stage, cell-wise patterns of identified dots or the NUMBRL codes, each representing a Braille character, are to be passed on to a Braille text printer for producing the Braille-text version of a line or circle.

Figure 2. (a) Dot positions, (b) Position values

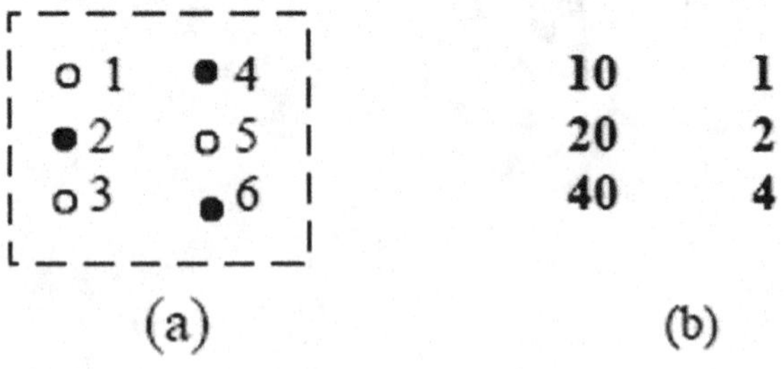

Graphics Algorithms for Braille

Let us consider a grid of pixels that resembles the actual spacing of dots of a 2D array of Braille characters or cells. We now discuss how dot positions can be identified algorithmically in the grid to best represent lines or circles.

Line Drawing

For embossing a straight line in Braille we have used the mid-point subdivision method. The mid-point subdivision method is based on a recursive algorithm (*Midpoint_line*) that keeps on finding the midpoints of bisected line segments and subsequently finds the nearest Braille dot from the newly found midpoint 'pm' (x,y) in each iteration. When the length of a divided line segment becomes less than the minimum distance between two adjacent Braille dots (say, n), the recursion unwinds. The arguments of the function are the line endpoints p1 (x1,y1) and p2 (x2,y2). Figure 3 illustrates the sequential selection of Braille dots in the grid while line p1p2 is processed.

Figure 3. Line drawing in Braille – selected Braille dots (shown in thick black dots) corresponds to midpoints pm1, pm2, pm3, pm4 found in the upper half of the line p1p2. Similarly for the lower half of the line there will be few more Braille dots selected.

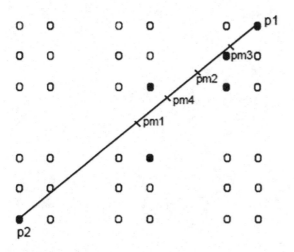

The functions *Midpoint()*, *Distance()* are standard functions to calculate the midpoint between two points and distance between two points respectively. *Find_nearest_Braille_dot()* is the function used to search a Braille dot that lies closest to the newly found midpoint 'pm' on the line path. The function measures and compares the distance of 'pm' from each of the Braille dots that fall within a small square region (2n x 2n) around 'pm'. The dot that gives the least distance is the nearest dot found in the search and its position is saved in a file. If there is more than one such dot, only the one found first will be selected as the nearest Braille dot.

It is to be noted that like the midpoint algorithm, other standard algorithms for drawing digital lines (e.g. *DDA* or *Bresenhams' algorithm* (Rogers, 1985)) can also be modified by applying the function *Find_nearest_Braille_dot()* to select nearest Braille dots corresponding to digital pixels generated by these algorithms.

Circle Drawing

As far as drawing curved line in Braille is concerned, the popular midpoint algorithm (Rogers, 1985) for drawing digital circle is suitably improvised to create the Braille function *Midpoint_circle()*. The change that we have made in the midpoint algorithm is in the function for generating 8 symmetric pixels (one in each octant) on the digital circle in every iteration. For every pixel position p (x,y) determined in the first octant, the function *Generate_symmetric_Braille_dot()* is called within *Midpoint_circle()*. This function then finds a Braille dot nearest to the circle path by calling the function *Find_nearest_Braille_dot()* corresponding to each of the eight symmetric pixel positions including p (see Figure 4).

Braille Mapping of Digital Diagram

In the previous sections we have shown how the standard computer graphics algorithms for drawing digital lines or circles (using pixels) are

Algorithm 1. Function Midpoint_line()

```
Midpoint_line(p1, p2)
Input: Coordinates of two pixels (p1 and p2) which are the end points of a
digital line
Output: A list of Braille dots (positions) representing the corresponding
Braille line
n: minimum distance between two adjacent Braille dots
{
   pm = Midpoint(p1,p2)
   Find_nearest_Braille_dot(pm)
   if Distance(pm,p1)>n
     Midpoint_line(p1,pm)
   end if
   if Distance(pm,p2)>n
     Midpoint_line(pm,p2)
   end if
}
```

Algorithm 2. Function Find_nearest_Braille_dot()

```
Find_nearest_Braille_dot(p)
Input: A pixel p whose x and y coordinates are p.x and p.y
Output: Position of the nearest Braille dot corresponding to p written to a
file
n: minimum distance between two adjacent Braille dots
{
 Set Dmin = max_value
 for (i = p.x - n to p.x + n)
   for(j = p.y - n to p.y + n)
     if Braille_dot(i,j) = TRUE
        D = Distance((p.x,p.y),(i,j))
        if D < Dmin
          Dmin = D
           Nearest_dot = (i,j)
         end if
      end if
      j = j + 1
   end for
   i = i + 1
 end for
 Save Nearest_dot to File
}
```

Figure 4. Circle drawing in Braille – The circle in blue represents the digital circle. The circle is divided into octants with dotted lines. Corresponding to pixel p (shown in red) on the circle in the first octant, p_1-p_7 are seven symmetric pixels in seven other octants. One Braille dot is selected nearest to each of these pixels. The thick black dots are all such selected dots that represent the Braille circle.

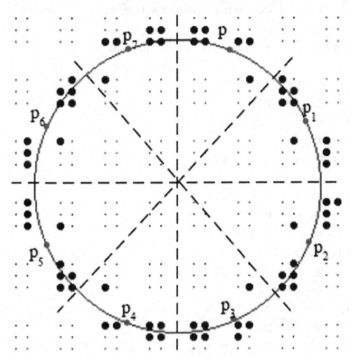

Algorithm 3. Function Midpoint_circle()

```
Midpoint_circle(c,r)
Input: center: c, radius: r
Output: A list of Braille dots (positions) representing the circle
p: a pixel on the digital circle whose x and y coordinates are p.x and p.y
{
  p.x = 0, p.y = r
  Q = 1 - r
  while p.x < p.y do
    if Q < 0
      p.x = p.x + 1
      Q = Q + 2*p.x + 1
    else
      p.x = p.x + 1
      p.y = p.y - 1
      Q = Q + 2*(p.x - p.y) + 1
    end if
    Generate_symmetric_Braille_dot(c,p)
  end while
}
```

Algorithm 4. Function Generate_symmetric_Braille_dot ()

```
Generate_symmetric_Braille_dot(c,p)
Input: center: c, a pixel on a circle: p
Output: Eight Braille dots corresponding to the eight symmetric pixels on the
digital circle
p1: a symmetric pixel on the circle corresponding to p
{
  p1.x = c.x + p.x; p1.y = c.y + p.y
  Find_nearest_Braille_dot(p1)
  p1.x = c.x + p.x; p1.y = c.y - p.y
  Find_nearest_Braille_dot(p1)
  p1.x = c.x - p.x; p1.y = c.y + p.y
  Find_nearest_Braille_dot(p1)
  p1.x = c.x - p.x; p1.y = c.y - p.y
  Find_nearest_Braille_dot(p1)
  p1.x = c.x + p.y; p1.y = c.y + p.x
  Find_nearest_Braille_dot(p1)
  p1.x = c.x + p.y; p1.y = c.y - p.x
  Find_nearest_Braille_dot(p1)
  p1.x = c.x - p.y; p1.y = c.y + p.x
  Find_nearest_Braille_dot(p1)
  p1.x = c.x - p.y; p1.y = c.y - p.x
  Find_nearest_Braille_dot(p1)
}
```

modified to represent lines or circles using Braille text characters. Now to demonstrate the actual implementation of the Braille mapping system we have made a simulation of Braille character mapping of geometric entities. The computer screen emulates the grid of Braille cells (each having 6 dots) printed by a traditional Braille printer; the array of 6-pixel groups displayed on the screen resembles the actual spacing of dots in the Braille grid. A standard size of Braille sheet is 11x11 inches and some Braille text printers can print 28 rows and 42 columns of Braille cells (or a periodic, but uneven grid of 84x84 dots) in a Braille sheet. One Braille dot having diameter of 1.5mm is represented by a pixel. The distance between two adjacent dots in a cell is kept uniform (2.4 mm) while the horizontal and vertical distances between two corresponding dots in adjacent cells are set unequal (6.8 mm and 10.1 mm respectively) as usually found in the traditional Braille system. In our experiment with the integrated system, we have used an Automatic Braille Embosser (BPRT) developed by Webel Mediatronics Limited (an India Govt. undertaking organization). This is basically a Perkins Brailler and it costs about US $3000.

Braille Mapping of Basic Entities

The functions *Midpoint_line()* or *Midpoint_circle()* generate a set of Braille dots that represent in Braille a digital line or circle respectively. Screen pixels at all such selected dot positions are marked with thick dots to emulate actual embossing of dots by a Braille text printer. By searching in an array that previously stores coordinates of all dots of all cells, it is then found which selected dot belongs to which cell. Position values of the selected dots in a cell are then added up to find the NUMBRL code of that cell. If there are no dots selected in a cell, the NUMBRL value of that cell is 0 which implies that the cell doesn't participate in Braille mapping. This process executed by the function *Find_NUMBRL()* is illustrated in Figure 5.

One row of NUMBRL codes in the output file correspond to one print line by Braille text printer. As the printer prints all the coded characters of the output file row-wise, the line or circle (or any Braille diagram) takes shape in Braille.

Braille Mapping of Problem Diagrams

The set of numerical values of the parameters of component lines and circles of a digital diagram (corresponding to a geometric statement or problem) is taken as input by the Braille mapping

module. For example, the numerical values of the endpoint coordinates of the four component lines of a digitally drawn parallelogram are, say:

```
(100,200),(50,100)
(50,100),(250,100)
(250,100),(300,200)
(300,200),(100,200)
```

These values are passed on as input (argument) to the *Midpoint_line()* function separately. This function along with the *Find_NUMBRL()* function then creates four Braille lines to produce the Braille version of the digital parallelogram.

A portion of the emulated Braille dot grid and embossed dots approximating different geometric shapes are shown in Figure 6. Initially we generated entities like straight line and circle (Figure 6(a) and (b) respectively) from corresponding digital representation. This is followed by generating simple geometric objects like parallelogram (as in Figure 6(c)), triangle (as in Figure 6(d)), rectangle, square, pentagon, hexagon, etc.

Figure 5. (a) Selection of nearest grid points (Braille dots) for representing a line in Braille, (b) The NUMBRL position values shown for selected dots in a Braille cell; The NUMBRL code for the cells having selected dots are (left to right, top to bottom): 0, 4, (20+40+1 =) 61, 40, 1, 0. The output list given by the function Find_NUMBRL() contains the following triplets: <1 1 0> <1 2 4> <1 3 61> <2 1 40> <2 2 1> <2 3 0>

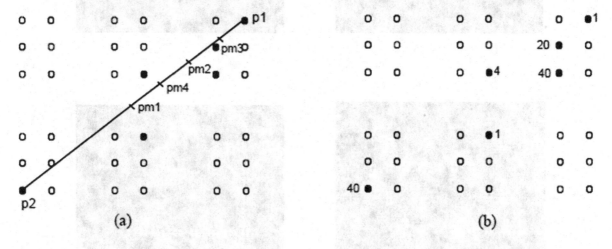

Algorithm 5. Function Find_NUMBRL() for finding NUMBRL code of a participating Braille cell

```
Find_NUMBRL()
Input: List of dots (positions) selected by the Braille drawing algorithm
Output: List of NUMBRL values of all Braille cells written to a file
i: Braille cell row position, j: Braille cell column position; pos: position
value of a dot
{
        for all (i,j) NUMBRL(i,j) = 0; end for
        for every dot d in the input list
            Find the Braille cell (i,j) corresponding to d
            pos = position value of d in cell(i,j)
            NUMBRL(i,j) += pos
        end for
        for all (i,j)
            write(i,j,NUMBRL(i,j)) to File
        end for
}
```

Figure 6. Computer simulation of Braille character grid and Braille-converted entities; the digital equivalents of the entities are shown in continuous lines while selected Braille dots are shown in solid dots. (a) line, (b) circle, (c) parallelogram, (d) triangle

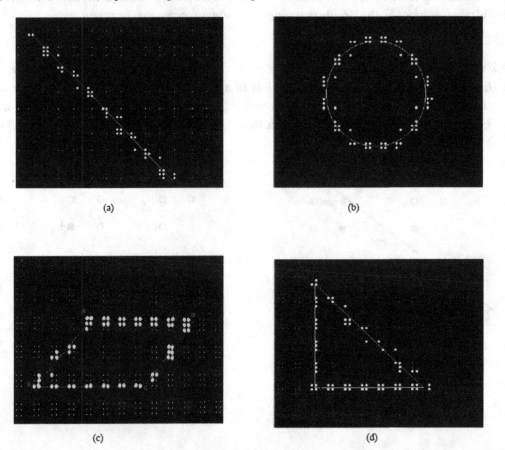

After generating simple objects, we tested our system for diagrams comprising multiple objects. The system, upon feeding the numerical values of the parameters defining the digital diagrams, yielded Braille diagrams for a test set of 32 geometry problems. The simulated Braille diagrams for 3 out of 32 problems are cited in Figure 7.

In the Braille objects (or diagrams) finally produced on Braille sheet, points are not labeled according to description and that is done intentionally to keep our study focused on the use of Braille for conveying a diagram rather than text. Labeling diagrams at this stage might confuse users and reduce their recognition accuracy. Once

Figure 7. Simulated Braille diagrams for the problems – (a) ABCD is a parallelogram. X and Y are the midpoints of AD and BC. BX and DY cuts AC at M and N respectively. Prove that AM = MN = NC, (b) PQ is a diameter of a circle centered at O. The tangents drawn at P and Q of the circle are APB and CQD. Prove that AB∥CD, (c) In triangle ABC, AB = AC. D is the midpoint of BC. From D, perpendiculars DM, DN are drawn to AB and AC respectively. Prove that DM = DN.

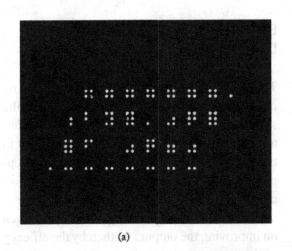

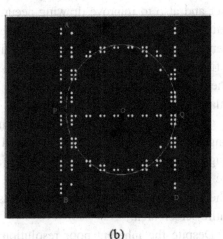

(a)

(b)

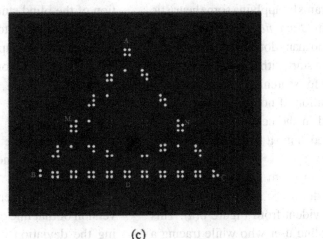

(c)

the users are familiar with Braille character chains as diagram elements, labels can be generated along with diagrams to better illustrate the problem description. We have put the labels of the points in the figures here for the sake of illustration only.

DESIGN OPTIMIZATION

It is seen that the numerical values passed as arguments of Braille drawing functions often cause entities produced in Braille too small in size to be separately recognized by touch only. To improve perception of a Braille-mapped figure by a blind user and also to improve drawing accuracy the better option is to generate figures in a larger scale. Hence, depending on the size, a digital diagram is first resized so that it can fit to the full-screen. Then digital to Braille mapping is done for the enlarged diagram causing the simulated Braille diagram also fit to the screen. This in turn yields longer lines and larger circles in the printed Braille diagram. It may be noted that Figures 6(a) - (d) are each screenshot of a portion of the screen whereas Figures 7(a) –(c) are screenshots of the entire screen area.

Despite the inherent poor resolution of the Braille system, we have tried to improve the quality of the Braille diagrams by applying some heuristic methods. Earlier the *Find_nearest_Braille_dot( )* function selected too many dots. To retain optimum number of dots, we start with a reduced range (in x and y direction) for searching of dots near to a selected pixel position. If no dot is selected, the range is increased in the next iteration and the process is repeated until a prefixed maximum range is attained.

Again, another problem noted was selection of more than one dot in the same row for an inclined line as is evident from Figure 6(a). This might confuse a blind user who while tracing a line path would expect a single raised dot at any position on the line path. This redundancy is eliminated by comparing the distances (from the line path) of all the selected dots in a row and retaining only the dot at minimum distance. However, the elimination of extra dots is avoided if it causes a wide gap between the retained dot and the next selected dot in the adjacent row along the same line path. The maximum allowable gap is the distance between two diagonally adjacent cells. Overall, the quality of the Braille figures has improved after implementing the design optimizations; the blind students could now recognize those figures with greater accuracy. The resultant simulated diagrams (e.g. those shown in Figure 8) reflect this optimization effect.

EVALUATION OF BRAILLE DIAGRAMS

The pixel resolution of computer display being much higher than the dot resolution of Braille system, the approximation of entities in the latter system is naturally much coarser than that in the former one. Another reason behind this approximation error is the uneven spacing of dots in the traditional Braille system. This error if quantified will have a bearing on future research on improving the output and thereby the efficacy of the system in supporting mathematics education of the blind students. Here we have applied a standard method to measure the approximation errors in Braille mapping of line and circle which are the basic components of geometry diagrams.

Error in Line

Figure 9 shows the simulated Braille version of a digital straight line. The original line is shown in red color.

The error between the actual line and the Braille version of that line can be found by first calculating the deviation or distance of each selected Braille dot from the actual line path and then finding the average of the squares of all such distances. This average is called the Mean Square

Algorithm 6. The optimized function Find_nearest_Braille_dot()

```
Find_nearest_Braille_dot(p)
Input: A pixel p whose x and y coordinates are p.x and p.y
Output: Position of the nearest Braille dot corresponding to p written to a
file
n: minimum distance between two adjacent Braille dots
w: length used to define the window for searching a Braille dot
Found: flag that indicates whether any dot is found within search window
{
set Dmin = max_value
set Found to 0
set w to n/2
while (NOT Found AND w <= 2*n) do
  for (i = p.x - w to p.x + w)
    for(j = p.y - w to p.y + w)
      if Braille_dot(i,j) = TRUE
        Found = 1
        D = Distance((p.x,p.y),(i,j))
        if D < Dmin
          Dmin = D
            Nearest_dot = (i,j)
          end if
        end if
        j = j + 1
      end for
      i = i + 1
    end for
    w = w + n/2
  end while
  If (Found) Save Nearest_dot to File
}
```

Error (MSE) of selected Braille dots with respect to the actual line. The general steps for finding the MSE of a Braille line is explained next.

Step 1: From endpoint coordinates (and slope) of the given line calculate y-value on the actual line corresponding to each sampling position or x-value.

Step 2: At every sampling position find the y-value(s) of the selected Braille dot(s).

Step 3: For every sampling position calculate the difference between the y-value on actual line and the y value of a selected dot on the Braille line. This difference is the deviation of the Braille line from the actual line or the approximation error at that sampling position.

Figure 8. Modified simulated diagram corresponding to - (a) Figure 7(a), (b) Figure 7(c)

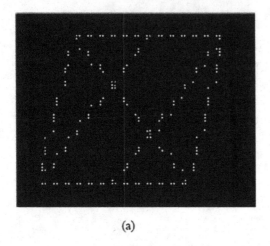

(a)

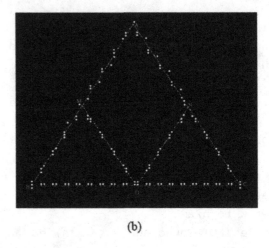

(b)

Step 4: Find the mean square of all the differences calculated in Step 3. This gives the MSE of the Braille approximation of the line.

The MSE of the line shown in Figure 9 turns out to be 0.035. It may be noted that there may be more than one selected Braille dot at a sampling position. In such case, error or difference should be calculated separately for all selected Braille dots having same x-value.

Error in Circle

Figure 10 shows the simulated Braille version of a digital circle. The original circle is shown in red color.

Similar to the Braille line, error of a Braille circle is found in terms of MSE of the selected Braille dots with respect to the actual circle.

Step 1: For each selected Braille dot calculate the difference between its (Euclidean) distance

Figure 9. A simulated Braille line represented by yellow Braille dots; the corresponding digital line (in red) is superimposed to show the deviation of the Braille dots from the line path

Figure 10. A simulated Braille circle represented by yellow Braille dots; corresponding digital circle (in red) is superimposed to show the deviation of the Braille dots from the circle path

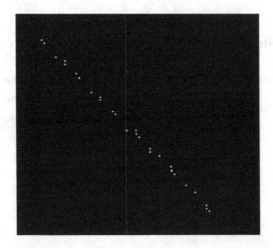

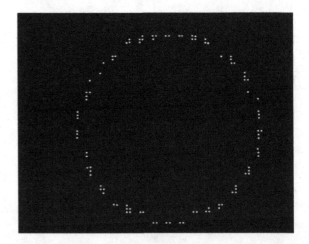

from the center of the circle and the actual radius of the circle. This difference is the deviation of that Braille dot from the actual circle path.

Step 2: Find the mean square of all the differences calculated in Step 1. This gives the MSE of the Braille approximation of the circle.

For the circle shown in Figure 10 the MSE calculated is 0.049.

Error in Diagrams

To find a measure of the errors in representing a geometric object (like triangle, parallelogram, etc.) or a diagram (e.g. diagrams shown in Figure 8) in Braille, we first evaluate the MSE of each constituent line and circle of a diagram. Then we find the cumulative MSE (of all the entities) which when divided by the number of entities gives the average MSE of a diagram (See Table 2).

We have evaluated Braille diagrams produced corresponding to 32 geometry word problems. The MSE for these 32 diagrams varied from 0 to 0.055. It is observed that the average MSE increases if number of inclined lines and circle increases whereas the increased number of vertical and horizontal lines effectively reduces the average MSE. For the individual geometric objects the error is mostly restricted within 0.020 (for parallelograms we find it worst i.e. 0.026).

Error Comparison with Other System

The literature does not provide any method of evaluation of accuracy of graphics generated using Braille text printer. To evaluate the effectiveness of our proposed method of Braille mapping of figures we have made a quantitative comparison of errors of Braille diagrams produced in our system to that produced using the method proposed by Rahman et al. (2010). We have calculated the MSE of a Braille line and a circle that can be produced by the latter system from the same set of input parameter values as used above. The MSE calculated for the simulated Braille line is 0.165 against 0.035 in our method whereas the MSE obtained for the simulated Braille circle is 0.147 against 0.049 in our case. In the other system the average errors (MSE) in Braille shapes/diagrams listed in Table 2 varies from 0 (for rectangle) to 0.104 (for parallelogram) and all the MSE values are 2 to 3 times greater or even more compared to the respective values obtained for our system. Thus,

Table 2. Average error of Braille diagrams

Shape/Diagram	Component Entity	Avg. MSE of Shape/Diagram
Equilateral Triangle	one horizontal line, two inclined lines	0.020
Right angled Triangle	one horizontal line, one vertical line, and one inclined line	0.012
Rectangle	two horizontal lines, two vertical lines	0
Parallelogram	two horizontal lines, two inclined lines	0.026
Hexagon	two vertical lines, four inclined lines	0.015
Figure . 7(b) (modified form)	one horizontal line, two vertical lines, and one circle	0.014
Figure . 8(a)	two horizontal lines, five inclined lines	0.023
Figure . 8(b)	one horizontal line, four inclined lines	0.022

empirically we find that as far as the accuracy of Braille figures is concerned, our system/method is more effective compared to that proposed by Rahman et al. (2010).

COMPUTATIONAL INTELLIGENCE IN DRAWING OF BRAILLE DIAGRAMS

As the method described in this chapter is capable of producing geometric diagrams on low-cost Braille text printer, it will certainly provide significant benefit to the blind students in accessing diagrams. But to enjoy the facility, assistance of a sighted person (may be the teacher) will be required who will have to create the digital diagram first (as the basic input to the Braille mapping system) upon reading a geometric description. Else, the blind students themselves will not be able to generate Braille diagrams according to a description to comprehend the description or solve a geometry word problem by their own. To address this issue we have further enhanced our Braille mapping module by integrating it with an earlier developed system (Mukherjee & Garain, 2009) that produces digital geometry diagrams directly from textual description (of the diagram) in natural language (English). As a result of this integration (refer Figure 11), given a geometry word problem as input, the system automatically generates the underlying diagram on Braille text

printer. This provides the proposed system with the much needed utility of a self-learning tool. The blind students simply need to type the text (a geometry word problem) using a Braille type writer to get the system-generated tactile diagram illustrating the text. This option is also helpful for the teacher who can just key in a text and easily generate multiple copies of the representative tactile diagram. This saves the teachers' effort wasted otherwise in creating and presenting accessible graphics for the blind students in a class.

The framework for drawing geometry diagrams directly from a geometry problem text comprises three logical parts - i) syntactic and to some extent semantic processing of the problem text in natural language (English), ii) machine understanding of the geometric meaning of the problem, and iii) applying standard graphics functions for drawing line or circle with necessary data to generate a diagram in computer.

It is the human experience and expertise in a subject domain (here geometry) and language domain (here English) that helps to figure out the essence of a word problem out of all lexical complexity and then attempt to draw/solve the problem. Simulating the logical and knowledge-based human approach one geometry knowledge base and two parsers are developed. *Parser 1* analyzes a problem-text, extracts the useful parts and correlates each part to generate a language-free *intermediate representation* while *Parser 2*

Figure 11. The connection between the earlier developed system of automatic diagram drawing from text and the Braille mapping system (within dotted boundary)

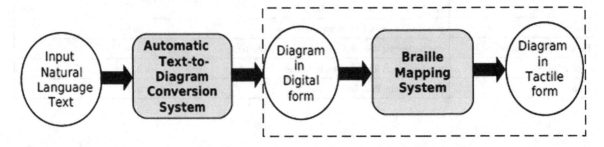

uses the intermediate representation for further processing i.e. machine understanding and diagram drawing.

A schematic diagram (refer Figure 12) illustrates the sequential execution of the functional modules of the framework. The *Parser 1* (Mukherjee et al., 2013) uses NLP tools (mainly parts-of-speech tagging) and a geometry knowledgebase namely *GeometryNet* (Mukherjee et al., 2007) to analyze the problem text and summarize the useful information extracted from the problem in a language-free formal representation in the form of a parse graph. Once the parse graph is produced it goes through a *Translator* which generates a graphics-friendly summary of the same parse graph. This summary is termed as intermediate representation which can be considered another language independent, unique, unambiguous representation of the input problem statements. A second parser, i.e. *Parser 2* acts on the intermediate representation of the problem statement, aided by the geometry knowledge base, to generate a set of arguments of graphics functions. A graphics module can then generate the required diagram through several calls to the graphics functions.

As the integration of the text-to-diagram conversion system is done with the Braille mapping module, the set of arguments (of the digital line/circle drawing functions) produced by Parser 2 is directly passed on as input arguments of the Braille line/circle drawing functions. This in-turn produces the Braille lines and circles and the diagram as a whole. Thus Braille diagrams are now directly produced from input geometric statements unlike the isolated Braille mapping system that can only recreate a diagram in Braille from its digital equivalent.

USER EVALUATION OF THE INTEGRATED SYSTEM

A user study (Mukherjee et al., 2013) was carried out at a Blind school in Kolkata, India with several groups of blind and sighted students and teachers over a span of nearly seven months to test their

Figure 12. Schematic diagram showing sequential execution of the modules of the text-diagram conversion system

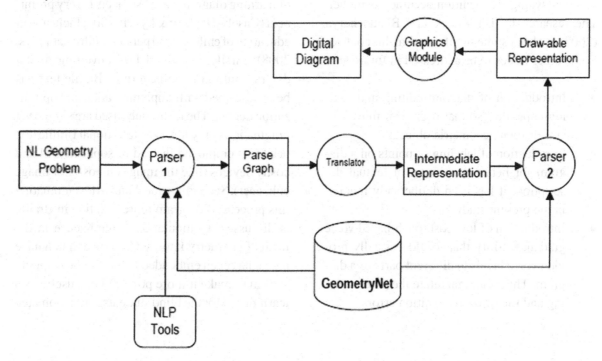

recognition of Braille diagrams automatically produced by our integrated system. The purpose was also to investigate the existing practice of classroom education of science subjects (including geometry), related problems or limitations, and most importantly, perceptions of the users towards the new system of diagram representation using Braille text. After overcoming the initial problem of confusing chain of Braille characters as text rather than outline of a geometric figure, the test subjects showed great interest in the training and diagram tracing process. Results showed that most participants could recognize most diagrams generated from text input after a series of training and most of the participants had positive impression about the system.

FUTURE SCOPE

Though the system described in this chapter is tested to be reasonably useful for the target users, there is much scope for improvement of the Braille mapping algorithms. In future, effort can be made towards even better representation of graphic entities so that approximation errors are less and average recognition accuracy is higher. The research by Bhowmick and Bhattacharya (2007) can be of some significance in this context. Some other issues to be addressed in future are:

- Introduction of diagram editing and scaling capability so that users can move, resize or rotate geometric objects.
- Introduction of labeling of points on a diagram for better illustration of textual description. It has been deliberately ignored in the present study.
- Introduction of low-cost touch-based voice guidance utility that would basically provide voice labels to different parts of a diagram. This would facilitate the object tracing and minimize recognition errors.

- Inclusion of better option for step-wise (statement-wise) diagram drawing to help the blind students in recognizing complex diagrams. This would render more self-control and learner-centric facility of the system.

Though geometry problems are taken as a case study, this work can be extended to address similar problems in other subject areas (e.g. physics, engineering drawings, etc.). Following similar approach as described here, simple electrical or electronic circuits, building diagrams, free body diagrams, etc. can be generated from the problem texts that describe such circuits or diagrams. However, this would require development of suitable knowledge bases containing descriptions of diagram-elements specific to a subject.

CONCLUSION

This chapter investigates an automated approach for generating low-cost tactile graphics for providing better science education to the blind students in the developing countries where inconvenience of learning diagram based subjects is very prominent (Casely-Hayford & Lynch, 2003; Inclusion in education of children and persons with disabilities, 2008). Firstly, a method for converting digital diagram into graphic pattern of Braille text has been described with implementation and optimization details. The techniques used are simple yet pragmatic as only low-cost traditional Braille text printer is employed instead of sophisticated and costly devices (like the image embosser or image enhancer). Secondly, a mechanism for automating this process of diagram representation in Braille is discussed. Computational intelligence in the form of geometry knowledge base and language parser has been embedded to the Braille mapping system to make it more powerful and useful as a learning aid for the blind students. The automated system can now be directly used by the blind students (without any assistance) - one can give (by typing) a geometry word problem as input to the system and get the corresponding diagram as Braille printout. Encouraging results obtained in the user study in a typical resource-constrained blind school in India attests the effectiveness of the system.

Though there are certain cases where the system fails to generate correct diagrams from geometric word problems, the reason of failure is determined and it no way undermines the logic and design of the approach. For each problem that produces correct result in digital form also produces correct result in tactile form. But it is a fact that the Braille lines or circles generated using our system are not as smooth as those which are manually set or embossed using image embossers. A method for evaluating the accuracy of Braille lines, circles and diagrams comprising multiple lines and circles is proposed in this chapter. The errors computed on a test set of Braille diagrams seem acceptable on all practical aspect; it is experienced that such errors do not affect much the effective cognition of a diagram by the target users. Again when compared with similar other systems, the mean errors of the diagrams are found lesser for our system – the design optimizations are probably the cause of this better quality.

Finally this chapter identifies the weak points of the system described and suggests probable methods to minimize the weaknesses in future. Additional utilities of the system are also envisaged which can provide some future research directions in the area of computational intelligence. As an outcome of future research endeavors on Braille mapping system we can expect development of a fully automated and intelligent teaching-learning utility available at low cost for the blind community of developing countries.

REFERENCES

Albert, P. (2006). Math class: An application for dynamic tactile graphics. In *Computers helping people with special needs (LNCS)* (Vol. 4061, pp. 1118–1121). Berlin: Springer. doi:10.1007/11788713_162

American Printing House for the Blind, Inc. (2013). *Shopping*. Retrieved June 30, 2013 from http://shop.aph.org/webapp/wcs/stores/servlet/Home1000111051

Barbieri, T., Mosca, L., & Sbattella, L. (2006). Learning math for visually impaired users. In *Computers helping people with special needs (LNCS)* (Vol. 5105, pp. 907–914). Berlin: Springer. doi:10.1007/978-3-540-70540-6_136

Batusic, M., & Urban, F. (2002). Preparing tactile graphics for traditional braille printers with Brl-GraphEditor. In *Computers helping people with special needs (LNCS)* (Vol. 2398, pp. 261–274). Berlin: Springer. doi:10.1007/3-540-45491-8_101

Bhowmick, P., & Bhattacharya, B. B. (2007). Fast polygonal approximation of digital curves using relaxed straightness properties. *IEEE Transactions on Pattern Analysis and Machine Intelligence*, 29(9), 1590–1602. doi:10.1109/TPAMI.2007.1082 PMID:17627046

Borges, J. A., & Jansen, L. R. (1999). Blind people and the computer: An interaction that explores drawing potentials. In *Proceedings of SEMENGE'99 - Seminário de Engenharia. Universidade Federal Fluminense Brazil*. SEMENGE.

Braille Geometry Kit. (2013). Retrieved June 30, 2013 from http://www.mathwindow.com/brl_geometry.html

Braille Graphics and Tactile Graphics from Repro-Tronics. (2013). Retrieved June 30, 2013 from http://www.Brailler.com/repro.htm

Bussel, L. (2003). Touch tiles: Elementary geometry software with a haptic and auditory interface for visually impaired children. In *Proceedings of EuroHaptics Conference* (pp. 512-515). EuroHaptics.

Casely-Hayford, L., & Lynch, P. (2003). *A review of good practice in ICT and special educational needs for Africa*. Retrieved June 30, 2013 from www.comp.dit.ie/dgordon/Publications/Contributor/Ghana/SENPHASE1FINAL.pdf

Duxbury Systems Products. (2013). Retrieved June 30, 2013 from http://www.duxburysystems.com/products.asp

Gouy-Pailler, C., Zijp-Rouzier, S., Vidal, S., & Chêne, D. (2007). A haptic based interface to ease visually impaired pupils' inclusion in geometry lessons. In *Proceedings of 4th International Conference on Universal Access in Human-Computer Interaction* (pp. 598-606). IEEE.

Guha, S. K., & Anand, S. (1992). Computer as a group teaching aid for persons who are blind. *Journal of Rehabilitation Research and Development*, *29*(3), 57–63. doi:10.1682/JRRD.1992.07.0057 PMID:1640382

Hesham, M. K., & James, A. L. (1999). The integrated communication 2 draw (IC2D), a drawing program for the visually impaired. In *Proceedings of Extended Abstracts on Human Factors in Computing Systems (CHI '99)* (pp. 222-223). ACM.

Horstmann, M., Lorenz, M., Watkowski, A., Ioannidis, G., Herzog, O., & King, A. et al. (2004). Automated interpretation and accessible presentation of technical diagrams for blind people. *New Review of Hypermedia and Multimedia*, *10*(2), 141–163. doi:10.1080/13614560512331326017

Inclusion in Education of Children and Persons with Disabilities. (2008). Retrieved June 30, 2013 from http://www.ibe.unesco.org/National_Reports/ICE_2008/india_NR08.pdf

Jayant, C., Renzelmann, M., Wen, D., Krisnandi, S., Ladner, R. E., & Comden, D. (2007). Automated tactile graphics translation: in the field. In *Proceedings of ASSETS* (pp. 75-82). ASSETS.

Krebs, B. M. (1977). *ABCs of Braille*. Braille Institute of America.

Krufka, S. E., & Barner, K. E. (2005). Automatic production of tactile graphics from scalable vector graphics. In *Proceedings of 7th International ACM SIGACCESS Conference on Computers and Accessibility*. ACM.

Kurze, M. (1996). Tdraw: A computer-based tactile drawing tool for blind people. In *Proceedings of Second Annual ACM Conference on Assistive Technologies* (pp. 131-138). Vancouver, Canada: ACM.

Lahav, O., & Mioduser, D. (2008). Haptic-feedback support for cognitive mapping of unknown spaces by people who are blind. *International Journal of Human-Computer Studies*, *66*, 23–35. doi:10.1016/j.ijhcs.2007.08.001

Lahiri, A., Chattopadhyay, S. J., & Basu, A. (2005). Sparsha: A comprehensive indian language toolset for the blind. In *Proceedings of 7th International ACM SIGACCESS Conference on Computers and Accessibility*. ACM.

Landau, S., & Gourgey, K. (2003). A new approach to interactive audio/tactile computing: the talking tactile tablet. In *Proceedings of Technology and Persons with Disabilities Conference*. California State Univ. Northridge.

Minagawa, H., & Ohnishi, N. (1996). Tactile-audio diagram for blind persons. *IEEE Transactions on Rehabilitation Engineering*, *4*(4), 431–437. doi:10.1109/86.547946 PMID:8973970

Mukherjee, A., & Garain, U. (2008). A review of the methods for automatic understanding of natural language mathematical problems. *Artificial Intelligence Review*, *29*(2), 93–122. doi:10.1007/s10462-009-9110-0

Mukherjee, A., & Garain, U. (2009). Understanding of natural language text for diagram drawing. In *Proceedings of IASTED International Conf. on Artificial Intelligence and Soft Computing* (pp. 138–145). Palma De Mallorca, Spain: IASTED.

Mukherjee, A., Garain, U., & Nasipuri, M. (2007). On construction of a GeometryNet. In *Proceedings of IASTED International Conference on Artificial Intelligence and Applications (AIA '07)* (pp. 530-536). IASTED.

Mukherjee, A., Sengupta, S., Sen, A., Chakraborty, D., & Garain, U. (2013). Text to diagram conversion: A method for formal representation of natural language geometry problems. In *Proceedings of IASTED International Conference on Artificial Intelligence and Applications (AIA '13)* (pp. 137-144). IASTED.

Parkes, D. (1991). Nomad: Enabling access to graphics and text-based information for blind and visually impaired and other disability groups. In *Proceedings of World Congress Tech. People Disabil* (pp. 689 - 716). Arlington, VA: IEEE.

PictureBraille. (2013). Retrieved June 30, 2013 from http://www.pentronics.com.au/index_files/PictureBraille.htm

Rahman, M. K., Sanghvi, S., Toyama, K., & Dias, M. B. (2010). Experiences with lower-cost access to tactile graphics in India. In *Proceedings of First ACM Symposium on Computing for Development*. ACM.

Refreshable Tactile Display, Assistive Technology Products. (2013). Retrieved June 30, 2013 from http://www.abledata.com/

Rogers, D. F. (1985). *Procedural elements for computer graphics*. New York: McGraw Hill Book Co.

Roth, P., Petrucci, L., & Pun, T. (2000). From dots to shape: an auditory haptic game platform for teaching geometry to blind pupils. [ICCHP.]. *Proceedings of ICCHP*, *2000*, 603–610.

Toennies, J. L., Burgner, J., Withrow, T. J., & Webster, R. J. (2011). Toward haptic/aural touchscreen display of graphical mathematics for the education of blind students. In Proceedings of *World Haptics Conference (WHC)* (pp. 373 - 378). IEEE.

Viewplus. (2013). Retrieved June 30, 2013 from http://www.viewplus.com/about/abstracts/05csungardner2.html

ViewPlus Tiger Software Suite. (2013). Retrieved June 30, 2013 from http://www.viewplus.com/products/software/Braille-translator/

Watanabe, T., Kobayashi, S., & Yokoyama, K. (2006). Practical use of interactive tactile graphic display system at a school for the blind. In *Current developments in technology-assisted education* (pp. 1111–1115). Academic Press.

Way, T. P., & Barner, K. E. (1997). Automatic visual to tactile translation, part 2: Evaluation of the tactile image creation system. *IEEE Transactions on Rehabilitation Engineering*, 5.

KEY TERMS AND DEFINITIONS

Braille: It is a tactile writing system used by the blind people for books, menus, signs, currency, etc. Braille is named after its creator, Frenchman Louis Braille who introduced the NUMBRL code to represent an alphanumeric character through different arrangement of six dots in a cell.

Braille Mapping of Digital Graphics: This refers to the process of representing digital graphic objects (generated in computer) in the Braille output system of dots. The mapping basically generates a pattern of Braille dots from a pattern of pixels maintaining the same representation as a whole.

Braille Printer: These are impact printers (also known as Braille embosser) which can produce on Braille papers tactile text or image with raised dots or lines. Traditional Braille printers cannot emboss images but the modern and costly printers can emboss high resolution images besides texts.

Computational Intelligence: It is a set of nature-inspired computational methodologies and approaches to address complex real-world problems. It involves automated reasoning and decision making by the machine using any or all of artificial neural networks, evolutionary computation, fuzzy logic, swarm intelligence, knowledge representation, machine learning, etc. and covers broader fields such as image processing, data mining, natural language processing, etc.

Computer Graphics: This field of computer science deals with the representation and manipulation of image data by a computer. Some of the procedures of computer graphics are: generation of line, circle, and other closed and open curves, geometric and viewing transformation of graphic objects, object clipping and area filling, texturing, illumination, surface modeling, etc.

Geometry Knowledge Base: It is a domain specific ontology for geometrical terminology. GeometryNet is such a knowledge base where the semantics of certain geometric terms are expressed in terms of equations involving their arguments. This is used for automated text-to-diagram conversion.

Natural Language Processing (NLP): It is a field of artificial intelligence and linguistics concerned with the interactions between computers and human (natural) languages. Many challenges in NLP involve natural language understanding i.e. enabling computers to derive meaning from human or natural language input.

Tactile Graphics: This refers to images that use raised surfaces so that a blind person can feel them. They are used to convey non-textual information such as maps, paintings, graphs and diagrams.

Text-to-Diagram Conversion: It is the process by which a diagram or figure is produced from a text that describes the diagram. Such texts are encountered very often in different science and engineering subjects. Automated text-to-diagram conversion requires knowledge base of the different terms and concepts of the domain the text refers to, machine understanding of the technical meaning of the text, and graphics procedures to draw the representative diagram.

Chapter 15
Application of Functional Approach to Lists for Development of Relational Model Databases and Petri Net Analysis

Sasanko Sekhar Gantayat
GMR Institute of Technology, India

B. K. Tripathy
VIT University, India

ABSTRACT

The concept of list is very important in functional programming and data structures in computer science. The classical definition of lists was redefined by Jena, Tripathy, and Ghosh (2001) by using the notion of position functions, which is an extension of the concept of count function of multisets and of characteristic function of sets. Several concepts related to lists have been defined from this new angle and properties are proved further in subsequent articles. In this chapter, the authors focus on crisp lists and present all the concepts and properties developed so far. Recently, the functional approach to realization of relational databases and realization of operations on them has been proposed. In this chapter, a list theory-based relational database model using position function approach is designed to illustrate how query processing can be realized for some of the relational algebraic operations. The authors also develop a list theoretic relational algebra (LRA) and realize analysis of Petri nets using this LRA.

INTRODUCTION

The concept of set introduced by G. Cantor (1883) is perhaps the most fundamental notion in mathematics. Although the formal definition of a set led to many antinomies (Reisig, 1983), the deviational cases occur in some artificial situations and so the mathematics basing upon this notion is a sound one for most of the situations. In a set the order of occurrences of elements as well the number of times an element occurs is of no importance. However, it was found later that

DOI: 10.4018/978-1-4666-4936-1.ch015

the number of times an element occurs in a collection is significant in many real life situations and cannot be avoided. This paved the way for the introduction of the notion of bags or multisets (Albert, 1991; Miyamoto, 2001; Yager, 1986). In a bag the number of times an element occurs is accounted for. However, the notions like queues and stacks, piles and racks of books, people seating in a vehicle all require the order of occurrence of elements as significant in modeling them. So, the notion of list was introduced to model such situations (Bird and Walder, 1988). In computer science the notion of arrays plays this role. In a list both the number of times and element occurs and their order of occurrence are important. The foundation of some topics like functional programming depends upon the notion of lists. The applications where arrangement of objects is of importance, the list is the most suitable model. Some other examples of lists can be as follows. Without the concept of list model, permutation cannot be represented. Arrangements of books on a shelf, arrangement of commodities in a ration shop, are better modeled through a list. Words used in natural languages are lists and sentences, paragraphs, pages and books are nothing but lists of characters. A computer program is a list of instructions.

A list is a linearly ordered collection of elements; one can talk about the first element of a list, the second element and so on. Lists are also called sequences in mathematics. Like sequences in mathematics, a list can contain an infinite number of elements. An important property of list is that all the elements of a given list must have the same type: one can have a list of numbers, a list of characters, even a list of lists (of values all of same type), but one cannot mix values of different types in the same list. One can put kind of a constraint on lists.

The concept of lists has long since been used in computer science. Lists are as important in functional programming as the sets are in many branches of mathematics. There was no formal definition of list in the same sense as for sets or multisets. In fact, a set is synonymous with its characteristic function and a bag is synonymous with its count function. However, the corresponding notion is the position unction introduced by Jena et al (2001). There are many advantages of this definition instead of the earlier non-formal definition of a list in the literature. The rich theory of functions could be used to define characteristics of lists and establish their properties in a more formal and concise manner.

The notion of database concept came from the principle of sequential files of data for information processing. Due to the computer system support for handling different types of files, it was required to process the information quickly based on a particular type of databases. Several types of databases have been developed for different applications and the structures of these databases are also different. The development of a database concept from sequential file to rough relational database model changed the world where vague and imprecise data can be handled. The relational database model, which is now used, is associated with the relation of attributes in the form of a table, where it is assumed that there is are duplicate tuples stored in the database. In fuzzy relational database model the information or the data stored is vague and imprecise. Whereas, in the bag database model, it is required to count the number of tuples of same type and stores in a counter, in which the duplicacy of tuples are considered.

In real life situation, it is important to know where and when a tuple or data is inserted in a database table, and how many times a tuple or a data occurs in a database table. So it is necessary to place a tuple or a data in a database table according to the position of occurrence, so that one can get the information about a tuple or a data that when it was stored and what is its position. Consider the example, where there are two employees joined in an organization in the same day. The organization is not interested to keep the joining time but interested in the sequential process of operation where the transaction takes place. Then it is difficult to take a decision to choose the employee who joined first. If the organization uses a sequential database where the position of the occurrence is important then it can be decided that which employee joined first.

It is also sometimes possible that the occurrence of multiple tuples in a database, for example the bag database model, where it is difficult to find the position of the occurrence of a tuple.

In this chapter we have proposed relational algebraic operations where the occurrence of a tuple or a data is based on the position of the occurrence with the duplicacy in the database model. The database model is based on the list theoretic operation (Tripathy and Gantayat, 2013). This article describes the list theoretic relational algebraic operations, which overcomes all the problems of the bag database model. The notations used for the algebraic operations are different for other notations like bags or multi sets and the relational database model (Tripathy and Pattnaik, 2004).

The overall structure of the chapter is as follows. In the beginning, we present some definitions and notations to be used throughout this chapter. Some important theorems on properties of lists which are to be used in this chapter have been also presented. After the theorems we present the important concept of filter and some of its properties. The proposed list theoretic relational model using the functional definition has been presented and many of the related concepts are defined using the lists with its functional definition. Some of these definitions are those of the operations;"insertion", "deletion" and "modification". We provide several examples to illustrate these operations. We define the unary operations on a relational database; like the "projection" and "selection" and illustrate their functioning through examples. In the next section we define and illustrate the binary opera-

tions, "union", "intersection" and "difference". Some of the issues related to implementation of this relational database are also discussed. Further, we discuss an important application of this approach by formalizing the theory of Petri nets using list theoretic relational algebra by the way extending the earlier approach using the extended bag theoretic relational algebra. At the end of this chapter, we summarise the contents of this chapter and provide some problems for further study on the topics of the chapter followed by a list of source materials consulted during the process of compilation of this piece of work.

DEFINITIONS AND PROPERTIES

We state below the definitions of several concepts, which are to be used in this chapter:

Definition 1: A list L drawn from a set X is characterized by its position function P_L defined as $P_L: X \rightarrow P(N)$, where $P(N)$ denotes power set of the set of non–negative integers N. For each $x \in L$, $P_L(x)$ is the set of positions in L where x occurs.

Definition 2: For any finite list L drawn from X, the cardinality or length of L is denoted by #L and is defined as

$$\#L = \sum_{x \in X} |P_L(x)|$$

whenever the right hand side exists. In this case L is said to be finite, otherwise L is said to be infinite.

Definition 3: Let L be a list drawn from X. We define the head of L, denoted by hd(L) as

$$hd(L) = x, \text{ if } 0 \in P_L(x).$$

Definition 4: A list L drawn from X is empty if $P_L(x) = \phi$ for each $x \in X$ and is denoted by [ ].

Definition 5: Let L_1 and L_2 be two finite lists drawn from X. Then the concatenation of L_1 and L_2 is denoted by $L_1 \# L_2$ and is given by the position function,

$$P_{(L_1 \# L_2)}(x) = P_{L_1}(x) \cup \left\{ \# L_1 + t : t \in P_{L_2}(x) \right\}, \; x \in X.$$

Definition 6: Let L_1 and L_2 be two lists drawn from X. Then we define the zip (L_1, L_2) of L_1 and L_2 by,

$$P_{zip(L_1, L_2)}(x, y) = \left\{ r : r \in P_{L_1}(x) \cap P_{L_2}(y) \right\}$$

$$= P_{L_1}(x) \cap P_{L_2}(y)$$

Definition 7: For a finite list L the functions init and last are given as

$$init(L) = rev\left(tl\left(rev(L)\right)\right),$$

and

$$last(L) = x, \; if \; (\# L - 1) \in P_L(x)$$

Definition 8: Let L be a finite list L drawn from X. Then the take operator on L, for any given $n \in N$, is denoted by take(n, L) and it is a list whose position function is given by

$$P_{take(n, L)}(x) =$$
$$\begin{cases} \phi, \; if \; n \leq \min P_L(x) \; or \; P_L(x) = \phi \\ \left\{ r : r < n \; and \, r \in P_L(x) \right\}, \; if \; n > P_L(x) \end{cases}$$

Definition 9: Let L be a finite list drawn from X. Then, for any $n \in N$ the drop operator on L is denoted by drop (n, L) and it is a list whose position function is given by

$$P_{drop(n, L)}(x) =$$
$$\begin{cases} \phi, \; if \; n > \max P_L(x) \\ \left\{ r - n : r \geq n \; and \; r \in P_L(x) \right\}, \\ \quad if \; n \leq \max P_L(x) \end{cases}$$

Definition 10: For any two lists L_1 and L_2 defined over X and Y respectively, we define their Cartesian product $L_1 \otimes L_2$ by

$$L_{\neg 1} \otimes L_2 = P_{(L_1 \otimes L_2)}(x, y) =$$
$$\left\{ \# L_2 . s + t : s \in P_{L_1}(x), t \in P_{L_2}(x) \right\}$$

Definition 11: Let L be a list drawn from X and f be a mapping from X to X. Then map(f, L) is a list whose position function is given by

$$P_{map(f, L)}(y) = \{r: y = f(x) \text{ for some } x \in X \text{ and } r \in P_L(x)\}.$$

The notion of zip of two lists defined above can be extended to a finite number of lists as follows:

Definition 12: Let $L_1, L_2, ...L_k$ be k lists drawn from X. Then $zip(L_1, L_2, ...L_k)$ is defined as a list on X^k whose position function is given by

$$P^{(x_1, x_2, ..., x_k)}_{zip(L_1, L_2, ..., L_k)} =$$

$$P_{L_1}(x_1) \cap P_{L_2}(x_2) \cap ... \cap P_{L_k}(x_k).$$

In some applications, it is required that the zip operation for lists be defined such that the length of all the lists be made up by adding null elements at the end and even there may be some positions in the lists which are blank. We denote elements in such positions in the lists by '*'. To distinguish this special type of zip from the original one we denote it by zip*.

SOME THEOREMS

Next, we state some theorems from (Tripathy and Gantayat, 2004) which are to be used in the sequel.

Theorem 1: (Tripathy, and Gantayat, 2004, Theorem 3.1) For any two functions f and g defined on X, and lists L, L_1 and L_2 drawn from X, we have:

1. map(fog, L) = map(f, map(g, L)), where o denotes the usual composition of functions.

Further, if the lists L, L_1, and L_2 are finite, then:

2. map(f, $L_1 \| L_2$) = map(f, L_1) $\|$ map(f, L_2).
3. map(f, rev(L)) = rev(map(f, L)).
4. hd(map(f, L)) = last(map(f, rev(L)))
5. map(f, []) = [].

Theorem 2: (Tripathy and Gantayat, 2004, Theorem 3.2) Let L be list drawn from X and f be a function X. Then for any $n \in N$,

1. map (f, take (n, L)) = take (n, map (f, L)) and
2. map (f, drop (n, L)) = drop (n, map (f, L))

Theorem 3: (Tripathy and Gantayat, 2004, Theorem 3.3) For any function f defined on X, and lists L_1, L_2 drawn from X,

map (f, zip(L_1, L_2))= zip (map (f, L_1), map (f, L_2)).

Theorem 4: (Tripathy and Gantayat, 2004, Theorem 3.4) Let L and L′ be two finite lists drawn from X where L′ is finite. 'f' be a one to one function from X to X. Then

1. map(f, L − [x]) = map(f, L) − map(f, [x]) and
2. map(f, L − L′) = map(f, L) − map(f, L′)

Theorem 5: (Tripathy and Gantayat, 2004, Theorem 3.1) For any $n \in N$ and finite lists L_1 and L_2 drawn from X, we have

Index(L1$\|$L2, n)=

$$\begin{cases} index(L_1, n), & if \; n < \#L_1; \\ index(L_2, n - \#L_1), & if \; n \geq \#L_1. \end{cases}$$

Theorem 6: (Tripathy and Pattnaik, 2004) Let L_1 and L_2 be two lists drawn from X. Then

take (n, zip(L_1, L_2)) = zip(take(n, L_1), take(n, L_2)).

Note 1: The above result can be extended to k-lists, that is take

(n, zip(L_1, L_2, ..., L_k)) = zip(take(n, L_1)

take

(n, L_2), ..., take(n, L_k)).

Also, zip can be replaced by zip*.

Theorem 7: (Tripathy and Pattnaik, 2004) For any two lists L_1 and L_2 of the same cardinality,

zip (take (n, L_1), take (n, L_2)) = take (n, zip (L_1, L_2)).

THE 'FILTER' OPERATOR AND ITS PROPERTIES

The function 'filter' takes a predicate p and a list L and returns the sublist L' of L whose elements satisfy p (Bird and Walder, 1988, p.65).

To define this important concept we require the following:

Definition 13: Let L be a finite list drawn from X. Then the *indexlist* (L, j), denoted by L_j is a singleton list containing the element at the jth position of L and is defined as

L_j = take(j +1, L) – take(j, L), $0 \leq j \leq$ # L.

Let L be a finite list drawn from X and p be a predicate on X. We define the Boolean function f_p as,

$f_p(x)$ = 1, if p(x) is true; = 0,

otherwise.

Now, for easier presentation, we use the notations,

L(p) = map (f_p, L) and P(L, p) = $P_{L(p)}(1)$.

Here L(p) is a binary list of 0s and 1s. $P_{L(p)}(1)$ provides the position of 1s in the list L(p).

Definition 14: Let L and p be as above. Then

$$filter\left(p,\ L\right)= \underset{j\ \in\ P(L,p)}{\#\#} L_j.$$

The following example illustrates the computation of filter using the above definition.

Example 1: Suppose L = [1, 2, 3, 4, 5, 6, 7, 8, 9, 10] and p be the predicate *'divisible by 4'*. Then

$$f_{divisible\ by\ 4}\left(x\right) = \begin{cases} 1, & \textit{if } x \textit{ is divisible by } 4; \\ 0, & \textit{otherwise.} \end{cases}$$

Here, we know that filter(*divisible by 4*, L) = [4, 8].

Now, map ($f_{divisible\ by\ 4}$, L) = [0, 0, 0, 1, 0, 0, 0, 1, 0, 0].

So, P(L, $f_{divisible\ by\ 4}$) =

$P_{map(f_{divisible\ by\ 4},L)}(1) = \{3,\ 7\}.$

Here, L_3 = [4] and L_7 = [8].

Now, filter (*divisible by 4*, L) =

$$\underset{j\ \in\ P(L,\ divisible\ by\ 4)}{\#\#} L_j =$$

$$\underset{j\ \in\ \{3,\ 7\}}{\#\#} L_j =$$

$L_3 \#\# L_7$ = [4] $\#\#$ [8] = [4, 8].

Lemma 1: Suppose L_1 and L_2 are two finite lists drawn from X. Then for any $j \in N$,

$$\left(L_1 \#\# L_2\right)_j = \begin{cases} (L_1)_j & \textit{if } j < \#L_1; \\ (L_2)_{j-\#L_1} & \textit{if } j \geq \#L_1. \end{cases}$$

LIST THEORETIC RELATIONAL MODEL

In the relational database model a database is a collection of relations, which is a table. Each row of a table consists of a collection of data values, one each from each of the domain values of different columns of which the table is comprised of. The table name and the column names are used to interpret the meaning of the values of each row of the table. It is assumed that each column has same data type.

As per Codd (1970), a row is called a tuple, and a column header is called an attribute and the relation is called a table. The data types that describe the values of each data in a column are called a domain of the corresponding attributes.

In the presented list theoretic relational model it is considered that each column is a list consisting of elements of the same data type and the column header is the name of the list, which is considered as the attribute name. Each column has a domain of some data type. The combination of lists form a relation schema T called as a table.

A relation schema T in our sense, $T (L_0, L_1, ..., L_{k-1})$ is composed of the relation T and the attributes which are lists $L_0, L_1, ..., L_{k-1}$. Each attribute or list L_i has some domain D and is denoted as $dom(L_i) = D_i$.

Definition 13: (Relation) Suppose $L_0, L_1, ..., L_{K-1}$ are the lists(attributes) drawn from a universe X. Then a *relation* r of T is a subset of the Cartesian product of the domains that are in T and

$$r(T) \subseteq dom(L_0) \times dom(L_1) \times .... \times dom(L_{k-1}).$$

In this case, the tuple t of the relation schema T is defined as $t = (t_0, t_1, ..., t_{k-1})$, where each $t_i \in L_i$ and the value of t_i is an element of $dom(L_i)$.

Generally, in a file or a database system there is a way to uniquely identify the distinguished data records or tuples and these unique identifications are made by a specific attribute or combination of attributes.

But, in list theoretic relational model the data records or the tuples are identified by the corresponding positional functions. The data records or the tuples may or may not be unique in the table T. So there are duplicate data items or tuples present and they can be accessed only by their positional values. We may note that duplication of tuples may not be there in the original tables. But it cannot be avoided in the derived tables. So, in case of original tables, the position function of a tuple provides a singleton set or an empty set.

When we study database systems it is necessary to use null values in attributes where there is no information to be stored. So we define the null values in the following manner.

Definition 14: (Null values) A null value of an attribute may be defined as the information that is either not available or unknown or does not exist. We define the null value as the symbol 'Δ' throughout this chapter. For example, consider the following information table, where there are some values of the attributes are unknown. These attribute values are mentioned by the symbol 'Δ'.

Table 1. Relation T (personal information)

Person	Data of Birth	Place	Hobbies	Experience
Roshan	12-12-1973	India	Singing, Writing	30
Polviz	01-04-1964	Spain	Jokes	38
Johnson	Δ	US	Tennis, Swimming	35
Hwang	06-08-1980	Japan	Δ	31

Definition 15: (Generalized zip) For the two elements x and y occurs in pairs based on the corresponding position functions, we can generalize the property of the zip function to k–lists in following manner.

Suppose $L_0, L_1, \ldots$ and L_{k-1} are k–lists drawn from the universe X.

Then zip* $(L_0, L_1, \ldots, L_{k-1})$ can be defined as follows.

$$P^{(x_0, x_1, \ldots, x_{k-1})}_{zip*(L_0, L_1, \ldots, L_{k-1})} =$$

$$P_{L_0}(x_0) \cap P_{L_1}(x_1) \cap \ldots \ldots \cap P_{L_{k-1}}(x_{k-1})$$

$$\forall x_j \in L_j, j = 0, 1, \ldots k{-}1$$

Definition 16: (Table or Relation) A table or a relation T over a universe X is defined as

$$T = zip* (L_0, L_1 \ldots L_{k-1}),$$

where L_j (j= 0, 1, …., k–1) are the attributes of the table T. Here T is also a list of composite elements of other lists.

Definition 17: (Tuple) If $L_0, L_1 \ldots L_{k-1}$ are the attributes of T, the elements of $L_0, L_1, \ldots, L_{k-1}$ together form a tuple of the table T with corresponding positional functions.

That is,

$$P_T(x_0, x_1, \ldots, x_{k-1}) =$$

$$P^{(x_0, x_1, \ldots, x_{k-1})}_{zip*(L_0, L_1, \ldots, L_{k-1})} =$$

$$P_{L_0}(x_0) \cap P_{L_1}(x_1) \cap \ldots \ldots \cap P_{L_{k-1}}(x_{k-1})$$

So here $(x_0, x_1, \ldots, x_{k-1})$ is a tuple of length k of the table T.

Example 2: Consider the database table T(patient) is now in the form shown in Table 2. where:

- Name = [Johny, Bevan, Jenia, Simon, Marry]
- Sex = [male, male, female, male, female]
- Blood_Pressure = [low, high, low, medium, low]
- Age_Group = [young, middle, young, old, middle]

Verification

$$P_T(\text{Jenia, Female, Low, Young}) = \{2\}$$

We have, P_T(Jenia, Female, Low, Young) = {2}.
  Now, P_{Name}(Jenia) ={ 2}, P_{Sex}(Male) = {2, 4}, $P_{Blood\_Pressure}$(Low) = {0, 2, 4}, and

$$P_{Age\_Group}(\text{Young}) = \{0, 2\}.$$

So, we get

Table 2. Database table T for patients

I	Name	Sex	Blood_Pressure	Age_Group
0	Johny	Male	low	Young
1	Bevan	Male	high	Middle
2	Jenia	Female	low	Young
3	Simon	Male	medium	Old
4	Marry	female	low	Middle

P_{Name}(Jenia) $\cap$ P_{Sex}(Female) $\cap$ $P_{Blood\_Pressure}$(Low) $\cap$ P_{Age_Group}(Young) = {2}.

This is true for the table T. Here, #T = the number of tuples = 5 and #A(T) = the number of attributes = 4.

Definition 18: In a table T, a tuple $(x_0, x_1, ..., x_{k-1})$ exists if $P_T (x_0, x_1, ..., x_{k-1}) \neq \phi$, otherwise the tuple does not exist in the table T.

The repetition of a tuple provides the information about where its position is, and how many times it is repeated.

Note 2: It will provide us correct answers to the queries where repetitions of elements are likely to occur, i.e. list gives the most suitable representation for the number of times and the places where a tuple is located. And it can also be tackled with bag theoretic approach where we get the number of times of repetition.

Definition 19: Suppose T is a table with k attributes, where T = zip* $(L_0, L_1, ..., L_{k-1})$. We define, #T is the number of tuples in a table, where #T = #L_i for each i = 0, 1, 2..., k–1 and #A(T) is the number of attributes in the table T = k. So, a table T is a matrix of order (#T × #A(T)).

Definition 20: (INSERTION) Suppose t is a tuple of T. Then we can insert the tuple t in any position of the table T. That is, we can insert the tuple t in an empty table or add the tuple t at the end of the table T or we can insert the tuple at any position of T.

Suppose t = $(t_0, t_1, ..., t_j, ..., t_{k-1})$.

1.　Inserting a tuple t in an empty table T:

The transformed table will be

$$T' = zip^*(L'_0, L'_1, ..., L'_{k-1})$$

where

$L'_i = [ ] \#\!\!\!+ [t_i]$ for each i = 0, 1, ..., k–1.

2.　Inserting a tuple t in a table T:

In this case the tuple t is appended with the present table T i.e. each attribute (list) of the table T will be appended at the end. The transformed table will be

$$T' = zip^*(L'_0, L'_1, ..., L'_{k-1})$$

where

$L'_i = L_i \#\!\!\!+ [t_i]$ for each i = 0, 1, ..., k–1.

3.　Inserting a tuple t at a particular position j of the table T:

The transformed table will be

$$T' = zip^*(L'_0, L'_1, ..., L'_{k-1}),$$

where

$L'_i = take(j{-}1, L_i) \#\!\!\!+ [t_i] \#\!\!\!+ drop(j{-}1, L_i)$

for each i = 0, 1, ..., k–1 and $j \geq 1$.

Definition 21: (DELETION) Suppose t is a tuple of T. Then we can delete the tuple t from any position of the table T. That is, we can delete t from the top of table or form the middle of the table T or we can delete the tuple t from the end of the table T.

Suppose $t = (t_0, t_1, ..., t_j, ..., t_{k-1})$.

1. *Deletion of the tuple t from the beginning (top) of the table T:* The transformed table will be

$T' = zip*(tl(L_0), tl(L_1), ..., tl(L_{k-1}))$.

2. *Deleting a tuple t from end of the table T:* In this case the tuple t is deleted from the end of the table T i.e. from end of each attribute (list) of the table T. The transformed table will be

$T' = zip*(init(L_0), init(L_1), ..., init(L_{k-1}))$.

3. *Deleting a tuple t from a particular position j of the table T:* The transformed table will be

$T' = zip*(L'_0, L'_1, ..., L'_{k-1})$,

where $L'_i = take(j-1, L_i) + drop(j, L_i)$ for each i = 0, 1, ..., k-1 and $1 \leq j \leq \#L_i$.

Definition 22: (MODIFICATION) A tuple t of T can be modified with another tuple t' at the position j of the table T with the following steps.

Suppose $T = zip*(L_0, L_1, ..., L_j, ..., L_{k-1})$ and $t = (t_0, t_1, ..., t_i, ..., t_{k-1})$. Let t will be modified with $t' = (t'_0, t'_1, ..., t'_i, ..., t'_{k-1})$.

Step 1: *Delete the corresponding tuple t from the table T from the position j. The temporary table will be T'. i.e.:*

$T' = zip*(L'_0, L'_1, ..., L'_j, ..., L'_{k-1})$

where

$L'_i = take(j-1, L_i) + drop(j, L_i)$

for each i = 0, 1, ..., k-1 and $1 \leq j \leq \#L_i$.

Step 2: *Insert the new tuple or modified tuple t at the position jth position.*

$T'' = zip*(L''_0, L''_1, ..., L''_j, ..., L''_{k-1})$

where

$L''_i = take(j-1, L'_i) + [t'_i] + drop(j-1, L'_i)$

for each i = 0, 1, ..., k-1 and $1 \leq j \leq \#L'_i$.

In this case we can change or modify a particular attribute(s) without affecting the other attributes to consume time and space.

Example 3: (The detailed database is given in next page) Consider the following sample relation table T of a flight schedule database of United Airlines, Airline ID: 20355 at the Airport: Reno-Sparks, NV - Reno-Tahoe International (RNO) for the month of January 2012, with six attributes mentioned below. (Source: *Bureau of Transportation Statistics, USA,* www.bts.gov)

Abbreviation used in the Flight Database:

- **Date:** Flight date,
- **FlightNo:** Flight number,
- **TailNo:** Tail number,
- **DAirport:** Destination airport,
- **SDTime:** Scheduled departure time,
- **ADTime:** Actual departure time.

The database table with attributes Date, FlightNo, TailNo, DAirport, SDTime, ADTime, is shown in Table 3.

Table 3. A sample flight database (T)

Flight = [Date, FlightNo, TailNo, DAirport, SDTime, ADTime]						
#	Date	FlightNo	TailNo	DAirport	SDTime	ADTime
0	01-01-2012	648	N831UA	DENVER	06:00	05:57
1	01-01-2012	270	N428UA	DENVER	07:36	07:24
2	01-01-2012	1519	N78511	HOUSTON	12:42	12:41
3	01-01-2012	507	N456UA	DENVER	13:35	13:30
4	02-01-2012	362	N832UA	DENVER	06:00	06:02
5	02-01-2012	270	N424UA	DENVER	07:30	07:24
6	02-01-2012	1519	N78511	HOUSTON	12:42	12:38

The data types are:

Date: *Date*, FlightNo: *Numeric*, TailNo: *Text*, DAirport: *Text*, SDTime: *Time*, ADTime: *Time*

Note 3: In this chapter we have considered the following database. A complete listing of airline and airport abbreviations is available. Times are reported in local time using a 24 hour clock.

- **Detailed Statistics:** Departures
- **Month(s):** January
- **Year(s):** 2012
- **Airport:** Reno-Sparks, NV - Reno-Tahoe International (RNO)
- **Airline:** United Airlines(UA)
- **Day(s):** 1, 2, 3, 4, 5, 6, 7, 8, 9, 10, 11, 12, 13, 14, 15, 16, 17, 18, 19, 20, 21, 22, 23, 24, 25

All Cause of Delay (in minutes) are referring to the Arrival Delay.

SOURCE: Bureau of Transportation Statistics, USA (www.bts.gov),

The table shows the data from 01.01.2012 to 17.01.2012

A. Inserting a Tuple

1. Insertion of the tuple t at the end of the table T.

Let

$t = (03\text{-}01\text{-}2012, 633, N415UA, DENVER, 13\text{:}27, 13\text{:}22)$,

where

$t_0 = 03\text{-}01\text{-}2012, t_1 = 633, t_2 = N415UA, t_3 = 13\text{:}27, t_4 = 13\text{:}22$

Now,

$L'_i = L_i \ \#\!\!\!| \ [t_i]$ for i = 0, 1, 2, 3, 4, 5,6

Date′ = Date $\#\!\!\!|$ [03-01-2012], FlightNo′ = FlightNo $\#\!\!\!|$ [633],

TailNo′ = TailNo $\#\!\!\!|$ [N415UA], DAirport′ = DAirport $\#\!\!\!|$ [N415UA],

SDTime′= SDTime $\#\!\!\!|$ [13:27], ADTime = ADTime $\#\!\!\!|$ [13:22]

So T′ = zip* ("Date′", "FlightNo′", "TailNo′", "DAirport′", "SDTime′", "ADTime′"), it will give the 8th tuple of the database at 7th position.(Table 5)

2. Suppose we want to insert a tuple at jth position then new tuple is inserted at jth position and jth tuple will be shifted to (j+1)th position.

Suppose, we want to insert a tuple

$t = (01\text{-}01\text{-}2012, 633, N415UA, DENVER, 13\text{:}47, 13\text{:}32)$,

where

Table 4. Structure of the flight database (T)

Carrier Code	Date (MM-DD-YYYY)	Flight Number	Tail Number	Destination Airport	Scheduled Departure Time	Actual Departure Time	Scheduled Elapsed Time (Minutes)	Actual Elapsed Time (Minutes)	Departure Delay (Minutes)	Wheels-off Time
UA	01-01-2012	270	N428UA	DEN	07:36	07:24	140	125	-12	07:40
UA	01-01-2012	507	N456UA	DEN	13:35	13:30	131	122	-5	13:38
UA	01-01-2012	648	N831UA	DEN	06:00	05:57	137	129	-3	06:09
UA	01-01-2012	1519	N78511	IAH	12:42	12:41	216	208	-1	12:52
UA	01-02-2012	270	N424UA	DEN	07:30	07:24	140	124	-6	07:37
UA	01-02-2012	362	N832UA	DEN	06:00	06:02	137	138	2	06:17
UA	01-02-2012	559	N498UA	DEN	13:35	13:32	131	130	-3	13:58
UA	01-02-2012	1519	N78511	IAH	12:42	12:38	216	235	-4	12:53
UA	01-03-2012	422	N831UA	DEN	06:00	05:53	134	120	-7	06:04
UA	01-03-2012	633	N415UA	DEN	13:27	13:22	134	123	-5	13:31
UA	01-03-2012	680	N813UA	DEN	07:28	07:20	134	136	-8	07:32
UA	01-04-2012	422	N854UA	DEN	06:00	05:58	134	121	-2	06:09
UA	01-04-2012	633	N464UA	DEN	13:27	13:24	134	125	-3	13:32
UA	01-05-2012	422	N442UA	DEN	06:00	06:02	134	116	2	06:13
UA	01-05-2012	633	N844UA	DEN	13:27	13:25	134	114	-2	13:32
UA	01-06-2012	422	N403UA	DEN	06:00	05:55	134	121	-5	06:07
UA	01-06-2012	633	N472UA	DEN	13:27	13:24	134	115	-3	13:31
UA	01-07-2012	281	N847UA	DEN	11:50	11:45	134	125	-5	11:56
UA	01-07-2012	422	N456UA	DEN	06:00	05:50	134	123	-10	06:05
UA	01-07-2012	452	N441UA	SFO	12:01	11:51	72	59	-10	12:00
UA	01-08-2012	422	N815UA	DEN	06:00	06:00	134	160	0	06:33
UA	01-08-2012	633	N435UA	DEN	13:21	13:14	134	134	-7	13:25

continued on following page

Table 4. Continued

Carrier Code	Date (MM-DD-YYYY)	Flight Number	Tail Number	Destination Airport	Scheduled Departure Time	Actual Departure Time	Scheduled Elapsed Time (Minutes)	Actual Elapsed Time (Minutes)	Departure Delay (Minutes)	Wheels-off Time
UA	01-08-2012	894	N471UA	SFO	05:33	05:26	72	54	-7	05:37
UA	01-08-2012	957	N488UA	SFO	20:30	20:24	68	54	-6	20:30
UA	01-09-2012	422	N485UA	DEN	06:00	05:52	134	126	-8	06:06
UA	01-09-2012	633	N482UA	DEN	13:27	13:18	134	117	-9	13:26
UA	01-10-2012	422	N441UA	DEN	06:00	05:55	134	121	-5	06:07
UA	01-10-2012	633	N442UA	DEN	13:27	13:16	134	116	-11	13:25
UA	01-11-2012	422	N462UA	DEN	06:00	05:50	134	138	-10	06:00
UA	01-11-2012	633	N438UA	DEN	13:27	14:43	134	134	76	14:53
UA	01-12-2012	422	N478UA	DEN	06:00	05:55	134	122	-5	06:06
UA	01-12-2012	633	N470UA	DEN	13:27	13:24	134	125	-3	13:33
UA	01-13-2012	422	N438UA	DEN	06:00	05:54	134	126	-6	06:05
UA	01-13-2012	633	N481UA	DEN	13:27	13:21	134	123	-6	13:31
UA	01-14-2012	281	N810UA	DEN	11:50	11:43	134	125	-7	11:54
UA	01-14-2012	422	N426UA	DEN	06:00	05:50	134	129	-10	06:10
UA	01-14-2012	452	N425UA	SFO	12:12	12:06	72	67	-6	12:14
UA	01-15-2012	422	N848UA	DEN	06:00	05:54	134	115	-6	06:05
UA	01-15-2012	633	N445UA	DEN	13:21	13:20	134	115	-1	13:31
UA	01-15-2012	894	N472UA	SFO	05:33	05:25	72	56	-8	05:35
UA	01-15-2012	957	N470UA	SFO	20:30	20:17	68	76	-13	20:32
UA	01-16-2012	422	N413UA	DEN	06:00	06:01	134	135	1	06:14
UA	01-16-2012	633	N469UA	DEN	13:27	13:21	134	128	-6	13:41
UA	01-17-2012	422	N405UA	DEN	06:00	05:55	134	137	-5	06:16
UA	01-17-2012	633	N459UA	DEN	13:27	13:23	134	124	-4	13:34

Table 5. Insertion at the end of the database table

#	Date	FlightNo	TailNo	DAirport	SDTime	ADTime
0	01-01-2012	648	N831UA	DENVER	06:00	05:57
1	01-01-2012	270	N428UA	DENVER	07:36	07:24
2	01-01-2012	1519	N78511	HOUSTON	12:42	12:41
3	01-01-2012	507	N456UA	DENVER	13:35	13:30
4	02-01-2012	362	N832UA	DENVER	06:00	06:02
5	02-01-2012	270	N424UA	DENVER	07:30	07:24
6	02-01-2012	1519	N78511	HOUSTON	12:42	12:38
7	**03-01-2012**	**633**	**N415UA**	**DENVER**	**13:27**	**13:22**

t_0 = 01-01-2012, t_1 =633, t_2 = N415UA, t_3 = DENVER, t_4 =13:47, t_5 = 13:32

at the position $j = 3$.

Here L'_i = take(j–1, L_i) $\Vert$ [t_i] $\Vert$ drop(j–1, L_i)

for each i = 0, 1, 2, 3.

Date' = take(3–1, L_0) $\Vert$ [t_0] $\Vert$ drop(3–1, L_0)

= take(2, L0) $\Vert$[01-01-2012] $\Vert$ drop(2, L0)

= [01-01-2012, 01-01-2012, 01-01-2012, 03-01-2012, 01-01-2012, 02-01-2012, 02-01-2012, 02-01-2012]

FlightNo' = take(3–1, L_1) $\Vert$ [t_1] $\Vert$ drop(3–1, L_1)
= take(2, L_1) $\Vert$ [633] $\Vert$ drop(2, L_1)

= [648, 270, 1519, 633, 507, 362, 270,1519]

Similarly, we can get,

TailNo' = [N831UA, N428UA, N78511, N415UA, N456UA, N832UA,N424UA, N78511]

DAirport' = [DENVER, DENVER, HOUSTON, DENVER, DENVER, DENVER, DENVER, HOUSTON]

SDTime' = [6:00,7:36, 12:42, 13:47, 13:35, 6:00, 7:30, 12:42]

ADTime' = [5:57, 7:24, 12:41, 13:32, 13:30, 6:02, 7:24, 12:38]

So, T' =zip* ("Date'", "FlightNo'", "TailNo'", "DAirport'", "SDTime'", "ADTime'"). The following table shows the updated information. (Table 6)

B. Deleting a Tuple

1.   Deleting a tuple from the end of the table T.

We use the formula,

T' = zip* (init(Date), init(FlightNo), init(TailNo), init(DAirport), init(SDTime), init(ADTime))

init(Date) = [01-01-2012, 01-01-2012, 03-01-2012, 01-01-2012, 02-01-2012, 02-01-2012]

init(FlightNo) = [648, 270, 1519, 507, 362,270]

init(TailNo) = [N831UA, N428UA, N78511, N456UA, N832UA,N424UA]

init(DAirport) = [DENVER, DENVER, HOUSTON, DENVER, DENVER]

Table 6. Insertion at the middle of the database table

#	Date	FlightNo	TailNo	DAirport	SDTime	ADTime
0	01-01-2012	648	N831UA	DENVER	6:00	5:57
1	01-01-2012	270	N428UA	DENVER	7:36	7:24
2	01-01-2012	1519	N78511	HOUSTON	12:42	12:41
3	**03-01-2012**	**633**	**N415UA**	**DENVER**	**13:47**	**13:32**
4	01-01-2012	507	N456UA	DENVER	13:35	13:30
5	02-01-2012	362	N832UA	DENVER	6:00	6:02
6	02-01-2012	270	N424UA	DENVER	7:30	7:24
7	02-01-2012	1519	N78511	HOUSTON	12:42	12:38

init(SDTime) = [6:00, 7:36, 12:42, 13:35, 6:00, 7:30]

init(ADTime) = [5:57, 7:24, 12:41, 13:30, 6:02, 7:24]

2. Deleting a tuple from the beginning of the table T.

We use the formula,

T' = zip* (tl(Date), tl(FlightNo), tl(TailNo), tl(DAirport), tl(SDTime)), tl(ADTime))

tl(Date) =[01-01-2012, 03-01-2012, 01-01-2012, 02-01-2012, 02-01-2012]

tl(FlightNo) = [270, 1519, 507, 362, 270,1519]

tl(TailNo) = [N831UA, N831UA, N831UA, N831UA, N831UA, N831UA]

tl(DAirport) = [DENVER, HOUSTON, DENVER, DENVER, DENVER, HOUSTON]

tl(SDTime) = [7:36, 12:42, 13:35, 6:00, 7:30, 12:42]

tl(ADTime) = [7:24, 12:41, 13:30, 6:02, 7:24, 12:38]

3. Deleting a tuple from any position the table T.

Suppose, we want to delete the 2nd tuple

t = [01-01-2012, 270, N428UA, DENVER, 7:36, 7:24]

from the table T.

Here $j = 2$ and T' = zip* (L'$_0$, L'$_1$, L'$_2$, L'$_3$, L'$_4$, L'$_5$), where

Table 7. Deletion from the end of the database table

#	Date	FlightNo	TailNo	DAirport	SDTime	ADTime
0	01-01-2012	648	N831UA	DENVER	06:00	05:57
1	01-01-2012	270	N428UA	DENVER	07:36	07:24
2	01-01-2012	1519	N78511	HOUSTON	12:42	12:41
3	01-01-2012	507	N456UA	DENVER	13:35	13:30
4	02-01-2012	362	N832UA	DENVER	06:00	06:02
5	02-01-2012	270	N424UA	DENVER	07:30	07:24

Table 8. Deletion from the beginning of the database table

#	Date	FlightNo	TailNo	DAirport	SDTime	ADTime
0	01-01-2012	270	N428UA	DENVER	7:36	7:24
1	01-01-2012	1519	N78511	HOUSTON	12:42	12:41
2	01-01-2012	507	N456UA	DENVER	13:35	13:30
3	02-01-2012	362	N832UA	DENVER	6:00	6:02
4	02-01-2012	270	N424UA	DENVER	7:30	7:24
5	02-01-2012	1519	N78511	HOUSTON	12:42	12:38

$L'_i = \text{take}(j-1, L_i) + \text{drop}(j, L_i)$ for each i = 0, 1, 2, 3, 4, 5

$= \text{take}(2-1, L_i) + \text{drop}(2, L_i)$ for each i = 0, 1, 2, 3, 4, 5

$= \text{take}(1, L_i) + \text{drop}(2, L_i)$ for each i = 0, 1, 2, 3, 4, 5

So, $\text{Date}' = \text{take}(1, \text{Date}) + \text{drop}(2, \text{Date})$

$= [01\text{-}01\text{-}2012] + [01\text{-}01\text{-}2012, 01\text{-}01\text{-}2012, 02\text{-}01\text{-}2012, 02\text{-}01\text{-}2012, 02\text{-}01\text{-}2012]$

$= [01\text{-}01\text{-}2012, 01\text{-}01\text{-}2012, 01\text{-}01\text{-}2012, 02\text{-}01\text{-}2012, 02\text{-}01\text{-}2012, 02\text{-}01\text{-}2012]$

Similarly, FlightNo′ = [648, 1519, 507, 362, 270, 1519],

TailNo′ = [N831UA, N831UA, N831UA, N831UA, N831UA, N831UA],

DAirport ′ = [DENVER, HOUSTON, DENVER, DENVER, DENVER, HOUSTON],

SDTime′ = [6:00, 12:42, 13:35, 6:00, 7:30, 12:42],

and

ADTime′ = [5:57, 12:41, 13:30, 6:02, 7:24, 12:38].

C. Modifying a Tuple

Suppose we want to modify a tuple at position 4, i.e. $j = 4$ and the tuple $t_3 = (01\text{-}01\text{-}2012, 507, N456UA, DENVER, 13:35, 13:30)$ will be changed to $t'_3 = (01\text{-}01\text{-}2012, 281, N847UA, DENVER, 13:35, 13:30)$. So we require to operations, i.e. deleting the tuple t_3 from the table T and inserting the new tuple t'_3 in the corresponding position $j = 4$. But, in this case only the two attributes *FlightNo* and *TailNo* are to be changed without affecting the other attributes, which minimizes the number of operations.

Table 9. Deletion from 3rd place of the database table

#	Date	FlightNo	TailNo	DAirport	SDTime	ADTime
0	01-01-2012	648	N831UA	DENVER	06:00	05:57
1	01-01-2012	1519	N78511	HOUSTON	12:42	12:41
2	01-01-2012	507	N456UA	DENVER	13:35	13:30
3	02-01-2012	362	N832UA	DENVER	06:00	06:02
4	02-01-2012	270	N424UA	DENVER	07:30	07:24
5	02-01-2012	1519	N78511	HOUSTON	12:42	12:38

That is, Date, DAirport, SDTime, ADTime will be unchanged and FlightNo and TailNo will be changed to FlightNo″ and TailNo″ and the new table will be T′ = zip* (Date, FlightNo″, TailNo″, DAirport, SDTime , ADTime).

Here $j = 4$, 507 and N456UA are replaced by 281 and N847UA respectively.

That is, $t_{31} = 507$ will be replaced by $t_{31} = 281$ and $t_{32} = N456UA$ will be replaced by $t_{32} = N847UA$.

1. At first we delete the corresponding attributes from the lists.

$L'_i = take(j–1, L_i) \# drop(j, L_i)$ for each i = 1,2

FlightNo′ = take(4–1, FlightNo) $\#$ drop(4, FlightNo) = take(3, FlightNo) $\#$ drop(4, FlightNo)

= [648, 270,1519] $\#$ [362, 270,1519] = [648, 270, 1519, 362, 270,1519]

TailNo′ = take(4–1, TailNo) $\#$ drop(4, TailNo) = take(3, TailNo) $\#$ drop(4, TailNo)

= [N831UA, N428UA, N78511] $\#$ [N832UA, N424UA, N78511]

= [N831UA, N428UA, N78511, N832UA, N424UA, N78511]

2. Now we will insert the new values at the position $j = 4$ in the selected tuple.

$L''_i = take(j–1, L'_i) \# [t_{3i}] \# drop(j–1, L'_i)$ for each i = 1,2

FlightNo″ = take(4–1, FlightNo′) $\#$ [281] $\#$ drop(4–1, FlightNo′)

= take(3, FlightNo′) $\#$ [281] $\#$ drop(3, FlightNo′)

= [648, 270,1519] $\#$ [281] $\#$ [362, 270,1519]

= [648, 270,1519, 281, 362, 270,1519]

TailNo″ = take(4–1, TailNo′) $\#$ [t_{32}] $\#$ drop(4–1, TailNo′)

= take(3, TailNo′) $\#$ [N847UA] $\#$ drop(3, TailNo′)

= [N831UA, N428UA, N78511] $\#$ [N847UA] $\#$ [N832UA, N424UA, N78511]

= [N831UA, N428UA, N78511, N847UA, N832UA, N424UA, N78511]

So T′ = zip* ("Date", "FlightNo″", "TailNo″", "DAirport", "SDTime", "ADTime") is given here.

Table 10. Modification of the database table at position j=4

#	Date	FlightNo	TailNo	DAirport	SDTime	ADTime
0	01-01-2012	648	N831UA	DENVER	06:00	05:57
1	01-01-2012	270	N428UA	DENVER	07:36	07:24
2	01-01-2012	1519	N78511	HOUSTON	12:42	12:41
3	01-01-2012	**281**	**N847UA**	DENVER	13:35	13:30
4	02-01-2012	362	N832UA	DENVER	06:00	06:02
5	02-01-2012	270	N424UA	DENVER	07:30	07:24
6	02-01-2012	1519	N78511	HOUSTON	12:42	12:38

Definition 23: (Cartesian Product) Suppose T_1 $(A_1, A_2, ..., A_M)$ and T_2 $(B_1, B_2, ..., B_N)$ are two tables and $x_i \in A_i$ for $i = 1, 2, .., M$ and $y_j \in B_j$ for $j = 1, 2, ..., N$, then we can define the Cartesian product of T_1 and T_2 in the following manner.

$$P_{T_1 \times T_2}(x_1, x_2, ..., x_M, y_1, y_2, ..., y_N) =$$

$$P_{zip^*(A_1, A_2, ..., A_M, B_1, B_2, ..., B_N)}^{(x_1, x_2, ..., x_M, y_1, y_2, ..., y_N)}$$

where

$$P_{zip^*(T_1, T_2)}(x_1, x_2, ..., x_M, y_1, y_2, ..., y_N) =$$

$$\{\#T_2 \cdot P_{T_1}(x_1, x_2, ..., x_M) + P_{T_2}(y_1, y_2, ..., y_N)\}$$

and

$$P_{T_1}(x_1, x_2, ..., x_M) =$$

$$P_{zip^*(A_1, A_2, ..., A_M)}^{(x_1, x_2, ..., x_M)}$$

$$P_{T_2}(y_1, y_2, ..., y_N) =$$

$$P_{zip^*(B_1, B_2, ..., B_N)}^{(y_1, y_2, ..., y_N)}$$

The number of attributes in $T_1 \times T_2 = \#A(T_1 \times T_2)$ $= \#A(T_1) + \#A(T_2) = M + N$ and the number of tuples in $T_1 \times T_2 = \#(T_1 \times T_2) = \#T_1 \times \#T_2$.

Example 4: Suppose T_1 and T_2 are given as follows. We have to find the Cartesian product of T_1 and T_2.

UNARY RELATIONAL OPERATIONS

In this section we introduce the unary operations on relational databases using the list theoretic approach.

Selection

The selection of an attribute(s) for a condition p, gives the position function of the attribute(s). The intersection of all the attributes for the corresponding position function gives the required tuple(s).

Definition 24: (SELECTION) Suppose T is a table with attributes $L_0, L_1, ..., L_j, ..., L_{k-1}$ in a universe X. We define a map $f_p: X \to \{0, 1\}$ where f is a function required for the implementation of the filter and $\forall x \in X$,

$$f_p(x) = \begin{cases} 1, & \text{if } p(x) \text{ is true;} \\ 0, & \text{otherwise.} \end{cases}$$

The selection operator

$$\sigma_{filter(p, L_i)}(T) = zip * (L_0^*, L_1^*, ..., L_{K-1}^*)$$

where

$$L_j^* = \underset{\substack{k \in P_{(1)} \\ map(f_p, L_i)}}{\#} L_{j,k}$$

and

$$Lj,_k = [index (L_{j, k}): k \in P_{map(f_p, L_i)}].$$

Using the above definitions, we can simplify the selection operator as follows.

Table 11. (a) Table of instance T_1 (b) Table of instance T_2 (c) Table of product $T_1 x T_2$

T_1	A_1	A_2	T_2	B_1	B_2	B_3
	a	b		1	2	3
	a	c		3	2	1
				2	3	2
(a)			**(b)**			

Here $\#T_1 = 2$, $\#T_2 = 3$ and $\#A(T_1) = 2$, $\#A(T_2) = 3$.

So the number of attributes in $T = T_1 \times T_2$ is

$$\#A(T_1 \times T_2) = \#A(T_1) + \#A(T_2) = 2+3 = 5$$

and the number of tuples in $T_1 \times T_2$ $= \#(T_1 \times T_2) = \#T_1 \times \#T_2 = 2 \times 3 = 6$.

$T = T_1 \times T_2$	A_1	A_2	B_1	B_2	B_3
	a	b	1	2	3
	a	b	3	2	1
	a	b	2	3	2
	a	c	1	2	3
	a	c	3	2	1
	a	c	2	3	2

(c)

$$\sigma_{filter(p,L_i)}(T) = zip * (L_0^*, L_1^*, ..., L_{K-1}^*),$$

where

$$L_j^* = \underset{\substack{k \in P^{(1)}_{map(f_p, L_i)}}}{\#} indexlist(L, k)$$

For multiple selections, we can define the SELECTION operator as follows.

$$\sigma_{\underset{i}{\cap} filter(p_i, L_i)}(T) = zip * (L_0^*, L_1^*, ..., L_{K-1}^*)$$

where $L_j^* =$

$$\underset{\substack{k \in \underset{i}{\cap} P^{(1)}_{map(f_{p_i}, L_i)}}}{\#} indexlist(L, k)$$

The selection of an attribute for condition p, gives the position function of the attribute. The intersection of all attributes for the corresponding position function gives the required tuple.

Definition 25: (PROJECTION) It is a specific operation to select specified columns from a given table without any duplicate tuples in the selection.

$\Pi_{<attribute\ list>}$ (T) gives the output in the same order as attributes appeared in the list. The commutative property of the projection does not hold in general. The number of attributes in the projection list does not exceed the number of attributes in the relation table T.

The non-key attributes of T occur in duplicates where as the project operation removes any duplicate tuples to form a set of tuples.

For the list of attributes

$$(L_{i_1}, L_{i_2}, \ldots\ldots, L_{i_k})$$

in the projection we define the projection operator as follows. We assume here that

$$D_{i_j} = \text{dom}(L_{i_j}) \text{ for } j = 1, 2, \ldots, k \text{ and } D =$$
$$D_{i_1} \times D_{i_2} \times \ldots\ldots \times D_{i_k}.$$

$$\Pi_{(L_{i_1}, L_{i_2}, \ldots, L_{i_k})} T' = T''$$

where

$$\sigma_{\bigcap_i \text{filter}(p_i, L_i)}(T) = T' \qquad (6.1)$$

where

$$T'' = \underset{(x_{i_1}, x_{i_2}, \ldots, x_{i_k}) \in D}{\bigparallel}$$
$$\text{take}(1, \underset{j \in P_{T'(x_{i_1}, x_{i_2}, \ldots, x_{i_k})}}{\bigparallel} \text{indexlist}(T', j))$$

and

$$P_{T'}(x_{i_1}, x_{i_2}, \ldots, x_{i_k}) =$$

$$P_{L_{i_1}}(x_{i_1}) \cap P_{L_{i_2}}(x_{i_2}) \cap \ldots \cap P_{L_{i_k}}(x_{i_k})$$

It may be noted here that if the number of non-repetitive elements in L_{i_j} is small comparison to D_{i_j} then in (6.1) we have performed the append operation of lists for appending only empty lists, which requires some computational time. So, one can think of defining this operation such that the above deficiency can be removed.

Example 5: Consider the following sample relation table T of a flight schedule database of United Airlines, Airline ID: 20355 at the Airport: Reno-Sparks, NV - Reno-Tahoe International (RNO) for the month of January 2012, with five attributes mentioned below. *(Source: Bureau of Transportation Statistics, USA).*

1. Suppose, we consider to get the details of a flight which is scheduled in different dates from the airport.

It's equivalent to the query, "*Find out the details of the flight number 633*".

So, $\sigma_C(T) = \text{zip}(\text{"Date*"}, \text{"FlightNo*"}, \text{"Tail-No*"}, \text{"DAirport*"}, \text{"SDTime*"}, \text{"ADTime*"})$ where C= "FlightNo=633" on the list FlightNo.

Now, map $(f_p, \text{FlightNo}) = \text{map}(\text{"=633"}, \text{FlightNo}) = \{0,0,0,0,0,0,0,0,0,0,1\}$.

This shows that at the index i=10, FlightNo=633 exists. So the index set=$\{10\}$.

Now the different information from the lists, Date, FlightNo, TailNo, DAirport, SDTime, ADTime are as follows.

Date* =

$$\underset{k \in \{10\}}{\bigparallel} \text{indexlist}(\text{Date}, k) =$$

Date(10) = [03-01-2012]

Table 12. A sample flight database

#	Date	FlightNo	TailNo	DAirport	SDTime	ADTime
0	01-01-2012	648	N831UA	DENVER	06:00	05:57
1	01-01-2012	270	N428UA	DENVER	07:36	07:24
2	01-01-2012	1519	N78511	HOUSTON	12:42	12:41
3	01-01-2012	507	N456UA	DENVER	13:35	13:30
4	02-01-2012	362	N832UA	DENVER	06:00	06:02
5	02-01-2012	270	N424UA	DENVER	07:30	07:24
6	02-01-2012	1519	N78511	HOUSTON	12:42	12:38
7	02-01-2012	559	N498UA	DENVER	13:35	13:32
8	03-01-2012	422	N831UA	DENVER	06:00	05:53
9	03-01-2012	680	N813UA	DENVER	07:28	07:20
10	03-01-2012	633	N415UA	DENVER	13:27	13:22

Since the index value for the FlightNo=633 is 10, the same index value is applied to find the information for other lists as follows..

FlightNo* = [633], TailNo* = [N415UA],

DAirport* = [DENVER], SDTime* = [13:27] and

ADTime* = [13:22].

Hence the table for $\sigma_{FlightNo=633}$ (T) is given as shown in Table 13(a).

2. Suppose that we have to find the details of the flights which are actually departured after a specific time from the airport.

It's equivalent to the query, *"Find out the details of the flights which are actually departured after 11.00 hours"*.

Table 13. Sample query

Date	FlightNo	TailNo	DAirport	SDTime	ADTime
03-01-2012	***633***	*N415UA*	*DENVER*	*13:27*	*13:22*

(a)

Date	FlightNo	TailNo	DAirport	SDTime	ADTime
01-01-2012	*1519*	*N78511*	*HOUSTON*	*12:42*	*12:41*
01-01-2012	*507*	*N456UA*	*DENVER*	*13:35*	*13:30*
02-01-2012	*1519*	*N78511*	*HOUSTON*	*12:42*	*12:38*
02-01-2012	*559*	*N498UA*	*DENVER*	*13:35*	*13:32*
03-01-2012	*633*	*N415UA*	*DENVER*	*13:27*	*13:22*

(b)

Date	FlightNo	SDTime	ADTime
02-01-2012	*362*	*06:00*	*06:02*

(c)

So, $\sigma_C(T)$ = zip("Date*", "FlightNo*", "Tail-No*", "DAirport*", "SDTime*", "ADTime*") where C= "ADTime > 11:00" on the list ADTime.

Now, map (f_p, ADTime) = map (">11:00", ADTime) = {0,0,1,1,0,0,1,1,0,0,1}.

This shows that at the index set i is {2, 3, 6, 7, 10}, where all the actual departure time is more than 11:00 hours.

So, ADTime* =

$$\underset{k \in \{2, 3, 6, 7, 10\}}{\#} \text{indexlist(ADTime, k)}$$

= ADTime(2) $\#$ ADTime(3) $\#$ ADTime(6) $\#$ ADTime(7) $\#$ ADTime(10)

= [12:41, 13:30, 12:38, 13:32, 13:22]

Similarly for the above index set, the different information from the lists, Date, FlightNo, TailNo, DAirport, SDTime are as follows.

Date* = [01-01-2012, 01-01-2012, 02-01-2012, 02-01-2012, 03-01-2012]

FlightNo* = [507,1519, 1519, 559,633]

TailNo* = [N456UA, N78511, N78511, N498UA, N415UA]

DAirport* = [DENVER, HOUSTON, HOUSTON, DENVER, DENVER]

SDTime* = [13:35, 12:42, 12:42, 13:35, 13:27]

Hence the table for $\sigma_{\text{ADTime} > 11:00}$ (T) is given as shown in Table 13(b).

3. To illustrate the composite condition case, let us consider to find out the actual departure time of the flights between a specific time period, say time1 and time2.

The condition here is the intersection of two conditions p = "actual departure time $\geq$ time1" and q = "actual departure time $\leq$ time2". So that the condition of the time period is "*time1 $\leq$ actual departure time $\leq$ time2*".

It's equivalent to the query, "*Find out the date, scheduled departure time and actual departure time of all the flights actually departured between 06.00 hours and 07:00 hours*".

So,

$\sigma_C(T)$ = zip("Date*", "FlightNo*", "SDTime*", "ADTime*")

where

C= "ADTime $\geq$ 06:00 and ADTime $\leq$ 07:00 "

on the list ADTime.

Now, map (f_p, ADTime) = map ("$\geq$ 06:00", ADTime) = {0,1,1,1,1,1,1,1,1,0,1,1}and map (f_q, ADTime) = map ("$\leq$ 07:00", ADTime) = {1,0,0,0,1,0,0,0,1,0,0}.

So, map $(f_p, \text{ADTime}) \cap$ map (f_q, ADTime) = {0,0,0,0,1,0,0,0,0,0,0}.

This shows that the index i = 4, where the actual time of departure is between 06:00 and 07:00 hours in the list ADTime.

So, ADTime* =

$$\underset{k \in \{4\}}{\#} \text{indexlist(ADTime, k)} =$$

ADTime(4) = [06:02]

This shows that at the index i = 4 for all the lists for the given condition. Similarly for the above index set, the different information from the lists, Date, FlightNo, SDTime are as follows.

Date* = [02-01-2012], FlightNo* = [362] and SDTime" = [06:00]

Hence the table for $\sigma_{06:00 \leq \text{ADTime} \leq 07:00}$ (T) is given as shown in Table 13(c).

In the following example we demonstrate the Projection operation on a supplier database table.

Example 6: Consider the following relation table T of suppliers, where L_0 is Person, L_1 is p# (Person id), L_2 is Place, L_3 is Item, and L_4 is Price in Rupees(Rs).

Here, $\text{dom}(L_0) = \{\text{Lohit, Bravo, Anush, Robin, Xavier, Riqvi}\}$,

$\text{dom}(L_1) = \{\#101, \#102, ..., \#201, ... \#205\}$,

$\text{dom}(L_2) = \{\text{India, France, USA, Spain, Australia, Sweden}\}$,

$\text{dom}(L_3) = \{A, B, C, D, E\}$ and $\text{dom}(L_4) = \{10, 15, 25, 30, 45\}$.

1. $\prod_{(L_1, L_3)} T = T''$ here $T' = T$ as no selection is used.

and

$$T'' = \underset{\substack{(x_1, x_3) \in D}}{+\!\!\!+} \text{take}(1, \underset{j \in P_T(x_1, x_3)}{+\!\!\!+} \text{indexlist}(T,j))$$

$D = \text{dom}(L_1) \times \text{dom}(L_3)$ and $|D| = |\text{dom}(L_1)| \times |\text{dom}(L_3)| = 105 \times 5 = 525$.

Table 14. Sample supplier table

Person	P#	Place	Item	Price(Rs.)
Lohit	#101	India	A	10
Bravo	#205	Spain	A	10
Anush	#108	UK	B	25
Bravo	#205	Spain	D	15
Lohit	#101	India	B	25
Bravo	#205	Spain	C	30
Riqvi	#200	Austria	E	45

$$T'' = \underset{\substack{x_1 \in L_1, x_3 \in L_3 \\ (x_1, x_3) \in D}}{+\!\!\!+} \text{take}(1, \underset{j \in P_T(x_1, x_3)}{+\!\!\!+} \text{indexlist}(T,j))$$

$$= \text{take}(1, \underset{j \in P_T(\#101, A)}{+\!\!\!+} \text{indexlist}(T,j)) +\!\!\!+ \text{take}(1,$$
$$\underset{j \in P_T(\#101, B)}{+\!\!\!+} \text{indexlist}(T,j)) +\!\!\!+ ..$$
$$...... +\!\!\!+ \text{take}(1, \underset{j \in P_T(\#108, B)}{+\!\!\!+} \text{indexlist}(T,j)) +\!\!\!+ ....$$

$$= \text{take}(1, \underset{j \in \{0\}}{+\!\!\!+} \text{indexlist}(T,j)) +\!\!\!+$$
$$\text{take}(1, \underset{j \in j}{+\!\!\!+} \text{indexlist}(T,j)) +\!\!\!+ ..$$
$$...... +\!\!\!+ \text{take}(1, \underset{j \in \{1\}}{+\!\!\!+} \text{indexlist}(T,j)) +\!\!\!+ ....$$

$= [(\#101, A)] +\!\!\!+ [] +\!\!\!+ ..... +\!\!\!+ [(\#101, B)]] ....+\!\!\!+ [(\#108, B)] +\!\!\!+ ... +\!\!\!+ [(\#200, E)] +\!\!\!+ .... +\!\!\!+ [(\#205, A)] +\!\!\!+ [(\#205, C)] +\!\!\!+ [(\#205, D)] +\!\!\!+ .... +\!\!\!+ []$

$= [(\#101, A), (\#101, B), (\#108, B), (\#200, E), (\#205, A), (\#205, C), (\#205, D)]$

2. $\prod_{(L_1 = \#101) \wedge (L_2 = \text{Spain})} T' = T''$

where

$$T' = \sigma_{(L_1 = \#101) \wedge (L_2 = \text{Spain})}(T)$$

Now $P_{L_1}(\#101) = \{0, 4\}$,
$P_{L_2}(\text{Spain}) = \{1, 3, 5\}$
This gives $P_{L_1}(\#101) \cap P_{L_2}(\text{Spain}) = \{0, 4\} \cap \{1, 3, 5\} = \phi$

So,

$$T' = \sigma_{(L_1 = \#101) \wedge (L_2 = \text{Spain})}(T) = [] \ .$$

Using it, we get the following result.

$$T'' = \underset{(x_1, x_2) \in D}{\#} take(1, \underset{j \in P_{T'}(x_1, x_2)}{\#} indexlist(T',j))$$

$$= \underset{(x_1, x_2) \in D}{\#} take(1, \underset{j \in \phi}{\#} indexlist([\,],j))$$

$$= \underset{(x_1, x_2) \in D}{\#} take(1, [\,]) = [\,] \# [\,] \# \cdots \# [\,] = [\,].$$

BINARY RELATIONAL OPERATIONS

In this section we introduce the binary operations on relational databases using the list theoretic approach.

UNION

The union operation gives all the tuples of two relations without duplication. Suppose, $T_1 = zip^*(A_1, A_2, \ldots, A_n)$ and $T_2 = zip^*(B_1, B_2, \ldots, B_n)$ are two relation tables. The two tables T_1 and T_2 are union compatible, if (i) they have the same degree and (ii) $dom(A_i) = dom(B_i)$ for $1 \leq i \leq n$. Also, it is important to note that the order of the attributes in T_1 and T_2 should be same.

Definition 24: (CONCATENATION OF TABLES) Suppose T_1 and T_2 are two relation tables with the attributes $(A_1, A_2, \ldots, A_n)$ and $(B_1, B_2, \ldots, B_n)$ respectively and $\#A(T_1) = \#A(T_2)$, where $T_1 = zip^*(A_1, A_2, \ldots, A_n)$ and $T_2 = zip^*(B_1, B_2, \ldots, B_n)$, A_i and B_i are lists and $dom(A_i) = dom(Bi)$ for $1 \leq i \leq n$. Then we define the concatenation of tables T_1 and T_2 as follows.

$$T_1 \# T_2 = zip^*(A_1 \# B_1, A_2 \# B_2, \ldots, A_n \# B_n).$$

The union operation defined on usual relation tables using set theoretic approach loses its meaning in the list theoretic approach. Here the operation 'U' is synonymous with the concatenation operation.

Definition 25: (UNION) Suppose T_1 and T_2 are two relation tables with the attributes $(A_1, A_2, \ldots, A_n)$ and $(B_1, B_2, \ldots, B_n)$ respectively. Then the union of T_1 and T_2, denoted as $T_1 \cup T_2$, is the collection of all the tuples of T_1 and T_2 without duplication. For $D = dom(A_1) \times dom(A_2) \times \ldots \times dom(A_n) = dom(B_1) \times dom(B_2) \times \ldots \times dom(B_n)$, suppose $T' = T_1 \# T_2$ and $T_1 \cup T_2 = T''$, where

$$T'' = \underset{(x_1, x_2, \ldots, x_n) \in D}{\#}$$

$$take(1, \underset{j \in P_{T'}(x_1, x_2, \ldots, x_n)}{\#} indexlist(T',j))$$

Note 4: In our case, $T_1 \cup T_2 \neq T_2 \cup T_1$, as the positional functions of the tuples of $(T_1 \cup T_2)$ and $(T_2 \cup T_1)$ are not same. This is also desirable that $(T_1 \cup T_2)$ and $(T_2 \cup T_1)$ have the same contents but they are not identical in all respect.

Example 7: Consider the following relation tables for the union operation.

INTERSECTION

Definition 26: (INTERSECTION) Suppose T_1 and T_2 are two relation tables with the attributes $(A_1, A_2, \ldots, A_n)$ and $(B_1, B_2, \ldots, B_n)$ respectively. Then the intersection of T_1 and T_2, denoted as $T_1 \cap T_2$, is the collection of all the common tuples of T_1 and T_2 without duplication.

Table 15. (a) Sample table for union operation (b) Table after union operation

T_1	A_1	A_2	A_3	T_2	B_1	B_2	B_3
	1101	Asit	Data Structure		1102	Lewis	C Program
	1102	Lewis	C Program		1101	Asit	Data Structure
	1101	Asit	Data Structure		1102	Asit	OOPs
	1103	Ali	Linux Internals		1102	Rameez	C Program

(a)

Then

$T = T_1 \cup T_2$	A_1	A_2	A_3
	1101	Asit	Data Structure
	1102	Lewis	C Program
	1101	Asit	Data Structure
	1103	Ali	Linux Internals
	1102	Lewis	C Program
	1101	Asit	Data Structure
	1102	Asit	OOPs
	1102	Rameez	C Program

(b)

$T_1 \cap T_2 = T_1' - (T_1' - T_2')$ where $T_j' = $ uniquelist (T_j) for $i = 1,2$.

DIFFERENCE

Definition 27: (DIFFERENCE) Suppose T_1 and T_2 are two relation tables with the attributes $(A_1, A_2 \ldots A_n)$ and $(B_1, B_2 \ldots B_n)$ respectively. Then the difference of T_1 and T_2, denoted as $T_1 \sim T_2$, is the collection of all the common tuples of T_1 and T_2.

$T_1 \sim T_2 = (T_1 \setminus T_2) \cup (T_2 \setminus T_1)$.

The definitions given above are theoretical consideration only, but in practice they may different.

THE IMPLEMENTATION ISSUE

Before the implementing the list theoretic relational algebraic operations to the database it is required to study the data for its normalization. The normalization of the data requires only the 1NF (1st Normal Form), where each tuple has atomic values (Codd, 1970). The further normalization is not considered here.

Another kind of implementation issue is the use of disk space required to handle the database. The list theoretic relational algebraic operation on a database is somewhat different from other database models. Here we consider that the lists i.e. the attributes used in a database table are stored in a physical storage and when the database is used as a result of zip, the zipped lists are transferred to the temporary memory to avoid the huge amount of space used by the database. A logical structure will be stored in the hard disk and it will be active at the time of operation of the database and the data will be fetched to the temporary memory.

But there may be problem to handle the '*Null Values*' in attributes or lists, which should be minimized using some technique.

Note 5: The following are the advantages of LRA over extended BRA, which justifies such a study:

Advantage 1: When a new tuple is added, in extended BRA, a search is mandatory, whether such a tuple exists. In case it can exist its # field is incremented by one or else the new tuple is to be added with # field being 'i', where as in LRA, we do not bother about the existence or non existence of the tuple. We simply add it at the end of table, which can be done by appending the element at the end of the table, which can be done by appending the element at the end of the list structure.

Advantage 2: We do not have to keep an additional field for #, which requires additional spaces. Simply, the required information is provided by $| P_L(\bar{x}) |$, where $\bar{x}$ is the tuple whose # field is required. As, $| P_L(\bar{x}) |$ is a well defined functions on lists, with simple query which uses its definitions can be obtained. However, we would like to note that it requires additional processing time.

Advantage 3: Orders of elements is very important in Petri net theory for study of properties like *liveness* and *reachability*. Also, position is important for occurrence of tuples for firing sequence.

So, with the above observation it is clear that LRA is an improved version of extended BRA and is capable of providing all the facilities for implementation of Petri nets, which is discussed in the next section.

FORMALIZATION OF PETRINETS USING LIST THEORETIC RELATIONAL ALGEBRA (LRA)

In the previous section it is discussed that the extended BRA can be replaced by list theoretic relational algebra (LRA) to formalize Petri nets to generate the Reachability tree.

PETRI NETS

Petri nets are a powerful tool for representing and studying systems that are being characterized as concurrent, asynchronous, distributed, parallel and/or non-deterministic. Strength of Petri nets is their support for analysis of many properties and problems associated with concurrent systems.

Petri net has its origin in the Doctoral dissertation of Carl Adam Petri (1962) which was prepared when he was a scientist at Institute fur Instrumentelle Mathematik in Bonn and was submitted to the Faculty of Mathematics and Physics at the Technical University of Dramstadt, Germany, in 1962. This work contained mainly a theoretic development of the basic concepts from which Petri nets have been developed. A.W. Holt et al. worked on a project on Information System Theory, which resulted in a project report (Holt, Saint, Shapiro and Warshall, 1968) containing much of the early theory, notation and representations of Petri nets. Another related work in the report "*Events and Conditions*" (Holt and Commoner, 1970), which showed Petri nets could be applied to the modeling and analysis of systems of concurrent component.

An excellent book on the history and development of the theory of Petri nets, their characteristics, modeling of systems through them and the analysis techniques to draw conclusions is by Peterson (1981). An annotated bibliography at the end adds more flavour to this treatise. However, those who are interested in rigour must refer to another excellent book by Riesig (1983), where mathematical proofs are provided in support of all the properties of Petri nets (Place Transition nets and their extensions). Many monographs and Lecturer Notes in Computer Science volumes have been devoted for the compilation and presentation of research works done so far, besides papers in different journals world over.

Petri nets are graphical and mathematical modeling tools applicable to many systems. In many fields of study, a phenomenon is not studied directly but indirectly through a model of the phenomenon. A model is a representation, often in mathematical terms, of what one felt to be the important features of the object or system under study. By the manipulation of the representation, it is hoped that new knowledge about the modeled phenomenon can be obtained without the danger, cost or inconvenience of manipulating the real phenomenon itself.

The formal definition of Petri net is as follows:

Definition 28: A Petri net, PN, is a five-tuple (P, T, I, O, M0); where

- P is a finite set of elements called places,
- T is a finite set of elements called transitions,
- I: $P \times T \rightarrow N$ is the input function, which associates with every pair of places and transition, a nonnegative integer representing the minimum number tokens in the place required for the transition to be fired.
- O: $T \times P \rightarrow N$ is the output function, which associates with every pair of transition and places, a nonnegative integer representing the exact number tokens to be added to the place in a single firing of the transition.
- M_0: $P \rightarrow N$ is the initial marking function, which associates with every place a nonnegative number of tokens. This captures and describes the initial state of the system.

The basic assumption is that $P \cap T = \phi$ and $P \cup T \neq \phi$.

Definition 29: Let PN = (P, T, I, O, M_0) be a Petri net.

A function M_k: $P \rightarrow N$, where k $\in$ N is called a marking of PN. $M_k(p)$ represents the number of tokens in the place p.

1. A transition t $\in$ T is enabled in marking Mk if and only if $I(p, t) \leq Mk(p)$, $\forall$ p $\in$ P. An enabled transition may or may not fire.
2. If t $\in$ T is a transition which is enabled at Mk then t may fire, yielding a new marking Mk' given by the equation:

$$M_{k'}(p) = M_k(p) - I(p, t) + O(t, p), \forall p \in P.$$

3. Firing t changes the marking Mk into the new marking $M_{k'}$, we denote this fact by $M_k \xrightarrow{t} M_{k'}$.
4. The set of all possible markings reachable from Mk in PN, denoted by $R(M_k)$, is the smallest set of markings of PN such that:
   a. $M_k \in R(M_k)$
   b. If $M_{k'} \in R(M_k)$ and $M_{k'} \xrightarrow{s} M_{k''}$ for some s $\in$ T then $M_{k''} \in R(M_k)$.

It may be noted that the markings of a Petri net depict the status of a system. By firing a transition the markings of a Petri net change. Firings of transitions provide dynamism to a Petri net. Of course, a transition can be fired only when sufficient numbers of tokens are available in its input places. The firing of a transition leads to reduction of number of tokens in its input places and addition of tokens in its output places. A transition is said to be enabled when sufficient number of tokens are there in its input places. But an enabled transition may or may not fire. When a set of transitions are in their enabled state their order of firing cannot be fixed.

Some measure problems associated with a Petri net are boundedness, conservation, liveness, reachability and coverability. These are different types of these problems. We define the concepts below.

Definition 30: (Boundedness)

1. $p \in P$ is *n-bounded* if and only if $\forall\, M_k \in R(M_0)$, $M_k(p) \leq n$;
2. PN is *n-bounded* if and only if $\forall p \in P$, p is n-bounded;
3. PN is *safe* if and only if PN is 1-bounded;
4. PN is *bounded* if and only if $\exists\, n \in N$, PN is n-bounded.

Definition 31: (Conservation)

1. PN is *strictly conservative* if and only if $\forall M_k \in R(M_0)$,

$$\sum_{p \in P} M_k(p) = \sum_{p \in P} M_0(p)$$

2. PN is *conservative* with respect to a weighting function W: $P \to N$, if and only if $\forall M_k \in R(M_0)$,

$$\sum_{p \in P} W(p).M_k(p) = \sum_{p \in P} W(p).M_0(p)$$

Definition 32: (Liveness)

1. $t \in T$ is *live* if and only if $\forall M_k \in R(M_0)$, $M_{k'} \in R(M_k)$, t is enabled at $M_{k'}$; PN is live if and only if $\forall t \in T$, t is live;
2. PN is *deadlock free* if and only if $\forall M_k \in R(M_0) \; \exists t \in T$, t is enabled at M_k.
3. There are two famous problems associated with a Petri net. These are important for the point of view of *system liveness*. We state these problems below:

1. **Reachability Problem:** Given a Petri net PN and a marking M_k, is $M_k \in R(M_0)$?

This means, starting from a given initial marking, can another marking by firing the transitions in some order? This provides an answer to a very practical problem, which is, *"Can the system reach a predetermined state from the present state?"* There are certain states from which the system can never came out. So, if one is confirmed about the non-reachability of such states from the current state then the system shall never enter a deadlock and it can be manipulated without such a danger.

2. **Coverability Problem:** Given a Petri net PN and a marking M_k, is there a Reachable marking $M_{k'} \in R(M_0)$ such that $M_{k'} \geq M_k$?

Given a marking in which the system is at present can there be a marking which is longer than the current one and is reachable from it?

Strength of Petri nets is their support for analysis of many properties and problems associated with concurrent systems. But a major weakness is that modeled Petri nets tend to become too large for analysis even for a modest-size system. For example, reachability analysis can be used in the protocol design phase to explore the global states of the system in order to detect undesirable behaviours such as unboundedness, deadlock and unreachable states. While reachability analysis has been used for formal verification of protocols of low complexity, the practical use of reachability analysis for more complex interactions has been constrained by the problem of state space explosion. The size of states space feasible for full search is known as approximately 105 states (Holzmann, 1991). This problem can be alleviated by the relational approach, because relational database management systems can handle large amounts of data efficiently. This approach has been used by Lee and Lai (1988) and Frieder and Herman (1989). However, formal methods used in both were finite state machines, not Petri nets. However, Kim and Kim (1996) have used bag-theoretical relational algebra as a formal basis.

In this chapter, a framework for the modeling and analysis of Petri nets has been proposed, using relational database technologies extended with bag theory.

Formalism of the framework is based on a bag-theoretic relational algebra. There has been some previous research in extending the relational model to bag-theoretic relational model (Albert, 1991; Dayal, Goodman and Katz, 1982). As discussed in (Kim and Kim, 1996), motivations behind such previous research are either to support the desired semantic modeling capability of the data model or to save the cost of duplicates elimination that is required to implement some set operations. However, Kim and Kim have followed the first approach. For this they had to take care of expressing the number of occurrences of tuples in bag relations by queries. This required an extension of the conventional bag-theoretic relational algebra to provide a much better expressive power. In their chapter a formal means for representing a Petri net using mathematical relations is defined in bag-theoretic relational algebra. Also, algorithms have been developed for generating a reachability tree from such formal relations. Finally, a set of queries on the relation of the reachability tree has been developed to analyze the Petri nets.

A new approach for Petri net for LRA is given below.

Definition 33: [Petri net in LRA] A Petri net in LRA (List theoretic Relational Algebra) is defined as a five-tuple of list theoretic relations PNLRA = (P, T, I, O, M), Where

1. P is a list theoretic relation on $\underline{P}$ = {pid} where dom(pid) is the set of place identifiers.
2. T is a list theoretic relation on $\underline{T}$ = {tid} where dom(tid) is the set of transition identifiers.

3. I is list theoretic relation on $\underline{I}$ = {pid, tid} where dom(pid), dom(tid) are the set of place identifiers, the set of transition identifiers respectively.
4. O is list theoretic relation on $\underline{O}$ = {tid, pid} where dom(pid), dom(tid) are the set of place identifiers, the set of transition identifiers respectively.
5. M is list theoretic relation on $\underline{M}$ = {mid, pid} where dom(mid), dom(pid) are the set of marking identifiers, the set of place identifiers respectively.

The following constraints are considered for the Petri net analysis.

1. dom(pid) $\rightarrow$ dom($|P_L(\overline{x})|$) in P.
2. dom(tid) $\rightarrow$ dom($|P_L(\overline{x})|$) in T.
3. dom(pid) $\times$ dom(tid) $\rightarrow$ dom($|P_L(\overline{x})|$) in I.
4. dom(tid) $\times$ dom(pid) $\rightarrow$ dom($|P_L(\overline{x})|$) in O.
5. dom(mid) $\times$ dom(pid) $\rightarrow$ dom($|P_L(\overline{x})|$) in M.
6. M_0 is the initial value of M.

Consider the Petri net PN_{LRA} with its tables as follows. Here a manufacturing system is considered with different places and different transitions in Figure 1, which is adopted from Kim & Kim(1996).

Tables for PN$_{LRA}$ for the flexible Manufacturing System

Definition 34: A *Reachability tree* in LRA is defined as a list relation RT_{LRA} = (R), where R is a relation on $\underline{R}$ = {pmid, tid, cmid, type} where dom(pmid), dom(tid), dom(cmid) and dom(type) are the set of place identifiers, the set of transition identifiers, the set of place identifiers and {INTERNAL, DUPLICATE, TERMINAL},

The following constraints are considered for reachability tree in LRA.

Figure 1. A flexible manufacturing system

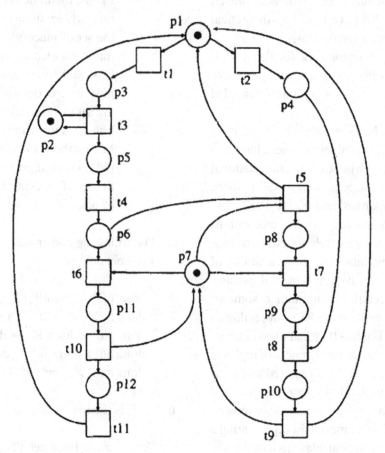

Table 16. Details of process ID (Pid), transaction ID(Tid) and relation M with Mid

P=	Pid	T=	Tid	M=	mid	pid
	1		1		0	1
	2		2		0	2
	3		3		0	7
	4		4			
	5		5			
	6		6			
	7		7			
	8		8			
	9		9			
	10		10			
	11		11			
	12					

Table 17. Input (I) and output (O) for Tid and Pid

I =	tid	Pid	O =	tid	pid
	1	1		1	3
	2	1		2	4
	3	2		3	2
	3	3		3	5
	4	4		4	6
	5	6		5	1
	5	7		5	8
	6	6		6	11
	6	7		7	9
	7	8		8	7
	8	4		8	10
	8	9		9	1
	9	10		10	7
	10	11		10	12
	11	12		11	1

1. $\text{dom(pmid)} \times \text{dom(tid)} \times \text{dom(cmid)}$
    $\rightarrow \text{dom(type)}$ in R,
2. $\text{dom(pmid)} \times \text{dom(tid)} \times \text{dom(cmid)}$
    $\rightarrow \text{dom}(|P_L(x)|)$ in R.

The formalized algorithm for generating the Reachability tree of a Petri net in LRA is used from Kim and Kim (1996), with the change '#' with '$|P_L(\overline{x})|$'. The Reachability tree of PN_{LRA} is given in the next page.

The Marking Table M and the Reachability Table R of PN_LRA

The advantages of LRA over extended BRA are as follows.

1. When a new tuple is added, in extended BRA, a search is mandatory whether such a tuple exists. Then its '#' field is incremented by 1 or else the new tuple is to be added with '#' field '1'. Where as in LRA, we do not bother about the existence or non-existence of the tuple. We simply add it at the end of the table.
2. We don't keep an additional field for '#'. Simply, it is provided by '$|P_L(\overline{x})|$', where $\overline{x}$ is the tuple where '#' is required. (Table 18)
3. The position and order are important factors for the safeness, boundedness, conservation, liveness, Reachability of the Petri net.

Note 6: In these tables $|P_L(\overline{x})|$ is for the illustrations, but need not be stored.

Note 7: Several algorithms have been developed or extended by Kim and Kim (1996) to verify Petri net properties. We would like to note that such algorithms can be used for implementation of LRA with the only modification of replacing # by $|P_L(\overline{x})|$ for each $\overline{x}$ in the tables. So we omit them.

CONCLUSION

Lists are one of the most important data structures (Aho, Ullman, and Hopcroft, 1987; Cormen, Leiserman, Rivest, and Stein, 2011; Quince, 1966; Syropoulos, 2012) in computer science. The classical definition of lists used in Functional programming was redefined by Tripathy et al (Tripathy, Jena and Ghosh, 2001) and it has many advantages over its counterpart. But also, it required redefining the earlier concepts from the new angle and also there is a necessity to establish properties which were there in the literature already. Also, new properties if any were also challenging.

In this chapter we have defined the list theoretic relational algebraic operations. Some important notions of relational operations like table, tuple, insertion, deletion, modification, Cartesian product, selection, projection, table concatenation, union, intersection, difference are studied and also some new properties of list like filter, generalized zip are introduced with theorems. At the end list theoretic relational algebra is studied using Petri net model.

SCOPE FOR FUTURE WORK

In this section we propose some problems which can be studied for further research in the direction of this chapter.

Table 18. Reachability (R) of the Petri net model

M=	mid	pid	$|P_L(\overline{x})|$	R=	pmid	Tid	cmid	type	$|P_L(\overline{x})|$
	0	1	1		Null	Null	0	INTERNAL	1
	0	2	2		0	1	1	INTERNAL	2
	0	7	3		0	2	2	TERMINAL	3
	1	2	4		1	3	3	INTERNAL	4
	1	3	5		3	4	4	INTERNAL	5
	1	7	6		4	5	5	INTERNAL	6
	2	2	7		4	6	6	INTERNAL	7
	2	4	8		5	1	7	INTERNAL	8
	2	7	9		5	2	8	INTERNAL	9
	3	2	10		5	7	9	INTERNAL	10
	3	5	11		6	10	10	INTERNAL	11
	3	7	12		7	3	11	INTERNAL	12
	4	2	13		7	7	12	INTERNAL	13
	4	6	14		8	7	13	INTERNAL	14
	4	7	15		9	1	14	DUPLICATE	15
	.	.	.		9	2	15	DUPLICATE	16
	.	.	.		10	11	16	DUPLICATE	17
	.	.	.		11	4	17	INTERNAL	18
	22	2	67		11	7	18	INTERNAL	19
	22	6	68		12	3	19	DUPLICATE	20
	22	9	69		13	8	20	INTERNAL	21
	23	1	70		17	7	21	TERMINAL	22
	23	2	71		18	4	22	DUPLICATE	23
	23	7	72		20	9	23	DUPLICATE	24

1. In order to capture imprecision in data many uncertainty based models have been introduced. Fuzzy sets, introduced by Zadeh (1965) are one of the earliest such models. In this model the concept of graded membership of elements is introduced. Using this concept, the fuzzy relational databases were introduced by Buckles and Petry (1982). Also, fuzzy lists have been defined by Tripathy et al (2004). So, one can use these definitions

Figure 2. The Marking table M and the Reachability Table R of PN$_{LRA}$

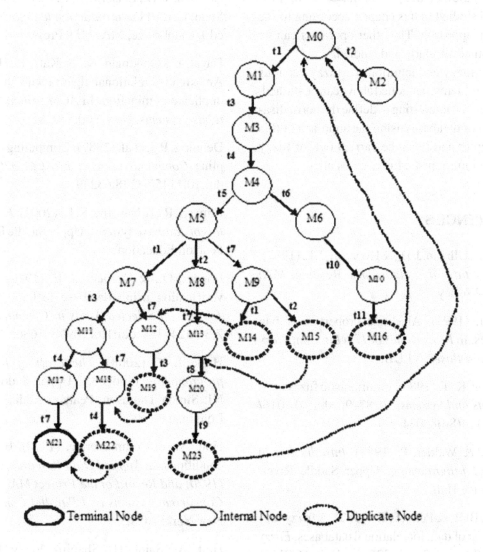

and follow the approach presented in this chapter to define fuzzy relational algebra through fuzzy lists and study their properties.

2. The concept of fuzzy sets has been extended by Atanassov, who introduced the concept of intuitionistic fuzzy sets (Atanassov, 1986). This concept has been generalised by the introduction of intuitionistic fuzzy bags and intuitionistic fuzzy lists (Tripathy and Choudhury, 2003). So far, the notion of intuitionistic fuzzy databases has not been fully explores. So, one can define the notion of Intuitionistic fuzzy relational databases through the intuitionistic fuzzy lists and study their properties.

3. Only a few of the operators have been defined and studied in this chapter according to the new approach. The other operators can be defined similarly and studied.
4. The fuzzy and intuitionistic fuzzy versions of problems mentioned above can be studied.
5. It will be interesting to define the normalisation of databases using the approach of this chapter and it can be carried out for fuzzy and intuitionistic fuzzy cases also.

REFERENCES

Aho, A. V., Ullman, J. D., & Hopcroft, J. E. (1987). *Data structures and algorithms*. Reading, MA: Addison-Wesley.

Albert, J. (1991). Algebraic properties of bag data types. In *Proceedings of 17th Int. Conf. Very Large Data Bases*. VLDB.

Atanassov, K. T. (1986). Intuitionistic fuzzy sets. *Fuzzy Sets and Systems*, *20*, 87–96. doi:10.1016/S0165-0114(86)80034-3

Bird, R., & Walder, P. (1988). *Introduction to functional programming*. Upper Saddle River, NJ: Prentice Hall.

Buckles, B. P., & Petry, F. E. (1982). A fuzzy representation of data for relational databases. *Fuzzy Sets and Systems*, *7*, 213–226. doi:10.1016/0165-0114(82)90052-5

Bureau of Transportation Statistics, USA. (2012). Retrieved from www.bts.gov

Cantor, G. (1883). *G. Grundlagen einer allgemeinen mannigfaltig-keitslehre*. Leipzig, Germany: B.G. Teubner.

Codd, E. (1970). A relational model of data for large shared data banks. *Communications of the ACM*, *13*, 377–387. doi:10.1145/362384.362685

Cormen, T. H., Leiserman, C. E., Rivest, R. L., & Stein, C. (2011). *Introduction to algorithms* (3rd ed.). Cambridge, MA: MIT Press.

Dayal, U., Goodman, N., & Katz, R. H. (1982). An extended relational algebra with control over duplicate elimination. In *ACM principles of database systems*. New York: ACM.

Denning, P. J. et al. (1989). Computing as a discipline. *Communications of the ACM*, *32*(1), 9–10. doi:10.1145/63238.63239

Elmasri, R., & Navathe, S. K. (2004). *Fundamentals of database systems*. Upper Saddle River, NJ: Pearson Education.

Frieder, O., & Herman, J. E. (1989). Protocol verification using database technology. *IEEE Journal on Selected Areas in Communications*, *7*(3), 324–334. doi:10.1109/49.16865

Haskell, R. (2008). *The craft of functional programming* (2nd ed.). Upper Saddle River, NJ: Simon Thomson, Pearson Addison Wesley Longman.

Holt, A., & Commoner, F. (1970). Events and conditions. In *Applied Data Research, New York (1970) and Record of the Project MAC Conf. on Concurrent Systems and Parallel Computation*. New York: ACM.

Holt, A., Saint, H., Shapiro, R., & Warshall, S. (1968). *Final report of the information system theory project* (Technical Report RADC-TR-68-305). New York: Rome Air Development Centre, Griffiss Air Force Base.

Holzmann, G. J. (1991). Design and validation of computer protocols. Englewood Cliffs, NJ: PH.

Kim, Y. C., & Kim, T. G. (1996). Petri nets modeling and analysis using extended bag-theoretic relational algebra. *IEEE Trans. on Systems, Man, and Cybernetics -Part B*, *26*(4), 599–605. doi:10.1109/3477.517034 PMID:18263057

Lee, T. T., & Lai, M. (1988). A relational approach to protocol verification. *IEEE Transactions on Software Engineering*, *14*(2), 184–193. doi:10.1109/32.4637

Miyamoto, S. (2001). Fuzzy multisets and their generalizations. In *Multiset Processing (LNCS)* (Vol. 2235, pp. 225–235). Berlin: Springer-Verlag. doi:10.1007/3-540-45523-X_11

Peterson, J. L. (1981). Petri net theory and the modeling of system. Englewood Cliffs, NJ: PH.

Petri, C. A. (1962). *Kommunikation mit automaten*. (Ph.D. Dissertation). University of Bonn, Bonn, Germany.

Quince, C. (1966). *LISP in small pieces*. Cambridge, UK: Cambridge University Press.

Rabhi, F. (2008). *Algorithms: A functional programming approach*. International Computer Science Series.

Reisig, W. (1983). *Petri nets: An introduction*. Berlin: Springer-Verlag.

Russell, B. (1937). *The principles of mathematics* (2nd ed.). London: George Allen & Unwin Ltd.

Syropoulos, A. (2012). On generalized fuzzy multisets and their use in computation. *Iranian Journal of Fuzzy Systems*, *9*(2), 113–125.

Tanimoto, S. L., & Tanimoto, S. (Eds.). (2008). The elements of artificial intelligence using common LISP (2nd ed.). Principles of Computer Science Series.

Tripathy, B. K., & Choudhury, P. K. (2003). Intuitionistic fuzzy lists. *Notes on Intuitionistic Fuzzy Sets*, *9*(2), 61–73.

Tripathy, B. K., & Gantayat, S. S. (2004). Some more properties of lists and fuzzy lists. *Information Sciences - Informatics and Computer Science*, *166*, 167-179.

Tripathy, B. K., & Gantayat, S. S. (2012). Conceptual application of list theory to data structures. In *Proceedings of the Second International Conference on Advances in Computing and Information Technology* (ACITY-2012), (pp. 551-560). Berlin: Springer-Verlag.

Tripathy, B. K., & Gantayat, S. S. (2013). Some new properties of lists and a framework of a list theoretic relation model. In *Proceedings of the Second International Conference on Computational Science, Engineering and Information Technology* (CCSEIT-2012). ACM.

Tripathy, B. K., Jena, S. P., & Ghosh, S. K. (2001). On the theory of bags and lists. *Information Sciences*, *132*, 241–254. doi:10.1016/S0020-0255(01)00066-4

Tripathy, B. K., & Pattnaik, G. P. (2004). On some properties of lists and fuzzy lists. *Information Sciences - Informatics and Computer Science*, *168*, 9-23.

Ullman, J. D. (1997). *Fundamentals of database systems*. New Delhi: Galgotia Publications.

Yager, R. R. (1986). On the theory of bags. *International Journal of General Systems*, *13*, 23–37. doi:10.1080/03081078608934952

Zadeh, L. A. (1965). Fuzzy sets. *Information and Control*, *8*(3), 338–353. doi:10.1016/S0019-9958(65)90241-X

APPENDIX

Table 19. Key terms and definitions

List	A list L drawn from a set X is characterized by its position function P_L defined as $P_L: X \rightarrow P(N)$, where $P(N)$ denotes power set of the set of non–negative integers N. For each $x \in L$, $P_L(x)$ is the set of positions in L where x occurs.
cardinality	For any finite list L drawn from X, the cardinality or length of L is denoted by #L and is defined as $$\#L = \sum_{x \in X} |P_L(x)|,$$ whenever the right hand side exists. In this case L is said to be finite, otherwise L is said to be infinite.
head	Let L be a list drawn from X. We define the head of L, denoted by hd(L) as hd(L) = x, if $0 \in P_L(x)$.
empty List	A list L drawn from X is empty if $P_L(x) = \phi$ for each $x \in X$ and is denoted by [ ].
concatenation	Let L_1 and L_2 be two finite lists drawn from X. Then the concatenation of L_1 and L_2 is denoted by $L_1 \# L_2$ and is given by the position function $P_{(L_1 \# L_2)}(x) = P_{L_1}(x) \cup \{\# L_1 + t : t \in P_{L_2}(x)\}, \forall x \in X$.
zip	Let L_1 and L_2 be two lists drawn from X. Then we define the zip (L_1, L_2) of L_1 and L_2 by, $$P_{zip(L_1, L_2)}(x, y) = \{r : r \in P_{L_1}(x) \cap P_{L_2}(y)\} = P_{L_1}(x) \cap P_{L_2}(y).$$
init	For a finite list L the functions init is given as $init(L) = rev\left(tl\left(rev(L)\right)\right)$,
last	For a finite list L the functions last are given as $last(L) = x$, if $(\# L - 1) \in P_L(x)$.
take	Let L be a finite list L drawn from X. Then the take operator on L, for any given $n \in N$, is denoted by take(n, L) and it is a list whose position function is given by $$P_{take(n, L)}(x) = \begin{cases} \phi, & \text{if } n \leq \min P_L(x) \text{ or } P_L(x) = \phi \\ \{r : r < n \text{ and } r \in P_L(x)\}, & \text{if } n > P_L(x) \end{cases}$$
drop	Let L be a finite list drawn from X. Then, for any $n \in N$ the drop operator on L is denoted by drop (n, L) and it is a list whose position function is given by $$P_{drop(n, L)}(x) = \begin{cases} \phi, & \text{if } n > \max P_L(x) \\ \{r - n : r \geq n \text{ and } r \in P_L(x)\}, & \text{if } n \leq \max P_L(x) \end{cases}$$
Cartesian product	For any two lists L_1 and L_2 defined over X and Y respectively, we define their Cartesian product $L_1 \otimes L_2$ by $$L_1 \otimes L_2 = P_{(L_1 \otimes L_2)}(x,y) = \{\# L_2.s + t : s \in P_{L_1}(x), t \in P_{L_2}(x)\}$$
map	Let L be a list drawn from X and f be a mapping from X to X. Then map(f, L) is a list whose position function is given by $P_{map(f, L)}(y) = \{r: y = f(x) \text{ for some } x \in X \text{ and } r \in P_L(x)\}$.

continued on following page

Table 19. Continued

indexlist	Let L be a finite list drawn from X. Then the *indexlist* (L, j), denoted by L_j is a singleton list containing the element at the jth position of L and is defined as L_j = take(j +1, L) – take(j, L), $0 \le j \le$ # L. Let L be a finite list drawn from X and *p* be a predicate on X. Boolean function f_p is defined as, $f_p(x) = 1$, if p(x) is true; = 0, otherwise. It is denoted as L(p) = map (f_p, L) and P(L, p) = $P_{L(p)}(1)$. Here L(p) is a binary list of 0s and 1s. $P_{L(p)}(1)$ provides the position of 1s in the list L(p).
filter	The filter from the indexlist is defined as: filter(p, L) = $\underset{j \in P(L,p)}{+\!\!\!+} L_j.$
Relation	Suppose $L_0, L_1, ..., L_{K-1}$ are the lists(attributes) drawn from a universe X. Then a *relation* r of T is a subset of the Cartesian product of the domains that are in T and $r(T) \subseteq dom(L_0) \times dom(L_1) \times .... \times dom(L_{k-1})$. In this case, the tuple t of the relation schema T is defined as $t = (t_0, t_1, ..., t_{k-1})$, where each $t_i \in L_i$ and the value of t_i is an element of $dom(L_i)$.
Generalized zip	Suppose $L_0, L_1, ...$ and L_{k-1} are k–lists drawn from the universe X. Then zip* $(L_0, L_1, ..., L_{k-1})$ can be defined as follows. $P_{zip*(L_0,L_1,.............,L_{k-1})}^{(x_0,x_1,.........,x_{k-1})} = P_{L_0}(x_0) \cap P_{L_1}(x_1) \cap .... \cap P_{L_{k-1}}(x_{k-1})$ $\forall x_j \in L_j, j = 0, 1, ... k-1$
Table/Relation	(A table or a relation T over a universe X is defined as $T = zip* (L_0, L_1, ..., L_{k-1})$, where L_j (j= 0, 1, ..., k–1) are the attributes of the table T. Here T is also a list of composite elements of other lists.
Tuple	If $L_0, L_1, ... L_{k-1}$ are the attributes of T, the elements of $L_0, L_1, ..., L_{k-1}$ together form a tuple of the table T with corresponding positional functions. That is, $P_T^{(x_0,x_1,.........,x_{k-1})} = P_{zip*(L_0,L_1,.............,L_{k-1})}^{(x_0,x_1,.........,x_{k-1})}$ $= P_{L_0}(x_0) \cap P_{L_1}(x_1) \cap .... \cap P_{L_{k-1}}(x_{k-1})$ So here $(x_0, x_1, ..., x_{k-1})$ is a tuple of length k of the table T.
INSERTION	Suppose t is a tuple of T. Then we can insert the tuple t in any position of the table T. That is, we can insert the tuple t in an empty table or add the tuple t at the end of the table T or we can insert the tuple at any position of T.
DELETION	Suppose t is a tuple of T. Then we can delete the tuple t from any position of the table T. That is, we can delete t from the top of table or form the middle of the table T or we can delete the tuple t from the end of the table T.
Cartesian Product	Suppose $T_1 (A_1, A_2, ..., A_M)$ and $T_2 (B_1, B_2, ..., B_N)$ are two tables and $x_i \in A_i$ for i = 1, 2, .., M and $y_j \in B_j$ for j = 1, 2, ..., N, then we can define the Cartesian product of T_1 and T_2 in the following manner. $P_{T_1 \times T_2}^{(x_1, x_2,......, x_M, y_1, y_2,......, y_N)} = P_{zip*(A_1, A_2,......, A_M, B_1, B_2,......, B_N)}^{(x_1, x_2,......, x_M, y_1, y_2,......, y_N)}$

continued on following page

Table 19. Continued

SELECTION	Suppose T is a table with attributes $L_0, L_1, ..., L_j, ..., L_{k-1}$ in a universe X. We define a map $f_p: X \to \{0, 1\}$ where f is a function required for the implementation of the filter and $\forall x \in X, f_p(x) = 1$, if p(x) is true; 0, otherwise. The selection operator $\sigma_{filter(p,L_i)}(T) = zip * (L_0^*, L_1^*, ..., L_{K-1}^*)$ where $L_j^* = \underset{k \in P_{map(f_p,L_i)}^{(1)}}{\text{\textbardbl}} L_{j,k}$ and $Lj_{,k} = [index (L_{j,k}): k \in P_{map(f_p,L_i)}]$. Using the above definitions, we can simplify the selection operator as follows. $\sigma_{filter(p,L_i)}(T) = zip * (L_0^*, L_1^*, ..., L_{K-1}^*)$, where $L_j^* = \underset{k \in P_{map(f_p,L_i)}^{(1)}}{\text{\textbardbl}} indexlist(L, k)$
PROJECTION	It is a specific operation to select specified columns from a given table without any duplicate tuples in the selection. $\prod_{<attribute list>}(T)$ gives the output in the same order as attributes appeared in the list. The commutative property of the projection does not hold in general. The number of attributes in the projection list does not exceed the number of attributes in the relation table T.
CONCATENATION OF TABLES	Suppose T_1 and T_2 are two relation tables with the attributes $(A_1, A_2, ..., A_n)$ and $(B_1, B_2, ..., B_n)$ respectively and $\#A(T_1) = \#A(T_2)$, where $T_1 = zip*(A_1, A_2, ..., A_n)$ and $T_2 = zip*(B_1, B_2, ..., B_n)$, A_i and B_i are lists and $dom(A_i) = dom(Bi)$ for $1 \le i \le n$. Then we define the concatenation of tables T_1 and T_2 as follows. $T_1 \text{\textbardbl} T_2 = zip*(A_1 \text{\textbardbl} B_1, A_2 \text{\textbardbl} B_2, ..., A_n \text{\textbardbl} B_n)$.
UNION	Suppose T_1 and T_2 are two relation tables with the attributes $(A_1, A_2, ..., A_n)$ and $(B_1, B_2, ..., B_n)$ respectively. Then the union of T_1 and T_2, denoted as $T_1 \cup T_2$, is the collection of all the tuples of T_1 and T_2 without duplication. For $D = dom(A_1) \times dom(A_2) \times .... \times dom(A_n) = dom(B_1) \times dom(B_2) \times .... \times dom(B_n)$, suppose $T' = T_1 \text{\textbardbl} T_2$ and $T_1 \cup T_2 = T''$, where $T'' = \underset{(x_1, x_2, ..., x_n) \in D}{\text{\textbardbl}} take(1, \underset{j \in P_{T'}(x_1, x_2, ..., x_n)}{\text{\textbardbl}} indexlist(T',j))$
INTERSECTION	Suppose T_1 and T_2 are two relation tables with the attributes $(A_1, A_2, ..., A_n)$ and $(B_1, B_2, ..., B_n)$ respectively. Then the intersection of T_1 and T_2, denoted as $T_1 \cap T_2$, is the collection of all the common tuples of T_1 and T_2 without duplication. $T_1 \cap T_2 = T_1' - (T_1' - T_2')$ where $T_j' = uniquelist (T_j)$ for $i = 1, 2$.
DIFFERENCE	Suppose T_1 and T_2 are two relation tables with the attributes $(A_1, A_2... A_n)$ and $(B_1, B_2... B_n)$ respectively. Then the difference of T_1 and T_2, denoted as $T_1 \sim T_2$, is the collection of all the common tuples of T_1 and T_2, $T_1 \sim T_2 = (T_1 \setminus T_2) \cup (T_2 \setminus T_1)$.
LRA	List Theoretic Relational Algebra
Petri net	A Petri net, PN, is a five-tuple (P, T, I, O, M0); where P is a finite set of elements called places, T is a finite set of elements called transitions, I: $P \times T \to N$ is the input function, which associates with every pair of places and transition, a nonnegative integer representing the minimum number tokens in the place required for the transition to be fired, O: $T \times P \to N$ is the output function, which associates with every pair of transition and places, a nonnegative integer representing the exact number tokens to be added to the place in a single firing of the transition, $M_0: P \to N$ is the initial marking function, which associates with every place a nonnegative number of tokens. This captures and describes the initial state of the system. The basic assumption is that $P \cap T = \phi$ and $P \cup T \ne \phi$.
Reachability Problem	Starting from a given initial marking, can another marking by firing the transitions in some order?
Coverability Problem	Given a marking in which the system is at present can there be a marking which is longer than the current one and is reachable from it?

Chapter 16
Soft Sets:
Theory and Applications

Pinaki Majumdar
M.U.C. Women's College, India & Visva-Bharati University, India

ABSTRACT

This chapter is about soft sets. A brief account of the developments that took place in last 14 years in the field of Soft Sets Theory (SST) has been presented. It begins with a brief introduction on soft sets and then it describes many generalizations of it. The notions of generalized fuzzy soft sets are defined and their properties are studied. After that, a notion of mapping, called soft mapping, in soft set setting is introduced. Later, algebraic structures on soft sets like soft group, soft ring, etc. are discussed. Then the next section deals with the concept of topology on soft sets. Here two notions of topology in soft sets are introduced, which are the topology of soft subsets and the soft topology, respectively. The idea of entropy for soft sets is defined in the later section. Next, some applications of hybrid soft sets in solving real life problems like medical diagnosis, decision-making, etc. are shown. Issues like measurement of similarity of soft sets are also addressed.

INTRODUCTION

Uncertainty is a common phenomenon of our daily existence because our world is full of uncertainties. In our daily life we encounter many situations where we do take account of these uncertainties. Therefore it is natural for man to understand and try to model this uncertainty prevailing in physi-

cal world. From centuries, in almost all branches of Science or in Philosophy, attempts have been made to understand and represent the features of uncertainty. Perhaps that is the main reason behind the development of Probability theory and Stochastic techniques which started in early eighteenth century. Till mid-twentieth century, Probability theory was the only tool for handling

DOI: 10.4018/978-1-4666-4936-1.ch016

certain type of uncertainty called "Randomness". But there are several other kinds of uncertainties; one such type is called "vagueness" or "imprecision" which is inherent in our natural languages. In 1965, L. A. Zadeh [Zadeh, 1965] coined his remarkable theory of Fuzzy sets that deals with a kind of uncertainty known as "Fuzziness" and which is due to partial membership of an element in a set. Later this "Fuzziness" concept leads to the highly acclaimed theory of Fuzzy Logic. This theory has been applied with a good deal of success to many areas of engineering, economics, medical science etc., to name a few, with great efficiency.

After the invention of fuzzy sets many other hybrid concepts begun to develop. In 1983, K. Atanassov [Atanasov, 1986] introduced the idea of Intuitionistic fuzzy sets, a set with each member having a degree of belongingness as well as a degree of non-belongingness. This is again a generalization of fuzzy set theory. Although Fuzzy set theory is very successful in handling uncertainties arising from vagueness or partial belongingness of an element in a set, it cannot model all sorts of uncertainties prevailing in different real physical problems. Thus search for new theories has been continued. In 1982, Z. Pawlak[41] came up with his Rough set theory. But there is one theory which is relatively new and having a lot of potential for being a major tool for modeling uncertainty, is the theory of Soft sets. In the year 1999, Russian mathematician Molodtsov [Molodtsov, 1999] initiated the theory of soft sets. His theory was primarily based on "parameterization of tools". In dealing with uncertain situations, fuzzy set theory was perhaps the most appropriate theory till then. But the main difficulty with fuzzy sets is to frame a suitable membership function for a specific problem. The reason behind this is possibly the inadequacy of the parameterization tool of the theory. In his remarkable paper, Molodtsov

proposed soft sets as a new mathematical tool for dealing with uncertainties and which is free from difficulties faced by previous fuzzy set theory.

A soft set is a classification of elements of the universe with respect to some given set of parameters. It has been shown that soft set is more general in nature and has more capabilities in handling uncertain information. Also a fuzzy set or a rough set can be considered as a special case of soft sets. Research involving soft sets and its application in various fields of science and technology are currently going on in a rapid pace.

This chapter deals with the theory of soft sets and is divided into several sections. In the first section some preliminary notions about soft sets and some operations on them are discussed. After the invention of soft sets in 1999, several generalizations of it came up in recent times. Here we have discussed a particular type of generalization of soft sets, called generalized fuzzy soft set in the second section. Section three describes an idea of soft mapping. Several algebraic structures like group, ring etc. have also extended in soft set settings. Some of these have been discussed in section four. A notion of soft topology has been discussed in section five. The notion of softness of a soft set or soft entropy has been discussed in section six. In the last section, some applications of soft sets have been shown.

THEORY OF SOFT SETS

A. Definitions

Definition 1: [Molodtsov, 1999] Let U be a classical set of elements, called the universe and E be a set of parameters, called the parameter set. Together they are often regarded as a soft universe. Members of the universe and the parameter set are generally denoted by x and e respectedly. A soft set [Molodtsov, 1999] over the soft universe (U, E) is denoted by (F, A), where

$$F : A \rightarrow P(U),$$

where

$A \subseteq E$ and $P(U)$

is the power set of U.

Actually in true sense a soft set is not a set; rather it is a parametrized collection of ordinary sets. Each $F(e), e \in A$ is called an $e -$ approximation or $e -$ elements of the soft set (F, A). To illustrate the notion of soft sets we present the following example.

Example 1: [Majumdar & Samanta, 2008] A soft set (F, E) describes the attractiveness of shirts which the author is going to wear for a party. Suppose a soft set (F, A). describes attractiveness of the shirts which the authors are going to wear.

Let U = the set of all shirts under consideration

=

$$\left\{ x_1, x_2, x_3, x_4, x_5 \right\}$$

A = the parameter set. Each parameter is a word or a sentence.

Let A = {colorful, bright, cheap, warm} =

$$\left\{ e_1, e_2, e_3, e_4 \right\}$$

Let

$$F(e_1) = \left\{ x_1, x_2 \right\},$$

$$F(e_2) = \left\{ x_1, x_2, x_3 \right\},$$

$$F(e_3) = \left\{ x_4 \right\},$$

$$F(e_4) = \left\{ x_2, x_5 \right\}$$

So, the soft set (F, A) is a subfamily

$$\left\{ F(e_i), i = 1, 2, 3, 4 \right\}$$

of $P(U)$.

Here to define a soft set means to point out colorful shirts, bright shirts, cheap shirts, and so on. It should be noted that the sets $F(e)$ may be arbitrary and some of them may be empty or may have non-empty intersection. A tabular representation of a soft set can be given as follows:

A fuzzy set may be considered as a special case of soft set. Let A be a fuzzy set, and μ_A be its membership function. So μ_A is a mapping of U into $[0,1]$. Now let us consider the family of $\alpha -$ level sets for function μ_A,

$$F(\alpha) = \{ x \in U \mid \mu_A(x) \geq \alpha \}, \alpha \in [0,1].$$

Table 1. Tabular representation of a soft set

U	colorful	bright	cheap	warm
x_1	1	1	0	0
x_2	1	1	0	1
x_3	0	1	0	0
x_4	0	0	1	0
x_5	0	0	0	1

Now if we know the family F, then we can find the function μ_A by means of the following formula:

$$\mu_A(x) = \underset{\substack{\alpha \in [0,1] \\ x \in F(\alpha)}}{Sup} \alpha.$$

Thus a fuzzy set may be considered as a soft set $(F, [0,1])$.

B. Set:Theoretic Operations

Now basic set theoretic operations are defined on soft sets as follows:

Definition 2: [Maji, Biswas, & Roy, 2003] For two soft sets (F, A) and (G, B) over a common universe U, we say that (F, A) is a soft subset of (G, B) if $(i) A \subset B$,

$(ii) \forall e \in A, F(e) \subseteq G(e)$.

Definition 3: [Maji, Biswas, & Roy, 2003] (Equality of two soft sets) Two soft sets (F, A) and (G, B) over a common universe U are said to be soft equal if (F, A) is a soft subset of (G, B) and (G, B) is a soft subset of (F, A) and this is denoted by $(F, A) = (G, B)$.

Definition 4: [Maji, Biswas, & Roy, 2003] Union of two soft sets (F, A) and (G, B) over a common universe U is the soft set (H, C), where $C = A \cup B$, and $\forall e \in C$,

$$H(e) = F(e),$$

$$if \ e \in A - B,$$

$$= G(e) \ if \ e \in B - A,$$

$$= F(e) \cup G(e) \ if \ e \in A \cap B,$$

This is denoted by

$$(F, A) \tilde{\cup} (G, B).$$

Definition 5: [Maji, Biswas, & Roy, 2003] Intersection of two soft sets (F, A) and (G, B) over a common universe U is the soft set (H, C), where $C = A \cap B$ and $\forall e \in C$,

$$H(e) = F(e) \cap G(e)$$

This is denoted by

$$(F, A) \tilde{\cap} (G, B).$$

Definition 6: [Majumdar & Samanta, 2008] The complement of a soft set (F, A) is denoted by $(F, A)^C$ and is defined by (F^c, A) where $F^c : A \to P(U)$ is a mapping given by

$$F^c(\alpha) = U - F(\alpha), \forall \alpha \in A.$$

Definition 7: [Maji, Biswas, & Roy, 2003] A soft set (F, A) over U is said to be a null soft set, denoted by $\tilde{\Phi}_A$, if $\forall e \in A, F(e) = \phi$, (null set).

Definition 8: [Maji, Biswas, & Roy, 2003] A soft set (F, A) over U is said to be a absolute soft set, denoted by $\tilde{A}$, if $\forall e \in A, F(e) = U$.

Let $P(U, E)$ *or* $P(U)^E$ denote the collection of all soft sets over U with parameters set E. Now the operations of union, intersection and complement defined above, the following properties hold.

Proposition 1: [Maji, Biswas, & Roy, 2003] For all

$$(F, A), (G, B), (H, C) \in P(U)^E,$$

the following holds:

1. Idempotency:

$$(F,A) \, \tilde{\cup} \, (F,A) = (F,A);$$
$$(F,A) \, \tilde{\cap} \, (F,A) = (F,A).$$

2. Identity:

$$(F,A) \, \tilde{\cup} \, \tilde{\Phi}_A = (F,A); (F,A) \, \tilde{\cap} \, \tilde{\Phi}_A = \tilde{\Phi}_A.$$

3. $(F,A) \, \tilde{\cup} \, \tilde{A} = \tilde{A}; (F,A) \, \tilde{\cap} \, \tilde{A} = (F,A).$

4. Commutative:

$$(F,A) \, \tilde{\cup} \, (G,B) = (G,B) \, \tilde{\cup} \, (F,A);$$
$$(F,A) \, \tilde{\cap} \, (G,B) = (G,B) \, \tilde{\cap} \, (F,A).$$

5. Associative:

$$((F,A) \, \tilde{\cup} \, (G,B)) \, \tilde{\cup} \, (H,C) =$$
$$(F,A) \, \tilde{\cup} \, ((G,B) \, \tilde{\cup} \, (H,C));$$
$$((F,A) \, \tilde{\cap} \, (G,B)) \, \tilde{\cap} \, (H,C) =$$
$$(F,A) \, \tilde{\cap} \, ((G,B) \, \tilde{\cap} \, (H,C))$$

6. Distributive:

$$(F,A) \, \tilde{\cup} \, ((G,B)) \, \tilde{\cap} \, (H,C)) =$$
$$((F,A) \, \tilde{\cup} \, (G,B)) \, \tilde{\cap} \, ((F,A) \, \tilde{\cup} \, (H,C));$$
$$(F,A) \, \tilde{\cap} \, ((G,B)) \, \tilde{\cup} \, (H,C)) =$$
$$((F,A) \, \tilde{\cap} \, (G,B)) \, \tilde{\cup} \, ((F,A) \, \tilde{\cap} \, (H,C)).$$

7. Involution:

$$((F,A)^c)^c = (F,A).$$

8. De Morgans:

$$((F,A) \, \tilde{\cup} \, (G,B))^c = (F,A)^c \, \tilde{\cap} \, (G,B)^c;$$
$$((F,A) \, \tilde{\cap} \, (G,B))^c = (F,A)^c \, \tilde{\cup} \, (G,B)^c.$$

- **Proof:** Proofs are left for the readers.

C. More Operations

Many other operations are operations on soft sets can be defined. Here we present AND, OR and NOT operations on soft sets.

Definition 9: [Maji, Biswas, & Roy, 2003] If (F,A) and (G,B) be two soft sets over a common universe U, then

"(F,A) *and* (G,B)"
denoted by $(F,A) \wedge (G,B)$

and is defined by

$$(F,A) \wedge (G,B) = (H, A \times B),$$

where

$$H(\alpha, \beta) =$$
$$F(\alpha) \cap G(\beta), \forall (\alpha, \beta) \in A \times B.$$

Definition 10: [Maji, Biswas, & Roy, 2003] If (F,A) or (G,B) be two soft sets over a common universe U, then

"(F,A) *or* (G,B)"
denoted by $(F,A) \vee (G,B)$

and is defined by

$$(F,A) \vee (G,B) = (O, A \times B),$$

where

$$O(\alpha, \beta) = F(\alpha) \cup G(\beta), \forall (\alpha, \beta) \in A \times B.$$

Example 2: Consider again the shirt selection problem discussed earlier.

Suppose the following two soft set (F, A) and (G, B) describes "attractiveness of the shirts" which the authors are going to wear and "the cost of the houses".

Let U = the set of all shirts under consideration $= \{x_1, x_2, x_3, x_4, x_5\}$

Let $A = \{\text{colorful}, \text{bright}, \text{warm}\} = \{e_1, e_2, e_3\}$

and $B = \{\text{costly, cheap}\} = \{f_1, f_2\}$.

Let $F(e_1) = \{x_1, x_2\}$,

$F(e_2) = \{x_1, x_2, x_3\}$,

$F(e_3) = \{x_4, x_5\}$.

So, the soft set (F, A) is a subfamily

$\{F(e_i), i = 1, 2, 3, 4\}$

of $P(U)$.

Similarly let

$G(f_1) = \{x_1, x_4, x_5\}, G(f_2) = \{x_2\}$.

Let

$(F, A) \wedge (G, B) = (O, A \times B)$

$(F, A) \vee (G, B) = (H, A \times B)$

Then

$(O, A \times B) = \{O(e_1, f_1) =$
$O(colorful, \cos tly) = \{x_1\}, O(e_1, f_2) = \{x_2\},$

$O(e_2, f_1) = \{x_1\}, O(e_2, f_2) =$
$\{x_2\}, O(e_3, f_1) = \{x_4, x_5\}, O(e_3, f_2) = \phi\}.$

Similarly,

$(H, A \times B) = \{H(e_1, f_1) =$
$H(\text{colorful,costly}) =$
$\{x_1, x_2, x_4, x_5\}, H(e_1, f_2) =$
$H(\text{colorful,cheap}) = \{x_1, x_2\},$

$H(e_2, f_1) = U, O(e_2, f_2) = \{x_1, x_2, x_3\},$
$O(e_3, f_1) = \{x_1, x_4, x_5\}, O(e_3, f_2) = \{x_2, x_4, x_5\}.$

Definition 11: [Maji, Biswas, & Roy, 2003] (NOT set of a parameter set) Let

$E = \{e_1, e_2, \ldots\ldots, e_n\}$

be a set of parameters. The NOT set of E denoted by $\sim E$ is defined by

$\sim E = \{\sim e_1, \sim e_2, \ldots\ldots\ldots, \sim e_n\}$

where

$\sim e_i = not\, e_i, \forall i.$

The following results are obvious.

Proposition 2: [Maji, Biswas, & Roy, 2003]

1. $\sim(\sim A) = A$
2. $\sim(A \cup B) = (\sim A) \cup (\sim B).$
3. $\sim(A \cap B) = (\sim A) \cap (\sim B).$

For example if the

$E = \{\text{expansive, beautiful, cheap}\}$

be a parameter set, then

$\sim E =$
$\{\text{not expansive, not beautiful, not cheap}\}.$

Next here is another notion of complement of a soft set based on the NOT set of a parameter.

Definition 12: [Maji, Biswas, & Roy, 2003] The complement of a soft set (F, A) is denoted by

$$(F, A)' = (F', \sim A),$$

where

$$F' : \sim A \to P(U)$$

is a mapping given by

$$F'(\alpha) = U - F(\sim \alpha), \forall \alpha \in \sim A.$$

We call F' to be the complementary function of F. Clearly

$$(F')' = F \ and \ ((F, A)')' = (F, A).$$

Then the following results hold.

Proposition 3: [Maji, Biswas, & Roy, 2003]

1. $((F, A) \vee (G, B))' = (F, A)' \wedge (G, B)'$.
2. $((F, A) \wedge (G, B))' = (F, A)' \vee (G, B)'$.

- **Proof:** Proofs are easy and left for the readers.

Also the following results trivially follow from definition.

Proposition 4: [Maji, Biswas, & Roy, 2003]

1. $((F, A) \vee (G, B)) \vee (H, C) =$ $(F, A) \vee ((G, B) \vee (H, C))$;
2. $((F, A) \wedge (G, B)) \wedge (H, C) =$ $(F, A) \wedge ((G, B) \wedge (H, C))$;
3. $(F, A) \vee ((G, B)) \wedge (H, C)) =$ $((F, A) \vee (G, B)) \wedge ((F, A) \vee (H, C))$;
4. $(F, A) \wedge ((G, B)) \vee (H, C)) =$ $((F, A) \wedge (G, B)) \vee ((F, A) \wedge (H, C))$.

GENERALIZATIONS OF SOFT SETS

A. From Crisp to Fuzzy Case

Several generalizations of soft sets have been done in recent years. In ordinary soft set, corresponding to each parameter there is an ordinary set. If instead we can associate a fuzzy set corresponding to each parameter, then what we would get is a fuzzy soft set. A formal definition with example is given below.

Definition 13: [Maji, Biswas, & Roy, 2001a] Let U be an initial universal set and let E be a set of parameters. Let I^U denote the power set of all fuzzy subsets of U. Let $A \subset E$. A pair (F, A) is called a fuzzy soft set over U, where F is a mapping given by $F : A \to I^U$.

Example 3: As an illustration, consider the example of soft set given earlier. We here give fuzzy version of it.

Suppose a soft set (F, E) describes attractiveness of the shirts which the authors are going to wear.

U = the set of all shirts under consideration =

$$\{x_1, x_2, x_3, x_4, x_5\}$$

Let I^U be the collection of all fuzzy subsets of U. Also let E = {colorful, bright, cheap, warm} = $\{e_1, e_2, e_3, e_4\}$.

Let

$$F(e_1) = \{\frac{x_1}{0.5}, \frac{x_2}{0.9}, \frac{x_3}{0}, \frac{x_4}{0}, \frac{x_5}{0}\}$$

$$F(e_2) = \{\frac{x_1}{1.0}, \frac{x_2}{0.8}, \frac{x_3}{0.7}, \frac{x_4}{0}, \frac{x_5}{0}\},$$

$$F(e_3) = \{\frac{x_1}{0}, \frac{x_2}{0}, \frac{x_3}{0}, \frac{x_4}{0.6}, \frac{x_5}{0}\},$$

$$F(e_4) = \{\frac{x_1}{0}, \frac{x_2}{1.0}, \frac{x_3}{0}, \frac{x_4}{0}, \frac{x_5}{0.3}\}.$$

So, the fuzzy soft set (F, E) is a family

$$\{F(e_i), i = 1, 2, 3, 4\}$$

of I^U.

B. From Fuzzy to Generalized Fuzzy Case

Fuzzy soft sets are further generalized to generalized fuzzy soft sets [Majumdar & Samanta, 2010a] which are more general in nature. Let

$$U = \{x_1, x_2, ..., x_n\}$$

be the universal set of elements and

$$E = \{e_1, e_2, ..., e_m\}$$

be the universal set of parameters. Let μ be a fuzzy subset of E, i.e.

$$\mu : E \to I = [0,1]$$

and I^U be the collection of all fuzzy subset of U. Let

$$F : E \to I(= [0,1])$$

be a mapping. Consider the mapping

$$F_\mu : E \to I^U \times I$$

defined as follows:

$$F_\mu(e) = (F(e), \mu(e))$$

Then F_μ is called a generalised fuzzy soft set (GFSS in short) over (U, E).

Here for each parameter e_i,

$$F_\mu(e_i) = (F(e_i), \mu(e_i))$$

indicates not only the degree of belongingness of the elements of U in $F(e_i)$ but also the degree of possibility of such belongingness.

Here is an example of generalized fuzzy soft sets.

Example 4: [Majumdar, & Samanta, 2010a] Let

$$U = \{x_1, x_2, x_3\}$$

be a set of three shirts under consideration. Let

$$E = \{e_1, e_2, e_3\}$$

be a set of qualities where

$$e_1 = bright, \ e_2 = cheap, \ e_3 = colorful$$

Let

$$\mu : E \to I = [0,1]$$

be defined as follows:-

$$\mu(e_1) = 0.1, \ \mu(e_2) = 0.4, \ \mu(e_3) = 0.6$$

We define a function $F_\mu : E \to I^U \times I$ as follows:

$$F_\mu(e_1) = \left(\left\{ \frac{x_1}{0.7}, \frac{x_2}{0.4}, \frac{x_3}{0.3} \right\}, 0.1 \right)$$

$$F_\mu(e_2) = \left(\left\{ \frac{x_1}{0.1}, \frac{x_2}{0.2}, \frac{x_3}{0.9} \right\}, 0.4 \right)$$

$$F_\mu(e_3) = \left(\left\{ \frac{x_1}{0.8}, \frac{x_2}{0.5}, \frac{x_3}{0.2} \right\}, 0.6 \right)$$

Then F_μ is a GFSS over (U,E). In matrix form this can be expressed as

$$F_\mu = \begin{pmatrix} & x_1 & x_2 & x_3 & \mu \\ e_1 & 0.7 & 0.4 & 0.3 & 0.1 \\ e_2 & 0.1 & 0.2 & 0.9 & 0.4 \\ e_3 & 0.8 & 0.5 & 0.2 & 0.6 \end{pmatrix}$$

Now operations like union, intersection and complement are defined on generalized fuzzy soft sets and which are as follows.

Definition 14: [Majumdar, & Samanta, 2010a] Let F_μ and G_δ be two GFSS over (U,E). Now F_μ is said to be a generalised fuzzy soft subset of G_δ if

1. μ is a fuzzy subset of δ
2. $F(e)$ is also a fuzzy subset of $G(e)$, $\forall e \in E$.

In this case we write $F_\mu \subseteq G_\delta$.

Example 5: [Majumdar, & Samanta, 2010a] Consider the GFSS F_μ over (U,E) given in example 4. Let G_δ be another GFSS over (U,E) defined as follows:

$$G_\delta(e_1) = \left(\left\{ \frac{x_1}{0.2}, \frac{x_2}{0.3}, \frac{x_3}{0.1} \right\}, 0.1 \right),$$

$$G_\mu(e_2) = \left(\left\{ \frac{x_1}{0.0}, \frac{x_2}{0.1}, \frac{x_3}{0.7} \right\}, 0.3 \right),$$

$$G_\delta(e_3) = \left(\left\{ \frac{x_1}{0.7}, \frac{x_2}{0.3}, \frac{x_3}{0.1} \right\}, 0.5 \right),$$

where $\delta \in I^E$ be defined as above.

Then G_δ is a generalised fuzzy soft subset of F_μ defined in example 4.

Definition 15: [Klier & Yuan, 1995] A function $c : [0,1] \to [0,1]$ which satisfy the following properties:

1. $c(0) = 1, c(1) = 0$
2. $\forall a,b \in [0,1]$, if $a \leq b$, then $c(a) \geq c(b)$
3. $c(c(a)) = a \forall a \in [0,1]$

is called an involutive fuzzy complement.

Theorem 1: [Klier & Yuan, 1995] Let $c : [0,1] \to [0,1]$ be a function. Then c is an involutive fuzzy complement iff there exists a continuous function $g : [0,1] \to R$ such that $g(0) = 0$, g is strictly increasing, and

$$c(a) = g^{-1}(g(1) - g(a)) \forall \, a \in [0,1]$$

Note 1: Let c be an involutive fuzzy complement and g be an increasing generator of c

Let $*$ and $\circ$ be two binary operations on $[0,1]$ defined as follows:

$$a * b = g^{-1}(g(a) + g(b) - g(1))$$

and

$$a \circ b = g^{-1}(g(a) + g(b))$$

Then $*$ is a $t - norm$ and $\circ$ is a $t - conorm$. Moreover $(*, \circ, c)$ becomes a dual triple.[1]

Henceforth in the rest of the paper we will take such an involutive dual triple to consider the general case.

Definition 16: [Majumdar, & Samanta, 2010a] Let F_μ be a GFSS over (U, E). Then the complement of F_μ, denoted by F_μ^c is defined by $F_\mu^c = G_\delta$ where

$$\delta(e) = c(\mu(e)), \forall e \in E$$

and

$$G(e) = c(F(e)), \forall e \in E$$

Note 2: Obviously $(F_\mu^C)^C = F_\mu$ as the fuzzy complement c is involutive in nature.

Definition 17: [Majumdar, & Samanta, 2010a] Union of two GFSS F_μ and G_δ, denoted by $F_\mu \tilde{\cup} G_\delta$, is a GFSS H_v, defined as

$$H_v : E \to I^U \times I$$

such that

$$H_v(e) = (H(e), v(e)),$$

where

$$H(e) = F(e) \circ \mathrm{G}(e)$$

and

$$v(e) = \mu(e) \circ \delta(e)$$

Definition 18: [Majumdar, & Samanta, 2010a] Intersection of two GFSS F_μ and G_δ, denoted by $F_\mu \tilde{\cap} G_\delta$, is a GFSS H_v, defined as

$$H_v : E \to I^U \times I$$

such that

$$H_v(e) = (H(e), v(e)),$$

where

$$H(e) = F(e) * G(e)$$

and

$$v(e) = \mu(e) * \delta(e)$$

Definition 19: [Majumdar, & Samanta, 2010a] A GFSS is said to be a generalised null fuzzy soft set, denoted by Φ_θ, if

$$\Phi_\theta : E \to I^U \times I$$

such that

$$\Phi_\theta(e) = (F(e), \theta(e)),$$

where

$F(e) = \overline{0} \forall e \in E$

and

$\theta(e) = 0 \forall e \in E$

Definition 20: [Majumdar, & Samanta, 2010a]
A GFSS is said to be a generalised absolute fuzzy soft set, denoted: by $\overline{A}_\alpha$, if

$\overline{A}_\alpha : E \to I^U \times I,$

where

$\overline{A}_\alpha(e) = (A(e), \alpha(e))$

is defined by

$A(e) = \overline{1} \forall e \in E,$

and

$\alpha(e) = 1 \forall e \in E$

Proposition 5: [Majumdar, & Samanta, 2010a]
Let F_μ be a GFSS over (U, E), then the following holds:

1. F_μ is a GF soft subset of $F_\mu \,\tilde{\cap}\, F_\mu$.
2. $F_\mu \,\tilde{\cap}\, F_\mu$ is a GF soft subset of F_μ.
3. $F_\mu \,\tilde{\cap}\, \Phi_\theta = F_\mu$
4. $F_\mu \,\tilde{\cap}\, \Phi_\theta = \Phi_\theta$
5. $F_\mu \,\tilde{\cap}\, \overline{A}_\alpha = \overline{A}_\alpha$
6. $F_\mu \,\tilde{\cap}\, \overline{A}_\alpha = F_\mu$

- **Proof:** We give the proofs for (i) and (ii) only, others are similarly follows from definition.

(i) For $e \in E$, $(F_\mu \,\tilde{\cup}\, F_\mu)(e) =$
$(F(e) \circ F(e), \mu(e) \circ \mu(e))$
Again for any t-conorm $\circ$,
we have $F(e) \circ F(e) \geq F(e)$
and $\mu(e) \circ \mu(e) \geq \mu(e)$.
Thus $F_\mu(e) \subseteq (F_\mu \,\tilde{\cup}\, F_\mu)(e) \forall e \in E$.
Hence (i) follows.

(ii) For $e \in E$, $(F_\mu \,\tilde{\cap}\, F_\mu)(e) =$
$(F(e) * F(e), \mu(e) * \mu(e))$
Again for any t-norm $*$, we have
$F(e) * F(e) \leq F(e)$ and $\mu(e) * \mu(e) \leq \mu(e)$.
Thus $F_\mu(e) \supseteq (F_\mu \,\tilde{\cap}\, F_\mu)(e) \forall e \in E$.
Hence (ii) follows.

The other results follow similarly from definition.

Note 3: Instead of taking any dual triple as described in note 1, if we take standard fuzzy operations (i.e. max, min and standard complement) then we get equality relation in (i) and (ii) above.

Proposition 6: [Majumdar, & Samanta, 2010a]
The following laws do not hold here:

1. $F_\mu \,\tilde{\cup}\, F_\mu^C = \overline{A}_\alpha$

and

2. $F_\mu \,\tilde{\cap}\, F_\mu^C = \Phi_\theta$

Note 4: The law of excluded middle and the law of contradiction holds here due to the properties of dual triple.

Proposition 7: [Majumdar, & Samanta, 2010a] Let F_μ, G_δ and H_λ be any three GFSS over (U, E), then the following holds:

1. $F_\mu \tilde{\cup} G_\delta = G_\delta \tilde{\cup} F_\mu$
2. $F_\mu \tilde{\cap} G_\delta = G_\delta \tilde{\cap} F_\mu$
3. $F_\mu \tilde{\cup} (G_\delta \tilde{\cup} H_\lambda) = (F_\mu \tilde{\cup} G_\delta)$
4. $F_\mu \tilde{\cap} (G_\delta \tilde{\cap} H_\lambda) = (F_\mu \tilde{\cap} G_\delta)$

- **Proof:** In any t-norm and t-conorm, the commutative law and associative law holds and therefore the above results automatically follow from definition.

Now we state an important result regarding dual triples.

Theorem 2: [Klier & Yuan, 1995] Let $< *, \circ, c >$ be a dual triple generated by note 1 and satisfies law of excluded middle and law of contradiction. Then the fuzzy operations $*, \circ, c$ does not satisfy distributive laws, i.e.

$$a * (b \circ d) = (a * b) \circ (a * d),$$

does not hold.

Now from note 3 and proposition 6 the next result follows:

Note 5: [Majumdar, & Samanta, 2010a] The following does not hold here:

1. $F_\mu \tilde{\cap} (G_\delta \tilde{\cup} H_\lambda) = (F_\mu \tilde{\cap} G_\delta) \tilde{\cup} (F_\mu \tilde{\cap} H_\lambda)$
2. $F_\mu \tilde{\cup} (G_\delta \tilde{\cap} H_\lambda) = (F_\mu \tilde{\cup} G_\delta) \tilde{\cap} (F \tilde{\cup} H_\lambda)$

But if we take standard fuzzy operations[2] then distributive property holds.

Here the De-Morgan laws will also hold due to the following property of dual triples:

Theorem 3: [Klier, & Yuan, 1995] Let $< *, \circ, c >$ be a dual triple generated by note 1. Then the fuzzy operations $*, \circ, c$ satisfy

$$c(a * b) = c(a) \circ c(b) \text{ and } c(a \circ b) = c(a) * c(b)$$

Proposition 8: [Majumdar, & Samanta, 2010a] Let F_μ and G_δ be two GFSS over (U, E), then the following holds:

1. $c(F_\mu) \tilde{\cup} c(G_\delta) = c(F_\mu \tilde{\cap} G_\delta)$
2. $c(F_\mu) \tilde{\cap} c(G_\delta) = c(F_\mu \tilde{\cup} G_\delta)$

- **Proof:** The proof follows from definitions of union, intersection and complement of generalized fuzzy soft sets and theorem 3.

Now we define fuzzy soft relation and generalised fuzzy soft relation in GFSS settings.

Definition 21: [Majumdar, & Samanta, 2010a] Let F_μ and G_δ be two GFSS over the parameterized universe (U, E) and $C \subseteq E^2$ Then a fuzzy soft relation R from F_μ to G_δ is a function $R : C \to I^U \times I$, defined as follows:

$$R(e, f) = F_\mu(e) \tilde{\cap} G_\delta(f)$$

for all $(e, f) \in C$

A Generalization of this may be:

Definition 22: [Majumdar, & Samanta, 2010a] Let

$$F = \{F^i_{\mu_i}, i \in \Delta\}$$

where Δ is some index set, be any collection of GFSS over (U, E) and $C \subseteq E^n$. Then an n-ary generalised fuzzy soft relation R on F is the mapping

$$R : C \to I^U \times I,$$

defined by

$$R(e_{i_1}, e_{i_2}, \ldots e_{i_n}) = \bigcap_{j=1}^{n} F_{\mu_j}^{i_j}(e_{i_j}),$$

where

$$(e_{i_1}, e_{i_2}, \ldots \ldots, e_{i_n}) \in C$$

C. Further Generalizations

Several other types of generalizations soft sets like intuitionistic fuzzy soft sets, vague soft sets, soft multisets etc., are also available and they have been used in solving many real life problems of decision making, medical diagnosis, forecasting etc. Here we present the notion of intuitionistic fuzzy soft sets only. An intuitionistic fuzzy soft set is a hybridization of soft set and Atanassov's intuitionistic fuzzy sets. These sets are introduced by Maji, Roy and Biswas in 2002.

First of all we give the definition of an intuitionistic fuzzy set as follows:

Definition 23: [Atanasov, 1986] Let a set U be the universe. An intuitionistic fuzzy set or IFS A in U is an object having the form

$$A = \{\langle x, \mu_A(x), \nu_A(x)\rangle \mid x \in U\}$$

where the function

$$\mu_A : U \to [0,1]$$

and

$$\nu_A : U \to [0,1]$$

define the degree of membership and the degree of non-membership respectively of the element $x \in U$ to the set A, and for every

$$x \in U, \ \ 0 \leq \mu_A(x) + \nu_A(x) \leq 1.$$

Definition 24: [Maji, Biswas & Roy, 2001, 2004] Let U and E be an initial universe and a set of parameters respectively. Let $I(U)$ denote the set of all intuitionistic fuzzy sets of U and $A \subseteq E$. Then the pair (F, A) is called an intuitionistic fuzzy soft set (IFSS in short) over U, where F is a mapping $F : A \to I(U)$.

Example 6: Consider the set

$$U = \{x_1, x_2, x_3, x_4\}$$

of four shirts the author is having in his collection. Let

$$E = \{e_1 = colourful, e_2 = \\ \cot ton, e_3 = warm, e_4 = cheap\}$$

be a collection of parameters regarding the quality of shirts. Let

$$A = \{e_1, e_2, e_3\}$$

Then we define a function

$$F : A \rightarrow I(U)$$

as follows:

$$F(e_1) = \{\frac{x_1}{(0.2, 0.4)}, \frac{x_2}{(0.8, 0.2)},$$

$$\frac{x_3}{(0.7, 0.2)}, \frac{x_4}{(0.3, 0.5)}\},$$

$$F(e_2) = \{\frac{x_1}{(0.9, 0.1)}, \frac{x_2}{(0.5, 0.3)},$$

$$\frac{x_3}{(0.2, 0.8)}, \frac{x_4}{(0.7, 0.3)}\},$$

$$F(e_3) = \{\frac{x_1}{(0.2, 0.4)}, \frac{x_2}{(0.8, 0.2)},$$

$$\frac{x_3}{(0.7, 0.3)}, \frac{x_4}{(0.3, 0.5)}\}.$$

Then (F, A) is an IFSS over U.

- **Further Reading:** One can study the following papers: [Ali, Feng, Liu, Min & Shabir, 2009], [Cagman, Citak, & Enginoglu, 2010], [Feng, Jun, Liu, & Li, 2010a], [Feng, Li, Davvaz, & Ali, 2010b], [Xiao, 2010], [Xu, Ma, Wang, & Hao, 2010], [Yang, 2011], [Yang, Lin, Yang, Li, & Yu, 2009] given in Reference section for further details.

SOFT MAPPING

A. Definitions

Let X be the universal set and E be a parameter set. Then the pair (X, E) will be called a soft universe. Throughout this section we assume that (X, E) is our soft universe.

Definition 25: [Majumdar, & Samanta, 2010b] Let A, B be two non-empty sets in X and E be the parameter set. Also let $E' \subset E$. Then the mapping

$$F : E' \rightarrow P(B^A)$$

is called a soft mapping from A to B under E', where B^A is the collection of all mappings from A to B.

Actually a soft mapping F from A to B under E' is a soft set over B^A.

Example 7: [Majumdar, & Samanta, 2010b] Let $X = \{x_1, x_2\}$ and $I = [0, 1]$. Then I^X is the collection of all fuzzy subsets of X. Let

$$C = \{f_i, i = 1, 2, ..5\} \subseteq I^X$$

where

$$f_1 = \{\frac{x_1}{0.8}, \frac{x_2}{0.4}\},$$

$$f_2 = \{\frac{x_1}{0.7}, \frac{x_2}{0.0}\},$$

$$f_3 = \{\frac{x_1}{0.1}, \frac{x_2}{0.8}\},$$

$$f_4 = \{\frac{x_1}{0.5}, \frac{x_2}{0.5}\},$$

and

$$f_5 = \{\frac{x_1}{0.2}, \frac{x_2}{0.3}\},$$

Let us define a function

$F : E \to (0,1) \to P(I^X)$

as follows:

For $\alpha \in E = (0,1)$, $F(\alpha)$ is the collection of members of C having same strong $\alpha -$ cuts

$(i.e.\{x \in X; f(x) > \alpha, for\ f \in I^X\})$

e.g.

$F(0.6) = \{f_1, f_2\},$

$F(0.1) = \{f_1, f_4, f_5\},$

$F(0.9) = C$ etc.

Then F is a soft mapping from X to I under E.

Example 8: [Majumdar, & Samanta, 2010b] Let

$E = \{e_1, e_2\}, A = \{x_1, x_2\}$

$B = \{x_3, x_4, x_5\}$

Let

$f_1, f_2, f_3, f_4 : A \to B$

be defined as follows:

$f_1(x_1) = x_3, f_1(x_2) = x_4$

$f_2(x_1) = x_4, f_2(x_2) = x_3$

$f_3(x_1) = x_4, f_3(x_2) = x_5$

and

$f_4(x_1) = x_5, f_4(x_2) = x_4$

Let

$F : E \to P(B^A)$

be defined as follows:

$F(e_1) = \{f_1, f_4\}, F(e_2) = \{f_1, f_2, f_3\}$

Then F is a soft mapping from A to B under E.

Note 6: [Dubois, 1983] It should be noted that if we consider the fuzzy functions of a non-fuzzy variable, then a fuzzy function can be looked as a soft function. In fact, fuzzy functions of a non-fuzzy variable can be of two types namely (i) fuzzifying function and (ii) fuzzy bunch of crisp functions. We will consider both the cases in detail.

1. A fuzzifying function $\tilde{f}$ from X to Y is an ordinary function from X to

$I^Y, i.e. \tilde{f} : X \to I^Y, where\ I = [0,1]$

Now $\tilde{f}$ can be thought of as a soft set over (I^Y, X) and also as a soft mapping

$F : X \to P(I^Y)$

From Y to I under the parameter set X by identifying the element

$\tilde{f}(x)(\& F(x))\ of\ I^Y$, for each $x \in X$,

the single pointic subset of I^Y.

2. Again a fuzzy bunch F of functions from X to Y is a fuzzy set in Y^X, that is, each

function f from X to Y has a membership value in F Again Aktaş & Cağman [2007] has shown that every fuzzy set in X can be considered as a soft set over X with parameter set [0,1] by means of its $\alpha -$ level sets. Therefore here a fuzzy bunch F can be considered as a soft set G over Y^X, with parameter set [0, 1]. And in Definition 25 we have shown that this type of soft set can be considered as a soft mapping from X to Y under [0, 1]. Hence F is a soft mapping.

Definition 26: [Majumdar, & Samanta, 2010b] Let

A, B, C

be non-empty sets and

E', E_1, E_2

be parameter sets. Then

The soft mapping

$F : E' \to P(A^A)$

defined by

$F(e) = \{i_A\} \forall e \in E'$

where $i_A : A \to A$ is the identity mapping on A, is called the identity soft mapping on A under E'.

A soft mapping

$F : E' \to P(\mathrm{B}^A)$

is said to be a constant soft mapping under

E' if $\forall e \in E', F(e)$

is a collection of constant mappings from A to B.

For two soft mappings

$F_1 : E_1 \to P(B^A)$

and

$F_2 : E_2 \to P(B^A)$

over (U, E), they are said to be equal (denoted by $F_1 = F_2$) if (i) $\mathrm{E}_1 = \mathrm{E}_2$ and

$(ii)\ F_1(e) = F_2(e), \forall e \in E_1 = E_2$

For a soft mapping

$F : E' \to P(\mathrm{B}^A)$

and for $E'' \subseteq E'$, the soft mapping

$F_{E''} : E'' \to P(B^A)$

defined by

$F_{E''}(e) = F(e), \forall e \in E''$

is called the restriction of F to E''.

For two soft mappings with

$F : E_1 \to P(\mathrm{B}^A)$

and

$G : E_2 \to P(C^B)$ with $E_1 \cap E_2 \neq \phi$

their composition

$$G * F : E_1 \cap E_2 \to P(C^A)$$

is defined by:

$$(G * F)(e) =$$
$$\{h^e = g^e \circ f^e : A \to C; g^e \in G(e), f^e \in F(e)\}$$

$$e \in E_1 \cap E_2$$

Example 9: [Majumdar, & Samanta, 2010b] Let

$$A = \{x_1, x_2\},$$

$$B = \{x_3, x_4, x_5\},$$

$$C = \{x_5, x_6, x_7\}$$

Also let

$$E_1 = \{e_1, e_2\} = E_2$$

Let

$$f_1, f_2 : A \to B$$

and

$$g_1, g_2 : B \to C$$

be ordinary mappings.
Let

$$F : E_1 \to P(B^A)$$

be a soft mapping defined as:

$$F(e_1) = \{f_1\}$$

and

$$F(e_2) = \{f_2\}$$

Again let

$$G : E_2 \to P(C^B)$$

be another soft mapping defined as:

$$G(e_1) = \{g_1, g_2\}$$

and

$$G(e_2) = \{g_2\}$$

Then the composition of F and G is possible and let

$$H = G * F : E_1 \cap E_2 \to P(C^A)$$

where

$$H(e_1) = \{g_1 \circ f_1, g_2 \circ f_1\}$$

and

$$H(e_2) = \{g_2 \circ f_2\}$$

Definition 27: [Majumdar, & Samanta, 2010b]
A soft mapping

$$F : E' \to P(B^A)$$

is said to be weakly injective if

$$\forall e, f \in E',$$

$$e \neq f \Rightarrow F(e) \neq F(f)$$

Again F is said to be strongly injective if

$\forall e, f \in E'$,

$e \neq f \Rightarrow F(e) \cap F(f) = \phi$

Definition 28: [Majumdar, & Samanta, 2010b] A soft mapping

$F : E' \to P(\mathrm{B}^A)$

is said to be weakly surjective if for any

$f \in B^A, \exists e \in E'$

such that $f \in F(e)$. F is said to be strongly surjective if

$f \in B^A \Rightarrow f \in F(e) \forall e \in E'$

Note 7: This is clear from the above definition that a strongly injective soft mapping is also a weakly injective soft mapping. Also a soft mapping is weakly surjective iff it is a full soft set[3].

Definition 29: [Majumdar, & Samanta, 2010b] A soft mapping

$F : E' \to P(\mathrm{B}^A)$

is said to be weakly (strongly) bijective if F is both weakly (strongly) injective and weakly (strongly) surjective.

Example 10: [Majumdar, & Samanta, 2010b] In example 9, the soft mapping F is strongly injective soft mapping but the soft mapping G is weakly injective.

Theorem 4: [Majumdar, & Samanta, 2010b] If

$F : E_1 \to P(B^A)$

is strongly surjective and

$G : E_2 \to P(C^B)$

be strongly surjective then $G * F$ is strongly surjective.

- **Proof:** Let

$F : E' \to P(\mathrm{B}^A)$

and

$G : E_2 \to P(C^B).$

Then

$H = G * F : E(= E_1 \cap E_2) \to P(C^A)$

Let $f \in C^A$, then f is a mapping from A to C.
Next we take a function $g : A \to B$. Define a function

$h : B \to C$

by

$h(g(x)) = f(x), \forall x \in A$

and

$h(y) = f(x_0)$

where x_0 is a fixed element of A, if $y \in B \setminus g(A)$.
Then

$g \in F(e)$ and $h \in G(e) \forall e \in E$

since F and G are strongly subjective.
Hence

$f = h \circ g \in (G * F)(e) \forall e \in E$

Also f is an arbitrary element of C^A. Thus $H = G * F$ is also strongly surjective.

- **A Corollary of the Theorem:** [Majumdar, & Samanta, 2010b] Let $E_1 = E_2 = E$. Then if F is weakly surjective and G is strongly surjective, then $G * F$ is weakly surjective.

Note 8: Composition of two weakly (strongly) injective soft mappings may not be weakly (strongly) injective.

To show this we present the following example:

Example 11: [Majumdar, & Samanta, 2010b] Let $E = \{e_1, e_2\}$,

$A = \{x_1, x_2\}, B = \{y_1, y_2\}, C = \{z_2, z_2\}$

Let $f_1, f_2 \in B^A$ be defined as follows:

$f_1(x_1) = y_1, f_1(x_2) = y_2;$

$f_2(x_1) = y_2, f_2(x_2) = y_1$

Also let $g_1, g_2 \in C^B$ be defined as follows:

$g_1(y_1) = z_1, g_1(y_2) = z_2;$

$g_2(y_1) = z_2, g_2(y_2) = z_1$

Further let

$F : E \to P(B^A)$

be a strongly injective soft mapping defined as follows:

$F(e_1) = \{f_1\}, F(e_2) = \{f_2\}$

Again let

$G : E \to P(C^B)$

be another strongly injective soft mapping defined as follows:

$G(e_1) = \{g_1\}, G\{e_2\} = \{g_2\}$

Then

$G * F : E \to P(C^A)$

is given by:

$(G * F)(e_1) = \{g_1 \circ f_1\}$

and

$(G * F)(e_2) = \{g_2 \circ f_2\}$

But

$(G * F)(e_1) = (G * F)(e_2)$

although $e_1 \neq e_2$.

Theorem 5: [Majumdar, & Samanta, 2010b] The composition operation of soft mappings is associative.

- **Proof:** Let

$$F : E \to P(C^B), G : E \to P(B^A), H : E \to P(A^C)$$

be three soft mappings such that the two composition mappings

$$(F * G) * H \text{ and } F * (G * H)$$

are defined. Let $e \in E$. Then

$$((F * G) * H)(e) =$$
$$\{t \circ h; t = f \circ g \in (F * G)(e), h \in H(e)\} =$$
$$\{(f \circ g) \circ h; f \in F(e), g \in G(e), h \in H(e)\}$$
$$= \{\{f \circ (g \circ h); f \in F(e), g \in G(e), h \in H(e)\}$$
(since crisp function
composition is associative)
$$= \{(f \circ s); f \in F(e),$$
$$s \in (G * H)(e)\} \subseteq (F * (G * H))(e).$$

So

$$(F * G) * H \subseteq F * (G * H)$$

Similarly it can be shown that

$$(F * (G * H)) \subseteq ((F * G) * H).$$

Hence the result.

Definition 30: [Majumdar, & Samanta, 2010b] A soft mapping

$$F : E \to P(B^A)$$

is said to be naturally injective (surjective) if $F(e)$ is a collection of injective (surjective) mappings from A to $B \forall e \in E$. If F is both naturally injective and naturally surjective then F will be called naturally bijective.

Let (X, E) be the soft universe. Let A be a non-empty subset of X. Let $\Im_E$ be the collection of all soft mappings from A to A. Now let '*', the composition of two soft mappings, be our binary operation. Then $(\Im_E, *)$ forms a monoid, since (i) by theorem 5 it follows that * is associative, (ii) the identity soft mapping I_A, over A exits. Hence $I_A \in \Im_E$ and for any $F \in \Im_E$,

$$F * I_A = I_A * F = F$$

Hence identity element exists in $(\Im_E, *)$.

B. Image of a Set Under a Soft Mapping

Definition 31: [Majumdar, & Samanta, 2010b] Let

$$F : E \to P(B^A)$$

be a soft mapping. Let $T \subseteq A$. Then $F(T)$ is a mapping from E to $P(B)$ such that

$$F(T)(e) = \bigcap_{f_e \in F(e)} f_e(T) = \bigcap_{f_e \in F(e)} \{f_e(t) : t \in T\}$$

Thus $F(T)$ is soft set over (B, E).

Example 12: [Majumdar, & Samanta, 2010b] Let

$$X = \{x_1, x_2, x_3, x_4, y_2, y_2, y_3, y_4\},$$

$$E = \{e_1, e_2\},$$

$$A = \{x_1, x_2, x_3\},$$

$$B = \{y_1, y_2, y_3\}$$

Let

$$F : E \rightarrow P(B^A)$$

be a soft mapping defined as follows:

$$F(e_1) = \{f_1, f_2\}, F(e_2) = \{f_3\}$$

where

$$f_1, f_2, f_3 : A \rightarrow B$$

are given as:

$$f_1(x_1) = y_1, f_1(x_2) = y_2, f_1(x_3) = y_3;$$

$$f_2(x_1) = y_2, f_2(x_2) = y_3, f_2(x_3) = y_1;$$

$$f_3(x_1) = y_3, f_3(x_2) = y_1, f_3(x_3) = y_2$$

Let

$$T = \{x_1, x_2\} \subseteq A$$

Then

$$F(T) : E \rightarrow P(B)$$

is such that

$$F(T)(e_1) = \{y_2\}$$

$$F(T)(e_2) = \{y_1, y_3\}$$

Theorem 6: [Majumdar, & Samanta, 2010b] Let

$$F : E \rightarrow P(B^A)$$

be a soft mapping and T_1, T_2 be two non-empty subsets of A, then the following holds:

(i) $T_1 \subset T_2 \Rightarrow F(T_1) \subset F(T_2)$

(ii) $F(T_1 \cup T_2) = F(T_1) \cup F(T_2)$

(iii) $F(T_1 \cap T_2) \subset F(T_1) \cap F(T_2)$

and if F is naturally injective,

$$F(T_1 \cap T_2) = F(T_1) \cap F(T_2)$$

(iv) $F(T_1^c) \subset [F(T_1)]^c,$

if F is naturally injective and equality holds for naturally bijective soft mappings.

- **Proof:** Let

$$F : E \rightarrow P(B^A)$$

be a soft mapping. Now for a given ordinary mapping

$f_e \in F(e)$ and $T_1, T_2 \subset A$
we have the followings :
$(a) T_1 \subset T_2 \Rightarrow f_e(T_1) \subset f_e(T_2),$
$(b) f_e(T_1 \cup T_2) = f_e(T_1) \cup f_e(T_2)$
$(c) f_e(T_1 \cap T_2) \subset f_e(T_1) \cap f_e(T_2)$
and if f_e is injective,
$f_e(T_1 \cap T_2) = f_e(T_1) \cap f_e(T_2).$
$(d) f_e(T_1^c) \subset [f_e(T_1)]^c,$ *if f_e*
is injective and
$(f_e(T_1))^c = f_e(T_1^c),$ *if f_e is bijective.*

Now the results (a)-(d) of this theorem will hold as because for each $e \in E, F(e)$ is a collection of ordinary mappings. We here only give the proof of (a) and (d). The proof of (b) and (c) is similar.

$(i) T_1 \subset T_2 \Rightarrow f_e(T_1) \subset f_e(T_2), \forall e \in E.$
$\therefore \bigcap_{f_e} f_e(T_1) \subset \bigcap_{f_e} f_e(T_2), \forall e \in E$
$\Rightarrow F(T_1)(e) \subset F(T_2)(e), \forall e \in E$
$\Rightarrow F(T_1) \subset F(T_2).$
$(iv) F(T_1^c) = \bigcap_{f_e \in F(e)} f_e(T_1^c) \subset \bigcap_{f_e \in F(e)} (f_e(T_1))^c =$
$(\bigcup_{f_e \in F(e)} f_e(T_1))^c = (F(T_1))^c.$

Definition 32: [Majumdar, & Samanta, 2010b] Let

$$F : E \to P(B^A)$$

be a soft mapping. Let $T \subset B$ Then the inverse image of T under F is defined as follows: For

$e \in E, F^{-1}(T)(e) =$
$\bigcup_{f_e \in F(e)} \{S : f_e(S) \subset T\} = \bigcup_{f_e \in F(e)} f_e^{-1}(T)$

Thus the inverse image $F^{-1}(T)$ is a soft set over A.

Theorem 7: [Majumdar, & Samanta, 2010b] Let

$$F : E \to P(B^A)$$

be a naturally surjective soft mapping. Let S, T be non-empty subsets of B. Then the following holds:

1. $S \subset T \Rightarrow F^{-1}(S) \subset F^{-1}(T)$
2. $F^{-1}(S \cup T) = F^{-1}(S) \cup F^{-1}(T)$
3. $F^{-1}(S \cap T) = F^{-1}(S) \cap F^{-1}(T)$
4. $F^{-1}(S^c) \supset (F^{-1}(s))^c$

- **Proof:** The proof easily follows from the analogous results on ordinary mappings. Here we give the proof on (i) and (ii), the rest is similar.

We have from definition 32,

1. $F^{-1}(T)(e) = \bigcup_{f_e \in F(e)} f_e^{-1}(T) \subset$
    $\bigcup_{f_e \in F(e)} f_e^{-1}(S) = F^{-1}(S)(e)$

    $F^{-1}(S \cup T) = \bigcup_{f_e \in F(e)} f_e^{-1}(S \cup T) =$
    $\bigcup_{f_e \in F(e)} [f_e^{-1}(S) \cup f_e^{-1}(T)]$

2. $= [\bigcup_{f_e \in F(e)} f_e^{-1}(S)] \cup [\bigcup_{f_e \in F(e)} f_e^{-1}(T)]$
    $= F^{-1}(S) \cup F^{-1}(T)$
    $\therefore F^{-1}(S \cup T) = F^{-1}(S) \cup F^{-1}(T).$

C. Image of a Soft Set Under a Soft Mapping

Definition 33: [Majumdar, & Samanta, 2010b] Let

$$F : E \to P(B^A)$$

be a soft mapping. Let $S = (P, E_1)$ be a soft set over A, where $E_1 \subset E$. Then the image of S under F, denoted by $F(S)$, is defined as follows:

For $\quad e \in E_1, F(S)(e) =$
$$\bigcap_{f_e \in F(e)} f_e(M(e)), \quad \text{if } M(e) \neq \phi$$
$$= \phi, \text{ if } M(e) = \phi$$

$$= \phi, \text{ if } P(e) = \phi$$

Hence $F(S)$ is a soft set over

B with respect to the parameter set E_1.

Example 13: [Majumdar, & Samanta, 2010b] Let

$$E = E_1 = \{e_1, e_2\},$$

$$A = \{x_1, x_2\},$$

$$B = \{y_1, y_2, y_3\}$$

Let $f_1, f_2 : A \to B$ be defined as follows:

$$f_1(x_1) = y_1, f_1(x_2) = y_2;$$

$$f_2(x_1) = y_3, f_2(x_2) = y_2$$

Also let $M : E \to P(A)$ be defined as follows:

$$M(e_1) = \{x_2\}, M(e_2) = \{x_1\}.$$

Then $S = (M, E)$ be a soft set over A.
Let

$$F : E \to P(B^A)$$

be defined as follows:

$$F(e_1) = f_1, F(e_2) = f_2$$

Then

$$F(S)(e_1) = f_1(M(e_1)) = \{y_2\}$$

and

$$F(S)(e_2) = f_2(M(e_2)) = \{y_3\}..$$

$$\therefore F(S) = \{\{y_2\}, \{y_3\}\},$$

which is a soft set over B.
The following theorem holds here.

Theorem 8: [Majumdar, & Samanta, 2010b] Let

$$F : E \to P(B^A)$$

be a soft mapping and

$$S_1 = (M_1, E_1), S_2 = (M_2, E_1), \text{ where } E_1 \subset E,$$

be two soft sets over A then the following holds:

1. $S_1 \subset S_2 \Rightarrow F(S_1) \subset F(S_2)$
2. $F(S_1 \cup S_2) \Rightarrow F(S_1) \cup F(S_2)$
3. $F(S_1 \cap S_2) \subset F(S_1) \cap F(S_2)$

and

$$F(S_1 \cap S_2) = F(S_1) \cap F(S_2)$$

if F is naturally injective.

4. $F(S_1^C) \subset F(S_1)^C$

- **Proof:** The result follows from theorem 6, definition 33 and the definition of soft set. Because for each

$e \in E_1$, $M_1(e)$ and $M_2(e)$

are crisp sets, the result follows from theorem 6.

Further Reading

One can study the followings [Babitha, & Sunil, 2010], [Kharal, & Ahmad, 2011], [Som, 2006] from Reference section for further details.

SOFT GROUPS

Let G be a group and A be a non-empty set. Here R will refer to an binary relation between an element of A and an element of G. A set valued function

$F : A \rightarrow P(G)$

can be defined as

$F(x) = \{y \in G : (x,y) \in R, x \in A \text{ and } y \in G\}.$

The pair (F, A) is a soft set over G.

Definition 34: [Aktas, & Cagman, 2007] Let (F, A) is a soft set over G. Then (F, A) is said to be a soft group over G if and only if $F(x) < G$, i.e. $F(x)$ is a subgroup of G, for all $x \in A$.

The following example illustrates the definition.

Example 14: [Aktas, & Cagman, 2007] Suppose

$G = A = S_3 = \{e, (12), (13), (23), (123), (132)\},$

and that we define the set-valued function

$F(x) = \{y \in G : xRy \Leftrightarrow y = x^n, n \in N\}.$

Then the soft group (F, A) is a parameterized family $\{F(x) : x \in A\}$ of subsets, which gives us a collection of subgroups of G. Now consider the particular mapping F defined above, which is also a subgroup of G. So the soft group (F, A) is the collection of subgroups of G given below:

$F(e) = \{e\}, F(12) = \{e, (12)\}, F(13) = \{e, (13)\}, F(23) = \{e, (23)\}, F(123) = F(132) = \{e, (123), (132)\}.$

Rosenfeld's Fuzzy groups [Rosenfeld, 1971] may be considered as a special case of soft groups. Let A be a fuzzy group of G with membership

μ_A, *i.e.* $\mu_A : G \rightarrow [0,1].$

Let us now consider the family of $\alpha -$ level subgroups of G for the function μ_A given by

$F(\alpha) = \{x \in G : \mu_A(x) \geq \alpha\}, \alpha \in [0,1].$

If we know the family F, then we can find the functions $\mu_A(x)$ by means of the formula

$\mu_A(x) = Sup\{\alpha : x \in F(\alpha)\}.$

Thus, each of Rosenfeld's fuzzy groups A is equivalent to the soft group $(F, [0, 1])$.

The following results hold for soft groups.

Theorem 9: [Aktas, & Cagman, 2007] Let (F, A) and (H, A) be two soft groups over G. Then the following results hold:

1. $(F, A) \tilde{\cap} (H, A)$ is a soft group over G.
2. $(F, A) \tilde{\cup} (H, B)$ is a soft group over G, if $A \cap B = \phi$.
3. $(F, A) \wedge (H, A)$ is a soft group over G.

- **Proof:** (i) Let

$(F, A) \tilde{\cap} (H, A) = (U, A)$

and

$\forall x \in A, U(x) = F(x)$ or $U(x) = H(x). U : A \rightarrow P(G)$

is a mapping. Therefore (U, A) is a soft set over G. For all

$x \in A, U(x) = F(x) < G$ or $U(x) = H(x) < G$

Since

(F, A) *and* (H, A)

are soft groups over G. Proofs of (ii) & (iii) are left for readers.

Further generalizations of soft groups have also been done. Fuzzy soft group is one of such generalizations. The definition of a fuzzy soft group is given below.

Definition 35: [Aygunoglu, & Aygun, 2009] Let X be a group and A be a set of parameters. Let $FP(X)$ denote the set of all fuzzy subsets of X. Then a fuzzy soft set (F, A) is said to be a fuzzy soft group over X iff $F(x)$ s a fuzzy subgroup of $X, \forall x \in A$.

An example of a fuzzy soft group is as follows:

Example 15: Suppose

$X = Z_4 = \{0, 1, 2, 3\}$

be the additive group of modulo 4 and $A = \{e, f, g\}$. The fuzzy set valued function F is defined by

$F(f) = \{ {}^0\!/\!_1, {}^1\!/\!_{0.5}, {}^2\!/\!_1, {}^3\!/\!_{0.5} \}, F(f) = \{ {}^0\!/\!_1, {}^1\!/\!_{0.4}, {}^2\!/\!_{0.5}, {}^3\!/\!_{0.4} \}$ *and* $F(f) = \{ {}^0\!/\!_1, {}^1\!/\!_{0.7}, {}^2\!/\!_{0.9}, {}^3\!/\!_{0.7} \}$.

Clearly F(x) is a fuzzy subgroup of X for all $x \in A$. .

Other algebraic structures like soft semiring and soft ring etc. have also been defined by many authors. Some of the concepts are defined as follows:

The notion of soft semiring was introduced by F. Feng et. al. in 2008. Their definition was as follows:

Definition 36: [Feng, Jun & Zhao, 2008] Let R be a semiring and A be a non-empty set. Let ρ be an arbitrary binary relation between an element of S. Let $\eta : A \rightarrow P(S)$ is defined as

$$\eta(x) = \{y \in S : (x,y) \in \rho\}$$

for all $x \in A$. Then the pair (η, A) is a soft set over S. Now let (η, A) be a non-null soft set over a semiring S. Then (η, A) is called a soft semiring over S if is a sub-semiring of S for all

$$x \in \text{Supp}(\eta, A) = \{x : \eta(x) \neq \phi\}.$$

An example of a soft semiring is given as follows:

Example 16: [Feng, Jun & Zhao, 2008] Let $Z_6 = \{0,1,2,3,4,5\}$ be the semiring of integers modulo 6. Let (η, A) be a soft set over Z_6, where $A = Z_6$ and $\eta : A \to P(Z_6)$ is a set valued function defined by

$$\eta(x) = \{y \in Z_6 : x\rho y = xy \in \{0,2,4\}\} \; \forall \, x \in A.$$

Then

$$\eta(0) = Z_6, \eta(1) = \{0,2,4\}, \eta(2) = Z_6, \eta(3) = \{0,2,4\}, \eta(4) = Z_6 \text{ and } \eta(5) = \{0,2,4\}$$

are sub-semirings of Z_6. Hence (η, A) is a soft semiring of Z_6.

Definition 37: Let (F, A) be a non-null soft set over a ring R. Then (F, A) is said to be a soft ring over R iff $F(a)$ is a sub-ring of R for each $a \in A$.

Further Reading

One can study [June & Park, 2009] and [Jun, 2008] in Reference section for further details.

SOFT TOPOLOGY

A. Topology of Soft Subsets Over the Universe (U, E)

Here definition of topology of soft subsets over (U, E) is given. Here it is assumed that in all soft subsets the parameter set is same and is equal to E for simplicity. Unless otherwise mentioned a soft subset (F, E) will be denoted by simply F.

First we investigate some properties of soft subsets of (U, E).

Definition 38: [Majumdar, Hazra, & Samanta, 2012] Let $\{F_i, i \in J\}$ be an indexed family of soft sets over (U, E). Then $\tilde{\bigcup_i} F_i$ is a soft set G defined as follows:

$$G(e) = \bigcup_i F_i(e) \; \forall e \in E$$

Similarly $\tilde{\bigcup_i} F_i(e)$ is again a soft set H defined as follows:

$$H(e) = \bigcap_i F_i(e) \; \forall e \in E$$

Theorem 10: [Majumdar, Hazra, & Samanta, 2012] The following holds in the case of soft subsets:

1. $F \tilde{\cap} G \subset F, G$
2. $F \tilde{\cap} (\tilde{\cup_i} G_i) = \tilde{\cup_i} (F \tilde{\cap} G_i)$
3. $F \tilde{\cup} (\cap_i G_i) = \cap_i (F \cup G_i)$
4. $F \subset G \Rightarrow F^C \supset G^C$
5. $\tilde{\Phi}^C = \tilde{A}$
6. $\tilde{A}^C = \Phi$
7. $(F^C)^C = F$
8. $(\cap_i F_i)^C = \cup_i F_i^C$

9. $(\underset{i}{\cup} F_i)^C = \underset{i}{\cap} F_i^C$

10. $F \,\tilde{\cap}\, F^C = \tilde{\Phi}$

11. $F \,\tilde{\cup}\, F^C = \tilde{A}$

- **Proof:** The proof are straightforward.

Definition 39: [Majumdar, Hazra, & Samanta, 2012] Let τ be a family of soft sets over (U, E).

Define

$$\tau(e) = \{F(e), F \in \tau\}$$

For $e \in E$.

Then τ is said to be a topology of soft subsets over (U, E) if $\tau(e)$ is a crisp topology on $U \ \forall e \in E$.

In this case $((U, E), \tau)$ is said to be a topological space of soft subsets.

If τ is a topology of soft subsets over (U, E), then the members of τ are called open soft sets and a soft set F over (U, E) is said to be closed soft set if $F^C \in \tau$.

Note 9: It is clear that the intersection of two topologies of soft subsets over (U, E) is also a topology of soft subsets over (U, E).

Theorem 11: [Majumdar, Hazra, & Samanta, 2012] Let Ω be a family of all closed soft sets over (U, E), then

1. $\tilde{\Phi}, \tilde{A} \in \Omega$,

2. $F_i \in \Omega \Rightarrow \underset{i}{\cap} F_i \in \Omega$

and

3. $F_1, F_2 \in \Omega \Rightarrow F_1 \cup F_2 \in \Omega$

- **Proof:** Trivial.

Example 17: [Majumdar, Hazra, & Samanta, 2012] Let

$$U = \{x_1, x_2, x_3\}$$

and

$$E = \{e_1, e_2\}$$

Also let

$$F_1 \in P(U)^E$$

be defined as follows:

$$F_1 = \{F_1(e_1) = \{x_1\}, F_1(e_2) = \{x_2, x_3\}\}$$

Here

$$\tau(e_1) = \{\phi, U, \{x_1\}\}$$

and

$$\tau(e_2) = \{\phi, U, \{x_2, x_3\}\}$$

are crisp topologies on U

Thus

$$\tau = \{\tilde{\Phi}, \tilde{A}, F_1\} \subset P(P(U)^E)$$

is a topology of soft subsets over (U, E).

Note 10: The collection $\tau_I = \{\tilde{\Phi}, \tilde{A}\}$ and $\tau_D =$ Collection of all soft sets of (U, E), are topologies of soft sets which are called respectively indiscrete and discrete topologies of soft sets over (U, E). Further the collection $\tau_{(U,E)}$ of all topologies of soft sets over (U, E) forms a lattice with respect to 'set inclusion' relation of which τ_I and τ_D are the smallest and the greatest elements respectively.

Definition 40: [Majumdar, Hazra, & Samanta, 2012] Let F be a soft set over (U, E). Then the closure of F in $((U, E), \tau)$, denoted by $Cl_\tau F$, and is defined by

$$(Cl_\tau F)(e) = Cl_\tau F(e), \text{ for } e \in E.$$

Proposition 9: [Majumdar, Hazra, & Samanta, 2012] Let $((U, E), \tau)$ be a topological space of soft subsets over (U, E). Then for $F \in P(U)^E$, the following holds:

1. $Cl_\tau \tilde{\Phi} = \tilde{\Phi}$,
2. $Cl_\tau \tilde{A} = \tilde{A}$,
3. $F \subset Cl_\tau F$
4. $Cl_\tau F$ is a closed soft set.
5. F is closed iff $F = Cl_\tau F$.
6. $Cl_\tau F$ is the smallest closed soft set containing F.
7. $Cl_\tau (F \cup G) = Cl_\tau F \cup Cl_\tau G$
8. $Cl_\tau (Cl_\tau F) = Cl_\tau F$.

- **Proof:**

$$(Cl_\tau \tilde{\Phi})(e) = Cl_{\tau(e)} \tilde{\Phi}(e) =$$

1. $Cl_{\tau(e)} \phi = \phi \forall e \in E$
   $\therefore Cl_\tau \tilde{\Phi} = \tilde{\Phi}$
   $(Cl_\tau \tilde{A})(e) = Cl_{\tau(e)} \tilde{A}(e) =$
2. $Cl_{\tau(e)} U = U \forall e \in E$
   $\therefore Cl_\tau \tilde{A} = \tilde{A}$
   $(Cl_\tau F)(e) = Cl_{\tau(e)} F(e) \supset F(e) \forall e \in E$
3. $Cl_\tau F \supset F$
4. $(Cl_\tau F)(e) = Cl_{\tau(e)} F(e)$

is a closed soft set in $(U, \tau(e))$ for each $e \in E$.
   $\therefore (Cl_\tau F)^C(e)$ is open in $(U, \tau(e))$ for each $e \in E$.
   $\therefore (Cl_\tau F)^C \in \tau$ and hence $Cl_\tau F$ is closed.

5. Let F be closed. Then $F(e)$ is closed for each $e \in E$.

$$\therefore Cl_{\tau(e)} F(e) = F(e) \forall e \in E$$

$$\therefore (Cl_\tau F)(e) = F(e) \forall e \in E$$

Hence $Cl_\tau F = F$.
Conversely let $Cl_\tau F = F$. Then F is closed.

6. Clearly $Cl_\tau F$ is a closed soft set containing F.
   Let G be a closed soft set containing F.

7. $\therefore G \supset F \Rightarrow Cl_\tau G \supset Cl_\tau F$
8. $G = Cl_\tau G \supset Cl_\tau F$.

Thus $Cl_\tau F$ is the smallest closed soft set containing F.
   7. and 8. can similarly be proved.

B. Soft Topology

Here we give the definition of another topology on soft sets, called soft topology and study some of its properties.

Definition 4: [Majumdar, Hazra, & Samanta, 2012] Let (U, E) be the universe. Let

$$\Im : E \to P(P(U)^E)$$

be a soft set over $(P(U)^E, E)$. Now $\Im$ is said to be a soft topology over (U, E) if for each $e \in E, \Im(e)$ is a topology of soft subsets over (U, E). In this case $((U, E), \Im)$ is called a soft topological space over (U, E).
   Elements of $\Im(e)$ are called e-open sets of $\Im$.

Note 11: It is to be noted that $\Im$ is a soft topology over (U, E) iff $\Im$ is a mapping from E to the collection $\tau_{(U, E)}$.

Note 12: A soft set F on (U, E) is called $e - closed$ of $\Im$ if $F^C \in \Im(e)$.

Then clearly $\tilde{\Phi}$ and $\tilde{A}$ are $e - open$ as well as $e - closed$, for all $e \in E$.

Example 18: [Majumdar, Hazra, & Samanta, 2012] Let

$$U = \{x_1, x_2, x_3\}$$

and

$$E = \{e_1, e_2, e_3\}$$

Let

$$F = \{\{x_1\}, \{x_1, x_2\}, \{x_3\}\}$$

and

$$G = \{\{x_1\}, \{x_1\}, \{x_3\}\}$$

be two soft sets over (U, E).
Further let

$$\Im : E \to P(P(U)^E)$$

be defined as follows:

$$\Im(e_1) = \{\tilde{\phi}, \tilde{A}\},$$

$$\Im(e_2) = \{\tilde{\phi}, \tilde{A}, F\},$$

$$\Im(e_3) = \{\tilde{\phi}, \tilde{A}, F, G\}.$$

Now

$$\Im(e_1)(e_i) = \{\phi, U\} \forall e_i, i = 1, 2, 3.$$

$$\Im(e_2)(e_i) = \{\phi, U, \{x_1\}\},$$

$$\Im(e_2)(e_2) = \{\phi, U, \{x_1, x_2\}\},$$

$$\Im(e_2)(e_3) = \{\phi, U, \{x_3\}\}.$$

$$\Im(e_3)(e_1) = \{\phi, U, \{x_1\}\}.$$

$$\Im(e_3)(e_2) = \{\phi, U, \{x_1, x_2\}, \{x_1\}\}.$$

$$\Im(e_3)(e_3) = \{\phi, U, \{x_3\}\},$$

Then $\Im$ is a soft topology over (U, E).

Example 19: [Majumdar, Hazra, & Samanta, 2012] Let (U, E) be the universe. Let us define functions

$$\Im_I, \Im_D : E \to P(P(U)^E)$$

as follows: For each

$$e \in E, \ \Im_I(e) = \tau_I, \Im_D(e) = \tau_D$$

(where τ_I, τ_D are as in Note 10) are soft topologies over (U, E), called soft indiscrete and soft discrete topologies over (U, E) respectively.

Definition 42: [Majumdar, Hazra, & Samanta, 2012] Let $\Im_1$ and $\Im_2$ be two soft topologies over (U, E). Then $\Im_1$ is said to be coarser than $\Im_2$ (denoted by $\Im_1 \prec \Im_2$) or in other words $\Im_2$ is finer than $\Im_1$ (denoted by $\Im_2 \succ \Im_1$) if

$$\forall e \in E, \Im_1(e) \subset \Im_2(e)$$

or

$\forall e \in E, \Im_2(e) \supset \Im_1(e)$

respectively.

Note 13: The collection $\Im_{(U,E)}$ of all soft topologies over (U, E) forms a lattice with respect to $'\prec'$ of which $\Im_I, \Im_D$ are smallest and greatest elements respectively.

Further Reading

One can study [Muhammad & Naz, 2011], [Tanay & Kandemir, 2011] from Reference section for further details.

SOFT ENTROPY

A fuzzy set or a rough set expresses different types of uncertainties and hence it is natural to measure the amount of uncertainty, whether fuzziness or imprecision etc, that is attached with it. But what type of uncertainty does a soft set represent? Soft sets actually deals with the uncertainty arising from the parameterized classification of elements of a universe. To illustrate the notion of soft set and the uncertainty associated with it, we here give an example:

Consider a collection

$$U = \{h_1, h_2, ..., h_5, h_6\}$$

of six houses that is sorted from others by a buyer willing to buy a house. Some parameters of a good house are selected and expressed as the parameter set

$E = \{e_1 = cheap, e_2 = well\ constructed,$
$e_3 = \cos tly, e_4 = in\ good\ neighbourhood,$
$e_5 = good\ location\}.$

A soft set is a mapping

$$F : E \rightarrow P(U)$$

which classify the elements of U according to the parameters given in E. For example here let us define the mapping

$$F : E \rightarrow P(U)$$

as follows:

Let

$F(e_1) = \{h_1, h_4\}, F(e_2) = \{h_2, h_3, h_5\}, F(e_3) = \{h_2, h_3\}, F(e_4) = \{h_1, h_2, h_3\}, F(e_5) = \{h_4\}$

Here apparently the situation may seem to be quite deterministic. But if we observe deeply we see the following facts: (i) This classification is dependent on E, (ii) Associated to each element of U, there are either no parameter, exactly one parameter or more than one parameter that is attached, e.g. consider the elements h_6, h_5 & h_2. (iii) From a buyers perspective there is always an uncertainty to select one particular house, especially that one which has several positive and negative parameters attached to it, e.g. h_3 (iv) Buyer may also be worried about other unknown parameters which may later affect him. (v) The situations where one house does not have any given parameters are very much uncertain, e.g. h_6. These are some of the points for which a soft set represents certain kind of uncertainty. Therefore it is significant to study the amount of uncertainty or 'softness' that is attached with a soft set.

A. Softness Measure of a Soft Set

In this section we introduce the notion of soft set entropy to measure the 'softness' of a soft set.

Throughout this paper we assume the universe U and parameter set E to be finite and denote $|A|$ as the cardinality of the set A. Here we give a set of axioms that should be satisfied by any measure of softness i.e. soft set entropy. For that purpose we give two new definitions, namely deterministic soft set and equivalent soft sets.

Definition 43: [Majumdar, & Samanta, 2013b] A soft set (F, A) is said to be a deterministic soft set over U if the following holds:

$$\bigcup_{e \in A} F(e) = U$$

$$F(e) \cap F(f) = \phi$$

where

$$e, f \in A, e \neq f$$

Definition 44: [Majumdar, & Samanta, 2013b] Let (F, A) be any soft set. Then another soft set (F^*, A) is said to be equivalent to (F, A) if there exists a bijective mapping σ from A to A defined as: $\sigma(F_x) = F_x^*$, where

$$F_x = \{e : x \in F(e)\} \text{ and } F_x^* = \{e : x \in F^*(e)\}.$$

Let $C(F)$ denote the collection of all soft sets which are equivalent with (F, A).

Example 20: [Majumdar, & Samanta, 2013b] Let the universe and parameter set be

$$U = \{x_1, x_2, x_3, x_4\} \text{ \&}$$

$$A = \{e_1, e_2, e_3\}$$

Then let us consider the following soft set (F, A) as follows:

$$F(e_1) = \{x_1, x_2\},$$

$$F(e_2) = \{x_2, x_3\},$$

$$F(e_3) = \{x_1, x_4\}$$

Then the following soft set (G, A) is equivalent to the soft set (F, A) where

$$G(e_1) = \{x_1, x_4\},$$

$$G(e_2) = \{x_1, x_2\},$$

$$G(e_3) = \{x_2, x_3\}$$

This is because there is a bijective mapping σ on A such that

$$\sigma(e_1) = e_2, \sigma(e_2) = e_3 \text{ \& } \sigma(e_3) = e_1$$

and

$$\sigma(F_x) = G_x \forall x \in U$$

From intuition we understand that the 'softness', i.e. the associated uncertainty of a soft set is maximum if either the elements cannot be classified at all w.r.t. the parameters or every element of the universe belong to every parameter, i.e. to every e-approximation. Again the softness of a soft set is minimum if each element of the universe is associated with only one parameter. Now for a superset of a soft set the uncertainty ultimately increases in comparison with its subset, as new elements being introduced in the set (i.e.

in e-approximations) which shares same parameters with other elements. The softness of a soft set and its equivalent soft sets are same because the amount of imperfectness or ambiguity of information is same in both cases. Based on the above discussion we have the following:

Definition 45: [Majumdar, & Samanta, 2013b] Let $\chi^*(U)$ be the collection of all soft sets over U. A mapping:

$$S : \chi^*(U) \to [0,1]$$

is said to be soft set entropy or softness measure if S satisfies the following properties:

$(S1)\, S(\tilde{\Phi}) = 1,\, S(\tilde{A}) = 1$

$(S2)\, S(F) = 0,\, \text{if } F \text{ is deterministic soft set}$

$(S3)\, S(F) \le S(G) \text{ if } F(\neq \Phi) \subseteq G$

$(S4)\, S(F^*) = S(F),\, \text{where } F^* \in C(F)$

Note that according to this definition an ordinary set has softness zero, as an ordinary set can be thought of as a soft set with a single parameter and thus is a deterministic soft set.

Then we have the following theorem:

Theorem 12: [Majumdar, & Samanta, 2013b] The function

$$S : \chi^*(U) \to [0,1]$$

defined below is an entropy (or measure of softness) of a soft set:

$$S(F) = 1 - \frac{|U|}{\displaystyle\sum_{x \in U} \left| \{e : x \in F(e)\} \right|}, if\ F \neq \tilde{\Phi}\ or\ \tilde{A}$$
$$= 1, if\ F = \tilde{\Phi}\ or\ \tilde{A}$$

- **Proof:** Here (S1) holds obviously from construction.

(S2) For a deterministic soft set

$$\sum_{x \in U} \left| \{e : x \in F(e)\} \right| = |U|$$

because each element is attached with exactly one parameter

$$\Rightarrow \left| \{e : x \in F(e)\} \right| = 1 \forall x \in U$$

Hence $S(F) = 0$
Thus (S2) holds.
Next let F & G be two soft sets such that

$$F(\neq \tilde{\Phi}) \subseteq G \Rightarrow \forall e \in E, F(e) \subseteq G(e) \Rightarrow$$
$$\{e : x \in F(e)\} \subseteq \{e : x \in G(e)\}$$

$$\therefore \sum_{x \in U} \left| \{e : x \in F(e)\} \right| \le \sum_{x \in U} \left| \{e : x \in G(e)\} \right| \Rightarrow$$
$$\frac{|U|}{\displaystyle\sum_{x \in U} \left| \{e : x \in F(e)\} \right|} \ge \frac{|U|}{\displaystyle\sum_{x \in U} \left| e : x \in G(e) \right|} \Rightarrow$$
$$S(F) \le S(G)$$

Thus (S3) also holds.
(S4) Let $F^* \in C(F)$
Then

$$\therefore \sum_{x \in U} \left| \{e : x \in F(e) \right| = \sum_{x \in U} \left| \{e : x \in F^*(e) \right|$$

$$\therefore S(F) = S(G)$$

Hence the theorem.

Next is an example of the previous theorem.

Example 21: [Majumdar & Samanta, 2013b] Consider the example of house selection discussed in the beginning of Section. Consider a collection

$$U = \{h_1, h_2, ..., h_5, h_6\}$$

of six houses that is sorted among others by a buyer willing to buy one house. Some parameters of a good house are collected and expressed as

$$E = \{e_1 = cheap, e_2 = well\ constructed,$$
$$e_3 = \cos tly, e_4 = in\ good\ neighbourhood,$$
$$e_5 = good\ location\}$$

A soft set is a mapping

$$F : E \to P(U)$$

which classify the elements of U according to the parameters given in E. Here we define the soft set

$$F : E \to P(U)$$

as follows:

Let

$$F(e_1) = \{h_1, h_4\}, F(e_2) = \{h_2, h_3, h_5\}, F(e_3) = \{h_2, h_3\}, F(e_4) = \{h_1, h_2, h_3\}, F(e_5) = \{h_4\}$$

Here

$$S(F) = 1 - \frac{|U|}{\sum_{x \in U} \left| \{e : x \in F(e)\} \right|} = 1 - \frac{6}{11} \approx 0.45$$

Further Reading

One can study [De Luca & Termini, 1972], [Kosko, 1986], [Szmidt & Kacprzyk, 2001] given in Reference section for further details.

APPLICATIONS

Here we present three possible applications of soft sets.

Similarity Measure of Soft Sets: [Majumdar & Samanta, 2008] a. Matching function based similarity measure

Let U be the universe. Throughout this section we will assume that the universe U and the set of parameters E are non-empty finite sets. Then we can express a soft set over U as a matrix. We illustrate the process with an example.

Let U be a set of 3 shirts x_1, x_2, x_3, i.e.

$$U = \{x_1, x_2, x_3\}$$

Let

$$E = \{e_1, e_2, e_3\},$$

where

$$e_1 = bright,$$

$$e_2 = colourful,$$

$$e_3 = fade.$$

Let (F, E) be a soft-set over U defined as

$$F(e_1) = \{x_1\},$$

$$F(e_2) = \{x_1, x_2\}$$

and

$$F(e_3) = \{x_3\}$$

This can be represented in the form of a matrix as follows:

The $(i, j)^{th}$ entry of the matrix is 1 if $x_i \in F(e_j)$ and it is equal to 0 if $x_i \notin F(e_j)$ Then we get a matrix called a membership matrix as below:

(F, E)	$F(e_1)$	$F(e_2)$	$F(e_3)$
x_1	1	1	0
x_2	0	1	0
x_3	0	0	1

Let

$$A = \begin{vmatrix} 1 & 1 & 0 \\ 0 & 1 & 0 \\ 0 & 0 & 1 \end{vmatrix}$$

Then with the above interpretation the soft set (F, E) is represented by the matrix A and we write $(F, E) = A$. Clearly, the complement of (F, E), i.e. $(F, E)^C$ will be represented by another matrix B where

$$B = \begin{vmatrix} 0 & 0 & 1 \\ 1 & 0 & 1 \\ 1 & 1 & 0 \end{vmatrix}$$

It is clear that for any given membership matrix A, we can retrieve the soft set (F, E) in an obvious way. Henceforth we will denote each column of the membership matrix by the vector $\vec{F}(e_i)$, or by simply $F(e_i)$, e.g. here

$$\vec{F}(e_i) = (1, 0, 0)$$

in A.

Now we define a matching function based measure of similarity of two soft sets.

Definition 46: [Majumdar & Samanta, 2008] If $E_1 = E_2$, then similarity between (F_1, E_1) and (F_2, E_2) is defined by

$$S(F_1, F_2) = \frac{\sum_i \vec{F}_1(e_i) \bullet \vec{F}_2(e_i)}{\sum_i [\vec{F}_1(e_i)^2 \vee \vec{F}_2(e_i)^2]} \qquad (1)$$

If $E_1 \neq E_2$ and

$$E = E_1 \cap E_2 \neq \phi,$$

then we first define $\vec{F}_1(e) = \underline{0}$ for $e \in E_2 \setminus E$ and $\bar{F}_2(f) = \underline{0}$ for $f \in E_1 \setminus E$. Then $S(F_1, F_2)$ is defined by the formula (4.1).

We observe that if

$$E_1 \cap E_2 = \phi,$$

then

$$S(F_1, F_2) = 0$$

One can also note that

$S(F_1, F_1^C) = 0$

as

$\vec{F}_1(e_i) \bullet \vec{F}_1^C(e_i) = 0 \forall i$

Example 22: [Majumdar & Samanta, 2008] Let us consider two soft sets (F, E) and (G, E) over U, where

$U = \{x_1, x_2, x_3\}$,

$E = \{e_1, e_2, e_3\}$

Let

$A = \begin{pmatrix} 1 & 1 & 0 \\ 0 & 1 & 0 \\ 0 & 0 & 1 \end{pmatrix}$

and

$B = \begin{pmatrix} 0 & 1 & 1 \\ 1 & 1 & 0 \\ 0 & 1 & 1 \end{pmatrix}$

be their representing matrices.
Then

$$S(F, G) = \frac{\sum_{i=1}^{3} \vec{F}(e_i) \bullet \vec{G}(e_i)}{\sum_{i=1}^{3} [\vec{F}(e_i)^2 \vee \vec{G}(e_i)^2]} = \frac{3}{6} = 0.5$$

Lemma 1: [Majumdar & Samanta, 2008] Let (F_1, E_1) and (F_2, E_2) be two soft sets over the same finite universe U. Then the following hold:

1. $S(F_1, F_2) = S(F_2, F_1)$
2. $0 \leq S(F_1, F_2) \leq 1$
3. $S(F_1, F_1) = 1$

Proof: Trivially follows from definition.

Lemma 2: [Majumdar & Samanta, 2008] Let (F, E), (G, E), (H, E) be three soft sets such that (F, E) is a soft subset of (G, E) and (G, E) is a soft subset of (H, E) then,

$S(F, H) \leq S(G, H)$

- **Proof:** Here

$(F, E) \subset (G, E) \subset (H, E)$.

Thus definition of subsets (see definition 3.1.3) of soft sets we have

$F(e) \subseteq G(e) \subseteq H(e) \ \forall e \in E$.

Thus we have

$\vec{F}(e) \bullet \vec{G}(e) \leq \vec{G}(e) \bullet \vec{H}(e)$

and

$\vec{F}(e)^2 \leq \vec{G}(e)^2 \leq \vec{H}(e)^2, \ \forall e \in E$.

Then

$\vec{F}(e)^2 \vee \vec{H}(e)^2 = \vec{H}(e)^2$

and

$\vec{G}(e)^2 \vee \vec{H}(e)^2 = \vec{H}(e)^2$

$$\therefore \frac{\sum\limits_{e \in E} \vec{F}(e) \bullet \vec{H}(e)}{\sum\limits_{e \in E} \vec{H}(e)^2} \leq \frac{\sum\limits_{e \in E} \vec{G}(e) \bullet \vec{H}(e)}{\sum\limits_{e \in E} \vec{H}(e)^2}$$

$$\therefore S(F, H) \leq S(G, H).$$

B. Weighted Similarity Measure between Two Soft Sets

Now we define the weighted similarity measure between two soft sets.

Definition 47: [Majumdar & Samanta, 2008] [Majumdar & Samanta, 2008] Let

$$U = \{u_1, u_2, \ldots, u_n\}$$

be the universe and let

$$E = \{e_1, e_2, \ldots, e_m\}$$

be the set of parameters. Again let w_i be the weight of u_i and $w_i \in [0,1]$, but not all zero, $1 \leq i \leq n$. Let (F, E) and (G, E) be two soft sets over U. Then their weighted similarity is defined as follows:

$$W(F, G) = \frac{\sum\limits_{i=1}^{m} T(\vec{F}(e_i) \bullet \vec{G}(e_i))}{\sum\limits_{i=1}^{m} (F(e_i)^2 \vee G(e_i)^2)} / (\sum\limits_{i=1}^{n} w_i) \quad (2)$$

where $T(\vec{F}(e_i) \bullet \vec{G}(e_i)) = \sum\limits_{j=1}^{n} w_j x_j^i y_j^i$, x_j^i's

and y_j^i's are either 0 or 1 such that
$F(e_i) = (x_1^i, x_2^i, \ldots, x_n^i)$
and $G(e_i) = (y_1^i, y_2^i, \ldots, y_n^i)$.

For the simplicity of the above expression, without loss of generality, we may take

$$\sum\limits_{i=1}^{n} w_i = 1$$

so that the expression 2 becomes.

$$W(F, G) = \frac{\sum\limits_{j=1}^{m} \sum\limits_{i=1}^{n} w_i x_i^j y_i^j}{\sum\limits_{j=1}^{m} [\vec{F}(e_j)^2 \vee \vec{G}(e_j)^2]}.$$

Example 23: [Majumdar & Samanta, 2008] Let

$$U = \{u_1, u_2, u_3\}$$

be the universe where $0.2, 0.6, 0.4$ are the weights of u_1, u_2, u_3 respectively. Let (F_1, E_1) and (F_2, E_2) be two soft sets on U whose associated membership matrices are

$$\begin{pmatrix} 1 & 1 & 0 \\ 0 & 1 & 0 \\ 0 & 0 & 1 \end{pmatrix}$$

and

$$\begin{pmatrix} 0 & 1 & 1 \\ 1 & 1 & 0 \\ 0 & 1 & 1 \end{pmatrix}$$

respectively.
Then

$$W(F_1, F_2) = \frac{0 + (0.2 + 0.4) + 0.6}{(1 + 3 + 2)} = 0.2.$$

Example 24: [Majumdar & Samanta, 2008] A graphical representation indicating the extent of similarity between two soft sets can be shown as follows:

Let

$$U = \{h_1, h_2, h_3, h_4, h_5\}$$

and

$$E = \{e_1, e_2, e_3, e_4, e_5\}$$

Let (F_1, E_1) and (F_2, E_2) be two soft sets which are represented by the matrices A and B as follows:

$$A = \begin{pmatrix} 0 & 1 & 0 & 1 & 1 \\ 1 & 0 & 0 & 0 & 0 \\ 0 & 1 & 1 & 1 & 0 \\ 1 & 0 & 1 & 0 & 0 \\ 0 & 0 & 1 & 1 & 0 \end{pmatrix}$$

and

$$B = \begin{pmatrix} 1 & 1 & 1 & 1 & 1 \\ 0 & 0 & 1 & 0 & 0 \\ 0 & 0 & 1 & 0 & 1 \\ 1 & 0 & 0 & 1 & 0 \\ 1 & 1 & 1 & 1 & 1 \end{pmatrix}$$

Definition 48: Let us define the set of all soft sets over U by $S(U)$. We define a relation $\overset{\alpha}{\approx}$ on $S(U)$, called $\alpha -$ similar, as follows:

Two soft sets (F_1, E_1) and (F_2, E_2) are said to be $\alpha -$ similar, denoted as

$$(F_1, E_1) \overset{\alpha}{\approx} (F_2, E_2),$$

if

$$S(F_1, F_2) \geq \alpha \; for \; \alpha \in (0,1)$$

It is well-known that similarity is a tolerance relation but not an equivalence one. Next lemma gives an evidence of this.

Lemma 3: [Majumdar & Samanta, 2008] $\overset{\alpha}{\approx}$ is reflexive and symmetric, but not transitive.

- **Proof:** The reflexivity and symmetry follows from definition of similarity measure defined in definition 46.

To prove that $\overset{\alpha}{\approx}$ is not transitive we give an example.

Example 25: [Majumdar & Samanta, 2008] Let

$$U = \{x_1, x_2, x_3\}$$

be the universe and

$$E = \{e_1, e_2, e_3\}$$

Box 1.

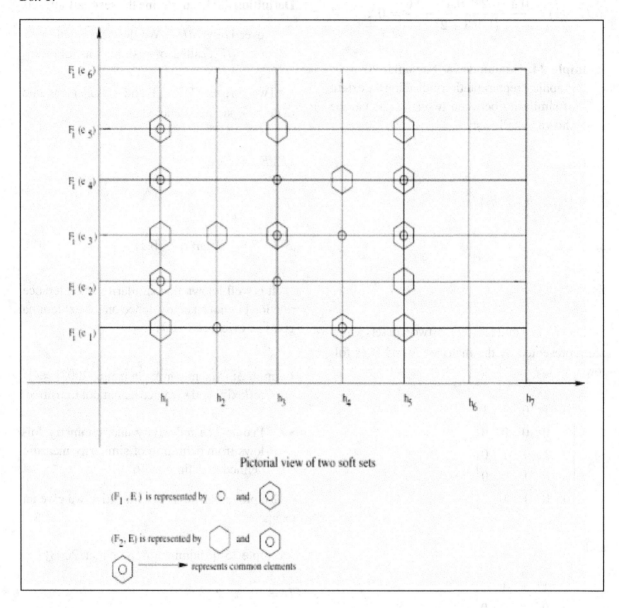

Pictorial view of two soft sets

(F_1, E) is represented by ◯ and ⬡

(F_2, E) is represented by ⬡ and ◯

◯ ──────▶ represents common elements

be the set of parameters.

Let

$$\alpha = \frac{1}{2}$$

We define three soft sets (F_1, E_1), (F_2, E_2) and (F_3, E_3) such that

$$E_1 = E_2 = E_3 = E$$

with A, B, C as membership matrices as follows:

$$A = \begin{vmatrix} 1 & 0 & 0 \\ 0 & 1 & 0 \\ 0 & 0 & 1 \end{vmatrix}$$

$$B = \begin{pmatrix} 1 & 0 & 0 \\ 0 & 1 & 0 \\ 0 & 0 & 0 \end{pmatrix}$$

and

$$C = \begin{pmatrix} 1 & 0 & 0 \\ 0 & 0 & 0 \\ 0 & 0 & 0 \end{pmatrix}$$

Then

$$S(F_1, F_2) = \frac{2}{3} > \frac{1}{2}$$

$$S(F_2, F_3) = \frac{1}{2}$$

but

$$S(F_1, F_3) = \frac{1}{3} < \frac{1}{2}$$

Definition 49: [Majumdar & Samanta, 2008] Let (F_1, E_1) and (F_2, E_2) be two soft sets over the same universe U. We call the two soft sets are significantly similar if

$$S(F_1, F_2) > \frac{1}{2}$$

In example 25 the soft sets (F_1, E_1) and (F_2, E_2) are significantly similar and the soft sets pairs

$$(F_2, E_2), (F_3, E_3) \, and \, (F_1, E_1), (F_3, E_3)$$

are not significantly similar.

C. Measuring Distances between Soft Sets

In this section we take our universe U to be finite, namely

$$U = \{x_1, x_2, ..., x_n\}$$

and universal parameter set

$$E = \{e_1, e_2, ..., e_m\}$$

Now for any soft set

$$(F, A) \in S(U),$$

A is a subset of E. Next we extend the soft set (F, A) to the soft set $(\hat{F}, E)$ where

$$\hat{F}(e) = \phi, \ \forall e \in A, \ i.e.$$

$$\hat{F}(e)(x_j) = 0$$

$$\forall j = 1, 2, .. n,$$

$$\forall e \notin A$$

Thus now on we will take the parameter subset of any soft set over $S(U)$ to be same with the parameter set E without loss of generality.

Then we define the following distances between two soft sets $(\hat{F}_1, E)$ and $(\hat{F}_2, E)$ as follows:

Definition 50: [Majumdar & Samanta, 2008] [Majumdar & Samanta, 2008] For two soft sets $(\hat{F}_1, E)$ and $(\hat{F}_2, E)$ we define the mean Hamming distance $D^S(\hat{F}_1, \hat{F}_2)$ between two soft sets as:

$$D^S(\hat{F_1}, \hat{F_2}) = \frac{1}{m} \left\{ \sum_{i=1}^{m} \sum_{j=1}^{n} \left| \hat{F_1}(e_j)(x_j) - \hat{F_2}(e_i)(x_j) \right| \right\}$$

(3)

the normalized Hamming distance $L^s(F_1, F_2)$ as:

$$L^S(\hat{F_1}, \hat{F_2}) = \frac{1}{m.n} \left\{ \sum_{i=1}^{m} \sum_{j=1}^{n} \left| \hat{F_1}(e_j)(x_j) - \hat{F_2}(e_i)(x_j) \right| \right\}$$

(4)

the Euclidean distance $E^S(\hat{F_1}, \hat{F_2})$ as:

$$E^S(\hat{F_1}, \hat{F_2}) = \sqrt{\frac{1}{m} \sum_{i=1}^{m} \sum_{j=1}^{n} \left(\hat{F_1}(e_1)(x_j) - \hat{F_2}(e_i)(x_j) \right)^2}$$

(5)

the normalized Euclidean distance $Q^S(\hat{F_1}, \hat{F_2})$ as:

$$Q^S(\hat{F_1}, \hat{F_2}) = \sqrt{\frac{1}{m.n} \sum_{i=1}^{m} \sum_{j=1}^{n} \left(\hat{F_1}(e_1)(x_j) - \hat{F_2}(e_i)(x_j) \right)^2}$$

(6)

For simplicity, from now on we will write $\hat{F_i}$ as F_i.

Example 26: [Majumdar & Samanta, 2008] Let

$$U = \{x_1, x_2, x_3\}$$

and

$$E = \{e_1, e_2, e_3\}$$

Let (F_1, E) and (F_2, E) be two soft sets defined below by their membership matrices

(F_1, E)	$F_1(e_1)$	$F_1(e_2)$	$F_1(e_3)$
x_1	1	1	0
x_2	0	1	0
x_3	0	0	1

and

(F_2, E)	$F_2(e_1)$	$F_2(e_2)$	$F_2(e_3)$
x_1	0	1	1
x_2	1	1	0
x_3	0	1	1

Then,

$$D^S(F_1, F_2) = \frac{4}{3}$$

$$L^S(F_1, F_2) = \frac{4}{9}$$

$$E^S(F_1, F_2) = \sqrt{\frac{4}{3}}$$

$$Q^S(F_1, F_2) = \sqrt{\frac{4}{9}} = \frac{2}{3}$$

Lemma 4: [Majumdar & Samanta, 2008] For any two soft sets (F_1, E) and (F_2, E) of $S(U)$, the following inequalities hold.

1. $D^S(F_1, F_2) \leq n$
2. $L^S(F_1, F_2) \leq 1$
3. $E^S(F_1, F_2) \leq \sqrt{n}$
4. $Q^S(F_1, F_2) \leq 1$

- **Proof:** Trivially follows from definition.

Now we define the equality of two soft sets.

Definition 51: [Majumdar & Samanta, 2008] Let (F_1, E_1) and

$$(F_2, E_2) \in S(U)$$

Then

$(F_1, E_2) = (F_2, E_2)$

if for every $e_i \in E$,

$F_1(e_i)(x_j) = F_2(e_i)(x_j)$

$\forall j = 1, 2, \ldots n.$

Theorem 13: [Majumdar & Samanta, 2008] The functions D^s, L^s, E^s,

$Q^s : S(U) \rightarrow R^+$

given by Equations (3)-(6), respectively are metrics, where R^+ is the set of all non-negative real numbers.

Proof: Here we will only prove for D^s, as the proofs are similar for the others.

For any two soft sets (F_1, E_1) and

$(F_2, E_2) \in S(U)$,

we have the followings:

1. $D^S(F_1, F_2) \geq 0$

   If

$(F_1, E_1) = (F_2, E_2) \Rightarrow (F_1(e_j)(x_i) - F_2(e_j)(x_i) = 0, \forall j = 1, 2, \ldots, n, \forall x_i \in U) \Rightarrow D^S(F_1, F_2) = 0$

   Conversely, let

$D^S(F_1, F_2) = 0 \Rightarrow$
$\frac{1}{m} \{ \sum_{i=1}^{m} \sum_{j=1}^{n} |F_1(e_i)(x_j) - F_2(e_i)(x_j)| \} = 0$
$\Rightarrow F_1(e_i)(x_j) = F_2(e_i)(x_j) \forall i = 1, 2, 3 \ldots, m$
$and \ \forall \ j = 1, 2, 3 \ldots, n$
$\Rightarrow (F_1, E_1) = (F_2, E_2)$

Clearly,

2. $D^S(F_1, F_2) = D^S(F_2, F_1)$

Triangle inequality follows easily from the observation that for any three soft sets

3. $(F_1, E_1), (F_2, E_2)$ and (F_3, E_3)

$|F_1(e_j)(x_i) - F_3(e_j)(x_i)| = $
$\left| \begin{array}{l} (F_1(e_j)(x_i) - F_2(e_j)(x_i)) + \\ (F_2(e_j)(x_i) - F_3(e_j)(x_i)) \end{array} \right| \leq$
$|(F_1(e_j)(x_i) - F_2(e_j)(x_i))|$
$+ |(F_2(e_j)(x_i) - F_3(e_j)(x_i))|$

Hence the result.

D. Distance Based Similarity Measure of Soft Sets

In the previous subsection we have defined several types of distances between a pair of soft sets. Now using these distances we can also define similarity measures for soft sets.

Based on Hamming distance a similarity measure can be defined, as:

$$S'(F_1, F_2) = \frac{1}{1 + D^S(F_1, F_2)} \qquad (7)$$

Similarly we can define another similarity measure as:

$$S'(F_1, F_2) = e^{-\alpha.D^S(F_1,F_2)} \qquad (8)$$

where α is a positive real number (parameter) called the steepness measure.

Similarly using Eucledian distance, two similarity measures has been defined, as:

$$S'(F_1, F_2) = \frac{1}{1 + E^S(F_1,F_2)} \qquad (9)$$

$$S'(F_1, F_2) = e^{-\alpha.E^S(F_1,F_2)} \qquad (10)$$

where α is a positive real number (parameter) called the steepness measure. Here (F_1, E_1) and (F_2, E_2) are assumed to be two soft sets over the same finite universe U.

It is clear that for distance based similarity measures, the similarity between a soft set and it's complement is never zero.

Lemma 5: [Majumdar & Samanta, 2008] For any two soft-sets (F_1, E) and (F_2, E), the following holds:

1. $0 \leq S'(F_1, F_2) \leq 1$
2. $S'(F_1, F_2) = S'(F_2, F_1)$
3. $S'(F_1, F_2) = 1 \Leftrightarrow (F_1, E_1) = (F_2, E_2)$

- **Proof:** Follows from definition.

E. A Medical Diagnosis Problem Using Similarity Measure of Two Soft Sets [Majumdar & Samanta, 2008]

This technique of similarity measure of two soft sets can be applied to detect whether an ill person is suffering from a certain disease or not.

In the following example we will try to estimate the possibility that an ill person having certain visible symptoms is suffering from pneumonia. For this we first construct a model soft set for pneumonia and the soft set for the ill person. Next we find the similarity measure of these two sets. If they are significantly similar then we conclude that the person is possibly suffering from pneumonia.

Let our universal set contains only two elements yes and no, i.e. $U = \{y, n\}$. Here the set of parameters E is the set of certain visible symptoms. Let

$$E = \{e_1, e_2, e_3, e_4, e_5, e_6, e_7, e_8\}$$

where $e_1 =$ high body temperature, $e_2 =$ low body temperature, $e_3 =$ cough with chest congestion, $e_4 =$ cough with no chest congestion, $e_5 =$ body ache, $e_6 =$ headache, $e_7 =$ loose motion, $e_8 =$ breathing trouble.

Our model soft set for pneumonia (F, E) is given below and this can be prepared with the help of a medical person:

Now the ill person is having fever, cough and headache. After talking to him we can construct his soft set (G, E) as follows:

Table 2. Model Soft set for pneumonia

(F,E)	e_1	e_2	e_3	e_4	e_5	e_6	e_7	e_8
Y	1	0	1	1	1	0	0	1
N	0	1	0	0	0	1	1	0

Table 3. First ill person

(G, E)	e_1	e_2	e_3	e_4	e_5	e_6	e_7	e_8
Y	0	1	0	1	0	1	1	0
N	1	0	1	0	1	0	0	1

Then we find the similarity measure of these two sets as:

$$S(F, G) = \frac{\sum_i \vec{F}(e_i) \bullet \vec{G}(e_i)}{\sum_i [\vec{F}(e_i)^2 \vee \vec{G}(e_i)^2]} = \frac{1}{8} < \frac{1}{2}$$

Hence the two soft sets, i.e. two symptoms (F, E) and (G, E) are not significantly similar. Therefore we conclude that the person is not possibly suffering from pneumonia. Whereas a person suffering from the following symptoms whose corresponding soft set (H, E) is given below:

Then

$$S(F, H) = \frac{6}{8} > \frac{1}{2}$$

Here the two soft sets, i.e. two symptoms (F, E) and (H, E) are significantly similar. Therefore we conclude that the person is possibly suffering from pneumonia.

This is only a simple example to show the possibility of using method for diagnosis of diseases which could be improved by incorporating clinical results and other competing diagnosis.

Medical Diagnosis System Based on Soft Mapping

A soft mapping [Majumdar & Samanta, 2010b] can be used to model a disease–symptom relationship in connection with medical diagnosis problems.

The problem: In interior places of a third world country, a patient comes with a certain symptoms to a physician and he often has to diagnose the disease by studying the symptoms only because in most of the cases proper clinical facilities are not available. So there is a possibility for human errors.

We want to device a mathematical system based on soft mapping which will help the physicians to diagnose the disease correctly.

For that we first have to construct a model soft mapping indicating the disease – symptom relationship. This model may be different depending upon different geographical regions etc.

Let

$$E = \{d_1, d_2, d_3, ..., d_m\}$$

denote the set of all diseases;

$$A = \{s_1, s_2, ..., s_n\}$$

Table 4. Second ill person

(H, E)	e_1	e_2	e_3	e_4	e_5	e_6	e_7	e_8
Y	1	0	1	1	1	1	1	1
N	0	1	0	0	0	0	0	0

denote the set of all known symptoms; $J = [0,1]$. Then we construct a soft mapping

$$F : E \rightarrow P(J^A)$$

such that $e \in E, F(e)$ is a singleton set $\{f_e\}$, where $f_e : A \rightarrow J$ is an injective function. This function f_e assigns a numeric value to each symptom with respect to a particular disease and this correspondence is one-one. Thus the soft mapping F represents a model of diseases and the occurring symptoms with a weight given to each symptom. The weights indicate the possibility of a particular disease with respect to a symptom. This model soft mapping can be constructed by consulting a group of specialist physicians.

Now suppose a patient comes with certain symptoms. We then construct the set S of his symptoms. Then to determine his disease we find $F(S)$.

Corresponding to each $d_j \in E$, we form the set

$$F(S)(d_j) \subset J$$

Now we calculate the score of a particular disease with respect to the symptoms S. The score of $d_j \in E$ is defined as follows:

$$Score : (d_j) = \sum_{s_i \in S} f_{d_j}(s_i).$$

We conclude that the person suffering with disease $d_k \in E$, if Score (d_k) is maximum.

We further illustrate the process with an example: Let here

$$E = \{d_1, d_2, d_3\},$$

where d_1 is influenza, d_2 is asthma and d_3 is pneumonia. We consider the following symptom set

$$A = \{s_1, s_2, \ldots, s_n\}$$

where s_1 is mild fever, s_2 is high fever, s_3 is acute breathing trouble, s_4 is sneezing, s_5 is loose motion, s_6 is body ache, s_7 is head ache, s_8 is wheeze cough, s_9 is mucus in lungs, s_{10} is whistle sound while breathing, s_{11} is running nose. We define three functions f_1, f_2 and f_3 in form of a table as shown in Table 5.

We construct the model soft mapping

$$F : E \rightarrow P(J^A)$$

defined as follows:

Table 5.

$f_1 =$	s_1	s_2	s_3	s_4	s_5	s_6	s_7	s_8	s_9	s_{10}	s_{11}
	0.8	0.2	0.1	0.7	0	0.4	0.9	0	0	0	1.0
$f_2 =$	s_1	s_2	s_3	s_4	s_5	s_6	s_7	s_8	s_9	s_{10}	s_{11}
	0.1	0	0.9	0.6	0.1	0	0.1	1.0	0.7	0.9	0.3
$f_3 =$	s_1	s_2	s_3	s_4	s_5	s_6	s_7	s_8	s_9	s_{10}	s_{11}
	0.3	0.6	0.5	0.1	0	0.8	0.6	0.4	1.0	0.4	0.1

$$F(\mathrm{d}_1) = \{f_1\}, F(d_2) = \{f_2\}, F(d_3) = \{f_3\}$$

A patient comes with the following symptoms

$$S = \{s_2, s_4, s_6, s_7, s_{11}\}$$

We find the image of S under F and find the respective scores:

Score $(d_1) = 3.2$, Score $(d_2) = 1.0$, Score $(d_3) = 2.2$.

Hence we conclude that the patient is suffering from d_1, i.e. from influenza.

This is a very preliminary model which may be improved by incorporating detailed disease – symptoms information and also clinical results.

Decision Making Using Generalised Fuzzy Soft Sets

An application of the Generalised fuzzy soft relation [Majumdar & Samanta, 2010a] in a decision making problem is shown below.

Suppose the universe consists of four machines,

$$x_1, x_2, x_3, x_4, \textit{i.e. } U = \{x_1, x_2, x_3, x_4\}$$

and there are three parameters

$$e_i, i = 1, 2, 3$$

which describe their performances according to certain specific task. Hence

$$E = \{e_1, e_2, e_3\}$$

Suppose a firm wants to buy one such machine depending on any two of the parameters only. Let there be two observations F_μ and G_δ by two experts A and B respectively.

Let their corresponding membership matrices are as follows:

$$F_\mu = (F, \mu) = \begin{pmatrix} 0.4 & 0.2 & 0.1 & 0.6 & 0.5 \\ 0.7 & 0.8 & 0.5 & 0.4 & 0.6 \\ 0.6 & 0.4 & 0.5 & 0.6 & 0.8 \end{pmatrix}$$

and

$$G_\delta = (\mathrm{G}, \delta) = \begin{pmatrix} 0.4 & 0.6 & 0.5 & 0.3 & 0.5 \\ 0.8 & 0.4 & 0.9 & 0.6 & 0.7 \\ 0.1 & 0.2 & 0.1 & 0.4 & 0.3 \end{pmatrix}$$

Let

$$R : C \to I^U \times I,$$

be the generalised fuzzy soft relation between F_μ and G_δ, defined as follows:

R	x_1	x_2	x_3	x_4	λ
(e_1, e_1)	(0.4)	0.2	0.1	0.3	0.5
(e_1, e_2)	0.1	0.2	0.1	(0.6)	0.5
(e_1, e_3)	0.1	0.2	0.1	(0.4)	0.3
(e_2, e_1)	0.4	(0.6)	0.5	0.3	0.5
(e_2, e_2)	(0.7)	0.4	0.5	0.4	0.6
(e_2, e_3)	0.1	0.2	0.1	(0.4)	0.3
(e_3, e_1)	0.4	0.4	(0.5)	0.3	0.5
(e_3, e_2)	0.6	0.4	0.5	(0.6)	0.7
(e_3, e_3)	0.1	0.2	0.1	(0.4)	0.3

Now to determine the best machine we first mark the highest numerical value (indicated in parenthesis) in each row excluding the last column which is the grade of such belongingness of a machine against each pair of parameters. Now the score of each of such machines is calculated by taking the product of the numerical value with the corresponding grade value. The machine with the highest score is the desired machine. We do not consider the numerical grades of the machines against the pairs

$$(e_i, e_i), i = 1, 2, 3,$$

as both the parameters are same.

Then the firm will select the machine with highest score. Hence they will buy machine x_3.

Further Reading

One can study the following papers: [Bojadziev & Bojadziev, 2007], [Chaudhuri, De & Chatterjee, 2009], [Chen, Tsang, Yeung & Xizhao, 2005], [Chen & Hsiao, 1995], [Feng, Jun, Liu, & Li, 2010a], [Grzegorzewski, 2004], [Hong & Kim, 1999], [Kong, Gao, Wang & Li, 2008], [Kong, Gao, & Wang, 2009], [Li, & Xu, 2001], [Lu, Yan, Yuan & Xu, 2005], [Maji, & Roy, 2002], [Majumdar, & Samanta, 2011], [Majumdar, & Samanta, 2010c], [Majumdar, & Samanta, 2013a] given in Reference section for further details.

CONCLUSION

"Uncertainty" is present in every sphere of our lives and it will remain there forever. Therefore conventional mathematics can no longer be the sole agent for modeling natural phenomenon. The need for a suitable tool for predicting the situations which are uncertain is legitimate and will continue in near future also. The recent techniques such as fuzzy sets, soft sets and their hybrid structures etc., those having greater powers of handling uncertainty, are currently being studied in detail and have been applied in solving many practical problems faced by the mankind.

Developments regarding soft sets have also been very significant and many application of this theory has been done. But lots of scopes are left for development of pure mathematics based on soft set theory. Ideas like soft metric and norm, soft topology and also other algebraic structures are currently being studied. Application of soft sets in solving real life problems is another area where a lot thrust is required. One can also study the similarity measurement of soft sets and its application. Several hybrid structures and generalizations are also possible involving fuzzy, rough and soft sets etc, which could be a good research problem. In this chapter I have addressed some of these issues and shown some possible applications of these theories. It is expected that the popularity of these non-conventional mathematics, i.e. fuzzy set theory, soft set theory and others, will increase tremendously in near future. With continuous advancements in these fields of non-conventional mathematics, I am confident that these new theories will be able to model and predict uncertainties more efficiently than as it is now.

Table 6. Score table

$$\begin{pmatrix} R & (e_1, e_1) & (e_1, e_2) & (e_1, e_3) & (e_2, e_1) & (e_2, e_2) & (e_2, e_3) & (e_3, e_1) & (e_3, e_2) & (e_3, e_3) \\ x_i & - & x_4 & x_4 & x_2 & - & x_4 & x_3 & x_3 & - \\ Score & - & 0.3 & 0.12 & 0.3 & - & 0.12 & 0.25 & 0.42 & - \end{pmatrix}$$

REFERENCES

Aktas, H., & Cagman, N. (2007). Soft sets and soft groups. *Information Science, 177,* 2726–2735. doi:10.1016/j.ins.2006.12.008

Ali, M. I., Feng, F., Liu, X., Min, W. K., & Shabir, M. (2009). On some new operations in soft set theory. *Computers & Mathematics with Applications (Oxford, England), 57,* 1547–1553. doi:10.1016/j.camwa.2008.11.009

Atanasov, K. T. (1986). Intuitionistic fuzzy sets. *Fuzzy Sets and Systems, 20,* 87–96. doi:10.1016/S0165-0114(86)80034-3

Aygunoglu, A., & Aygun, H. (2009). Introduction to soft groups. *Computers & Mathematics with Applications (Oxford, England), 58,* 1279–1286. doi:10.1016/j.camwa.2009.07.047

Babitha, K. B., & Sunil, J. J. (2010). Soft set relations and functions. *Computers & Mathematics with Applications (Oxford, England), 60*(7), 1840–1849. doi:10.1016/j.camwa.2010.07.014

Bojadziev, G., & Bojadziev, M. (2007). *Fuzzy logic for business, finance, and management* (2nd ed.). Singapore: World Scientific Press.

Cagman, N., Citak, F., & Enginoglu, S. (2010). Fuzzy parameterized fuzzy soft set theory and its applications. *Turkish Journal of Fuzzy Systems, 1*(1), 21–35.

Chaudhuri, A., De, K., & Chatterjee, D. (2009). Solution of the decision making problems using fuzzy soft relations. *International Journal of Information Technology, 15*(1), 78–107.

Chen, D. G., Tsang, E. C. C., Yeung, D. S., & Xizhao, W. (2005). The parameterization reduction of soft sets and its applications. *Computers & Mathematics with Applications (Oxford, England), 49,* 757–763. doi:10.1016/j.camwa.2004.10.036

Chen, S. M., & Hsiao, P. H. (1995). A comparison of similarity measures of fuzzy values. *Fuzzy Sets and Systems, 72,* 79–89. doi:10.1016/0165-0114(94)00284-E

De Luca, A., & Termini, S. (1972). A definition of a non-probabilistic entropy in the setting of fuzzy sets theory. *Information and Control, 20,* 301–312. doi:10.1016/S0019-9958(72)90199-4

Dubois, D. J. (1983). *Fuzzy sets and systems* (4th ed.). New York: Academic Press Inc.

Feng, F., Jun, B. Y., Liu, X., & Li, L. (2010a). An adjustable approach to fuzzy soft based decision making. *Journal of Computational and Applied Mathematics, 234*(1), 10–20. doi:10.1016/j.cam.2009.11.055

Feng, F., Jun, Y. B., & Zhao, X. Z. (2008). Soft semirings. *Computers & Mathematics with Applications (Oxford, England), 56*(10), 2621–2628. doi:10.1016/j.camwa.2008.05.011

Feng, F., Li, C., Davvaz, B., & Ali, M. I. (2010b). Soft sets combined with fuzzy sets and rough sets: a tentative approach. *Soft Computing, 14,* 899–911. doi:10.1007/s00500-009-0465-6

Grzegorzewski, P. (2004). Distances between intuitionistic fuzzy sets and/or interval-valued fuzzy sets based on the Hausdorff metric. *Fuzzy Sets and Systems, 148,* 319–328. doi:10.1016/j.fss.2003.08.005

Hong, D. H., & Kim, C. A. (1999). Note on similarity measure between vague sets and elements. *Information Sciences, 115,* 83–96. doi:10.1016/S0020-0255(98)10083-X

Jun, Y. B. (2008). Soft BCK/BCI-algebras. *Computers & Mathematics with Applications (Oxford, England), 56*(5), 1408–1413. doi:10.1016/j.camwa.2008.02.035

Jun, Y. B., & Park, C. H. (2008). Applications of soft sets in ideal theory of BCK/BCI algebras. *Information Sciences, 178*(11), 2466–2475.

Jun, Y. B., & Park, C. H. (2009). Application of soft sets in Hilbert algebras. *Iranian Journal of Fuzzy Systems, 6*(2), 75–86.

Kharal, A., & Ahmad, B. (2011). Mapping on soft classes. *New Mathematics & Natural Computation, 7*(3), 471–481. doi:10.1142/S1793005711002025

Klier, G. J., & Yuan, B. (1995). *Fuzzy sets and fuzzy logic: Theory and applications* (6th ed.). Upper Saddle River, NJ: Prentice-Hall.

Kong, Z., Gao, L., Wang, L., & Li, S. (2008). The normal parameter reduction of soft sets and its algorithm. *Computers & Mathematics with Applications (Oxford, England), 56*, 3029–3037. doi:10.1016/j.camwa.2008.07.013

Kong, Z., Gao, L. Q., & Wang, L. F. (2009). Comment on a fuzzy soft set theoretic approach to decision making problems. *Journal of Computational and Applied Mathematics, 223*, 540–542. doi:10.1016/j.cam.2008.01.011

Kosko, B. (1986). Fuzzy entropy and conditioning. *Information Sciences, 40*(2), 165–174. doi:10.1016/0020-0255(86)90006-X

Li, F., & Xu, Z. Y. (2001). Similarity measure between vague sets. *Chinese Jr. of Software, 12*(6), 922–927.

Lu, J., Yan, X., Yuan, D., & Xu, Z. (2005). A new similarity measure for vague sets. *IEEE Intelligent Informatics Bulletin, 6*(2), 14–18.

Maji, P. K., Biswas, R., & Roy, A. R. (2001a). Fuzzy soft-sets. *The Jr. of Fuzzy Math., 9*(3), 589–602.

Maji, P. K., Biswas, R., & Roy, A. R. (2001b). Intuitionistic fuzzy soft sets. *The Jr. of Fuzzy Math., 9*(3), 677–691.

Maji, P. K., Biswas, R., & Roy, A. R. (2003). Soft set theory. *Computers & Mathematics with Applications (Oxford, England), 45*, 555–562. doi:10.1016/S0898-1221(03)00016-6

Maji, P. K., & Roy, A. R. (2002). An application of soft sets in a decision making problem. *Computers & Mathematics with Applications (Oxford, England), 44*, 1077–1083. doi:10.1016/S0898-1221(02)00216-X

Maji, P. K., & Roy, A. R. (2004). On intuitionistic fuzzy soft sets. *The Jr. of Fuzzy Math., 12*(3), 669–683.

Majumdar, P., Hazra, H., & Samanta, S. K. (2012). Soft topology. *Fuzzy Inform., &. Engineering, 3*(1), 105–115.

Majumdar, P., & Samanta, S. K. (2008). Similarity measure of soft sets. *New Mathematics and Natural Computation, 4*(1), 1–12. doi:10.1142/S1793005708000908

Majumdar, P., & Samanta, S. K. (2010a). Generalised fuzzy soft set. *Computers & Mathematics with Applications (Oxford, England), 59*(4), 1425–1432. doi:10.1016/j.camwa.2009.12.006

Majumdar, P., & Samanta, S. K. (2010b). On soft mappings. *Computers & Mathematics with Applications (Oxford, England), 60*(9), 2666–2672. doi:10.1016/j.camwa.2010.09.004

Majumdar, P., & Samanta, S. K. (2010c). On distance based similarity measure between intuitionistic fuzzy soft sets. *Anusandhan, 12*(22), 41–50.

Majumdar, P., & Samanta, S. K. (2011). On similarity measure of fuzzy soft sets. *Int. J. Advance. Soft Comput. Appl., 3*(2), 1–8.

Majumdar, P., & Samanta, S. K. (2013a). Decision making based on similarity measure of vague soft sets. *J. Intelligent and Fuzzy Systems, 24*, 637–646.

Majumdar, P., & Samanta, S. K. (2013b). Softness of a soft set: Soft set entropy. *Annals of Fuzzy Mathematics and Informatics*, *6*(1), 59–68.

Molodtsov, D. (1999). Soft set theory –First results. *Computers & Mathematics with Applications (Oxford, England)*, *37*, 19–31. doi:10.1016/S0898-1221(99)00056-5

Muhammad, S., & Naz, M. (2011). On soft topological spaces. *Computers & Mathematics with Applications (Oxford, England)*, *61*(7), 1786–1799. doi:10.1016/j.camwa.2011.02.006

Pawlak, Z. (1982). Rough sets. *Int. Jr. Computation & Information Science*, *11*, 341–356.

Rosenfeld, A. (1971). Fuzzy groups. *Journal of Mathematical Analysis and Applications*, *35*, 512–517. doi:10.1016/0022-247X(71)90199-5

Som, T. (2006). On soft relation and fuzzy soft relation. In *Proceedings of UAMA-2006*. Burdwan, India: UAMA.

Szmidt, E., & Kacprzyk, J. (2001). Entropy for intuitionistic fuzzy sets. *Fuzzy Sets and Systems*, *118*, 467–477. doi:10.1016/S0165-0114(98)00402-3

Tanay, B., & Kandemir, M. B. (2011). Topological structure of fuzzy soft sets. *Computers & Mathematics with Applications (Oxford, England)*, *61*, 2952–2957. doi:10.1016/j.camwa.2011.03.056

Xiao, Z. (2010). Exclusive disjunctive soft sets. *Computers & Mathematics with Applications (Oxford, England)*, *59*(6), 2128–2137. doi:10.1016/j.camwa.2009.12.018

Xu, W., Ma, J., Wang, S., & Hao, G. (2010). Vague soft sets and their properties. *Computers & Mathematics with Applications (Oxford, England)*, *59*, 787–794. doi:10.1016/j.camwa.2009.10.015

Yang, H. L. (2011). Notes on generalised fuzzy soft sets. *J. of Math. Research & Exposition*, *31*(3), 567–570.

Yang, X., Lin, T. Y., Yang, J., Li, Y., & Yu, D. (2009). Combination of interval-valued fuzzy set and soft set. *Computers & Mathematics with Applications (Oxford, England)*, *58*, 521–527. doi:10.1016/j.camwa.2009.04.019

Yang, X., Yang, J., & Wu, C. (2007). Generalization of soft set theory: From crisp to fuzzy case. In B. Y. Cao (Ed.), *Fuzzy Information & Engineering (ICFIE)* (pp. 345–354). ICFIE. doi:10.1007/978-3-540-71441-5_39

Zadeh, L. A. (1965). Fuzzy sets. *Information and Control*, *8*, 338–353. doi:10.1016/S0019-9958(65)90241-X

KEY TERMS AND DEFINITIONS

Let U be an initial universal set and let E be a set of parameters and $A \subset E$.:

Fuzzy Set: A fuzzy set F of U is defined by the mapping $F : U \to I = [0,1]$.

Fuzzy Soft Set: Let I^U denote the power set of all fuzzy subsets of U. Let $A \subset E$. A pair (F, A) is called a fuzzy soft set over U, where F is a mapping given by $F : A \to I^U$.

Generalised Fuzzy Soft Set: Let U be an initial universal set and let E be a set of parameters. Let I^U denote the power set of all fuzzy subsets of U. Let $A \subset E$. A pair (F, A) is called a fuzzy soft set over U, where F is a mapping given by $F : A \to I^U$.

Similarity Measure of Soft Sets: Amount of similarity between two soft sets.

Soft Entropy: It is a measure of uncertainty expressed by a soft set.

Soft Group: Let (F, A) is a soft set over G. Then (F, A) is said to be a soft group over G if and only if $F(x) < G$, i.e. $F(x)$ is a subgroup of G, for all $x \in A$.

Soft Mapping: Let A, B be two non-empty sets in X and E be the parameter set. Also let $E' \subset E$. Then the mapping $F : E' \to P(B^A)$ is called a soft mapping from A to B under E', where B^A is the collection of all mappings from A to B.

Soft Set: A soft set is a parametrized family of subsets of U. A soft set over the soft universe (U, E) is denoted by (F, A), where $F : A \to P(U)$, where $A \subseteq E$ and $P(U)$ is the power set of U.

Soft Topology: It is a parametrized family of crisp topologies. But there are several other types of soft topologies. Mainly it indicates the topological structure on soft sets.

ENDNOTES

[1] $(*, \circ, c)$ is called a dual triple if $c(a * b) = c(a) \circ c(b)$ and $c(a \circ b) = c(a) * c(b)$.

[2] $(A * B)(x) = \min[A(x), B(x)]$, $(A \circ B)(x) = \max[A(x), B(x)]$ and $c(A(x)) = 1 - A(x), \forall x \in U$

are called standard fuzzy operations.

[3] A soft set (F, E) is said to be a full soft set if $\bigcup_{a \in A} F(a) = U$.

Section 4
Information Science and Neural Network

Chapter 17
Adaptive and Neural pH Neutralization for Strong Acid–Strong Base System

J. Abdul Jaleel
Al Azhar College of Engineering and Technology, India

Anish Benny
Amal Jyothi College of Engineering, India

David K. Daniel
VIT University, India

ABSTRACT

The control of pH is of great importance in chemical processes, biotechnological industries, and many other areas. High performance and robust control of pH neutralization is difficult to achieve due to the nonlinear and time-varying process characteristics. The process gain varies at higher order of magnitude over a small range of pH. This chapter uses the adaptive and neural control techniques for the pH neutralization process for a strong acid-strong base system. The simulation results are analyzed to show that an adaptive controller can be perfectly tuned and a properly trained neural network controller may outperform an adaptive controller.

INTRODUCTION

Effective modeling of a pH neutralization plant is not a recent issue. However, due to the nonlinear characteristics and complexity of this type of system, research on how to provide a good dynamic model of pH neutralization process, which was first started in the 1970's or earlier, still continues. The pH process can be mainly classified into four groups and they are strong acid-strong base system, strong acid-weak base system, weak acid-strong base system and weak acid-weak base system. The strong acid-strong base pH process is the most highly nonlinear process among the

DOI: 10.4018/978-1-4666-4936-1.ch017

group. The pH value versus the reagent flow has a logarithmic relationship. Away from neutrality, the process gain is relatively small. Near neutrality where pH = 7, the process gain can be a few thousand times higher. Hence it is impossible for a fixed controller like PID to effectively control this process.

pH control is an interesting and challenging research subject which has led to a large number of motivating and interesting published papers. The control of pH process is a classic and difficult nonlinear control problem encountered in the chemical process industry. Various control strategies used for pH control are classified as non-adaptive linear, adaptive linear, model based, non-adaptive non-linear and adaptive nonlinear. For years there has been researches using various control approaches, such as simple PID control, adaptive control, nonlinear linearization control and various model-based control. Conventional control methods rely on the exact mathematical modeling of the plant, which may be tremendously difficult to obtain in many cases.

LITERATURE REVIEW

Ahmmed (2010) illustrated a modified dynamic structure model which takes into account the presence of acid and alkali in the reaction with ions which depend on chemical reactions of acid and alkali concentration feeds. Model simulations indicated that it was capable of predicting reactor performance indicators as well as calculating the changes of ions through the chemical reaction. Thomas et al., (1972) presented a rigorous and generally applicable method of deriving dynamic equations for pH in continuous stirred tank reactors (CSTRs). A specific example of neutralizing sodium hydroxide with acetic acid was discussed in detail. Experimental results on a laboratory-sized CSTR verified the accuracy of the derived model. Commonly available linear controllers carry out well in the linear range of the process for which

they have been tuned. But they are unsuitable and unstable in nonlinear ranges due to time varying process gain. Hence the linear control designing methods are limited in many real-world processes. The conventional PI or PID controller provides poor controlling performance for pH process and needs frequent tuning of the controller while parameters are not estimated. The PID controllers are tuned based on the highest gain at the equivalence point of pH equal to 7 in order to make a closed loop stable system. Hence the controllers will be working around the neutralization point which results in wasteful consumption of reagents due to process oscillation or sluggish response of the process variable [Shinskey (1996)]. From this it is concluded that linear controlling techniques are not appropriate for highly nonlinear pH process. Waller and Gustafsson (1983) investigated the fundamental properties of continuous pH control. Their experimental results suggest that taking into account the capacity of the reactor tank during plant design is important in order to have fast and efficient mixing in the tank. Gustafsson and Waller (1992) have discussed the issues in dynamics and control that arise in this nonlinear control applications. Further reviews were also carried out by Gustafsson et al., (1995). The non-adaptive linear PI or PID controller provides poor performance for pH process or requires frequent tuning (which is impractical) of a controller when parameters are uncertain. The sliding mode PID controller has problems of chattering of manipulated variable. Linear model based techniques are not suitable for highly nonlinear pH process. Many nonlinear control methods which use empirical models or rigorous physiochemical models are available. Several control algorithms have been proposed in the literature to design a good pH control system. Many of them use non-linear model-based algorithms combined with some kind of adaptive feature. In this context, the controller design methods usually consider the process nonlinear characteristics. This non-linearity can be seen as a time-varying gain that leads to linear adaptive controllers. Qinghui and Zongze (2010) stated that it was significant to control pH value rapidly and accurately for neutralization reaction process, which was characterized by critical nonlinearity and strong disturbance. On the base of nonlinear compensator, a single closed-loop PI control scheme was applied in pH neutralization reaction process. Accepting the flow of the modulated liquid as main disturbance, the simulation results suggested that the proposed scheme had good steady state and dynamic performance. Wright et al., (1991) have published several papers on pH control applications. They introduced a new method of modelling and design of a nonlinear controller based on the concept of the strong acid equivalent. Wright (1991) provided a comprehensive review of previous research work on pH modeling and control. The strong acid equivalent was one state variable of a reduced model which could be calculated online from the pH measurements, given a nominal titration curve of the process stream. The formulation of the new approach transformed the control problem into an equivalent linear control problem which was expressed in terms of the strong acid equivalent. The focus was on the implementation of the strong acid equivalent method on a laboratory-scale pH neutralization process. Their experimental results showed that in addition to a nominal process stream titration curve the proposed control algorithm required no chemical information, such as the dissociation constant and chemical species involved. These two main papers provided a foundation for further research to explore this subject in greater detail and this then led to some more interesting papers in later years from the same group.

The family of intelligent controllers includes those based on neural nets, fuzzy logic, and the genetic algorithm. Fuzzy logic is now recognized as one of the most successful technologies for developing and implementing control systems for a wide range of industrial applications. This is due to the fact that fuzzy logic is capable of managing complex applications efficiently, even with uncertainties or vague information about the system to be controlled. The fuzzy logic concept has also been shown to be capable of mimicking human decision making processes for applications where manual control is known to produce acceptable control performance. Thus the successful application of fuzzy control concepts in other fields has encouraged this research activity to investigate the benefits and limitations of fuzzy control in the pH neutralization process. These research activities also reflect interest in improving the operation and control of systems involving highly nonlinear process plant. Kelkar and Postlethwaite (1994) stated that the inherent nonlinearity of the pH process often renders conventional control difficulty. This non-linearity suggested that pH control would be a suitable application area for a fuzzy control system, whose ability to handle non-linearities is well known. Many fuzzy controllers are of the rule based type where the controller's output response is described by a series of control rules. However, the controller described in this chapter is of a fuzzy-model based type which means that a fuzzy model of the process itself is embedded into the predictive control structure. Ranganath and Elamin (2003) illustrated that for nonlinear systems, fuzzy logic control provided a better alternative to the classical proportional plus integral (PI) controller. Xie (2010) proposed a novel parameter self-adjusting Fuzzy-PID control method in the view of the nonlinear and time-delay characteristics in acid and alkali neutral reaction process. The fuzzy controller can adjust PID controller's parameters online according to the real-time deviation of pH value. There are two main methods to obtain the expected control index. Firstly, through enhancing the sensitivity of the linguistic value, it can adapt the big change rate of pH value nearby the neutral point when the deviation is small. Secondly, by analyzing the magnitude and symbol of the deviation and change rate of deviation, fuzzy rules can be well established. The simulation results showed that the method can not only adapt to the change of pH value in large scale, but also overcome the flow fluctuation. Zeybek and Alpbaz (2005) developed a simple fuzzy model for dye waste water treatment. Several factors may play critical roles in the dye removal, such as coagulant type, application dosages, pH level and temperature. Due to the difficulty in expressing the treatment processes mathematically, a Fuzzy-DMC controller becomes an attractive approach to tackle above mentioned problems. Kwok and Wang (1993) proposed a new control strategy consisting of three different parts: a fuzzy controller which represents the proportional and derivative control action, an integrator and a Smith predictor. The simulation results demonstrated the effectiveness of the proposed controller in comparison with the classical control approach involving the conventional PID controller. Parekh et al., (1994) proposed a new form of advanced control system involving a technique based on the fuzzy logic approach. The main advantages of the controller included a wider operation range, robustness of the controller in handling random disturbances as well as a relatively simple implementation. Nie et al., (1996) presented fuzzy-neural approach. During the formulation of the FLC, experimental data and practical experience of the real process play an important role. They showed that the proposed form of fuzzy logic controller worked very well and provides good control performance. The use of neural network's learning ability avoids complex mathematical analysis in solving control problems when plant dynamics are complex and highly nonlinear, which is a distinct advantage over traditional control methods. Artificial neural networks (ANN) may be a better way to solve nonlinear system control problems since they have the parallel processing and learning capabilities. Hence, it has received considerable attention in the field of chemical process control and controller design. Gomm et al., (1996) presented the control of an experimental in-line pH process exhibiting varying nonlinearity and dead time. A radial basis function (RBF)

ANN was used to model the nonlinear dynamics of the process. Accommodation of the varying process dead time in the neural model was achieved by the generation of a feed-forward signal, for input to the neural network, from a downstream pH measurement. The feed forward signal is derived from a variable delay model based on process knowledge and a flow measurement. The neural model was then used to realize a predictive control scheme for the process. Li and Ning (2010) presented a double neuron model-free control method for pH processes. In this control system, the principal neuron controller was designed to control pH process, and the subordinate neuron controller was used to compensate for the nonlinear characteristic. The purpose of improving response speed and reducing errors was reached. Simulation results showed the efficiency, good disturbance resistability and very strong robustness of the proposed method. Bernt et al., (2005) utilised a neuro-fuzzy modelling technique which was also referred to as quasi-ARMAX to model the nonlinear characteristic of the pH neutralization process. They developed neuro-fuzzy model capable of representing the behaviour of a highly nonlinear pH neutralization process to a high level of accuracy. The simulation results for the nonlinear model predictive controller showed that the controller worked very well not only for set point changes but also with feed flow concentration disturbances. However, the weaknesses of neural networks, such as complex training algorithm, slow learning speed and the long weight convergence time limit their applications. In order to achieve effectiveness and high control performance of highly nonlinear processes, several schemes of neural controllers were proposed in the past. Amongst the most popular schemes of neural network control architectures are: Internal Model Control (IMC), Model Predictive Control (MPC) and Model Reference Adaptive Control (MRAC). Woei et al., (2001) aimed at utilizing computational intelligence techniques, such as genetic algorithm (GA) and multi-objective evolutionary algorithm (MOEA), to design a Wiener-model controller for regulating the pH level in an acid-base titration process. A Wiener-model control structure comprises of an inverse model of the system non-linearity, and a simple linear controller. The inverse model serves to simplify the control problem by eliminating the bulk of the non-linear characteristics from the pH control loop. A PID controller can then be used to control the linearized system. GA was employed to identify the parameters of the inverse titration equation while the PID parameters were obtained using MOEA. Karr and Gentry (1993) presented the use of GA in a fuzzy control approach for a pH process. Their paper basically described work done by researchers at the U.S. Bureau of Mines as an extension of previous investigations on adaptive fuzzy logic controllers. The GA approach was employed to alter membership functions in response to changes in the process. The idea presented utilized the ability of GA in terms of optimizing the membership functions for different requirements in terms of set point or concentration disturbances. The experimental results showed that the performance of this form of controller is very encouraging. Barve and Nataraj (1998) stated the robust regulatory controller for highly nonlinear pH process synthesized using Non-Linear Equivalent Disturbance Attenuation (NLEDA) technique of Quantitative Feedback Theory (QFT). The controller was designed to regulate the pH of the outlet stream within (7.0 ± 0.2) in the presence of significant parameter uncertainties and load disturbances. The robust stability of the control system was guaranteed by the QFT design procedure.

In adaptive control system the controller parameters are adjusted automatically to compensate for varying process conditions. It is used when more precise control over pH is required, for example in a production stage where a small deviation band is the norm. Several adaptive nonlinear controllers have been proposed like gain scheduling, self tuning and model reference control. Hong

et al., (1996) illustrated a nonlinear predictive control scheme using adaptive NARX models. The simulated process had a time delay of four time units in the dynamic part of mathematical model whilst the laboratory-scale neutralization process was shown to have a time delay of two time units. This indicated that it may be more difficult to control the simulated system than the laboratory scale plant. Jin-Yong and Rhinehart (1987) illustrated a new strategy for the control of waste water pH neutralization. The internal adaptive-model controller required adaptation of two model parameters and it was rapidly parameterized, remaining a true process simulator during rapid process change. The simulated flow-through control efficacy suggested that process water can be effectively neutralized with low capital cost processes. Dhruba et al., (2000) illustrated a MRAC scheme in which the control and parameter estimation laws were derived based on a reference model approach for nonlinearly parameterized systems. By suitably choosing the parameter update and control laws, the algorithms were much simplified for this pH problem. Global stability and zero tracking error could be achieved with this new adaptive controller. Manuel et al., (2002) presented an experimental evaluation of the CMRAC applied to control the pH in a chemical reactor in which water reacts with acetic acid (weak acid) and sodium hydroxide (strong base). Its performance was compared with a classical PID controller and with another adaptive control strategy (DMRAC). Comparing the different control strategies under set point changes, all of them resulted in a stable operation bringing the pH to the desired value even in the critical case of pH 7.2. The PID controller presents oscillations, which is not the case in the adaptive controllers. Nevertheless, the latter was slower than the PID controller. In the case of step perturbations, the PID controller performed better than the adaptive ones, since the latter exhibit large overshoot. Ehsan et al., (2008) designed and evaluated two conventional and advanced adaptive controllers from industrial point of view. The advanced controllers control pH of the effluent stream, while a classical PI controller with smaller sampling time controlled the level of solution in the tank at a constant value. Both advanced controllers belong to indirect adaptive control schemes. It is obvious that the multiple-model approach outperforms the conventional adaptive one when pH crosses from or stays at equivalence point having the greatest gain. The exact tracking of the desired output using these algorithms without buffering stream to make the titration curve smoother is a very difficult task. On the other hand, the multiple-model approach rejected load disturbances better than the other. Gustafsson and Waller (1982) have produced several interesting papers concerning modeling and control of the pH neutralization process and a number of these have been reviewed and cited by others as providing good reference material. They introduced a new concept concerning the averaging pH value of a mixture of solutions. The idea was to utilize reaction invariant variables in calculating the pH value of mixtures of solutions instead of using a direct calculation involving a simple averaging of hydrogen ions. They introduced the concept of invariants species which represent the species that remain chemically unchanged by the governing of reactions in the neutralization process. They suggested that the final pH value of a mixture of solutions needs to take into consideration the concentration of all variables involved in the reaction process. Waller and Gustafsson (1983) published a systematic method for the modeling of the dynamics of the pH neutralization process. It was based on this concept of invariant species and the development of the dynamic nonlinear section involved mass balances of all the invariant species involved in the neutralization reaction process. They presented some simulation results which highlight the possible use of this pH model in implementing an adaptive pH control scheme. They also developed an adaptive controller where the developed model was incorporated in the

controller in order to provide relevant information necessary for the controller. They used hypothetical species estimation to obtain the inverse titration curve so that overall linearization of the control loop can be utilized. Henson and Seborg (1994) published work on adaptive nonlinear control applied to a pH neutralization process. A nonlinear controller was developed by applying an input-output linearization approach to a reaction invariant model of the process. The controller also utilized an open-loop nonlinear state observer and a recursive least squares parameter estimator. Their paper highlighted results for three different tests carried out to investigate the performance of the main types of controllers considered (i.e. a PI controller, and non-adaptive and adaptive forms of nonlinear controller). The first test involved set point changes; the second test involved buffer flow rate disturbances and finally the third test included acid flow rate disturbances. Based on the results from these tests the adaptive nonlinear pH control was found to provide the best results for the three controllers considered. Pajunen (1987) compared linear and nonlinear adaptive control of a pH process. She presented two different schemes of adaptive control involving linear and nonlinear adaptive controllers. The case involving the linear adaptive controller was based on flow and mixing models that were initially assumed to be known. The second scheme utilized piecewise-polynomial approximation to obtain an inverse of the titration curve for the pH process. The performance of the nonlinear adaptive controller was found to be better than that of the linear controller. However in the case of frequent step disturbances she suggests the use of linear controller instead. Nayeem and Geoff (2003) considered a model reference non-linear controller developed earlier and the method was tested using a CSTR to neutralise a strong acid using a strong alkaline solution. Experimental results confirm that a robust control of the process is achievable. Sandra et al., (1999) stated that pH control was recognized as an industrially important, yet notoriously difficult control problem. Wiener models, consisting of a linear dynamic element followed in series by a static nonlinear element, were considered to be ideal for representing this and several other nonlinear processes. Wiener models require little more effort in development than a standard linear step-response model, yet offer superior characterization of systems with highly nonlinear gains. These models may be incorporated into MPC schemes in a unique way which effectively removes the nonlinearity from the control problem, preserving many of the favourable properties of linear MPC. Wiener model predictive control (WMPC) was evaluated experimentally, and also compared with benchmark proportional integral derivative (PID) and linear MPC strategies, considering the effects of output constraints and modelling error.

Simon and Igor (2007) showed a method of nonlinear continuous-time MPC. In the derivation procedure the method implicitly incorporated a fuzzy-system static nonlinear-mapping approximation. The control law was in compact analytical form; furthermore, adaptation of the control parameters as a response to nonlinear behaviour of the process was only a matter of scalar-product computation. As a consequence, the computational burden was low and the proposed method was suitable for real-time applications where high-quality control is desired. They showed that the proposed method exhibited quality control that outperforms a robust nonlinear method. Balaji and Vasudevan (2009) applied MPC technique in order to improve the control performance on the reactor that could not be controlled satisfactorily using PID controls. The MPC technique not only controlled the status of the valve but was also used to control the stirrer, whereas PID could be used only to control the status of the valve. The automatic control of the pH enabled the plant to reduce the batch cycle time, to increase the plant productivity. They showed that the response of MPC was accurate and nearer to the ideal response, when compared to PID. Syafiie et al., (2009) demonstrated a simple learning control approach

for controlling a pH neutralization process. A one-step-ahead Q-learning, namely Q(A)-learning, using a lookup table was developed and applied to a weak base - strong acid process. The application at a laboratory pilot plant showed that the proposed Q(A)-learning regulates the process well, even in the presence of reference changes. Hermansson et al., (2010) showed the control of nonlinear systems using linear models. The control strategy utilized a piecewise linear description of the process, considered the model bank. The model bank was then combined at each sampling interval, through the application of a Bayesian weight calculator, to render a single linear model describing the system. The linear model was used in MPC setting to render the optimal control move. The performance of the setup demonstrated a good following of set point changes and quick reduction of oscillations. Galip and Omer, (1996), proposed an adaptive fuzzy controller for a class of continuous time nonlinear dynamic systems. In their model, an explicit linear parameterization of the uncertainty in the dynamic was either unknown or impossible. The controller developed was capable of incorporating fuzzy if-then rules into the controller and guaranteed the global stability of the resulting closed loop system in the sense that all signals involved were uniformly bounded. The multi region FLC used an auxiliary variable to indicate different nonlinear region of processes and yield better control performance than a 1-region fuzzy controller. Simulation results showed that the multi region fuzzy controller performed well in controlling a pH CSTR which is highly nonlinear process. Zhandong and Jiangtao (2005) presented the pH neutralization process in alkali-terminal tank of poly-acrylonitrile which is typical process of strong alkali titrating multiple weak acids. An adaptive singularity-free control approach by neural compensation was presented. In order to avoid the zero crossing of the estimated control gains, a novel quasi-weighted Lyapunov function was modified in the design. The result of the simulation meant that the controller was robust to some nonlinear uncertainties and bounded disturbance, and the control scheme could guarantee the global boundedness of all closed-loop signals. Feng et al., (2006) stated the one-step-ahead adaptive fuzzy control scheme which was applied for control of a pH process. The process was modeled by a standard Mamdani fuzzy system with the equally- spaced triangular membership functions. Human knowledge about the process could be easily put into the fuzzy model, and also the input-output data of the process could affect the fuzzy model through the least square parameter tuning algorithm with dead zone. The control action was computed by making use of the special internal property of the fuzzy system, which globally minimized the cost function comprising the errors between the predicted outputs of the process and the reference trajectory. Simulation results demonstrate the effectiveness of the controller for both tracking and regulation problems and the benefit from the linguistic information. Valarmathi et al., (2007) applied fuzzy logic to many applications in control with uncertainties successfully. The system performance could be improved by tuning the membership functions. In a fuzzy system the membership functions and rule set are codependent, they are encoded into the chromosome and evolved simultaneously using genetic algorithm. The performance of the proposed approach was demonstrated through development of fuzzy controller for a bench mark pH process. In both set point tracking and disturbance rejection, simulation results showed a better performance when compared to fuzzy logic controller. Lou and Dai (2008) stated that in order to tackle the deficiency, the Minimal Re-source Allocation (MRA) network was introduced in predictive control system and a novel predictive control algorithm based on MRAN was presented. MRAN is a sequential learning RBF network and has ability to grow and prune the hidden neurons to ensure a parsimonious structure and is well suited for real-time processing applications. The neural predictive

controller was able to eliminate the most significant obstacles by facilitating the development of non-linear models. It provided a better generalization and rapid real-time ability to the control algorithm and presented a better real-time control effect. Shahin et al., (2009) presented an adaptive control scheme for pH neutralization processes. The controller was designed such that no composition measurement was required. Meanwhile to cope with uncertainties and unknown system nonlinearities, a fuzzy logic system was employed as an approximator. The proposed controller had few tuning parameters, simple design and could be implemented easily. The effectiveness of the proposed controller in set-point tracking and load rejection was demonstrated through computer simulation and experimental studies. The results also indicated that the performance of proposed controller was much better than that of a tuned PI controller. Martin et al., (2009) presented the design, setup and application of a real time control system. Due to its flexibility, this system had a broad range of potential application fields: from production sites to teaching. As at the design stage several configurations were discussed, the reader could tailor own systems to ones needs, preferences, and budget. Solved issues included DAQ boards drivers availability, modified operating systems distributions, and software package incompatibility. As a proof of functionality the proposed real-time controller was successfully applied to control the pH of a bio reactor. Sonali and Bodhe (2009) stated the case of development of a neuro fuzzy logic based pH controller to illustrate the complete controller design process. This controller could be used to control the pH of any process/plant exhibiting non-linearity, large settling time and time lag. A tolerance limit of $\pm$ 0.02 in control of final pH was achieved by employing NFLC controller. The performance of NFLC was superior for nonlinear system as compared to FLC and any other conventional controllers. It was robust, stable and accurate over complete range of operation. Also, the logic is simple, versatile and powerful. Ireneus and Sudchai (2010) presented a nonlinear experimental pH neutralization plant which was controlled using a neural networks based approximate predictive control (APC) strategy. First closed-loop identification was performed, further, using neural networks, a black-box modeling of the experimental plant was conducted. Then the APC was realized, where a linear model of the plant was extracted at each sampling period from the neural network model. This strategy was used to control the experimental neutralization plant for set point tracking and disturbance rejection. To deal with the pH neutralization process in a PID controller based on a neural network model was presented, which used a GA to tune the parameters of the PID controller off-line on the nonlinear neural network model. In this problem an adaptive nonlinear control strategy was used.

Most process plants generate a waste water effluent that must be neutralized prior to discharge or reuse. Consequently, pH control is needed in just about every process plant, and yet a large percentage of pH loops perform poorly. Results are inferior product quality, environmental pollution, and material waste. With ever increasing pressure to improve plant efficiency and tighter regulations in environmental protection, effective and continuous pH control is highly desirable. However, implementing a pH system is like putting a puzzle together. It will only work when all the components are in place. The pH puzzle includes effective pH probes, actuators, and controllers. While various pH probes and actuators for pH control are available, commercial adaptive pH controllers are still in demand. The challenge is to provide a controller that is able to deal with large nonlinear gain changes in the pH loop. It will be useful for not only waste water neutralization, but also chemical concentration control, since concentration is a key quality variable. In these circumstances, conventional linear controllers no longer provide adequate and achievable control performance over the whole operating range. Thus,

designing a nonlinear controller which is robust in terms of its performance for different operating conditions is essential.

There is also increasing interest in the potential of intelligent control methods for process applications. Intelligent control can be described as a control approach or solution that tries to imitate important characteristics of the human way of thinking, especially in terms of decision making processes and uncertainty. It is also a term that is commonly used to describe most forms of control systems that are based on artificial neural networks (ANN) or fuzzy logic (FL). The central theme of this research concerns problems of system modeling, control system development, implementation and testing for a specific application which involves a pH neutralization process. The control of a pH neutralization process presents a significant challenge due to the time-varying and highly nonlinear dynamic characteristics of the process.

In practice, most pH loops are in a bang-bang type of control with pumps cycling on and off, which causes large oscillations. Since acid and caustic neutralize each other, overdosing acid and caustic is prohibitively expensive. Statistics show that a poorly controlled pH process can cost tens of thousands of dollars in chemical usage each month, not counting the penalties imposed by violating environmental protection agency or local government discharge codes. To avoid these difficulties, a new and efficient control system has to be designed with the help of latest computer tools.

THE pH PROCESS: PROBLEM DESCRIPTION

The process consists of a strong acid flowing into a CSTR which is thoroughly mixed with a strong base. As shown in Figure 1 the CSTR has two input streams, one containing sodium hydroxide (NaOH) and the other containing hydrochloric acid (HCl) for a strong acid – strong base (SASB)

Figure 1. The schematic diagram of a pH neutralization process CSTR

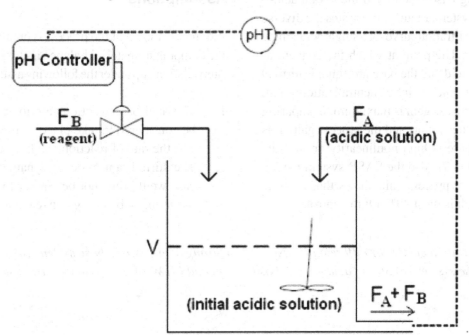

system. Let F_A and F_B be the flow rates of the acid and the reagent streams respectively and C_A and C_B be the corresponding concentrations. The volume of the total solution in the CSTR is denoted as V.

The flow rate and concentration changes of the acid are taken into account as the disturbances. The concentration of the base, C_B is kept constant to make the system simpler. The pH measurement is done on the outlet flow. A controller is to be designed to control the feed flow rate of the base, so as to neutralize the pH value for any change in the flow rate and concentration of the acid flow. The sum of F_A and F_B is the flow rate of the outlet stream.

Modeling of the pH Process

The principle of physio-chemical modelling of a pH process was first stated by Thomas et al., (1972). They used a weak acid – strong base model (WASB) for the pH process simulation. Gustafsson

and Waller (1983) developed a reaction invariant pH process formulation which could be used for practical processes.

Titration Curves

Titration curves provide information about acids and bases in addition to analyzing the quantity that is present. They can provide information about the strength of the acid or base, the number of ionizable groups, ionization and hydrolysis constants, and molecular weights. A titration curve is a graph of pH vs. volume of the acid and/or base added. Because of the logarithmic nonlinearity, it is possible for the gain of a pH process to change by as much as a factor of 10 per pH unit. Based on the type of acid-base mixture and titration curve characteristics, there are four types of pH systems. The weak acid – weak base system and the strong acid – weak base systems are basically easier to control whereas it is difficult to control the strong acid – strong base system and the strong acid – weak base system. Figure 2 illustrates the diverse shapes of the titration curve for a single acid/single base system. The point at which the concentrations of the acid and the base are equal is termed as the equivalence point or neutralization point, where the process gain is maximum. Comparing the equivalence points and the process gain, it is clear that there is high nonlinearity around the value of pH = 7. Also the SASB system having the maximum process gain shows that it is the system which is most difficult to control.

Assumptions

A dynamic model of the process is obtained from the component material balance and the equilibrium relationship under the following assumptions:

1. The acid-base reactions are ionic and can be considered to take place, with the result that the rate of reaction can be considered. The stirred tank process dynamics in this case would thus not be similar to the case of mixing or blending non reacting streams.

Figure 2. Titration curves for different pH systems: (a) Strong acid – strong base system, (b) Weak acid – strong base system, (c) Strong acid – weak base system and (d) Weak acid – weak base system

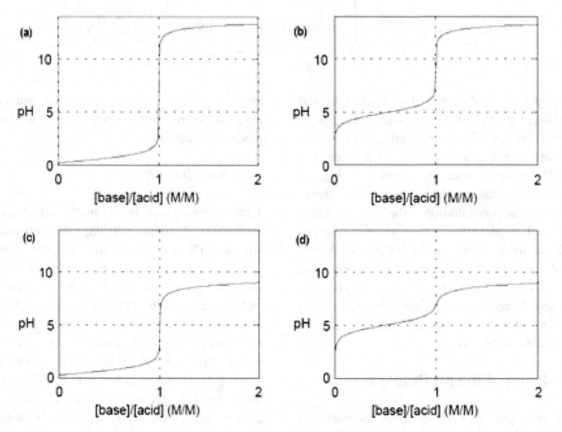

2. The system is in an ideal condition without any pollutant influence.
3. Perfect mixing.
4. No valve dynamics. Usually, the valve dynamics are much faster than the process dynamics and, thus, can be ignored.
5. The volume of the reacting mixture in the tank is constant and equal to V.

STRONG ACID: STRONG BASE SYSTEM MODELING

Consider a process stream of strong acid, HCl entering into a CSTR and is neutralized by a strong base, NaOH. The process equation is given by

$$\dot{x} = \left(\frac{F_A}{V}\right)x - \frac{1}{V}F_B(x + C_B) + \left(\frac{F_A}{V}\right)C_A \quad (1)$$

where, x is the deviation of pH from neutrality and x dot is the time derivative of deviation of pH from neutrality. The pH value y and the deviation of pH from neutrality are related by the nonlinear equation:

$$x(t) = 10^{-y(t)} - 10^{y(t)}K_w \quad (2)$$

where K_w, the water equilibrium constant $= 10^{-14}$. The other variables denote the same parameters as in a WASB system. The output equation is

$$h(x, y) = x + 10^{y-14} - 10^{-y} = 0 \quad (3)$$

Design of Controllers

We can design conventional linear controllers like PI and PID for pH neutralization process. For that, the titration curve is divided into four zones with nominal operating points at pH 5, 7, 9 and 11. The system is approximated as a first order in each zone and the process parameters are evaluated from simulation results on the nonlinear system from the transient response for step change in base flow rate [Thomas et al., 1972]. Hence a PI or PID controller designed for a particular zone cannot be used for the pH range which does not belong to that zone.

Adaptive Control

Figure 3 shows the structure of one of our proposed controller. It consists of the CSTR process, reference model and the controller block. The desired behavior of the closed loop system is specified by a reference model. The parameters of the controller are adjusted based on the error between the output of the closed-loop system and the reference model. The control objective is to track the reference model output, such that the closed-loop system will provide the neutralized pH value for any disturbance.

Figure 3. The block diagram of a model reference adaptive pH control

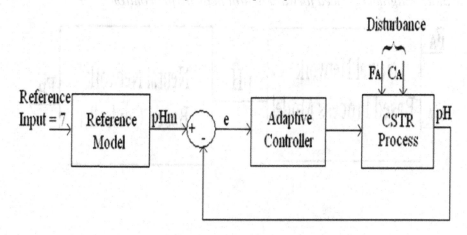

Here the reference input is pH = 7 for neutralization, *pHm* is the pH value calculated from the reference model. The error, *e* is fed to the adaptive controller and the controller forces the error vector to become zero. If the error is zero, it means the process tracks the reference model output.

Neural Network Control

The feed forward neural network (NN) controller can be implemented as shown in Figure 4. The control objective is to achieve the pH neutralization by employing two networks, one to predict the reactor pH based on the acid flow rate and acid concentration, while the other network predict the base flow rate required to bring the pH value to 7.

The two networks were trained using the NN tool box in MATLAB. The algorithm used for training is Levenberg - Marquardt back propagation algorithm. Both the neural networks use 1 hidden layer comprising of 20 neurons.

Parameter Values

The disturbances applied and other parameters for the open loop and closed loop control are given in Table 1.

The simulation was run for 200 seconds as indicated in the Table 1. The base flow rate is the manipulated variable and its value is provided by the corresponding controllers.

Table 1. CSTR process parameters

Symbol	Parameter	Value
V	CSTR liquid volume	5 l
F_A	Acid flow rate	0 - 0.501 l/s
F_B	Base flow rate	Manipulated variable
C_A	Acid concentration	0-0.501 M
C_B	Base concentration	0.2 M
K_W	Water dissociation constant	10^{-14}
t	Simulation time	200 s

Simulation Results

In order to plot the titration curve, the base flow rate and the base concentration are held constant in the open loop system. Both the acid flow rate and concentration are varied from 0 – 0.5 range of values. Then the curve is obtained by plotting the pH value along the y axis and the acid flow rate along the x axis as in Figure 5. Since the base flow rate is constant and the acid flow rate is varied from a minimum value to maximum, the initial pH level lies along the base region (close to pH 14) and goes on decreasing till the acidic region (close to pH 1).

For the simulation purpose, a step disturbance is applied to both the acid flow rate and the acid concentration. The disturbances acid flow rate and the acid concentration are shown in Figures 6 and 7 respectively.

Figure 4. The block diagram of a feed forward neural network pH control

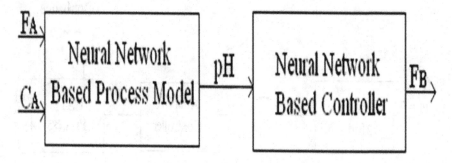

Figure 5. The titration curve for the SASB system for acid flow variation

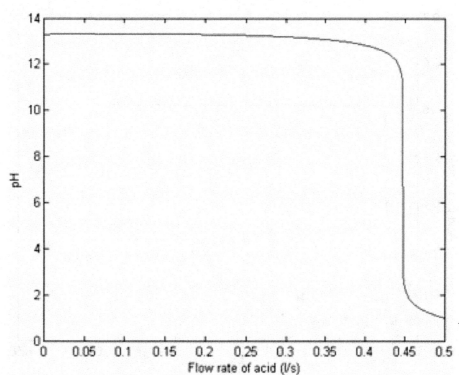

Figure 6. The step disturbance applied to the acid flow rate

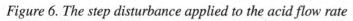

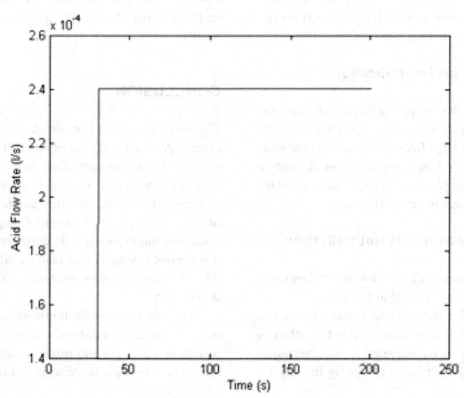

Figure 7. The step disturbance applied to the acid concentration

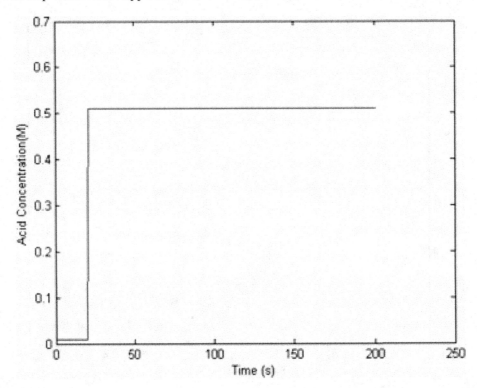

Since the process gain at neutralization point is very high, even a small change in acid flow rate will affect the neutralization process.

Adaptive pH Neutralization

Figure 8 shows the pH variation with time after the CSTR process is adaptively controlled. We can observe large fluctuations at the initial point of time which shows the time lag for the neutralization of the pH value. If the disturbance is too high it requires more time to settle.

Neural Network pH Neutralization

The pH change with time for an NN controlled CSTR process is plotted in Figure 9.

The NN controller can identify the disturbances at the initial stage itself before affecting the plant. Also it is quick reacting since the random fluctuations which were exhibited by the adaptive

controller are removed. More accurate training on the NN controller can produce more accurate results.

CONCLUSION

This work emphasizes on simulation based pH control. A strong acid – strong base pH process is controlled using two controllers: model reference adaptive control and neural network control. In both cases the pH value is settled around the value of 7.0 with very small deviation. Comparison of both controllers reveal that the design of the adaptive control is a bit tedious than the NN control. Also the cost of implementation of NN control will be very less.

Typically, pH neutralization plant can be found in a wide range of industries such as waste water treatment, oil & gas and petrochemicals. It is a known fact that a pH process plant of this kind is

Figure 8. The pH vs. time graph of the adaptive controlled SASB system

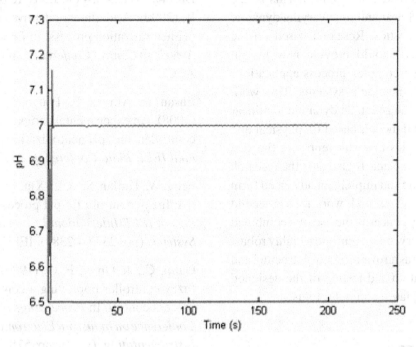

Figure 9. The pH vs. time graph of the NN controlled SASB system

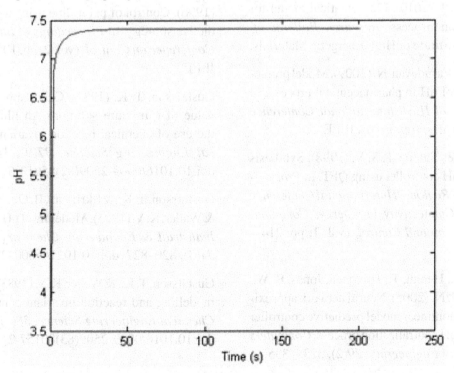

very difficult to model and control. This is due to its highly nonlinear and time varying dynamic process characteristics. Research based on the pH process plant should provide new insight of value for other complex process applications involving highly nonlinear systems. This work helps to provide an adequate dynamic nonlinear pH neutralization model, based on physical and chemical principles that can represent the real pH neutralization plant. It also aids the research to design, develop and implement advanced form of controllers. The research work for the second objective mainly concerns the use of a combined feedback/feed forward system and a highly robust feedback system as an overall control structure and the implementation and testing of the designed controller using latest computer tools.

REFERENCES

Ahmmed, S. I. (2010). Mathematical model for neutralization process. *Research Bulletin of. Australian Institute of High Energetic Materials.*

Balaji, V., & Vasudevan, N. (2009). Model predictive control of pH in pharmaceutical process. In *Proceedings of IEEE International Conference on Mechatronics,* (pp. 1 – 6). IEEE.

Barve, J. J., & Nataraj, P. S. V. (1998). Synthesis of a robust pH controller using QFT. In *Proceedings of IEEE Region 10 International Conference on Global Connectivity in Energy, Computer, Communication and Control,* (vol. 1, pp. 214 – 217). IEEE.

Bernt, M. A., Hannu, T., Toivonen, Jonas, B. W., & Rasmus H. N. (2005). Neural network approximation of a nonlinear model predictive controller applied to a pH neutralization process. *Computers and Chemical Engineering, 29*(2), 323 – 335.

Dhruba, S. D., Ai-Poh, L., & Krishnaswamy, P. R. (2000). A nonlinear adaptive controller for a pH neutralization process. In *Proceedings of the American Control Conference,* (pp. 2250 – 2254). ACC.

Ehsan, P., Alireza, F., Pouya, B., & Ali, K. S. (2008). An experimental comparison of adaptive controllers on a pH neutralization pilot plant. *Annual IEEE India Conference, 2*, 377 – 382.

Feng, W., Huilan, S., & Li-Xin, W. (2006). Adaptive fuzzy control of a pH process. In *Proceedings of IEEE International Conference on Fuzzy Systems,* (pp. 2377 – 2384). IEEE.

Galip, C., & Omer, F. O. (1996). An adaptive fuzzy controller improving a control system for process control. In *Proceedings of International Conference on Industrial Electronics, Control and Instrumentation,* (vol. 1, pp. 578 – 583). IEEE.

Gomm, J. B., Doherty, S. K., & Williams, D. (1996). Control of pH in-line using a neural predictive strategy. In *Proceedings of International Conference on Control,* (vol. 2, pp. 1058 – 1063). IEEE.

Gustafsson, T. K. (1982). Calculation of the pH value of a mixture solutions-An illustration of the use of chemical reaction invariants. *Chemical Engineering Science, 37*(9), 1419–1421. doi:10.1016/0009-2509(82)85013-6

Gustafsson, T. K., & Skrifvars, B. O., Sandstroem, & Waller, K. V. (1995). Modeling of pH for control. *Industrial & Engineering Chemistry Research, 34*(3), 820–827. doi:10.1021/ie00042a014

Gustafsson, T. K., & Waller, K. V. (1983). Dynamic modelling and reaction invariant control of pH. *Chemical Engineering Science, 38*(3), 389–398. doi:10.1016/0009-2509(83)80157-2

Gustafsson, T. K., & Waller, K. V. (1992). Nonlinear and adaptive control of pH. *Industrial & Engineering Chemistry Research*, *31*(12), 2681–2693. doi:10.1021/ie00012a009

Henson, M. A., & Seborg, D. E. (1994). Adaptive nonlinear control of a pH neutralization process. *IEEE Transactions on Control Systems Technology*, *2*(3), 169–182. doi:10.1109/87.317975

Hermansson, A. W., Syafiie, S., & Mohd Noor, S. B. (2010). Multiple model predictive control of nonlinear pH neutralization system. In *Proceedings of IEEE International Conference on Industrial Engineering and Engineering Management*, (pp. 301 – 304). IEEE.

Hong, T., Morris, A. J., Karim, M. N., Zhang, J., & Luo, W. (1996). Nonlinear control of a wastewater pH neutralisation process using adaptive NARX models. *IEEE International Conference on Systems, Man, and Cybernetics*, *2*, 911 – 916.

Ireneus, W., & Sudchai, B. (2010). *Modeling and control of an experimental pH neutralization plant using neural networks based approximate predictive control*. Academic Press.

Jin-Yong, C., & Rhinehart, R. R. (1987). Internal adaptive-model control of waste water pH. In *Proceedings of IEEE American Control Conference*, (pp. 2084 –2089). IEEE.

Karr, C. L., & Gentry, E. J. (1993). Fuzzy control of pH using genetic algorithms. *IEEE Transactions on Fuzzy Systems*, *1*(1), 46–53. doi:10.1109/TFUZZ.1993.390283

Kelkar, B., & Postlethwaite, B. (1994). Study of pH control process using fuzzy modeling. *International Conference on Control*, *1*, 272 – 275.

Li, Z., & Ning, W. (2010). Double neuron model-free control for pH processes. In *Proceedings of Chinese Control and Decision Conference*, (pp. 2867 – 2871). IEEE.

Lou, H., & Dai, W. (2008). A novel non-linear model predictive controller based on minimal resource allocation network and its application in CSTR pH process. In *Proceedings of the 7th World Congress on Intelligent Control and Automation*, (pp. 5672 – 5676). IEEE.

Manuel, A., Duarte-Mermoud, Franklin, A. R., & Ricardo, P. (2002). Experimental evaluation of combined model reference adaptive controller in a pH regulation process. *International Journal of Adaptive Control and Signal Processing*, *16*, 85–106. doi:10.1002/acs.674

Martin, J. W., Ralph, S., Adrian, G., Winfried, S., & Essameddin, B. (2009). On setting-up a portable low-cost real-time control system for research and teaching with application to bioprocess pH control. In *Proceedings of IEEE Control Applications and Intelligent Control*, (pp. 1631 – 1636). IEEE.

Nayeem, N. K., & Geoff, W. (2003). Non-linear model reference control of pH process: An experimental study. In *Proceedings 15th European Simulation Symposium*. IEEE.

Nie, J., Loh, A. P., & Hang, C. C. (1996). Modeling pH neutralization processes using fuzzy-neural approaches. *Fuzzy Sets and Systems*, *78*(1), 5–22. doi:10.1016/0165-0114(95)00118-2

Pajunen, G. A. (1987). Comparison of linear and nonlinear adaptive control of pH process. *IEEE Control Systems Magazine*, *7*(1), 39–44. doi:10.1109/MCS.1987.1105238

Parekh, M., Desai, M., Li, H., & Rhinehart, R. R. (1994). In-line control of nonlinear pH neutralization based on fuzzy logic. *IEEE Transactions on Components Packaging & Manufacturing Technology Part A, 17*(2), 192–201. doi:10.1109/95.296400

Qinghui, W., & Zongze, C. (2010). Nonlinear compensator based PI controller for pH neutralization reaction process. In *Proceedings of Second International Conference on Industrial and Information Systems,* (vol. 2, pp. 71 – 74). IEEE.

Ranganath, M., & Elamin, E. K. (2003). Fuzzy logic control of a pH neutralization process. In *Proceedings of the 2003 10th IEEE International Conference on Electronics, Circuits and Systems,* (vol. 3, pp. 1066 – 1069). IEEE.

Sandra, J. N., Ahmet, P., & Jose, A. R. (1999). Application of Wiener model predictive control (WMPC) to a pH neutralization experiment. *IEEE Transactions on Control Systems Technology, 7*(4), 437–445. doi:10.1109/87.772159

Shahin, S., Mohammad, S., & Ali, N. (2009). Adaptive nonlinear control of pH neutralization processes using fuzzy approximators. *Control Engineering Practice, 17*(11), 1329–1337. doi:10.1016/j.conengprac.2009.06.007

Shinskey, F. G. (1996). *Process control systems: Application, design and tuning* (4th ed.). New York: McGraw-Hill.

Simon, O., & Igor, S. (2007). Continuous-time wiener-model predictive control of a pH process. In *Proceedings of 29th International Conference on Information Technology Interfaces,* (pp. 771 – 776). IEEE.

Sonali, N., & Bodhe, G. L. (2009). Design and implementation of real time neuro-fuzzy based pH controller. In *Proceedings of Second International Conference on Emerging Trends in Engineering and Technology,* (pp. 946 – 952). IEEE.

Syafiie, S., Tadeo, F., & Martinez, E. (2009). Q(A) learning technique for pH control. In *Proceedings of IEEE International Conference on Industrial Engineering and Engineering Management,* (pp. 712 – 716). IEEE.

Thomas, J. M., Elmer, H. S. U., & Lowenthal, S. (1972). Dynamics of pH in controlled stirred tank reactor. *Industrial & Engineering Chemistry Process Design and Development, 11*(1), 68–70. doi:10.1021/i260041a013

Valarmathi, K., Kanmani, J., Devaraj, D., & Radhakrishnan, T. K. (2007). Hybrid GA fuzzy controller for pH process. In *Proceedings of International Conference on Computational Intelligence and Multimedia Applications,* (pp. 13 – 18). IEEE.

Waller, K. V., & Gustafsson, T. K. (1983). Fundamental properties of continuous pH control. *ISA Transactions, 22*(1), 25–34.

Woei, W. T., Fengwei, L. U., & Ai-Poh, L. (2001). An application of genetic algorithm for designing a Wiener-model controller to regulate the pH value in a pilot plant. *Proceedings of the Congress on Evolutionary Computation, 2,* 1055 – 1061.

Wright, R. A. (1991). Nonlinear control of pH processes using the strong acid equivalent. *Industrial & Engineering Chemistry Research, 30*(7), 1561–1572. doi:10.1021/ie00055a022

Wright, R. A., Soroush, M., & Kravaris, C. (1991). Strong acid equivalent control of pH processes: An experimental study. *Industrial & Engineering Chemistry Research*, *30*(11), 2437–2444. doi:10.1021/ie00059a012

Xie, S. (2010). Research about fuzzy-PID control method of pH value in chemical industry process. In *Proceedings of International Conference on Electrical and Control Engineering*, (pp. 1554 – 1557). IEEE.

Zeybek, Z., & Alpbaz, M. (2005). Fuzzy-dynamic matrix pH control for treatment of dye waste water plant. In *Proceedings of Sixth International Conference on Computational Intelligence and Multimedia Applications*, (pp. 118 – 123). IEEE.

Zhandong, Y., & Jiangtao, X. (2005). Adaptive singularity-free controller by neural compensation for pH process in alkali-terminal tank of polyacrylonitrile. In *Proceedings of International Conference on Neural Networks and Brain*, (vol. 3, pp. 1836 – 1839). IEEE.

KEY TERMS AND DEFINITIONS

Adaptive: Changing in order to deal with new situations.

Artificial Neural Network: The use of computing system that is designed to think and work in the same way as the human brain.

pH Control: pH is defined as the decimal logarithm of the reciprocal of the hydrogen ion activity in a solution. pH control is the ability to limit the acidity or alkalinity of a substance as desired in the range of 0 to 14.

Strong Acid – Strong Base System: A strong acid is one that completely dissociates in solution by losing one proton. A strong base is one that completely dissociates in water into the cation and hydroxide ion.

Chapter 18

A Shannon–Like Solution for the Fundamental Equation of Information Science

Alexandre de Castro

Embrapa Agriculture Informatics, Brazilian Agricultural Research Corporation, Brazil

ABSTRACT

In a seminal paper published in the early 1980s titled "Information Technology and the Science of Information," Bertram C. Brookes theorized that a Shannon-Hartley's logarithmic-like measure could be applied to both information and recipient knowledge structure in order to satisfy his "Fundamental Equation of Information Science." To date, this idea has remained almost forgotten, but, in what follows, the authors introduce a novel quantitative approach that shows that a Shannon-Hartley's log-like model can represent a feasible solution for the cognitive process of retention of information described by Brookes. They also show that if, and only if, the amount of information approaches 1 bit, the "Fundamental Equation" can be considered an equality in stricto sensu, as Brookes required.

INTRODUCTION

In the last few years, several studies in the literature have addressed information and knowledge from the concepts proposed by Brookes (Brookes, 1981; Cole, 2011; Bawden, 2011; Castro, 2013a; Castro, 2013b). After more than three decades, Brookes' contributions to Information Science are indisputable. Numerous updates have been based on his

equality for the information-knowledge duality, widely known as the Fundamental Equation of Information Science (Cole, 2011).

Brookes' contributions to foundations of information science are indisputable, and numerous works have been based on his representational model for the knowledge-information duality. This underlying equation to cognitive perceptual behavior is commonly defined as

DOI: 10.4018/978-1-4666-4936-1.ch018

$$K(S) + I = K(S + \Delta S)$$

where a knowledge framework, $K(S)$, is changed into an altered structure, $K(S + \Delta S)$, by an input of information, I, being ΔS an indicator of the effect of the modification (Brookes, 1981; Cole, 2011; Bawden, 2011).

Notably, Brookes' work provides a quantitative sharp bias, albeit a seldom examined from this viewpoint. Most of the works found in the literature refer to Equation Fundamental of Information Science merely how a pseudo-mathematical shorthand description of knowledge transformation. However, in a pioneering paper published in the early 1980's and entitled "Information technology and the science of information", Brookes suggested outright that his representational equation could be treated how a quantitative problem, so much so that he even probed, in field of what he called perspective space, a possible logarithmic solution similar to Shannon-Hartley's measure (Brookes,1981).

That nontrivial idea has been long forgotten, but in a recent paper, Bawden (2011) suggested that a model based on the Power Law (PL) (Newman, 2005; Clauset et al., 2009) could be used to account the I input term in the Brookes equality. Bawden's hypothesis takes into account that the input, I, should not be treated as a number, but as a function (Bawden, 2011). This author maintains the following: "We do not know, a priori, what this function is; not even its general nature. But we may take an educated guess that the most likely form of such a function would be that of a Power Law. This seems likely, simply because Power Laws are very commonly found in many aspects of the biological and social domains; it is difficult to see any rationale for choosing any other form of function".

Inspired by Brookes' quest for an analytics solution that satisfies the $\Delta K = I$ equality, we show in this piece that a first-order ordinary differential equation based on premises of meaningful learning converges accurately to a Shannon-Hartley's log-like model for the I input, as Brookes (1981) required. This continuous-time log-measure, once treated as an infinite sum of terms calculated from the values of the I function's derivatives, exhibits a behavior how Power Law, according to Bawden's hypothesis.

THEORETICAL BACKGROUND

Based on Brookes' premises, information (an outside stimulus) is considered as an element that provokes changes in the cognitive structure (framework) of an individual (Neill & Brookes, 1982; Todd, 1994; Todd, 1999; Cornelius, 2002; Capurro & Hjorland, 2003; Bawden, 2008). Information is received by an individual as a code that can be interpreted/assimilated according to an idiosyncratic affinity model (matching), i.e., an individual produces knowledge only when receiving stimuli that make sense to them (Cognitive-Meaningful Learning Theory) (Ausubel, 1963; Ausubel, 1978; Novak & Mosunda, 1991; Wadsworth, 2003; Wadsworth, 2004;Novak, 2010).

This matching can be mathematically translated using an approach based on the well-known Law of Mass Action (LMA), which is widely used by physicists, mathematicians, and theoretical biologists to quantitatively describe the relationships between biological entities (Jong, 1995;Knell et al.,1996; Devaney et al., 2004; Adleman et al. 2008; Bacaër, 2011).

The LMA originated in chemical equilibrium analysis, Guldberg-Waage Law (Adleman et al. 2008), where the reaction speed is proportional to the product of the concentrations of the reactants. The implementation of this approach in epidemiology, for example, is based on the assumption that infectious agents interact mathematically with susceptible populations by means of multiplicative operation. In our approach, the information and cognitive state are treated as analogous to the infectious agent and the susceptible entity of epidemiological modeling.

A QUANTITATVE TREATMENT FOR ΔI

Considering Brookes' variables and a LMA-based approach, a change rate in the cognitive structure can be defined, in a first approximation:

$$\frac{dS}{dt} \alpha S(\bar{\sigma}, t) \Delta I(\sigma, t),$$

where

$$S(\bar{\sigma}, t) = S(\bar{\sigma})$$

is the initial framework into a short range time, and dS is a small change (shift) in the cognitive structure provoked by a small bit of information (or bit of knowledge, according to Brookes' definition), $dI(\sigma)$. The change in the cognitive structure is proportional to the product (interaction) of a bit of information and the initial framework (the *status quo*). This change is dependent on the degree of affinity between the external information and the individual. In our approach, the information term $\Delta I(\sigma)$ is characterized by a shape σ (e.g. a binary string) that represents distinct outside stimuli, and the information-framework affinity (matching) is represented by the complementarity between σ and $\bar{\sigma}$ [Castro, 2006; Castro, 2009).

Let $\Delta I(\sigma)$ be a matching (interaction) with $S(\bar{\sigma})$, provoking a cognitive structure change in accordance with both the Cognitive-Meaningful Learning Theory and the assimilation quantitative process proposed by Wadsworth (2003,2004).

In this case – when there is matching between σ and $\bar{\sigma}$ – a change rate in the cognitive structure can be mathematically modeled by

$$\frac{dS}{dt} \alpha S \Delta I$$

or by rearranging

$$S \, \Delta I \, dt = \mu(S,I) \, dS$$

where $\mu(S,t)$ is a proportionality parameter that depends on the individual's instantaneous cognitive structure.

In a short time range, it is possible to regard

$$\mu(S,t) \overset{def}{=} \mu(\text{constant})$$

Integrating ΔI over time, we obtain

$$\int_{\Delta t} \Delta I dt = \mu \int_{S}^{S+\Delta S} \frac{dS}{S}$$

Considering Brookes' premises, a bit of knowledge (information) should occur in a short time range. Thus, it is expected that , in a time range equal to unity.

Consequently:

$$\Delta I \int_{t}^{t+1} dt = \mu \int_{S}^{S+\Delta S} \frac{dS}{S}$$

This equation can be rewritten as

$$\Delta I = \mu \ln(\frac{S + \Delta S}{S}) = \mu \ln(1 + \frac{\Delta S}{S})$$

or rearranging:

$$\Delta I = \ln(1 + \frac{\Delta S}{S})^{\mu}$$

where ΔI is the information per unit time, and in our approach, $\frac{\Delta S}{S}$ is a mathematical representation of the relative cognitive change. The $\frac{\Delta S}{S}$ term depends on both the amount of information assimilated and the characteristics of the individual's cognitive framework. The measurement of the relative cognitive change has also been proposed by Murray et al. (2011).

This latter logarithmic equation is a Boltzmann-Planck entropy-like expression (Downarowicz, 2011), and can be expanded by a Taylor-Maclaurin series (Larson et at., 2008):

$$\Delta I = \mu \ln(1 + \frac{\Delta S}{S}) = \mu \sum_{n=1}^{\infty} \frac{1}{n}(-1)^{n+1}(\frac{\Delta S}{S})^{n}$$

where n denotes the nth term in sequence.

Thus, the equation for ΔI can be rewritten as follows:

$$\Delta I = \mu \frac{\Delta S}{S} - \frac{\mu}{2}(\frac{\Delta S}{S})^{2} + \frac{\mu}{3}(\frac{\Delta S}{S})^{3} + O(\frac{\Delta S}{S})^{4}$$

Figure 1(a) shows the natural logarithmic curve. The Taylor-Maclaurin approximation for ΔI converges to the logarithmic function only in the interval:

Figure 1. Logarithmic curve (a) for the $1 + \Delta S / S$ argument. In (b), a pictorial representation of the cognitive shift is presented.

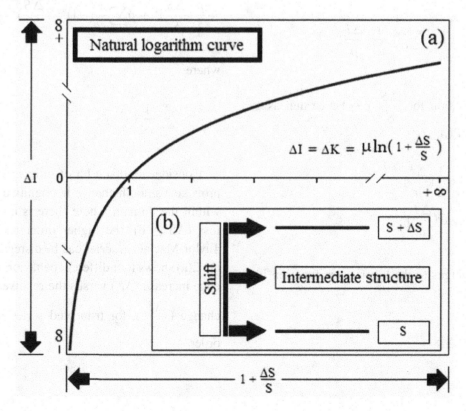

$$-1 < \frac{\Delta S}{S} \leq 1$$

outside this interval, the higher degree Taylor-Maclaurin polynomials are worse approximations of the function.

If the ΔS term in the Brookes' equation represents an internal shift in the cognitive structure upwards or downwards from an initial frame or intermediate structure (see Figure 1(b)), the effect a bit of information (ΔI) on the knowledge framework depends on the individual. Then, the relative cognitive change can be mathematically represented by:

$$\frac{\Delta I}{\mu} = \ln(1 + \frac{\Delta S}{S}) \rightarrow \frac{\Delta S}{S} = e^{\frac{\Delta I}{\mu}} - 1$$

which, using the Taylor-Maclaurin expansion, leads to the relative shift (percentage gain) in the cognitive structure:

$$\frac{\Delta S}{S} = e^{\frac{\Delta I}{\mu}} - 1 = \sum_{n=1}^{\infty} \frac{1}{n!} (\frac{\Delta I}{\mu})^n$$

This equation for $\frac{\Delta S}{S}$ can be written as a power law (PL):

$$\frac{\Delta S}{S} = \frac{\Delta I}{\mu} + \frac{1}{2} (\frac{\Delta I}{\mu})^2 + \frac{1}{3} (\frac{\Delta I}{\mu})^3 + O(\frac{\Delta I}{\mu})^4$$

which converges to the logarithmic function in the interval

$$-\infty < \frac{\Delta I}{\mu} \leq \infty$$

Finally, the Brookes' equality

$$K(S) + \Delta I = K(S + \Delta S)$$

can be written as:

$$K(S) + \ln(1 + \frac{\Delta S}{S})^{\mu} = K(S + \Delta S)$$

or in Power Law (PL) form proposed by Bawden (2011):

$$K(S) + \mu \frac{\Delta S}{S} - \frac{\mu}{2} (\frac{\Delta S}{S})^2 + \frac{\mu}{3} (\frac{\Delta S}{S})^3 + O(\frac{\Delta S}{S})^4 = K(S + \Delta S)$$

or

$$\Delta K = \mu \frac{\Delta S}{S} - \frac{\mu}{2} (\frac{\Delta S}{S})^2 + \frac{\mu}{3} (\frac{\Delta S}{S})^3 + \frac{\mu}{4} (\frac{\Delta S}{S})^4 + \mu \sum_{n=S}^{\infty} \frac{1}{n} (-1)^{n+1} (\frac{\Delta S}{S})^n$$

where

$$\frac{\Delta S}{S} = \sum_{n=1}^{\infty} \frac{1}{n!} (\frac{\Delta I}{\mu})^n$$

Considering that a bit of information should provoke a smooth change in cognitive structure, within the domain where there is no cognitive loss ($\Delta S \geq 0$), the higher order terms in the Taylor-Maclaurin series can be disregarded. Figure 2(a) shows four different behaviors of knowledge increase (ΔK) versus the relative cognitive change ($\frac{\Delta S}{S}$), for truncated series' until 4th-order.

Figure 2. Linear and nonlinear curves (a) versus $\Delta S / S$. In (b), a pictorial frame for knowledge acquisition.

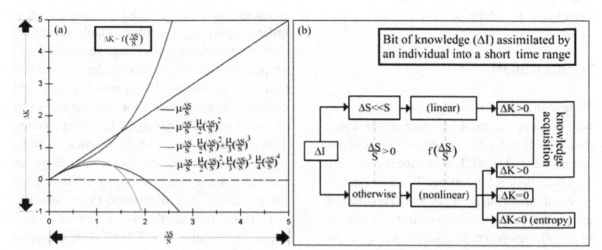

It is possible to note from Fig. 2(a) that an information amount which produces a small change in cognitive structure (smooth change) causes a linear knowledge increase. Yet for major relative cognitive changes, nonlinear behaviors arise because the higher order terms should be considered in Taylor-Maclaurin sequence. The linear behavior shows that, in a small time range, small changes in cognitive structure lead to a smooth assimilation of information and to a monotonic acquisition of knowledge, therefore producing a more uniform learning. However, abrupt cognitive changes can lead to nontrivial behaviors where, even though there exist positive cognitive change, entropy (disorder) increases ($\Delta K < 0$), or there is no knowledge acquisition ($\Delta K = 0$). These results indicate that in a small time range a better knowledge acquisition occurs when there are small cognitive changes. A scheme for knowledge acquisition is presented in Fig. 2(b). This pictorial framework shows that the same bit of information can provoke both linear and nonlinear behavior.

Recently, Jansen and Rieh (2010) wrote the following: "Depending on the situation, information has a physical aspect, a cognitive aspect, or an affective aspect. Being influenced by Shannon (1948), information from a physical view involves little or no cognitive processing". More recently, Cole [4] stated the following "In information science, information use is firmly linked to information (versus an objective notion of information), which Brookes (1981) defined in his fundamental equation of information science as that which modifies a user's knowledge structure. Information and knowledge in Brookes' equation are measured in the same units and are therefore of the same kind". In this sense, Bawden (2011) also suggests that a quantitative treatment for information can be done. In Bawden's words: "Brookes' equation, which has hitherto been regarded as a kind of non-mathematical shorthand description of information use, is extended so as to show the qualitative pattern of information access. Information inputs are represented by a simple power law, and changes in knowledge structure by possible changes to a simple mental map. The resulting pattern shows seven forms of information input and three forms of change in knowledge structure, giving 21 categories overall. These have the potential for use as an explanatory tool and taxonomy for studying and summarizing information behavior, and offer the possibility of being developed into more sophisticated and quantitative treatments".

CONCLUSION

We here presented a possible quantitative treatment for information, in accordance with a suggestion by Bawden [5], combining physical and cognitive aspects [30]. This treatment shows that there is a relationship between Brookes' qualitative equation and Shannon's quantitative equation, and that this relationship can indicate the similarity of both viewpoints. In conclusion, a quantitative treatment for the information and cognitive approach based on Law of Mass Action (LMA) leads to a Boltzmann-Planck entropy-like model (Shannon, 1948; Downarowicz, 2011; Gray, 2011), which results in a Power Law (PL)-like quantitative expression for ΔI, according to a hypothesis recently published by Bawden (2011). Our calculations show that in the Brookes' equation, when a bit of information ($\Delta I > 0$) is assimilated by the cognitive structure of an individual, a potential cognitive gain ($\Delta S > 0$) is induced, in accordance with Cognitive-Meaningful Learning Theory. Nevertheless, if $\Delta I \leq 0$, it is expected, theoretically, that no significant cognitive shift occurs, although the framework can experience a potential disorganization (anomalous state) when $\Delta I < 0$. Such inferences are consistent with the Shannon entropy for a definition of measurable information. Based on the Boltzmann-Plank entropy, the Shannon entropy is the amount of information about an object that corresponds to the number of binary decisions that are necessary to identify it. Thus, the amount of information contained in an observed phenomenon is equal to the amount of disorganization (entropy) that can be eliminated by restructuring the system. The process of information gain ($\Delta K > 0$) proceeds in the opposite direction of the process of increasing entropy ($\Delta I < 0$). Therefore, information gain is a process of entropy reduction, a process of increasing order: $S + \Delta S > S$. However, in order to apply the Boltzmann-Plank entropy for the communication processing, Shannon (1948) proposed a logarithmic measure for the information without relating it to a possible structural cognitive change, which is the fundamental focus of the Cognitive-Meaningful Learning Theory. Taking into account Von Neumann's analysis, which shows that the change in knowledge (or information) can be quantitatively tied to entropy (Stapp, 2007), our Boltzmann-Planck-like entropy model suggests that, consistent with a first approximation approach (LMA), there is a direct relationship between the relative cognitive change ($\dfrac{\Delta S}{S}$) and an outside stimulus (information). This relationship leads to a logarithmic expression for knowledge,

$$K(S) + \ln(1 + \frac{\Delta S}{S})^{\mu} = K(S + \Delta S)$$

as being a possible "solution" for the Brookes' equation in limit where $K(S)$ approaches 1 bit (the least possible amount), namely, when it can be considered *per se* a mathematical equality (Castro, 2013b). Thereby, this finding can contribute to a more detailed understanding of the potentially quantitative behavior of the information-knowledge duality.

REFERENCES

Adleman, L., Gopalkrishnan, M., Huang, M. D., Moisset, P., & Reishus, D. (2008). *On the mathematics of the law of mass action*. Available from arXiv:0810.1108.

Ausubel, D. (1963). *The psychology of meaningful verbal learning*. New York: Grune & Stratton.

Ausubel, D. (1978). In defense of advance organizers: A reply to the critics. *Review of Educational Research, 48,* 251–257. doi:10.3102/00346543048002251

Bacaër, N. (2011). *A short history of mathematical population dynamics.* London, UK: Springer-Verlag. doi:10.1007/978-0-85729-115-8

Bawden, D. (2008). Smoother pebbles and the shoulders of giants: The developing foundations of information science. *Journal of Information Science, 34*(4), 415–426. doi:10.1177/0165551508089717

Bawden, D. (2011). Brookes equation: The basis for a qualitative characterization of information behaviours. *Journal of Information Science, 37*(1), 101–108. doi:10.1177/0165551510395351

Brookes, B. C. (1981). Information technology and the science of information. In *Information retrieval research.* London: Butterworths.

Capurro, R., & Hjorland, B. (2003). The concept of information. *Annual Review of Information Science & Technology, 37,* 343–411. doi:10.1002/aris.1440370109

Castro, A. (2006). Antibodies production and the maintenance of the immunological memory. *The European Physical Journal Applied Physics, 33*(2), 147–150. doi:10.1051/epjap:2006015

Castro, A. (2013a). On the quantum principles of cognitive learning. Commentary on Pothos & Busemeyer. *Behavioral and Brain Sciences, 36,* 281–282. doi:10.1017/S0140525X12002919 PMID:23673028

Castro, A. (2013b). *The thermodynamic cost of fast thought, minds and machines, 23,* 473. doi:10.1007/s11023-013-9302-x

Castro, A., & Alves, D. (2009). Viral mutation and its influence in the time evolution of the immunizations. *The European Physical Journal Applied Physics, 47,* 31401–31406. doi:10.1051/epjap/2009098

Clauset, A., Shalizi, C. R., & Newman, M. E. J. (2009). Power-law distributions in empirical data. *SIAM Review, 51*(4), 661–703. doi:10.1137/070710111

Cole, S. (2011). A theory of information need for information retrieval that connects information to knowledge. *Journal of the American Society for Information Science and Technology, 62*(7), 1216–1231. doi:10.1002/asi.21541

Cornelius, I. (2002). Theorizing information for information science. *Annual Review of Information Science & Technology, 36,* 393–425.

Devaney, R. L., Hirsch, M. W., & Smale, S. (2004). *Differential equations, dynamical systems, and an introduction to chaos* (2nd ed.). Amsterdam, The Netherlands: Elsevier Academic Press.

Downarowicz, T. (2011). *Entropy in dynamical systems 2011.* Cambridge, UK: Cambridge University Press. doi:10.1017/CBO9780511976155

Gray, R. M. (2011). *Entropy and information theory* (2nd ed.). New York: Springer Verlag. doi:10.1007/978-1-4419-7970-4

Jansen, B. J., & Rieh, S. Y. (2010). The seventeen theoretical constructs of information searching and information retrieval. *Journal of the American Society for Information Science and Technology, 61*(8), 1517–1534.

Jong, M. C. M. (1995). Mathematical modelling in veterinary epidemiology: Why model building is important. *Preventive Veterinary Medicine, 25,* 183–193. doi:10.1016/0167-5877(95)00538-2

Knell, R. J., Begon, M., & Thompson, D. J. (1996). Transmission dynamics of bacillus thuringiensis infecting Plodia inter-punctella: A test of the mass action assumption with an insect pathogen. *Proceedings. Biological Sciences*, *263*(1366), 75–81. doi:10.1098/rspb.1996.0013

Larson, R., Hostetler, R., & Edwards, B. H. (2008). *Essential calculus - Early transcendental functions*. Boston: Houghton Mifflin Company.

Murray, C., Johnson, W., Wolf, M. S., & Deary, I. J. (2011). The association between cognitive ability across the lifespan and health literacy in old age: The lothian birth cohort 1936. *Intelligence*, *39*, 178–187. doi:10.1016/j.intell.2011.04.001

Neill, S. B. (1982). Popper and objective knowledge. *Journal of Information Science*, *4*(1), 33–39. doi:10.1177/016555158200400105

Newman, M. E. J. (2005). Power laws: Pareto distributions and Zipf's law. *Contemporary Physics*, *46*(5), 323–351. doi:10.1080/00107510500052444

Novak, J. D. (2010). *Learning, creating, and using knowledge: Concept maps as facilitative tools in schools and corporations* (2nd ed.). New York: Lawrence Erlbaum. Associentes, Inc.

Novak, J. D., & Mosunda, D. (1991). A twelve-year longitudinal study of science concept learning. *American Educational Research Journal*, *28*(1), 117–153. doi:10.3102/00028312028001117

Shannon, C.E. (1948). A mathematical theory of communication. *Bell Sysytem Technical Journal*, *27*, 379-423, 623-656.

Stapp, H. P. (2007). *Mindful universe: Quantum mechanics and the participating observer*. New York: Springer-Verlag.

Todd, R. J. (1994). Back to our beginnings: Information utilization, Bertram Brookes and the fundamental equation of information science. *Information Processing & Management*, *35*(6), 851–870. doi:10.1016/S0306-4573(99)00030-8

Todd, R. J. (1999). Utilization of heroin information by adolescent girls in Australia: A cognitive analysis. *Journal of the American Society for Information Science American Society for Information Science*, *50*(1), 10–23. doi:10.1002/(SICI)1097-4571(1999)50:1<10::AID-ASI4>3.0.CO;2-B

Wadsworth, B. J. (2003). *Inteligência e afetividade da criança na teoria de Piaget* (5th ed.). São Paulo: Pioneira Thomsom Learning.

Wadsworth, B. J. (2004). *Piaget's theory of cognitive and affective development* (5th ed.). Boston: Allyn & Bacon.

KEY TERMS AND DEFINITIONS

Bit of Knowledge-Information: Here it is treated how smallest unit of classical here it is treated how smallest unit of information.information.

Brookes' Equation: Shorthand description of knowledge transformation known as undamental equation of information science.

Cognitive Change: Shift in the state of knowledge when the individual acquires information.

Cognitive Structure: Individual's knowledge structure or framework of meaning and concepts in individual's mind.

Cognitive-Meaningful Learning Theory: Refers to a sort of learning proposed by David Ausubel where the new knowledge to acquire is related with previous knowledges.

Idiosyncratic Affinity Model: Representation of interaction that considers the individual's own characteristics.

Law of Mass Action: Process used by physicists, mathematicians to quantitatively describe the relationships between biological entities.

Compilation of References

Aamodt, A., & Plaza, E. (1994). Case-based reasoning: Foundational issues, methodological variations, and system approaches. *AI Communications, 7*(1), 39–59.

Abdel-Kader, R. F. (2010). Genetically improved PSO algorithm for efficient data clustering. In *Proceedings of the 2010 Second International Conference on Machine Learning and Computing,* (pp. 71-75). ICMLC.

Aber, M. M., et al. (2013). Analysis of machine learning techniques for gene selection and classification of microarray data. In *Proceedings of the 6th International Conference on Information Technology.* ICIT.

Adleman, L., Gopalkrishnan, M., Huang, M. D., Moisset, P., & Reishus, D. (2008). *On the mathematics of the law of mass action.* Available from arXiv:0810.1108.

Adomavicius, G., & Kwon, Y. O. (2007). New recommendation techniques for multi criteria rating systems. *IEEE Intelligent Systems, 22*(3), 48–55. doi:10.1109/MIS.2007.58

Adomavicius, G., & Tuzhilin, A. (2005). Toward the next generation of recommender systems: A survey of the state-of-the-art and possible extensions. *IEEE Transactions on Knowledge and Data Engineering, 17*(6), 734–749. doi:10.1109/TKDE.2005.99

Aggarwal, C., Procopiuc, C., Wolf, J. L., Yu, P. S., & Park, J. S. (1999). Fast algorithms for projected clustering. In *Proceedings of ACM SIGMOD International Conference on Management of Data* (pp. 61-72). ACM.

Agrawaal, R., & Srikant, R. (1994). Fast algorithm for mining association rules. In *Proceedings of 20ᵗʰ International Conference on Very Large Databases* (pp. 487-99). VLDB.

Agrawal, R., Imieliński, T., & Swami, A. (1993). Mining association rules between sets of items in large databases. *SIGMOD Record, 22*(2), 207–216. doi:10.1145/170036.170072

Ahmmed, S. I. (2010). *Mathematical model for neutralization process. Research Bulletin of.* Australian Institute of High Energetic Materials.

Aho, A. V., Hopcroft, J. E., & Ullman, J. D. (1983). *Data structures and algorithms.* Amsterdam: Addison Wesley.

Akhtar, S., Tai, K., & Ray, T. (2002). A socio-behavioral simulation model for engineering design optimization. *Journal of Engineering Optimization, Taylor & Francis, 34*(4), 341–354. doi:10.1080/03052150212723

Aktas, H., & Cagman, N. (2007). Soft sets and soft groups. *Information Science, 177,* 2726–2735. doi:10.1016/j.ins.2006.12.008

Albert, J. (1991). Algebraic properties of bag data types. In *Proceedings of 17th Int. Conf. Very Large Data Bases.* VLDB.

Albert, P. (2006). Math class: An application for dynamic tactile graphics. In *Computers helping people with special needs (LNCS)* (Vol. 4061, pp. 1118–1121). Berlin: Springer. doi:10.1007/11788713_162

Alcalá, R., Alcalá-Fdez, J., Gacto, M. J., & Herrera, F. (2007). A multi-objective evolutionary algorithm for rule selection and tuning on fuzzy rule-based systems. In *Proceedings of Fuzzy Systems Conference,* (pp. 1-6). IEEE.

Alcala-Fdez, J., Alcalá, R., Gacto, M. J., & Herrera, F. (2009). Learning the membership function contexts for mining fuzzy association rules by using genetic algorithms. *Fuzzy Sets and Systems, 160*(7), 905–921. doi:10.1016/j.fss.2008.05.012

Alcalá, R., Nojima, Y., Herrera, F., & Ishibuchi, H. (2009). Generating single granularity-based fuzzy classification rules for multi-objective genetic fuzzy rule selection. In *Proceedings of Fuzzy Systems* (pp. 1718–1723). IEEE.

Alexandrini, F., & Krechel, D. (2003). Integrating CBR into health care organization. In *Proceedings of the 16th IEEE Symposium on Computer-Based Medical Systems,* (pp. 130-135). IEEE.

Ali, M. I., Feng, F., Liu, W. K., & Shabir, M. (2009). On some new operations in soft set theory. *Computers & Mathematics with Applications (Oxford, England), 57,* 1547–1553. doi:10.1016/j.camwa.2008.11.009

Alizadeh, A. A., Eisen, M. B., & Davis, R. E. et al. (2000). Distinct types of diffuse large B-cell lymphoma identified by gene expression profiling. *Nature, 403,* 503–511. doi:10.1038/35000501 PMID:10676951

Alizadeh, A. A., Ross, D. T., Perou, C. M., & Rijn, M. (2001). Towards a novel classification of human malignancies based on gene expression patterns. *The Journal of Pathology, 195,* 41–52. doi:10.1002/path.889 PMID:11568890

Al-Sultan, K. S. (1995). A tabu search approach to the clustering algorithm. *Pattern Recognition, 28*(9), 1443–1451. doi:10.1016/0031-3203(95)00022-R

Alteanu, D., Ristic, D., & Graser, A. (2005). Content based threshold adaptation for image processing in industrial application. In *Proceedings of 2005 International Conference Control and Automation.* Budapest, Hungary: IEEE.

American Printing House for the Blind, Inc. (2013). *Shopping.* Retrieved June 30, 2013 from http://shop.aph.org/webapp/wcs/stores/servlet/Home1000111051

Anagnostopoulos, G. (n.d.). SVM-based target recognition from synthetic aperture radar images using target region outline descriptors. *Methods & Applications, 71,* 2934–2939.

Androutsos, D., Plataniotis, K. N., & Venetsanopoulos, A. N. (1998). Distance measures for color image retrieval. *Proceedings IEEE Conference Image Processing, 2,* 770-774.

Angeline, P. J. (1998). Evolutionary optimization versus particle swarm optimization: Philosophy and performance differences. In *Proceedings of the 7th International Conference on Evolutionary Programming VII,* (pp. 601-610). Springer-Verlag.

Antonelli, M., Ducange, P., & Marcelloni, F. (2011). A new approach to handle high dimensional and large datasets in multi-objective evolutionary fuzzy systems. In Proceedings of Fuzzy Systems (FUZZ), (pp. 1286-1293). IEEE.

Antonelli, M., Ducange, P., Lazzerini, B., & Marcelloni, F. (2011). Learning knowledge bases of multi-objective evolutionary fuzzy systems by simultaneously optimizing accuracy, complexity and partition integrity. *Soft Computing, 15*(12), 2335–2354. doi:10.1007/s00500-010-0665-0

Araújo, A. R. F., & Costa, D. C. (2009). Local adaptive receptive field self-organizing map for image color segmentation. *Image and Vision Computing, 27*(9), 1229–1239. doi:10.1016/j.imavis.2008.11.014

Araujo, T., Nedjah, N., & Mourelle, L. (2008). Quantum-inspired evolutionary state assignment for synchronous finite state machines. *Journal of Universal Computer Science, 14*(15), 2532–2548.

Atanassov, K. T. (1986). Intuitionistic fuzzy sets. *Fuzzy Sets and Systems, 20,* 87–96. doi:10.1016/S0165-0114(86)80034-3

Atkins, M., & Mackiewich, B. (1998). Fully automatic segmentation of the brain in MRI. *IEEE Transactions on Medical Imaging, 17*(1), 98–107. doi:10.1109/42.668699 PMID:9617911

Ausubel, D. (1963). *The psychology of meaningful verbal learning.* New York: Grune & Stratton.

Ausubel, D. (1978). In defense of advance organizers: A reply to the critics. *Review of Educational Research, 48,* 251–257. doi:10.3102/00346543048002251

Aviv, Y. (2003). A time series framework for supply-chain inventory management. *Operations Research, 51,* 210–227. doi:10.1287/opre.51.2.210.12780

Aygunoglu, A., & Aygun, H. (2009). Introduction to soft groups. *Computers & Mathematics with Applications (Oxford, England), 58,* 1279–1286. doi:10.1016/j.camwa.2009.07.047

Azimi-Sadjadi, M. R., Ghaloum, S., & Zoughi, R. (1993). Terrain classification in SAR images using principal component analysis and neural networks. *IEEE Transactions on Geoscience and Remote Sensing, 31*(2), 511–515. doi:10.1109/36.214928

Babitha, K. B., & Sunil, J. J. (2010). Soft set relations and functions. *Computers & Mathematics with Applications (Oxford, England), 60*(7), 1840–1849. doi:10.1016/j.camwa.2010.07.014

Bacaër, N. (2011). *A short history of mathematical population dynamics.* London, UK: Springer-Verlag. doi:10.1007/978-0-85729-115-8

Back, T. (1996). *Evolutionary algorithms in theory and practice.* New York: Oxford University Press.

Baixeries, J., Szathmary, L., Vatchel, P., & Godibn, R. (2009). Yet a faster algorithm for building the hasse diagram of concept lattice. In *International Conference on Formal Concept Analysis* (LNAI), (vol. 5548, pp. 162-177). Berlin: Springer -Verlag.

Balaji, V., & Vasudevan, N. (2009). Model predictive control of pH in pharmaceutical process. In *Proceedings of IEEE International Conference on Mechatronics,* (pp. 1 – 6). IEEE.

Ballerini, L., Bocchi, L., & Johansson, C. (2004). Image segmentation by a genetic fuzzy *c*-means algorithm using color and spatial information. *Applications of Evolutionary Computing, 3005,* 260–269. doi:10.1007/978-3-540-24653-4_27

Ballini, R., & Gomide, F. (2002). Learning in recurrent, hybrid neuro-fuzzy networks.[]. IEEE.]. *Proceedings of Fuzzy Systems, 1,* 785–790.

Barbieri, T., Mosca, L., & Sbattella, L. (2006). Learning math for visually impaired users. In *Computers helping people with special needs (LNCS)* (Vol. 5105, pp. 907–914). Berlin: Springer. doi:10.1007/978-3-540-70540-6_136

Barve, J. J., & Nataraj, P. S. V. (1998). Synthesis of a robust pH controller using QFT. In *Proceedings of IEEE Region 10 International Conference on Global Connectivity in Energy, Computer, Communication and Control,* (vol. 1, pp. 214 – 217). IEEE.

Batusic, M., & Urban, F. (2002). Preparing tactile graphics for traditional braille printers with BrlGraphEditor. In *Computers helping people with special needs (LNCS)* (Vol. 2398, pp. 261–274). Berlin: Springer. doi:10.1007/3-540-45491-8_101

Bawden, D. (2008). Smoother pebbles and the shoulders of giants: The developing foundations of information science. *Journal of Information Science, 34*(4), 415–426. doi:10.1177/0165551508089717

Bawden, D. (2011). Brookes equation: The basis for a qualitative characterization of information behaviours. *Journal of Information Science, 37*(1), 101–108. doi:10.1177/0165551510395351

Bayer, R. (1972). Symmetric binary B-trees, data structures and maintenance algorithms. *Acta Informatica, 1,* 290–306. doi:10.1007/BF00289509

Bayer, R., & McCreight, E. M. (1972). Organization and maintenance of large ordered indexes. *Acta Informatica, 1*(3), 173–189. doi:10.1007/BF00288683

Bazi, Y., Bruzzone, L., & Melgani, F. (2007). Image thresholding based on the EM algorithm and the generalized Gaussian distribution. *Pattern Recognition, 40,* 619–634. doi:10.1016/j.patcog.2006.05.006

Belecheanu, R., Pawar, K. S., Barson, R. J., Bredehorst, B., & Weber, F. (2003). The application of case based reasoning to decision support in new product development. *Integrated Manufacturing Systems, 14*(1), 36–45. doi:10.1108/09576060310453335

Belohlavek, R., & Vychodil, V. (2006). Replacing full rectangles by dense rectangles: Concepts lattices and attribute implications. In *Proceedings of IEEE International Conference Information Reuse & Integration* (pp. 117-22). IEEE.

Belohlavek, R., Sklenar, V., & Zacpal, J. (2004). Formal concept analysis with hierarchically ordered attributes. *International Journal of General Systems*, *33*, 383–394. doi:10.1080/03081070410001679715

Belohlavek, R., & Vychodil, V. (2009). Formal concept analysis with background knowledge: Attribute priorities. *IEEE Transactions on Systems, Man, and Cybernetics*, *39*(4), 399–409. doi:10.1109/TSMCC.2008.2012168 PMID:19109092

Bernt, M. A., Hannu, T., Toivonen, Jonas, B. W., & Rasmus H. N. (n.d.). Neural network approximation of a nonlinear model predictive controller applied to a pH neutralization process. *Computers and Chemical Engineering, 29*(2), 323 – 335.

Berry, A., Bordat, J. P., & Cogis, O. (2000). Generating all minimal separator of a graph. *International Journal of Foundations of Computer Science*, *11*, 397–404. doi:10.1142/S0129054100000211

Berry, A., Bordat, J. P., & Sigayret, A. (2007). A local approach to concept generation. *Annals of Mathematics and Artificial Intelligence*, *49*(1/4), 117–136. doi:10.1007/s10472-007-9063-4

Bezdek, J. C., Boggavaparu, S., Hall, L. O., & Bensaid, A. (1994). Genetic algorithm guided clustering. In *Proceedings of IEEE Congress on Evolutionary Computation* (pp. 34-40). IEEE.

Bezdek, J., & Hathaway, R. (1988). Recent convergence results for the fuzzy c-means clustering algorithms. *Journal of Classification*, *5*(2), 237–247. doi:10.1007/BF01897166

Bhanu, B., Lee, S., & Ming, J. (1995). Adaptive image segmentation using a genetic algorithm. *IEEE Transactions on Systems, Man, and Cybernetics*, *25*(12), 1543–1567. doi:10.1109/21.478442

Bhattacharyya, S., & Dasgupta, K. (2003). Color object extraction from a noisy background using parallel multilayer self-organizing neural networks. *Proceedings of CSI-YITPA (E), 2003*, 32-36.

Bhattacharyya, S., & Dey, S. (2011). An efficient quantum inspired genetic algorithm with chaotic map model based interference and fuzzy objective function for gray level image thresholding. In *Proceedings of 2011, International Conference on Computational Intelligence and Communication Systems*. IEEE.

Bhattacharyya, S. (2011). A brief survey of color image preprocessing and segmentation techniques. *Journal of Pattern Recognition Research*, *1*(1), 120–129. doi:10.13176/11.191

Bhattacharyya, S., Dutta, P., & Maulik, U. (2008). Self organizing neural network (SONN) based gray scale object extractor with a multilevel sigmoidal (MUSIG) activation function. *Foundations of Computing and Decision Sciences*, *33*(2), 131–165.

Bhattacharyya, S., Dutta, P., Maulik, U., & Nandi, P. K. (2007). Multilevel activation functions for true color image segmentation using a self supervised parallel self organizing neural network (PSONN) architecture: A comparative study. *International Journal on Computer Sciences*, *2*(1).

Bhattacharyya, S., Maulik, U., & Dutta, P. (2011). Multilevel image segmentation with adaptive image context based thresholding. *Applied Soft Computing*, *11*, 946–962. doi:10.1016/j.asoc.2010.01.015

B-Hillel. A., & Weinshall, D. (2006). Subordinate class recognition using relational object models. In Advances in Neural Information Processing Systems. Cambridge, MA: MIT Press.

B-Hillel. A., Hertz, T., Shental, N., & Weinshall, D. (2003). Learning distance functions using equivalence relations. In *Proceedings of the 20th International Conference on Machine Learning (ICML-2003)*. Washington, DC: ICML.

Bhowmick, P., & Bhattacharya, B. B. (2007). Fast polygonal approximation of digital curves using relaxed straightness properties. *IEEE Transactions on Pattern Analysis and Machine Intelligence*, *29*(9), 1590–1602. doi:10.1109/TPAMI.2007.1082 PMID:17627046

Billah, B., King, M. L., Snyder, R. D., & Koehler, A. B. (2006). Exponential smoothing model selection for forecasting. *International Journal of Forecasting, 22,* 239–247. doi:10.1016/j.ijforecast.2005.08.002

Bird, R., & Walder, P. (1988). *Introduction to functional programming.* Upper Saddle River, NJ: Prentice Hall.

Birkhoff, G. (1940). *Lattice theory.* Washington, DC: American Mathematical Society, Colloquium Publication.

Biswas, R. (2011). r-Train (train): A new flexible dynamic data structure. *Information: An International Journal, 14*(4), 1231–1246.

Biswas, R. (2012). Heterogeneous data structure r-Atrain. *Information: An International Journal, 15*(2), 879–902.

Biswas, S. S., Alam, B., & Doja, M. N. (2012). A theoretical characterization of the data structure 'multigraph'. *Journal of Contemporary Applied Mathematics, 2*(2).

Biswas, S. S., Alam, B., & Doja, M. N. (2013). Generalization of Dijkstra's algorithm for extraction of shortest paths in directed multigraphs. *Journal of Computer Science, 9*(3), 377–382. doi:10.3844/jcssp.2013.377.382

Biswas, S. S., Alam, B., & Doja, M. N. (2013). Real time multigraphs for communication networks: An intuitionistic fuzzy mathematical model. *Journal of Computer Science, 9*(7), 847–855. doi:10.3844/jcssp.2013.847.855

Bojadziev, G., & Bojadziev, M. (2007). *Fuzzy logic for business, finance, and management* (2nd ed.). Singapore: World Scientific Press.

Bonikowski, Z., Bryniarski, E., & Wybraniec, U. (1998). Extensions and intensions in the rough set theory. *Journal of Information Science, 107,* 149–167. doi:10.1016/S0020-0255(97)10046-9

Bonzano, A., Cunningham, P., & Meckiff, C. (1996). ISAC: A CBR system for decision support in air traffic control. In *Advances in case-based reasoning (LNCS)* (Vol. 1168, pp. 44–57). Berlin: Springer. doi:10.1007/BFb0020601

Booker, L. B., Goldberg, D. E., & Holland, J. H. (1989). Classifier systems and genetic algorithms. *Artificial Intelligence, 40*(1-3), 235–282. doi:10.1016/0004-3702(89)90050-7

Boongoen, T., Shang, C., Iam-On, N., & Shen, Q. (2011). Extending data reliability measure to a filter approach for soft subspace clustering. *IEEE Transactions on Systems, Man and Cybernetics. Part B, 41*(6), 1705–1714.

Boongoen, T., & Shen, Q. (2010). Nearest-neighbor guided evaluation of data reliability and its applications. *IEEE Transactions on Systems, Man and Cybernetics. Part B, 40*(6), 1622–1633.

Bordat, J. P. (1986). Calcul pratique du trellis de galois d'une correspondance. *Mathematiques et Sciences Humaines, 96,* 31–47.

Borges, J. A., & Jansen, L. R. (1999). Blind people and the computer: An interaction that explores drawing potentials. In *Proceedings of SEMENGE'99 - Seminário de Engenharia. Universidade Federal Fluminense Brazil.* SEMENGE.

Borsotti, M., Campadelli, P., & Schettini, R. (1998). Quantitative evaluation of color image segmentation results. *Pattern Recognition Letters, 19,* 741–747. doi:10.1016/S0167-8655(98)00052-X

Boulicaut, J. F., & Besson, J. (2008). Actionability and formal concepts: A data mining perspective. In *International Conference on Formal Concept Analysis* (LNAI), (vol. 4933, pp. 14-31). Berlin: Springer-Verlag.

Boyarsky, A., & G'ora, P. (2010). A random map model for quantum interference. *Communications in Nonlinear Science and Numerical Simulation, 15,* 1974–1979. doi:10.1016/j.cnsns.2009.08.018

Braga-Neto, & Dougherty. (2004). Is cross-validation valid for small sample microarray classification? *Bioinformatics (Oxford, England), 20,* 374–380. doi:10.1093/bioinformatics/btg419 PMID:14960464

Braille Geometry Kit. (2013). Retrieved June 30, 2013 from http://www.mathwindow.com/brl_geometry.html

Braille Graphics and Tactile Graphics from Repro-Tronics. (2013). Retrieved June 30, 2013 from http://www.Brailler.com/repro.htm

Bremermann, H. (1962). Optimization through evolution and recombination. In *Self-organizing systems.* Washington, DC: Spartan Books.

Brookes, B. C. (1981). Information technology and the science of information. In *Information retrieval research*. London: Butterworths.

Bryant, S. M. (1997). A case-based reasoning approach to bankruptcy prediction modeling. *International Journal of Intelligent Systems in Accounting Finance & Management*, *6*(3), 195–214. doi:10.1002/(SICI)1099-1174(199709)6:3<195::AID-ISAF132>3.0.CO;2-F

Buckles, B. P., & Petry, F. E. (1982). A fuzzy representation of data for relational databases. *Fuzzy Sets and Systems*, *7*, 213–226. doi:10.1016/0165-0114(82)90052-5

Bureau of Transportation Statistics, USA. (2012). Retrieved from www.bts.gov

Burgmann, C., & Wille, R. (2006). The basic theorem in preconcept lattices. In *International Conference on Formal Concept Analysis* (LNCS), (vol. 3874, pp. 80-88). Berlin: Springer—Verlag.

Bussel, L. (2003). Touch tiles: Elementary geometry software with a haptic and auditory interface for visually impaired children. In *Proceedings of EuroHaptics Conference* (pp. 512-515). EuroHaptics.

Buta, P. (1994). Mining for financial knowledge with CBR. *AI Expert*, *9*(2), 34–41.

Cagman, N., Citak, F., & Enginoglu, S. (2010). Fuzzy parameterized fuzzy soft set theory and its applications. *Turkish Journal of Fuzzy Systems*, *1*(1), 21–35.

Cagman, N., & Enginoglu, S. (2010). Soft matrix theory and its decision making. *Computers & Mathematics with Applications (Oxford, England)*, *59*, 3308–3314. doi:10.1016/j.camwa.2010.03.015

Cannone, R., Alonso, J. M., & Magdalena, L. (2011). Multi-objective design of highly interpretable fuzzy rule-based classifiers with semantic cointension. In Proceedings of Genetic and Evolutionary Fuzzy Systems (GEFS), (pp. 1-8). IEEE.

Cantor, G. (1883). *G. Grundlagen einer allgemeinen mannigfaltig-keitslehre*. Leipzig, Germany: B.G. Teubner.

Cantor, G. (1883). *Grundlagen einer allgemeinen mannigfaltig-keitslehre*. Leipzig, Germany: B.G. Teubner.

Cao, L., & Zhang, C. (2007). Domain-driven data mining: A framework. *IEEE Intelligent Systems*, *22*(4), 78–79. doi:10.1109/MIS.2007.67

Capurro, R., & Hjorland, B. (2003). The concept of information. *Annual Review of Information Science & Technology*, *37*, 343–411. doi:10.1002/aris.1440370109

Carkacioglu, L., Atalay, R. C., Konu, O., Atalay, V., & Can, T. (2010). Bi-k-bi clustering: Mining large scale gene expression data using two-level biclustering. *International Journal of Data Mining and Bioinformatics*, *4*(6), 701–721. doi:10.1504/IJDMB.2010.037548 PMID:21355502

Carmona, C. J., González, P., Del Jesús, M. J., & Herrera, F. (2009). Non-dominated multi-objective evolutionary algorithm based on fuzzy rules extraction for subgroup discovery. In *Hybrid artificial intelligence systems* (pp. 573–580). Berlin: Springer. doi:10.1007/978-3-642-02319-4_69

Carpineto, C., & Romano, G. (1996). A lattice conceptual clustering system and its application to browsing retrieval. *Machine Learning*, *24*, 95–122. doi:10.1007/BF00058654

Carpineto, C., & Romano, G. (2004). *Concept data analysis: Theory and applications*. Hoboken, NJ: John Wiley & Sons. doi:10.1002/0470011297

Carvalho, D. R., & Freitas, A. A. (2004). A hybrid decision tree/ genetic algorithm method for data mining. *Information Science*, *163*(1-3), 13–35. doi:10.1016/j.ins.2003.03.013

Casely-Hayford, L., & Lynch, P. (2003). *A review of good practice in ICT and special educational needs for Africa*. Retrieved June 30, 2013 from www.comp.dit.ie/dgordon/Publications/Contributor/Ghana/SENPHASE-1FINAL.pdf

Casillas, J., & Martínez-López, F. J. (2009). Mining uncertain data with multi-objective genetic fuzzy systems to be applied in consumer behavior modeling. *Expert Systems with Applications*, *36*, 1645–1659. doi:10.1016/j.eswa.2007.11.035

Castillo, O., Trujillo, L., & Melin, P. (2007). Multiple objective genetic algorithms for path-planning optimization in autonomous mobile robots. *Soft Computing*, *11*(3), 269–279. doi:10.1007/s00500-006-0068-4

Castro, A. (2006). Antibodies production and the maintenance of the immunological memory. *The European Physical Journal Applied Physics, 33*(2), 147–150. doi:10.1051/epjap:2006015

Castro, A. (2013). On the quantum principles of cognitive learning. *The Behavioral and Brain Sciences, 36*, 281–282. doi:10.1017/S0140525X12002919 PMID:23673028

Castro, A. (2013). *The thermodynamic cost of fast thought.* Mins and Machines.

Castro, A., & Alves, D. (2009). Viral mutation and its influence in the time evolution of the immunizations. *The European Physical Journal Applied Physics, 47*, 31401–31406. doi:10.1051/epjap/2009098

Cawley, G. C., Talbot, N. L. C., & Girolami, M. (2007). Sparse multinomial logistic regression via Bayesian l1 regularisation. In *Proceedings of NIPS*. NIPS.

Ceccarelli, M., & Petrosino, A. (1997). Multi-feature adaptive classifiers segmentation for SAR image. *Journal of Neuro-Computing, 14*, 345–363.

Chakrabarti, K., & Mehrotra, S. (2000). Local dimensionality reduction: A new approach to indexing high dimensional spaces. In *Proceedings of International Conference on VLDB* (pp. 89-100). VLDB.

Chakraborty, B., Ghosh, D., & Ranjan, R. (2010). Knowledge management with case-based reasoning applied on fire emer handling. In *Proceedings of 8th IEEE International Conference on Industrial Informatics* (INDIN 2010) (pp. 708-713). IEEE.

Chang, C. L. (2005). Using case-based reasoning to diagnostic screening of children with developmental delay. *Expert Systems with Applications, 28*, 237–240. doi:10.1016/j.eswa.2004.09.002

Chang, P. C., & Lai, C. Y. (2005). A hybrid system combining self-organizing maps with case-based reasoning in wholesaler's new-release book for forecasting. *Expert Systems with Applications, 29*, 183–192. doi:10.1016/j.eswa.2005.01.018

Chatterjee, S., & Hadi, A. S. (2006). *Regression analysis of example* (4th ed.). Hoboken, NJ: Wiley-Interscience. doi:10.1002/0470055464

Chaudhuri, A., De, K., & Chatterjee, D. (2009). Solution of the decision making problems using fuzzy soft relations. *International Journal of Information Technology, 15*(1), 78–107.

Chawla, S. (2010). Feature selection, association rules network and theory building. In *Proceedings of the 4th Workshop on Feature Selection in Data Mining*. IEEE.

Chen, C. H., Hong, T. P., & Tseng, V. S. (2010). A SPEA2-based genetic-fuzzy mining algorithm. In Proceedings of Fuzzy Systems (FUZZ), (pp. 1-5). IEEE.

Chen, D. G., Tsang, E. C. C., Yeung, D. S., & Xizhao, W. (2005). The parameterization reduction of soft sets and its applications. *Computers & Mathematics with Applications (Oxford, England), 49*, 757–763. doi:10.1016/j.camwa.2004.10.036

Cheng, H., Hua, K. A., & Vu, K. (2008). Constrained locally weighted clustering. In *Proceedings of International Conference on VLDB* (pp. 90-101). VLDB.

Cheng, Y., & Church, G. M. (2000). Biclustering of expression data. In *Proceedings of International Conference on Intelligent Systems for Molecular Biology* (pp. 93-103). IEEE.

Cheng, H. D., Jiang, X. H., Sun, Y., & Wang, J. (2001). Color image segmentation: Advances and prospects. *Pattern Recognition, 34*(12), 2259–2281. doi:10.1016/S0031-3203(00)00149-7

Chen, H.-C., Chien, W.-J., & Wang, S.-J. (2004). Contrast-based color image segmentation. *IEEE Signal Processing Letters, 11*(7), 641–644. doi:10.1109/LSP.2004.830116

Chen, L. C., Yu, P. S., & Tseng, V. S. (2011). WF-MSB: A weighted fuzzy-based biclustering method for gene expression data. *International Journal of Data Mining and Bioinformatics, 5*(1), 89–109. doi:10.1504/IJDMB.2011.038579 PMID:21491846

Chen, S. M., & Hsiao, P. H. (1995). A comparison of similarity measures of fuzzy values. *Fuzzy Sets and Systems, 72,* 79–89. doi:10.1016/0165-0114(94)00284-E

Chen, S., Huang, Y., Hsieh, B., Ma, S., & Chen, L. (2004). Fast video segmentation algorithm with shadow cancellation: Global motion compensation and adaptive threshold techniques. *IEEE Transactions on Multimedia, 6,* 732–748. doi:10.1109/TMM.2004.834868

Chen, Y. K., Wang, C.-Y., & Feng, Y.-Y. (2010). Application of a 3NN+1 based CBR system to segmentation of the notebook computers market. *Expert Systems with Applications, 37*(1), 276–281. doi:10.1016/j.eswa.2009.05.002

Chi, D. (2011). Self-organizing map-based color image segmentation with k-means clustering and saliency map. *ISRN Signal Processing, 2011.* doi:10.5402/2011/393891

Chiu, C. (2002). A case-based customer classification approach for direct marketing. *Expert Systems with Applications, 22*(2), 163–168. doi:10.1016/S0957-4174(01)00052-5

Chiu, C., Chang, P. C., & Chiu, N. H. (2003). A case-based expert support system for due-date assignment in a water fabrication factory. *Journal of Intelligent Manufacturing, 14*(3–4), 287–296. doi:10.1023/A:1024693524603

Chootinan, P., & Chen, A. (2006). Constraint handling in genetic algorithms using a gradient-based repair method. *Computers & Operations Research, 33,* 2263–2281. doi:10.1016/j.cor.2005.02.002

Chuzhanova, N. A., Jones, A. J., & Margetts, S. (1998). Feature selection for genetic sequence classification. *Bioinformatics (Oxford, England), 14*(2), 139–143. doi:10.1093/bioinformatics/14.2.139 PMID:9545445

Cios, K. J., Pedrycz, W., Swiniarski, R. W., & Kurgan, L. A. (2012). *Data mining: A knowledge discovery approach.* New York: Springer-Verlag.

Cirovic, G., & Cekic, Z. (2002). Case-based reasoning model applied as a decision support for construction projects. *Kybernete, 31*(5/6), 896–908. doi:10.1108/03684920210432844

Clauset, A., Shalizi, C. R., & Newman, M. E. J. (2009). Power-law distributions in empirical data. *SIAM Review, 51*(4), 661–703. doi:10.1137/070710111

Cleator, S., & Ashworth, A. (2004). Molecular profiling of breast cancer: Clinical implications. *British Journal of Cancer, 90,* 1120–1124. doi:10.1038/sj.bjc.6601667 PMID:15026788

Codd, E. (1970). A relational model of data for large shared data banks. *Communications of the ACM, 13,* 377–387. doi:10.1145/362384.362685

Coello, C. A. (2000). An updated survey of GA-based multi objective optimization techniques. *ACM Computing Surveys, 32*(2), 109–143. doi:10.1145/358923.358929

Coello, C. A. C. (2006). Evolutionary multi-objective optimization: A historical view of the field. *IEEE Computational Intelligence Magazine, 1*(1), 28–36. doi:10.1109/MCI.2006.1597059

Coello, C. A., & Mezura, M. E. (2002). Constraint-handling in genetic algorithms through the use of dominance-based tournament selection. *Advanced Engineering Informatics, 16,* 193–203. doi:10.1016/S1474-0346(02)00011-3

Cohen, D. S., & Blum, M. (1995). On the problem of sorting burnt pancakes. *Discrete Applied Mathematics, 61,* 105–120. doi:10.1016/0166-218X(94)00009-3

Cohen, J. L. (1978). *Multi-objective programming and planning.* New York: Academic Press.

Cole, S. (2011). A theory of information need for information retrieval that connects information to knowledge. *Journal of the American Society for Information Science and Technology, 62*(7), 1216–1231. doi:10.1002/asi.21541

Contreras, J., Espnola, R., Nogales, F. J., & Conejo, A. J. (2003). ARIMA models to predict next day electricity prices. *IEEE Transactions on Power Systems, 18*(3), 1014–1021. doi:10.1109/TPWRS.2002.804943

Cormen, T. H., Leiserson, C. E., Rivest, R. L., & Stein, C. (2001). *Introduction to algorithms* (2nd ed.). Cambridge, MA: MIT Press and McGraw-Hill.

Cornelius, I. (2002). Theorizing information for information science. *Annual Review of Information Science & Technology, 36*, 393–425.

Cvetković, D., Parmee, I., & Webb, E. (1998). Multi-objective optimization and preliminary airframe design. In *Adaptive computing in design and manufacture* (pp. 255–267). London: Springer. doi:10.1007/978-1-4471-1589-2_20

Daelemans, W., Hoste, V., De Meulder, F., & Naudts, B. (2003). Combined optimization of feature selection and algorithm parameter interaction in machine learning of language. In *Proceedings of the 14th European Conference on Machine Learning (ECML-2003)* (pp. 84–95). ECML.

Das, S. (2001). Filters, wrappers and a boosting-based hybrid for feature selection. In *Proceedings of the 18th Int'l Conf. Machine Learning* (pp. 74- 81). IEEE.

Dash, M., Choi, K., Scheuermann, P., & Liu, H. (2002). Feature selection for clustering- A filter solution. In *Proceedings of the Second Int'l Conf. Data Mining* (pp. 115-122). IEEE.

Dash, S., & Patra, B. N. (2012). Rough set aided gene selection for cancer classification. In *Proceedings of the 7th International Conference on Computer Sciences and Convergence Information Technology.* IEEE.

Dash, S., & Patra, B. N. (2012). Study of classification accuracy of microarray data for cancer classification using hybrid, wrapper and filter feature selection method. In *Proceedings of the 2012 International Conference on Bioinformatics & Computational Biology, WORLDCOMP'12.* WORLDCOMP.

Dash, S., & Patra, B.N. (2013). Redundant gene selection based on genetic and quick-reduct algorithms. *International Journal on Data Mining and Intelligent Information Technology Application.*

Dash, M., & Liu, H. (1997). Feature selection for classification. *Intelligent Data Analysis, 1*(3), 131–156. doi:10.1016/S1088-467X(97)00008-5

Das, S., Abraham, A., & Konar, A. (2008). Automatic clustering using an improved differential evolution algorithm. *IEEE Transactions on Systems, Man, and Cybernetics. Part A, Systems and Humans, 38*(1), 218–237. doi:10.1109/TSMCA.2007.909595

Davey, B. A., & Priestley, M. A. (2002). *Introduction of lattices and order.* Cambridge, UK: Cambridge University Press. doi:10.1017/CBO9780511809088

Dayal, U., Goodman, N., & Katz, R. H. (1982). An extended relational algebra with control over duplicate elimination. In *ACM principles of database systems.* New York: ACM.

De Luca, A., & Termini, S. (1972). A definition of a non-probabilistic entropy in the setting of fuzzy sets theory. *Information and Control, 20*, 301–312. doi:10.1016/S0019-9958(72)90199-4

de Souto, M., Costa, I., de Araujo, D., Ludermir, T., & Schliep, A. (2008). Clustering cancer gene expression data: A comparative study. *BMC Bioinformatics, 9*, 497. doi:10.1186/1471-2105-9-497 PMID:19038021

De, S., Bhattacharyya, S., & Chakraborty, S. (2010). True color image segmentation by an optimized multilevel activation function. In *Proceedings of 2010 IEEE International Conference on Computational Intelligence and Computing Research,* (pp. 545-548). IEEE.

Deb, K., & Agarwal, S. (1999). A niched-penalty approach for constraint handling in genetic algorithms. In *Proceedings of the ICANNGA.* Portoroz, Slovenia: ICANNGA.

Deb, K. (1995). *Optimization for engineering design: Algorithms and examples.* New Delhi: Prentice-Hall of India.

Deb, K. (1997). A robust optimal design technique for mechanical component design. In *Evolutionary algorithms in engineering applications.* Berlin: Springer Verlag. doi:10.1007/978-3-662-03423-1_27

Deb, K. (2001). *Multi-objective optimization using evolutionary algorithms.* New York: John Wiley and Sons.

Deb, K., Mohan, M., & Mishra, S. (2005). Evaluating the ε-domination based multi-objective evolutionary algorithm for a quick computation of Pareto-optimal solutions. *Evolutionary Computation, 13*(4), 501–525. doi:10.1162/106365605774666895 PMID:16297281

Deb, K., Pratap, A., Agarwal, S., & Meyarivan, T. (2002). A fast and elitist multi-objective genetic algorithm: NSGA-II. *IEEE Transactions on Evolutionary Computation, 6*(2), 182–197. doi:10.1109/4235.996017

Deep, K., & Das, K. N. (2008). Quadratic approximation based hybrid genetic algorithm for function optimization. *AMC*, *203*, 86–98.

Deep, K., & Das, K. N. (2013). A novel hybrid genetic algorithm for constrained optimization. *International Journal of System Assurance Engineering and Management, 4*(1).

Deep, K., & Thakur, M. (2007). A new crossover operator for real coded genetic algorithms. *Applied Mathematics and Computation, 188*(1), 895–911. doi:10.1016/j.amc.2006.10.047

Deep, K., & Thakur, M. (2007). A new mutation operator for real coded genetic algorithms. *Applied Mathematics and Computation, 193*(1), 211–230. doi:10.1016/j.amc.2007.03.046

Degang, C., Changzhong, W., & Qinghua, H. (2007). A new approach to attribute reduction of consistent and inconsistent covering decision systems with covering rough sets. *Journal of Information Science, 177*, 3500–3518. doi:10.1016/j.ins.2007.02.041

Degang, C., Wenxiu, Z., Yeung, D., & Tsang, E. C. C. (2006). Rough approximations on a complete completely distributive lattice with applications to generalized rough sets. *Journal of Information Science, 176*, 1829–1848. doi:10.1016/j.ins.2005.05.009

Dehuri, S., & Mall, R. (2004). Mining predictive and comprehensible classification rules using multi-objective genetic algorithm. In *Proceedings of the ADCOM*, (pp. 99-104). ADCOM.

Dehuri, S., Ghosh, A., & Mall, R. (2006). Genetic algorithms for multi-criterion classification and clustering in data mining. *International Journal of Computing & Information Sciences, 4*(3), 143–154.

Dehuri, S., Jagadev, A. K., Ghosh, A., & Mall, R. (2006). Multi-objective genetic algorithm for association rule mining using a homogeneous dedicated cluster of workstations. *American Journal of Applied Sciences, 3*(11), 2086–2095. doi:10.3844/ajassp.2006.2086.2095

Delp, E., & Mitchell, O. (1991). Moment-preserving quantization. *IEEE Transactions on Communications, 39*, 1549–1558. doi:10.1109/26.111432

Dempster, A., Laird, N., & Rubin, D. (1977). Maximum likelihood from incomplete data via the EM algorithm. *Journal of the Royal Statistical Society. Series B. Methodological, 39*(1).

Dempster, R. T. (1974). The measurement and modelling of iceberg drift. *IEEE Ocean, 74*(1), 125–129.

Deng, Y., Manjunath, B. S., & Shin, H. (1999). Color image segmentation. In *Proceedings of IEEE Conference Computer Vision Pattern Recognition*, (pp. 1021-1025). IEEE.

Denning, P. J. et al. (1989). Computing as a discipline. *Communications of the ACM, 32*(1), 9–10. doi:10.1145/63238.63239

Deogun, J. S., & Saquer, J. (2004). Monotone concept for formal concept analysis. *Discrete Applied Mathematics, 144*, 70–78. doi:10.1016/j.dam.2004.05.001

De, S., Bhattacharyya, S., & Chakraborty, S. (2012). Color image segmentation using parallel OptiMUSIG activation function. *Applied Soft Computing Journal, 12*(10), 3228–3236. doi:10.1016/j.asoc.2012.05.011

De, S., Bhattacharyya, S., & Dutta, P. (2010). Efficient gray level image segmentation using an optimized MUSIG (OptiMUSIG) activation function. *International Journal of Parallel. Emergent and Distributed Systems, 26*(1), 1–39.

Deutsch, D., & Jozsa, R. (1992). Rapid solution of problems by quantum computation. *Royal Society of London Proceedings Series, 439*(1907), 553–558.

Devaney, R. L., Hirsch, M. W., & Smale, S. (2004). *Differential equations, dynamical systems, and an introduction to chaos* (2nd ed.). Amsterdam, The Netherlands: Elsevier Academic Press.

Deyashi, S., Banerjee, D., & Chakraborty, B. (2012). Fever-type detection system: A combination of CBR and bottom up approach. In *Proceedings of 10th IEEE International Conference on Industrial Informatics (INDIN)*, (pp. 962 – 967). IEEE.

Deyashi, S., Banerjee, D., Chakraborty, B., Ghosh, D., & Debnath, J. (2011). Application of CBR on viral fever detection system (VFDS). In *Proceedings of IEEE INDIN 2011*. Lisbon, Portugal: IEEE.

Dhruba, S. D., Ai-Poh, L., & Krishnaswamy, P. R. (2000). A nonlinear adaptive controller for a pH neutralization process. In *Proceedings of the American Control Conference,* (pp. 2250 – 2254). ACC.

Di Nuovo, A. G., & Catania, V. (2009). Linguistic modifiers to improve the accuracy-interpretability trade-off in multi-objective genetic design of fuzzy rule based classifier systems. In *Proceedings of Intelligent Systems Design and Applications* (pp. 128–133). IEEE. doi:10.1109/ISDA.2009.97

Dias, S. M., & Viera, J. (2013). Applying the JBOS reduction method for relevant knowledge extraction. *Expert Systems with Applications, 40*(5), 1880–1887. doi:10.1016/j.eswa.2012.10.010

Ding, H., Trajeevski, G., Scheuermann, P., Wang, X., & Keogh, E. (2008). Querying and mining of time series data: Experimental comparison of representations and distance measures. *Proceedings VLDB Endow., 1*, 1542–1552.

Ding, J. et al. (2012). Feature based classifiers for somatic mutation detection in tumour-normal paired sequencing data. *Bioinformatics (Oxford, England), 28*(2), 167–175. doi:10.1093/bioinformatics/btr629 PMID:22084253

Dixena, D., Chakraborty, B., & Debnath, N. (2011). Application of case-based reasoning for ship turning emergency to prevent collision. In *Proceedings of 9th IEEE International Conference on Industrial Informatics (INDIN),* (pp. 654 – 659). IEEE.

Dobbin, K., & Simon, R. (2005). Sample size determination in microarray experiments for class comparison and prognostic classification. *Biostatistics (Oxford, England), 6*, 27–38. doi:10.1093/biostatistics/kxh015 PMID:15618525

Doelken, M., Stefan, H., Pauli, E., Stadlbauer, A., Struffert, T., & Engelhorn, T. et al. (2008). Hammen. T. 1H-MRS profile in MRI positive-versus MRI negative patients with temporal lobe epilepsy. *Seizure, 17*, 490–497. doi:10.1016/j.seizure.2008.01.008 PMID:18337128

Dohare, D., & Devi, V. S. (2011). Combination of similarity measures for time series classification using genetic algorithms. In *Proceedings of IEEE Congress on Evolutionary Computation.* New Orleans, LA: IEEE.

Domeniconi, C., Gunopulos, D., Ma, S., Yan, B., Al-Razgan, M., & Papadopoulos, D. (2007). Locally adaptive metrics for clustering high dimensional data. *Data Mining and Knowledge Discovery, 14*(1), 63–97. doi:10.1007/s10618-006-0060-8

Downarowicz, T. (2011). *Entropy in dynamical systems 2011.* Cambridge, UK: Cambridge University Press. doi:10.1017/CBO9780511976155

Dubois, D. J. (1983). *Fuzzy sets and systems* (4th ed.). New York: Academic Press Inc.

Dubois, D., & Prade, H. (1990). Rough fuzzy sets and Fuzzy rough sets. *International Journal of General Systems, 17*(1), 191–209. doi:10.1080/03081079008935107

Duda, R., Hart, P., & Stork, D. (2001). *Pattern classification* (2nd ed.). New York: Wiley.

Dummett, M. (1967). Gottlob Frege (1848-1925). In P. Edwards (Ed.), *The encyclopedia of philosophy* (Vol. 3, pp. 225–237). New York: Academic Press.

Duxbury Systems Products. (2013). Retrieved June 30, 2013 from http://www.duxburysystems.com/products.asp

Dy, J. G., & Brodley, C. E. (2004). Feature selection for unsupervised learning. *Journal of Machine Learning Research, 5*, 845–889.

Ebada, A., & Maksoud, M. A. (2005). Applying neural networks to predict ship turning track manoeuvring. In *Proceedings of 8th Numerical Towing Tank Symposium.* Academic Press.

Eberhart, R. C., & Kennedy, J. (1995). A new optimizer using particle swarm theory. In *Proceedings of Sixth International Symposium on Micro Machine and Human Science* (pp. 39-43). Academic Press.

Edgeworth, F. Y. (1881). *Mathematical physics.* London: P. Keagan.

Efron, B., Hastie, T., Johnstone, I., & Tibshirani, R. (2004). Least angle regression. *Annals of Statistics, 32*, 407–449. doi:10.1214/009053604000000067

Egmont-Petersen, M., & de Ridder, D. (2002). Image processing using neural networks - A review. *Pattern Recognition, 35*(10), 2279–2301. doi:10.1016/S0031-3203(01)00178-9

Ehsan, P., Alireza, F., Pouya, B., & Ali, K. S. (2008). An experimental comparison of adaptive controllers on a pH neutralization pilot plant. *Annual IEEE India Conference, 2*, 377 – 382.

Elmasri, R., & Navathe, S. K. (2004). *Fundamentals of database systems*. Upper Saddle River, NJ: Pearson Education.

Eshelman, L. J., Mathias, K. E., & Schaffer, J. D. (1997). Convergence controlled variation. In R. Belew, & M. Vose (Eds.), *Foundations of genetic algorithms* (Vol. 4, pp. 203–224). San Francisco: Morgan Kaufmann.

Esseghir, M. A. (2010). Effective wrapper-filter hybridization through grasp schemata. In *Proceedings of the 4th Workshop on Feature Selection in Data Mining*. IEEE.

Estevez, P. A., Flores, R. J., & Perez, C. A. (2005). Color image segmentation using fuzzy min-max neural networks. *Proceedings of IEEE International Joint Conference on Neural Networks, 5*, 3052-3057.

Fan, J., Samworth, R., & Wu, Y. (2009). Ultrahigh dimensional feature selection: Beyond the linear model. *Journal of Machine Learning Research, 10*, 2013–2038. PMID:21603590

Fayyad, U. M., Piatetsky-Shapiro, G., & Smyth, P. (1996). From data mining to knowledge discovery: An overview. In *Advances in knowledge discovery and data mining* (pp. 1–34). Cambridge, MA: MIT Press.

Feng, L., & Liu, Z. (2006). Effects of multi-objective genetic rule selection on short-term load forecasting for anomalous days. In *Proceedings of Power Engineering Society General Meeting*. IEEE.

Feng, W., Huilan, S., & Li-Xin, W. (2006). Adaptive fuzzy control of a pH process. In *Proceedings of IEEE International Conference on Fuzzy Systems*, (pp. 2377 – 2384). IEEE.

Feng, F., Jun, B. Y., Liu, X., & Li, L. (2010). An adjustable approach to fuzzy soft based decision making. *Journal of Computational and Applied Mathematics, 234*(1), 10–20. doi:10.1016/j.cam.2009.11.055

Feng, F., Jun, Y. B., & Zhao, X. Z. (2008). Soft semirings. *Computers & Mathematics with Applications (Oxford, England), 56*(10), 2621–2628. doi:10.1016/j.camwa.2008.05.011

Feng, F., Li, C., Davvaz, B., & Irfan Ali, M. (2010). Soft sets combined with fuzzy sets and rough sets-A tentative approach. *Soft Computing, 14*, 899–911. doi:10.1007/s00500-009-0465-6

Feng, F., Liu, X., Fotea, V. L., & Jun, Y. B. (2011). Soft sets and soft rough sets. *Information Sciences, 181*, 1125–1137. doi:10.1016/j.ins.2010.11.004

Fern, X. Z., & Brodley, C. E. (2003). Random projection for high dimensional data clustering: A cluster ensemble approach. In *Proceedings of International Conference on Machine Learning* (pp. 186-193). IEEE.

Fern, X. Z., & Brodley, C. E. (2004). Solving cluster ensemble problems by bipartite graph partitioning. In *Proceedings of International Conference on Machine Learning* (pp. 36-43). IEEE.

Fernandez, A., Garcia, S., Luengo, J., Bernado-Mansilla, E., & Francisco, H. (2010). Genetic-based machine learning for rule induction: State of art, taxonomy and comparative study. *IEEE Transactions on Evolutionary Computation, 14*(6), 913–943. doi:10.1109/TEVC.2009.2039140

Fink, E., & Pratt, K. B. (2004). Indexing of compressed time series. In *Data mining in time series databases* (pp. 51–78). Singapore: World Scientific. doi:10.1142/9789812565402_0003

Firestone, J. M., & Elroy, M. (2003). *Key issues in the future of knowledge management*. London: Butterworth – Heinemann.

Fischer, B., & Buhmann, J. M. (2003). Bagging for path-based clustering. *IEEE Transactions on Pattern Analysis and Machine Intelligence, 25*(11), 1411–1415. doi:10.1109/TPAMI.2003.1240115

Floudas, C. A., & Pardalos, P. M. (1990). *A collection of test problems for constrained global optimization algorithms*. Belin. Springer Verlag. doi:10.1007/3-540-53032-0

Fogel, L., Owens, A., & Walsh, M. (1966). *Artificial intelligence through simulated evolution*. New York: Wiley.

Fonseca, C. M., & Fleming, P. L. (1995). An overview of evolutionary algorithms in multi-objective optimization. *Evolutionary Computation, 3*, 1–16. doi:10.1162/evco.1995.3.1.1

Fraser, A. (1957). Simulation of genetic systems by automatic digital computers. *Australian Journal of Biological Sciences, 10*, 484–491.

Fred, A. L. N., & Jain, A. K. (2005). Combining multiple clusterings using evidence accumulation. *IEEE Transactions on Pattern Analysis and Machine Intelligence, 27*(6), 835–850. doi:10.1109/TPAMI.2005.113 PMID:15943417

Freitas, A. A. (2003). A survey of evolutionary algorithms for data mining and knowledge discovery. In *Advances in evolutionary computing* (pp. 819–845). Academic Press. doi:10.1007/978-3-642-18965-4_33

Freudenberg, J., Boriss, H., & Hasenclever, D. (2004). Comparison of pre processing procedures for oligonucleotide micro-arrays by parametric bootstrap simulation of spike-in experiments. *Methods of Information in Medicine, 43*, 434–438. PMID:15702196

Frieder, O., & Herman, J. E. (1989). Protocol verification using database technology. *IEEE Journal on Selected Areas in Communications, 7*(3), 324–334. doi:10.1109/49.16865

Friedman, J. H., & Meulman, J. J. (2004). Clustering objects on subsets of attributes. *Journal of the Royal Statistical Society. Series B. Methodological, 66*(4), 825–849. doi:10.1111/j.1467-9868.2004.02059.x

Fu, Y., & Shen, R. (2004). GA based CBR approach in Q&A system. *Expert Systems with Applications, 26*(2), 167–170. doi:10.1016/S0957-4174(03)00117-9

Gacto, M. J., Alcalá, R., & Herrera, F. (2009). A multi-objective evolutionary algorithm for tuning fuzzy rule based systems with measures for preserving interpretability. In *Proceedings of IFSA/EUSFLAT Conf.* (pp. 1146-1151). IFSA.

Gacto, M. J., Alcalá, R., & Herrera, F. (2010). Integration of an index to preserve the semantic interpretability in the multi-objective evolutionary rule selection and tuning of linguistic fuzzy systems. *IEEE Transactions on Fuzzy Systems, 18*(3), 515–531. doi:10.1109/TFUZZ.2010.2041008

Gacto, M. J., Alcala, R., & Herrera, F. (2012). A multi-objective evolutionary algorithms for an effective tuning of fuzzy logic controllers in heating, ventilating and air conditioning systems. *Applied Intelligence, 36*(2), 330–347. doi:10.1007/s10489-010-0264-x

Galip, C., & Omer, F. O. (1996). An adaptive fuzzy controller improving a control system for process control. In *Proceedings of International Conference on Industrial Electronics, Control and Instrumentation,* (vol. 1, pp. 578 – 583). IEEE.

Gan, G. J., & Wu, J. H. (2008). A convergence theorem for the fuzzy subspace clustering (FSC) algorithm. *Pattern Recognition, 41*, 1939–1947. doi:10.1016/j.patcog.2007.11.011

Ganter, B. (1984). *Two basic algorithms in concept analysis (Technical Report No-831)*. Technishe Hoschule Darmstadt.

Ganter, B. (2002). *Formal concept analysis: Algorithmic aspects (Technical Report)*. Technical University Dresden.

Ganter, B., Stumme, G., & Wille, R. (2005). *Formal concept analysis: Foundations and applications*. Berlin: Springer Verlag.

Ganter, B., & Wille, R. (1999). *Formal concept analysis: Mathematical foundations*. Berlin: Springer Verlag. doi:10.1007/978-3-642-59830-2

Garcia, E., Romero, C., Ventura, S., & De Castro, C. (2009). An architecture for making recommendations to courseware authors using association rule mining and collaborative filtering. *User Modeling and User-Adapted Interaction, 19*(1-2), 99–132. doi:10.1007/s11257-008-9047-z

Gardner, E. S., McKenzie, J. R., & McKenzie, E. D. (1989). Seasonal exponential smoothing with damped trends. *Management Science, 35*(3), 372–376. doi:10.1287/mnsc.35.3.372

Garrell, J. M., Golobardes, E., Bernado, E., & Llora, X. (1999). Automatic diagnosis with genetic algorithms and case-based reasoning. *Artificial Intelligence in Engineering, 13*(4), 367–372. doi:10.1016/S0954-1810(99)00009-6

Gen, M., & Cheng, R. (1997). *Genetic algorithms and engineering design.* New York: Wiley.

Gershenfeld, N. A., & Weigend, A. S. (1993). The future of time series. In *Time series prediction: Forecasting the future and understanding the past.* Reading, MA: Addison-Wesley.

Getz, G., & Domany, E. (2003). Coupled two-way clustering server. *Bioinformatics (Oxford, England), 19,* 1153–1154. doi:10.1093/bioinformatics/btg143 PMID:12801877

Ghandar, A., & Michalewicz, Z. (2011). An experimental study of multi-objective evolutionary algorithms for balancing interpretability and accuracy in fuzzy rule base classifiers for financial prediction. In *Proceedings of Computational Intelligence for Financial Engineering and Economics (CIFEr)* (pp. 1–6). IEEE.

Ghosh, A., & Das, M. K. (2008). Non-dominated rank based sorting genetic algorithms. *Fundamenta Informaticae, 83*(3), 231–252.

Ghosh, A., & Nath, B. (2004). Multi-objective rule mining using genetic algorithms. *Information Sciences, 163,* 123–133. doi:10.1016/j.ins.2003.03.021

Ghosh, A., Pal, N. R., & Pal, S. K. (1993). Self-organization for object extraction using a multilayer neural network and fuzziness measures. *IEEE Transactions on Fuzzy Systems, 1*(1), 54–68. doi:10.1109/TFUZZ.1993.390285

Ghosh, P., Kundu, K., & Sarkar, D. (2010). Fuzzy graph representation of fuzzy concept lattice. *Fuzzy Sets and Systems, 161,* 1669–1675. doi:10.1016/j.fss.2009.10.027

Gionis, A., Mannila, H., & Tsaparas, P. (2005). Clustering aggregation. In *Proceedings of International Conference on Data Engineering* (pp. 341-352). IEEE.

Godin, R., & Missaoui, R. (1994). An incremental concept formation approach for learning from databases. *Theoretical Computer Science, 133,* 387–419. doi:10.1016/0304-3975(94)90195-3

Goldberg, D. E. (1989). *Genetic algorithm in search optimization and machine learning.* Reading, MA: Addison-Wesley.

Golobardes, E., Llora, X., Salamo, M., & Marti, J. (2002). Computer aided diagnosis with case-based reasoning and genetic algorithms. *Knowledge-Based Systems, 15,* 45–52. doi:10.1016/S0950-7051(01)00120-4

Golub, T., Slonim, D., Tamayo, P., Huard, C., Gaasenbeek, M., & Mesirov, J. et al. (1999). Molecular classification of cancer: Class discovery and class prediction by gene expression monitoring. *Science, 286,* 531–537. doi:10.1126/science.286.5439.531 PMID:10521349

Gomm, J. B., Doherty, S. K., & Williams, D. (1996). Control of pH in-line using a neural predictive strategy. In *Proceedings of International Conference on Control,* (vol. 2, pp. 1058 – 1063). IEEE.

Gonzalez, R. C., & Woods, R. E. (2002). *Digital image processing.* Upper Saddle River, NJ: Prentice Hall.

Goodchild, A. V., & Daganzo, C. F. (2004). *Reducing ship turn-around time using double-cycling, research reports.* Berkeley, CA: UC Berkeley.

Goodrich, M. T., & Kloss, J. G., II. (1999). Tiered vectors: Efficient dynamic arrays for rank-based sequences. In *Proceedings of the Workshop on Algorithms and Data Structures* (vol. 1663, pp. 205–216). IEEE. doi:10.1007/3-540-48447-7_21

Gorodetsky, V., & Samoylov, V. (2010). Feature extraction for machine learning: Logic probabilistic approach. In *Proceedings of the 4th Workshop on Feature Selection in Data Mining.* IEEE.

Gouy-Pailler, C., Zijp-Rouzier, S., Vidal, S., & Chêne, D. (2007). A haptic based interface to ease visually impaired pupils' inclusion in geometry lessons. In *Proceedings of 4th International Conference on Universal Access in Human-Computer Interaction* (pp. 598-606). IEEE.

Govedarova, N., Stoyanov, S., & Popchev, I. (2003). An ontology based CBR architecture for knowledge management in BULCHINO catalogue. In *Proceedings of International Conference on Computer Systems and Technologies.* CompSysTech.

Gray, R. M. (2011). *Entropy and information theory* (2nd ed.). New York: Springer Verlag. doi:10.1007/978-1-4419-7970-4

Greene, D. P., & Smith, S. F. (1993). Competition-based induction of decision models from examples. *Machine Learning*, *13*(23), 229–257. doi:10.1023/A:1022622013558

Gronau, N., & Laskowski, F. (2003). Using case-based reasoning to improve. In *Spring Information Retrieval in Knowledge Management Systems (LNCS)* (Vol. 2663, p. 954). Berlin: Springer.

Grover, L. (1996). A fast quantum mechanical algorithm for database search. In *Proceedings of 28th ACM Symposium on Theory of Computing*, (pp. 212–219). ACM.

Grzegorzewski, P. (2004). Distances between intuitionistic fuzzy sets and/or interval-valued fuzzy sets based on the Hausdorff metric. *Fuzzy Sets and Systems*, *148*, 319–328. doi:10.1016/j.fss.2003.08.005

Guha, S. K., & Anand, S. (1992). Computer as a group teaching aid for persons who are blind. *Journal of Rehabilitation Research and Development*, *29*(3), 57–63. doi:10.1682/JRRD.1992.07.0057 PMID:1640382

Gu, J., & Liu, J. S. (2008). Bayesian biclustering of gene expression data. *BMC Genomics*, *9*(Suppl 1), S4. doi:10.1186/1471-2164-9-S1-S4 PMID:18366617

Gustafsson, T. K. (1982). Calculation of the pH value of a mixture solutions-An illustration of the use of chemical reaction invariants. *Chemical Engineering Science*, *37*(9), 1419–1421. doi:10.1016/0009-2509(82)85013-6

Gustafsson, T. K., & Skrifvars, B. O., Sandstroem, & Waller, K. V. (1995). Modeling of pH for control. *Industrial & Engineering Chemistry Research*, *34*(3), 820–827. doi:10.1021/ie00042a014

Gustafsson, T. K., & Waller, K. V. (1983). Dynamic modelling and reaction invariant control of pH. *Chemical Engineering Science*, *38*(3), 389–398. doi:10.1016/0009-2509(83)80157-2

Gustafsson, T. K., & Waller, K. V. (1992). Nonlinear and adaptive control of pH. *Industrial & Engineering Chemistry Research*, *31*(12), 2681–2693. doi:10.1021/ie00012a009

Gyenesei, A., & Teuhola, J. (2001). Interestingness measures for fuzzy association rules. In *Principles of data mining and knowledge discovery* (pp. 152–164). Berlin: Springer. doi:10.1007/3-540-44794-6_13

Hall, M. A. (2000). Correlation-based feature selection for discrete and numeric class machine learning. In *Proceedings of the 17th Int'l Conf. Machine Learning* (pp. 359-366). IEEE.

Halvorsen, O. J., Oyan, A. M., & Bo, T. H. et al. (2005). Gene expression profiles in prostate cancer: Association with patient subgroups and tumour differentiation. *International Journal of Oncology*, *26*, 329–336. PMID:15645116

Han, J., & Kamber, M. (2001). *Data mining: Concepts and techniques*. San Francisco: Morgan Kaufman.

Han, J., & Kamber, M. (2006). *Data mining concepts and techniques* (2nd ed.). San Francisco: Morgan Kaufmann.

Han, J., Pei, J., & Yin, Y. (2000). Mining frequent patterns without candidate generation. *SIGMOD Record*, *29*(2), 1–12. doi:10.1145/335191.335372

Han, K., & Kim, J. (2002). Quantum-inspired evolutionary algorithm for a class combinational optimization. *IEEE Transactions on Evolutionary Computation*, *6*(6), 580–593. doi:10.1109/TEVC.2002.804320

Harrison, P. J. (1967). Exponential smoothing and short-term sales forecasting. *Management Science*, *13*(11), 821–842. doi:10.1287/mnsc.13.11.821

Haskell, R. (2008). *The craft of functional programming* (2nd ed.). Upper Saddle River, NJ: Simon Thomson, Pearson Addison Wesley Longman.

Haykin, S. (1999). *Neural networks: A comprehensive foundation*. Upper Saddle River, NJ: Prentice Hall.

Henson, M. A., & Seborg, D. E. (1994). Adaptive nonlinear control of a pH neutralization process. *IEEE Transactions on Control Systems Technology*, *2*(3), 169–182. doi:10.1109/87.317975

Hermann, M., & Sertkaya, B. (2008). On the complexity of computing generators of closed sets. In *International Conference on Formal Concept Analysis* (LNAI), (vol. 4933, pp. 158-168). Berlin: Springer-Verlag.

Hermansson, A. W., Syafiie, S., & Mohd Noor, S. B. (2010). Multiple model predictive control of nonlinear pH neutralization system. In *Proceedings of IEEE International Conference on Industrial Engineering and Engineering Management,* (pp. 301 – 304). IEEE.

Herrera, F. (2008). Genetic fuzzy systems: taxonomy, current research trends and prospects. *Evolutionary Intelligence, 1,* 27–46. doi:10.1007/s12065-007-0001-5

Hesham, M. K., & James, A. L. (1999). The integrated communication 2 draw (IC2D), a drawing program for the visually impaired. In *Proceedings of Extended Abstracts on Human Factors in Computing Systems (CHI '99)* (pp. 222-223). ACM.

Hey, T. (1999). Quantum computing: An introduction. *IEEE Computing & Control Engineering, 10,* 105–112. doi:10.1049/cce:19990303

Himmelblau, D. M. (1997). *Applied nonlinear programming.* New York: McGraw-Hill.

Hinterding, R. (1999). Representation, constraint satisfaction and the knapsack problem. In *Proceedings of 2008 Congress on Evolutionary Computation. Piscataway.* IEEE Press.

Hochbaum, D. S., & Shmoys, D. B. (1985). A best possible heuristic for the k-center problem. *Mathematics of Operations Research, 10*(2), 180–184. doi:10.1287/moor.10.2.180

Hogarth, R. M., & Makridakis, S. (1981). Forecasting and planning: An evaluation. *Management Science, 27*(2), 115–138. doi:10.1287/mnsc.27.2.115

Holland, J. (1975). *Adaptation in natural and artificial systems.* Ann Arbor, MI: University of Michigan Press.

Holland, J. H., & Reitman, J. S. (1978). Cognitive systems based on adaptive algorithms. In *Pattern-directed inference systems.* Academic Press.

Holt, A., & Commoner, F. (1970). Events and conditions. In *Applied Data Research, New York (1970) and Record of the Project MAC Conf. on Concurrent Systems and Parallel Computation.* New York: ACM.

Holt, A., Saint, H., Shapiro, R., & Warshall, S. (1968). *Final report of the information system theory project* (Technical Report RADC-TR-68-305). New York: Rome Air Development Centre, Griffiss Air Force Base.

Holzmann, G. J. (1991). Design and validation of computer protocols. Englewood Cliffs, NJ: PH.

Hong, T., Morris, A. J., Karim, M. N., Zhang, J., & Luo, W. (1996). Nonlinear control of a wastewater pH neutralisation process using adaptive NARX models. *IEEE International Conference on Systems, Man, and Cybernetics, 2,* 911 – 916.

Hong, D. H., & Kim, C. A. (1999). Note on similarity measure between vague sets and elements. *Information Sciences, 115,* 83–96. doi:10.1016/S0020-0255(98)10083-X

Horstmann, M., Lorenz, M., Watkowski, A., Ioannidis, G., Herzog, O., & King, A. et al. (2004). Automated interpretation and accessible presentation of technical diagrams for blind people. *New Review of Hypermedia and Multimedia, 10*(2), 141–163. doi:10.1080/1361456 0512331326017

Hossain, M., Hossain, M., & Hashem, M. (2010). A generalizes hybrid real-coded quantum evolutionary algorithm based on particle swarm theory with arithmetic crossover. [IJCSIT]. *International Journal of Computer Science & Information TECHNOLOGY, 2*(4). doi:10.5121/ijcsit.2010.2415

Hsu, C. I., Chiu, C., & Hsu, P. L. (2004). Predicting information systems outsourcing success using a hierarchical design of case-based reasoning. *Expert Systems with Applications, 26*(3), 435–441. doi:10.1016/j.eswa.2003.10.002

Huang, L., & Wang, G. M. (1995). Image thresholding by minimizing the measures of fuzziness. *Pattern Recognition, 28,* 41–51. doi:10.1016/0031-3203(94)E0043-K

Iam-On, N., & Boongoen, T. (2012). New soft subspace method to gene expression data clustering. In *Proceedings of IEEE-EMBS International Conference on Biomedical and Health Informatics* (pp. 984-987). IEEE.

Iam-On, N., Boongoen, T., & Garrett, S. (2010). LCE: A link-based cluster ensemble method for improved gene expression data analysis. *Bioinformatics (Oxford, England), 26*(12), 1513–1519. doi:10.1093/bioinformatics/btq226 PMID:20444838

Iam-On, N., Boongoen, T., Garrett, S., & Price, C. (2011). A link-based approach to the cluster ensemble problem. *IEEE Transactions on Pattern Analysis and Machine Intelligence, 33*(12), 2396–2409. doi:10.1109/TPAMI.2011.84 PMID:21576752

Iam-On, N., & Garrett, S. (2010). LinkCluE: A MATLAB package for link-based cluster ensembles. *Journal of Statistical Software, 36*(9).

Inclusion in Education of Children and Persons with Disabilities. (2008). Retrieved June 30, 2013 from http://www.ibe.unesco.org/National_Reports/ICE_2008/india_NR08.pdf

Inza, I., Larranaga, P., Blanco, R., & Cerrolaza, A. (2004). Filter versus wrapper gene selection approaches in DNA microarray domains. *Artificial Intelligence in Medicine, 31*, 91–103. doi:10.1016/j.artmed.2004.01.007 PMID:15219288

Iordache, O. (2011). Formal concept analysis. *Modelling Multilevel Systems, 9*, 143–162. doi:10.1007/978-3-642-17946-4_9

Ireneus, W., & Sudchai, B. (2010). *Modeling and control of an experimental pH neutralization plant using neural networks based approximate predictive control.* Academic Press.

Irizarry, R. A., Bolstad, B. M., Collin, F., Cope, L. M., Hobbs, B., & Speed, T. P. (2003). Summaries of affymetrix GeneChip probe level data. *Nucleic Acids Research, 31*, e15. doi:10.1093/nar/gng015 PMID:12582260

Ishibuchi, H., Kuwajima, I., & Nojima, Y. (2007). Use of Pareto-optimal and near Pareto-optimal candidate rules in genetic fuzzy rule selection. In *Analysis and design of intelligent systems using soft computing techniques* (pp. 387–396). Berlin: Springer. doi:10.1007/978-3-540-72432-2_39

Ishibuchi, H., Murata, T., & Turksen, I. B. (1997). Single-objective and two-objective genetic algorithms for selecting linguistic rules for pattern classification problems. *Fuzzy Sets and Systems, 89*(2), 135–150. doi:10.1016/S0165-0114(96)00098-X

Ishibuchi, H., Nakashima, T., & Murata, T. (2001). Three objective genetic-based machine learning for linguistic rule extraction. *Information Science, 136*, 109–133. doi:10.1016/S0020-0255(01)00144-X

Ishibuchi, H., & Yamamoto, T. (2004). Fuzzy rule selection by multi-objective genetic local search algorithms and rule evaluation measures in data mining. *Fuzzy Sets and Systems, 141*(1), 59–88. doi:10.1016/S0165-0114(03)00114-3

Isibuchi, H., & Nojima, Y. (2007). Analysis of interpretability-accuracy tradeoff of fuzzy systems by multi-objective genetic-based machine learning. *International Journal of Approximate Reasoning, 44*, 4–31. doi:10.1016/j.ijar.2006.01.004

Jacobs, D. W., Weinshall, D., & Gdalyahu, Y. (2000). Classification with nonmetric distances: Image retrieval and class representation. *IEEE Transactions on Pattern Analysis and Machine Intelligence, 22*(6), 583–600. doi:10.1109/34.862197

Jaeger, J., Weichenhan, D., Ivandic, B., & Spang, R. (2005). Early diagnostic marker panel determination for microarray based clinical studies. *Statistical Applications in Genetics and Molecular Biology, 4*(9). PMID:16646862

Jafar, O. A. M., & Shivakumar, R. (2010). Ant-based clustering algorithms: A brief survey. *International Journal of Computer Theory and Engineering, 2*(5), 1793–8201.

Jain, A. K., & Dubes, R. C. (1988). *Algorithms for clustering data.* Upper Saddle River, NJ: Prentice Hall.

Jalali-Heravi, M., & Zaïane, O. R. (2010). A study on interestingness measures for associative classifiers. In *Proceedings of the 2010 ACM Symposium on Applied Computing* (pp. 1039-1046). ACM.

Jansen, B. J., & Rieh, S. Y. (2010). The seventeen theoretical constructs of information searching and information retrieval. *Journal of the American Society for Information Science and Technology*, *61*(8), 1517–1534.

Jawahar, C., Biswas, P., & Ray, A. (1997). Investigations on fuzzy thresholding based on fuzzy clustering. *Pattern Recognition*, *30*, 1605–1613. doi:10.1016/S0031-3203(97)00004-6

Jayant, C., Renzelmann, M., Wen, D., Krisnandi, S., Ladner, R. E., & Comden, D. (2007). Automated tactile graphics translation: in the field. In *Proceedings of AS-SETS* (pp. 75-82). ASSETS.

Jiang, D., Pei, J., & Zhang, A. (2003). DHC: A density-based hierarchical clustering method for time-series gene expression data. In *Proceedings of the BIBE 2003: Third IEEE Intl Symp Bioinformatics and Bioeng* (pp. 393-400). IEEE.

Jiang, Y., Chen, K. J., & Zhou, Z. H. (2003). SOM-based image segmentation. In *Proceedings of 9th Conf. Rough Sets, Fuzzy Sets, Data Mining and Granular Computing*, (pp. 640-643). IEEE.

Jiang, D., Tang, C., & Zhang, A. (2004). Cluster analysis for gene expression data: A survey. *IEEE Transactions on Knowledge and Data Engineering*, *16*(11), 1370–1386. doi:10.1109/TKDE.2004.68

Jiang, Y., & Zhou, Z. (2004). SOM ensemble-based image segmentation. *Neural Processing Letters*, *20*(3), 171–178. doi:10.1007/s11063-004-2022-8

Ji-Lin, C., Yuan-Long, H., Zong-Yi, X., Li-Min, J., & Zhong-Zhi, T. (2006). A multi-objective genetic-based method for designing fuzzy classification systems. *International Journal of Computer Science and Network Security*, *6*(8A), 110–117.

Jing, L., Ng, M. K., & Huang, J. Z. (2007). An entropy weighting k-means algorithm for subspace clustering of high-dimensional sparse data. *IEEE Transactions on Knowledge and Data Engineering*, *19*(8), 1026–1041. doi:10.1109/TKDE.2007.1048

Jin, Y. (2000). Fuzzy modeling of high-dimensional systems: complexity reduction and interpretability improvement. *IEEE Transactions on Fuzzy Systems*, *8*, 212–222. doi:10.1109/91.842154

Jin-Yong, C., & Rhinehart, R. R. (1987). Internal adaptive-model control of waste water pH. In *Proceedings of IEEE American Control Conference*, (pp. 2084 –2089). IEEE.

Jo, H., & Han, I. (1996). Integration of case-based forecasting, neural network, and discriminate analysis for bankruptcy prediction. *Expert Systems with Applications*, *11*(4), 415–422. doi:10.1016/S0957-4174(96)00056-5

Johannsen, G., & Bille, J. (1982). A threshold selection method using information measures.[ICPR.]. *Proceedings of ICPR*, *82*, 140–143.

John, G. H., Kohavi, R., & Pfleger, K. (1994). Irrelevant feature and the subset selection problem. In *Proceedings of the 11th Int'l Conference on Machine Learning* (pp. 121-129). IEEE.

Joliffe, I. (1986). *Principal component analysis*. New York: Springer. doi:10.1007/978-1-4757-1904-8

Jong, M. C. M. (1995). Mathematical modelling in veterinary epidemiology: Why model building is important. *Preventive Veterinary Medicine*, *25*, 183–193. doi:10.1016/0167-5877(95)00538-2

Joshi, M., Lingras, P., Wani, G., & Zheng, P. (2011). Clustering based stability despite of temporal variations. In *Proceedings of the International Conference on Information Technology, Systems and Management (ITSM 2011)*, (pp. 306-311). Macmillan Publisher.

Juan, Y. K., Shin, S. G., & Perng, Y. H. (2006). Decision support for housing customization: A hybrid approach using case-based reasoning and genetic algorithm. *Expert Systems with Applications*, *31*(1), 83–93. doi:10.1016/j.eswa.2005.09.010

Jun, Y. B. (2008). Soft BCK/BCI-algebras. *Computers & Mathematics with Applications (Oxford, England)*, *56*(5), 1408–1413. doi:10.1016/j.camwa.2008.02.035

Jun, Y. B., & Park, C. H. (2008). Applications of soft sets in ideal theory of BCK/BCI algebras. *Information Sciences*, *178*(11), 2466–2475.

Jun, Y. B., & Park, C. H. (2009). Application of soft sets in Hilbert algebras. *Iranian Journal of Fuzzy Systems*, *6*(2), 75–86.

Jurekevicius, D., & Vasilecas, O. (2009). Formal concept analysis for concept collecting and their analysis. *Scientific Paper*, *751*, 22–39.

Kang, C. C., & Wang, W. J. (2009). *Fuzzy based seeded region growing for image segmentation*. Paper presented at the 2009 Annual Meeting of the North American Fuzzy Information Processing Society. New York, NY.

Karl, E. W. (1994). A first course in formal concept analysis: How to understand line diagram. In Soft Stat'93 Advances in Statistical Software, (vol. 4, pp. 429-438). Gustav Fisher Verlag.

Karr, C. L., & Gentry, E. J. (1993). Fuzzy control of pH using genetic algorithms. *IEEE Transactions on Fuzzy Systems*, *1*(1), 46–53. doi:10.1109/TFUZZ.1993.390283

Kaur, H., & Wasan, S. K. (2006). Empirical study on applications of data mining techniques in healthcare. *Journal of Computer Science*, *2*(2), 194–200. doi:10.3844/jcssp.2006.194.200

Kaya, M. (2006). Multi-objective genetic algorithm based approaches for mining optimized fuzzy association rules. *Soft Computing*, *10*, 578–586. doi:10.1007/s00500-005-0509-5

Kaya, M., & Alhajj, R. (2004). Integrating multi-objective genetic algorithms into clustering for fuzzy association rules mining. In *Proceedings of Data Mining* (pp. 431–434). IEEE. doi:10.1109/ICDM.2004.10050

Kaya, M., & Alhajj, R. (2004). Multi-objective genetic algorithm based method for mining optimized fuzzy association rules. In *Proceedings of Intelligent Data Engineering and Automated Learning* (pp. 758–764). Berlin: Springer. doi:10.1007/978-3-540-28651-6_113

Kaytoue, M., Kuznetsov, S. O., Napoli, A., & Duplessis, S. (2011). Mining gene expression data with pattern structures in formal concept analysis. *Information Sciences*, *181*, 1989–2001. doi:10.1016/j.ins.2010.07.007

Kelkar, B., & Postlethwaite, B. (1994). Study of pH control process using fuzzy modeling. *International Conference on Control*, *1*, 272 – 275.

Kennedy, J., & Eberhart, R. C. (1995). Particle swarm optimization. *Neural Networks*, *4*, 1942–1948.

Keogh, E., & Kasetty, S. (2002). On the need for time series data mining benchmark: A survey and empirical demonstration.[ACM.]. *Proceedings of SIGKDD*, *02*, 102–111.

Khalili-Damghari, K., Sadi-Nezhad, S., Lotfi, F. H., & Tavana, M. (2013). A hybrid fuzzy rule-based multi-criteria framework for sustainable project portfolio selection. *Journal of Information Science*, *220*, 442–462. doi:10.1016/j.ins.2012.07.024

Kharal, A., & Ahmad, B. (2011). Mapping on soft classes. *New Mathematics & Natural Computation*, *7*(3), 471–481. doi:10.1142/S1793005711002025

Kilama, W., & Ntoumi, F. (2009). Malaria: A research agenda for the eradication era. *Lancet*, *374*(9700), 1480–1482. doi:10.1016/S0140-6736(09)61884-5 PMID:19880004

Kilic, K., & Casillas, J. (2012). Hybrid genetic-fuzzy system modeling application in innovation management. In J. Casillas et al. (Eds.), *Management intelligent systems* (pp. 25–34). Berlin: Springer-Verlag. doi:10.1007/978-3-642-30864-2_3

Kim, J. H., & Myung, H. (1996). A two phase evolutionary programming for general constrained optimization problem. In *Proceedings of the Fifth Annual Conference on Evolutionary Programming*. San Diego, CA: Academic Press.

Kim, Y., Kim, J., & Han, K. (2006). Quantum-inspired multiobjective evolutionary algorithm for multiobjective 0/1 knapsack problems. In *Proceedings of 2006 IEEE Congress on Evolutionary Computation*. IEEE.

Kim, Y., Street, W., & Menczer, F. (2000). Feature selection for unsupervised learning via evolutionary search. In *Proceedings of the Sixth ACM SIGKDD Int'l Conf. Knowledge Discovery and Data Mining* (pp. 365-369). ACM.

Kim, J. H., & Myung, H. (1997). Evolutionary programming techniques for constrained optimization problems. *IEEE Transactions on Evolutionary Computation*, *1*(2), 129–140. doi:10.1109/4235.687880

Kim, K. (2004). Toward global optimization of case-based reasoning systems for financial forecasting. *Applied Intelligence*, *21*(3), 239–249. doi:10.1023/B:APIN.0000043557.93085.72

Kim, K., & Han, I. (2001). Maintaining case-based reasoning systems using a genetic algorithms approach. *Expert Systems with Applications*, *21*(3), 139–145. doi:10.1016/S0957-4174(01)00035-5

Kim, Y. C., & Kim, T. G. (1996). Petri nets modeling and analysis using extended bag-theoretic relational algebra. *IEEE Trans. on Systems, Man, and Cybernetics -Part B*, *26*(4), 599–605. doi:10.1109/3477.517034 PMID:18263057

King, B. (1967). Step-wise clustering procedures. *Journal of the American Statistical Association*, *69*, 86–101. doi:10.1080/01621459.1967.10482890

Kittler, J., Hatef, M., Duin, R., & Matas, J. (1998). On combining classifiers. *IEEE Transactions on Pattern Analysis and Machine Intelligence*, *20*(3), 226–239. doi:10.1109/34.667881

Klier, G. J., & Yuan, B. (1995). *Fuzzy sets and fuzzy logic: Theory and applications* (6th ed.). Upper Saddle River, NJ: Prentice-Hall.

Knell, R. J., Begon, M., & Thompson, D. J. (1996). Transmission dynamics of bacillus thuringiensis infecting Plodia inter-punctella: A test of the mass action assumption with an insect pathogen. *Proceedings. Biological Sciences*, *263*(1366), 75–81. doi:10.1098/rspb.1996.0013

Knuth, D. E. (1968). *The art of computer programming*. Reading, MA: Addison Wesley.

Kolodner, J. (1983). Reconstructive memory: A computer model. *Cognitive Science*, *7*, 281–328. doi:10.1207/s15516709cog0704_2

Kolodner, J. L. (1993). *Case-based reasoning: Techniques for enterprise systems*. San Mateo, CA: Morgan Kaufman.

Kong, Z., Gao, L. Q., & Wang, L. F. (2009). Comment on a fuzzy soft set theoretic approach to decision making problems. *Journal of Computational and Applied Mathematics*, *223*, 540–542. doi:10.1016/j.cam.2008.01.011

Kong, Z., Gao, L., Wang, L., & Li, S. (2008). The normal parameter reduction of soft sets and its algorithm. *Computers & Mathematics with Applications (Oxford, England)*, *56*, 3029–3037. doi:10.1016/j.camwa.2008.07.013

Kosko, B. (1986). Fuzzy entropy and conditioning. *Information Sciences*, *40*(2), 165–174. doi:10.1016/0020-0255(86)90006-X

Kouk, C. M., Fu, A., & Wong, M. H. (1998). Fuzzy association rules in databases. *SIGMOD*, *27*(1), 41–46. doi:10.1145/273244.273257

Krajca, P., Outrata, J., & Vychodil, V. (2010). Advances in algorithms based on CBO. In *Proceedings of CLA* (pp. 325-337). CLA.

Krebs, B. M. (1977). *ABCs of Braille*. Braille Institute of America.

Kriegel, H. P., Kroger, P., & Zimek, A. (2009). Clustering high-dimensional data: A survey on subspace clustering, pattern-based clustering, and correlation clustering.[-ex.]. *ACM Transactions on KDD*, *3*(1), 1.

Krohn, U., Davies, N. J., & Weeks, R. (1999). Concept lattices for knowledge management. *BT Technology Journal*, *17*(4), 108–116. doi:10.1023/A:1009607427957

Krufka, S. E., & Barner, K. E. (2005). Automatic production of tactile graphics from scalable vector graphics. In *Proceedings of 7th International ACM SIGACCESS Conference on Computers and Accessibility*. ACM.

Kruger, G. A. (2005). A statistician looks at inventory management. *Quality Progress*, *38*(2), 36.

Krupka, J., Kasparova, M., & Jirava, P. (2009). Case-based reasoning model in process of emergency management. *Advances in Soft. Computing*, *59*, 77–84.

Kumar, C. A. (2011). Mining association rules using non-negative matrix factorization and formal concept analysis. In *5th International Conference on Information Processing*, (vol. 157, pp. 31-39). Berlin: Springer --Verlag.

Kumar, C. A., & Sumangali, K. (2012). A performance of evaluation of employees of an organization using formal concept analysis. In *Proceedings of International Conference on Pattern Recognition, Informatics & Medical Engineering* (pp. 94-98). IEEE.

Kumar, P., Gopalan, S., & Sridhar, V. (2005). Context enabled multi-CBR based recommendation engine for e-commerce. In *Proceedings of the IEEE international conference on e-business engineering (ICEBE)* (pp. 237–244). IEEE Press.

Kumar, C. A. (2011). Knowledge discovery in data using formal concept analysis and random projections. *International Journal of Applied Mathematics and Computer Science, 21*(4), 745–756. doi:10.2478/v10006-011-0059-1

Kumar, C. A. (2012). Fuzzy clustering based formal concept analysis for associaton rules mining. *Applied Artificial Intelligence, 26*(3), 274–301. doi:10.1080/08839514.2012.648457

Kumar, C. A. (2013). Designing role-based access model using formal concept analysis. *Security and Communication Networks, 6,* 373–383. doi:10.1002/sec.589

Kumar, C. A., Radvansky, M., & Annapurna, J. (2012). Analysis of vector space model, latent semantic indexing and formal concept analysis for information retrieval. *Cybernetics and Information Technologies, 12*(1), 34–48.

Kumar, C. A., & Srinivas, S. (2010). Mining associations in health care data using formal concept analysis and singular value decomposition. *Journal of Biological System, 18*(4), 787–807. doi:10.1142/S0218339010003512

Kumar, C. A., & Srinivas, S. (2010). Concept lattice reduction using fuzzy k-means clustering. *Expert Systems with Applications, 37,* 2696–2704. doi:10.1016/j.eswa.2009.09.026

Kumar, M., & Patel, N. (2010). Using clustering to improve sales forecasts in retail merchandising. *Annals of Operations Research, 174*(1), 33–46. doi:10.1007/s10479-008-0417-z

Kuncheva, L. I., & Hadjitodorov, S. T. (2004). Using diversity in cluster ensembles. In *Proceedings of the IEEE International Conference on Systems, Man & Cybernetics* (pp. 1214-1219). IEEE.

Kuncheva, L. I. (2000). *Fuzzy classifier design.* Berlin: Springer. doi:10.1007/978-3-7908-1850-5

Kuncheva, L. I., & Vetrov, D. (2006). Evaluation of stability of k-means cluster ensembles with respect to random initialization. *IEEE Transactions on Pattern Analysis and Machine Intelligence, 28*(11), 1798–1808. doi:10.1109/TPAMI.2006.226 PMID:17063684

Kundu, S., & Osyczka, A. (1996). Genetic multicriteria optimization of structural systems. In *Proceedings of the 19th International Congress on Theoretical and Applied Mechanics (ICTAM).* Kyoto, Japan: IUTAM.

Kurze, M. (1996). Tdraw: A computer-based tactile drawing tool for blind people. In *Proceedings of Second Annual ACM Conference on Assistive Technologies* (pp. 131-138). Vancouver, Canada: ACM.

Kuznetsov, S. O. (2004). Machine learning and formal concept analysis. In *Proceedings of International Conference on Formal Concept Analysis* (pp. 287-312). IEEE.

Kuznetsov, S. O., & Obiedkov, S. A. (2000). *Algorithm for construction of the set of all concepts and their line diagram (Preprint MATH-AI-05).* Dresden, Germany: TU-Dresden.

Kuznetsov, S. O., & Obiedkov, S. A. (2002). Comparing performance of algorithms for generating concept lattices. *Journal of Experimental & Theoretical Artificial Intelligence, 14*(2/3), 189–216. doi:10.1080/09528130210164170

L`azaro, J., Mart`ın, J., Arias, J., Astarloa, A., & Cuadrado, C. (2010). Neuro semantic thresholding using OCR software for high precision OCR applications. *Image and Vision Computing, 28*(4), 571–578. doi:10.1016/j.imavis.2009.09.011

Lahav, O., & Mioduser, D. (2008). Haptic-feedback support for cognitive mapping of unknown spaces by people who are blind. *International Journal of Human-Computer Studies, 66,* 23–35. doi:10.1016/j.ijhcs.2007.08.001

Lahiri, A., Chattopadhyay, S. J., & Basu, A. (2005). Sparsha: A comprehensive indian language toolset for the blind. In *Proceedings of 7th International ACM SIGACCESS Conference on Computers and Accessibility.* ACM.

Landau, S., & Gourgey, K. (2003). A new approach to interactive audio/tactile computing: the talking tactile tablet. In *Proceedings of Technology and Persons with Disabilities Conference.* California State Univ. Northridge.

Larson, R., Hostetler, R., & Edwards, B. H. (2008). *Essential calculus - Early transcendental functions.* Boston: Houghton Mifflin Company.

Laumanns, M., Thiele, L., Deb, K., & Zitzler, E. (2002). Combining convergence and diversity in evolutionary multi-objective optimization. *Evolutionary Computation, 10*(3), 263–282. doi:10.1162/106365602760234108 PMID:12227996

Law, M. H. C., Figueiredo, M. A. T., & Jain, A. K. (2004). Simultaneous feature selection and clustering using mixture models. *Pattern Analysis and Machine Intelligence, 26,* 1154–1166. doi:10.1109/TPAMI.2004.71 PMID:15742891

Lawrence, J. (1993). *Introduction to neural networks: Design, theory, and applications.* California Scientific Software Press.

Lebowitz, M. (1983). Memory-based parsing. *Artificial Intelligence, 21,* 363–404. doi:10.1016/S0004-3702(83)80019-8

Lee, H., Hong, S., & Kim, E. (2009). Neural network ensemble with probabilistic fusion and its application to gait recognition. *Neurocomputing, 72,* 1557–1564. doi:10.1016/j.neucom.2008.09.009

Lee, J. W., Lee, J. B., Park, M., & Song, S. H. (2005). An extensive comparison of recent classification tools applied to microarray data. *Computational Statistics & Data Analysis, 48,* 869–885. doi:10.1016/j.csda.2004.03.017

Lee, M. C., Chen, H. H., & Li, S. Y. (2011). FCA based concept constructing and similarity measurement algorithms. *International Journal of Advancements in computing. Technology (Elmsford, N.Y.), 3*(1).

Lee, T. T., & Lai, M. (1988). A relational approach to protocol verification. *IEEE Transactions on Software Engineering, 14*(2), 184–193. doi:10.1109/32.4637

Lee, T., & Chen, I. (2005). A two-stage hybrid credit scoring model using artificial neural networks and multivariate adaptive regression splines. *Expert Systems with Applications, 28*(4), 743–752. doi:10.1016/j.eswa.2004.12.031

Lee, W., Stolfo, S. J., & Mok, K. W. (2000). Adaptive intrusion detection: A data mining approach. *AI Rev., 14*(6), 533–567.

Lenz, M., Bartsch-Sporl, B., Burkhard, H., & Wess, S. (1998). Case-based reasoning technology – From foundation to applications. *Lecture Notes in Artificial Intelligence, 1400,* 273–297.

Leopold, E., & Kindermann, J. (2002). Text categorization with support vector machines: How to represent texts in input space? *Machine Learning, 46,* 423–444. doi:10.1023/A:1012491419635

Lesh, N., Zaki, M.J., & Ogihara, M. (1999). Mining features for sequence classification. In *Proceedings of the Fifth ACM SIGKDD International Conference on Knowledge Discovery and Data Mining,* (pp. 342-346). New York: ACM.

Leung, K., Cheong, F., & Cheong, C. (2007). Consumer credit scoring using an artificial immune system algorithm. In *Proceedings of the IEEE International Conference on Evolutionary Computation (CEC 2007)* (pp. 3377–3384). IEEE Press.

Levy, A. V., & Montalvo, A. (1985). The tunneling algorithm for the global minimization of functions. *Society for Industrial and Applied Mathematics, 6,* 15–29.

Lewis, D. D. (1998). Naive (Bayes) at forty: The independence assumption in information retrieval. In *Proceedings of the 10th European Conference on Machine Learning* (pp. 4-15). London, UK: Academic Press.

Li, J., Mei, C., Kumar, C.A., & Zhang, X. (2013). On rule acquisition in decision formal context. *International Journal of Machine Learning and Cybernetics.*

Li, Z., & Ning, W. (2010). Double neuron model-free control for pH processes. In *Proceedings of Chinese Control and Decision Conference,* (pp. 2867 – 2871). IEEE.

Liang, Z., & Shi, P. (2003). Similarity measures on intuitionistic fuzzy sets. *Pattern Recognition Letters*, *24*(15), 2687–2693. doi:10.1016/S0167-8655(03)00111-9

Liao, T. W., Zhang, Z., & Mount, C. R. (1998). Similarity measures for retrieval in case based reasoning systems. *Applied Artificial Intelligence*, *12*, 267–288. doi:10.1080/088395198117730

Li, F., & Jiaju, Q. (2005). Electrical load forecasting based on load patterns. *Power System Technology*, *29*(4), 23–26.

Li, F., & Xu, Z. Y. (2001). Similarity measure between vague sets. *Chinese Jr. of Software*, *12*(6), 922–927.

Li, H., & Sun, J. (2010). Business failure prediction using hybrid2 case-based reasoning (H2CBR). *Computers & Operations Research*, *37*(1), 137–151. doi:10.1016/j.cor.2009.04.003

Li, H., Sun, J., & Sun, B. L. (2009). Financial distress prediction based on OR-CBR in the principle of k-nearest neighbors. *Expert Systems with Applications*, *36*(1), 643–659. doi:10.1016/j.eswa.2007.09.038

Li, J., Mei, C., & Lv, Y. (2011). A heuristic knowledge reduction method for decision formal contexts. *Computers & Mathematics with Applications (Oxford, England)*, *61*(4), 1096–1106. doi:10.1016/j.camwa.2010.12.060

Li, J., Mei, C., & Lv, Y. (2012). Knowledge reduction in formal decision contexts based on an order preserving mapping. *International Journal of General Systems*, *41*(2), 143–161. doi:10.1080/03081079.2011.634410

Li, J., Mei, C., & Lv, Y. (2012). Knowledge reduction in real decision formal contexts. *Information Sciences*, *189*, 191–207. doi:10.1016/j.ins.2011.11.041

Li, J., Mei, C., & Lv, Y. (2013). Incomplete decision contexts: Approximate construction, rule acquisition and knowledge reduction. *International Journal of Approximate Reasoning*, *54*(1), 149–165. doi:10.1016/j.ijar.2012.07.005

Lindig, C. (2000). Fast concept analysis. In *ICCS (LNCS)* (Vol. 1867, pp. 152–161). Berlin: Springer.

Lingras, P., Zhong, M., & Sharma, S. (2008). Evolutionary regression and neural imputations of missing values. *STUDFUZZ*, *226*, 151–163.

Li, T., Zhang, C., & Ogihara, M. (2004). A comparative study of feature selection and multiclass classification methods for tissue classification based on gene expression. *Bioinformatics (Oxford, England)*, *20*(15), 2429–2437. doi:10.1093/bioinformatics/bth267 PMID:15087314

Liu, B., Hsu, W., & Ma, Y. (1998). Integrating classification and association rule mining. In *Proceedings of 4th ACM SIGKDD International Conference on Knowledge Discovery and Data Mining* (pp. 80-86). New York, NY: ACM.

Liu, B., Hsu, W., & Ma, Y. (1999). Mining association rules with multiple minimum supports. In *Proceedings of the Fifth ACM SIGKDD International Conference on Knowledge Discovery and Data Mining* (pp. 337-341). ACM.

Liu, J., Ji, S., & Ye, J. (2009). Multi-task feature learning via efficient l2,1-norm minimization. In *Proceedings of the Twenty-Fifth Conference on Uncertainty in Artificial Intelligence*. IEEE.

Liu, M. Setiono, & Zhao. (2011). Feature selection: An ever evolving frontier in data mining. In *Proceedings of JMLR: Workshop and Conference The Fourth Workshop on Feature Selection in Data Mining*. JMLR.

Liu, Y., & Srihari, S. (1994). Document image binarization based on texture analysis. *Proceedings of 1994 SPIE*, *2181*, 254–263.

Liu, C. L. (1985). *Elements of discrete mathematics* (2nd ed.). New York: McGraw-Hill.

Liu, H., Li, J., & Wong, L. (2002). A comparative study on feature selection and classification methods using gene expression profiles and proteomic patterns. *Genome Inform*, *13*, 51–60. PMID:14571374

Liu, H., & Motoda, H. (1998). *Feature selection for knowledge discovery and data mining*. Boston: Kluwer Academic. doi:10.1007/978-1-4615-5689-3

Liu, H., & Motoda, H. (Eds.). (2007). *Computational methods of feature selection*. New York: Chapman and Hall/CRC Press.

Liu, H., & Yu, L. (2005). Toward integrating feature selection algorithms for classification and clustering. *IEEE Transactions on Knowledge and Data Engineering, 17*(4), 491–502. doi:10.1109/TKDE.2005.66

Liu, J., & Yang, Y. H. (1994). Multi-resolution color image segmentation. *IEEE Transactions on Pattern Analysis and Machine Intelligence, 16*(7), 689–700. doi:10.1109/34.297949

Liu, Y. C., Yang, Y. Y., Lin, F., & Du, X. (2009). Case learning in CBR based agent systems for ship collision avoidance. In *Principles of Practice in Multi-Agent Systems (LNCS)* (Vol. 5925, pp. 542–551). Berlin: Springer. doi:10.1007/978-3-642-11161-7_40

Lopez, M., McSherry, R., Bridge, D. D., Leake, D., Smyth, B., & Craw, S. (2005). Retrieval, reuse, revision, and retention in case-based reasoning. *The Knowledge Engineering Review, 20*(3), 215–240. doi:10.1017/S0269888906000646

Lou, H., & Dai, W. (2008) A novel non-linear model predictive controller based on minimal resource allocation network and its application in CSTR pH process. In *Proceedings of the 7th World Congress on Intelligent Control and Automation,* (pp. 5672 – 5676). IEEE.

Lucchese, L., & Mitra, S. K. (2001). Color image segmentation: A state-of-art survey. *Image Processing, Vision, and Pattern Recognition, 67*(2), 207–221.

Lu, J., Yan, X., Yuan, D., & Xu, Z. (2005). A new similarity measure for vague sets. *IEEE Intelligent Informatics Bulletin, 6*(2), 14–18.

Lynch, N. A. (1996). *Distributed algorithms*. San Francisco: Morgan Kaufmann Publishers.

MacQueen, J. (1967). Some methods for classification and analysis of multivariate observations. In *Proceedings of Fifth Berkeley Symposium on Mathematical Statistics and Probability,* (pp. 281-297). IEEE.

Maddouri, M. (2005). A formal concept analysis approach to discover association rules from data. In *Concept lattices and their applications* (pp. 10–21). Academic Press.

Maeda, M., Shimakawa, M., & Murakami, S. (1995). Predictive fuzzy control of an autonomous mobile robot with forecast learning function. *Fuzzy Sets and Systems, 72*(1), 51–60. doi:10.1016/0165-0114(94)00271-8

Mahajan, S., & Reshamwala, A. (2011). An approach to optimize fuzzy time-interval sequential patterns using multi-objective genetic algorithm. In *Technology systems and management* (pp. 115–120). Berlin: Springer. doi:10.1007/978-3-642-20209-4_16

Maio, C. D., Fenza, G., Loia, V., & Senatore, S. (2012). Hierarchical web resources retrieval by exploiting fuzzy formal concept analysis. *Information Processing & Management, 48*(3), 399–418. doi:10.1016/j.ipm.2011.04.003

Maji, P. K., Biswas, R., & Roy, A. R. (2001). Fuzzy soft-sets. *The Jr. of Fuzzy Math., 9*(3), 589–602.

Maji, P. K., Biswas, R., & Roy, A. R. (2001). Intuitionistic fuzzy soft sets. *The Jr. of Fuzzy Math., 9*(3), 677–691.

Maji, P. K., & Roy, A. R. (2004). On intuitionistic fuzzy soft sets. *The Jr. of Fuzzy Math., 12*(3), 669–683.

Maji, P. K., & Roy, A. R. (2007). A fuzzy soft set theoretic approach to decision making problems. *Journal of Computational and Applied Mathematics, 203*(2), 412–418. doi:10.1016/j.cam.2006.04.008

Maji, P. K., Roy, A. R., & Biswas, R. (2002). An application of soft sets in a decision making problem. *Computers & Mathematics with Applications (Oxford, England), 44*(8-9), 1077–1083. doi:10.1016/S0898-1221(02)00216-X

Maji, P. K., Roy, A. R., & Biswas, R. (2003). Soft set theory. *Computers & Mathematics with Applications (Oxford, England), 45*(4-5), 555–562. doi:10.1016/S0898-1221(03)00016-6

Majumdar, P., Hazra, H., & Samanta, S. K. (2012). Soft topology. *Fuzzy Inform., &. Engineering, 3*(1), 105–115.

Majumdar, P., & Samanta, S. K. (2008). Similarity measure of soft sets. *New Mathematics and Natural Computation, 4*(1), 1–12. doi:10.1142/S1793005708000908

Majumdar, P., & Samanta, S. K. (2010). Generalised fuzzy soft set. *Computers & Mathematics with Applications (Oxford, England), 59*(4), 1425–1432. doi:10.1016/j.camwa.2009.12.006

Majumdar, P., & Samanta, S. K. (2010). On soft mappings. *Computers & Mathematics with Applications (Oxford, England)*, *60*(9), 2666–2672. doi:10.1016/j.camwa.2010.09.004

Majumdar, P., & Samanta, S. K. (2010). On distance based similarity measure between intuitionistic fuzzy soft sets. *Anusandhan*, *12*(22), 41–50.

Majumdar, P., & Samanta, S. K. (2011). On similarity measure of fuzzy soft sets. *Int. J. Advance. Soft Comput. Appl.*, *3*(2), 1–8.

Majumdar, P., & Samanta, S. K. (2013). Decision making based on similarity measure of vague soft sets. *J. Intelligent and Fuzzy Systems*, *24*, 637–646.

Majumdar, P., & Samanta, S. K. (2013). Softness of a soft set: Soft set entropy. *Annals of Fuzzy Mathematics and Informatics*, *6*(1), 59–68.

Maldague, X. (1994). *Advances in signal processing for non destructive evaluation of materials IV*. Berlin: Springer. doi:10.1007/978-94-011-1056-3

Manuel, A., Duarte-Mermoud, Franklin, A. R., & Ricardo, P. (2002). Experimental evaluation of combined model reference adaptive controller in a pH regulation process. *International Journal of Adaptive Control and Signal Processing*, *16*, 85–106. doi:10.1002/acs.674

Martin, J. W., Ralph, S., Adrian, G., Winfried, S., & Essameddin, B. (2009). On setting-up a portable low-cost real-time control system for research and teaching with application to bioprocess pH control. In *Proceedings of IEEE Control Applications and Intelligent Control*, (pp. 1631 – 1636). IEEE.

Ma, S. (2006). Empirical study of supervised gene screening. *BMC Bioinformatics*, *7*, 537. doi:10.1186/1471-2105-7-537 PMID:17176468

Maulik, U. (2009). Medical image segmentation using genetic algorithms. *Proceedings of 16th Annual International Conference of the IEEE Engineering in Medicine and Biology Society*, *13*(2), 166-173.

Maxwell, B. A., & Brubaker, S. J. (2003). Texture edge detection using the compass operator. *University of Pennsylvania Law Review in British Machine Vision Conference*, *154*(3), 477.

McQueen, J. (1967). Some methods for classification and analysis of multivariate observations. In *Proceedings of the Fifth Berkeley Symposium on Mathematical Statistics and Probability* (pp. 281-297). IEEE.

Mehrez, A., & Hu, M. Y. (1992). A clustering analysis of forecasting methods in a multiobjective inventory system. *International Journal of Production Economics*, *27*(1), 1–8. doi:10.1016/0925-5273(92)90121-M

Mephu, N. E., & Njiwoua, P. (1998). Using lattice – based framework as a tool for feature extraction. In *Feature extraction construction and selection: A data mining perspective* (pp. 205–216). Boston: Kluwer Academic Publishers.

Michalewicz, Z., & Naguib, F. A. (1994). Evolutionary optimization of constrained problems. In *Proceedings of the 3rd Annual Conference on Evolutionary Programming*, (pp. 98–108). World Scientific.

Michalewicz, Z. (1992). *Genetic algorithms + data structures = evolution programs*. New York: Springer-Verlag. doi:10.1007/978-3-662-02830-8

Michalewicz, Z., & Schoenauer, M. (1996). Evolutionary algorithms for constrained parameter optimization problems. *Evolutionary Computation*, *4*(1), 1–32. doi:10.1162/evco.1996.4.1.1

Milasi, R. M., Jamali, M. R., & Lucas, C. (2007). Intelligent washing machine: A bio-inspired and multi-objective approach. *International Journal Control. Automation and Systems*, *5*(4), 436–443.

Minagawa, H., & Ohnishi, N. (1996). Tactile-audio diagram for blind persons. *IEEE Transactions on Rehabilitation Engineering*, *4*(4), 431–437. doi:10.1109/86.547946 PMID:8973970

Mitchell, M. (1996). *An introduction to genetic algorithms*. Cambridge, MA: MIT Press.

Mitra, P., Murthy, C. A., & Pal, S. K. (2002). Unsupervised feature selection using feature similarity. *IEEE Transactions on Pattern Analysis and Machine Intelligence*, *24*(3), 301–312. doi:10.1109/34.990133

Miyamoto, S. (2001). Fuzzy multisets and their generalizations. In *Multiset Processing (LNCS)* (Vol. 2235, pp. 225–235). Berlin: Springer-Verlag. doi:10.1007/3-540-45523-X_11

Mohan, C., & Nguyen, H. T. (2004). A controlled random search technique incorporating the simulating annealing concept for solving integer and mixed integer global optimization problems. *Int. Jr. of Computational Optimization and Applications, 14*, 103–132. doi:10.1023/A:1008761113491

Mohan, C., & Shanker, K. (1994). A random search technique for global optimization based on quadratic approximation. *Asia Pacific Journal of Operation Research, 11*, 93–101.

Mohanty, D. (2010). Rough set on generalized covering approximation space. *International Journal of Comp. Science and Research, 1*(1), 432–449.

Mohanty, D., Kalia, N. R., Pattanayak, L., & Nayak, B. B. (2012). An introduction to rough soft set. *Mathematical Sciences, 1*(3), 927–936.

Molodtsov, D. (1999). Soft set theory—First results. *Computers & Mathematics with Applications (Oxford, England), 37*(4-5), 19 31. doi:10.1016/S0898-1221(99)00056-5

Montazemi, A. R., & Gupta, K. M. (1997). A framework for retrieval in case-based reasoning systems. *Annals of Operations Research, 72*, 51–73. doi:10.1023/A:1018960607821

Monti, S., Tamayo, P., Mesirov, J. P., & Golub, T. R. (2003). Consensus clustering: A resampling-based method for class discovery and visualization of gene expression microarray data. *Machine Learning, 52*(1-2), 91–118. doi:10.1023/A:1023949509487

Moorthy, K., Mohamad, M. S. B., & Deris, S. (2013). Multiple gene sets for cancer classification using gene range selection based on random forest. In *Proceedings of ACIIDS 2013* (LNAI), (vol. 7802, pp. 385–393). Berlin: Springer.

Morgan Kaufmman. Crossley, W. A., & Williams, E. A. (1997). A study of adaptive penalty functions for constrained genetic algorithm based optimization. In *Proceedings of AIAA 35th Aerospace Sciences Meeting and Exhibit*. Reno, NV: AIAA.

Muhammad, S., & Naz, M. (2011). On soft topological spaces. *Computers & Mathematics with Applications (Oxford, England), 61*(7), 1786–1799. doi:10.1016/j.camwa.2011.02.006

Mukherjee, A., & Garain, U. (2009). Understanding of natural language text for diagram drawing. In *Proceedings of IASTED International Conf. on Artificial Intelligence and Soft Computing* (pp. 138–145). Palma De Mallorca, Spain: IASTED.

Mukherjee, A., Garain, U., & Nasipuri, M. (2007). On construction of a GeometryNet. In *Proceedings of IASTED International Conference on Artificial Intelligence and Applications (AIA '07)* (pp. 530-536). IASTED.

Mukherjee, A., Sengupta, S., Sen, A., Chakraborty, D., & Garain, U. (2013). Text to diagram conversion: A method for formal representation of natural language geometry problems. In *Proceedings of IASTED International Conference on Artificial Intelligence and Applications (AIA '13)* (pp. 137-144). IASTED.

Mukherjee, A., & Garain, U. (2008). A review of the methods for automatic understanding of natural language mathematical problems. *Artificial Intelligence Review, 29*(2), 93–122. doi:10.1007/s10462-009-9110-0

Munoz-Salinas, R., Aguirre, E., Cordon, O., & Garcia-Silvente, M. (2008). Automatic tuning of a fuzzy visual system using evolutionary algorithms: Single-objective vs. multi-objective approaches. *IEEE Transactions on Fuzzy Systems, 16*(2), 485–501. doi:10.1109/TFUZZ.2006.889954

Murie, C., Woody, O., Lee, A., & Nadon, R. (2009). Comparison of small n statistical tests of differential expression applied to microarrays. *BMC Bioinformatics, 10*, 45. doi:10.1186/1471-2105-10-45 PMID:19192265

Murray, C., Johnson, W., Wolf, M. S., & Deary, I. J. (2011). The association between cognitive ability across the lifespan and health literacy in old age: The lothian birth cohort 1936. *Intelligence, 39*, 178–187. doi:10.1016/j.intell.2011.04.001

Myung, H., & Kim, J. H. (1996). Hybrid evolutionary programming for heavily constrained problems. *Bio Systems, 38*, 29–43. doi:10.1016/0303-2647(95)01564-7 PMID:8833746

Nayeem, N. K., & Geoff, W. (2003). Non-linear model reference control of pH process: An experimental study. In *Proceedings 15th European Simulation Symposium*. IEEE.

Neill, S. B. (1982). Popper and objective knowledge. *Journal of Information Science, 4*(1), 33–39. doi:10.1177/016555158200400105

Newman, M. E. J. (2005). Power laws: Pareto distributions and Zipf's law. *Contemporary Physics, 46*(5), 323–351. doi:10.1080/00107510500052444

Ng, A., Jordan, M., & Weiss, Y. (2001). On spectral clustering: Analysis and an algorithm. *Advances in NIPS, 14.*

Ng, k.s., & Liu, H. (2000). Customer retention via data mining. *AI Rev., 14*(6), 569-590.

Nguyen, H. V., & Gopalkrishnan, V. (2010). Feature extraction for outlier detection in high-dimensional spaces. In *Proceedings of the 4th Workshop on Feature Selection in Data Mining*. IEEE.

Nguyen, N., & Caruana, R. (2007). Consensus clusterings. In *Proceedings of IEEE International Conference on Data Mining* (pp. 607-612). IEEE.

Niblack, W. (1986). *An introduction to image processing.* Englewood Cliffs, NJ: Prentice-Hall.

Nie, J., Loh, A. P., & Hang, C. C. (1996). Modeling pH neutralization processes using fuzzy-neural approaches. *Fuzzy Sets and Systems, 78*(1), 5–22. doi:10.1016/0165-0114(95)00118-2

Nigam, K., Mccallum, A. K., Thrun, S., & Mitchell, T. (2000). Text classification from labeled and unlabeled documents using EM. *Machine Learning, 39*, 103–134. doi:10.1023/A:1007692713085

Nojima, Y., Kaisho, Y., & Ishibuchi, H. (2010). Accuracy improvement of genetic fuzzy rule selection with candidate rule addition and membership tuning. In Proceedings of Fuzzy Systems (FUZZ), (pp. 1-8). IEEE.

Nojima, Y., & Ishibuchi, H. (2006). Designing fuzzy ensemble classifiers by evolutionary multi-objective optimization with an entropy-based diversity criterion. In *Proceedings of Hybrid Intelligent Systems* (pp. 59–59). IEEE.

Nojima, Y., & Ishibuchi, H. (2009). Incorporation of user preference into multi-objective genetic fuzzy rule selection for pattern classification problems. *Artificial Life and Robotics, 14*(3), 418–421. doi:10.1007/s10015-009-0700-3

Norris, E. M. (1974). An algorithm for computing the maximal rectangle in a binary relation. *Journal of the ACM, 21*, 356–366.

No-urine, L., & Reynaud, O. (1999). A fast algorithm for building lattices. *Information Processing Letters, 71*, 199–204. doi:10.1016/S0020-0190(99)00108-8

Novak, J. D. (2010). *Learning, creating, and using knowledge: Concept maps as facilitative tools in schools and corporations* (2nd ed.). New York: Lawrence Erlbaum. Associentes, Inc.

Novak, J. D., & Mosunda, D. (1991). A twelve-year longitudinal study of science concept learning. *American Educational Research Journal, 28*(1), 117–153. doi:10.3102/00028312028001117

Novotny, M., & Pawlak, Z. (1985). Characterization of rough top equalities and rough bottom equalities. *Bull. Polish Acad. Sci. Math., 33*, 91–97.

Novotny, M., & Pawlak, Z. (1985). On rough equalities. *Bull. Polish Acad. Sci. Math., 33*, 99–104.

Novotny, M., & Pawlak, Z. (1985). Black box analysis and rough top equality. *Bull. Polish Acad. Sci. Math., 33*, 105–113.

O'Gorman, L. (1994). Binarization and multithresholding of document images using connectivity. *Graph. Models Image Process, 56*, 494–506. doi:10.1006/cgip.1994.1044

Omran, M. G. H., Engelbrecht, A. P., & Salman, A. (2006). Particle swarm optimization for pattern recognition and image processing. *Studies in Computational Intelligence, 34*, 125–151. doi:10.1007/978-3-540-34956-3_6

Ong, S. H., Yeo, N. C., Lee, K. H., Venkatesh, Y. V., & Cao, D. M. (2002). Segmentation of color images using a two-stage self-organizing network. *Image and Vision Computing, 20*, 279–289. doi:10.1016/S0262-8856(02)00021-5

Orvosh, D., & Davis, L. (1995). Using a genetic algorithm to optimize problems with feasibility constraints. In *Proceedings of the Sixth International Conference on Genetic Algorithms* (pp. 548-552). Echelman.

Osyczka, A. (1985). Multi-criteria optimization for engineering design. In J. S. Gero (Ed.), *Design optimization* (pp. 193–227). Academic Press.

Pajunen, G. A. (1987). Comparison of linear and nonlinear adaptive control of pH process. *IEEE Control Systems Magazine, 7*(1), 39–44. doi:10.1109/MCS.1987.1105238

Pal, S. K., & Shiu, S. C. K. (2004). Foundations of soft case-based reasoning. CH-1, ISBN 0-471-08635-5

Pal, N., & Bhandari, D. (1993). Image thresholding: Some new techniques. *Signal Processing, 33*, 139–158. doi:10.1016/0165-1684(93)90107-L

Pal, S., & Rosenfeld, A. (1988). Image enhancement and thresholding by optimization of fuzzy compactness. *Pattern Recognition Letters, 7*, 77–86. doi:10.1016/0167-8655(88)90122-5

Parekh, M., Desai, M., Li, H., & Rhinehart, R. R. (1994). In-line control of nonlinear pH neutralization based on fuzzy logic. *IEEE Transactions on Components Packaging & Manufacturing Technology Part A, 17*(2), 192–201. doi:10.1109/95.296400

Pareto, V. (1896). *Cours d'economie politique*. Lausanne: F. Rouge.

Parkes, D. (1991). Nomad: Enabling access to graphics and text-based information for blind and visually impaired and other disability groups. In *Proceedings of World Congress Tech. People Disabil* (pp. 689 - 716). Arlington, VA: IEEE.

Park, S. B., Lee, J. W., & Kim, S. K. (2004). Content-based image classification using a neural network. *Pattern Recognition Letters, 25*, 287–300. doi:10.1016/j.patrec.2003.10.015

Pawlak, Z. (1982). Rough sets. *Int. Jour. of Computer and Information Sciences, 11*, 341–356. doi:10.1007/BF01001956

Pawlak, Z. (1991). *Rough sets: Theoretical aspects of reasoning about data*. London: Kluwer Academic Publishers.

Peterson, J. L. (1981). Petri net theory and the modeling of system. Englewood Cliffs, NJ: PH.

Petri, C. A. (1962). *Kommunikation mit automaten*. (Ph.D. Dissertation). University of Bonn, Bonn, Germany.

Pham, D. T., & Pham, P. T. N. (1999). Artificial intelligence in engineering. *International Journal of Machine Tools & Manufacture, 39*(6), 937–949. doi:10.1016/S0890-6955(98)00076-5

PictureBraille. (2013). Retrieved June 30, 2013 from http://www.pentronics.com.au/index_files/PictureBraille.htm

Pignalberi, G., Cucchiara, R., Cinque, L., & Levialdi, S. (2003). Tuning range image segmentation by genetic algorithm. *EURASIP Journal on Applied Signal Processing, 8*, 780–790. doi:10.1155/S1110865703303087

Poelmans, J., Elzinga, P., Viaene, S., & Dedene, G. (2010). Formal concept analysis in knowledge discovery: A survey. In *Proceedings of 18th International Conference on Conceptual Structures* (pp. 139-53). IEEE.

Prelic, A., Bleuler, S., Zimmermann, P., Wille, A., Buhlmann, P., & Gruissem, W. et al. (2006). A systematic comparison and evaluation of biclustering methods for gene expression data. *Bioinformatics (Oxford, England), 22*(9), 1122–1129. doi:10.1093/bioinformatics/btl060 PMID:16500941

Priss, U., Polovina, S., & Hill, R. (2007). Conceptual structures: Knowledge architectures for smart applications. In *Proceeding of 15 International Conferences on Conceptual Structures* (LNAI), (Vol. 4604). Sheffield, UK: Springer Verlag.

Priss, U. (2006). Formal concept analysis in information science. *Annual Review of Information Science & Technology, 40*, 521–543. doi:10.1002/aris.1440400120

Priss, U., & Old, L. J. (2004). Modelling lexical databases with formal concept analysis. *Journal of Universal Computer, 10*(8), 967–984.

Pulkkinen, P. (2009). A multi-objective genetic fuzzy system for obtaining compact and accurate fuzzy classifiers with transparent fuzzy partitions. In *Proceedings of Machine Learning and Applications* (pp. 89–94). IEEE.

Pulkkinen, P., Hytonen, J., & Koivisto, H. (2008). Developing a bioaerosol detector using hybrid genetic fuzzy systems. *Engineering Applications of Artificial Intelligence, 21*(8), 1330–1346. doi:10.1016/j.engappai.2008.01.006

Qian, Y. H., & Liang, J. Y. (2006). Rough set method based on multi-granulations. In *Proceedings of the 5th IEEE Conference on Cognitive Informatics*, (vol. 1, pp. 297 – 304). IEEE.

Qian, Y. H., Liang, J. Y., & Dang, C. Y. (2010). Pessimistic rough decision. In *Proceedings of RST 2010*. Zhoushan, China: RST.

Qinghui, W., & Zongze, C. (2010). Nonlinear compensator based PI controller for pH neutralization reaction process. In *Proceedings of Second International Conference on Industrial and Information Systems,* (vol. 2, pp. 71 – 74). IEEE.

Quince, C. (1966). *LISP in small pieces*. Cambridge, UK: Cambridge University Press.

Quinlan, J. R. (1993). *C4.5: Programs for machine learning*. San Francisco: Morgan Kaufmann.

Rabhi, F. (2008). *Algorithms: A functional programming approach*. International Computer Science Series.

Rahman, M. K., Sanghvi, S., Toyama, K., & Dias, M. B. (2010). Experiences with lower-cost access to tactile graphics in India. In *Proceedings of First ACM Symposium on Computing for Development*. ACM.

Rajasekaran, S., & Pai, G. A. V (2003). *Neural networks, fuzzy logic, and genetic algorithms: Synthesis and applications*. New Delhi: Prentice-Hall of India Pvt. Ltd.

Ramaswamy, S., Ross, K., Lander, E., & Golub, T. (2003). A molecular signature of metastasis in primary solid tumours. *Nature Genetics, 33*, 49–54. doi:10.1038/ng1060 PMID:12469122

Ramos, V., & Muge, F. (2004). Image colour segmentation by genetic algorithms. *Pattern Recognition*, 125–129.

Ranganath, M., & Elamin, E. K. (2003). Fuzzy logic control of a pH neutralization process. In *Proceedings of the 2003 10th IEEE International Conference on Electronics, Circuits and Systems,* (vol. 3, pp. 1066 – 1069). IEEE.

Ratanamahatana, C. A., & Keogh, E. (2004). Making time-series classification more accurate using learned constraints. In *Proceedings of SDM 04: SIAM International Conference on Data Mining*. SIAM.

Raudys, S. J., & Jain, A. K. (1991). Small sample size effects in statistical pattern recognition: Recommendations for practitioners. *IEEE Transactions on Pattern Analysis and Machine Intelligence, 13*, 252–264. doi:10.1109/34.75512

Ray, W. D. (1982). ARIMA forecasting models in inventory control. *The Journal of the Operational Research Society, 33*(6), 567–574.

Rechenberg, I. (1973). *Evolutionsstrategie: Optimierung technischer systeme nach prinzipien der biologishen evolution*. Stuttgart, Germany: Frommann-Holzbog.

Reeves, C. (1993). Using genetic algorithms with small populations. In *Proceedings of Fifth International Conference on Genetic Algorithms*. Morgan Kaufman.

Refreshable Tactile Display, Assistive Technology Products. (2013). Retrieved June 30, 2013 from http://www.abledata.com/

Reiffel, E., & Polak, W. (2000). *An introduction to quantum computing for non-physicists*. Retrieved from arxive.org. quant-ph/9809016v2

Reisig, W. (1983). *Petri nets: An introduction*. Berlin: Springer-Verlag.

Roger, S. (1982). *Dynamic memory: A theory of learning in computers and people*. New York: Cambridge University Press.

Rogers, D. F. (1985). *Procedural elements for computer graphics*. New York: McGraw Hill Book Co.

Rojas, R. (1996). *Neural networks: A systematic introduction*. Berlin: Springer-Verlag.

Rosenfeld, A. (1971). Fuzzy groups. *Journal of Mathematical Analysis and Applications, 35*, 512–517. doi:10.1016/0022-247X(71)90199-5

Roth, P., Petrucci, L., & Pun, T. (2000). From dots to shape: an auditory haptic game platform for teaching geometry to blind pupils.[ICCHP.]. *Proceedings of ICCHP, 2000*, 603–610.

Rouane, H. M., Huchard, M., Napoli, A., & Valtchev, P. (2010). Using formal concept analysis for discovering knowledge patterns. In *Proceedings of 7th International Conference of Concept Lattices & Their Applications* (pp. 223-34). IEEE.

Rubner, Y., Tomasi, C., & Guibas, L. J. (1998). A metric for distributions with applications to image databases. In *Proceedings International Conference on Computer Vision*, (pp. 59-66). ICV.

Ruiz, D., Cantón, J., María Nougués, J., Espuña, A., & Puigjaner, L. (2001). On-line fault diagnosis system support for reactive scheduling in multipurpose batch chemical plants. *Computers & Chemical Engineering*, *25*(4), 829–837. doi:10.1016/S0098-1354(01)00657-3

Russell, B. (1937). *The principles of mathematics* (2nd ed.). London: George Allen & Unwin Ltd.

Russ, J. (1987). Automatic discrimination of features in gray-scale images. *Journal of Microscopy*, *148*, 263–277. doi:10.1111/j.1365-2818.1987.tb02872.x

Ruzon, M. A., & Tomasi, C. (1999). Color edge detection with the compass operator. *Computer Vision Pattern Recognition*, *2*, 511–514.

Saber, M. E., Ruhul, A. S., & Daryl, L. E. (2011). Improved genetic algorithm for constrained optimization. In *Proceeding of International Conference on Computer Engineering & Systems (ICCES)* (pp. 111-115). ICCES.

Saeys, Y., Inza, I., & Larraaga, P. (2007). A review of feature selection techniques in bioinformatics. *Bioinformatics (Oxford, England)*, *23*(19), 2507–2517. doi:10.1093/bioinformatics/btm344 PMID:17720704

Sahoo, P., Wilkins, C., & Yeager, J. (1997). Threshold selection using Renyi's entropy. *Pattern Recognition*, *30*, 71–84. doi:10.1016/S0031-3203(96)00065-9

Salkin, H. M. (1975). *Integer programming*. Amsterdam: Edison Wesley Publishing Com.

Salleh, A. R. (2011). From soft sets to intuitionistic fuzzy soft sets: A brief survey. In *Proceedings of the International Seminar on the Current Research Progress in Sciences and Technology (ISSTech '11)*. Universiti Kebangsaan Malaysia—Universitas Indonesia.

Sammouda, M., Sammouda, R., Niki, N., & Benaichouche, M. (2004). Tissue color images segmentation using artificial neural networks. In *Proceedings of IEEE International Symposium on Biomedical Imaging: Nano to Macro*, (pp. 145-148). IEEE.

Sandra, J. N., Ahmet, P., & Jose, A. R. (1999). Application of Wiener model predictive control (WMPC) to a pH neutralization experiment. *IEEE Transactions on Control Systems Technology*, *7*(4), 437–445. doi:10.1109/87.772159

Sathya, P., & Kayalvizhi, R. (2010). Development of a new optimal multilevel thresholding using improved particle swarm optimization algorithm for image segmentation. *International Journal of Electronics Engineering*, *1*(2), 63–67.

Sauvola, J., & Pietaksinen, M. (2000). Adaptive document image binarization. *Pattern Recognition*, *33*, 225–236. doi:10.1016/S0031-3203(99)00055-2

Schittkowski, K. (1987). More examples for mathematical programming codes. *Lecture Notes in Economics and Mathematical Systems, 282*.

Schmidt, R., & Gierl, L. (2001). Case-based reasoning for medical knowledge-based systems. *International Journal of Medical Informatics*, *64*(2-3), 355–367. doi:10.1016/S1386-5056(01)00221-0 PMID:11734397

Schwefel, H. (1995). *Evolution and optimum seeking*. New York: Wiley.

Seidel, R., & Aragon, C. R. (1996). Randomized search trees. *Algorithmica*, *16*, 464–497. doi:10.1007/BF01940876

Selim, S. Z., & Alsultan, K. (1991). A simulated annealing algorithm for the clustering problem. *Pattern Recognition*, *24*(10), 1003–1008. doi:10.1016/0031-3203(91)90097-O

Sezgin, M., & Sankur, B. (2004). Survey over image thresholding techniques and quantitative performance evaluation. *Journal of Electronic Imaging*, *13*(1), 146–165. doi:10.1117/1.1631315

Shaffer, C. A. (2001). *A practical introduction to data structures and algorithm analysis*. Upper Saddle River, NJ: Prentice Hall.

Shaffer, M. J., & Brodahl, M. K. (1998). Rule-based management for simulation in agricultural decision support systems. *Computers and Electronics in Agriculture*, *21*(2), 135–152. doi:10.1016/S0168-1699(98)00031-3

Shahin, S., Mohammad, S., & Ali, N. (2009). Adaptive nonlinear control of pH neutralization processes using fuzzy approximators. *Control Engineering Practice*, *17*(11), 1329–1337. doi:10.1016/j.conengprac.2009.06.007

Shannon, C.E. (1948). A mathematical theory of communication. *Bell Sysytem Technical Journal*, *27*, 379-423, 623-656.

Shelokar, P. S., Jayaraman, V. K., & Kulkarni, B. D. (2004). An ant colony approach for clustering. *Analytica Chimica Acta*, *509*(2), 187–195. doi:10.1016/j.aca.2003.12.032

Shen, Z., Guo, C., & Yan, Y. (2008). Mathematical modelling and simulation of ultra large container ship motion. In *Proceedings of 7th International Conference on System Simulation and Scientific Computing, ICSC 2008*, (pp. 693-696). ICSC.

Shi, H. F., Hua, Q., & Zhang, P. (2007). The formal concept analysis of the document clusters. In *Proceedings of 6th International Conference on Machine Learning and Cybernetic* (pp. 3381-3385). IEEE.

Shi, J., & Malik, J. (2000). Normalized cuts and image segmentation. *IEEE Transactions on Pattern Analysis and Machine Intelligence*, *22*(8), 888–905. doi:10.1109/34.868688

Shimazu, H. (2002). ExpertClerk: A conversational case-based reasoning tool for developing salesclerk agents in e-commerce webshops. *Artificial Intelligence Review*, *18*(3/4), 223–244. doi:10.1023/A:1020757023711

Shimazu, H., Shibata, A., & Nihei, K. (2001). Expert guide: A conversational case based reasoning tool for developing mentor in knowledge space. *Applied Intelligence*, *14*(1), 33–48. doi:10.1023/A:1008350923935

Shin, K. S., & Han, I. (1999). Case-based reasoning supported by genetic algorithms for corporate bond rating. *Expert Systems with Applications*, *16*, 85–95. doi:10.1016/S0957-4174(98)00063-3

Shin, K. S., & Han, I. (2001). A case-based approach using inductive indexing for corporate bond rating. *Decision Support Systems*, *32*(1), 41–52. doi:10.1016/S0167-9236(01)00099-9

Shinskey, F. G. (1996). *Process control systems: Application, design, and tuning* (4th ed.). New York: McGraw-Hill.

Shiu, C. K., & Pal, S. K. (2001). Case-based reasoning: concepts, features and soft computing. *Applied Intelligence*, *21*(3), 233–238. doi:10.1023/B:APIN.0000043556.29968.81

Shor, P. (1998). *Quantum computing*. Retrieved from http://east.camel.math.ca/EMIS/journals/DMJDMV/xvolicm/00/Shor.MAN.html

Shoumei, C., & Chengming, Q. (2008). Incremental formation algorithm based on concept semilattice. In *Proceedings of International Symposium on Computational Intelligence and Design* (pp. 148-151). IEEE.

Silva, J., Lins, R., & Rocha, V., Jr. (2006). Binarizing and filtering historical documents with back-to-front interference. In *Proceedings of SAC ACM Symposium on Applied Computing*. ACM.

Silver, E. A., Pyke, D. F., & Peterson, R. (1998). *Inventory management and production planning and scheduling* (3rd ed.). Hoboken, NJ: John Wiley & Sons.

Simon, O., & Igor, S. (2007). Continuous-time wiener-model predictive control of a pH process. In *Proceedings of 29th International Conference on Information Technology Interfaces*, (pp. 771 – 776). IEEE.

Simon, R. (2003). Diagnostic and prognostic prediction using gene expression profiles in high-dimensional microarray data. *British Journal of Cancer*, *89*, 1599–1604. doi:10.1038/sj.bjc.6601326 PMID:14583755

Singh, P. K., & Kumar, C. A. (2012). A method for reduction of fuzzy relation in fuzzy formal context. In *Proceedings of International Conference on Mathematical Modelling and Scientific Computation*, (vol. 283, pp. 343-350). Berlin: Springer-Verlag.

Singh, P. K., & Kumar, C. A. (2012). Interval-valued fuzzy graph representation of concept lattice. In *Proceedings of 12th International Conference on Intelligent System Design and Application* (pp. 1852-1857). IEEE.

Singh, P. K., & Kumar, C. A. (2012). A method for decomposition of fuzzy formal context. *Procedia Engineering, 38*, 1852–1857. doi:10.1016/j.proeng.2012.06.228

Sitarski, E. (1996). Algorithm alley, HATs: Hashed array trees. *Dr. Dobb's Journal, 21*(11).

Sleator, D. D., & Tarjan, R. E. (1983). A data structure for dynamic trees. *Journal of Computer and System Sciences, 26*(3). doi:10.1016/0022-0000(83)90006-5

Sleator, D. D., & Tarjan, R. E. (1985). Self-adjusting binary search trees. *Journal of the ACM, 32*(3), 652–686. doi:10.1145/3828.3835

Smith, S. F. (1980). *A learning system based on genetic algorithms*. (Ph. D. Dissertation). University of Pittsburgh, Pittsburgh, PA.

Smyth, B., Keane, M., & Cunningham, P. (2001). Hierarchical case-based reasoning integrating case-based and decomposition problem-solving techniques for plant-control software design. *IEEE Transactions on Knowledge and Data Engineering, 13*(5), 793–812. doi:10.1109/69.956101

Snyder, R. D., Koehler, A. B., & Ord, J. K. (2002). Forecasting for inventory control with exponential smoothing. *International Journal of Forecasting, 18*(1), 5–18. doi:10.1016/S0169-2070(01)00109-1

Som, T. (2006). On soft relation and fuzzy soft relation. In *Proceedings of UAMA-2006*. Burdwan, India: UAMA.

Sonali, N., & Bodhe, G. L. (2009). Design and implementation of real time neuro-fuzzy based pH controller. In *Proceedings of Second International Conference on Emerging Trends in Engineering and Technology*, (pp. 946 – 952). IEEE.

Song, L., Smola, A., Gretton, A., Borgwardt, K., & Bedo, J. (2007). Supervised feature selection via dependence estimation. In *Proceedings of the International Conference on Machine Learning*. IEEE.

Sorjamaa, A., Hao, J., Reyhani, N., Ji, Y., & Lendasse, A. (2007). Methodology for long-term prediction of time series. *Neurocomputing, 70*(16-18), 2861–2869. doi:10.1016/j.neucom.2006.06.015

Spang, R. (2003). Diagnostic signatures from microarrays: A bioinformatics concept for personalized medicine. *BIOSILICO, 1*, 264–268. doi:10.1016/S1478-5382(03)02329-1

Srikanthan, T., & Asari, K. (2001). Automatic segmentation algorithm for the extraction of lumen region and boundary from endoscopic images. *Medical & Biological Engineering & Computing, 39*, 8–14. doi:10.1007/BF02345260 PMID:11214277

Srikant, R., & Agrawal, R. (1996). Mining quantitative association rules in large relational tables. *SIGMOD Record, 25*(2), 1–12. doi:10.1145/235968.233311

Stapp, H. P. (2007). *Mindful universe: Quantum mechanics and the participating observer*. New York: Springer-Verlag.

Stefanovic, N., Stefanovic, D., & Radenkovic, B. (n.d.). Application of data mining for supply chain inventory forecasting. *Applications and Innovations in Intelligent Systems, 15*, 175-188.

Stockwell, D. (1999). The GARP modeling system: Problems and solutions to automated spatial prediction. *International Journal of Geographical Information Science, 13*(2), 143–158. doi:10.1080/136588199241391

Strehl, A., & Ghosh, J. (2002). Cluster ensembles: A knowledge reuse framework for combining multiple partitions. *Journal of Machine Learning Research, 3*, 583–617.

Strok, F., & Neznanov, A. (2010). Comparing and analyzing the computational complexity of FCA algorithms. In *Proceedings of Annual Research Conference of the South African Institute of Computer Scientists and Information Technologists* (pp. 417-420). IEEE.

Stumme, G. (2002). Efficient data mining based on formal concept analysis. In *Proceedings of 13th International Conference on Database and Expert System Applications* (LNCS), (vol. 2453, pp. 3-22). Berlin: Springer-Verlag.

Stumme, G. (2002). Formal concept analysis on its way from mathematics to computer science. In *Conceptual Structures Integration & Interfaces, 10th International Conferences on Conceptual Structures* (LNAI), (vol. 2393, pp. 2-19). Berlin: Springer Verlag.

Stumme, G. (1995). Attribute exploration with background implications and exceptions. In *Data analysis and information system* (pp. 457–466). New York: Springer.

Stumme, G. (2009). Formal concept analysis. In *Handbook on ontologies* (pp. 177–200). Academic Press. doi:10.1007/978-3-540-92673-3_8

Stumme, G., Taouil, R., Bastide, Y., Pasquier, N., & Lakhal, L. (2001). Intelligent structuring and reducing of association rules with formal concept analysis.[LNAI]. *Advances in Artificial Intelligence, 2174*, 335–350.

Stumme, G., Taouil, R., Bastide, Y., Pasquier, N., & Lakhal, L. (2002). Computing iceberg concept lattice with titanic. *Data & Knowledge Engineering, 42*, 189–222. doi:10.1016/S0169-023X(02)00057-5

Stumme, G., Wille, R., & Wille, U. (1998). Conceptual knowledge discovery in databases using formal concept analysis methods. In *Principles of data mining and knowledge discovery (LNAI)* (Vol. 1510, pp. 450–458). Berlin: Springer-Verlag. doi:10.1007/BFb0094849

Su, C., & Amer, A. (2006). A real-time adaptive thresholding for video change detection. In *Proceedings of 2006 IEEE International Conference, Image Processing*. Atlanta, GA: IEEE.

Sun, Y., Babbs, C. F., & Delp, E. J. (2005). A comparison of feature selection methods for the detection of breast cancers in mammograms: Adaptive sequential floating search vs. genetic algorithm. *IEEE Eng Med Biol Soc, 6*, 6532–6535. PMID:17281766

Swartz, M. D., Yu, R. K., & Shete, S. (2008). Finding factors influencing risk: Comparing Bayesian stochastic search and standard variable selection methods applied to logistic regression models of cases and controls. *Statistics in Medicine, 27*(29), 6158–6174. doi:10.1002/sim.3434 PMID:18937224

Swetha, K. P., & Devi, V. S. (2012). Modified particle swarm optimization for pattern clustering. In *Proceedings of the International Conference on Neural Information Processing*, (pp. 496-503). Doha, Qatar: ICONIP.

Swetha, K. P., & Devi, V. S. (2012). Simultaneous feature selection and clustering using particle swarm optimization. In *Proceedings of the International Conference on Neural Information Processing*, (pp. 509-515). Doha, Qatar: ICONIP.

Swetha, K. P., & Devi, V. S. (2012). Feature weighting for clustering by particle swarm optimization. In *Proceedings of the Sixth International Conference on Genetic and Evolutionary Computing*, (pp. 441-444). ICGEC.

Syafiie, S., Tadeo, F., & Martinez, E. (2009). Q(A) learning technique for pH control. In *Proceedings of IEEE International Conference on Industrial Engineering and Engineering Management*, (pp. 712 – 716). IEEE.

Sycara, K. (1988). Using case-based reasoning for plan adaptation and repair. In *Proceedings Case-Based Reasoning Workshop*. Morgan Kaufmann.

Syropoulos, A. (2012). On generalized fuzzy multisets and their use in computation. *Iranian Journal of Fuzzy Systems, 9*(2), 113–125.

Szmidt, E., & Kacprzyk, J. (2001). Entropy for intuitionistic fuzzy sets. *Fuzzy Sets and Systems, 118*, 467–477. doi:10.1016/S0165-0114(98)00402-3

Talbi, H., Draa, A., & Batouche, M. (2004). A new quantum-inspired genetic algorithm for solving the travelling salesman problem. In *Proceedings of IEEE International Conference on Industrial Technology*. IEEE.

Talbi, H., Draa, A., & Batouche, M. (2006). A novel quantum-inspired evolutionary algorithm for multi-sensor image registration. *The International Arab Journal of Information Technology, 3*(1), 9–15.

Tanay, A., Sharan, R., & Shamir, R. (2002). Discovering statistically significant biclusters in gene expression data. *Bioinformatics (Oxford, England), 18*(1), 136–144. doi:10.1093/bioinformatics/18.suppl_1.S136 PMID:12169541

Tanay, B., & Kandemir, M. B. (2011). Topological structure of fuzzy soft sets. *Computers & Mathematics with Applications (Oxford, England), 61*, 2952–2957. doi:10.1016/j.camwa.2011.03.056

Tang, Y., Xu, F., Wan, X., & Zhang, Y. Q. (2002). Web-based fuzzy neural networks for stock prediction. In *Proceedings of Second International Workshop on Intelligent Systems Design and Application,* (pp. 169-174). IEEE.

Tanimoto, S. L., & Tanimoto, S. (Eds.). (2008). The elements of artificial intelligence using common LISP (2nd ed.). Principles of Computer Science Series.

Tan, K. S., & Isa, N. A. M. (2011). Color image segmentation using histogram thresholdingFuzzy *C*-means hybrid approach. *Pattern Recognition, 44,* 1–15.

Tao, W., Jin, H., & Zhang, Y. (2007). Color image segmentation based on mean shift and normalized cuts. *IEEE Transactions on Systems, Man, and Cybernetics. Part B, Cybernetics, 37*(5), 1382–1389. doi:10.1109/TSMCB.2007.902249 PMID:17926718

Taskar, B., Obozinski, G., & Jordan, M. I. (2006). *Multi-task feature selection.* Berkeley, CA: UC Berkeley.

Taylor, J. W. (2003). Short-term electricity demand forecasting using double seasonal exponential smoothing. *The Journal of the Operational Research Society, 54*(8), 799–805. doi:10.1057/palgrave.jors.2601589

Thilagam, P. S., & Ananthanarayana, V. S. (2008). Extraction and optimization of fuzzy association rules using multi-objective genetic algorithm. *Pattern Analysis & Applications, 11*(2), 159–168. doi:10.1007/s10044-007-0090-x

Thomas, J. M., Elmer, H. S. U., & Lowenthal, S. (1972). Dynamics of pH in controlled stirred tank reactor. *Industrial & Engineering Chemistry Process Design and Development, 11*(1), 68–70. doi:10.1021/i260041a013

Tizhoosh, H. (2005). Image thresholding using type II fuzzy sets. *Pattern Recognition, 38,* 2363–2372. doi:10.1016/j.patcog.2005.02.014

Todd, R. J. (1994). Back to our beginnings: Information utilization, Bertram Brookes and the fundamental equation of information science. *Information Processing & Management, 35*(6), 851–870. doi:10.1016/S0306-4573(99)00030-8

Todd, R. J. (1999). Utilization of heroin information by adolescent girls in Australia: A cognitive analysis. *Journal of the American Society for Information Science American Society for Information Science, 50*(1), 10–23. doi:10.1002/(SICI)1097-4571(1999)50:1<10::AID-ASI4>3.0.CO;2-B

Toennies, J. L., Burgner, J., Withrow, T. J., & Webster, R. J. (2011). Toward haptic/aural touchscreen display of graphical mathematics for the education of blind students. In Proceedings of *World Haptics Conference (WHC)* (pp. 373 - 378). IEEE.

Topchy, A. P., Jain, A. K., & Punch, W. F. (2005). Clustering ensembles: Models of consensus and weak partitions. *IEEE Transactions on Pattern Analysis and Machine Intelligence, 27*(12), 1866–1881. doi:10.1109/TPAMI.2005.237 PMID:16355656

Tran, K. D. (2009). An improved multi-objective evolutionary algorithm with adaptable parameters. *International Journal of Intelligent Systems Technologies and Application Archive, 7*(4), 347–369. doi:10.1504/IJISTA.2009.028052

Trier, O., & Jain, A. (1995). Goal-directed evaluation of binarization methods. *IEEE Transactions on Pattern Analysis and Machine Intelligence, 17,* 1191–1201. doi:10.1109/34.476511

Tripathy, B. K., & Gantayat, S. S. (2004). Some more properties of lists and fuzzy lists. *Information Sciences - Informatics and Computer Science, 166,* 167–179.

Tripathy, B. K., & Gantayat, S. S. (2012). Conceptual application of list theory to data structures. In *Proceedings of the Second International Conference on Advances in Computing and Information Technology* (ACITY-2012), (pp. 551-560). Berlin: Springer-Verlag.

Tripathy, B. K., & Gantayat, S. S. (2013). Some new properties of lists and a framework of a list theoretic relation model. In *Proceedings of the Second International Conference on Computational Science, Engineering and Information Technology* (CCSEIT-2012). ACM.

Tripathy, B. K., & Mitra, A. (2013). On the approximate equalities of multigranular rough sets and approximate reasoning. In *Proceedings, 4ᵗʰ IEEE International Conference on Computing, Communication and Networking Technologies* (ICCCNT 2013). IEEE.

Tripathy, B. K., & Pattnaik, G. P. (2004). On some properties of lists and fuzzy lists. *Information Sciences - Informatics and Computer Science, 168*, 9-23.

Tripathy, B. K., & Tripathy, H. K. (2009). Covering based rough equivalence of sets and comparison of knowledge. In *Proceedings of the IACSIT Spring Conference 2009*. IACSIT.

Tripathy, B. K., Jhawar, A., & Vats, E. (2012). An analysis of generalised approximate equalities based on rough fuzzy sets. In *Proceedings of the International Conf. on SocPros 2011*. SocPros.

Tripathy, B. K., Panda, G. K., & Mitra, A. (2009). Covering based rough equality of sets and comparison of knowledge. In *Proceedings of the Inter. Conf. in Mathematics and Computer Science* (ICMCS 2009). ICMCS.

Tripathy, B.K. (2011). An analysis of approximate equalities based on rough set theory. *International Journal of Advanced Science and Technology, 31*.

Tripathy, B.K., Mitra, A., & Ojha, J. (2009). Rough equivalence and algebraic properties of rough sets. *International Journal of Artificial Intelligence and Soft Computing, 1*(2/3/4), 271 – 289.

Tripathy, B. K. (2009). On approximation of classifications, rough equalities and rough equivalences. *Springer International Studies in Computational Intelligence, 174*, 85–133. doi:10.1007/978-3-540-89921-1_4

Tripathy, B. K., & Choudhury, P. K. (2003). Intuitionistic fuzzy lists. *Notes on Intuitionistic Fuzzy Sets, 9*(2), 61–73.

Tripathy, B. K., Jena, S. P., & Ghosh, S. K. (2001). On the theory of bags and lists. *Information Sciences, 132*, 241–254. doi:10.1016/S0020-0255(01)00066-4

Tripathy, B. K., & Mitra, A. (2013). On approximate equivalences of multigranular rough sets and approximate reasoning. *International Journal of Information Technology and Computer Science, 10*, 103–113. doi:10.5815/ijitcs.2013.10.11

Tripathy, B. K., Mitra, A., & Ojha, J. (2008). On rough equalities and rough equivalences of sets. In *RSCTC 2008 (LNAI)* (Vol. 5306, pp. 92–102). Akron, OH: Springer-Verlag. doi:10.1007/978-3-540-88425-5_10

Tripathy, B. K., & Panda, G. K. (2012). Approximate equalities on rough intuitionistic fuzzy sets and an analysis of approximate equalities. *International Journal of Computer Science Issues, 9*(2), 371–380.

Tripathy, B. K., Rawat, R., Divya, V., & Parida, S. C. (2013). *On multigranular approximate rough equalities and approximate reasoning*. VIT University.

Tsang, C. H., Kwong, S., & Wang, H. (2005). Anomaly intrusion detection using multi-objective genetic fuzzy system and agent-based evolutionary computation framework. In *Proceedings of Data Mining* (pp. 789–792). IEEE.

Tsang, E., Yung, P., & Li, J. (2004). EDDIE-automation, a decision support tool for financial forecasting. *Decision Support Systems, 37*(4), 559–565. doi:10.1016/S0167-9236(03)00087-3

Tseng, F. M., Yu, H. C., & Tzeng, G. H. (2002). Combining neural network model with seasonal time series ARIMA model. *Technological Forecasting and Social Change, 69*, 71–87. doi:10.1016/S0040-1625(00)00113-X

Tseng, G., & Wong, W. (2005). Tight clustering: A resampling-based approach for identifying stable and tight patterns in data. *Biometrics, 61*, 10–16. doi:10.1111/j.0006-341X.2005.031032.x PMID:15737073

Tseng, H. E., Chang, C. C., & Chang, S. H. (2005). Applying case-based reasoning for product configuration in mass customization environments. *Expert Systems with Applications, 29*(4), 913–925. doi:10.1016/j.eswa.2005.06.026

Tseng, L. Y., & Yang, S. B. (2001). A genetic approach to the automatic clustering problem. *Pattern Recognition, 34*, 415–424. doi:10.1016/S0031-3203(00)00005-4

Tsutsui, S., & Fujimoto, Y. (1993). Forking genetic algorithm with blocking and shrinking modes. In *Proceedings of the Fifth Int. Conf. on Genetic Algorithms* (pp. 206-213).

Tusher, V., Tibshirani, R., & Chu, G. (2001). Significance analysis of microarrays applied to the ionizing radiation response. *Proceedings of the National Academy of Sciences of the United States of America*, *98*(9), 5116–5121. doi:10.1073/pnas.091062498 PMID:11309499

Uchiyama, T., & Arbib, M. A. (1994). Color image segmentation using competitive learning. *IEEE Transactions on Pattern Analysis and Machine Intelligence*, *16*(12), 1197–1206. doi:10.1109/34.387488

Valarmathi, K., Kanmani, J., Devaraj, D., & Radhakrishnan, T. K. (2007). Hybrid GA fuzzy controller for pH process. In *Proceedings of International Conference on Computational Intelligence and Multimedia Applications*, (pp. 13 – 18). IEEE.

Valtchev, P., Missaousi, R., & Godin, R. (2004). Formal concept analysis for knowledge discovery and data mining: The new challenges. In *Proceedings of 2ⁿᵈ International Conference on Formal Concept Analysis* (LNAI), (vol. 2961, pp. 352-371). Berlin: Springer.

Valtchev, P., Missaoui, R., Godin, R., & Meridji, M. (2002). A framework for incremental generation of frequent closed item sets using Galois (concept) lattices. *Journal of Experimental & Theoretical Artificial Intelligence*, *14*(2/3), 115–142. doi:10.1080/09528130210164198

Valtchev, P., Missaoui, R., & Lebrun, P. (2002). A partition based approach towards constructing Galois (concept) lattices. *Discrete Mathematics*, *256*(3), 801–829. doi:10.1016/S0012-365X(02)00349-7

van der Merwe, D. W., & Engelbrecht, A. P. (2003). Data clustering using particle swarm optimization. *Congress on Evolutionary Computation*, *1*, 215–220.

Van der, M. F., Obiedkov. S., & Kourie, D. (2004). Add intent: A new incremental algorithm for conctructing concept lattices. In *Proceedings of ICFCA 2004* (pp. 372-385). ICFCA.

Van Der, M. F., Obiedkov, S., & Kourie, D. (2004). Add intent: A new incremental algorithm for constructing concept lattices. In *ICFCA (LNAI)* (Vol. 2961, pp. 342–385). Berlin: Springer-Verlag.

Vandenbroucke, N., Macaire, L., & Postaire, J. G. (2003). Color image segmentation by pixel classification in an adapted hybrid color space: Application to soccer image analysis. *Computer Vision and Image Understanding*, *90*(2), 190–216. doi:10.1016/S1077-3142(03)00025-0

Veloso, M. M., & Carbonell, J. (1993). Derivational analogy in prodigy. *Machine Learning*, *10*(3), 249–278. doi:10.1023/A:1022686910523

Velskii, G. M., & Landis, E. M. (1962). An algorithm for the organization of information. *Soviet Mathematics Doklady*, *3*, 1259–1263.

Venkatamaran, S., Krishnan, R., & Rao, K. K. (1993). A rule-rule-case based system for image analysis. In *Proceedings of First European Workshop on Case-Based Reasoning*. University of Kaiserslautern.

Venkatesh, S., Rosin, P., & Hanqing, L. (1995). Dynamic threshold determination by local and global edge evaluation. *CVGIP: Graph. Models Image Process.*, *57*, 146–160. doi:10.1006/gmip.1995.1015

Venter, F. J., Oosthuizen, G. D., & Ross, J. D. (1997). Knowledge discovery in databases using concept lattices. *Expert Systems with Applications*, *13*(4), 259–264. doi:10.1016/S0957-4174(97)00047-X

Venturini, G. (1993). SIA: A supervised inductive algorithm with genetic search for learning attributes based concepts.[Berlin: Springer.]. *Proceedings of Machine Learning, ECML-93*, 280–296.

Vesanto, J., & Alhoniemi, E. (2000). Clustering of the self-organizing map. *IEEE Transactions on Pattern Analysis and Machine Intelligence*, *11*(3), 586–600. PMID:18249787

ViewPlus Tiger Software Suite. (2013). Retrieved June 30, 2013 from http://www.viewplus.com/products/software/Braille-translator/

Viewplus. (2013). Retrieved June 30, 2013 from http://www.viewplus.com/about/abstracts/05csungardner2.html

Wadsworth, B. J. (2003). *Inteligência e afetividade da criança na teoria de Piaget* (5th ed.). São Paulo: Pioneira Thomsom Learning.

Wadsworth, B. J. (2004). *Piaget's theory of cognitive and affective development* (5th ed.). Boston: Allyn & Bacon.

Wagstaf, K., Cardie, C., Rogers, S., & Schroedl, S. (2001). Constrained K-means clustering with back-ground knowledge. In *Proceedings of the 18th International Conference on Machine Learning*. San Francisco: Morgan Kaufmann.

Waller, K. V., & Gustafsson, T. K. (1983). Fundamental properties of continuous pH control. *ISA Transactions*, *22*(1), 25–34.

Wallqvist, A., Rabow, A., Shoemaker, R., Sausville, E., & Covell, D. (2002). Establishing connections between microarray expression data and chemotherapeutic cancer pharmacology. *Molecular Cancer Therapeutics*, *1*, 311–320. PMID:12489847

Wang, J., Bo, T. H., Jonassen, I., Myklebost, O., & Hovig, E. (2003). Tumor classification and marker gene prediction by feature selection and fuzzy c-means clustering using microarray data. *BMC Bioinformatics*, *4*, 60. doi:10.1186/1471-2105-4-60 PMID:14651757

Wang, J.-H., Rau, J.-D., & Liu, W.-J. (2003). Two-stage clustering via neural networks. *IEEE Transactions on Neural Networks*, *14*(3), 606–615. doi:10.1109/TNN.2003.811354 PMID:18238042

Wang, S., Hao, G., Ma, J., & Xu, W. (2010). Vague soft sets & their properties. *Computers & Mathematics with Applications (Oxford, England)*, *59*, 787–794. doi:10.1016/j.camwa.2009.10.015

Wang, S., & Siskind, J. M. (2003). Image segmentation with ratio cut. *IEEE Transactions on Pattern Analysis and Machine Intelligence*, *25*(6), 675–690. doi:10.1109/TPAMI.2003.1201819

Wan, S.-Y., & Higgins, W. E. (2003). Symmetric region growing. *IEEE Transactions on Image Processing*, *12*(8), 1–9. PMID:18237875

Wasto, I. (1997). *Applying case-based reasoning: Techniques for enterprise systems*. San Francisco, CA: Morgan Kaufmann.

Watanabe, S., Hiroyasu, T., & Miki, M. (2003). Multi-objective rectangular packing problem and its applications. In *Evolutionary multi-criterion optimization* (pp. 565–577). Berlin: Springer. doi:10.1007/3-540-36970-8_40

Watanabe, T., Kobayashi, S., & Yokoyama, K. (2006). Practical use of interactive tactile graphic display system at a school for the blind. In *Current developments in technology-assisted education* (pp. 1111–1115). Academic Press.

Watson, I. (2011). Knowledge management and case based reasoning: A perfect match? In *Proceedings of the Fourteenth International Florida Artificial Intelligence Research Society Conference*, (pp. 118-122). Academic Press.

Way, T. P., & Barner, K. E. (1997). Automatic visual to tactile translation, part 2: Evaluation of the tactile image creation system. *IEEE Transactions on Rehabilitation Engineering*, *5*.

WebSource. (2000). Retrieved from http://www.math.tau.ac.il/~turkel/images.html

Weigang, H., & Xiuli, S. (2011). A fuzzy associative classification method based on multi-objective evolutionary algorithm. *Journal of Computer Research and Development*, *48*(4), 567–575.

Weiss, S. M., & Indurkhya, N. (1998). *Predictive data mining: A practical guide*. San Francisco: Morgan Kaufmann.

Weston, J., Elisse, A., Schoelkopf, B., & Tipping, M. (2003). Use of the zero norm with linear models and kernel methods. *Journal of Machine Learning Research*, *3*, 1439–1461.

Wille, R. (2008). Formal concept analysis as applied lattice theory. In *Proceedings of 4th International Conferences on Concept Lattices and Their Applications* (pp. 42-67). Berlin: Springer-Verlag.

Wille, R. (1982). Restructuring lattice theory: An approach based on hierarchy of concepts. In I. Rival (Ed.), *Ordered sets* (pp. 445–470). Boston: Reidel. doi:10.1007/978-94-009-7798-3_15

Wille, R. (2002). Why can concept lattice support knowledge discovery in databases. *Journal of Experimental & Theoretical Artificial Intelligence, 14*(2/3), 81–92. doi:10.1080/09528130210164161

Woei, W. T., Fengwei, L. U., & Ai-Poh, L. (2001). An application of genetic algorithm for designing a Wiener-model controller to regulate the pH value in a pilot plant. *Proceedings of the Congress on Evolutionary Computation, 2*, 1055 – 1061.

Wolpert, D. H., & Macready, W. G. (1995). *No free lunch theorems for search* (Technical Report SFI-TR-95-02-010). Santa Fe, NM: Santa Fe Institute.

Wong, C.-C., & Chen, C.-C. (2000). A GA-based method for constructing fuzzy systems directly from numerical data. *IEEE Transactions on Systems, Man and Cybernetics. Part B, 30*, 904–911.

Wright, R. A. (1991). Nonlinear control of pH processes using the strong acid equivalent. *Industrial & Engineering Chemistry Research, 30*(7), 1561–1572. doi:10.1021/ie00055a022

Wright, R. A., Soroush, M., & Kravaris, C. (1991). Strong acid equivalent control of pH processes: An experimental study. *Industrial & Engineering Chemistry Research, 30*(11), 2437–2444. doi:10.1021/ie00059a012

Wu, L., Songde, M., & Hanqing, L. (1998). An effective entropic thresholding for ultrasonic imaging. In *Proceedings of 1998 Intl. Conf. Patt. Recog.*, (pp. 1522–1524). IEEE.

Wu, W. Z., Leung, Y., & Mi, J. S. (2009). Granular computing and knowledge reduction in formal contexts. *IEEE Transactions on Knowledge and Data Engineering, 21*(10), 1461–1474. doi:10.1109/TKDE.2008.223

Xi, X., Keogh, E., Shelton, C., Wei, L., & Ratanamahatana, C. A. (2006). Fast time series classification using numerosity reduction. In *Proceedings of ICML06* (pp. 1033-1040). ICML.

Xiao, Z. (2010). Exclusive disjunctive soft sets. *Computers & Mathematics with Applications (Oxford, England), 59*(6), 2128–2137. doi:10.1016/j.camwa.2009.12.018

Xie, S. (2010). Research about fuzzy-PID control method of pH value in chemical industry process. In *Proceedings of International Conference on Electrical and Control Engineering,* (pp. 1554 – 1557). IEEE.

Xing, E., Jordan, M., & Karp, R. (2001). Feature selection for high-dimensional genomic microarray data. In *Proceedings of the 15th Int'l Conf. Machine Learning* (pp. 601-608). IEEE.

Xu, Z., Jin, R., Ye, J., Michael, J., Lyu, R., & King, I. (2009). Discriminative semi-supervised feature selection via manifold regularization. In *Proceedings of the 21st International Joint Conference on Artificial Intelligence IJCAI' 09*. IEEE.

Xue, H., Chen, S., & Yang, Q. (2009). Discriminatively regularized least-squares classification. *Pattern Recognition, 42*(1), 93–104. doi:10.1016/j.patcog.2008.07.010

Yager, R. R. (1986). On the theory of bags. *International Journal of General Systems, 13*, 23–37. doi:10.1080/03081078608934952

Yakhnenko, O., Silvescu, A., & Honavar, V. (2005). Discriminatively trained Markov model for sequence classification. In *Proceedings of the Fifth IEEE International Conference on Data Mining,* (pp. 498-505). Washington, DC: IEEE.

Yang, J., Wang, H., Wang, W., & Yu, P. (2003). Enhanced bi-clustering on expression data. In *Proceedings of the Third IEEE Symposium on Bioinformatics and Bioengineering* (pp. 321-327). IEEE.

Yang, J., Wang, W., Wang, H., & Yu, P. (2002). Delta-clusters: Capturing subspace correlation in a large data set. In *Proceedings of the 18th International Conference on Data Engineering* (pp. 517-528). IEEE.

Yang, H. L. (2011). Notes on generalised fuzzy soft sets. *J. of Math. Research & Exposition, 31*(3), 567–570.

Yang, H. L., & Wang, C. S. (2008). Two stages of case-based reasoning – Integrating genetic algorithm with data mining mechanisms. *Expert Systems with Applications, 35*(1–2), 262–272. doi:10.1016/j.eswa.2007.06.027

Yang, H. L., & Wang, C. S. (2009). Personalized recommendation for IT certification test in e-learning environment. *Journal of Research and Practice in Information Technology, 41*(4), 295–306.

Yang, H. L., & Wang, C. S. (2009). Recommender system for software project planning – One application of revised CBR algorithm. *Expert Systems with Applications, 36*(5), 8938–8945. doi:10.1016/j.eswa.2008.11.050

Yang, J., Hao, S., & Chung, P. (2002). Color image segmentation using fuzzy *C*-means and eigenspace projections. *Signal Processing, 82*(3), 461–472. doi:10.1016/S0165-1684(01)00196-7

Yang, Q. (2007). Learning actions from data mining models. *IEEE Intelligent Systems, 22*(4), 79–81.

Yang, X., Lin, T. Y., Yang, J., Li, Y., & Yu, D. (2009). Combination of interval-valued fuzzy set and soft set. *Computers & Mathematics with Applications (Oxford, England), 58*, 521–527. doi:10.1016/j.camwa.2009.04.019

Yang, X., Yang, J., & Wu, C. (2007). Generalization of soft set theory: From crisp to fuzzy case. In B. Y. Cao (Ed.), *Fuzzy Information & Engineering (ICFIE)* (pp. 345–354). ICFIE. doi:10.1007/978-3-540-71441-5_39

Yanni, M., & Horne, E. (1994). A new approach to dynamic thresholding. In *Proceedings of 1994 EUSIPCO' 94: 9th European Conf. Sig. Process.,* (pp. 34–44). EUSIPCO.

Yao, Y. Y. (1998). Relational interpretations neighbourhood operators and rough set approximation operators. *Information Science, 3*, 239–259. doi:10.1016/S0020-0255(98)10006-3

Yeh, P., Antoy, S., Litcher, A., & Rosenfeld, A. (1986). *Address location on envelopes.* University of Maryland.

Yen, J., Chang, F., & Chang, S. (1995). A new criterion for automatic multilevel thresholding. *IEEE Transactions on Image Processing, 4*, 370–378. doi:10.1109/83.366472 PMID:18289986

Yu, J., Xi, L., & Zhou, X. (2008). Intelligent monitoring and diagnosis of manufacturing processes using an integrated approach of KBANN and GA. *Computers in Industry, 59*(5), 489–501. doi:10.1016/j.compind.2007.12.005

Yun, L., Yunhao, Y., Xin, G., Yen, S., & Ling, C. (2008). A fast algorithm for generating concepts. In *Proceedings of International Conference on Information and Automation* (pp. 1728-1733). IEEE.

Zadeh, L. A. (1965). Fuzzy sets. *Information and Control, 8*(11), 338–353. doi:10.1016/S0019-9958(65)90241-X

Zadeh, L. A. (1975). The concept of a linguistic variable and its application to approximate reasoning-I. *Information Sciences, 8*, 199–249. doi:10.1016/0020-0255(75)90036-5

Zadeh, L. A. (1988). Fuzzy logic. *IEEE Computer, 21*(4), 88–91. doi:10.1109/2.53

Zainal, A., Maarof, M. A., & Shamsuddin, S. M. (2009). Ensemble classifiers for network intrusion detection system. *Journal of Information Assurance and Security, 4*, 217–225.

Zakowski, W. (1983). Approximation in space. *Demonstratio Mathematica, 16*, 761–769.

Zeybek, Z., & Alpbaz, M. (2005). Fuzzy-dynamic matrix pH control for treatment of dye waste water plant. In *Proceedings of Sixth International Conference on Computational Intelligence and Multimedia Applications,* (pp. 118 – 123). IEEE.

Zhandong, Y., & Jiangtao, X. (2005). Adaptive singularity-free controller by neural compensation for pH process in alkali-terminal tank of polyacrylonitrile. In *Proceedings of International Conference on Neural Networks and Brain,* (vol. 3, pp. 1836 – 1839). IEEE.

Zhang, H., Fritts, J. E., & Goldman, S. A. (2004). An entropy-based objective evaluation method for image segmentation. In *Proceedings of SPIE Storage and Retrieval Methods and Applications for Multimedia,* (pp. 38–49). SPIE.

Zhang, P., Joshi, M., & Lingras, P. (2011). Use of stability and seasonality analysis for optimal inventory prediction models. *Journal of Intelligent Systems, 20*(2), 20. doi:10.1515/jisys.2011.009

Zhang, S., & Wu, X. (2011). Fundamentals of associations rules in data mining and knowledge discovery. *Wiley Interdisciplinary Reviews: Data Mining & Knowledge Discovery, 1*(2), 97–116. doi:10.1002/widm.10

Zhang, X., Mei, C., Ched, D., & Li, J. (2013). Multi-confidence rule acquisition oriented attribute reduction of covering decision systems via combinatorial optimization. *Knowledge-Based Systems*. doi:10.1016/j. knosys.2013.06.012

Zhang, Y., Ding, C., & Li, T. (2008). Gene selection algorithm by combining relief and mrmr. *BMC Genomics, 9*, S27. doi:10.1186/1471-2164-9-S2-S27 PMID:18831793

Zhang, Y., Wu, X. B., Xing, Z. Y., & Hu, W. L. (2011). On generating interpretable and precise fuzzy systems based on Pareto multi-objective cooperative co-evolutionary algorithm. *Applied Soft Computing, 11*(1), 1284–1294. doi:10.1016/j.asoc.2010.03.005

Zhao, Z., & Liu, H. (2007). Spectral feature selection for supervised and unsupervised learning. In *Proceedings of the International Conference on Machine Learning (ICML)*. ICML.

Zhao, Z., Wang, L., & Liu, H. (2010). Efficient spectral feature selection with minimum redundancy. In *Proceedings of the 24th AAAI Conference on Artificial Intelligence*. AAAI.

Zhu, J., Rosset, S., Hastie, T., & Tibshirani, R. (2003). 1-norm support vector machines. In Advances in Neural Information Processing Systems. Academic Press.

Zhu, W. (2007). Basic concepts in covering-based rough sets. In *Proceedings of 3rd IEEE International Conference on Natural Computation*. IEEE Computer Society.

Zhu, W., & Wang, F. Y. (2006). Relationships among three types of covering rough Sets. In *Proceedings of IEEE GrC*, (pp. 43-48). IEEE.

Zhu, W. (2007). Topological approaches to covering rough sets. *Journal of Information Science, 177*, 1499–1508. doi:10.1016/j.ins.2006.06.009

Zhu, W. (2007). On three types of covering-based rough sets. *IEEE Transactions on Knowledge and Data Engineering, 19*(8), 1131–1143. doi:10.1109/TKDE.2007.1044

Zhu, W., & Wang, F. Y. (2003). Reduction and axiomization of covering generalized rough sets. *Journal of Information Science, 152*, 217–230. doi:10.1016/S0020-0255(03)00056-2

Zimmermann, H. J. (1996). *Fuzzy set theory and its applications* (3rd ed.). Dordrecht, The Netherlands: Kluwer. doi:10.1007/978-94-015-8702-0

Zingaretti, P., Tascini, G., & Regini, L. (2002). Optimising the colour image segmentation. In *Proceedings VIII Convegno dell Associazione Italiana per Intelligenza Artificiale*. Academic Press.

Zitzler, E., Laumanns, M., & Thiele, L. (2001). *SEPA2: Improving the performance of the strength of pareto evolutionary algorithm*. Zurich, Switzerland: Swiss Federal Institute of Technology.

Zitzler, E., & Thiele, L. (1999). Multi-objective evolutionary algorithms: A comparative case study and the strength Pareto approach. *IEEE Transactions on Evolutionary Computation, 3*(4), 257–271. doi:10.1109/4235.797969

Zong-Yi, X., Yong, Z., Yuan-Long, H., & Guo-Qiang, C. (2008). Multi-objective fuzzy modeling using NSGA-II. In *Proceedings of Cybernetics and Intelligent Systems* (pp. 119–124). IEEE.

About the Contributors

B. K. Tripathy a senior professor in the school of computing sciences and engineering, VIT University, at Vellore, India. He has published more than 190 technical papers in various international journals, conferences, and book chapters and has guided 14 scholars for their Ph.D degrees in both mathematics and computer science. He is associated with many professional bodies like IEEE, ACEEE, ACM, IRSS, AISTC, ISTP, CSI, AMS, and IMS. He is in the editorial board of several international journals like CTA, ITTA, AMMS, IJCTE, AISS, AIT, and IJPS, and is a reviewer of over 40 international journals like *Mathematical Reviews, Information Sciences, Analysis of Neural Networks, Journal of Knowledge Engineering, Mathematical Communications, IEEE Transactions on Fuzzy Systems,* and *Journal of Analysis.* His research interest includes fuzzy sets and systems, rough sets and knowledge engineering, data clustering, soft computing, granular computing, theory of multisets, list theory, content-based learning, remote laboratories and social networks.

D. P. Acharjya received his Ph. D in computer science from Berhampur University, India; M. Tech. degree in computer science from Utkal University, India in 2002; and M. Sc. from NIT, Rourkela, India. He has been awarded with Gold Medal in M. Sc. Currently, he is an Associate Professor in the school of computing sciences and engineering, VIT University, Vellore, India. He has authored many national and international journal papers and five books: *Fundamental Approach to Discrete Mathematics; Computer Based on Mathematics; Theory of Computation; Rough Set in Knowledge Representation and Granular Computing; Introduction to Information Technology;* and *Computer Programming* to his credit. He is associated with many professional bodies CSI, ISTE, IMS, AMTI, ISIAM, OITS, IACSIT, CSTA, IEEE, and IAENG. He was founder secretary of OITS Rourkela chapter. His current research interests include rough sets, formal concept analysis, knowledge representation, data mining, granular computing, and business intelligence.

* * *

Anish Benny received B. Tech (ECE) from College of Engineering, University of Kerala, India and M. Tech (Industrial Instrumentation & Control) from TKM College of Engineering, University of Kerala. Currently he is working as Assistant Professor in the electrical and electronics department, at Amal Jyothi College of Engineering, Kerala, India. His areas of interest are in systems control, instrumentation, sensor systems, modeling and simulation, biomedical instrumentation and mixed circuit design. He has rich industrial experience and has published papers in several national and international conferences.

Siddhartha Bhattacharyya did his B. Sc. (Physics), B. Sc. (Optics and Optoelectronics), and M. Sc. (Optics and Optoelectronics) from University of Calcutta, India in 1995, 1998, and 2000, respectively. He completed Ph. D. (CSE) from Jadavpur University, India. He is the recipient of the university gold medal from the University of Calcutta for his Masters. At present, he is working as an associate professor in the department of information technology, RCC Institute of Information Technology, Kolkata, India. He has published many books, edited books and more than 80 research papers. He was the convener of many national and international conferences. His name appears in editorial board of many international journals. His research interests include soft computing, pattern recognition and quantum computing. Dr. Bhattacharyya is a senior member of IEEE and is associated with many professional bodies like ACM, IRSS, IAENG, OSI, and ISTE.

Arindam Biswas graduated from Jadavpur University, Kolkata, India, and received his Masters and Doctorate degree from the Indian Statistical Institute, Kolkata, India. He is currently an associate professor in the department of information technology, Bengal Engineering and Science University, Shibpur, India. His research interests include digital geometry, image processing, approximate shape matching and analysis, medical image analysis, and biometrics. He has published over 50 research papers in international journals, edited volumes, and refereed conference proceedings, and holds one US patent.

Ranjit Biswas obtained his M. Tech. (Comp. Sc.) from IIT, Kharagpur and Ph.D. (Engg.) in Computer Science from Jadavpur University, Calcutta, India. He has guided twelve Ph.D.s (degrees conferred), more than 100 M. Tech. thesis and published more than 120 research papers all being in foreign journals of international repute. He is having about 32 years of teaching experience in India and abroad at renowned universities which include Calcutta University, IIT Kharagpur, Philadelphia University, IGNOU, NIT, etc. He is a member in editorial board of 14 journals of high esteem international repute published from various countries. His main areas of research include soft computing, fuzzy theory, rough theory, DBMS, data structures, algorithms, graph theory, discrete mathematics, optimization, approximation theory, decision theory, and computer architecture, etc. At present, he is working as a professor in the department of CSE, Jamia Hamdard University, Hamdard Nagar, New Delhi, India.

Tossapon Boongoen is an assistant professor with the department of mathematics and computer science, Royal Thai Air Force Academy, Thailand. Prior to this appointment, he obtained a PhD in artificial intelligence from Cranfield University and worked as postdoctoral research associate at Aberystwyth University. His research interests include data mining, link analysis, data clustering, fuzzy aggregation, and classification systems.

Alexandre de Castro is a research scientist at the Brazilian Agricultural Research Corporation (Embrapa) with experience in computational modeling and simulation. Currently, he is working in modeling of collective and cooperative behaviors in biological and organizational systems. His research about computational modeling and simulation has appeared in *Behavioral and Brain Sciences, Minds and Machines, International Journal of Information Management, Computer Modeling in Engineering & Sciences, Simulation Modelling Practice and Theory, Physica A: Statistical Mechanics and its Applications, Lecture Notes in Computer Science*, and *The European Physical Journal*.

Baisakhi Chakraborty received her Ph.D. (CSE) from National Institute of Technology, Durgapur, India, in 2011. Her research interest includes knowledge systems, engineering and management, database systems, data mining, and software engineering. She has published 20 research articles in international and national journals and conferences. She has a decade of industrial and 12 years of academic experience.

Susanta Chakraborty received his B. Tech, M. Tech. and Ph. D in computer science from the University of Calcutta, India. He is currently working as a professor in the department of CST, Bengal Engineering Science and University, West Bengal, India. He has published around 31 research papers in very reputed international journals like *IEEE Transactions on CAD* and international conference proceedings of IEEE. He is a recipient of INSA-JSPS Fellowship in the session 2003-2004. He has worked with many international universities such as University of Potsdam, University of Michigan in various capacities. His 25 years research interest primarily focused on logic synthesis and testing of VLSI circuits, DFT, BIST design test-pattern generation, fault-tolerant computing, image processing, fault diagnosis, low power design and synthesis. In addition, he has served as program chair for various international conferences.

David K. Daniel obtained his B. Tech (Chemical Engineering) from the University of Kerala, India, M. Tech (Chemical Engineering) from Calicut University, India. He received his Ph. D (Biotechnology) from the IIT-Kharagpur, India. At present, he is working as professor in the chemical engineering division, School of Mechanical and Building Sciences, at VIT University, Vellore, India. His research interests include bioprocess development, optimization and modeling, alternate fuels, microbial fuel cells and biosensors development. He is the recipient of the best teacher award by the VIT University followed by the certificate of appreciation from VIT University in recognition of the research efforts for publishing in refereed journals. He has also received JEC-Asia 2013 innovation award for recycling category. Dr. David is an active member of the IE, IICE and Biotech Research Society of India.

Kedar Nath Das is recently working as an assistant professor in the department of mathematics, NIT Silchar, Assam, India. He obtained his Ph. D from IIT Roorkee in 2008. Before joining NIT, he served with BIT, Mesra, India, and KIIT University, Bhunaneswar, India. He has published 20 national and international publications. He has published two books. He has visited many countries like Las Vegas (USA), Sarawak (Malaysia), and Dubai for delivering guest lecturers. He has also delivered guest lecturers at various institutes of national repute. He is the life member of ORSI, ISTE, and OMS.

Sujata Dash received her Ph.D. (Computational Modeling and Simulation) from Berhampur University, Odisha, India. She is a senior professor in computer science at Gandhi Institute for Technology, Biju Pattnaik University of Technology, Odisha, India. She has published more than 55 technical papers in international journals, proceedings of international conferences, book chapters of reputed publications. Her current research interests include machine learning, data mining, bio-informatics, intelligent agent, Web data mining, image processing, and cloud computing.

Sourav De did his Bachelors in Information Technology from The University of Burdwan, Burdwan, India; and Masters in Information Technology from West Bengal University of Technology, Kolkata, India. Presently, he is an associate professor in the department of computer science and information technology of University Institute of Technology, The University of Burdwan, Burdwan, India. He has industrial experience and published several papers. His research interests include soft computing, pattern recognition, and image processing. He is a member of IAENG and ISTE.

Satchidananda Dehuri is an associate professor in the department of systems engineering, Ajou University, Suwon, Republic of Korea. He received his M. Sc. (Mathematics) from Sambalpur University, Odisha, India; M. Tech. and Ph. D. degrees in computer science from Utkal University, Odisha, India. He completed his postdoctoral research in soft computing laboratory, Yonsei University, Seoul, Korea under the BOYSCAST Fellowship Program of DST, Govt. of India. He received young scientist award in engineering and technology from Odisha Vigyan Academy, Department of Science and Technology, Govt. of Odisha. His research interest includes evolutionary computation and data mining.

V. Susheela Devi completed her Ph.D. from the Indian Institute of Science, Bangalore, India. She works in the department of computer science and automation at the Indian Institute of Science, India. She has taught a number of courses including data structures and algorithms, data mining, artificial intelligence, and linear and nonlinear optimization. She works in the field of pattern recognition and soft computing. She is the author of a book and a Web course on pattern recognition. She also has a number of papers in international journals and conferences. She is a member of IEEE and IEEE computational intelligence society.

Sandip Dey did his Bachelors in Mathematics in 1999. He completed B-level from DOEACC society and M. Tech. (Software Engineering) from West Bengal University of Technology in 2005 and 2008 respectively. Currently, he is pursuing Ph. D from Jadavpur University. He is currently working as an assistant professor in the department of information technology, Cammelia Institute of Technology, Kolkata, India. Prior to this, he worked as a lecturer in computer application of Narula Institute of Technology, Kolkata, India.

Sasanko Sekhar Gantayat is working as an Associate Professor in the department of computer science & engineering, GMR Institute of Technology, Rajam, Andhra Pradesh, India. He has published many research papers in national, international journals and conferences. He is a reviewer of many referred international journals, and his name appears in the editorial board of *American Journal of Database Theory and Application* (USA). He is a life member of IE (I), ISTE, CSI, AIRCC, IRSS, OITS, IACSIT, ISIAM, IMS, and SSI. His research interests include fuzzy sets and systems, rough set theory and knowledge discovery, list theory and applications, soft computing, cryptography, and discrete mathematics.

Utpal Garain received his bachelor and master degrees in computer science and engineering from Jadavpur University, India; and Ph. D. degree from Indian Statistical Institute, India. He is, at present, serving as an associate professor at ISI, India. His research interest includes document image analysis including OCRs and handwriting analysis, computational forensics and language engineering. He has been regularly reviewing papers for several international journals including IEEE PAMI, SMC, EvC, IJDAR, PR, PRL, *Image & Vision Computing*, etc. For his significant contribution in pattern recognition and its applications for language engineering, he has received the Young Engineer Award from the Indian National Academy of Engineering and the prestigious Indo-US Research Fellowship. In addition, he has co-authored two research monographs on language technology and about 90 peer-reviewed journal and conference papers.

Ashish Ghosh is a Professor with the Machine Intelligence Unit, ISI, Kolkata. He has already published more than 150 research papers in internationally reputed journals and refereed conferences, and has edited eight books. His current research interests include pattern recognition and machine learning, data mining, image analysis, remotely sensed image analysis, video image analysis, soft computing, fuzzy sets and uncertainty analysis, neural networks, evolutionary computation, and bioinformatics. Dr. Ghosh received the most coveted Young Scientists Award in Engineering Sciences from the Indian National Science Academy in 1995, and in Computer Science from the Indian Science Congress Association in 1992. He was selected as an Associate of the Indian Academy of Sciences, Bangalore, India, in 1997. He is a member of the founding team that established the National Centre for Soft Computing Research at the ISI, Kolkata, in 2004 and currently he is the In-charge of the centre. He is acting as a member of the editorial boards of various international journals.

Natthakan Iam-On received her PhD in Computer Science from Aberystwyth University, UK. Currently, she is a lecturer at School of Information Technology, Mae Fah Luang University, Chiang Rai, Thailand. Her research focuses on data clustering, cluster ensembles, data transformation, classification systems, applications of pattern recognition techniques to biomedical data analysis, business intelligence, and business analytics.

J. Abdul Jaleel received his B.E (Electrical Engineering) from University of Kerala, India, and the M. Tech (Energetics) from Regional Engineering College Calicut, India. He obtained his Ph. D. from Washington International University, USA. Currently he is working as Principal, AL Azhar College of Engineering and Technology, Thodupuzha, Kerala, India. His main areas of interest are application of artificial intelligence, image processing, industrial instrumentation and control, power system control and optimization, power system reliability, voltage stability, and computer aided design and analysis. Dr. Jaleel is the recipient of many awards and is a certified value engineer and auditor for quality management systems. He is an active member of professional societies like ISTE, CSI, IETE, and Saudi Council of Engineers.

Manish Ratnakar Joshi completed his post graduation (MCS) from Pune University, and Ph. D. from North Maharashtra University, India. He has also worked with faculty of Computer Science, University of New Brunswick, Fredericton, Canada as Post Doctoral Fellowship. At present, he is working in the department of computer science, North Maharashtra University, India. His current research interests include rough set based machine intelligence, knowledge discovery, and natural language processing. He has published more than 50 research papers in journals and international conference proceedings and delivered several invited talks. He is also edited an open access e-book. He is a committee member of various International conferences and reviewer of many international journals. He is one of the executive council members of Indian Society for Rough Sets.

Harihar Kalia is working as an assistant professor in the department of computer science and engineering, Seemanta Engineering College, Mayurbhanj, Odisha, India. He received his M. Sc. (Mathematics) from Ravenshaw University, Odisha; M. Tech. (CS) from Utkal University, Odisha, India. Now he is perusing his PhD in the area of Multi-Objective Fuzzy Rule Mining in department information and communication technology, Fakir Mohan University, Balasore, Odisha, India. His area of interest includes data mining, multi-objective optimization, fuzzy logic, evolutionary algorithms, and hybrid systems.

Ch. Aswani Kumar is working as a professor of network and information security division, School of Information Technology and Engineering, VIT University, Vellore, India. Ch. Aswani Kumar holds a PhD degree in Computer Science from VIT University, India. His current research interests are data mining, formal concept analysis, information security, and machine intelligence. Aswani Kumar has published 50 refereed research papers so far in various national, international journals and conferences. Aswani Kumar is a senior member of ACM and is associated with other professional bodies including ISC, CSI, and ISTE.

Pawan Lingras is a Professor in the Department of Mathematics and Computing Science at Saint Mary's University, Halifax, Canada. He was a Visiting Professor at IIT Gandhinagar from December 2011-May 2012. From January-June 2011, he has served as a University Grant Commission appointed Scholar-in-Residence at Swami Ramanand Teerth Marathwada University, Nanded, India. His undergraduate education from IIT Bombay was followed by graduate studies at the University of Regina, Canada. He has authored more than 160 research papers in various international journals and conferences. He has also co-authored two textbooks and co-edited two collections of research papers, and a number of volumes of conference proceedings. His areas of interests include artificial intelligence, information retrieval, data mining, Web intelligence, and intelligent transportation systems. He has served as the general co-chair, program co-chair, review committee chair, program committee member, and reviewer for various international conferences on artificial intelligence and data mining.

Pinaki Majumdar is an assistant professor and head of the department of Mathematics of M.U.C Women's College under University of Burdwan in INDIA. He is also a guest faculty in the department of Integrated Science Education and Research of Visva-Bharati University, India. His research interest includes soft set theory and its application, fuzzy set theory, fuzzy and soft topology, and fuzzy functional analysis. He has published many research papers in reputed international journals and acted reviewer of more than a dozen of international journals. He has completed few projects sponsored by UGC of India.

Ujjwal Maulik is a Professor in the department of computer science and engineering, Jadavpur University, Kolkata, India. He did his B. Sc. (Physics) and B. Sc. (Computer Science) in 1986 and 1989, respectively. Subsequently, he did his Masters and Ph. D. in Computer Science in 1992 and 1997, respectively. Dr. Maulik has worked with many international universities and laboratories. He has also visited many universities around the world for invited lectures, collaborative research. In addition, he is a co-author of 7 books and more than 250 research publications. He is the editorial board member of many journals and is a senior member of IEEE, CSI, IETE, and IE (I). He is the founder member of IEEE computational intelligence society (CIS) chapter, Calcutta Section and currently working as the chair. His research interests include computational intelligence, bioinformatics, combinatorial optimization, pattern recognition and data mining.

Debadutta Mohanty has completed his Ph.D. degree in 1996 from Berhampur University, Odisha, He has 27 years of teaching experience at under graduate level and 7 years in P.G. level. He has completed one Minor Research Project and one Major Research Project successfully under UGC (New Delhi, India) assistance. He has published more than twenty research papers in the national and international journals and conference proceedings. At present three Research Scholars are doing their research work under his guidance for Ph.D. degree.

Anirban Mukherjee received his BE (Civil Engineering) from Jadavpur University, India, and at present pursuing Ph. D at Bengal Engineering and Science University, Shibpur, India. He is currently an assistant professor in the department of information technology, RCC Institute of Information Technology, Kolkata, India. His research interest includes computer graphics, artificial intelligence, and assistive technology. He has co-authored two engineering textbooks: *Computer Graphics and Multimedia* and *Engineering Mechanics*. He has some international journal and conference papers to his credit.

Bichitrananda Patra is an associate professor at the department of computer science engineering, at KMBB College of Engineering and Technology, Biju Patnaik University of Technology, Odisha, India. He received his master degree in Physics and Computer Science from the Utkal University, Bhubaneswar, Odisha, India. He is currently pursuing his Ph.D. (Computer Science) at Berhampur University, Odisha, India. He has published many research papers in international and national journals and conferences. He is associated with different professional bodies like ISTE, CSI, etc.

Durga Prasad Roy received his B. Tech. (CSE) from Bankura Unnayani Institute of Engineering, west Bengal in 2009 and his M. Tech. (Multimedia and Software System) from National Institute of Technical Teachers' Training Institute and Research Kolkata, west Bengal in 2012. Presently he is pursuing PhD in Information Technology at National Institute of Technology Durgapur, West Bengal, and working on knowledge management and case-based reasoning.

Prem Kumar Singh is a research scholar at the School of Information Technology and Engineering, VIT University, India. He holds a master's degree in computer application from CSJM University, Kanpur, as well as a bachelor's degree in computer science from University of Allahabad, India. His research interests include data mining, fuzzy logic, and formal concept analysis. He has published three refereed research papers so far in various international conferences.

Gajendra R. Wani is a research scholar of school of computer science, North Maharashtra University, Jalgaon. He completed post graduation (MCS) from Pune University, Maharashtra (India). At present, he is heading the department of computer science and information technology. He is also working as a coordinator of Institute of Management and Career Development. His research interest includes data warehouse and data mining, artificial intelligence and operating system.

Peng Zhang is a part time professor in the department of mathematics and computing science at Saint Mary's University, Halifax, Canada. He has been teaching in department of mathematics and computer science at Saint Mary's University (Halifax) since 2010. His undergraduate education and graduate studies were accomplished at Saint Mary's University, Halifax, Canada. He authored and co-authored a few research papers in journals and conferences. His areas of interests include artificial intelligence, data mining, business intelligence, and business analysis. He also works as an IT consultant in the areas of business analysis and system analysis. In addition, he serves as the Vice President of International Institution of Business Analyst Halifax Chapter.

Index